DATE DUE

OCT 2 1 2009		

HIGHSMITH #45115

D1564192

THE
SOUTHERN STRATEGY

THE
SOUTHERN STRATEGY

BRITAIN'S CONQUEST OF
SOUTH CAROLINA AND GEORGIA
1775–1780

David K. Wilson

University of South Carolina Press

© 2005 University of South Carolina

Published in Columbia, South Carolina,
by the University of South Carolina Press

Manufactured in the United States of America

09 08 07 06 05   5 4 3 2 1

Library of Congress Cataloging-in-Publication Data

Wilson, David K., 1966–
   The southern strategy : Britain's conquest of South Carolina and Georgia, 1775–1780 / David K.
Wilson.
     p. cm.
Includes bibliographical references and index.
ISBN 1-57003-573-3 (alk. paper)
   1. Southern States—History—Revolution, 1775–1783—Campaigns. 2. United States—History—
Revolution, 1775–1783—British forces. 3. Strategy—History—18th century. 4. South Carolina—
History—Revolution, 1775–1783—Campaigns. 5. Georgia—History—Revolution, 1775–1783—
Campaigns. 6. United States—History—Revolution, 1775–1783—Campaigns. I. Title.
   E230.5.S7W55 2005
   973.3'3'0975—dc22

                                                                                    2004025510

This work is dedicated to the men and women of the American armed forces, past and present, who have fought to defend the lives and liberty of the people of the United States.

———⟫◆⟪———

"Who would have thought a hundred years ago that out of this multitude of rabble would arise a people who could defy kings?"

CAPTAIN JOHANN EWALD,
HESSIAN FIELD-JAEGER CORPS
YORKTOWN, VIRGINIA, 1781

Contents

List of Maps and Illustrations   ix
Preface   xi
Introduction   xiii

ONE
Making the Southern Strategy   1

TWO
Great Bridge: The Battle for Norfolk   5
Order of Battle: Great Bridge   17

THREE
Moore's Creek Bridge   19
Order of Battle: Moore's Creek Bridge   33

FOUR
Charlestown, 1776: The Battle of Sullivan's Island   36
Order of Battle: Sullivan's Island   56

FIVE
Remaking the Southern Strategy   59

SIX
Savannah, 1778   65
Order of Battle: Savannah, 1778   78

SEVEN
Briar Creek   81
Order of Battle: Briar Creek   98

EIGHT
Charlestown, 1779   100
Order of Battle: Charlestown, 1779   113

NINE
Stono Ferry   116
Order of Battle: Stono Ferry   130
American Casualty Return: Stono Ferry, 20 June 1779   132

TEN
The Siege of Savannah, 1779   133
Order of Battle: Savannah, 1779   177
French Orders of Attack: Savannah, 9 October 1779   182
American Orders of Attack: Savannah, 9 October 1779   184
British Commissary Return: Savannah, 11–20 October 1779   185
American Casualty Return: Savannah, 9 October 1779   189
American and French Camp Organization: Savannah, 1779   190

ELEVEN
The Siege of Charlestown, 1780   193
Order of Battle: Charlestown, 1780   238

TWELVE
Waxhaws   242
Order of Battle: Waxhaws   260

THIRTEEN
The End of the Beginning   262

Author's Note and Historiography   267
Notes   287
Selected Bibliography   323
Index   329

Maps and Illustrations

Maps

Strategic map of battles in the Southern Strategy   xiv
The battle of Great Bridge   6
The Moore's Creek Bridge campaign   20
The battle of Fort Sullivan   38
The battle of Savannah, 1778   68
The battle of Briar Creek   85
The battle of Stono Ferry   120
The siege of Savannah, 1779   136
The Charlestown campaign, 1780   197
The siege of Charlestown, 1780   217
The battle of Waxhaws   245

Illustrations *following page 132*

Great Bridge
Charles Lee
William Moultrie
Fort Moultrie
Henry Clinton
Benjamin Lincoln
Casimir Pulaski
Henri d'Estaing
Death of Pulaski
Spring Hill redoubt
Charlestown, 1780

Preface

This book is an examination of the British plan to conquer the American South during the Revolutionary War, a plan that modern historians have come to call the "Southern Strategy." I started this book with the intention of telling the story of the Southern Strategy from its beginning in 1775 to its end at Yorktown in 1781. However, as I progressed in my research, I realized that the history of the Revolutionary War in the South prior to Cornwallis's taking charge of British forces in the summer of 1780 had been woefully underreported. In addition, much of what had been written about this era was inaccurate—sometimes extremely so. The foundations of the failure of the Southern Strategy were established during this time, and it soon became clear to me that this fascinating period of the war deserved—and required—its own volume.

The British Southern Strategy was based on the idea of a counterrevolution by Loyalists who, it was argued by British officers in America, comprised the majority of the population in the South. However, did the British have sufficient intelligence to initiate military operations on this basis? Moreover, did British leaders ignore evidence that accumulated in their campaigns that contradicted the assumption that the majority of Southerners were Loyalists? Could they have modified the Southern Strategy to match the facts on the ground?

In addition to answering these questions, this book examines individual battles and campaigns in unprecedented detail. For the first time, the full and accurate story of the critical siege of Savannah is told. Significant, yet historically neglected engagements such as Great Bridge and Stono Ferry are given their most thorough narrative treatment to date; and surprising revelations are made regarding even relatively well-chronicled battles such as Moore's Creek Bridge and the siege of Charleston. Equally important, the battles, command decisions, politics, and policy are all evaluated with regard to how they helped or hindered Britain's strategy to conquer the South.

Several people have earned my thanks for support they gave in providing research materials, constructive comments, or moral encouragement to finish the work. Brian Leigh Dunnigan, curator of maps at the William L. Clements Library, was especially helpful in researching and copying items from the Clinton Papers held at the University of Michigan. Angie Sierra, at the Manuscripts and Archives Division of the New York Public Library, was of great help in retrieving and copying strength returns and letters from the Thomas Addis Emmet Collection. I appreciate Nancy Myers's proofreading of the early drafts of the manuscript, and I thank Dave Nighswonger for his constructive comments. I am very grateful to the staff of the University of South Carolina Press for their indefatigable efforts during the production of this book. Special thanks also go to Scott Bowden—his incisive and knowledgeable observations were of immense help.

I am grateful for the love and support of my wife Amy, my daughter Sarah, my son Alex, and my parents, Glenn and Edna. I thank Kevin Muldoon and Fred Stovall for their encouragement and friendship over the years. I owe a special debt to Robert Thielemann, my friend, for his comradeship and because his ill-timed death motivated an end to my procrastination in writing this book.

Introduction

On a hazy September morning in 1775, Lieutenant Colonel William Moultrie raised a new blue and white flag over Fort Johnson overlooking Charlestown harbor. "On its first being hoisted," Moultrie wrote, "it gave some uneasiness to our timid friends who were looking forward to reconciliation. They said that it had the appearance of a declaration of war . . . and [the British] would look upon it as an insult, and a flag of defiance."[1] The flag, designed by Moultrie, consisted of a white crescent moon in the upper left corner on a blue field. It was the first national flag of South Carolina, and its raising heralded the beginning of the end of British sovereignty in the American South.

The American Revolutionary War is popularly remembered as a war fought in the northern states. The imagery of New England minutemen facing down redcoats at Concord Bridge and the stories of Washington's frostbitten soldiers enduring the frigid winter at Valley Forge are seared into Americans' collective historical subconscious. However, the war of the Revolution was also fought in America's southern states; the ramparts of Savannah were no less bloodstained than Bunker Hill, and the siege of Charlestown was no less important than the battle for New York. Public and academic interest in the American Revolution in the South has enjoyed a recent renaissance, and yet scholarship on the southern campaigns has focused on the period following the British capture of Charlestown, South Carolina, in 1780. (The city was renamed "Charleston" in 1783. I have retained the archaic name throughout.) This was the period that Americans enjoyed their greatest success in the southern theater that concluded with the decisive victory at Yorktown in 1781. However, this was only the last chapter in the long story of the Revolutionary War in the South.

This book seeks to examine the critical period of the Revolutionary War in the South from 1775 to the spring of 1780—when Crown armies crushed all organized resistance in South Carolina and Georgia. The paradox of British defeat in 1781—after apparent unqualified success in 1780—only makes sense if one understands the fundamental flaws in what modern historians have come to call Britain's "Southern Strategy" (see "Author's Notes and Historiography"). The British had based the Southern Strategy on the erroneous premise that the majority of the population in the southern colonies was loyal to the king. The ministers in London held to this mistaken belief notwithstanding the accumulation of considerable evidence to the contrary during the course of the war. In addition, not only was the Southern Strategy flawed, but the implementation of the strategy was often flawed as well. The British would ultimately prove incapable

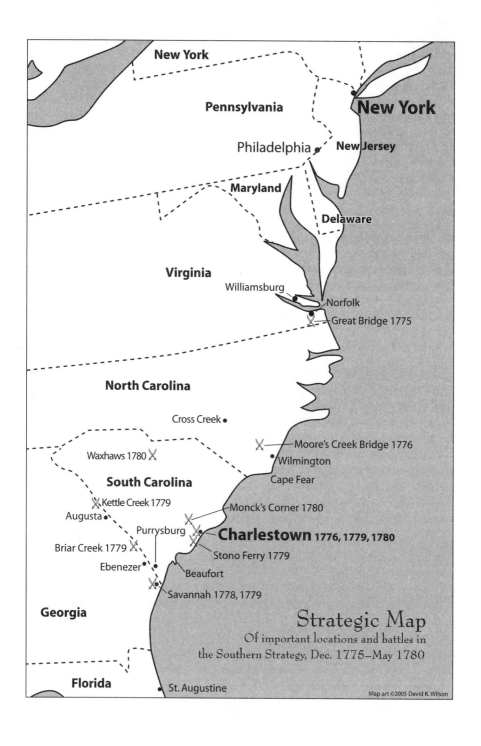

New York

Pennsylvania

New York

Philadelphia

New Jersey

Maryland

Delaware

Virginia

Williamsburg

Norfolk

Great Bridge 1775

North Carolina

Cross Creek

Moore's Creek Bridge 1776

Waxhaws 1780

Wilmington

South Carolina

Cape Fear

Kettle Creek 1779

Monck's Corner 1780

Augusta

Purrysburg

Charlestown 1776, 1779, 1780

Briar Creek 1779

Stono Ferry 1779

Ebenezer

Beaufort

Georgia

Savannah 1778, 1779

Strategic Map

Of important locations and battles in
the Southern Strategy, Dec. 1775–May 1780

Florida

St. Augustine

Map art ©2005 David K. Wilson

of adapting their plans to the reality of the situation on the ground. Yet, in spite of a flawed strategy and inflexible thinking, the British came very close to winning the southern campaigns—a fact that can be credited to the professionalism of the British military and the superior resources of the British state.

The Southern Strategy was based on the concept of counterrevolution; it was a sociomilitary approach that relied on the Loyalists of the southern states to provide the bulk of the manpower to achieve victory. The strategy called for a relatively small force of British regulars to invade a state and subdue the Patriot forces there with the help of the local Loyalists. (I use the terms "Americans," "Whigs," and "Patriots" when referring to Americans who favored independence from Britain; while the terms "Loyalists" and "Tories" are used to indicate those inhabitants of America who wished to remain British subjects.) Once that state was secure and protected by Loyalist militiamen, the British regulars would move on to the next state and repeat the process in an eighteenth-century version of the domino theory.

The student of recent military history will no doubt recognize the similarity between Britain's eighteenth-century strategy to conquer the American South and the United States' twenty-first-century strategy to overthrow the Taliban government in Afghanistan. In each case a state with superior military resources intended to project its power to a distant part of the globe using a handful of professional soldiers in support of an indigenous militia. However, the similarity ends at the planning stages. American operations in twenty-first-century Afghanistan succeeded because American intelligence was correct in its determination that the majority of Afghans did not support the Taliban government. British operations in the American South during the eighteenth century failed because the British presumption that the majority of southerners was loyal to the Crown was false.

Britain's first southern campaign ended in abject failure in the summer of 1776, but this did not shake the royal government's belief in the basic soundness of the Southern Strategy. In last days of 1778 Britain launched a new invasion of the South. From that time to the spring of 1780, the British Southern Army enjoyed an unbroken winning streak that culminated in two of the largest battles of the war—at Savannah in October 1779 and at Charlestown in May 1780. In the weeks that followed the British capture of Charlestown, the king's troops fanned out over both South Carolina and Georgia, occupying towns and ruthlessly destroying all opposition. However, because the British never found the Loyalist majority that supposedly existed in the South, the Americans were able to recover, and within a year they achieved a monumental victory over the British at Yorktown.

It was an extraordinary turnabout. Even with the benefit of historical hindsight, the American victory in the War of Independence is difficult to appreciate fully. It is important for modern readers to remember that at the time of the Revolution, Britain was the "Superpower" and America was the eighteenth-century equivalent of a "third-world" country. Victory for the nascent United States of America, bereft of resources and short on cash, was anything but certain. Ultimately, overconfident British generals and aloof ministers in London allowed success on the battlefield to blind them to deficiencies in their strategy. The other factor in American victory was the professionalism of the Continental Army and the perseverance of the American militiamen. Even during their darkest days the Americans continued to fight—much to the surprise of the British, who repeatedly believed their adversary to have been defeated beyond the possibility of recovery. Yet time and again, as Nathanael Greene described it, the Americans would rise and fight again until final victory was achieved.

THE
⊹⊱SOUTHERN STRATEGY⊰⊹

ONE

Making the Southern Strategy

I N 1774 THE BRITISH PARLIAMENT retaliated against the perpetrators of the Boston Tea Party by enacting a series of laws that the English called the "Coercive Acts." These laws, known as the "Intolerable Acts" in America, closed the port of Boston and essentially placed the colony of Massachusetts under martial law. Parliament hoped that this punishment of Massachusetts would serve to discourage other colonies from defying parliamentary rule. However, the British had miscalculated badly; instead of intimidating the Americans, the acts infuriated them. The colonies sent representatives to the first Continental Congress in order to coordinate their resistance against Britain's provocative measures. At the same time many colonies began drilling their militias more frequently in anticipation of hostilities with the mother country.

The first military clash of the Revolution occurred on 19 April 1775, when the British botched a raid on an American arms cache in Concord, Massachusetts. (The first shots of the war were fired at the town of Lexington, which lay along the route of march to Concord.) At this time Britain's American colonies stretched along the entire length of the Atlantic seaboard. By the spring of 1775 all of these colonies except Canada and Florida had rebelled against the authority of the British Crown. Parliament and King George III were unwilling to compromise or redress American grievances; instead they chose to pursue a military campaign to punish the colonials and reassert the supremacy of home rule over the colonies. The British focused their early military efforts against New England, which they regarded as the geographic and intellectual center of American discontent; however, it was not long before British strategists began contemplating military prospects in America's southern colonies.

Josiah Martin, the royal governor of North Carolina, was responsible for generating early British interest in a southern campaign. Governor Martin was confident that the majority of North Carolinians were loyal to the Crown, and that with proper arms and support they could reassert royal authority in the colony. In the summer of 1775 Martin sent his plan to Lord Dartmouth, the secretary of state for the American colonies. In a letter dated 30 June 1775, Martin claimed that with only minimal assistance he could "reduce to order and obedience every colony to the southward of Pennsylvania." To accomplish this scheme, Martin requested that Lord Dartmouth send to North

Carolina a handful of artillery, ten thousand muskets, ammunition, "and a supply of money as might be necessary for the support of such a force."[1]

Martin said that with proper support he would "restore order here and in South Carolina and hold Virginia in such awe as to prevent that province sending any succor to the northward." Moreover, Martin's belief in American weakness and Tory strength in the southern colonies was universally supported by other royal officials and military officers in the American South. John Murray, Earl of Dunmore, the governor of Virginia, wrote in 1775 that only a few hundred regulars would "reduce, without the smallest doubt the whole of this southern Continent to a perfect state of obedience."[2] Matthew Squire, an officer in the Royal Navy stationed in Virginia in 1775, wrote, "I am well convinced that had we a few more troops, and one or two more Ships, that the Rebels in these parts would be very soon quieted."[3] Likewise, Lord William Campbell, the royal governor of South Carolina, bragged, "Three regiments, a proper detachment of artillery, with a couple of good frigates . . . would do the whole business here."[4] Ironically, all of the men making these assertions of American impotence had been reduced to executing their royal duties from the safety of Royal Navy vessels offshore.

Initially, Dartmouth was dubious of Governor Martin's claim that he could retake their provinces from the American rebels with so little assistance. However, after many similar reports came in from other royal officials in the South, Dartmouth changed his mind. He wrote, "I confess that it appeared to me at the first view of the propositions made by Lord Dunmore and Governor Martin that they were too sanguine in their expectations; but later advices confirm what they represented of the temper and disposition of the people, and there is good ground to believe that the appearance of a respectable force to the southward . . . will have the effect to restore order and government in those four provinces [North and South Carolina, Virginia, and Georgia]."[5]

Lord Dartmouth agreed to give Martin the arms and financing he requested. Dartmouth ordered General William Howe in Boston to send officers to lead the regiments that Martin promised to raise. The British ministry also supplied a war chest of several thousand pounds sterling to finance operations in North Carolina—specifically funds for recruiting soldiers. Dartmouth also ordered Howe to send several companies of regulars to Virginia as Governor Dunmore had requested. Howe was reluctant to divide his force at a time when he needed every available soldier for operations in the North, but he of course complied with his superior's request and sent two companies of the 14th Regiment to Norfolk.

Then Secretary Dartmouth upped the ante: He would send six infantry regiments and a full battalion of Royal Marines to support the Loyalists in North Carolina and the other southern colonies. The expedition was scheduled to depart from Cork, Ireland, on 1 December 1775 and sail to Cape Fear off the coast of North Carolina. Dartmouth figured that once Crown rule was restored "in any one of the southern colonies the troops may proceed to another, leaving the support and protection of that which has been reduced to a corps formed out of the well-affected provincials who shall have taken up arms in the King's cause."[6]

Dartmouth had thus expanded significantly on Governor Martin's original plan of a counterrevolution relying only on Loyalists. His new strategy called for British regulars

—in conjunction with thousands of southern Loyalists—to eliminate Whig military forces in North Carolina. Josiah Martin claimed that at least two-thirds of the backcountry settlers of North Carolina were loyal to the British Crown. These Loyalists would be armed to defend the colony, which would allow the regulars to march to liberate the next colony in line. The strategy relied on two critical assumptions: that the amateur armies of the colonials could be easily brushed aside by England's professional soldiers and that a majority of southerners were loyal to the Crown. Dartmouth was hopeful on both accounts. "It is possible," the secretary wrote, that "the people [rebels] may be rash enough to appear in the open field against the King's troops and to hazard an action; but should that be the case, I trust the matter will soon be decided to the advantage of [the king's] government." Dartmouth also put his faith in the "encouragement of the King's governors" that when a respectable force appeared in the South, the Loyalists would soon prevail over the rebels. Dartmouth nevertheless still held some lingering doubts regarding the promises of the royal governors, which he communicated to General Howe: "I hope we are not deceived in the assurances we have been given, for if we are and there should be no appearance of a disposition in the inhabitants of the southern colonies to join the King's army, I fear little more will be effected than gaining the possession of some respectable post to the southward where the officers and servants of government may find protection and from which the rebels may be annoyed."[7]

During the early stages of the conflict, royal officials adhered to the simplistic notion that the southern colonies, far away from the hotbed of radicalism in New England, would contain fewer Patriots and more Loyalists. In addition, it was believed that the southern colonies, particularly Virginia and South Carolina, were more vulnerable because of the large number of slaves that they held when compared to the North. Some British officials would attempt to take advantage of the South's slaves by arming them to fight against their Whig masters (though the practice ultimately proved more harmful to the royal cause than helpful). Martin's prediction proved to be at least partially correct because the threat of a slave insurrection (and/or Indian attacks in the case of frontier counties) usually kept half of a southern county's militia at home. This halved the number of militia from the countryside that could be used freely to reinforce areas threatened by the British. Even prominent southern Whigs admitted that the presence of slaves in the South inhibited their ability to raise troops since many slave owners "were afraid to leave their slaves behind unguarded."[8]

In November 1775 Lord George Germain took over the post of secretary of state for the American colonies from Dartmouth. Germain had fought as a major at Minden, but after an ignominious retreat he resigned from the army in disgrace. After clawing his way back into the political graces, Germain finally earned enough favor with the king to be appointed to a ministerial position in the government. Germain approved of Martin's and Dartmouth's plans for a southern expedition. In December of that year Germain sent the following secret communiqué to royal authorities in America: "An armament consisting of seven regiments, with a fleet of frigates and small ships, is now in readiness to proceed to the southern Colonies, in order to attempt the restoration of legal Government in that part of America. It will proceed, in the first place, to North

Carolina, and from thence either to South-Carolina or Virginia, as circumstances of greater or less advantage shall point out."[9]

Writing in 1903, the British historian Sir John Fortescue was highly critical of British policy makers staking the fate of America on promises of Loyalist support: "It was therefore concluded that the mere presence of British troops in certain quarters would be sufficient to rally the entire population to the royal standard; and it was resolved in effect to base the military operations on the presumed support of a section of the inhabitants. Of all the foundations whereon to build the conduct of a campaign this is the loosest, the most treacherous, the fullest of peril and delusion; yet, as shall be seen in the years before us, there is none that has been in more favour with British ministers, with the invariable consequence of failure and disaster."[10]

Fortescue's analysis is of course correct, but at the time Lord Dartmouth and Lord Germain had little reason not to trust the opinions of Martin and the other royal governors who had, after all, spent years governing and living in the American southern provinces. Major General Henry Clinton was appointed commander of the southern expedition. He was ordered to sail from Boston with only a small escort and link up off Cape Fear with the main fleet from England carrying over two thousand troops.

Germain told Clinton that, after securing North Carolina, he was at liberty to pursue the campaign into South Carolina or Virginia as he saw fit. "If you should think fit to proceed first to Virginia," Lord Germain wrote, "the whole plan of your operations must be directed by such information and opinion as you shall receive from Lord Dunmore whose knowledge of the state of that province will be of great use and advantage to you."[11] Following his orders, Clinton scheduled a visit to Virginia on his way south from Boston. The British general would find, however, that by the time he met with Governor Dunmore off the coast near Norfolk, the situation in Virginia had ceased to be favorable to the British cause.

---TWO---

Great Bridge

THE BATTLE FOR NORFOLK

"Boys! Stand to your arms!"

GEORGE WASHINGTON warned Congress in late 1775 that "the fate of America a good deal depends on [the British] being obliged to evacuate Norfolk this winter."[1] The American commander in chief knew that Norfolk, the wealthiest and most populous city in Virginia, possessed many unique advantages for the British in America. With over six thousand inhabitants in 1775, Norfolk was the second-largest city (Charlestown was the largest) in all the southern colonies. Most important, Norfolk had a reputation as a Loyalist stronghold. The town's commerce was dominated by Scottish merchants from Glasgow who benefited from the trade produced by Britain's system of mercantilism. Norfolk sits on the south bank of the James River, just inside the Chesapeake Bay. Being protected by the river to the north and the morass of the Great Dismal Swamp to the south, the town seemed a safe gathering place for Virginia Loyalists who were otherwise outnumbered and overawed by their Whig opponents. General Washington understood that if the British were allowed to fortify and garrison Norfolk, it would be difficult for the Americans to dislodge them, and the British could then use the city as a base for military operations in the South.

A mere eight months before Washington penned his cautionary note to Congress about the importance of Norfolk, America was not even at war. It was only in March 1775 that the Virginia House of Burgesses resolved to put the colony "into a posture of defense" after hearing Patrick Henry's defining "Liberty or Death" oratory. At the time of the Revolution, Virginia's government was dominated by a political faction known as Whigs, as were most of Britain's colonial governments in America. The Whigs favored limiting the authority of the king and his ministers in favor of democratic institutions such as the British Parliament and elected colonial legislatures. The Tory faction was more conservative and gave greater support to Crown rule. Virginia's Whig legislators voted to mobilize the colony's military by establishing sixteen "Minute" battalions of militia (based on sixteen recruiting districts) and two regiments of professional troops. John Murray, the royal governor of Virginia and Earl of Dunmore (better

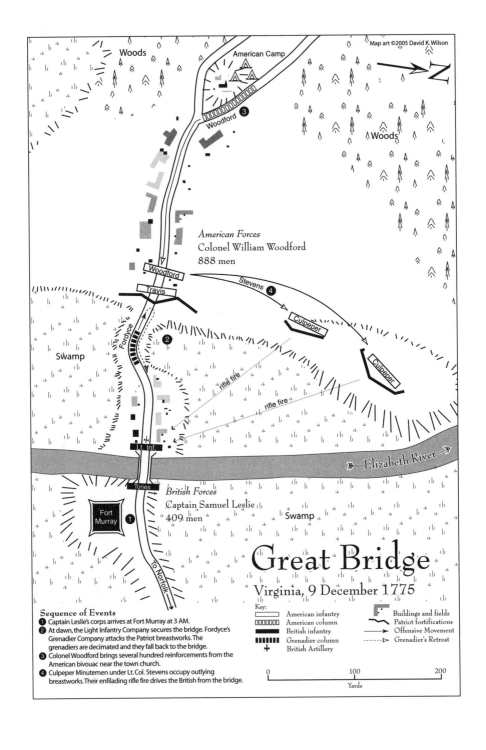

Map art ©2005 David K. Wilson

Woods

American Camp

Woods

Woodford ③

Woods

American Forces
Colonel William Woodford
888 men

Woodford

Stevens ④

Travis

Culpeper

Fordyce

Swamp

②

Culpeper

rifle fire

rifle fire

Lt. Inf.

Elizabeth River

Tories

British Forces
Captain Samuel Leslie
409 men

Swamp

Fort
Murray ①

Great Bridge

Virginia, 9 December 1775

To Norfolk

Sequence of Events
① Captain Leslie's corps arrives at Fort Murray at 3 AM.
② At dawn, the Light Infantry Company secures the bridge. Fordyce's
   Grenadier Company attacks the Patriot breastworks. The
   grenadiers are decimated and they fall back to the bridge.
③ Colonel Woodford brings several hundred reinforcements from the
   American bivouac near the town church.
④ Culpeper Minutemen under Lt. Col. Stevens occupy outlying
   breastworks. Their enfilading rifle fire drives the British from the bridge.

Key:
▭▭▭ American infantry
▢▢▢▢ American column
▬▬▬ British infantry
▮▮▮▮ Grenadier column
✚ British Artillery

◥ Buildings and fields
∿ Patriot fortifications
→ Offensive Movement
----▷ Grenadier's Retreat

0   100   200
          Yards

known as Lord Dunmore), was convinced by the actions of the House of Burgesses that Virginia Whigs were already in rebellion against the Crown.

In an attempt to deny the Whigs access to the colony's military stores, Lord Dunmore sent a party of Royal Marines to seize a depot of gunpowder in the capital of Williamsburg on the night of 20–21 April 1775. The marines successfully secreted the powder out of the city and put it aboard a vessel of the Royal Navy offshore. This powder raid occurred only one day after General Thomas Gage, the governor of Massachusetts, attempted the same maneuver at Lexington and Concord with less successful results. Gage's men met with stiff resistance, with the ensuing battles igniting the Revolutionary War. While Lord Dunmore's action at Williamsburg did not result in bloodshed, it did rouse the Whigs of Virginia to arms.

Within a week Patrick Henry, now a colonel in the colonial militia, had assembled Whig troops at Williamsburg and demanded the return of the powder that Dunmore had taken. The governor reacted to Henry's impertinent demands with the declaration that "if an insult is offered to me or to those who have obeyed my orders, I will declare freedom to the slaves and lay the town in ashes!"[2] Despite his imperious rhetoric, Dunmore was ill prepared to confront Henry at that time, having only a handful of soldiers available to defend the royal government. Eventually the governor compromised with the Whigs by agreeing to pay the colonial treasury for the powder. Patrick Henry soon left military service to serve a term in Congress, and thereafter he became the first governor of the independent state of Virginia.

Tensions in Williamsburg continued to intensify between Lord Dunmore and the Whig legislators. On 8 June 1775 the governor, "fearing personal violence," left the capital. He took his family to Yorktown, where they boarded the Royal Navy vessel *Fowey* in the York River.[3] Dunmore's flight from Williamsburg effectively terminated royal government in the colony, and from that moment onward Virginia acted as an independent state. Soon after, on 16 June 1775, the first set-piece battle of the war was fought on Bunker Hill, overlooking Boston harbor. It was a sanguinary fight that eliminated any hope that the disagreements between England and the American colonies could be resolved without war. Friction in Virginia continued to increase until October 1775, when a storm blew a small ship of the Royal Navy ashore on the north bank of the James River near the town of Hampton. A swarm of opportunistic Patriots quickly descended on the hapless vessel, which they immediately plundered and burned. Dunmore retaliated by sending a naval task force to attack Hampton.

On hearing reports that British ships were threatening Hampton, the Virginia legislature ordered troops to the defense of the town. This force consisted of Colonel William Woodford's four-hundred-man 2nd Virginia Regiment, reinforced by about one hundred Culpeper County Minutemen. The Culpeper men were backwoods riflemen and sharpshooters of renown; they were also conspicuous for having Patrick Henry's motto "Liberty or Death" emblazoned in large, stark white stitches on their buckskin shirts. It is also worth mentioning that the future first Chief Justice of the Supreme Court, John Marshall, and his father were volunteers in the Culpeper Minute battalion.

The militia was the force of citizen-soldiers on which America depended for the bulk of its military. The British tended to dismiss the colonial militia as rabble. English officers generally believed that the militia, drilling infrequently and lacking adequate arms, could never hold their own against the well-equipped, professional soldiers of the British army. British regulars lived and breathed the art of war, and most of the red-coated soldiers served for life. To address the deficiencies of the normal militia, the New England colonies created an elite class of militia called "minutemen." In this way they hoped to produce a force capable of confronting British regulars. Minutemen were still citizen-soldiers—not professionals—but they drilled frequently and could therefore be ready for combat on a "minute's" notice. The Culpeper battalion was perhaps one of the finest units of minutemen fielded in the early days of the Revolution.

Captain Matthew Squire, commander of the Royal Navy squadron in the Chesapeake, led a small flotilla of four armed "tenders"—small craft used to shuttle supplies between the shore and larger ships—to the waters off Hampton on 24 October 1775. Captain Squire spent most of the 24th trading ineffective gunshots with the rebels on Hampton's shore while his men cleared a path through the debris-blocked harbor. On the morning of 25 October, Squire maneuvered his vessels into Hampton harbor and opened fire on the town. Squire intended to soften up the town with a cannonade and then land raiding parties under the protection of his ships' guns. However, when Squire's vessels came within musket and rifle range, Woodford's regiment and the Culpeper riflemen unleashed a withering fire against them. The Virginians shot several sailors dead and pinned down the ships' remaining complements.[4] Captain Squire made a judicious retreat, but not before one of his tenders drifted within the range of the riflemen ashore. Under a devastating fusillade of rifle shots, several sailors abandoned the hapless ship and swam to Captain Squire's flagship to seek safety. The rest of the tender's crew surrendered when a party of Woodford's regiment waded into the shallow water to seize the vessel.[5]

Dunmore was enraged and embarrassed by the setback at Hampton. To retaliate against the Whigs, the furious governor declared martial law on 7 November and announced the emancipation of all slaves in Virginia who would serve in Crown armies. Dunmore had declared war on the Virginia Whigs, but his emancipation proclamation stunned *all* Virginians, including the colony's loyal Tories. Slave owning is recognized today as an obviously cruel and immoral institution; but at the time of the Revolution it was practiced in all of England's colonies and many other nations around the world. In the American South, politically powerful slave owners perceived Dunmore's emancipation as an affront to their property rights. Dunmore's impolitic announcement therefore alienated many slave-owning Tories who might otherwise have supported the royal cause. In addition, Dunmore did not merely free the slaves—he sought to arm them against their former Whig masters. There was no more frightening scenario for white southerners than that Dunmore would arm the colony's Negroes, and once again Dunmore lost much support among Tories by this action. The reaction of the Whig-controlled Virginia legislature to Dunmore's pronouncements was a swift deployment of troops toward the governor's base at Norfolk.

Part of the 14th Regiment of Foot (Bedfordshire) had recently been assigned to Dunmore. These troops were mostly from the two flank companies, the grenadiers and the light infantry, and were thus the elite soldiers of the regiment.[6] The governor sought to reinforce these professional soldiers by assembling two regiments of Loyalists: one of white Tories called the Queen's Own Loyal Virginia Regiment; the other of blacks called Lord Dunmore's Royal Ethiopians. The irony of the Virginia Whigs' war for "liberty" was that they kept slaves themselves, and this fact was not lost on the blacks of the Ethiopian Regiment. They sought to remind their opponents of the paradox of their position by stitching on their uniforms the words "Liberty to Slaves." This satirical derivative of Patrick Henry's battle cry was also meant to hold up an ironic mirror to the uniforms of the Culpeper Minutemen.

Running south from Norfolk was the primary road between Virginia and North Carolina. This road formed the only practical landward route into and out of town because it lay atop a narrow strip of relatively dry ground that threaded its way through the great Dismal Swamp, which lay south of the city. A little village called Great Bridge lay on this vital causeway about nine miles from Norfolk. The town's namesake bridge was the best means of communication over the south branch of the Elizabeth River. Dunmore said that Great Bridge "is by nature a very strong pass and the only one by which they can enter Princess Anne County by land and a great part of Norfolk County. I immediately ordered a fort to be erected there and put an officer with 25 [soldiers] of the 14th regiment to garrison it."[7] The fort was built on the east bank of the river in position to cover the bridge. The soldiers removed the planking of the bridge to help secure their position against attack.

The village of Great Bridge consisted of only about twenty buildings west of the river, with the most prominent structure being a church at the west end of town. The bridge was of simple wood rail and plank construction, about forty yards long. While touring the town in 1848, the historian Benson Lossing wrote, "Great Bridge is the name for a comparatively insignificant structure, unless the causeways connected with it may be included in the term."[8]

Moving to confront Dunmore, Colonel Woodford crossed the James River and established his camp at Great Bridge across the river from the British fort on 2 December 1775. The English had named their little stronghold Fort Murray in honor of the governor (John Murray, Earl of Dunmore). Woodford described the structure as a "stockade fort" mounting "two four pounders, some swivells & Wall Peices [*sic*];" his men derisively called it the "hog pen."[9]

Colonel Woodford, commanding close to seven hundred men, initially considered mounting an assault on the British position, but he instead settled on fortifying the ground west of the bridge. "The Enemy's Fort, I think, might have been taken," Woodford wrote, "but not without the loss of many of our Men; their Situation is very advantageous, & no way to Attack them but by exposing most of the Troops to their Fire upon a large open Marsh."[10]

Woodford estimated the British garrison at 250 regulars. There were actually only about 40 to 80 men in the fort, these being a mixture of regulars, white Tories, and blacks of the Ethiopian Regiment.[11] Over the next few days the British burned the homes closest to the fort to allow for a clear field of fire for both their cannons and small arms. During this time the Patriot troops skirmished with the garrison but did not attempt any assault. The situation was thus a stalemate. Both sides were in good defensive positions, but neither party believed that they had the means to press an effective attack.

Colonel Woodford was not sure how to proceed. Reinforcements were arriving from both Virginia and North Carolina, but few came with weapons and none with supplies; so rather than being a help, the additional men only added to Woodford's already difficult logistic situation. The Patriots had the upper hand numerically, but they were ill-equipped and inexperienced, and they lacked ammunition and supplies. Woodford protested to the Virginia legislature that many of his muskets were "rather to be considered as lumber, than fit to be put in men's hands."[12] The Carolinians had brought cannons, but they were not operational because they had no mountings or carriages. Along with everything else, a rumor had spread that 500 Scottish Highlanders had recently reinforced Dunmore. The "Highlanders" were actually 120 families (about 300 people including women and children) of peaceable Scottish émigrés. A rebel spy later described them as "very poor Raw creatures [knowing] Nothing of the Gun nor Sword"; but Colonel Woodford, lacking this intelligence at the time, had to take the threat seriously.[13]

As poor as the American position seemed to be, the British soldiers were no better off—and maybe worse. Fort Murray had only a few lightweight cannons, and the structure was isolated and far removed from the main defenses being erected around Norfolk. The fort's garrison was outnumbered by the Americans, who were receiving reinforcements regularly. Lord Dunmore received intelligence indicating that the Americans had procured artillery, but he did not know the guns were not operational. Afraid that the Americans would blow Fort Murray to bits with their cannons, the governor decided that he had to act quickly to attack Great Bridge and drive the Americans out: "Being informed that the Rebels had procured some cannon from North Carolina, and they were also to be reinforced from Williamsburg, and knowing that our little Fort was not in a condition to withstand any thing heavier than a Musquet shot, I thought it advisable to risque something to save the Fort."[14]

Dunmore concocted a straightforward plan to defeat the Americans. Several companies of the Ethiopian Regiment would make a demonstration downstream to lure the Patriot soldiers away from their fortifications. While Colonel Woodford was distracted by the feint, the British regulars would launch a frontal assault against the American earthworks and then drive Woodford's soldiers from the town. Captain Samuel Leslie of the 14th Regiment was the most senior British military officer in Virginia and so had charge of the operation. He commanded all the regular troops in the city, which primarily consisted of the light infantry and grenadier companies of the 14th Regiment —roughly 163 effectives of which about 120 were available for duty.[15] The light infantry company was designated to lead the crossing of the bridge, while the grenadiers were detailed to mount the assault on the rebel earthworks. Supporting the regulars were approximately 230 former slaves and white Tories from the two provincial battalions. Captain

Squire donated a handful of Royal Navy gunners to service the two four-pounders that accompanied the sortie. The British attack force therefore totaled roughly 400 troops including supporting militia. Dunmore had told the regulars that they could expect only 300 Virginia "shirtmen" to oppose them.[16] However, Woodford's command had actually accrued by this time to about 900, with 760 fit for duty.[17]

⟫⟫◆⟪⟪

Captain Leslie's column left Norfolk the night of 8 December 1775, arriving at Great Bridge at about three o'clock the next morning. However, things started to go wrong immediately. "By some mistake," the two companies of black soldiers that were supposed to mount the diversionary attack were not at the fort.[18] The Ethiopian companies had made a routine tactical redeployment to another pass on the river, but no one had informed Dunmore in Norfolk, nor had Dunmore sent any orders to the Ethiopians notifying them ahead of time of their role in the upcoming attack. It was a bilateral communications failure. The diversion was a key element of the planned attack, but no one was available to execute it. Captain Leslie made a bold decision to continue with the operation anyway.

Having marched nine miles overnight, Leslie rested his men on the east side of the river until just before dawn. At first light, the light infantry replaced the missing planks on the bridge and crossed the river. After establishing a bridgehead on the west bank, the light infantrymen were joined by the navy gunners, who placed their two four-pounders in front of the bridge facing the rebel earthworks. Somehow all this activity went undetected by the Americans in the dim light of the early dawn.

Once the bridge was secure, the light infantry held their position while Captain Charles Fordyce[19] led the sixty-man grenadier company of the 14th Foot across the bridge and toward the American camp. The Tory reserve, under Captain Leslie's personal command, took up position at the bridge to hold open the vital link with the fort and Norfolk. The Patriot works were protected by impassable swamps accessible only by the narrow road leading from the bridge. A British officer described the situation with dismay: "Figure to yourself a strong breastwork built across a causeway, on which six men only could advance abreast; a large swamp almost surrounded them, at the back of which were two small breastworks to flank us in our attack on their intrenchments [*sic*]. Under these disadvantages it was impossible to succeed."[20]

The grenadiers advanced in narrow column down the causeway. About halfway to the breastworks they came upon a three-man American picket. The picket briefly skirmished with a British platoon and then fell back toward the American earthworks. The picket men had done their duty, however, having both slowed the British advance and given the Americans warning of the attack by the sound of their guns firing.

Major Alexander Spotswood, one of Woodford's officers, was in his tent just getting up when he heard the sound of the skirmishing. Assuming that it was merely the customary "morning salute" the British discharged to greet them each dawn, the major did not take serious note of the gunfire until he heard a fellow officer cry out, "Boys! Stand to your arms!"[21] The Americans were surprised, but this British advantage was negated because the attack came just after a Patriot drummer had completed beating reveille. "Lucky time for us," Woodford said later, "all our men must be under arms."[22]

The distance from the bridge to the Patriot breastworks was 160 yards. Lieutenant Travis commanded sixty men in the forward earthworks. Watching the red column snake its way down the road toward his position, Travis told his troops to open fire when the enemy was at 50 yards. Once the grenadiers reached that mark, Travis's men unleashed a deadly fusillade that ripped apart the front ranks of the British column. The grenadiers who survived the first volley staggered and hesitated. Captain Fordyce knew that his only hope was to close with the rebels so his troops could employ their bayonets and overrun the American breastwork. In the best tradition of his profession, the captain took his hat off, waved it above his head, and rushed forward. The grenadiers struggled down the narrow road after their captain, but the weight of fire was too much for them. Fordyce took his first bullet in the knee. After falling he stood back up and shouted at his troops to remember their regiment's "ancient glory" and that "the day was their own."[23] The brave captain came to within fifteen steps of the earthwork before a rebel bullet felled him a second time. He did not rise again. Many Americans later expressed admiration for Fordyce. One American newspaper said that the captain's death "would have been that of a hero had he met it in a better cause."[24] Colonel Woodford also wrote of Fordyce with respect: "Captain Fordyce, of the Grenadiers, led the van with his company, who for coolness and bravery, deserved a better fate, as well as the brave fellows who fell with him, who behaved like heroes. They marched up to our breastwork with fixed bayonets, and perhaps a hotter fire never happened or a greater carnage, for the number of troops."[25]

With Fordyce dead, the attack disintegrated under a hail of Patriot musket balls. Over half the grenadiers had fallen killed or severely wounded, and of those who still stood nearly all had been wounded. These brave men reluctantly gave up the assault and returned to the bridge where Captain Leslie was attempting to reform for another attack.

Not more than ninety men of Woodford's regiment had engaged the enemy up to this time. Lying before them were more than fifteen British dead and at least as many wounded. The British cannons provided covering fire for the retiring grenadiers, but the small guns had little effect on the Patriot earthworks. Seeing that the British were attempting to reform, Colonel Woodford ran to retrieve reinforcements. Most of the small Patriot army was bivouacked in and about the church, which was four hundred yards away at the other end of town. Once at the church, Woodford gathered hundreds of Virginia and Carolina troops behind him and led the march back to the front. As the large American column came into view from the bridge, it was immediately bombarded with fire from British cannons and small arms, and the Americans answered in kind. The effective range of an eighteenth-century musket was about eighty yards, but the two sides were exchanging fire from well over one hundred. Thus, neither side suffered any casualties despite the impressive display generated by the discharge of hundreds of muskets.

Woodford had to face the dilemma of how to press the advantage he had gained. If he advanced down the narrow road to attack the British at the bridge, his troops would face the same disadvantages—and probably meet the same fate—that the grenadiers had met minutes earlier. The decision was therefore made to use the crack-shot Culpeper riflemen. Lieutenant Colonel Edward Stevens led one hundred of his minutemen in a daring dash across exposed ground to occupy some of the Patriots' outlying fortifications north of the main works.

Once in position, the minutemen rained rifle fire on the right flank of the British forces. The Pennsylvania rifles that the Culpeper men carried had more than twice the effective range of the redcoats' smoothbore muskets. Thus, the British infantry was unable to respond to this new threat effectively, while the two small cannons being served by the sailors could not suppress a hundred riflemen firing from behind earthworks. As the British troops began to suffer more casualties, Captain Leslie ordered the Tory militia and what remained of the 14th Regiment to fall back to the fort. They left behind most of their dead as well as many of their wounded. The navy gunners abandoned their two fieldpieces on the American side of the bridge, but only after spiking the guns.[26] A few American officers urged an immediate counterattack against the demoralized British, but Woodford—still wary of the difficulties inherent in assaulting the British fort—refused. He also feared that the rumored Highlanders might be waiting nearby. The American commander therefore decided to hold up and wait for reinforcements. The battle was over.

Based on the amount of "blood on the bridge," Major Spotswood believed that the British had lost half their men.[27] Woodford reported recovering 15 dead and 18 wounded on the field.[28] An American spy reported British losses at 102 killed and wounded; this same source claimed that when Dunmore received news of the defeat, "He raved like the mad man he is, & swore to hang the boy who gave him the information [of the supposed weakness of the American forces]."[29] Dunmore officially reported 17 dead and 44 wounded in the 14th Regiment, but he failed to report the casualties among the Tories, if there were any.[30] In any case, the losses were severe for the regulars, who sustained 61 casualties out of a starting force of 120 men fit for duty—a staggering casualty rate of over 50 percent. Including the two Tory regiments, however, the overall British casualty rate was about 15 percent.

The Americans went to great lengths to aid the British wounded; in fact, Woodford's men deserve as much credit for their humanity as for their courage under fire. During the action several Patriot soldiers left the breastwork and braved British gunfire to bring to safety fallen grenadiers, who they feared would perish without immediate aid from a surgeon. One wounded grenadier, seeing a Whig soldier rushing toward him, cried out "For God's sake, do not murder us!"[31] The American simply placed the grenadier's arm around his own neck and carried the man to safety. Woodford's men suffered almost no casualties. "I have the pleasure to inform you," Woodford proclaimed in a letter to Patrick Henry, "that the victory was complete. . . . This was a second Bunker's Hill affair, in miniature, with this difference, that we kept our post and had only one man wounded in the hand."[32]

—————◆•◆————

Great Bridge was one of many small but important battles fought early in the Revolution. Compared to the titanic clashes of later American conflicts, many Revolutionary War engagements seem like war in miniature. The small number of casualties at Great Bridge, for example, would not warrant mention in most Civil War battles, where casualty counts often reached into the tens of thousands. However, the import of military actions should not be judged simply by the volume of blood spilt, but by their influence on subsequent events. It should be noted that in the Revolutionary War both sides had great difficulties in deploying large numbers of men into the field. America was a young country at the time without a strong central government and no central taxing authority. It therefore had little means to put men in uniform. Britain likewise had to project its power across the sea and had to protect its many other colonies around the globe. These problems naturally inhibited Britain's ability to deploy large armies in North America except with great effort.

In 1789 David Ramsay—one of America's first historians and a prominent southern Patriot—made some cogent remarks regarding the scale of Revolutionary War battles:

> To those who are acquainted with European wars, [the size of American Revolutionary War battles] must appear inconsiderable, but such is the difference in the state of society and of the population in the old and new world, that in America, a few hundreds decided objects of equal magnitude with those, which in Europe would have called into the field as many thousands. The prize contended for was nothing less than the Sovereignty of three millions of people, and of five hundred millions of acres of land, and yet from the remote situation of the invading powers, and the thin population of the invaded States, especially in the southern extreme of the union, this momentous question was materially affected by the consequences of battles, in which only a few hundreds engaged.[33]

This is not to say that there were not any large battles in the South. The siege of Savannah in 1779 involved over twelve thousand men, while the siege of Charlestown in 1780 had almost twenty thousand combatants. Yet, the small skirmish at Great Bridge was the decisive action for control of Norfolk—the largest and most important city in Virginia. The cream of the 14th Regiment of Foot, the only body of regular troops the British had in the South, had been decimated. With a growing American presence, there was nothing left for Dunmore to do now but evacuate. That evening Leslie spiked the guns at Fort Murray and immediately withdrew his men to Norfolk. Two days later most of Dunmore's little army evacuated the city for the safety of the ships of the Royal Navy in the Chesapeake Bay. The soldiers were soon joined by many of Norfolk's Tory civilians who sought to escape the advancing rebels.

Most historians have been highly critical of Dunmore's decision to attack. However, given his limited information regarding the American artillery, the governor's action was bold but not unreasonable. Dunmore's real mistake was failing to understand until it was too late that the critical pass over the Elizabeth River at Great Bridge was the key to the defense of Norfolk. It was the one spot where the small number of troops under his command could stop the larger Patriot forces from approaching the city. Rather than build a substantial fort at Great Bridge that could withstand rebel cannon fire, Dunmore instead wasted time building extensive fortifications around Norfolk that he could not defend with the limited number of troops at his disposal.

Lord Dunmore blamed Captain Leslie[34] for the debacle at the bridge, accusing him of "imprudently" choosing to proceed with the attack when the troops meant to divert the rebels were not available.[35] While Leslie's decision to continue the operation without the diversion was questionable, it probably would have made little difference given that there were so many more Patriot troops at Great Bridge than Dunmore had expected. In addition, it was Dunmore—a former military officer and the man who planned the operation—who failed to send advance word to the troops intended to make the diversion of their role in his plan.

While Dunmore deflected blame for the disaster, Colonel Robert Howe, commanding the 2nd North Carolina Regiment, arrived to reinforce Woodford. Howe was senior to Woodford and held a commission in the Continental Army. He therefore assumed overall command of the combined American army—somewhat to Colonel Woodford's chagrin. (Woodford would later be made a brigadier general in the Continental Army and would go on to command a brigade of Virginians through many important battles in the war.) The American forces outside Norfolk now numbered close to two thousand men. On 14 December the last British troops remaining in the city evacuated and Colonel Howe took the city without encountering resistance.

For several weeks the Patriots entrenched themselves in Norfolk while the British patrolled the waters around the city. However, on 30 December, Colonel Howe received a communication from the British naval commander, Captain Henry Bellew, informing him that the American troops should "avoid being seen" in the streets. It was a ridiculous request since the Patriots controlled the town. Hinting at his plans, Bellew also told Colonel Howe that he would be wise to evacuate the women and children from the city. Two days later, on 1 January 1776, the Royal Navy began a fierce cannonade of the city. Dunmore sent landing parties to set fire to the docks, from which the American riflemen had been "annoying" passing British vessels. Within a few hours the flames were out of control and the town burned to the ground.

Dunmore, for his part, claimed that he did not intend to burn the entire town. Indeed, it did not make political or strategic sense for him to have done so. However, it did not make sense for the British to have fired on the town at all. Dunmore lacked the strength to retake the city, so to open fire on and burn any part of the town could only be considered desultory and spiteful. Nevertheless, in his frustration Dunmore handed torches to his soldiers, who were equally frustrated and vengeful after a series of defeats in battle. Even if Dunmore is taken at his word that he did not want the whole city burned, he still should have expected the holocaust that followed.[36]

It is also obvious that Captain Bellew, who had only recently arrived to take command of the British naval forces in the Chesapeake, did not understand the complex political landscape in America. Bellew made little distinction between Tory and Whig —all Americans appearing as the enemy to him. Idly drifting in the waters around Norfolk while the enemy impudently sniped at the fleet was unpleasant duty for the Royal Navy, and Captain Bellew was eager to retaliate by firing on Norfolk. After the city was razed, one British naval officer gleefully remarked, "The detested town of Norfolk is no more!"[37] His feelings were certainly not unique in the fleet.

Some believe that, once the conflagration had begun, the Patriots encouraged it. It is likely that at least some Tory-owned shops and homes met with Whig torches that New Year's Day—if only out of misguided retaliation for the British torching of the docks and warehouses. However, Lord Dunmore had repeatedly threatened to leave Virginia's cities "in ashes," and he is the one who sent British soldiers into the city with torches. In addition, Captain Bellew had threatened several times to destroy the town before he began his cannonade on 1 January 1776. Ultimately, the British must bear the responsibility for the destruction of the city.

The loss of Norfolk had terrible consequences for the British. Though Lord Dunmore had only achieved minor success in recruiting both black slaves and white Tories into loyal militia regiments, given more time and support Norfolk might have been made into a formidable Tory stronghold. Had the royal governor managed to hold Norfolk only a few months longer until Major General Henry Clinton arrived in March 1776 with additional troops, Washington's warning of terrible consequences for America might have come true. As it was, by the time Clinton arrived in Virginia he found Dunmore's situation irrecoverable: "Driven from the shore, and the whole country in arms against him, I could not see the use of His Lordship's remaining longer there, especially after the failure of his attack . . . at the Great Bridge."[38]

Nevertheless, Clinton did see the potential of the region around Norfolk as a base for future British operations and as a refuge for Loyalists. Clinton made up his mind that operations in Virginia would someday prove advantageous for Britain—though it would be many years before an opportunity to launch such operations arose again. For now, Clinton had more immediate concerns. He took his leave of Lord Dunmore and headed south for Cape Fear, North Carolina. Dunmore derided this course of action, calling North Carolina "a most insignificant province." The governor argued that Virginia was the "first colony on the continent both for its riches and power," and thus should have been first on Clinton's list for aid.[39]

Events at Norfolk foreshadowed the difficulty the British would have in getting southern Loyalists to turn out in significant numbers to fight for the king. After all, there were six thousand inhabitants of Norfolk, and both sides agreed that most of them were Loyalists. Why did only a few hundred men volunteer for service in Dunmore's regiments? Dunmore claimed that more than three thousand Tories in the Norfolk area had signed loyalty oaths, but he also admitted that only a small portion of this number was capable of bearing arms. By contrast, the Patriots had little problem getting thousands of arms-bearing men to come forth and serve in the American military establishment. It can therefore be concluded that there were fewer Loyalists in the Norfolk area than either side calculated, or that the Virginia Tories lacked the same fighting spirit and motivation that their Whig counterparts possessed.

Surprisingly, Dunmore was undeterred by the lackluster Tory turnout. Instead he believed that alleged Patriot oppression of Tories in Princess Anne and Norfolk counties would create a favorable environment for Tory recruitment at some future date.

Shortly after the battle Dunmore wrote, "I only want a few troops to ensure them [the Loyalists] of protection, [then] I am sure numbers would flock to the King's standard."[40]

In the spring of 1776, driven from Norfolk and having received no aid from Clinton, Dunmore chose to establish a small base at Gwynn Island—about five hundred yards off the banks of the Rappahannock River inside Chesapeake Bay. From there he stubbornly continued to launch nuisance raids against the Virginia Patriots until he was driven from the post on 8 July 1776. As a parting insult, Dunmore suffered a painful gunshot wound to the knee during the withdrawal from the island. Finally admitting the futility of his remaining in Virginia, Dunmore sailed north to join the main British fleet off the coast of New York. After depositing with General Howe those few ships and troops he commanded, Dunmore left for England, never to return to America. Virginia was secure for the Americans and would not again be the seat of war for several years to come.

ORDER OF BATTLE: GREAT BRIDGE

Virginia, 9 December 1775

American Forces[41]
Col. William Woodford

	MEN	ARTILLERY
2nd Virginia Regiment—Col. Wm. Woodford	396	
1st Battalion, Culpeper Minutemen—		
Lt. Col. Edward Stevens	287	
North Carolina Volunteer Militia	178	
Total	**861**	**0**

British Forces[42]
Capt. Samuel Leslie

	MEN	ARTILLERY
14th Regiment of Foot—Capt. Samuel Leslie	169	
Light Infantry Company		
Grenadier Company—		
Capt. Charles Fordyce		
Tories	230	
Queen's Own Loyal Virginians		
Lord Dunmore's Royal Ethiopians		
Royal Navy gunners (4-lb. cannon)	10	2
Total	**409**	**2**

Casualties[43]

	AMERICAN	BRITISH
Killed	–	17
Wounded & Captured	1	44
Missing	–	–
Total	**1**	**61**

Order of Battle: Great Bridge (*continued*)

**American Forces Occupying Norfolk,
  29 December 1775 (not engaged)**[44]

Col. Robert Howe

	MEN	ARTILLERY
2nd North Carolina Continental Regiment—Col. Robert Howe	421	
2nd Virginia Regiment—Col. William Woodford	376	
1st Virginia Regiment (detachment)	206	
1st Battalion, Culpeper Minutemen (detachment)—Lt. Col. Edward Stevens	164	
Southern District Minute Battalion	197	
Total	**1,364**	?

THREE

Moore's Creek Bridge

"King George and Broadswords!"

THE YEAR 1775 had been a disagreeable one for Josiah Martin, the royal governor of North Carolina. As in every other British colony in America (except Canada and Florida), North Carolina's Whig legislators had usurped control from Crown authorities. In late May 1775 Governor Martin became fearful that the ever more belligerent Whigs would arrest him. He decided to abandon the gubernatorial mansion in New Bern for the safety of a British man-of-war offshore. However, the fact that he had fled did not mean that Martin had given up.

In early January 1776—only a few days after Norfolk, Virginia, had burned to the ground—Governor Martin received a letter from Lord Germain informing him that Martin's plan to reassert Crown rule over North Carolina had been approved. The letter, dated 1 November 1775, said that an expedition of seven regiments of regulars (over two thousand men) would depart for America from Cork, Ireland. Per Martin's request, the fleet carried ten thousand muskets to arm the thousands of Loyalist he had promised to provide. Martin had already received some aid from General William Howe in Boston in the form of several Scottish officers and a large war chest to pay new recruits. To fulfill his part of the bargain, the governor planned to make use of two disaffected segments of the Carolina population: Highland Scots immigrants and an enigmatic group of settlers who called themselves "Regulators."

Governor Martin felt confident that he could rely on the Highlanders to support the royal government: "I could collect immediately among the emigrants from the Highlands of Scotland who are settled here and immovably attached to His Majesty and his government, that I am assured by the best authority I may compute at 3,000 men; but should be able to draw together under that protection out of the interior counties of this province, where the people are in general well-affected and much attached to me, at least two-thirds of the fighting men in the whole country, which may be computed according to my best information to exceed thirty thousand."[1]

In other words, Governor Martin believed that twenty thousand men of gun-bearing age were Loyalists, and of this number his agents inside Loyalist communities had already

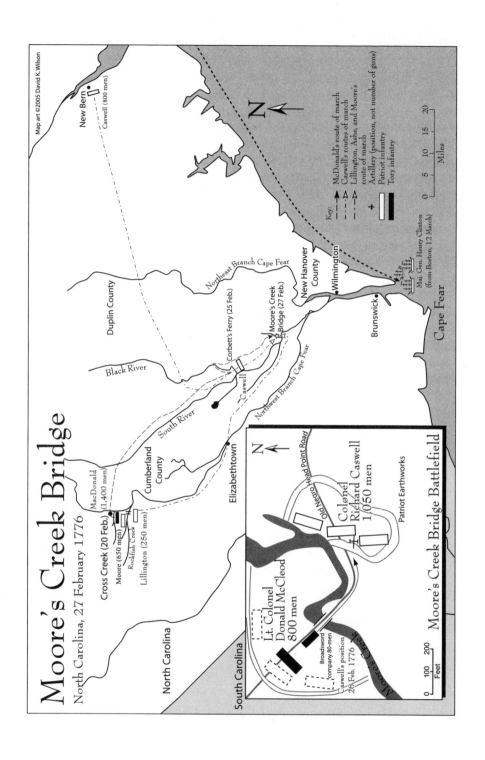

Moore's Creek Bridge

North Carolina, 27 February 1776

Map art ©2005 David K. Wilson

New Bern

Caswell (800 men)

North Carolina

Duplin County

Northeast Branch Cape Fear

New Hanover County

Wilmington

Brunswick

Cape Fear

Maj. Gen. Henry Clinton
(from Boston, 12 March)

Black River

Corbett's Ferry (25 Feb.)

Moore's Creek
Bridge (27 Feb.)

Caswell

Northwest Branch Cape Fear

South River

MacDonald
(1,400 men)

Cross Creek (20 Feb.)

Moore (650 men)

Rockfish Creek

Lillington (250 men)

Cumberland County

Elizabethtown

Key:
McDonald's route of march
Caswell's routes of march
Lillington, Ashe, and Moore's
route of march
Artillery (position, not number of guns)
Patriot infantry
Tory infantry

0   5   10   15   20
Miles

Moore's Creek Bridge Battlefield

South Carolina

North Carolina

N

Old Negro Head Point Road

Lt. Colonel
Donald McLeod
800 men

Broadsword
company 80-men

Caswell's position
26 Feb. 1776

Colonel
Richard Caswell
1,050 men

Patriot Earthworks

Moore's Creek

0   100 200
Feet

promised that three thousand would be ready when called. The fact that Martin asked for ten thousand muskets to be sent from England indicates his expectation that at least seven thousand more Loyalists could eventually be recruited to serve under the king's banner. To explain why Martin thought he would find so much support in the back-country requires a brief examination of the geopolitical map of the Carolinas in the 1770s.

Revolutionary politics in the Carolinas was linked to the region's three geographic regions: the tidewater, the piedmont, and the frontier. The tidewater is the fertile, swamp-ridden land near the coast; the piedmont[2] or backcountry is a vast, relatively flat inland region that lies between the tidewater and the mountains; while the frontier consisted of the Blue Ridge chain of the Appalachians and the "over-the-mountain" or back-water region. The region was called "backwater" because the rivers to the east of the mountains flowed east to the Atlantic, while rivers to the west of the mountains flowed west, or "back" toward the Mississippi drainage basin. To oversimplify the political situation in 1776: the tidewater was mostly Patriot; the piedmont had a large Loyalist population (but also had many Patriots); and the frontier was almost entirely Patriot.

The modern aphorism that "all politics are local politics,"[3] was as true in the eighteenth century as it is today and helps explain the political leanings of the various regions. When the British government attempted to impose its will on the colonists with regard to taxes and trade, the tidewater-dominated southern legislatures immediately resisted. The merchant classes of the coastal cities did not like the rules and restrictions that Britain's mercantile system placed on their trade. Therefore, the tidewater population tended to be Patriots. Likewise, the frontiersmen of the mountain areas were almost universally Patriots. Their dislike of royal government was based on favorable British policies toward the Indians and limits on colonial westward expansion set up by the Proclamation of 1763. The over-the-mountain men were determined to settle and expand the western frontier, regardless of royal proclamations.

In between the frontier and the tidewater was the piedmont or backcountry. Many backcountry citizens felt neglected by the tidewater-dominated legislatures. Lawless-ness was rampant in the backcountry, and yet the problem was ignored by those in power on the coasts. At the same time the backcountry settlements bore the brunt of keeping the Indian nations in check—something the backcountry settlers felt that the tidewater elites failed to appreciate. In the late 1760s thousands of piedmont citizens of both Carolinas banded together in loosely organized paramilitary groups known as the Regulators in order to restore order to the backcountry. However, the Regulators did much more than chase out lawless elements; soon they were combating the legal authority of the tidewater-dominated legislature and courts. They arbitrarily stopped foreclosures and other legal proceedings against fellow Regulators and sent several judges packing for the coast.

William Tryon, the royal governor of North Carolina in 1771, called up the colonial militia to restore the authority of legal government in the backcountry. On 16 May 1771 Tryon crushed the Regulators at the Battle of Alamance Court House. Though defeated, the former Regulators remained a significant dissatisfied bloc within the colony at the time of the Revolution. Also, while it was a royal governor who put down the Regulators, it was perceived that he was acting in the interests of the tidewater-dominated legislature. (In South Carolina the Regulators dissolved more or less peacefully after internal disputes fractured the movement into competing factions.[4]) When the "time of troubles" came, in the mid-1770s, many—though by no means all—of the former Regulators and backcountry residents saw the revolutionary fervor as being fomented by the merchant classes on the coast. They felt that the tax and trade disputes were distant issues that had little meaning for the average piedmont farmer.[5]

The Highlanders were similarly disaffected with the colony's tidewater-dominated legislature. After the English defeated the last Scottish uprising at Culloden Moor in 1746, many Highland Scots came to settle in North Carolina along the Cape Fear River, where they had received bounties of land in exchange for their service in the British military. "There were plenty of newly arrived Scotsmen in the area, their wrists bearing the scars of the Blood Oath they had taken before coming to America."[6] The town of Cross Creek, deep in the interior of the province, formed the capital of the Scottish enclave. At the time of the Revolution, the Scots were still treated like an alien colony within North Carolina. Like the Regulators, the Highlanders wanted a strong central British government to help check the power of the tidewater-controlled courts and legislature. The common opinion at the time was that the inhabitants of the southern backcountry were "in general warmly attached to the [Crown] government."[7]

For months Governor Martin had been sending spies and agents into the backcountry to organize the Highlanders and Regulators to support the royal cause. In the summer of 1775 the secretary of state for the American colonies, Lord Dartmouth, approved Martin's plan to retake North Carolina using the Highlanders and Regulators. He agreed to send money, Scottish military officers, weapons, and later troops to aid North Carolina's Loyalists in retaking their colony.

Lord George Germain, who succeeded Dartmouth as secretary of state for the American colonies in the fall of 1775, was even more enthusiastic about Governor Martin's proposals. In November 1775 Germain sent a letter to Martin informing him that an expedition of over two thousand regulars was being sent to North Carolina. When Martin received this news in January 1776, he was ecstatic. Martin's own plan had not called for *any* professional troops to support his counterrevolution. Major General Henry Clinton was to command the expedition, which should have been "on its way from Cork from the very beginning of December [1775], or sooner."[8] Given that departure date and an eight-week Atlantic crossing, Martin figured that the expedition would arrive sometime in early February 1776.

With a February arrival date for the expedition in mind, Governor Martin issued a proclamation on 10 January 1776 demanding that all loyal citizens of North Carolina rise in support of the Crown or be declared traitors and rebels. He then called on his agents in the backcountry to rally the loyal inhabitants and bring them to him at Wilmington by 15 February, "or as soon afterwards as might be possible."[9] Martin relied primarily on two men, Alex McLean and Lieutenant Colonel Donald MacDonald, for the success of his plan. Variously reported to be between fifty and eighty years old, MacDonald had been sent to North Carolina by General Gage six months earlier with orders to raise a battalion for the Royal Highland Emigrants Regiment. Alex McLean was a Scotch immigrant who acted as the governor's chief agent provocateur in the backcountry.

McLean and MacDonald organized a secret meeting of the leadership of the Regulators and Highlanders at Cross Creek on 5 February 1776. The Scottish leaders argued that it was best not to assemble their men before 1 March or until the British expedition arrived in the colony, whichever came first. That way they could coordinate with the regular troops and stand a better chance of achieving their goals. However, the Scots were overruled by the representatives of the "country-born" (i.e., American-born) Tories and Regulators, who "insisted upon taking up arms immediately."[10] McLean was disappointed to discover that many of the older, established Scottish families in the colony were unwilling to commit to the royal cause out of fear that they would have their extensive landholdings confiscated by the Patriots. The historian Hugh F. Rankin wrote that the only Scots who would enlist were the "late arrivals and the poor."[11] As a result, the Highlanders could only promise to contribute six hundred to seven hundred men. The Tory and Regulator leaders said that they could make up the deficit, declaring that "instead of the 3,000 they promised, they made themselves sure of bringing 5,000 men to the field, and that they even then had 500 men in a body."[12]

At the end of the meeting, the leaders of the Regulators took their leave of the Scots and, after promising to return in a few days with their troops, disappeared into the backcountry. Donald MacDonald then raised the royal standard and issued a proclamation calling for all the king's loyal subjects to gather at Cross Creek. Though MacDonald held the commission of a lieutenant colonel in the Royal Army, Governor Martin promoted him to the local rank of brigadier general in charge of all Loyalist military forces in North Carolina. It was believed that MacDonald, who had commanded a contingent fighting the British at Culloden in 1746, had the necessary military prestige to rally and lead the Carolina Highlanders. Perhaps more important than his résumé, the venerable Scotsman brought a large war chest to pay the recruits; in addition, all who enlisted in the new Royal Highland Emigrants Regiment would receive a bonus of two hundred acres of land and a twenty-year tax exemption at the end of the war. (The land for the bonuses was to be confiscated from the rebels.)

Based on the promises of the leaders of the Regulators, McLean sent word back to Governor Martin at Wilmington that they would soon have as many as six thousand men in the field (five thousand Tories and about one thousand Scots). However, three days later McLean received a message from a Scottish officer assigned to escort the Regulators to Cross Creek. The news was not good. According to the officer, "All the loyalists [had] dispersed, and he could not even get amongst them a guide to conduct him back." McLean sent another man to the homes of some of the Tory leaders, but there was no sign of them; their neighbors said that "they were skulking and hiding themselves through swamps and such concealed places." On 10 February, McLean went to the town of Cross Hill, deep in the backcountry, where the Regulators promised to assemble. Instead of finding the promised five thousand Tories ready to march, there were only five hundred Regulators and a few Highlanders gathered under a miscellany of Tory and Scotch leaders. McLean conveyed the group to Cross Creek, where they joined with another five hundred Highlanders commanded by Thomas Rutherford. A former representative in the Patriot provincial congress, Rutherford had changed sides and joined Governor Martin's Loyalist forces.[13]

MacDonald delayed at Cross Creek for almost a week, hoping that more men would come in; but through various accidents, enemy deceptions, and a myriad of other obstacles, the old general was mostly frustrated in this hope. Small handfuls of Tories came in, but not enough. On 14 February 1776 Dr. John Pyle[14] brought in about 130 Loyalists, but it was apparent that this was the last large body of men that could be expected to join.

On 15 February 1776 MacDonald decided that it was time to call roll. "An order was issued to all the captains to make a return of the strength of their companies," Alex McLean wrote. "The army was found to consist of 1,400 men with only 520 stand of arms." Of those present, about six hundred were recent Highland immigrants wearing kilts and plaids, and the remaining eight hundred were country-born Tories.[15]

Because the army was so deficient in firearms, a company of horsemen was then sent out to "bring in all the arms they could find belonging to the rebels." The riders returned three days later with an additional 130 guns taken from the populace and a substantial amount of powder confiscated from the Committee of Safety of Cumberland County. The Loyal army in Cross Creek was now equipped with 650 guns and about 150 broadswords and dirks (a Scottish long, straight-bladed dagger). "All the broadswords in the army," McLean wrote, "[were] given to 80 able-bodied Highlanders who turned out volunteers and put themselves under the command of Captain John Campbell." On 18 February, General MacDonald decided that he could delay no longer and ordered the men to break camp and begin the march to the sea.[16]

North Carolina Patriots had been nervously eyeing the Tory gathering at Cross Creek. Much of the Carolina Whig military, including the 2nd North Carolina Continentals, was still away at Norfolk aiding the Virginia Whigs in the aftermath of Great Bridge. The primary responsibility for countering the Scots therefore fell to Colonel James Moore's 1st North Carolina Continentals. The professional soldiers of America were called Continentals because the units were commissioned by the Continental Congress, which was the national government of the rebellion. By law each state in the confederation was obligated to contribute a certain number of regiments to the national army based on that state's population. Since the Continental Congress had no power to tax, this was the only way the national government could acquire an army. While the states raised and outfitted the Continental regiments, Congress paid and commanded the forces.

In theory, Continental soldiers were uniformed, well drilled, and armed with military muskets equipped with bayonets. However, due to a perennial lack of congressional funds for clothing and equipment, in practice many Continental regiments appeared little different from average militia. Nevertheless, all the Continentals shared a great advantage over their "weekend-warrior" militia allies: they were full-time soldiers who trained and served together for long periods. In order to block MacDonald's advance to the sea, Moore moved his regiment of Continentals to Rockfish Creek, seven miles south of Cross Creek. There he was joined by several hundred Patriot militia, bringing the American strength up to about eleven hundred soldiers.[17]

Probably due to a lack of a sufficient number of boats, and the difficulties of navigating a narrow river lined with rifle-armed enemies, MacDonald had resolved to take his troops overland to the sea. His intended line of march was roughly along the right or southern bank of the Cape Fear River. The unavoidable problem with the route lay in crossing the river's tributaries, which could only be traversed at isolated bridges and ferries. These natural choke points were key to Colonel Moore's strategy to stop the Loyalists from reaching the coast.

———◆———

In mid-February, Colonel Moore moved his Continentals to Rockfish Creek, where he fortified the area around at a crossing point there. However, Moore had apparently made an error in the disposition of his troops, stationing most of them with the deep Rockfish Creek at their rear. On 19 February, General MacDonald saw the vulnerability of the American position and prepared to attack. As was often the custom in eighteenth-century warfare, the two opposing officers exchanged words of warning before setting about the business of preparing to fight. When rumor of the attack filtered down to the rank and file of the makeshift royal army, many of the common foot soldiers decided that they were not up for that task. "One Captain Sneed with two companies of Colonel Cotton's corps ran off with their arms very early that night," Captain Alex McLean wrote. The day after this incident General MacDonald addressed his troops in an attempt to raise their spirits. He encouraged them to "consider the glorious cause" in which they were engaged, adding: "If any amongst them there was so fainted hearted as not to serve with the resolution of conquering or dying, this was the time for such to declare themselves. Upon which, there was a general 'huzza' for the King, except from about 20 men of Colonel Cotton's corps who laid down their arms and declared their courage was not warproof."[18]

Including the company that had just departed, General MacDonald had already lost almost one hundred men from desertions—and he was only one day out of Cross Creek. Now he received intelligence of the approach of more American troops under Richard Caswell. Realizing how deficient his little army was in both arms and morale, General MacDonald chose discretion as the better part of valor. He canceled his plans to attack and marched his army in the other direction on the night of 20 February. MacDonald sidestepped Colonel Moore's troops and crossed over the Northwest Branch of the Cape Fear River at Cross Creek (which some also called "Campbelltown"). Destroying the ferryboats behind him, he proceeded southeast toward the sea via the Black River Road on the left bank (north side) of the Cape Fear River.

It was not until the next day that Colonel Moore realized the Loyalists had departed and stolen a march on him. The best chance to intercept MacDonald now lay with Colonel Richard Caswell, who was marching west from New Bern with eight hundred Patriot militiamen. Moore sent orders to Caswell to take up a blocking position on the

Black River at Corbett's Ferry. If MacDonald could be stopped at the ferry, Colonel Moore's Continentals could fall on the rear of the Tory army, trapping it between two Patriot forces.

As a precaution against MacDonald's slipping by Caswell, Colonel Moore decided to send a detachment to the next river crossing further southeast at Moore's Creek Bridge. Colonel Alexander Lillington and 150 of his Wilmington Minutemen along with Colonel John Ashe's New Hanover Volunteer Company of Rangers (100 men) immediately left Moore's camp and proceeded by force marches to occupy a defensive position at the bridge. The small force was under the overall command of Lillington. This would prove to be a wise and prescient deployment by Moore.

The rest of Moore's force followed behind Lillington as quickly as possible; however, the Continentals, burdened with baggage and artillery, would necessarily be a couple of days behind Lillington's lightly armed minutemen and rangers. Both Moore and Lillington would march along the right bank of the Northwest Branch of the Cape Fear River, crossing to the left bank at Elizabethtown, and then proceed to the North East Cape Fear River branch, crossing near its confluence with Moore's Creek.

MacDonald's army was the largest single armed force in North Carolina, but his troops were outnumbered by the combined Patriot forces that were converging on him from every direction. Unknown to MacDonald, the 4th North Carolina Continentals had already occupied Cross Creek, leaving him no safe place to retreat, and Patriot authorities were arresting Regulators and other "disaffected" individuals in the colony.[19] All hope for the Tory cause in North Carolina lay in the old Scottish general's ability to find a way to the coast where Governor Martin had promised that an English army would soon be landing.

Lieutenant Colonel Donald McLeod commanded a company of one hundred horsemen who had the duty of scouting the road and securing passes over the rivers ahead of the main Loyalist column. When McLeod's scouts reached Corbett's Ferry, they found Caswell's militia in firm control of the crossing. Knowing no other way around, MacDonald reluctantly prepared to assault the strong rebel position. Shortly before the attack was to begin, a black slave informed them of another, little-known ferry about five miles upstream. The rebels had sunk the flatboat there, but the slave said that it could easily be raised again to form a makeshift bridge across the stream. This was perhaps the first of many instances during the war in the South when black slaves aided British armies by supplying them with intelligence and by acting as guides.

Armed with this new information, MacDonald at once canceled the attack and ordered his rear guard under Alex McLean to make a demonstration in front of the Americans at Corbett's Ferry. McLean's orders were to "amuse Caswell as if the army meant to cross the river and force his entrenchments."[20] McLean's men played bagpipes, beat drums, fired muskets, and marched to and fro in a convincing show while the rest of the column crossed the river upstream.

Once Caswell realized that MacDonald had given him the slip, he sent word to General Moore of his situation and at the same time rushed his troops east in order to occupy "Widow Moore's Creek Bridge."[21] Following the old Negro Point Head Road, Caswell's men covered the ten miles to Moore's Creek quickly, arriving at the bridge on the afternoon of 26 February 1776. Caswell found Alexander Lillington's men already entrenched on the east side of the creek. MacDonald also pushed hard for the bridge but lost the race to Caswell by just a few hours. By the time the Loyalists arrived, more than a thousand Patriots were in defensive positions at the bridge.

In a week's worth of hard marching, MacDonald's men had covered more than sixty miles of rough terrain. Wilmington was almost within grasp—merely seventeen more miles away—but there was one more river crossing to make at Moore's Creek Bridge. Crossing a defended water obstacle is one of the toughest scenarios a military commander can face, and MacDonald had already successfully accomplished this task twice in the last few days. Perhaps he could outwit the Patriots a third time. To gain better intelligence of the enemy's strength and position, MacDonald sent one of his officers, James Hepburn, to the Patriot camp under a flag of truce. Arriving just before dark on 26 February, Hepburn demanded Caswell's submission. Caswell refused, of course, and sent the Highlander packing; but the false embassy had accomplished his goal, and Hepburn returned to camp with a detailed description of the American position. The Whigs had placed their fortifications on the near side of the creek, forming a small defensive pocket around the western bridgehead.

To the delight of the Scots, it seemed that the inexperienced Whig commander had blundered. When Lillington arrived at Moore's Creek the previous day, he had constructed a small earthwork on the east side of the creek, facing the bridge. When Caswell arrived, he unwisely decided to expand the defenses by erecting an earthwork on the west side of the bridge, much as Moore had arrayed his troops at Rockfish Creek the week before. This was a poor arrangement since it denied the Patriots the defensive advantages of the creek. In addition, the bridge had to be kept intact in order to allow the Whigs an avenue of retreat. In effect, Caswell was positioning his men to fight with a river at their backs and only a narrow bridge as an escape route. It seemed an ideal situation for the Highlanders, who could rush out of the tree line and, without the creek as an obstacle, close quickly with the Whigs in order to use their broadswords at close quarters.

Thirty years earlier at Culloden the hopes for Scottish supremacy were thwarted by the English bayonet, which revolutionized eighteenth-century warfare by allowing the musket to double as a pike. The Highlanders were confident of success now, however, because few of Caswell's infantry were equipped with bayonets. Muskets with bayonets were military weapons, but the Patriot militiamen were mostly armed with civilian "fowling pieces" (essentially light muskets) and rifles that were incapable of mounting bayonets. Due to the slow reloading rate of a musket, the Patriots were vulnerable to a close-in weapon such as the broadsword—vulnerable, that is, if the Scots got close enough for hand-to-hand combat.

The Scottish commanders held council of war on the night of 26 February to decide how to proceed. (The Regulator leaders had deferred command to the Scots.) There were only two choices: they could attack the rebels or they could attempt to find another crossing somewhere further upstream. Both courses held dangers. Despite the vulnerability of the rebels' position, attacking the bridge would still present a challenge for the untried Highlanders and Regulators, who had never trained or drilled together before.

However, Colonel Moore's Continentals were not far away, and the time it took to find an undefended crossing might allow Moore time to fall on the rear of the Tory column. Therefore, the council of war voted unanimously to attack.

The Loyalist army was in bad shape due to rampant desertions that had started when the march began and continued daily "as danger and difficulty increased upon them."[22] Out of a starting force of fourteen hundred, the Loyalist army was now reduced to only six hundred Highlanders and one hundred or two hundred Regulators. Even worse, the aged General MacDonald had fallen ill. Overall command fell to Lieutenant Colonel Donald McLeod, who now ordered his officers to make ready to attack the rebels. At one o'clock in the morning on 27 February 1776, the army broke camp and marched six miles to the bridge. Their pace was slowed by the darkness, muddy swamps, and thick fog, and they only reached Caswell's campsite about an hour before daybreak. The Patriot campfires were burning weakly, which made the Highlanders suspicious. Cautiously ascending the American parapets, they were surprised to find the fortifications abandoned! Caswell had thought better about the position during the night and moved his men to the east side of the creek, and they had taken up the planking of the bridge behind them as they left.

Lieutenant Colonel McLeod was somewhat at a loss about how to proceed. After a few minutes he ordered his troops to fall back to a nearby line of trees and form a line of battle. However, just as the Loyalists began to retire, a shot rang out from the direction of the bridge: a Patriot picket had fired to warn Caswell of the enemy's approach. The Loyalist army immediately faced about, and Lieutenant Colonel McLeod ordered the signal for the attack, which was "three cheers, the drum to beat, the pipes to play."[23]

It was still predawn and quite dark; this fact along with the morning mist made it difficult to distinguish friend from foe. As a company of Highlanders led by Captain Alex McLean neared the bridge, some shadowy figures shouted at them from the opposite bank. Asked to identify himself, McLean replied that he was "a friend." The unseen men asked "to whom" he was a friend, to which McLean replied "The King."[24] To this last remark there was no response. Wanting to be sure his inquisitors were not some of his own people who had managed to cross the creek, McLean challenged them in Gaelic. When there was again no response, McLean ordered his men to fire a volley. Their fire was returned in kind by their well-shrouded opponents on the other side of the creek: Patriot picket men.

As the firing between McLean's party and the pickets continued, Captain John Campbell approached the bridge with his company of eighty picked swordsmen. Shouting "King George and Broadswords!" the courageous Campbell charged onto the bridge. The commander of all the Highlanders, Lieutenant Colonel Donald McLeod, accompanied Campbell in his reckless dash. Moore's Creek was thirty-five feet wide and five to ten feet deep. The planking having been removed from the bridge,[25] the only way across was to walk on the structure's rails and stringers. The half-light of predawn revealed the two men scrambling across the thin railings—their way made more difficult by the fact that the Patriots had greased the sleepers. The men of Campbell's volunteer company followed diligently behind, echoing their commander's battle cry. It is possible that Campbell and McLeod thought the rebels had panicked and fled—little else explains why they decided to continue their attack in the face of such daunting obstacles.

Caswell and his men waited behind the earthworks they had constructed overnight. The Patriot fortifications, about one hundred yards east of the bridge, formed a rough semicircle around the eastern bridgehead. Caswell placed his two small artillery pieces —a two-pounder nicknamed "Mother Covington" and her "daughter," a one-pound swivel gun—on the road in position ready to blast anyone coming across bridge. The sound of the initial exchange of gunfire was still echoing in the woods when the Highlanders came storming out of the thick morning mist. The Scottish swordsmen "advanced in a most furious manner over the bridge," and as each man reached the opposite bank, he brandished his broadsword above his head and charged.[26] The sound of drums and bagpipes filled the air as Campbell's company, many dressed in traditional kilts and plaids, rushed the rebel fortifications.

The Patriot militia steadied themselves, and when the Highlanders were "within thirty paces of the breastworks they were received with a very heavy fire, which did great execution."[27] A sheet of flame and smoke from a thousand rebel muskets covered the battlefield. The Patriot artillery contributed to the terrible slaughter, lighting up the murky forest with terrific flashes of light and sparks. It is said that Mother Covington, the Patriot two-pounder, refused to fire until Colonel Caswell shot his pistols into the touchholes. Many of the Scots were dropped in their steps; others fell seconds later as the Patriot militia released volley after volley. "Captain McLeod and Captain Campbell," according to a report made by Colonel Moore "fell within a few paces of the breastwork, the former of whom received upwards of twenty balls through his body."[28]

As the smoke and fog cleared, the rebels could see the remains of thirty bodies on the ground. It is generally accepted that more were shot while crossing the bridge, their bodies falling into the deep creek never to be recovered. What remained of Campbell's company fled back across the bridge. One of Caswell's officers, Lieutenant Slocum, forded the creek with a small party to outflank the retreating Scots. He succeeded, and Slocum's men "fell with vigor upon the rear of the Loyalists."[29] In an exuberant tide Caswell's militia now sallied from their defenses, replaced the planks on the bridge, and set off in hot pursuit of the fleeing Scots. What happened next was astonishing. The main body of the Highlanders simply melted as the Americans pursued them. Some Scottish officers tried to rally the fleeing masses at their camp six miles distant from the bridge. However, when the common soldiery found out that the army's food stocks had been reduced to only two barrels of flour, there was no stopping the rout. Panic-stricken and bereft of supplies, the Scotsmen and Regulators fled. Some soldiers mounted up two or three to a horse and then cut the wagons loose to make best speed away from the Americans. Those who could not find a horse took off on foot, pausing only to fire an occasional, poorly aimed shot at their Patriot pursuers.

Colonel Moore and his Continentals arrived at the bridge a few hours after the battle ended, having made their way in boats down the Cape Fear River and by foot up the banks of the Black River to the bridge. "The loss of the enemy in this action," Moore wrote, "is about thirty killed and wounded; but as numbers of them must have fallen into the creek, besides more that were carried off, I suppose their loss may be estimated at fifty."[30] The Americans suffered only one wounded and one killed. (The single fatal casualty was Private John Grady, who was killed during the pursuit; a monument stands today in his memory at the Moore's Creek National Battlefield.) Donald MacDonald and most of the senior Scotch officers were captured that day or shortly thereafter. Over the next few days over 850 Highlanders and Regulators were apprehended.[31] Most of the Loyalist rank and file were temporarily imprisoned and then released on parole. However, the leaders and officers were sent to jails in Halifax and then on to a prison in Philadelphia under the care of the Continental Congress. Colonel Moore remarked afterward that the battle would, "I trust, put an effectual check to Toryism in this country."[32]

It has generally been accepted that at the time of the battle at Moore's Creek Bridge the Loyalists had sixteen hundred troops. The acknowledged authority on this engagement, historian Hugh F. Rankin, put the number of Loyalists in the battle at this amount, as does the National Parks Service.[33] The number sixteen hundred came from Caswell's after-action report, which said that General MacDonald testified as a prisoner that the Loyalist strength was about "fifteen or sixteen hundred."[34] However, if MacDonald did give that number to Caswell, he must have been stating the number of men he commanded at the start of the campaign, rather than the number that was at the bridge.

Both Governor Martin and Alex McLean, who organized or participated in the campaign, reported that the Loyalists started their march at Cross Creek with no more than 1,400 troops. According to Martin, the number of Loyalists had "daily diminished" until no more than 600 Highlanders and 100 Regulators were present on the day of battle.[35] Alex McLean likewise testified that only 800 men were in the force that attacked at the bridge.[36] Caswell said that 850 Loyalists were captured within two days of battle, supporting the figure of 700 to 800 men given in McLean's and Martin's accounts. The excess of prisoners can be accounted for by the fact that the Patriots had probably rounded up many British deserters as well as some Scottish immigrants who were not in MacDonald's army.

In addition to there being fewer Loyalists at the battle than has previously been accepted, it is likely that the Patriots had a few more men than many historians have traditionally stated. Previous histories of the battle state that the Patriot forces at the bridge consisted of 800 militia under Caswell and 150 minutemen under Lillington. However, Colonel Moore's correspondence says that in addition to Lillington's 150 men, he sent John Ashe's 100 rangers to Moore's Creek. While Caswell's own report only mentions Lillington's troops being present, he may have grouped Ashe's troops with those of Lillington. Thus, the Patriots were probably about 100 men stronger than was previously believed.

Traditional accounts of this battle have portrayed the Loyalists as outnumbering the Patriots by a large margin (1,600 to 1,000). However, the correspondence of Governor Josiah Martin, Alex McLean, and Colonel James Moore show not only that the Patriots outnumbered the Loyalists (1,050 to 800), but also that the latter army was highly demoralized due to the massive desertion of almost one-half of its force over the course of the week-long march. This obviously helps explain why the battle was so one-sided, and certainly casts the engagement in a new light.

As for the number of weapons that MacDonald's men had on the day of the battle, we know from McLean's account that at the start of the campaign they had 650 guns. A Patriot account also said that 150 broadswords and dirks were seized after the battle. Though MacDonald's force had about 800 men at the bridge, far fewer than that actually saw action. It is doubtful that anyone without a weapon would have participated in the attack, so it may thus be safely assumed that all the Highlanders and Loyalists who actually took part in the assault were armed with firearms, broadswords, or dirks.[37]

The Patriots reported capturing 1,500 rifles (these were probably a variety of civilian firearms) and 350 muskets after the battle. Hugh F. Rankin believes that the large number of firearms confiscated—greater than the number of Loyalist soldiers at the start of the campaign and far more than McLean claimed the Loyalists possessed—can be explained by the fact that the Patriots took weapons from Scots and former Regulators in the region who did not actually participate in the campaign.[38] This conclusion is further supported by a statement made by Colonel Caswell after the battle: "We have flying parties out, taking in the ringleaders and all suspected persons, and disarming the common soldiers throughout the whole back country."[39] In addition to the haul of prisoners and weapons, the Patriots took thirteen wagons full of stores, and they confiscated a significant amount of gold and specie valued at fifteen thousand pounds from MacDonald's baggage train and hidden caches at Cross Creek.[40]

Exuberant after their success at Moore's Creek, the North Carolina Whigs told their delegation to the second Continental Congress that the time had come for a complete separation with Britain. Accordingly, the North Carolina delegation became the first colony at that Continental Congress to vote for complete independence. Richard Caswell's political career was boosted by his triumph on the battlefield, and shortly thereafter he would make a successful run for governor. A relatively minor controversy has persisted since the battle regarding whether Caswell or Alexander Lillington (who first took up position at Moore's Creek Bridge) deserved credit for the victory. A folk song written long after the battle says, "Lillington fought for Caswell's glory," but this probably overrates Lillington's contribution. Lillington certainly deserves credit for first establishing the earthworks on the more secure east side of the river; however, it is clear that Caswell was in command at the engagement. More important, both Caswell and Lillington were at Moore's Creek on Colonel James Moore's orders. Moore handled the campaign "like a skilled chess player";[41] however, because he was not present at the actual battle, he received less popular recognition for the victory than Caswell did. Moore was promoted to brigadier general only days after the battle, but his military career was cut short when he died from a stomach illness only a year later.

Historians have generally blamed Josiah Martin for the failure of the Moore's Creek campaign. The traditional criticism has been that he issued his proclamation calling for the uprising of the Scots too early—that he should have waited for the British troops to land first. Governor Martin defended his decision to call out the Loyalists on the grounds that he had been told that the southern expedition was to sail from Ireland no later than 1 December 1775, meaning that it should have arrived in North Carolina sometime in early February 1776. Martin thus believed that the date of his proclamation calling up the Loyalists (10 January) and the date he set for the Loyalist gathering at Wilmington (15 February) were in accord with the strategic schedule set by Lord Germain. As it was, Major General Henry Clinton only left Boston on 10 January 1776. After a two-month voyage, Clinton arrived at Wilmington on 12 March—more than two weeks after the battle at Moore's Creek Bridge.

Even if Clinton had been on time, his little flotilla of four ships carried only two hundred light infantry—far too few to have marched inland to save the Loyalists. The fleet from England carrying over two thousand redcoats should have been waiting for Clinton, but that venture had only left Ireland in mid-February of 1776, *more than ten weeks later* than it should have and about the time it should have been *arriving* in America! Martin claimed, with much justification, that it was not he but rather the British government that failed to live up to its own plan.

Nevertheless, Governor Martin was perfectly aware of the difficulties in coordinating transatlantic operations at that time in history. Why did he not take the safe approach and wait to issue his proclamation when the British fleet arrived in North Carolina? Governor Martin said that he feared his scheme had been betrayed to the Patriots by a turncoat spy, and he thought that his plot would be foiled by the Whig authorities if he did not act quickly. "The raising of a large body of men in this country . . . is not to be effected without communicating the purpose to each individual to be engaged. . . . Wherefore, it being almost impossible to conduct with secrecy a design of this nature, it can only succeed in the present state of things by the prompt execution of the purpose after it is broached."[42]

Martin attributed the disaster at Moore's Creek to such things as false rumors of his being at Cross Creek with one thousand redcoats (which supposedly disheartened the Loyalists who found it not to be true). The arrests of some Tory leaders and broken promises by others also prevented the assembly of as many Loyalists as he anticipated.

On 12 March, Clinton met at sea with Governor Martin, who had for many months been exiled aboard HMS *Syreen*. Martin tried to convince Clinton that the defeat at Moore's Creek was merely a "little check," and that the Scots and Regulators would rise again if Clinton would march with his regulars into the interior of the colony. Alex McLean seconded Martin on this subject, saying that he believed the inhabitants of the backcountry "will still readily embrace the first opportunity (when properly supported) of raising and taking up arms in support of His Majesty's government."[43]

Both Martin and McLean seemed oblivious to the reality of the situation; the fact was that the same conditions and difficulties that prevented their success the first time would still be present for a second attempt. Indeed, future conditions for a Loyalist uprising could only be worse after the Moore's Creek debacle because the Patriots had arrested most of North Carolina's Tory leaders and confiscated the property of many Loyalists who took part in MacDonald's ill-fated march to the sea.

Clinton found Martin's and McLean's platitudes unconvincing, saying that it was his "well founded conviction that the friends of the [royal] government in the Carolinas were at too great a distance from the coast" to be relied on as means of reestablishing the "King's authority."[44] Before leaving for South Carolina, General Clinton issued a proclamation announcing the reestablishment of royal authority in North Carolina and amnesty for all but the most well-known Whigs who pledged fealty to the king. The proclamation was just a formality; no one responded. As a parting gesture, Clinton allowed some of the British troops to plunder and set fire to the town of Brunswick (and the nearby plantation of Brigadier General Robert Howe, who was still away at Norfolk). North Carolina's Patriots—and probably many Tories—sighed with relief as Clinton's armada finally disappeared over the horizon, leaving the province in peace for over four years.

The action at Moore's Creek Bridge demonstrated that the North Carolina Whigs were more numerous, better organized, and more willing to fight than were their opponents. At the end of February there were more than nine thousand North Carolina Patriots in arms (more than ten times the number of Tories that reached Moore's Creek). In this respect, the battle at Moore's Creek Bridge established the permanent ascendancy of Patriot military and political power in North Carolina.

Lord George Germain seemed unconcerned about Governor Martin's failure to deliver twenty thousand Loyalists as promised. Instead, he remained a believer in Martin's argument that the Carolina backcountry was an untapped reserve of Loyalist strength merely waiting for the right conditions and proper support to be released. His Lordship seemed also not to understand that the defeat at Moore's Creek Bridge, and the failure of the British army to come when promised, might affect the future willingness of the backcountry Loyalists to volunteer for duty. Germain chose to see the glass as half full, taking heart in the fact that fourteen hundred Tories had taken up arms for the king with almost no help from the royal government. How many more, Germain wondered, would join the royal cause if they were given proper backing? The lessons of the Moore's Creek campaign were therefore lost on the British leadership, and the chimera of Tory support in the piedmont would become the driving force behind further British misadventures in the Carolinas in the years to come.

ORDER OF BATTLE: MOORE'S CREEK BRIDGE
North Carolina, 27 February 1776

American Forces[45]
Col. Richard Caswell

	MEN	ARTILLERY
New Bern Minutemen—		
Col. Richard Caswell	800	
Cannon (2-lb.) "Mother Covington"		1
Cannon (swivel, 1-lb.?) "Her Daughter"		1
Wilmington Minutemen—		
Col. Alexander Lillington	150	

Order of Battle: Moore's Creek Bridge (*continued*)

	MEN	ARTILLERY
New Hanover Volunteer Company of Rangers—		
Col. John Ashe	100	
Total engaged	**ca. 1050**	**2**

British Forces
Lt. Col. Donald McLeod

	MEN	ARTILLERY
Royal Highland Emigrants		
Volunteer Broadsword Company—		
Capt. John Campbell	80	
Main body	520	
Tories and Regulators[46]	ca. 100–200	
Total engaged	**ca. 700–800**	**0**

Casualties[47]

	AMERICAN	BRITISH
Killed	1	ca. 30 (killed and wounded)
Wounded	1	see above
Missing	–	ca. 20
Total Casualties	**2**	**ca. 50**
Captured	–	850
Total Losses	**2**	**ca. 900**

All American Forces Involved in the Campaign
Col. James Moore

	MEN	ARTILLERY
1st North Carolina Regiment—		
Col. James Moore	650	
Fieldpieces (4-lb.?)		5
Duplin County Militia—		
Col. James Keenan	200	
Wilmington Minutemen—		
Col. Alexander Lillington	150	
New Hanover Volunteer Company of Rangers—		
Col. John Ashe	100	
New Bern Minutemen—Col. Richard Caswell	800	
Cannon (2-lb.) "Mother Covington"		1
Cannon (swivel, 1-lb.?) "Her Daughter"		1
Total	**ca. 1,900**	**7**

British (Loyalist) Forces at Campaign Start[48]
Brig. Gen. Donald MacDonald

	MEN	ARTILLERY
Royal Highland Emigrants	600	
Volunteer Broadsword Company—		
Capt. John Campbell (80 taken		
from Rutherford's)		
Light Horse—Capt. Donald McLeod (100)		
Highlanders—Col. Thomas Rutherford (420)		
Regulators and Tories	800	
Capt. Dr. John Pyle (130)		
Lt. Col. Cotton		
Capt. Alex McLeod		
Capt. McDonald		
Total	1,400	0

FOUR

Charlestown, 1776

THE BATTLE OF SULLIVAN'S ISLAND

"One continual blaze and roar"

MAJOR GENERAL HENRY CLINTON, commander of the first British expedition to the southern provinces, sailed south from Boston on 10 January 1776. Clinton was to rendezvous at Cape Fear, North Carolina, with a British fleet under the command of Commodore Sir Peter Parker. The fleet was scheduled to depart Cork, Ireland, on 1 December 1775. Given a standard two-month transatlantic crossing, Parker and Clinton should have been able to rendezvous off the North Carolina coast no later than mid-February. Clinton was delayed, however, by a prolonged stop in New York and so did not reach the Carolina coast until 12 March 1776. Due to his tardy arrival, he expected to find Commodore Parker waiting for him at Cape Fear; instead he found only empty ocean. It was an ominous sign.

General Clinton waited for over a month, "casting an anxious eye every day toward the cape in expectation of a signal for the fleet."[1] In the meantime he rendezvoused with the ships carrying the royal governors of North and South Carolina, Josiah Martin and William Campbell. Both men, like Governor Dunmore in Virginia, had been reduced to a state of watery exile aboard Royal Navy frigates. Clinton learned from Martin of the debacle at Moore's Creek, which thus ended his mission to retake North Carolina before it had properly begun. Likewise, Governor Campbell said that the backcountry Tories in South Carolina had been defeated by Whig partisans in late 1775 in a series of skirmishes that came to be called the "Snow Campaign."[2] As a result of these incidents, along with the crushing of Lord Dunmore's forces at Great Bridge, the Patriots had gained complete superiority over the Tories in all the southern provinces. "These were but gloomy forebodings of my future success," Clinton later wrote.[3]

Governors Martin and Campbell "were not dispirited" by the sorry state of their affairs, and both men looked to Clinton to set matters right. However, with just two companies of light infantry, Clinton could only make short beach excursions to give the waterlogged governors "an opportunity of stretching their legs on shore."[4] Meanwhile, Clinton puzzled and worried about the fate of Commodore Parker's fleet. Unknown to him, the fleet's departure from Ireland had been delayed by several *months* due to a bureaucratic disagreement between London and Dublin over the legal disposition of the troops of the Irish Establishment that were to be used in the expedition. It was 13 February 1776 when the bureaucratic red tape was finally resolved and Parker's fleet departed from Cork. The delay was inexcusable given that Lord Germain had promised his subordinates in America that "the armament should sail from [Cork] by the 1st of December [1775]."[5]

Once the "Irish" fleet got under way it had the bad luck to run into a violent storm that scattered its ships over the Atlantic. This act of God further delayed the expedition, and it was 18 April 1776 when the first transport of the Irish fleet finally arrived off Cape Fear (a full two months after the defeat of the North Carolina Loyalists with whom they were to have rendezvoused). The whole episode was a grim lesson in the difficulties of coordinating a transoceanic war in the eighteenth century.

Commodore Parker's fleet arrived slowly, one storm-battered ship at a time. On 3 May 1776 the bulk of the armada finally arrived at Cape Fear along with the commodore. (The last straggling ships of the fleet would not complete the Atlantic crossing until 31 May.) With sufficient force finally under his command, Clinton began to formulate plans for his next move. His primary concern was General Howe's stipulation that, whatever Clinton decided to do, southern operations had to be concluded by the summer so that his troops could be used for a projected attack on New York. Howe based his orders on Germain's and Dartmouth's recommendations, as both men assumed that southern operations would be concluded, for better or worse, by the end of spring 1776. These orders were indicative of the fallacy inherent in General Howe's implementation of the Southern Strategy: the British regulars were not going to stay in the South; they were going to aid the Loyalists in retaking their colonies and then return northward.

Clinton was not convinced that this was wise policy. He told Howe that once the British regulars left, the southern Tories would be left exposed "to the resentment and malice of their enemies."[6] In addition, since Commodore Parker's fleet had not arrived until late spring, if Clinton were to accomplish anything of value in the South he would need more time. Responding to these concerns, General Howe issued revised orders to Clinton in May that removed him from the obligation to rejoin the main army before summer—though he was still expected to return sometime that year. In his letter Howe suggested that Charlestown, South Carolina, was an "object of importance," but he did not directly order Clinton to attack the city.

Thus empowered, Clinton briefly entertained the notion of returning to Virginia. Though initially unimpressed by the arguments of Lord Dunmore to come to Virginia's aid, Clinton changed his mind after considering the advantages that the waterways of the Chesapeake Bay would afford his forces, given British naval superiority. The counties of Norfolk and Princess Anne, which lay behind the Great Dismal Swamp, would afford a secure place for Tories to repair if they were guarded by a small force of regulars and a squadron of the Royal Navy, and the area was agriculturally rich enough to support a large number of refugees. However, Clinton seemed to be the only British officer who did not assume that Charlestown, South Carolina, was the target of the southern expedition.

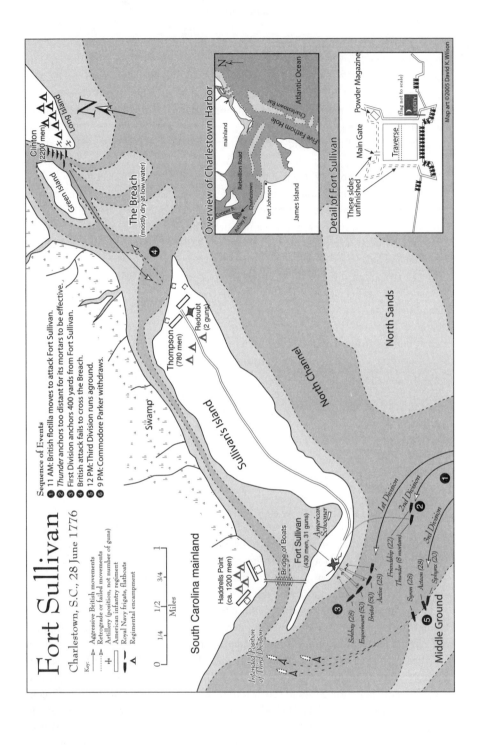

Fort Sullivan

Charlestown, S.C., 28 June 1776

Key:

→ Aggressive British movements
┈┈▷ Retrograde or failed movements
╬ Artillery (position, not number of guns)
◢ American infantry regiment
◣ Royal Navy frigate, flatboats
▲ Regimental encampment

0   1/4   1/2   3/4   1
Miles

Sequence of Events

① 11 AM: British flotilla moves to attack Fort Sullivan.
② *Thunder* anchors too distant for its mortars to be effective.
③ First Division anchors 400 yards from Fort Sullivan.
④ British attack fails to cross the Breach.
⑤ 12 PM: Third Division runs aground.
⑥ 9 PM: Commodore Parker withdraws.

Clinton
(2200 men)
Long Island

Green Island

The Breach
(mostly dry at low water)

④

Thompson
(780 men)

Redoubt
(2 guns)

Swamp

Sullivan's Island

North Channel

North Sands

South Carolina mainland

Haddrells Point
(ca. 1200 men)

Intended Position of Third Division

Bridge of Boats

Fort Sullivan
(430 men, 31 guns)

American Schooner

③

Solebay (28)
Experiment (50)
Bristol (50)
Active (28)
Friendship (22)
Thunder (8 mortars)
Syren (28)
Acteon (28)
Sphynx (20)

1st Division

2nd Division

②

3rd Division

⑤

①

Middle Ground

Overview of Charlestown Harbor

N

mainland

Rebellion Road

Cooper R.
Charlestown
Ashley R.

Fort Johnson

James Island

Five Fathom Hole

Charlestown Bar

Atlantic Ocean

Detail of Fort Sullivan

These sides
unfinished

Powder Magazine

Main Gate

Traverse

(flag not to scale)

Map art ©2005 David K. Wilson

Clinton's orders on where he was to campaign had been somewhat muddied by the change in secretaries at the Colonial Office. Lord George Germain, the current secretary of state for the American colonies, had told Clinton that he had discretion on whether to pursue operations in Virginia or South Carolina after matters in North Carolina were concluded. However, Lord Dartmouth, Germain's predecessor, had earlier sent orders that implied or directly stated that Charlestown was to be attacked after North Carolina. Moreover, Dartmouth sent these orders to all the officers involved in the operation (as was common practice in an era when no one could be sure that any one letter would reach its destination), including General Howe, Commodore Parker, and the royal governors. Therefore, nearly everyone involved in the expedition had good reason to suppose that Clinton would choose to attack Charlestown after finding North Carolina to be a lost cause.

When Commodore Parker finally joined Clinton off Cape Fear, he was dismayed to find Clinton disposed to invade Virginia. Was not Charlestown the greatest prize in the southern colonies? Why would Clinton want to seize some insignificant swampland in Virginia? In fact, Parker had already sent two frigates on a reconnaissance mission to Charlestown. The scouts had observed that a large fort on Sullivan's Island, near the entrance to Charlestown harbor, was incomplete on two sides and therefore vulnerable to attack. A large coastal fortification was a target worthy of the Royal Navy! If the fort were attacked before the rebels finished it, it might be taken by a coup de main.

Parker reported these findings to General Clinton. The commodore argued that the fort, if taken, could be used to control access to the shipping channels and so blockade all of Charlestown's trade. Politically this would be an impressive accomplishment —much more so than merely establishing a small base of operations on an obscure bit of Virginia coastline. Moreover, sanguine reports from British officials in the South said that the Patriot army in South Carolina was in low spirits and would crumble when faced with the prospect of combat. "By the account I have the men [of the South Carolina regiments] will certainly rise on their officers," wrote Patrick Tonyn, the royal governor of British Florida. "I dare think the battery at Sullivan's Island will not discharge two rounds."[7]

However, attacking the trade of South Carolina would not afford any real opportunity to aid the southern Loyalists in a counterrevolution—which was the key to Lord Germain's strategy. Despite this fact, Clinton ultimately accepted Parker's recommendation to attack South Carolina, a decision reinforced by General Howe's suggestion that Charlestown was an important objective. Clinton rationalized that Sullivan's Island could be used as a refuge and rallying point for South Carolina Loyalists—thus fulfilling Lord Germain's strategic objective to aid the Loyalists in retaking the southern provinces.

However, Clinton was fooling himself if he genuinely thought that Sullivan's Island would make a good base for southern Tories. The island was located right next to a Patriot stronghold (Charlestown), and the surrounding countryside was notoriously Whig. Any Loyalists who could actually make it safely to the island would be cut off and surrounded. Sullivan's Island was terribly vulnerable to attack from the landward side, and provisions on the sandy island were not sufficient for large numbers of refugees.

Clinton had essentially been strong-armed by Commodore Parker into giving up his own plan to invade Virginia in order to participate in a naval operation that carried political importance but had little relevance to furthering Germain's Southern Strategy.

Clinton was undoubtedly an enigma. He seemed to have two personalities: one aggressive and cock-sure, the other timid and full of self-doubt. He described himself as a shy man, but he also had a reputation for being quarrelsome and difficult. Clinton never held his superiors in the Royal Army in high esteem. He felt that his plans were better than theirs; and while he was often right, he gained a reputation for arrogance that worked against him politically. Nevertheless, Lord Germain liked the straightforward competence of Clinton, and by 1778 the general would be knighted and promoted to commander in chief of all British military forces in North America.

Clinton had served with distinction in Europe during the Seven Years' War, rising to the rank of colonel. After the war he fell in love and married. Clinton's wife, Harriet, died shortly after giving birth to their fifth child—something all too common before the age of modern medicine. A devoted husband, Henry was crushed by his wife's death and for some time was unable to function normally in society. He even forewent a seat in Parliament to which he had been elected.[8] Clinton's recovery from the loss of his wife was a slow process. In 1774 he took a sabbatical in Europe. The ostensible purpose of his trip was to serve as an English observer in the Russian army during Catherine the Great's war against the Turks. The trip reinvigorated Clinton, who was ready for new challenges after he returned to England. He was promoted to the rank of major general and assigned to the staff of General Gage, commander of His Majesty's armed forces in North America.

Clinton arrived in America just in time to take part in the battle at Bunker Hill on 16 June 1776. He had been left in charge of the Boston garrison, but on seeing the disastrous assaults on Breed's Hill, Clinton decided to "exceed the limits" of his orders and join the fray.[9] He "rowed" to the sound of the guns, crossing the harbor in a boat with reinforcements while under enemy fire, arriving at Breed's Hill just in time to rally the British left flank. Clinton received much praise for his actions, both in England and from his fellow officers in America. However, the insecure general worried for some time that he would be censured by General Gage for having left his post in Boston without orders, and he never again exercised such bold initiative.

The battles around Boston and the invasion of Canada commanded nearly all the attention of Congress during the early war years of 1775 and 1776. When Henry Clinton and his small flotilla left Boston, Washington was unsure of his ultimate destination, although he suspected that it was bound for either New York or the southern colonies. Accordingly, Washington dispatched Major General Charles Lee for New York in order to counter the British move. Lee arrived on Manhattan on 4 February 1776, just a few hours after Clinton's ship entered the harbor. The Patriot citizens of New York were very much bothered by the British warships off their shore, but after a few weeks the ships sailed on without firing a shot or landing any troops. Clinton had only stopped to consult with the royal governor of New York, William Tryon, who had fled the governor's house for the safety of a British warship in the waters off Manhattan. Tryon was formerly the governor of North Carolina and was the man who had put down the first Regulator uprising at the battle of Alamance Court House in 1771. Certainly Tryon's knowledge of North Carolina politics was an invaluable resource, though it seems unlikely that whatever Tryon told Clinton could be worth the long delay of his mission.

Assuming that the southern colonies were now Clinton's target, Congress appointed Lee to command the Southern Department. This military district encompassed Virginia, the Carolinas, Georgia, and later Maryland and Delaware. Congress believed that the appointment of such a prestigious general to command in this theater would show how important they considered the security of the southern colonies to be. At that time General Charles Lee was regarded as the most experienced military officer in America. Born in England in 1731, Lee had a reputation as a soldier of fortune with broad military knowledge. Lee served during the Seven Years' War (known in America as the French and Indian War) in both the American and European theaters. Lee was severely wounded when his regiment unsuccessfully assaulted French-held Ticonderoga in 1758. Four years later he would perform his greatest personal feat of arms when he led a night assault on a Spanish strongpoint in Portugal, capturing the post.

By the end of the Seven Years' War, Lee was addicted to military life. Not content to wait for Britain's next war, he chose to sell his services abroad. The young Englishman became an aide-de-camp to Stanislaus, the king of Poland, and rose to the rank of major general in the Polish army. He went on to join the Russian army and in their service fought against the Turks.

Because of his extensive experience, Charles Lee considered himself the most qualified soldier in America. When he joined the Continental Army, he chafed at being made a subordinate to George Washington—a man who, until the Revolution, had only fought as a colonel in backwoods frontier battles. However, Washington was a native-born American and a member of the Virginia gentry with an impeccable reputation. Unlike Lee's, Washington's roots were unquestionably American. The fact that Washington was a southerner sealed his destiny, as his appointment to command of the Continental Army helped cement the southern states to their northern counterparts. Despite his considerable military reputation, the English-born Charles Lee had no political allies in the American Congress that could promote him past Washington.

Whereas Washington took the mantle of leadership with some reluctance, Lee looked at the war as an opportunity for advancement. He encouraged the Continental Congress to raise armies and declare independence. In this respect he was an advocate of the cause of liberty. However, events subsequent to this story would come to show that Lee's true loyalty was to himself. While Charles Lee was a prisoner of the British in New York in 1777, he presented to his British captors a plan that described how he felt the United States could best be conquered.[10] This treasonous act went undiscovered for seventy years, however, and so was unknown by his contemporaries on the American side. (The British ignored Lee's advice and returned him to American service after he was exchanged for a British prisoner in American custody in April 1778.) It should be noted that whether the enigmatic Lee was truly a traitor is a subject of historical controversy that lies outside the scope of this study, and that during the term of his involvement in the southern campaigns he consistently acted as an American patriot whose interest was defending the independence of the United States.[11]

Traitor or not, Lee was seen as egotistical and abrasive by all who met him, and the two dogs he kept constantly at his side annoyed many a visitor. Lee prided himself as a man of letters, and as such he could hardly correspond with anyone without quoting Shakespeare or quipping some military aphorism. However, Lee's pen was more pleasant than his tongue. The condescending general constantly reminded those around him that he was the most knowledgeable military officer in America. This was probably true, but a dose of humility would have attracted more political allies.

After assuming command of the Southern Department, Lee immediately repaired to Williamsburg, then the capital of Virginia. Arriving in March 1776, Lee, with his usual lack of tact, set about providing for the defense of the colony by practically assuming dominion of the state. Robert Morris (the "financier of the Revolution") declared in a letter to General Horatio Gates, "Our friend Lee has taken possession of the Palace at Williamsburgh, which I fancy will not be much approved by the gentlemen of that country."[12]

Lee now had to face what was the greatest challenge to American strategic planning during the Revolution: British control of the sea. By the time Lee reached Virginia on horseback, Henry Clinton's flotilla had already come and gone and was now menacing North Carolina. Lee expressed his frustration in a letter to Washington: "My command (as you may easily conceive) is extremely perplexing from the consideration of the vast extent of vulnerable parts of this country, intersected by such a variety of navigable waters, and the expedition with which the enemy (furnished with canvass wings) can fly from one spot to another."[13]

General Lee had a lucky break when an American privateer captured a British transport carrying a secret letter from Lord Germain to royal officers in America. The letter revealed the details of the expedition, including the information that North Carolina was the initial target, to be followed by Virginia or South Carolina. The information was confirmed as genuine when Commodore Parker's fleet was seen arriving off Cape Fear.

Armed with this intelligence, Lee left Virginia and arrived in North Carolina in mid-May 1776. He asked Governor Thomas Burke to order the state's militia out to defend the coast. However, the call to arms generated a lackluster response, and Governor Burke was forced to make sheepish excuses for the militia's dawdling. The piedmont militia, the governor said, were "chiefly wheat farmers, and if obliged to leave their crops before they can save that necessary grain, a dearth in the next year could scarcely be avoided." The governor similarly excused the tidewater militia, saying that they had been "in unremitting service so long that it has become irksome, and exceedingly burdensome to them."[14]

The behavior of the North Carolina militia during 1776 was illustrative of the strengths and weaknesses of such forces. Whereas the militia had turned out with vigor earlier in the year to deal with the Highlanders and the Regulators, they were unable to keep the enthusiasm up to stay in the field for long; they shortly wanted to return to their fields and shops. Depending on militia, Washington said, was akin to "resting upon a broken staff."[15] America would become increasingly reliant on regulars, rather than militia, in what would become a protracted war for independence.

When the British fleet departed the North Carolina coast at the end of May, General Lee had to guess if they were headed to Virginia or South Carolina. After a couple of days Lee made up his mind: "I shall myself set out for Charlestown," he told Washington, "but at the same time confess I know not whether I shall go to or from the enemy." Lee based his decision to head south on the fact that South Carolina, unlike Virginia, possessed a strategic center in the form of Charlestown. Lee reasoned that if a major city was their target, then "their operations will be more regular, and, consequently, my presence as Commander-in-Chief of the district more requisite."[16]

Events proved that Lee had chosen correctly. The Patriots of Charlestown had been busy gathering gunpowder, ammunition, and all the other necessities of war since the conflict with Britain began in 1775. When the Continental Congress informed the city in January 1776 that it was probably the target of Clinton's military expedition, an expanded series of defensive works were begun in and around the town. Charlestown sat then, as today, on the tip of a peninsula formed by the confluence of the Ashley and Cooper rivers. The city of twelve thousand souls (almost half of whom were slaves) was the undisputed trading capital of the southern colonies and by some measures the wealthiest city in America. The South Carolina gentry who controlled Charlestown had made their fortunes trading rice, indigo, and tobacco with Europe.

Charlestown harbor was protected by two barrier islands: James to the south and Sullivan's to the north. Fort Johnson, an existing fortification on James Island, had been occupied by Patriot forces the previous year (and is where William Moultrie first raised the South Carolina state flag in 1775). The Americans soon decided to strengthen the harbor defenses by building a new fort on the southern tip of Sullivan's Island. This position was especially advantageous since it covered Rebellion Road—the narrow channel that all ships headed into Charlestown had to pass. Colonel William Moultrie, a well-respected Carolina militia officer now in command of the 2nd South Carolina Continentals, was given the important duty of overseeing the construction of the fort (which had no official name but was usually referred to as Fort Sullivan). The fortress was designed to hold one thousand men and over thirty guns. The immense size of the building prolonged the construction process, and only two of the fort's four massive sides would be complete by the time the British fleet arrived. The layout of the fort was conventional, a square with diamond-shaped bastions jutting out from each corner. The walls of the fort were made of logs cut from the state's abundant palmetto trees— a material that, like the untested American troops, would soon prove to be more resilient than anyone could have guessed. Despite having ample warning of an impending attack, the citizens of Charlestown were still panic-stricken when Commodore Parker's fleet appeared outside the harbor on 4 June 1776: "Men [were] running about the town looking for horses, carriages, and boats to send their families into the country; and as they were going out . . . they met the militia from the country marching into town; traverses were made in the principal streets; fleches thrown up at every place where troops could land."[17]

Even the Patriot president of South Carolina, John Rutledge, was not immune to the contagious fear. He immediately sent an anxious plea to General Lee for help. "I wish you and a powerful reinforcement were now here," Rutledge wrote. "For God's sake lose not a moment."[18] The message was copied and sent by several couriers along different routes so that Lee would not be missed. When Lee finally arrived in the South Carolina capital on 8 June,[19] he brought with him an element of sanity. Thousands of reinforcements from North Carolina and Virginia were close behind him, Lee told the city. Just as important as the troops he brought, General Lee brought his reputation. "His presence gave us great spirits," Moultrie attested. Despite Lee's "hasty and rough" manners, Moultrie conceded that his coming "was equal to a reinforcement of 1,000 men."[20]

Lee immediately began an examination of the defensive works of the city, and not surprisingly, the infamously fastidious general was not impressed by what he found. Giving "spur to all our actions," as Moultrie put it, Lee set about fixing everything. "He was every day and every hour of the day on horse back, or in boats viewing our situation and directing small works to be thrown up at different places."[21]

William Moultrie was a backwoods militia captain and Indian fighter with an affable personality. Charles Lee, on the other hand, was a sophisticated, world-traveled soldier and scholar infamous for his snobbish attitude. Predictably, the two did not get along. The two officers first clashed when Lee inspected Moultrie's fort: "When he came to Sullivan's Island, he did not like the post at all, he said there was no way to retreat, that the garrison would be sacrificed; nay he called it a 'slaughter pen,' and wished to withdraw the garrison and give up the post, but Rutledge insisted that it should not be given up."[22]

To comply with Rutledge's demand that the fort not be abandoned, General Lee ordered that a bridge of boats be constructed between Sullivan's Island and the mainland. The bridge would allow a means of escape for the garrison in case the fort was attacked with overwhelming force. However, the distance to shore was over a mile, and the Charlestonians did not have enough boats to complete the task. Moultrie constructed a thin, wood plank bridge floating on empty barrels, but it proved too flimsy to support the weight of more than a few men at a time. At this point Lee became obsessed with constructing an avenue of retreat for Moultrie's garrison, so certain was he that they would need one. "For my part," Moultrie stated, "I never was uneasy on not having a retreat because I never imagined that the enemy could force me to that necessity."[23]

Lee had reconciled himself to maintaining the post at Sullivan's Island only because John Rutledge, the president of South Carolina, insisted on it. Rutledge had, in fact, sent secret instructions to Moultrie telling him not to abandon Sullivan's Island without his explicit order, adding, "I will cut off my right hand sooner than write it." At the same time, in order to placate Lee, Rutledge issued a public order to Moultrie stating that all regular and militia forces in South Carolina were under General Lee's command and that "orders issued by him are to be obeyed."[24]

Rutledge's secret orders to Moultrie reveal that his cooperation with General Lee would last only as long as the general's command decisions were in accordance with his own. This subtle undermining of the authority of the Southern Department's Continental commander by the Charlestown civil authorities would be repeated with disastrous results when the city came under threat again in 1779 and 1780.

Attempting to mollify General Lee, Moultrie suggested that if a retreat were forced on him, the garrison could withdraw by boat. It seemed a satisfactory solution, but Lee refused to be satisfied: "I do not . . . much like the scheme of retreating by boats, it cannot, I think be done without confusion."[25] After that time Lee would hardly let a day go by without remonstrating Colonel Moultrie about the bridge. "Finish the bridge," one communiqué said; "I am in hopes your bridge will be finished this night," said another; "I must beg that you will be expeditious in finishing the bridge," he ordered yet again; "I hope your bridge is finished," and so on day after day. Although Moultrie began its construction, he never did complete the bridge, his reason being that he did not have enough boats. Lee, however, felt that the colonel was simply being obstinate.[26]

General Lee was probably correct in his assessment of the vulnerability of Fort Sullivan. The British certainly thought that the fort was vulnerable. Indeed, the only reason they were there was because of the incomplete state of the fortress. Moreover, Lee was not the only American officer who thought that the post was indefensible. One day in June, Captain Clement Lemprière, a respected Patriot privateer, inspected Fort Sullivan escorted by Moultrie. Standing on a rampart, the captain gestured toward the armada of British warships arrayed before them and asked, "Well Colonel what do you think of it now?" Moultrie said simply, "We should beat them." The mariner pointed to the fleet and said, "Sir, when those ships come to lay along side your fort, they will knock it down in half an hour." Moultrie coolly replied, "[Then] we will lay behind the ruins and prevent their men from landing."[27]

⟫◆⟪

The navigation of Charlestown harbor was notoriously tricky. Commodore Parker spent the first few days of June sounding the harbor and placing buoys to mark channels for his frigates. Parker's flagship, the fifty-gun *Bristol*, burdened by the weight of her armament, could not cross the Charlestown bar without first lightening her load. As a result the Royal Navy busied itself for a few days removing cannons from the frigate. On 10 June the ship was light enough to cross the bar and take up station with the rest of the warships in Five-Fathom Hole, an anchorage just past the bar but still out of range of Fort Sullivan.

During this time Clinton fitted out a small sloop and spent two days reconnoitering Sullivan's Island and Long Island. He became convinced that making an opposed landing on Sullivan's Island would involve "considerable hazard." Clinton consulted with his second in command, Lord Cornwallis, who had headed up the seven regiments that came from England. The two decided that the British troops would make an unopposed landing on Long Island (known today as the Isle of Palms), just to the north of Sullivan's Island. The two islands were separated at that time by a seventy-five-yard inlet known as the "Breach." Clinton had been told, apparently by a local, that the Breach was only eighteen inches deep at low tide, and thus easily forded.

Troop landings began on 9 June, and over the next nine days most of the British infantry (roughly twenty-two hundred men) had disembarked and bivouacked on Long
Island. The initial assault plan called for Parker's flotilla to begin a cannonade, at which
point Clinton's troops would sortie across the Breach and make a landward attack
against Fort Sullivan in concert with the naval bombardment. The plan immediately
unraveled when Clinton discovered that the Breach was not eighteen inches deep at low
tide, but rather a swampy morass up to seven feet deep in places: too deep to ford. Clinton could still attempt to cross the Breach by boat, but he only had enough craft to carry
seven hundred men at a time. In addition, shallow spots in the water made a crossing
by boat a slow and tedious affair, a particularly dangerous proposition while under
enemy observation.

Once the British had landed, General Lee's job became much easier. It was obvious
that Fort Sullivan was Clinton's intended target, and not Charlestown proper. Lee immediately reinforced points near Long Island in order to contain the British landing.
At one point Lee ordered one of his regiments to counterattack the British beachhead,
but he later canceled the order (good thing for him, too, as Lee did not realize the strength
of Clinton's force). Colonel William Thompson was placed in charge of the American
defense of the Breach with 780 Carolina troops and two cannons. Initially, Thompson
placed his force at the extreme northern tip of Sullivan's Island, near the water's edge
—an exposed position within range of the British artillery on Long Island. The British
commanders were encouraged by the sloppy disposition of the American defenses. Clinton and Cornwallis were hopeful that they could use their field pieces to bombard the
Americans and force them to withdraw from their works; the British could then use their
flatboats to land their troops on Sullivan's Island under the cover of their fieldpieces.

On one of his numerous inspection tours, General Lee noticed the poor disposition of Thompson's detachment and ordered the men to take up a stronger post to the
rear. Thompson accordingly retrenched himself five hundred yards back from the Breach
and out of range of British cannons. It was a smart and—unbeknownst to the Patriots
—timely move as the British were almost ready to attack. "They removed themselves
from this [vulnerable] station," Clinton wrote, "and took up some very strong ground
500 yards back, in a much more extended front than the narrow spit of land on which
they had first placed themselves, having a battery on their right and a morass on their
left."[28] It was now impossible for Clinton and Cornwallis to use their fieldpieces to bombard the Americans, whereas any landing on Sullivan's Island would have to be done
under the fire of Thompson's cannons. The two British generals concluded that they
could not force a crossing of the Breach without suffering unacceptable losses. In effect,
the British army had been neutralized.

The lavish attention that General Lee paid to the green Carolina troops has been
called both "henpecking" and "micromanagement" by James Buchanan in *The Road to
Guilford Court House* (11). Charles Lee was certainly effete, overbearing, and arrogant;
yet even his rival William Moultrie had to admit that Lee played a valuable role teach-
ing the inexperienced South Carolina troops war-fighting skills. The newly minted American officer corps had had little formal military training. Even those officers who had

seen action in the field were mostly experienced at skirmishing with Indians—not battling professional, world-class military powers. In other words, the young American military *needed* some henpecking from experienced officers such as Lee. The general's "micromanagement" of Thompson's corps saved them from bombardment and assault, and prevented the British army from playing any significant role in the upcoming battle.

Commodore Parker was not overly concerned with Clinton's sticky predicament on Long Island. Letters that the commodore sent to Clinton at this time reveal that the naval commander believed his ships could pummel Fort Sullivan into submission without help from the army. Parker informed Clinton that his plan was first to silence the fort's batteries by naval gunfire, after which he would "land seamen and marines (which I have practiced for the purpose) under the guns to get in through the embrasures." Emphasizing his belief that he needed no assistance from Clinton's infantry, Parker added, "Should this happen, we [the marines and sailors] may keep possession till you send as many troops as you think proper."[29]

On 24 June, Parker attempted to close with the fort, but a sudden squall prevented the attack. This was just as well for the British since it allowed time for HMS *Experiment,* another fifty-gun frigate, to join Parker's fleet on the 25th. Between Clinton's ineffective maneuvering, unfavorable winds, and other factors, the British had hovered nearly a month outside of Charlestown. This delay gave the rebels, as one British observer put it, "every opportunity they could have asked for to extend their lines . . . [and] they were not idle."[30] There was some grumbling among the British troops ashore that the fleet was not being sufficiently aggressive, to which Parker was said to have replied, "Lord Cornwallis might march his troops when he pleased, but the fleet required a fair wind."[31] At about half past ten on the morning of 28 June 1776, the winds finally favored the commodore, and he flew the signal to weigh anchor.

Parker sent nine frigates against the fort in three divisions. The first division, commanded by the commodore personally, consisted of four frigates: *Bristol* (Parker's flagship) and *Experiment,* each rated at fifty guns; and *Active* and *Solebay,* each carrying twenty-eight guns. These ships were to hammer the southeastern face of the fortress and its bastions. This side of the fortress had a dominant view of the harbor and was therefore where the Americans had placed their biggest guns.

The second division consisted of *Friendship* and *Thunder,* the latter being a "bomb" ship that carried eight mortars capable of firing explosive shells. The mortar shells could arc over the walls of the fort, while normal cannons could only fire solid shot in a flat trajectory. *Friendship,* a transport recently converted to carry twenty-two cannons, was assigned to *Thunder* as an escort.

The third division consisted of the twenty-eight-gun frigates *Syren* and *Acteon,* as well as the twenty-gun *Sphynx.* These ships had the critical task of outflanking the fort in order to fire on its unfinished west side. Parker's plan was for the first division to drive the rebels out of the fort with cannon fire, supported by *Thunder's* mortars. The third division would then cut off or destroy the garrison as it made its escape, be that by boats or bridge.[32]

On 27 June 1776 General Lee made up his mind to relieve Colonel Moultrie of his command. Moultrie had not completed the bridge as ordered, nor had he finished other improvements to the fort that Lee had commanded. That night Lee sent orders to Colonel Francis Nash of the 1st North Carolina Continentals to come see him the next day. It was Lee's intention to replace Moultrie with Nash as commander of Fort Sullivan. The next morning was 28 June. Colonel Nash was coming to see Lee as ordered when he saw something that stopped him dead in his tracks: the British fleet was bearing down on Sullivan's Island. When General Lee heard this news, he realized that it was now too late to switch commanders at Fort Sullivan. In an ironic twist of fate, Moultrie's command had been saved by the British attack!

That morning a flare-up in William Moultrie's gout kept the forty-five-year-old colonel from sleeping. Moultrie decided to make his insomnia useful. He rode three miles to the opposite end of Sullivan's Island in order to inspect Colonel Thompson's post at the Breach. About midmorning Moultrie noticed some of Clinton's boats on Long Island preparing, apparently, to make an assault on Thompson's position. Moultrie then looked to the south and saw that the British warships had loosed their topsails and were beginning to move toward Sullivan's Island. Moultrie realized that the decisive day had come—and he was three miles from the fort! Expecting an attack by Clinton across the Breach, Moultrie grabbed Thompson and told him to hold his position as long as possible but to fall back to the fort if necessary. Mounting his horse, Fort Sullivan's commander rushed back to his post.

Leaving a trail of mud and dust behind him, Moultrie reached Fort Sullivan before the British ships. Dashing through the gate, he "ordered the long roll to beat, and officers and men to their posts."[33] The soldiers of the garrison spilled out of their bunks and took their places on the ramparts and at the cannons. Morale was high, and the men were ready to begin the long anticipated fight. Unlike many American units, the 413 men of the 2nd South Carolina Regiment were smartly uniformed in blue coats faced with red. The silver crescent moon of South Carolina was affixed to the front of each soldier's black cap. In addition, 22 men of the 4th South Carolina Regiment of Artillery helped man the artillery batteries. The flag that flew above the fort was of Moultrie's own design. It had a blue field with a pale crescent located in the upper left corner and the word "LIBERTY" emblazoned in large white letters along the bottom.

The day was clear and hot. At about eleven o'clock *Thunder* opened the battle with a salvo of shells intended to cover the approach of Commodore Parker's division. *Solebay, Experiment, Bristol,* and *Active* approached the island head on and in that order. "[They] came sailing up," Moultrie remembered, "as if in confidence of victory; as soon as they came within reach of our guns, we began to fire."[34] When they were about four hundred yards from the fort, the commodore's four ships dropped anchor and swung around to present their starboard (right) sides to the island.[35] Each of the four ships then unleashed a broadside at the fort. They continued to fire broadside after broadside until the air in the harbor was filled with billowing clouds of white smoke.

Hundreds of shots smashed into the fortress, but they made almost no impression on the walls. To most everyone's surprise, the soft palmetto logs (backed by sixteen feet of earth) easily absorbed or deflected the heavy cannonballs.

Thunder fired its explosive shells with great accuracy but, as Moultrie described it, without much effect. "Most of [the shells] fell within the fort," he wrote, "but we had a morass in the middle, that swallowed them up instantly, and those that fell in the sand in and about the fort, were immediately buried, so that very few of them bursted amongst us."[36] *Thunder* lost her voice early in the conflict because the vessel had been situated too far away from its target. The ship's engineer increased the range of the mortars by adding more powder to each shot, but after about twenty volleys the recoil of the overcharged guns broke their beds and left them disabled for the rest of the battle. As this ship was the only one capable of firing over the fort's walls, the loss of its firepower was sorely felt by Commodore Parker.

The soldiers of the 2nd South Carolina Regiment were trained to fire the cannons in addition to their small arms. They therefore served as matrosses, or assistants, to the dedicated artillerymen of the 4th South Carolina Regiment of Artillery. The fort was equipped with thirty-one guns, mostly French-made eighteen- and twenty-six-pounders.[37] The American cannoneers fired round after round into the wooden hulls of the British men-of-war. Balls smashed into the rigging and raked the decks of all the ships, but most of the fire was concentrated on the two fifty-gun frigates.

At about noon the third division of British ships—*Sphynx, Acteon,* and *Syren*—approached the battle area and began their planned movement to outflank the fort. Seeing the drubbing the rest of the fleet was getting, the pilots of the third division tried to keep their distance from the fort as they maneuvered through the channel. Paying too much attention to the American guns and not enough to their craft, these pilots accidentally steered the division into the "Middle Ground," a well-known bar in the center of the ship channel that would later become the foundation of Fort Sumter.[38] All three ships ran aground, but *Sphynx* and *Acteon* also became fouled with each other. In order to untangle the two ships, *Sphynx* had to cut off its bowsprit. Eventually *Sphynx* and *Syren* were able to refloat, but too late to attempt their original mission. *Acteon,* however, would remain stuck fast on the Middle Ground throughout the battle.

The flanking movement by the third division was the best chance the British had to win. Only through conspicuous bad judgment on the part of the ship's pilots and captains did the maneuver fail. Even Colonel Moultrie admitted that fact. "Had these three ships effected their purpose," he wrote, "they would have enfiladed us in such a manner, as to have driven us from our guns." Despite this setback, Commodore Parker still thought that he could drive the rebels out of the fort using sheer firepower. He kept the remainder of his ships on station for the rest of the day attempting to batter the fortress apart. "At one time," Moultrie recalled, "3 or 4 of the men-of-war's [*sic*] broadsides struck the fort at the same instant, which gave the merlons [walls] such a tremor, that I was apprehensive that a few more such would tumble them down." But the walls never yielded.[39]

The Americans made the two largest ships their primary targets, the officers and men on the gun platform shouting, "Mind the Commodore, mind the two fifty gun ships!"

At one point in the action, the spring of one of *Bristol*'s anchor cables was shot away. The vessel swung around uncontrolled until the stern of the ship faced the fort, leaving it vulnerable and unable to return fire. The ship would regain control, but not before the Americans perceived *Bristol*'s difficulty and fired "all the guns that could bear on her."[40]

The *Bristol*'s surgeon described the horror of the American cannonade: "The spring of her cable shot away—of course she lay end on to the battery and was raked fore and aft; she lost upwards of one hundred men killed and wounded. Captain Morris, who commanded her, lost his arm; the worthy man, however, died a week after on board the *Pigot*. Perhaps an instance of such slaughter cannot be produced; twice the quarter-deck was cleared of every person except Sir Peter [Parker], and he was slightly wounded. She had nine thirty-two-pound shot in her mainmast, which is so much damaged as to be obliged to be shortened; the mizzen had seven thirty-two-pound shot and was obliged, being shattered, to be entirely cut away."[41]

The commodore's wound was the result of a large splinter that was kicked up by a nearby hit. The blast tore Parker's breeches off and "laid his backside bare, his thigh and knee wounded, and he walks only with the support of two men."[42] For a critical period of time the "backsides" of both the *Bristol* and the commodore were literally hanging in the wind.

Lord William Campbell, the royal governor of South Carolina, had volunteered to man a cannon aboard the *Bristol*. The governor had once said that two frigates could easily conquer Charlestown and that the American soldiers at Fort Sullivan would run after the second British volley was fired at them. He was relieved of this notion when the concussion from an American cannonball knocked him from his gun and gave him a severe contusion on his left side. At the time Campbell's injury was not thought to be of "much consequence."[43] However, the former governor died two years later in England from complications attributed to this wound.

As the battle wore on into the afternoon, the heat became oppressive. The thirst of the 2nd South Carolina Regiment of Foot was quenched by fire buckets of grog. "We partook of [the grog] very heartily; I never had a more agreeable draught than that which I took out of one of those buckets at the time." Spirits in the fort were generally high through the action. "Never did men fight more bravely," Moultrie said, "and never were men more cool."[44]

The biggest worry for the Patriots was their dwindling supply of ammunition. They began the day with forty-six hundred pounds of powder, enough for about twenty-eight rounds for each of their twenty-six largest guns. However, as the action dragged on hour after hour into the afternoon, it became apparent that the scarcity of powder might be their undoing. At about three o'clock in the afternoon, Moultrie received an erroneous report that Clinton had effected a landing in between Colonel Thompson's position and the fort. Moultrie decided to stop the cannonade of the fleet in order to save powder for grapeshot and small arms that would be needed to repel an infantry assault; at the same time, he applied to the mainland for more powder.

The pause in the American fire puzzled the British. Commodore Parker finally concluded that the Patriots had abandoned the fort, and he later accused Clinton of failing to seize the structure while it was "undefended." Of course, it is not clear why Parker did not land his own marines, as was his stated plan, if he truly thought the defenders had fled. In any case, both Clinton and Parker failed to take advantage of the slack in the American cannonade. About an hour passed before Moultrie decided that the report of the British landing was in error. He then ordered his big guns to resume firing at the fleet. "The fire [from the fort] became exceedingly severe when it was renewed again," a British sailor observed, "and did amazing execution."[45]

Responding to Moultrie's request for additional ammunition, President Rutledge dipped into the city's reserves to resupply the fort. At the height of the engagement, Moultrie received the badly needed powder accompanied by a note that read: "I send you 500 pounds of powder. . . . You know our collection is not very great. HONOR and VICTORY, my good sir, to you, and our worthy countrymen with you. P.S. Do not make too free with your cannon. Cool and do mischief."[46] Yet another 200 pounds of powder was appropriated from a Whig schooner lying behind Sullivan's Island.

General Lee watched the action closely from the mainland. Though he had fought in wars all over Europe and America, Lee still called the fight "one of the most furious and incessant fires I ever saw or heard."[47] Moultrie described the hours of bombardment as "one continual blaze and roar."[48] At about five o'clock in the afternoon, Lee decided to visit the island himself. Riding in a boat packed with gunpowder to resupply the fort, Lee braved numerous British cannonballs that overshot the fort and landed in the water on the landward side of the island.

When Colonel Moultrie heard that Lee was coming, he sent Lieutenant Colonel Francis Marion (later to become a famous partisan leader known as the "Swamp Fox") to unbar the gate. When Lee entered the fort, Moultrie and his officers quickly extinguished their pipes, knowing that their demanding commander would not approve of such informal behavior in front of the enlisted men during battle. Moultrie greeted Lee and offered to show him around the post, completely unaware that just a few hours earlier his superior had come close to relieving him of his command. Taking a quick tour of the fort, Lee took the time to aim two or three guns and then turned to Moultrie, saying, "Colonel, I see you are doing very well here, you have no occasion for me, I will go up to town again."[49]

The Americans within the fort suffered surprisingly few losses considering the intensity of the combat. Moultrie reported twelve killed and twenty-four wounded (and at least five of the wounded died within a few days).[50] All of the Patriot casualties were from cannonballs that passed through the embrasures (ports for the cannons). At one point three men were ripped apart by a British cannon shot as they stood in a line positioning a cannon. Not one man made a sound during the split second it took for them all to be killed.

Others took longer to die. Sergeant McDaniel was hit by a cannonball that took off his shoulder and "scouped out his stomach." Knowing his wound was mortal, he shouted to the other men: "Fight on, my brave boys; don't let liberty expire with me today!"[51] General Lee said that the maimed and wounded soldiers "enthusiastically encouraged their comrades never to abandon the standard of liberty and their country. This I do assure you, is not in the style of gasconading romance usual after every successful action, but literally a fact."[52]

The battle raged hour after hour. The citizens of Charlestown watched the spectacle from the rooftops and the wharves. "Looking on with anxious hopes and fears," Moultrie wrote, "[their] hearts must have been pierced at every broadside."[53] During the course of the fight a British cannonball snapped the fort's flagstaff, and the flag fluttered down outside the walls. Many in the city thought that the fort had struck its colors. Sergeant William Jasper called out to Moultrie, "Colonel, don't let us fight without a flag!" The colonel replied, "What can you do? The staff is broke."[54] The brave sergeant then leaped through one of the embrasures, cannonballs ripping through the air around him, and retrieved the flag. He immediately tied it to a sponge staff and planted it atop the bastion closest to the enemy ships.[55] "Our flag once more waving in the air," Moultrie recalled, "revived the drooping spirits of our friends; and they continued looking on, till night had closed the scene, and hid us from their view; only the appearance of a heavy storm, with continual flashes and peals of thunder."[56] At about nine o'clock that night, after almost ten hours of combat, the thunder stopped and what must have seemed an eternity of battle to the participants finally ended. Parker's ships quietly slipped their anchor cables and took up position again in the safety of Five-Fathom Hole.

The next morning the British surveyed the damage and licked their wounds. The *Bristol*, Parker's flagship, had suffered forty killed and seventy-one wounded. *Bristol's* damaged mizzenmast fell overboard the next day, and twenty-two feet had to be cut off the main mast. The vessel's hull had been holed more than seventy times, and the ship had been set afire three times by hot shot fired from the fort.[57] "If the water had not been very smooth," one observer remarked, "it would have been impossible to have kept her from sinking."[58] *Experiment's* crew had twenty-three killed and fifty-six wounded and, like *Bristol*, "suffered much in her hull, masts, yards and rigging."[59] Of course, many of the injured on both sides died of their wounds within days of the action. Both of the fifty-gun frigates numbered their captains among the casualties. Captain Alexander Scott of *Experiment* lost his left arm during the action; the wound forced his retirement from the service.[60] Captain Morris of *Bristol* lost his right arm during the battle and died two days later.

Dawn revealed *Acteon* still stuck fast on the Middle Ground on 29 June; with the light coming up, her captain decided to scuttle the ship. The officers set the ship ablaze and evacuated the vessel. With more than a bit of daring, an American boarding party rowed out from the fort and took possession of the smoldering vessel. These men even had the audacity to fire some of *Acteon's* cannons at *Bristol* during their brief occupation. Counting the ship's bell among their loot, the raiders had scarcely evacuated the burning hulk when the fire reached the ship's powder magazine. A terrific blast tore the frigate apart and shook the harbor and city. "The explosion," Moultrie said, "issued a grand pillar of smoke, which soon expanded itself at the top, and to appearance, formed the figure of a palmetto tree."[61]

The action was of unusual duration and severity considering the number of ships and men involved. More than twelve hundred shots and shells would be plucked from in and around Moultrie's fortress. The British had expended more than seven times the amount of powder that the Americans used: thirty-four thousand pounds against forty-seven hundred pounds. Moultrie insisted that if he had more powder he would have undoubtedly sunk the British fleet. The question must be asked why Commodore Parker persisted in the attack for so long when it was apparent after the first few hours that they could not batter the fort into submission. Moultrie believes that the British could not withdraw for most of the day because the wind and the tide were against them; but it is likely that Parker was also being stubborn. He did not want to admit to defeat by an opponent he considered second-rate.[62]

Clinton had watched the battle impotently from Long Island. Two or three times he attempted an amphibious assault across the Breach, but he was turned back each time by rifle and cannon fire from Thompson's corps. Clinton later claimed that he was opposed by "3 or 4000 men," though Thompson's command actually numbered just 780 troops. Clinton might have attempted a landing further up the shore to the north, in order to attempt an attack on Haddrells Point and so cut off the fort from resupply and reinforcement. However, Lee had anticipated this possibility, and fifteen hundred men were in position to cover that approach. In the end, the danger of moving in open boats under the guns of the enemy was too intimidating for Clinton—he retired to Long Island having accomplished nothing.[63]

Recriminations began immediately between the British army and the Royal Navy over responsibility for the defeat, but both Parker and Clinton made mistakes. Clinton failed to conduct a proper reconnaissance of the Breach before he landed all of his troops on Long Island, effectively removing them from the conflict. Ultimately, though, Commodore Parker must bear the greatest blame for the defeat. Parker had underestimated the resilience of the Americans. He assumed that after a few broadsides the inexperienced American soldiers would flee; but when they failed to run, the commodore was at a loss to know how to proceed.

Clinton stated in his official report to Lord Germain that Parker had stationed his ships too far away from the fort for their attack to be effective. On this point Clinton was correct. Had Parker maneuvered his ships to within seventy yards of the fort as he had originally planned, his vessels would have been able to employ grapeshot from their cannons, which would have been more effective in silencing the American guns. Also, at this closer range Parker might have been able to place sharpshooters in the masts and yardarms so that they could fire muskets over the walls directly down into the fort. Moultrie claimed that the walls of the fort were high enough to cover his men from fire from the ships' tops, though it is perhaps fortunate for the garrison that his belief was not put to the test.[64]

Parker admitted that the ships were posted too far away, but he put the blame on his pilots: local blacks who had been pressed into British service. Despite Parker's orders to move in closer, the pilots refused for fear of running aground. Parker might have anticipated that civilian pilots, who had no desire or duty to put themselves in harm's way, would not want to steer their ships to within point-blank range of the fort. Parker could have moved his ships closer to the fort against the advice of the pilots, but he had obviously been afraid to do so. To run aground so close to the fort would have sealed the ships' fate. Furthermore, Parker's reliance on civilian pilots caused the failure of his flanking maneuver. Afraid of the fort's fire, the pilots steered the three ships of the third division as far away from the island as possible, ultimately running them aground on a well-known bar. Indeed, it is hard to shake the suspicion that the pilots—who were intimately familiar with every detail of the harbor—deliberately steered the ships into the bar in order to escape the more hazardous station they were to have taken up.

Parker's ships would probably not have received much damage if they had merely sailed past Sullivan's Island and into the harbor. In 1780 a British fleet would do just that, suffering little damage because they sailed in and out of range of Fort Sullivan's guns so quickly. However, in 1776 the British had insufficient force to take the city, and Fort Sullivan was the British object.

On 21 July 1776 Clinton and Cornwallis evacuated South Carolina and the British fleet began its journey northward. As a postscript to the battle, the British transport *Glasgow*, with fifty-six Scottish soldiers aboard, ran aground as it attempted to depart the waters off Long Island. The Americans quickly sent an armed galley with a boarding party to take control of the stranded vessel. After taking the Highlanders captive, along with the ship's crew, the Americans burned the ship.[65] The rest of the British fleet departed South Carolina's waters safely and joined Admiral Richard Howe's armada near the New York coast in time for Clinton's troops to participate in the British assault on New York in August.

Despite Parker's culpability in the disaster at Charlestown, he won a public war of letters and pamphlets in England with Clinton over who was responsible. Parker went on to become admiral of the fleet and was eventually knighted for the personal courage he displayed at Charlestown in 1776. Clinton was quietly exonerated of any wrongdoing in the matter by the government. However, in the public eye Clinton was to blame for the debacle. The discredited general would somewhat redeem himself a little over a month later by leading a brilliant flanking attack at the battle of Harlem Heights in New York.

The battle for Charlestown generated a great deal of interest in Britain. Accounts of the engagement and illustrated maps of the action were eagerly consumed by the literate classes. The reason for this interest was that the battle was the first naval defeat of the war. In some ways the fight for Sullivan's Island was the Royal Navy's Bunker Hill—except that the Americans kept their ground. Like General Gage at Boston, Commodore Parker underestimated American spirit and fighting skill at Sullivan's Island —and his men suffered heavily for the error. "This will not be believed when it is first reported in England," the *Bristol*'s surgeon wrote; "I can scarcely believe what I myself saw on that day. . . . One would have imagined no battery could have resisted [the Royal Navy's] incessant fire."[66]

While the British were busy trading recriminations for a disaster, the Americans were happy to share the fruits of victory with one another. Everyone in the city celebrated: "Old and young, high and low, rich and poor, white and black, one with another."[67] Indeed, black slaves deserve as much credit for the victory as anyone, for they were mostly the ones who had toiled so hard to create the impermeable ramparts on which Colonel Moultrie stood so firmly. In addition to the white soldiers, a black servant of one of the fort's officers was killed by a British cannonball during the battle.

Charles Lee received due praise in Congress and from the Charlestonians for his work in shoring up the city's weak defenses on his arrival. Of course, the greatest laurels went to Colonel Moultrie; for him, the victory was a vindication of his men, his fort, and his judgment. Moultrie took great pleasure watching his rival Lee eat his words about the fort being a "slaughter pen." Moultrie said, "after the 28th of June, [Lee] made me his bosom friend."[68] The South Carolina legislature finally officially named the fort on Sullivan's Island, dubbing it "Fort Moultrie" in the colonel's honor. Moultrie remained popular with the citizens of South Carolina, and after the war he served two terms as governor of the state.

Sergeant William Jasper became a folk hero for his bravery in saving the fort's flag. President John Rutledge, who many years later became chief justice of the Supreme Court of South Carolina (and who was nominated to serve as chief justice of the U.S. Supreme Court but was rejected by the Senate), presented the young sergeant with a sword. Rutledge then offered to promote the youthful hero to the rank of lieutenant, but Jasper, citing his lack of education and literacy, declined the commission, saying, "I am not fit to keep officer's company; I am but a sergeant."[69]

The 2nd South Carolina Regiment of Foot was given many gifts—including a barrel of Antigua rum—but none was as treasured as the two regimental colors presented to them on 1 July 1776. They were sewn with care by Susannah Elliot, the wife of one of the unit's officers, Major Barnard Elliot. Mrs. Elliot handed the flags, one blue and the other red, to Colonel Moultrie and Lieutenant Colonel Francis Marion, saying, "I make not the least doubt, under heaven's protection, you will stand by them as long as they can wave in the air of LIBERTY."[70] Three years later Sergeant Jasper and two other color bearers of the 2nd South Carolina would meet their deaths attempting to place these colors atop the British ramparts at Savannah in 1779.

The battle of Sullivan's Island would be the first and last action that General Charles Lee would see in the South. Lee was uncharacteristically magnanimous in his praise of Moultrie and the Carolina troops. He freely gave them credit for the victory. However, Lee's limitless ego and lack of tact would eventually become his undoing. He commanded in several important engagements in the coming years, but in June 1778 Lee put in a disgraceful performance leading the American vanguard at the battle of Monmouth Court House in Pennsylvania. Washington did little more than scold and censure Lee for his conduct, but Lee's ego was so bruised that he wrote letters disrespectful of Washington and demanded a court-martial to clear his name. Congress and Washington obliged Lee, found him guilty of disobeying orders, and terminated his career. He died soon after being dismissed from service in 1782, a man little loved by others.

On 4 July 1776, only six days after the battle at Sullivan's Island, the Continental Congress declared independence from England. The United States of America was now a sovereign nation. The previous spring the British had evacuated Boston, and after Clinton's retreat from Charlestown in July, the newborn American nation was free from the presence of any British troops on its soil. In August, however, the strategic situation changed dramatically. The British attacked and captured the city of New York, which became their principal base in America until the end of the war. For the time being, however, the South was safe. The repulse of the Royal Navy at Charlestown represented an early end to the first attempt by the British to implement their Southern Strategy. The efforts of men such as William Woodford in Virginia, Richard Caswell in North Carolina, and William Moultrie in South Carolina bought the southern states an extended respite. For the next two and a half years the secure South was able to send military aid to the North. Even more important, the South was free to trade goods such as tobacco and indigo with Europe in order to generate hard currency for the war effort. The British had lost the first southern campaign, but they would be back.

ORDER OF BATTLE: SULLIVAN'S ISLAND
South Carolina, 28 June 1776

American Forces
Maj. Gen. Charles Lee

	MEN	ARTILLERY
Fort Sullivan —Col. William Moultrie		
2nd S.C. Regiment of Foot	413	
4th S.C. Regiment of Artillery (detachment)	22	
Cannon (9-lb.)		ca. 7
Cannon (12-lb.)		ca. 9
Cannon (18-lb.)		6
Cannon (26-lb.)		9
Total	**435**	**ca. 31**
The Breach on Sullivan's Island—		
Lt. Col. William Thompson		
3rd S.C. Rifle Regiment (Rangers)—		
Lt. Col. William Thompson	300	
1st N.C. Regiment (detachment)—		
Lt. Col. Thomas Clark	200	
S.C. Militia—Lt. Col. Daniel Horry	200	
"Raccoon" Company—Capt. John Allston	50	
Charleston Militia	30	
Artillery		
Cannon (18-lb.)		1
Cannon (6-lb.)		1
Total	**780**	**2**
Haddrells Point—Brig. Gen. James Armstrong		
5th S.C. Rifle Regiment—Col. Isaac Huger	268	
6th S.C. Rifle Regiment—Col. Thomas Sumter	160	
1st N.C. Regiment (detachment)—		
Col. Francis Nash	ca. 221	
2nd N.C. Regiment—Col. Alexander Martin	345	
8th Virginia Regiment[71] Peter Mulhenburg	535	

	MEN	ARTILLERY
Charlestown Artillery	40	?
Total	**ca. 1,569**	**?**

James Island—Col. Christopher Gadsden
Fort Johnson
    1st S.C. Regiment of Foot

	MEN	ARTILLERY
(Cannon 18–26-lb.)	380	ca. 20
Detached Battery		
Company of 1st S.C. (Cannon "heavy")—		
Capt. Thomas Pinckney	60	12
Total	440	ca. 32

Charlestown and Environs—
  Maj. Gen. Charles Lee

	MEN	ARTILLERY
S.C. "Country" Militia	1,972	
Charleston Militia	700	
3rd N.C. Regiment—Col. Jethro Sumner	397	
4th S.C. Artillery Regiment—		
Lt. Col. Owen Roberts	200	?
Total	3,269	?
American Grand Total	**ca. 6,493**	**ca. 65**

British Forces

Royal Navy—Commodore Sir Peter Parker

	GUNS	KILLED	WOUNDED
Bristol (frigate)—			
Capt. John Morris (killed)	50	40	71
Experiment (frigate)—			
Capt. Alexander Scott (wounded)	50	23	56
Active (frigate)—Capt. William Williams	28	1	6
Solebay (frigate)—Capt. Thomas Symons	28		8
Acteon (frigate)—Capt. Christopher Atkins	28		
Syren (frigate)—Capt. Tobias Furneaux	28		
Sphynx (frigate)—Capt. Anthony Hunt	20		
Friendship (armed transport)—			
Capt. Charles Hope	22		
Thunder (bombship w/mortars)—			
Capt. James Reid	8		
Ranger (sloop)—Capt. Roger Wills	8		
St. Lawrence (schooner)—			
Lt. John Graves	8		
Total	278	64	141

Order of Battle: Sullivan's Island (*continued*)

Royal Army & Marines—Maj. Gen. Henry Clinton

	MEN	ARTILLERY
15th, 33rd, 37th, 42nd, 54th, 57th Regiments of Foot	ca. 2,200	
Royal Marines	est. 700	
Total	**ca. 2,900**	?

Casualties

	AMERICAN	BRITISH
Killed	12	64
Wounded	26	141
Missing	–	–
Total Casualties	**37**	**205**
Captured[72]	–	5
Total Losses	**37**	**210**

⊹≒ F I V E ≒⊹

Remaking the Southern Strategy

*"Conquest of these provinces is considered by
the King as an object of great importance."*

THE END OF CLINTON'S southern expedition of 1776 marked the beginning of a long respite from war for the American South. In fact, the region was virtually ignored by the British military for the next two and a half years. British strategists had determined early in the war that New England was the heart of the rebellion, and their initial strategic focus was centered on isolating and subduing that region. Their logic was that if this hotbed of rebellion could be pacified, the remaining colonies would soon give up the fight.

For the first half of 1776 things had gone well for the Americans. George Washington forced the British to evacuate Boston in March, an event that so boosted American spirits that only a few months later the United States declared its independence on 4 July. However, this was the apogee of American fortunes for the year. In August the British theater commander, General William Howe, attacked and captured the city of New York, which became the primary British base in America for the remainder of the war. A series of defeats at Long Island, Fort Washington, and White Plains sapped the American army of its strength and morale. Forced to retreat into New Jersey, the Americans were on the verge of utter despair and defeat. Had it not been for Washington's brilliant and daring counterattacks at Trenton and Princeton at the end of 1776, the Continental Army might have disintegrated and the British possibly could have won the war then and there. As it was, the spring of 1777 saw a rebuilt American army ready to fight again.

Superior resources and naval mobility allowed the British to retain the initiative, which they used to mount two major offensives in the spring and summer of 1777. General William Howe led an expedition against Philadelphia, which he captured in September after a sharp fight with Washington at Brandywine Creek. A second offensive commanded by General John Burgoyne was launched from Canada into upstate New York with the ultimate goal of isolating and subjugating New England. However, Burgoyne's army was defeated and captured in October by Generals Horatio Gates and Benedict Arnold at Saratoga. This world-changing victory secured America's northern frontier with Canada and—most important—convinced the French to enter the war on America's side.

France had been discreetly supporting the Americans with arms, munitions, and money for years—but they had been reluctant to ally openly with the United States. King Louis XVI was unsure if the nascent American military could compete with the English, especially after the disastrous 1776 New York campaign. However, Saratoga eliminated all doubt and established America as a serious local military power. Another major action was fought at Germantown, just outside of Philadelphia, in October 1777. Though the battle was inconclusive, the Americans made a good showing and for a time even had the British on the run. Germantown thus served as a morale booster for the American cause and was further proof for the French that the professionalism exhibited by U.S. forces at Saratoga was not a fluke. On 6 February 1778 King Louis XVI signed a treaty of alliance with the United States.

General Henry Clinton officially succeeded William Howe as commander in chief of the British army in America in spring 1778. Despite his dismal performance at Charles-town in 1776, Clinton performed well in the North. He conceived and commanded the battle-winning flank attack at Long Island, and his well-executed capture of New-port, Rhode Island, was also appreciated by London. As a result, Clinton was knighted and promoted to lieutenant general in 1777. (He was also given the "local" rank of full general in America.) Clinton accepted the senior position in America with some reluc-tance since the military situation was obviously not as favorable at that time as it had been in the preceding years. The entry of France into the war had drastically changed the strategic outlook for England. Britain now had to fight a global war that included America, the Caribbean, and distant India—all the while guarding against the very real possibility of an invasion of the home islands.

The war having taken on a more ominous demeanor, the British king and his min-isters decided that it was time to attempt to reconcile with their American brethren so that the greater threat of France could be dealt with more effectively. Parliament re-pealed the Tea Act and most of the provisions of the Intolerable Acts that had prompted the rebellion. A peace commission under Lord Carlisle (which became known as the Carlisle Commission) was then appointed and sent to America with orders to recon-cile the conflict.

Clinton was told to assume a defensive posture while the Carlisle Commission was attempting to negotiate with Congress. Lord Germain instructed Clinton to withdraw his army from Philadelphia and move it to New York in order to release men for opera-tions in the Caribbean against the French. Conveyance by sea was judged impractical due to the lack of sufficient transport and the fear of French naval attack, so Clinton chose to walk to New York. During the march, Washington engaged the extended British column at Monmouth Court House in New Jersey on 28 June 1778. What began as a sharp rearguard action turned into an all-out battle involving twelve thousand Ameri-cans and eleven thousand Britons. The fighting seesawed back and forth; however, the British withdrew after dark to leave Washington holding the field in victory.

Monmouth Court House was a strategic turning point in the war and the last major action fought in the northern states. Before leaving Philadelphia, Clinton claimed that he hoped to engage Washington so that he could destroy the American army. However, when given the opportunity to fight at Monmouth, Clinton chose to withdraw and assume a defensive posture in New York. Clinton's strategic withdrawal from Philadelphia and his tactical retreat at Monmouth proved that the British army in America was stretched beyond its means. The Americans were still too weak to take the initiative, but for the first time in the war the British could not claim it either.

⇒◆⇐

The Carlisle Commission arrived in America in early June 1778, empowered by the British king to give Congress nearly anything it wanted to end the rebellion—anything *except* independence. Had the British taken this step in 1775, it is almost certain that the American colonies would have reconciled with the mother country. However, the recent victory at Saratoga and the consummation of the alliance with France had Congress in a confident mood; the Americans were not going to accept anything *less* than full independence now. By the time Clinton's army reached New York at the end of June, it was apparent that Lord Carlisle had failed since Congress refused even to meet with his commission.

Lord Germain had previously given instructions to Clinton on how to prosecute the war in the event that the Carlisle Commission failed in its mission to end the war through negotiations. That now being the case, Clinton proceeded to implement Germain's new war plans. The secretary had detailed his strategy in two letters, dated 8 and 21 March 1778. Germain ordered Clinton to attempt quickly to bring Washington into a decisive engagement where he might destroy the Continental Army. (As previously noted, Clinton had this opportunity at Monmouth Court House on 28 June, but he chose to withdraw.) Germain's letters told Clinton that if Washington would not engage him on favorable terms, then Clinton should "give up every idea of offensive operations" in the North and instead shift the focus of the war southward. "The King was tempted by the thought of retaining the southern provinces," the British historian Fortescue wrote, "even if he should be forced to part with New England."[1]

The American secretary told Clinton that, "after the month of October [he was] to proceed to the conquest of Georgia and the Carolinas, and make at the same time every cooperating diversion in Virginia and Maryland, in the expectation they might lead to the entire reduction of all the colonies to the southward of [the] Susquehanna." If the southern operations were successful, Germain wrote, "the intention was to leave those to the northward to their own feelings, and make them suffer every distress which cutting off their supplies and blocking up their ports might occasion."[2]

The king and his ministers put their faith in men such as former royal governors Dunmore of Virginia, Campbell of South Carolina, and—of course—Josiah Martin of North Carolina. All of these men, who were now in England, continued to insist that the majority of southerners were Loyalists who would rise up in support of the Crown when and if British troops showed up to support them. The fact that all three of these royal officials had been run forcibly out of their gubernatorial mandates by vastly superior Whig armies seemed to be of no consequence to their thinking. The failure of Henry Clinton's 1776 southern expedition had likewise done little to reduce the interest of the king and his ministers in a new southern campaign. Indeed, the first British southern campaign had been such a debacle and was defeated so quickly that the belief developed that the Southern Strategy had not been given "a fair trial."

Unlike the southern campaign of 1776, which was to have started with an invasion of North Carolina, Germain's new Southern Strategy called for an invasion of Georgia, the southernmost American state. This approach had the advantage of helping to secure British Florida's northern border, and it would allow British forces in Florida to aid in subduing Georgia. Once Georgia was occupied, each state to the northward would be taken in turn, starting with South Carolina.

As was the case with the first southern expedition, the new southern campaign was justified by the principle of economy of force: Land a few thousand regular troops and receive manyfold Tory militia in return. Given the shortage of manpower that Britain faced, the potential return on investment seemed too lucrative not to try. Lord Germain thought that only a "small corps" would be needed to capture Georgia. The American secretary went so far as to speculate that "possession [of the Carolinas] might be easily maintained."[3]

It was also believed that the southern Indian nations, such as the Cherokee and Creeks, which were ostensibly allied to Britain, would be of help in subduing Georgia's and South Carolina's frontier. The Cherokee had launched a war against South Carolina in the summer of 1776 shortly after the British attack on Charlestown. Most Americans assumed that the Indian raids were timed to coincide with the British attack, but this was not the case. The Cherokee War of 1776 was coincidental with the first British southern campaign and not coordinated with it.

The Cherokee were swiftly crushed by Patriot militia and forced to make peace on terms favorable to the Americans. Nevertheless, John Stuart, the British superintendent for Indian affairs, promised Germain that the southern Indians would turn out in great numbers to support British military operations in the South. Based on Stuart's assurances, Germain funneled large amounts of gifts and cash to the Indian nations. However, when the time came, Stuart proved completely incapable of delivering on his promises. The Cherokee in South Carolina were unwilling to risk another war with the Americans, and the other southern Indian nations were no more eager to court destruction. In any case, Indian cooperation was never an essential feature of the Southern Strategy, which turned out to be a dead end for the British cause in the South.

The American secretary also thought that southern military operations would cripple the American economy. Since the nascent American government had no hard money, southern cash crops represented a substantial portion of the currency that the United States used to purchase weapons, ammunition, uniforms, and other war goods. Germain wanted to shut down the economic engine of the southern states: "A very valuable branch of commerce would be restored to this country and the rebels deprived of a principal resource for the support of their foreign credit. . . . The seizing or destroying [of] their shipping would also be attended with the important consequence of preventing the Congress from availing themselves, as they have done, of their staple commodity, tobacco, on which, and the rice and indigo of [South] Carolina and Georgia, they entirely depend for making remittances to Europe."[4]

Germain believed not only that the provender in Georgia alone would be enough to supply the British army forces deployed there, but also that "the British West India Islands may avail themselves of the supplies of provisions & lumber that province is capable of furnishing."[5] The American secretary also wanted Clinton to mount raids on Virginia and Maryland ports in order to destroy the tobacco trade there, as well as to prevent Washington's army from moving south to interfere with operations in the Carolinas. Germain left the details of prosecuting the war up to Clinton, but he also warned the British commander, "The conquest of these provinces is considered by the King as an object of great importance in the scale of the war."[6]

Attacking the weaker states in the South was part of a long-term strategy. Even if successful, it would take years for the Royal Army to work its way from Georgia to the northern states. The advantage to the scenario was that the southern states were much less populous and generally less wealthy than were their northern counterparts. The Americans would have difficulty deploying armies southward, distant from their centers of power. However, if the idea of strong Loyalist support is removed from the equation, this strategy would obviously take a large commitment of force, something that was not economically or politically palatable to the British government at the time. The new Southern Strategy was adopted only because Germain believed that there were sufficient numbers of Tories in the South to change the strategic balance of manpower in America decisively in Britain's favor.

Hindsight shows that there was not a Loyalist majority in the South; yet it was entirely possible for Lord Germain and the king to have reached the same conclusion had they been willing to learn from the failure of their first southern campaign. In the Moore's Creek Bridge campaign of 1776, only slightly fewer than fourteen hundred Loyalists were ever embodied, and even this number dwindled to fewer than eight hundred by the time of their defeat. During this same time North Carolina Patriots had been able to embody more than nine thousand regulars and militia to oppose the Loyalists. Likewise, in 1775 Governor Dunmore was only able to recruit a few hundred white Virginians to support the royal cause, while Virginia Whigs were able to form thousands into battalions that easily brushed Dunmore's troops aside and then went on to aid the other colonies in their struggle against Britain. Similar lackluster recruiting of Tories in South Carolina had resulted in a crushing defeat of Crown rule in that colony as well, months before Commodore Parker's ships were nearly blasted to kingdom come in Charlestown harbor.

Defeat of Britain's first southern campaign in 1776 made General Clinton wary of relying too much on Loyalists. He remained open to the prospect of renewed southern operations if sufficient resources could be allocated to the endeavor, but Clinton was uneasy about expanding the war at a time when Britain's military was becoming stretched ever more thin. Clinton's army had increased responsibilities and decreased manpower due to the entry of France into the war. Insufficient land and naval resources were, after all, why the British chose to give up Philadelphia. Clinton justifiably complained that Germain expected him to invade the South while keeping New York and Halifax secure even though he had fewer troops than his predecessors (Gage and Howe) who had no orders to open a southern front and no threat of French intervention.

Clinton was also unhappy with the way Germain framed his orders as "recommendations." This rhetorical tactic allowed the American secretary the ability to take credit for successes that came of his recommendations while at the same time retaining the capability to defer responsibility for the failures back to Clinton, who was the commander "on the spot." Because of these fundamental disagreements with Lord Germain's strategy and command style, Clinton attempted to resign as commander in chief in America. However, he was soon told that the king respected Clinton and would have no one else in the job. The king's compliment somewhat mollified Clinton, who set about the task of organizing an invasion of the South that would begin in Georgia, as Lord Germain had instructed.

Clinton understood the military and political landscape of the South better than Lord Germain and even Governor Martin did. The astute general had concluded at the end of the failed southern expedition of 1776 that the Loyalists could not reestablish royal government in the South by themselves. "To bring those poor people forward," Clinton wrote, "only exposed them to the resentment and malice of their enemies." Clinton recognized the need to establish safe havens for southern Loyalists *before* calling them to arms. He therefore cautioned the officers he was sending southward not to call up the Tories of Georgia and the Carolinas without being certain that they could rally in security. Whether or not Clinton's officers understood this critical point would prove questionable. In addition, the caution Clinton exhibited in regard to southern Loyalists seemed to be a tacit admission that they were not the majority the royal governors claimed them to be. Nevertheless, it was now time for the Southern Strategy to have its second trial.

+≽SIX≼+

Savannah, 1778

*"First . . . to [rend] a stripe and
star from the rebel flag of Congress"*

A S THE WHIGS secured the governments of the Carolinas and Georgia
during 1775 and 1776, the most notorious of the defeated Tories fled to
British-held East Florida. This diaspora was a bonanza for Patrick Tonyn,
the royal governor of Florida in St. Augustine. He organized the refugees into his own
private military to conduct raids in neighboring Georgia and even into South Carolina. One Georgia refugee, Thomas Brown, was a particularly effective leader. Governor Tonyn appointed him colonel of a partisan force formally titled the "King's Rangers"[1]
but which was most commonly called "Brown's Florida Rangers." Brown was a recent
immigrant from England, having arrived in Georgia in 1774. Since he was an intractable
and belligerent Tory, equally intractable and belligerent Georgia Whigs tarred and
feathered him before running him out of Augusta.

After taking command of the Florida Rangers in 1776, Brown began a guerrilla
campaign against Patriots in southern Georgia. He soon became a thorn in the side of
his former tormentors and remained so for years to come. The Patriots in Georgia and
South Carolina considered these raids a nuisance, but the incursions also hinted at the
genuine threat that British Florida represented to southern security.

Though the usefulness of Brown's corps of 120 rangers was undeniable, they also
proved to be troublesome for Major General Augustine Prevost, commander of the
regular British military in Florida. This was because Colonel Brown was a militia officer, and by law the militia reported directly to Governor Tonyn. Brown and his militia officers often refused to obey General Prevost's orders, even in combat situations.
In addition, Brown's officers frequently flaunted their brevetted rank before the British
regulars. Brown's men had only a few weeks or months in service, whereas similarly
ranked British regular officers had served for as many years. Even so, Brown's militia
officers had the gall to demand salutes from lower-ranked British regulars even though
the latter might have seen many years more service.

Brown's Rangers finally became such an annoyance that General Prevost threatened
to cut off all support to Tory partisans in the field unless they agreed to follow his orders.

Governor Tonyn claimed that all militia forces, including Brown's Rangers, were legally under his command—and that they only volunteered to serve because of this fact. To put the militia under the control of regular officers, Tonyn argued, would harm efforts to recruit Loyalists into military service. The situation was not fully resolved until the Florida Rangers were transferred from Governor Tonyn's militia to the Royal Army as provincials in the "American Establishment" in 1779.

It probably would have comforted Prevost little to know that the Americans were experiencing even worse divisions of military authority in the South. While Brown's renegade attitude was irritating to Prevost, it never represented a real threat to the supremacy of his command. This was primarily because the bulk of the royal military in America consisted of British regulars. Since the Continental Congress lacked sufficient funds to maintain an adequate regular army, the Americans relied more heavily on the militia, which was entirely financed by the state and local governments.

There existed a legal gray area in regard to superiority of command when the Continental Army had to cooperate with the militia. State militia officers generally accepted that same-ranked officers in the Continental Army had "seniority" in most military situations, but the primacy of Continental command had never been codified in law. Therefore, disputes over command supremacy often occurred whenever there were mixed Continental and militia armies (which was the majority of the time). This "command indecision" was exacerbated by the dependence of the state governments on charismatic local celebrities to help raise and lead their militia forces. These small-town stars tended to be egocentric and temperamental men who were often more concerned about the microcosm of their own local politics than about promoting American strategic interests. Local militia leaders sometimes even equipped their troops using their own funds, a fact that increased these militia officers' sense of independence. In addition, Patriot commanders had to coddle militiamen who were loath to serve far from home or for long periods. Militiamen were therefore usually ineffective on the offense, since their short enlistments (typically three months) would often expire just as they were about to engage the enemy.

Early American attempts to invade East Florida were good examples of the problems involving the militia's performance of offensive operations. Thomas Brown's depredatory raids into southern Georgia convinced the state's Patriot leaders that they needed to eliminate the British military threat in Florida. In 1776 General Charles Lee began organizing an expedition to attack Florida. However, Lee was recalled to the North by Congress before the expedition was fully under way. Soon after Lee's departure, Georgia's first "invasion" of Florida devolved into a mere border skirmish.

In 1777 Button Gwinnett, one of Georgia's most prominent politicians and a signer of the Declaration of Independence, decided to plan an attack on Florida. However, Gwinnett was only able to convince about two hundred militiamen to join his expedition. For Gwinnett's proposed invasion to succeed, he needed the assistance of Georgia's Continentals, which were commanded by Brigadier General Lachlan McIntosh. However, the two men could not agree on who was to command the expedition, which got no further south than Sunbury before it fell apart. Thus, Georgia's second "invasion" of Florida also fizzled before it had properly begun. The failure of the expedition (among other issues) led to a personal feud between McIntosh and Gwinnett. Eventually the two rivals agreed to a duel, which resulted in Gwinnett's death. Obviously, the military establishment in Georgia was fragmented, to say the least.

The task of eliminating the British threat in Florida then fell to Major General Robert Howe of the Continental Army, who had taken command of the Southern Department after Charles Lee's departure. Howe was a wealthy North Carolinian who had been educated in Europe. A longtime adherent to the American cause, Howe had helped to raise Patriot militia forces early in the crisis with Britain. He had been the officer in charge of the Patriot defenses of Norfolk when Governor Dunmore attacked and burned the city. His handling of the operations during that crisis was well regarded by the Continental Congress, and in 1776 he was made a brigadier general in the Continental line.

Robert Howe had a reputation for straight talk, and for being a ladies' man. One Tory woman from North Carolina described him as follows: "He is however very like a Gentleman, much so indeed than anything I have seen in the Country. He is deemed a horrid animal, a sort of woman-eater that devours everything that comes in his way, and that no woman can resist him. . . . I do assure you they overrate his merits and as I am certain it would be in the power of mortal woman to withstand him, so I am convinced he is not so voracious as he is represented. But he has a general polite gallantry, which every man of good breeding ought to have."[2]

Unfortunately for Howe, his womanizing would eventually prove a liability that provided ammunition for his political opponents. His personal reputation aside, Congress thought highly enough of Howe to promote him to major general and appoint him commander of the Southern Department in October 1777. Though Howe was a southerner, his appointment was not popular in South Carolina as the leaders in that state wanted one of their own officers to have the theater command.

In early 1778 the Americans received intelligence that the British were reinforcing Prevost in East Florida. Howe thought it best to preempt any British plans by striking at St. Augustine before the British could launch their own attack. Having only about one thousand Continentals in the theater necessitated an appeal to the governor of Georgia, John Houstoun, for support from the state's militia. The governor complied with the request, albeit too slowly for Howe's taste. Worse still for Howe, Governor Houstoun insisted on leading Georgia's militia himself. A contingent of the South Carolina militia under Andrew Williamson also accompanied the expedition.

On 20 May 1778 the small American army reached the Altamaha River, about sixty miles south of Savannah. The march thereafter proceeded slowly, and it was July before the army reached the Georgia-Florida border. At about this time the militia commanders, led by Governor Houstoun, rebelled against General Howe's authority as commander of the expedition. The governor insisted that neither he nor the militia was obligated to follow Howe's orders. Howe argued with Houstoun about the importance of unity of command, but to no avail. Indeed, Howe's rough manner served only to earn the enmity of the stubborn Georgians.

The argument over command was made moot when rampant sickness among the American troops reduced the invasion force to a mere 350 healthy men in mid-July.

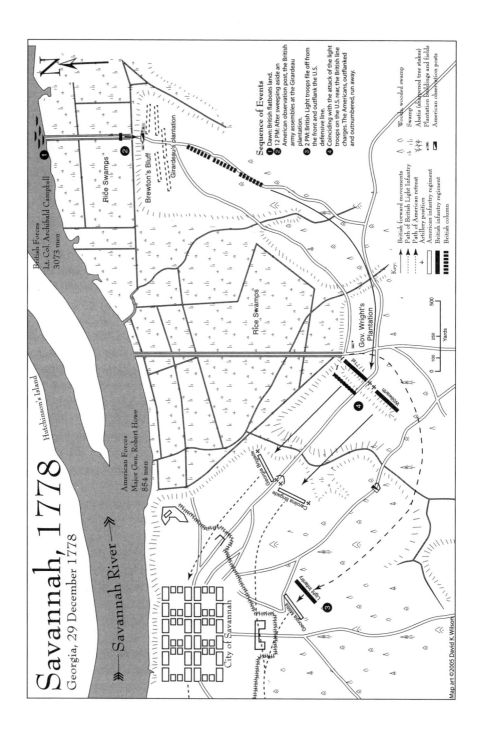

Savannah, 1778

Georgia, 29 December 1778

Savannah River →

Hutchinson's Island

British Forces
Lt. Col. Archibald Campbell
3073 men

American Forces
Major Gen. Robert Howe
854 men

Rice Swamps

Brewton's Bluff

Girardeau's plantation

Rice Swamps

Gov. Wright's
Plantation

City of Savannah

Carolina Brigade

Georgia Brigade

1st

Woolworth

Light Infantry

Georgia Militia

Sequence of Events

1. Dawn: British flatboats land.
2. 12 PM: After sweeping aside an American observation post, the British army assembles at the Girardeau plantation.
3. 2 PM: British Light troops file off from the front and outflank the U.S. defensive line.
4. Coinciding with the attack of the light troops on the U.S. rear, the British line charges. The Americans, outflanked and outnumbered, run away.

Key:

→ British forward movements
→ Path of British Light Infantry
→ Path of American retreat
+ Artillery position
▬ American infantry regiment
▬ British infantry regiment
▬ British column

Λ Woods, wooded swamp
ılı Swamp
ΥΛΥ Abatis (sharpened tree stakes)
▬ Plantation buildings and fields
▬ American observation posts

0   100   250   500
         Yards

Map art ©2005 David K. Wilson

The expedition had to be abandoned, but General Howe never forgave Governor Houstoun and the other militia commanders for their insubordination. He later wrote, "If I am ever again to depend upon operations I have no right to guide and men I have no right to command, I shall deem it then, as now I do, one of the most unfortunate accidents of my life."[3]

The civilian leadership of Georgia and South Carolina used the botched invasion of British Florida against Howe, whom they derided as incompetent. Christopher Gadsden, a popular political and military figure in Charlestown, was particularly vehement in his criticism of the beleaguered general. Gadsden had been a brigadier general in the Continental Army, but he became jealous when command of the Southern Department went to Howe instead of himself. Refusing to acknowledge General Howe's right to command, Gadsden resigned his commission in protest and then proceeded to write decidedly unfair public letters impugning Howe's character. The general from North Carolina was not a man to have his honor besmirched, however, and Howe summarily challenged Gadsden to a duel, which was fought on 30 August 1778.[4]

Once again a Continental officer challenged a prominent southern politician to a death match. However, unlike the fatal results of the duel between Lachlan McIntosh and Button Gwinnett, Howe's bullet only grazed Gadsden's ear during their duel. The South Carolinian acknowledged that he had wronged Howe by firing his own pistol into the air and then asking Howe to fire again. Howe refused, and honor was served. "Colonel Barnard Elliot, Gadsden's second, said that he did not think Gadsden could have made a handsomer apology or Howe shown a higher degree of honor. Walking up to Howe after the duel, Gadsden explained that he had not apologized for having challenged Howe's right to command, but only for publicly having used abusive language toward him."[5]

Gadsden and Howe later became good friends. Despite the happy outcome of the duel, Howe was still politically vulnerable. He had been involved in a feud with the governor of Georgia, had fought a duel with a prominent South Carolina politician, and had alienated most of the region's militia. If Howe's terminal lack of diplomatic panache was not bad enough, his performance as theater commander was lackluster and without accomplishment. To top it all, Howe's womanizing caught up with him, and the congressional delegates from South Carolina and Georgia demanded his removal from the theater command because of a "ridiculous matter he has been concerned in S.C.—with regard to a female."[6] Congress had no choice but to acquiesce to the South Carolina and Georgia faction, and in September 1778 the legislative body voted to replace Robert Howe with the Saratoga veteran Benjamin Lincoln as commander of the Southern Department. This switch was made just as the course of the war in the South was about to change radically.

⟫⧫⟪

While Congress was choosing a new commander for the Southern Department, Sir Henry Clinton was similarly looking for someone to lead his expedition to conquer Georgia. The man he chose was Lieutenant Colonel Archibald Campbell, commander of the 2nd Battalion of the 71st Regiment of Foot, also known as Fraser's Highlanders.[7] Campbell had returned to duty in March 1778 after enduring two years as an American prisoner of war. He had been exchanged for Ethan Allen, the famous New Englander who had captured Fort Ticonderoga but who had been taken captive in a failed attack on Montreal in 1775.

The 71st Regiment had been raised in the Scottish Highlands, a region of the British Empire where the men were renowned for their fighting spirit and skills. Wearing red-plaid bonnets and green-tartan trousers, the men of the 71st would play an important role throughout all of the southern campaigns, winning nearly every engagement they fought.[8] (The most notable exception was at Cowpens in 1781, where the entire 1st Battalion was captured by Daniel Morgan.) The 71st experienced a rough start in the war. In June 1776 elements of the 71st sailed to Boston to reinforce the British garrison there, only to find that the British had abandoned the city to the Americans two months earlier. It was yet another example of the difficulties of coordinating a transoceanic war in the eighteenth century. The company Campbell accompanied was captured in Boston harbor, and four more companies were captured shortly thereafter off the Massachusetts coast.[9] Campbell said that while he was imprisoned he was treated in a manner that "disgraced human Nature" and with "unprecedented Barbarity."[10] According to the historian Mark Boatner, Campbell's ill treatment was in "retaliation for cruelties suffered by American prisoners,"[11] although this is specious justification.

To address the reduction of Georgia, Clinton organized a force of about three thousand British troops. This force, commanded by Lieutenant Colonel Campbell, would sail from New York directly to Georgia in order to attack Savannah. At the same time, Clinton ordered General Augustine Prevost to sortie from Florida to join Campbell in Georgia. Once the two armies had rendezvoused, Prevost would take overall command. The historian Craig L. Symonds, in *A Battlefield Atlas of the American Revolution,* accuses Campbell of "stretching the letter of his orders" when he attacked Savannah without waiting for Prevost (p. 75). Likewise, Dan Morrill asserts in *Southern Campaigns of the American Revolution* that upon landing in Georgia, Lieutenant Colonel Campbell "abandoned his intention of waiting" for Prevost (p. 44). However, these assertions are in error. Sir Henry Clinton's orders to Campbell, dated 8 November 1778, tell him to sail directly to Savannah and take possession of the city. The orders do not tell him to wait for Prevost, though they do instruct him to yield command as soon as the senior general joined him in Savannah. In anticipation of success, Campbell was even given a "secret" commission to act as civilian governor of the colony.[12]

As a lieutenant colonel, Campbell's authority to command more than one regiment was tenuous. Clinton therefore wanted to promote Campbell to the rank of brigadier general, at least on a brevetted or temporary basis. However, the protests of other officers who were senior to Campbell dissuaded Clinton from proceeding with the promotion. Campbell would retain his current rank, but as a compromise he would receive the pay of a brigadier general while in command of the Georgia expedition. The situation did not please Campbell, and he was quite bitter about being passed up for the promotion. By being retained at his lower rank, Campbell believed that his ability to command the expedition might effectively be compromised.

Assigned to Campbell's expedition were the first two battalions of the 71st Highland Regiment (the third battalion remained in New York), the German von Wöllwarth and von Wissenbach regiments,[13] and four battalions of Tory "provincials," the latter of which consisted of the New York Volunteers, two battalions of DeLancy's[14] Regiment (also raised in New York), and one battalion of Skinner's Regiment from New Jersey. The Tory units had seen little action, but the experience of the 71st and the Hessians compensated for this. The 71st had participated in the battles of Long Island and Fort Washington in 1776 and at Brandywine in 1777. The Wöllwarth Regiment was the reconstituted regiment von Rall that Washington had captured at Trenton in 1776. The Wissenbach regiment had fought at Fort Washington in 1776, where it helped hand the Americans what was arguably the most devastating defeat they suffered during the war.

There was a two-week delay departing New York while waiting for proper transport for the artillery. Campbell's fleet finally departed Sandy Hook on 26 November 1778 escorted by a small flotilla of warships.[15] Clinton wanted the expedition to leave in the autumn in order to execute a winter campaign in a region known for its enervating and "sickly" summers.[16] The journey by sea to Georgia was typically harrowing, with massive storms tossing the fleet about and scattering the ships to and fro.[17] Despite these difficulties, Campbell's fleet arrived safely on 23 December off Tybee Island at the mouth of the Savannah River.

Even though he was a lame-duck commander, Major General Robert Howe continued to look after the Southern Department's defenses pending the arrival of his replacement. Howe was a committed Patriot even in the face of what he believed was unfair persecution. Waiting in Charlestown, Howe wanted to turn over his command personally to Lincoln. However, as British raids into Georgia became more threatening, Howe realized that he would not have the luxury of a leisurely end to his administration; instead, he was forced to hurry south with two regiments of Continentals. Leaving Charlestown on 18 November 1778, Howe was determined to hand the Southern Department over to Lincoln intact.

Howe's little army consisted of Colonel Isaac Huger's (pronounced "Yu-Gee") 5th South Carolina Regiment and Lieutenant Colonel William Thompson's 3rd South Carolina Rangers. Thompson's riflemen had defended the Breach at Sullivan's Island in 1776, but aside from that light duty, both regiments had seen little action and on the whole were inexperienced.

On 25 November elements of the British 60th Regiment under Lieutenant Colonel Lewis Valentine Fuser approached Sunbury, a town about twenty miles south of Savannah. General Prevost had not left St. Augustine yet (and would not do so for another month), but the enterprising Fuser thought that he could bluff the Americans into surrender. The town of Sunbury was guarded by a small bastion known as Fort Morris.

The commander of the American garrison was John McIntosh, a colonel in the Georgia Continentals.[18] The British commander sent a message to McIntosh stating that British reinforcements were on the way and that it was therefore useless to defend the fort. McIntosh replied that the nearness of British reinforcements was "entirely chimerical" and then added, "We, sir, are fighting the battles of America. . . . As to surrendering the fort, receive this laconic reply, 'Come and take it!'"[19] Fuser declined the offer and withdrew on hearing of the approach of Robert Howe's army. The fort's commander was known ever after as "Come'n Take It McIntosh."

At Sunbury, Howe reinforced Fort Morris with regulars from his own army to bring the garrison up to two hundred men. These men were expected to delay the British army that was advancing out of St. Augustine under General Prevost. Having received intelligence that Georgia was the target of a British expedition from New York, Howe then turned north to establish the defenses of what was then the state's capital.

The city of Savannah was founded in 1733 by James Oglethorpe, who had intended Georgia to be a refuge for formerly imprisoned debtors. Oglethorpe established the city on the sandy banks of the Savannah River about fifteen miles from where it empties into the Atlantic Ocean. Unlike many cities in America, Savannah was well planned from the beginning. The town was laid out in a large rectangle with straight, intersecting streets. Fine homes and shops dotted the quiet streets and picturesque squares.

In 1778 Savannah was surrounded by a series of dilapidated, twenty-year-old fortifications built to defend the city from the Spanish during the Seven Years' War. General Howe and the civilian government should have shored up the fortifications much earlier, but it was too late for that now. Howe correctly concluded that it would be futile to defend the town from within the city's decrepit "walls," which would only serve to trap the American forces when the British arrived.

Howe assumed that he would be heavily outnumbered, given that he had so few troops at his disposal. Indeed, his numbers were so anemic that he considered giving up Savannah without a fight and withdrawing his troops to fight another day. The American commander called a council of war on Christmas Eve of 1778 to solicit the opinions of his senior officers. These officers, many of whom lived in the city or in other parts of Georgia, thought that Savannah ought to be defended. They argued that if Savannah could be defended even for a few days, General Lincoln might arrive in time to relieve the town with the forces he was known to be gathering at Charlestown. Howe found this argument compelling. He resolved to attempt a defense of Savannah, or at least to fight a delaying action there before falling back to South Carolina.

As the Americans planned their defense, Lieutenant Colonel Campbell's expedition arrived off Tybee Island at the mouth of the Savannah River on 23 December 1778. Campbell immediately sent a light infantry company of the 71st ashore to capture some locals and procure intelligence. A black slave and his taskmaster were captured and interrogated. The slave, named Peter, told Campbell that Howe's army had eighteen hundred men (roughly twice its actual size) and was disposed to defend Savannah.[20] Acting on this information, Campbell decided to disembark his troops about two miles from the city at Girardeau's plantation, "the first practicable landing-place on the Savannah

River."[21] The fleet took two days to navigate the muddy river. Two small American galleys fired on the lumbering column in a futile attempt to delay its advance upriver, but a single shot from a British man-of-war sent the little American boats running. The fleet reached the landing at Girardeau's plantation early in the morning of 29 December 1779, and Campbell ordered his officers to begin landing their troops at first light.

Colonel Samuel Elbert, the commander of Georgia's Continentals, purportedly told General Howe that he thought the American army should make a stand at Brewton's Hill, the bluff that overlooked the rice fields of the plantation where the British troops were landing.[22] From that vantage point the Americans would be able to pour artillery and musket fire down on the disembarking British troops; the steep bluff would also give the defending Americans the advantage in close combat. Howe rejected Colonel Elbert's advice, however, because he thought that the landings at Girardeau's might be a feint. Instead, Howe sent just one company of South Carolina Continentals to occupy Brewton's Hill with orders to delay the British advance off the beachhead. The American commander then deployed the rest of his army in an open field about one-half mile southwest of Savannah.

Lieutenant Colonel Campbell designated the two light infantry companies of the 71st Regiment, led by Sir James Baird and Captain Charles Cameron, to act as the vanguard to the army. The boats of Baird's company grounded before they could reach shore, so Captain Cameron's light company went ashore by themselves. Cameron moved immediately to execute his orders to "take Possession of the Commanding Grounds in Front of the Disembarkation."[23]

Lieutenant Colonel Campbell organized his Light Infantry Corps during the sea voyage from New York. He supplemented the light infantry companies of the 71st Regiment with picked men from the Tory units. When creating this formation, Campbell asked that "the Officers selected for this Purpose have been accustomed to active Service; and that the Men shall be such who have distinguished themselves as good Marksmen, and who have Health, Activity and Resolution for Enterprize." Events would show that Campbell was wise in his preparation of this corps, which would play a pivotal role in upcoming operations.[24]

Campbell accompanied Cameron's men as they waded ashore. The lieutenant colonel personally dressed the troops' battle line and began them marching toward Brewton's Hill, which was about six hundred yards from the river. The bluff rose about forty feet above the rice swamps, and the view from buildings that dotted its crest dominated the landing area. The British could not safely disembark the rest of their troops and supplies without possession of the bluff. Cameron ordered his troops to advance in three lines: leading the way was a "forlorn hope"[25] of 5 men, about fifty yards behind were 13 men acting as skirmishers, with the rest of the 120-man company in battle order following close behind.

Captain John Carraway Smith commanded the company of fifty South Carolina Continentals on the bluff. His men occupied a series of buildings on the bluff and "knocked out Planks for their Firelocks to look through." When the British light infantry came within about one hundred yards of the buildings, Smith's company fired a volley. The British did not fire back but instead advanced rapidly to attack with their bayonets.

The rapid charge left no time for a second volley by the Americans, and in less than three minutes Cameron's men were in possession of the bluff. "The Rebels retreated with precipitation by the Back Doors and Windows," Campbell reported. Captain Smith's Continentals withdrew in good order and suffered no casualties, but they had yielded an important piece of ground. The British suffered four killed and five wounded, including Captain Cameron, who was mortally injured leading the attack. Campbell lamented the loss of Cameron, calling him "an Officer of Distinguished Merit and Bravery."[26]

Campbell thought it foolish of the Americans not to have invested more in the defense of the bluff (exactly as Colonel Elbert had argued). "Had the Rebels stationed four Pieces of Cannon on this Bluff with 500 Men for its Defense," Campbell wrote later, "it is more than probable, they would have destroyed the greatest part of this Division of our little Army."[27]

After hearing of Captain Smith's retreat from Brewton's Hill, General Howe held another council of war at ten o'clock that morning. The enemy had landed in force, and the Americans were heavily outnumbered. The question Howe put before the council was whether they should abandon the town. Howe's senior officers decided that, considering the proximity of the enemy (only a few miles distant), they should stand and fight, and retreat if necessary.[28] The British landing, meanwhile, proceeded at a slow pace. It was only at midday, five or six hours after the first men had waded onto the banks, that the majority of the British made it ashore. During this critical time the Americans did not attempt to counterattack or otherwise hinder the disembarkation. Howe later claimed that the scout he had assigned to watch the British disembarkation had run off on a "private errand," leaving him ignorant of the situation there.

Shortly after noon, elements of the British army proceeded carefully down the road toward Savannah. At about two o'clock they finally arrived at the plantation of former governor James Wright, near the main American battle line. Clambering up a tall tree, the energetic Lieutenant Colonel Campbell surveyed the situation. From his new perspective Campbell was able to discover the American dispositions: "The Rebel Army were formed on a level Piece of Ground, across the Savannah Road with their Front towards the West, their Right to Tatnel's House joining a thick Wood. . . . Their Left was nearly extended to the Rice Swamps on the South east Quarter."[29]

Howe's deployment was just as Campbell had observed. The American battle line was roughly one-half mile southeast of Savannah in a shallow "V" shape, with the open end facing the British line and both ends anchored by woods and swamps. Owing to the lay of the land and the defensive works the Americans had made, the "V" shape was a good defensive formation. If the British charged the American center, Howe's entire line would have a good angle from which to shoot. A small trench had been dug across the American front, behind which Howe arrayed his troops. On his left, Howe had placed Colonel Samuel Elbert's Georgia Brigade, a mix of about 200 Georgia militia and Continentals. Howe's right consisted of approximately 464 South Carolina Continentals composed of Colonel Isaac Huger's 5th South Carolina Regiment and Lieutenant Colonel William Thompson's 3rd South Carolina Rangers.[30] The 4th South Carolina Regiment of Artillery supported the line with four fieldpieces; one piece was deployed on either end of the main line and two pieces together in the center behind a small breastwork.

To guard his flanks, Howe detached troops from the line companies to act as light infantry—Georgians on the left and South Carolinians on the right.

About one hundred yards in front of the American line was a small, marshy rivulet. While not a significant water barrier, the marshy steam would slow down anyone passing through it—and just when they were coming within musket range of the Americans. Spanning the stream at the road was a bridge, which the Americans had set on fire. A line of riflemen acted as skirmishers ahead of the main American line.

Baird's light infantry led the British column as it filed down the road toward Savannah. About eight hundred yards from the American position the light troops deployed along a rail fence that extended perpendicular to the road. About this time the American artillery began to fire at the British light troops, but with little effect. Meanwhile, the rest of the British column held up behind the plantation, out of sight of the American guns.

Howe had chosen a strong defensive position. If Campbell attempted a frontal assault, there is little doubt that the British would have met stiff resistance. The British were saved from this necessity through the cooperation of a slave found on Wright's plantation. The man, whom some have identified as "Quamino Dolly,"[31] told Campbell that "he could lead the Troops without Artillery through the Swamp upon the Enemy's Right."[32]

Campbell ordered Sir James Baird to take the Light Infantry Corps, follow the slave through the wooded swamp on the Patriots' right, and attack the American army in the flank. Campbell then redeployed his forces: "I ordered the first battalion of the 71st to form on our right of the road and move up to the rear of the light-infantry, whilst I drew off that corps to the right as if I meant to extend my front to that quarter, where a happy fall of ground favored the concealment of this manoeuver [*sic*], and increased the jealously of the enemy with regard to their left."[33]

Baird's 350 light infantry filed off to their right and circled around the rear of the British army, following their guide down a narrow path through the swamp on the British left (the American right). The New York Volunteers followed the light infantry in a supporting role, bringing the total strength of the flanking column to 588 men. Campbell placed one of his officers—one Major Skelly—in a tall tree to observe the movements of the light infantry. Skelly was ordered to signal when he saw that Baird had begun his attack. Campbell then arranged his main battle line. He formed his artillery and the Wöllwarth Regiment behind a "swell of ground" on the left of the road, while the 1st Battalion of the 71st Regiment held the ground to the right at the rail fence. Thus deployed, nearly the entire British line was hidden from the Americans' view by the small bluff to its front.

Baird's corps quickly and quietly followed their black scout through the quagmire that formed the right flank of the American line. The trail eventually terminated just where the slave said it would: at the barracks in the American rear. Howe had placed no pickets in the area, and so the Americans were completely unaware they were being flanked. Colonel George Walton and one hundred Georgian militiamen guarded the barracks. It is said that Walton, a signer of the Declaration of Independence, attempted to warn Howe to guard the side path around the American right flank before the battle began.[34] This warning was apparently ignored out of the belief that the British would never find the obscure route.

Baird's men charged out of the overgrown morass and furiously fell on the unsuspecting Georgians. Sitting high in his tree, Major Skelly saw the powder smoke in the American rear. He waved his hat to alert Lieutenant Colonel Campbell that Baird's attack had begun. On that signal, Campbell ordered the British artillery to the hilltop to his front. When these guns opened fire on the American line, 437 men of the 71st Highlanders and another 442 troops of the Wöllwarth Regiment were ordered to advance across eight hundred yards of no-man's-land. They did so, according to Campbell, with "alacrity."[35]

Near the center of the main American line, General Howe heard the unexpected sound of musket shots coming from the direction of the barracks to his rear. At the same time British cannonballs began to crash about him, causing casualties. The American line had been standing to their arms for the better part of the day. Suddenly cannonballs were flying about them, and the inexperienced American troops began to shift and twitch nervously under the British bombardment. Then came the sight of the red-coated British and blue-uniformed German troops surging over the hill in front of the American position. Howe suddenly realized that he was caught between the hammer and the anvil. He immediately ordered a general retreat. The American troops began an orderly march to the rear, but as the king's forces crossed the marshy rivulet and charged with their bayonets, the retreat turned into a rout. Few Americans, regulars or militia, bothered to fire a shot. Many flung their weapons aside in their desperation to escape. "It was scarcely possible to come up with them," Campbell later wrote; "their Retreat was rapid beyond Conception."[36]

As the main American line crumbled, Baird's light infantry drove into George Walton's militia who were guarding the barracks in the rear. The heavily outnumbered militia ran, and Walton took a bullet in the thigh and fell from his horse. Walton was captured by the advancing British, who apparently never found out that he was a signer of the Declaration of Independence (an act that in British eyes made him a certified traitor, punishable by death).[37]

Sweeping past the barracks, the light infantry took control of the Augusta road, an act that sealed the main escape route out of the city. The trap had been closed. The redcoats and Hessians, particularly the 1st Battalion of the 71st Regiment, kept a close pursuit of the Americans. Howe's troops fled the battlefield and made a mad scramble into the city. Hundreds of soldiers from both sides charged through the lovely streets and squares of Savannah. As the Highlanders tore through the town, many terrified Patriot citizens who had taken up arms in the city militia grounded their weapons and surrendered.

Colonel Campbell claimed to have treated the town's Whig population with civility, a fact that is generally well accepted. There were some claims to the contrary, however, and according to some Patriot observers, any militiamen who did not surrender instantly "were bayoneted in the streets by their victorious pursuers."[38] John Houstoun, the Patriot governor of the state, said that the townspeople suffered brutal acts at the hands of their conquerors. The Georgians regarded the Highlanders with special horror. Indeed, after the war was over, the Georgia legislature passed a law prohibiting Scots from settling in the state unless they had fought on the Patriot side during the war.

Colonel Huger mounted a desperate rearguard action, aided by the American artillery under Colonel Owen Roberts. They were able to hold off the pursuing British long enough for many American soldiers to get out of the city. Colonel Roberts was able to bring off three fieldpieces before all the roads out of the city were closed off.[39] Despite Colonel Huger's valiant efforts, he was forced to fall back before the tide of British troops. Many Patriot soldiers attempted to swim Yamacraw Creek to escape. Tossing their weapons aside, soldiers and officers alike leaped into the water and made for the safety of the opposite shore. Campbell estimated that 30 men drowned trying to cross, but there is no way of knowing the true number. General Howe, along with Colonels Thompson and Huger, were forced to abandon their horses and brave the dangerous waters. Once on the other side, Howe fled with what was left of his army and regrouped eight miles away at Cherokee Hill. From there he fell back to Zubly's Ferry, crossed the Savannah River into South Carolina, and made camp at Purrysburg. Only about 342 men remained of Howe's army, less than half the force he had at the start of the day. Colonel Elbert's Georgia brigade had suffered particularly badly, with only 30 soldiers escaping capture out of 200.[40]

In one quick stroke Campbell had taken the capital of Georgia. The spoils of war included 48 cannons in the city's defensive works, 23 mortars and howitzers, 817 muskets, a number of ships, and large quantities of goods and foodstuffs.[41] The loss of small arms was a particularly hard-felt loss for the Patriots, as military-grade weapons were difficult to come by for the Americans. The British captured 453 men of all ranks and found 83 Americans dead on the field. There were at least 11, and probably many more, Americans wounded.[42] The British sustained negligible losses: 7 killed and 17 wounded. A contemporary American officer, Colonel Henry "Light Horse Harry" Lee, said of the battle: "Never was a victory of such magnitude so completely gained with so little loss."[43]

Campbell's success, however, made him even more bitter about the promotion he was denied. It was now obvious to all that he was deserving of advancement, yet it would be many years before the honor would be bestowed on him. The lieutenant colonel was so embarrassed about his low rank that he placed Commodore Hyde Parker's name above his own when issuing proclamations at Savannah. Campbell thought that this was necessary because in America "a cobbler is on footing with a lieutenant-colonel." Nevertheless, the universal acclaim he received for his conduct of the battle went a long way toward healing his injured ego. Campbell fancied that he would soon be "the first British officer to rent [*sic,* rend] a stripe and star from the rebel flag of Congress."[44]

On the American side, William Moultrie held Howe responsible for the defeat, arguing that he should never have attempted to stand simply on the defensive against Campbell's larger, seasoned army. In hindsight, Moultrie was of course correct in this opinion. Howe either should have opposed the British landing at Girardeau's plantation or should have abandoned Savannah to the British without a fight in order to hand his 850-man army over to Major General Lincoln intact. The nearly 550 men killed, wounded, or captured would have been a great help to Lincoln, who arrived at Purrysburg on 3 January 1779—only four days after Howe's defeat—with 1,500 troops.

General Howe was later court-martialed for his conduct of the battle. During this trial Pierre Colomb, a Frenchman serving in the American army, stated that Howe should have made his stand on Brewton's Hill—the bluff above Girardeau's plantation —as Campbell essentially wrote later in his journal.[45] In his own defense, Howe said that he could not be sure that the landing at Girardeau's was not a diversion. If he had placed his army at the bluff, it would have been out of position to counter landings elsewhere. Howe's judges agreed with this conclusion and acquitted him of any wrongdoing. However, Howe was not acquitted in the court of public opinion. Losing a battle was acceptable, perhaps even expected, in the ill-equipped and undermanned American military; but failing to make a respectable fight was not. Searching for excuses for his defeat, Howe complained bitterly about the failure of the Georgia militia to support him more vigorously. Of course, it may have occurred to Howe that the militia's apathy was perhaps a result of the animosity he had accumulated with them earlier in the war.

Ultimately, the cause of the American defeat was not the choice of battleground or the imbalance of troops, but rather Howe's failure to gather adequate battlefield intelligence and anticipate enemy actions. "How happens it," asked the soldier-historian Henry Lee, "that [Howe], who had been in command in that country for many months, should not have discovered the by-way passing to his rear, when Lieutenant-Colonel Campbell contrived to discover it in a few hours?"[46]

Campbell, in contrast with Howe, scouted the terrain, interrogated the locals, and even climbed a tree to get a better look at the rebel troops. If the American commander had applied similar energy to planning his defense of Savannah, things might have gone very differently. Such was not the case, however, and the British had captured a valuable port city where they could gather men and supplies, rally local Tory support, and carry the war to the interior of Georgia and South Carolina. Savannah seemed to be everything the British could want from a base in the South, and the ease of their victory seemed to bode well for future operations. The second attempt at Lord Germain's Southern Strategy was off to a good start.

ORDER OF BATTLE: SAVANNAH, 1778
Georgia, 29 December 1778

American Forces[47]
Maj. Gen. Robert Howe

	MEN	ARTILLERY
South Carolina Brigade—Col. Isaac Huger		
5th S.C. Regiment—Col. Isaac Huger	ca. 169	

	MEN	ARTILLERY
3rd S.C. Rangers—		
Lt. Col. William Thompson	ca. 295	
Georgia "Brigade"—Col. Samuel Elbert		
Militia and Continentals	ca. 200	
4th S.C. Artillery Regiment (4-lb.)—		
Col. Owen Roberts	est. 40	ca. 9
Georgia Militia at the New Barracks—		
Col. George Walton	ca. 100	
City of Savannah Militia at Savannah Fort	est. 50	
Total	**ca. 854**	**ca. 9**

British Forces
Lt. Col. Archibald Campbell

	MEN	ARTILLERY
71st Regiment—		
Lt. Col. John Maitland		
1st Battalion	437	
2nd Battalion	507	
Light Infantry Corps[48]		
Captain James Baird's		
Light Infantry Company	184	
Captain Charles Cameron's Light		
Infantry Company	170	
Regiment von Wöllwarth—		
Lt. Col. von Kettle	442	
Regiment von Wissenbach—		
Lt. Col. Fredrick von Porbeck	448	
New York Volunteers—		
Lt. Col. George Turnbull	234	
DeLancy's New York Regiment—		
Lt. Col. DeLancy		
1st Battalion	219	
2nd Battalion	160	
3rd Battalion, Skinner's New Jersey Regiment	242	
Royal Artillery matrosses and gunners[49] (3-lb.?)	36	8
Total	**3,079**	**8**

Casualties

	AMERICAN	BRITISH
Killed	83	7
Wounded	>11	17

Order of Battle: Savannah, 1778 (*continued*)

	AMERICAN	BRITISH
Missing	n/a	–
Total Casualties	**ca. 94**	**24**
Captured	453	–
Total Losses[50]	**ca. 547**	**24**

⊹≒SEVEN≒⊹

Briar Creek

"Now my boys, remember poor MacAlister!"

A S THE CALENDAR TURNED TO 1779, both the Americans and the British found themselves with new commanders and new strategic possibilities in the southern theater. Despite his brilliant performance wresting Savannah from the Americans, Lieutenant Colonel Archibald Campbell had to yield theater command to Major General Augustine Prevost, who arrived at Savannah after a long march from St. Augustine, Florida. On the American side, Major General Benjamin Lincoln succeeded Major General Robert Howe as commander of the Southern Department.

Benjamin Lincoln had been a lieutenant colonel in the Massachusetts militia when war broke out in 1775. After being promoted to major general, Lincoln commanded his state's militia in the disastrous New York campaign of 1776. It was there that George Washington came to know Lincoln as an able leader with exceptional administrative skills. Lincoln had a couple of physical failings, the most salient of which was his odd habit of falling into a deep, brief sleep at peculiar times. Some historians have suggested that General Lincoln had narcolepsy; however, it is more likely—given the symptoms —that Lincoln actually had sleep apnea, a condition often afflicting those who are extremely overweight. Lincoln fit this description easily; some said in jest that he was wider than he was tall.

General Washington was impressed with Lincoln's handling of his forces in New York in 1776 (despite the disappointing outcome for the Americans), and he asked Congress to adopt him into the national military. Congress not only drafted Lincoln into Continental service but also allowed the New Englander to retain his rank of major general. Thus Lincoln, a relatively obscure militia officer, had suddenly become one of the nation's top military leaders. Lincoln was even promoted ahead of Benedict Arnold, despite Arnold's longer service and greater distinction in the Continental Army. The promotion of Lincoln (and four other officers made major general along with him on 19 February 1777) became one of Arnold's chief grievances with Congress before he committed treason later in the war.

81

In 1777 Lincoln was given command of the New England militia that was at that time gathering to oppose Burgoyne's offensive in upstate New York. During this period Lincoln demonstrated his talent for diplomacy as well as administration. He was able to mollify headstrong militia leaders such as John Stark of New Hampshire, one of the heroes of the battle of Bunker Hill. Stark had left Continental service after being passed over for promotion (again, in favor of men such as Lincoln). To accommodate Stark, Lincoln allowed him wide latitude in commanding his volunteer troops.

Lincoln's policy paid off when Stark led his militia to a brilliant victory over part of Burgoyne's army at Bennington, Vermont. Later in the campaign Lincoln bagged the British bateaux as they sat virtually unguarded on the banks of Lake Champlain near Fort Ticonderoga. This action completely cut off Burgoyne's communications with his supply base at St. Johns, Canada. At the battle of Saratoga, Lincoln accompanied the Massachusetts brigade in the field. Like Benedict Arnold, Lincoln took a British bullet in his leg during combat on 7 October 1777 (the battle of Bemis Heights); unlike Arnold, Lincoln's patriotism survived the wound.

By 1778 Lincoln had recovered sufficiently from his injury to return to service. Congress decided that Lincoln would make a good replacement for Robert Howe as head of the Southern Department, and Washington approved of the choice. As previously described, Howe had alienated the southern leaders and militia commanders. Unlike his hot-blooded predecessor, Benjamin Lincoln was not a man who dueled in the street. He was coolheaded and even-tempered, and it was said that a curse word never passed his lips. Congress hoped that Lincoln could mend the broken relationship between the Continental Army and the state officials in the South much as he had done in New York with John Stark.

When Lincoln arrived at Charlestown in late 1778, the new theater commander discovered a military department exceedingly short of all the articles necessary for fighting a war: equipment, money, and personnel. Lincoln complained to Washington that the Continental Army in the theater was so utterly destitute that it was impossible to move the Continental regiments without the aid and permission of the government of South Carolina. Over the course of his tenure Lincoln attempted to rectify the situation, and he displayed a talent for administration. However, he was never able to completely fulfill his goal of making the Continentals independent of South Carolina's support (and therefore control). This would have an important effect on military operations and relations between the civilian and military leaders for the remainder of the war.

Lincoln had to leave his logistical problems to be solved later, since haste was now required to rescue the situation in Georgia. He grabbed what fighting men he could and rushed southward. On 3 January 1779 Lincoln and his army arrived at the town of Purrysburg, which lay on the South Carolina–Georgia border. Lincoln found Major General Robert Howe and the remnants of the Savannah garrison waiting for him at Purrysburg, where they had withdrawn after being driven from Georgia's capital in disarray. Lincoln listened to the story of Howe's trouncing with a sympathetic ear, grimly realizing that he was now saddled with the same handicaps as his defeated predecessor had been.

The Savannah River now formed the primary defensive barrier between the British in Georgia and the Americans in South Carolina. Purrysburg lay twenty miles from Savannah on the east bank of the river, and the town's position commanded the main ferry and the primary road between the two sister states. Lincoln was therefore in an ideal position both to observe the British in Georgia and to block their advance into the Carolinas. Within a few days Lincoln had reconstituted a motley army of about seventeen hundred men. However, of this number only five hundred were Continentals; the remainder of the force consisting of ill-disciplined and poorly equipped Carolina militia.

Lincoln's antagonist in the upcoming struggle was General Augustine Prevost. Prevost's father was a Swede serving in the British army. According to Mark Boatner's *Encyclopedia of the American Revolution,* Prevost was born in Geneva in 1723. Prevost's father was an officer in the Royal Army and helped found the 60th Regiment of Foot, later known as the Royal Americans, in 1755. The following year young Augustine followed his father's example and became a major in the 60th Regiment. During the Seven Years' War, Prevost was severely wounded while serving under General James Wolfe at Quebec in 1759. After the end of that war, he accompanied the 60th to Florida as its colonel. Prevost was promoted to brigadier general when the rebellion in America began, and at the beginning of 1779 he was advanced to the prestigious rank of major general.

In January 1779 General Prevost took command in Georgia from Lieutenant Colonel Archibald Campbell, the latter holding the jealous opinion that Prevost was too old and infirm to command. Prevost later admitted as much, however, and in a few months he would request to be relieved from his command because "gout and former wounds does [*sic*] not afford me those resources of activity necessary for this important service."[1] For now, though, Prevost accepted the responsibility willingly.

The four-thousand-man army that Prevost commanded in Georgia was an eclectic mix of British redcoats, German regulars, Tory auxiliaries from the North, and southern Loyalist refugees. Prevost held a thin and ever shrinking numeric advantage over Lincoln, whose army grew stronger every day as large numbers of militia and Continentals joined the American camp. Of course, the whole purpose behind the British expedition to Georgia was to exploit what the British Crown hoped was a vast untapped reservoir of Tory manpower. After the capture of Savannah, the city's residents were forced to sign an oath of loyalty to the Crown that essentially drafted them into the Loyalist militia. Most of Savannah's inhabitants signed the document, though it is hard to establish how willingly they did so. It is known that when they were needed later, not many residents of Savannah shouldered weapons to fight for King George.

Prevost, however, was not looking for substantial support along the coast. It had been long assumed by British authorities that the southern backcountry was where they would find those well affected to Crown rule. Backcountry Loyalists who had come into Savannah to greet Prevost told him exactly what he wanted to hear: Send a brigade to the frontier, and the king's friends would come quickly to their aid. Encouraged by these reports, Prevost sent word back to Lord Germain. "The frontier inhabitants of Carolina," the general wrote, "give the strongest hopes of joining heartily whenever they find that they are to be supported." Accordingly, plans were made for an expedition to Augusta, the principal city of Georgia's piedmont.[2]

Augusta lay on the south side of the Savannah River, about 120 miles as the crow flies from the sea. An attack on this place seemed a logical way for the British to sustain their initiative and give their friends in the backcountry a safe location to rally. Lieutenant Colonel Archibald Campbell received permission from General Prevost to lead a force of light troops to take the town. The expedition was composed of Sir James Baird's Light Infantry Corps (299 men); the New York Volunteers (175 men); the 1st Battalion of the 71st Regiment (356 men—their light company still with Baird's corps); and a contingent of Royal Artillery with 25 men, five cannons, and two mortars. Two units of southern provincials also joined Campbell's expedition: a newly raised unit of Loyalists commanded by Colonel Alexander Innes called the Carolina Loyalists (75 men); and, of course, Colonel Thomas Brown and 72 of his Florida Rangers. A troop of 42 light dragoons also accompanied the column, amounting to a total force of 1,044 British and Tory soldiers—about one-quarter of the total British force in Georgia.

The Florida Rangers had been transferred from the Florida militia into the British army as a "provincial" unit. This move eliminated any confusion regarding General Prevost's right to command Brown and his men. Though the regulars despised them, Brown's motley troop of mounted partisans was thought to be invaluable for frontier operations because of their knowledge of the land. Lieutenant Colonel Campbell called the Rangers a "mere Rabble of undisciplined Freebooters."[3]

The mission was risky. The expedition ran the obvious danger of being cut off from the main body at Savannah by the rebel troops gathering at Purrysburg. The Americans were weak at the moment, but their numbers were fast increasing. The only hope of British success lay in the swift capture of Augusta and the quick formation of a substantial Tory militia. Campbell had been told—by whom it is not clear—that he would find as many as six thousand recruits in the backcountry of Georgia and South Carolina.[4] If this turned out to be true, the British would soon have enough men to move against Charlestown.

The expedition began its march into the backcountry on 24 January 1779, encountering only light resistance along the way. A handful of Georgia Continentals under Brigadier General Samuel Elbert[5] and some militia under Colonels John Twiggs and William Few did harass Campbell's troops on their march, but they failed to slow the British column substantially. On 31 January, Campbell's army neared Augusta. The British commander sent Thomas Brown's light horse (cavalry) ahead to scout for the enemy. Colonel Brown reported back that General Andrew Williamson had about one thousand South Carolina and Georgia militia in the town. Williamson was one of the rebellious militia officers who had taken part in Robert Howe's ill-fated Florida expedition the previous year. As Campbell approached the city, Williamson withdrew all but a token force of his militia across the Savannah River into South Carolina, content to observe the British while gathering his strength.

84

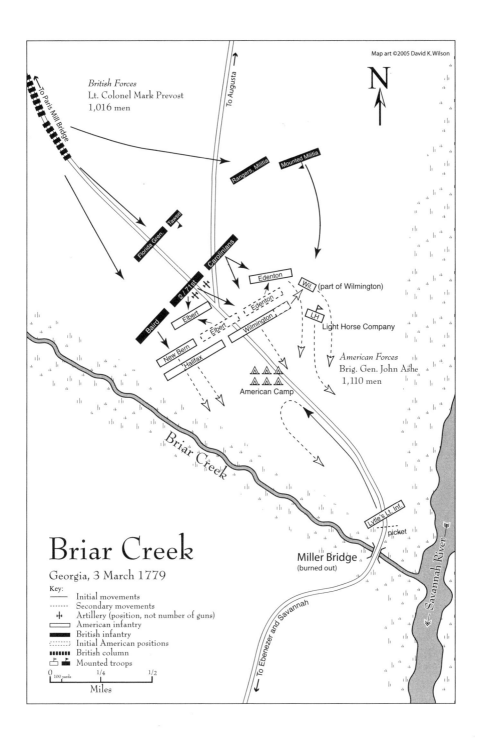

Map art ©2005 David K. Wilson

N

British Forces
Lt. Colonel Mark Prevost
1,016 men

To Paris Mill Bridge

To Augusta

Rangers, Militia

Mounted Militia

Florida Gren.

Tawse

2d 71st

Carolinians

Baird

Edenton

Elbert

Edenton

Wil (part of Wilmington)

Elbert

Edenton

New Bern

Wilmington

LH

Halifax

Light Horse Company

American Camp

American Forces
Brig. Gen. John Ashe
1,110 men

Briar Creek

Lytle's Lt. Inf.

picket

Briar Creek

Georgia, 3 March 1779

Miller Bridge
(burned out)

Savannah River

Key:
——— Initial movements
········· Secondary movements
⊹ Artillery (position, not number of guns)
▭ American infantry
▬ British infantry
▭ Initial American positions
▮▮▮▮ British column
◖▸ Mounted troops

To Ebenezer and Savannah

0 1/4 1/2
100 yards
Miles

After a brief skirmish with the American rear guard, Campbell took possession of Augusta. General Williamson's corps was still nearby, however, and the British had to keep constantly under arms to guard against surprise. Campbell's men were therefore unable to get much rest or receive much advantage from taking the city. The number of rebel militia near Augusta fluctuated between eight hundred and twelve hundred men. In the following days, the two sides constantly maneuvered and skirmished. While Campbell was able to send a few detachments to occupy some frontier forts and settlements, because of the proximity of Williamson's army neither the British military nor the backcountry Loyalists ever really felt secure.

It soon became obvious to the local inhabitants that Lieutenant Colonel Campbell had too few troops to risk engaging Williamson. As a result, the British occupation of Augusta failed to inspire confidence on the part of the local Tories. Though Campbell signed up about eleven hundred of the "King's friends" at Augusta, no more than a few hundred ever formed into actual military units. In an attempt to generate more support, Campbell administered an oath of loyalty to the inhabitants of the areas he had under his control. Failing to sign the oath meant the forfeiture of one's property: slaves, plantations, or homes. Many local property owners were therefore inclined to give an insincere oath to Campbell in order to save their possessions; however, most Georgians who took the oath quickly rushed across the river to reassure General Williamson that their true loyalty was to the Patriot cause. In fact, far more backcountry residents—about two or three times as many—actually took up arms against the British than were raised by Campbell to fight for the Crown. It was a conspicuous indication that the southern backcountry did not have the Tory majority that Lord Germain and the southern royal governors claimed—and was ominously reminiscent of the failed British effort to conquer North Carolina in 1776.

The failure of Lieutenant Colonel Campbell's recruiting efforts made the situation look increasingly bleak for the little British army at Augusta. Campbell's best hope at retrieving the situation lay in a covert operation being run by a mysterious Tory colonel named Boyd, who accompanied Campbell from New York and was supposedly a man of some influence in the Carolina backcountry. When Campbell started on his journey to Augusta, he dispatched Colonel Boyd into the Carolina piedmont with secret orders to provoke a counterrebellion among the Loyalist population and mobilize a force of Tories to march to Augusta. Men of today's special forces and intelligence services will no doubt recognize the similarity of their duties to Boyd's mission.

Colonel Boyd successfully made his way to Anson County, North Carolina, along the southern border of the state. Many of the Scottish immigrants who had participated in the ill-fated Moore's Creek campaign three years earlier lived in this county. Apparently Boyd *did* have some influence in the region, as several hundred Scottish Loyalists in Anson County immediately volunteered to follow him to Georgia. As the Loyalist column wormed its way through South Carolina toward Augusta, hundreds more of the "King's Friends" joined under Boyd's banner. By the time he reached Red Creek in central South Carolina, Boyd's command numbered six hundred to eight hundred men.

Despite the British victories in Georgia, it was no small thing for a Carolina Loyalist to pick up a gun and defy the American Congress. Having a private opinion in favor of the king was one thing, but openly taking up arms left a man's family and property without protection against Patriot retaliation. The homes of many Tories met with Whig torches after they left to join the British in Georgia. James Fergus, a Patriot militiaman, cavalierly remarked at the end of one such partisan patrol: "After burning a number of the Tories' houses [whose owners] were gone, we returned home."[6]

Boyd's Tories also faced a 150-mile trek through enemy territory in order to get to Augusta. Given these facts, it is perhaps no wonder the British found it difficult to rally more support for the Crown. It is also not surprising that many of those who did join Boyd were nonpropertied vagabonds who had little to lose. This same comment may be applied to many Tory armies that rose in the South, as the propertied Tory families tended to be much more conservative in displaying their loyalty to the Crown. Many of Boyd's men used the march through South Carolina as an opportunity to fill their own pockets by "confiscating" property from "rebels" during the march. The rapacious Tory column looted and burned its way through South Carolina with the predictable result that it made more enemies to the Crown than friends. South Carolina Patriots called Boyd's men a "plundering banditti, more solicitous for booty, than for the honor and interest of their royal master."[7] Even discounting the Patriots' obvious bias, it is certain that Colonel Boyd's column had to live off the land as it marched since Boyd lacked the time or resources to organize a supply train.

Captain John Hamilton had been sent by Campbell with 300 local Tories to secure a few posts outlying Augusta. To oppose Hamilton, Colonel Andrew Pickens gathered 350 South Carolina Whigs and marched to Georgia. Born in Pennsylvania of Scotch-Irish parents, Pickens moved to Waxhaws, South Carolina, at age thirteen. He received his military education at age twenty-two when he took part in a punitive expedition against the Carolina Cherokees in 1761. More recently Pickens also played an important role in the 1776–77 Cherokee border war.

On the approach of Pickens's militia, Hamilton holed up in a small redoubt called Carr's Fort. While in the process of besieging the fort, Pickens received word from his brother of the passage of Boyd's column through Ninety Six,[8] a prominent trading town in an area of southwestern South Carolina known for its Tory sentiment. Pickens abandoned the siege to intercept the new threat. Colonel Boyd angled for Cherokee Ford, about ten miles north of Pickens's position. The ford was guarded by eight Patriots in a small redoubt. Outnumbered about one hundred to one, the Americans were able to fend off Boyd's column using two swivel guns. Boyd, lacking artillery, thought it senseless to force the position; he and his men instead detoured five miles upstream and crossed the Savannah River into Georgia on rafts. Pickens had only just crossed the Savannah in the opposite direction when he found out that Boyd had already advanced into Georgia. Pickens did an about-face, recrossed the river, and fell in behind the Loyalists.

On 14 February, Boyd's column camped on the north side of Kettle Creek, a tributary of the Savannah River. Apparently unaware of the proximity of his pursuers, Boyd took no special precautions when making his bivouac. He nonchalantly sent off his horses to graze and dispatched many of his men to slaughter some of their looted cattle for provisions. Gunshots from his pickets were Boyd's first indications that he was under attack.

The outnumbered Americans were advancing in three divisions against the Tory camp. The American center was commanded by Pickens, the left divisions by Lieutenant Colonel Elijah Clark, and the right division by Colonel John Dooly. Most accounts say that the Americans mustered about 300 to 350 men, while the number of Tories reported to have been present varies from 600 to 800. Whether or not the strengths of the two sides were actually this imbalanced, it is certain that Boyd's men never fully recovered from the initial surprise of the American assault. After one to two hours of hard fighting, the Americans emerged victorious. Most of the Tory army fled the field, leaving behind 70 killed and 75 made prisoner. Boyd was mortally wounded and died that evening. The Americans achieved the victory at the cost of only 9 killed and 23 mortally wounded.[9] Five of the captured Tories were hung by the Patriots for violating a "test oath" to South Carolina that they had allegedly made earlier.[10] The effect of the battle and its aftermath was to send a powerful message to the backcountry Tories: Rise up against Patriot authority at your own peril.

The same day that the Patriots stifled the Tories at Kettle Creek, Lieutenant Colonel Campbell had made up his mind to evacuate Augusta and withdraw southward toward Savannah. Many historians make a post hoc argument that since Campbell withdrew from Augusta on 14 February, the same day as the battle at Kettle Creek, his retreat must have been prompted by Colonel Boyd's defeat. However, this was not the case. In his journal Campbell says that he only learned of the affair at Kettle Creek the day *after* the event and that his withdrawal from Augusta was prompted by the approach of the North Carolina militia commanded by Brigadier General John Ashe.[11]

Another error that some historians have made with regard to Kettle Creek is to assume that the Patriot victory swelled the ranks of Lincoln's army. In fact, the American militia that was then gathering at Purrysburg had been organized, supplied, and dispatched to South Carolina weeks earlier by the governments of the Carolinas in response to the British invasion of Georgia. (The popular notion that American militias sprang up from the woods on the approach of enemy troops is exaggerated; the formation of most militia forces required coordination and financing by the state governments.) Therefore, the action at Kettle Creek did not drive Campbell from Augusta, nor did it dramatically increase the ranks of the Whig militia. Colonel Boyd's defeat was, however, a graphic example of the British regulars' inability to control territory beyond the range of their muskets. The detachments that Lieutenant Colonel Campbell had sent out to protect Boyd's approach proved only barely able to defend themselves and powerless to protect others.

On General Ashe's arrival at Augusta, Campbell estimated the total number of Americans opposing him at about thirty-eight hundred. (The actual number was closer to twenty-four hundred—still twice as large as Campbell's force.) Faced with a lackluster response from local Tories and no word as to the fate of Colonel Boyd's column,

Campbell felt that he had to retreat or risk being surrounded and destroyed. After only a brief two-week stay, Campbell marched his troops south. Augusta would not again come under British control until after the fall of Charlestown and the collapse of American resistance throughout Georgia and South Carolina in the spring of 1780.[12]

The British expedition to Augusta turned out to be nothing more than a raid. Instead of finding six thousand eager Tory militiamen in the backcountry, Lieutenant Colonel Campbell was able to recruit only a thousand men, not all of whom were actually willing to take up arms. On the other hand, the Patriots easily raised and deployed thousands of militiamen from Georgia and the Carolinas against the British, driving Campbell out of the backcountry. Campbell refused to admit that the mission was a failure. Instead, he claimed victory on the dubious ground that he left Augusta with more supplies than he had when he arrived. The only solace the British could salvage from their shameful withdrawal was that they only lost one man during the expedition, a light infantryman of the 71st Regiment named MacAlister.

MacAlister's death was particularly infuriating to the British troops because he had been killed by Patriot partisans while performing the role of *sauveguarde,* or "safeguard." Safeguards were soldiers or noncommissioned officers left by a passing army at homes of vulnerable civilians. In this case the killing was even more ironic because MacAlister had been guarding the wife and home of an American officer who was being held captive by the British in Augusta. The rebel prisoner had entreated Archibald Campbell to post a safeguard at his home to protect his wife and family. Campbell assented, and MacAlister was assigned. The role of safeguard was considered sacred by the rules of eighteenth-century warfare; but the piedmont militiamen rarely adhered to European martial traditions, and in most cases probably did not know or care about them. The British officers were dismayed at the lack of couth among their opponents; nevertheless, they continued the practice of assigning safeguards throughout the war.

When he learned of the incident, Lieutenant Colonel Campbell insisted that General Williamson punish MacAlister's murderers, but Williamson only agreed to send the offending militiamen to be judged by General Lincoln at Purrysburg, and Lincoln declined to prosecute the suspects. (He was probably afraid that if he did so, he would alienate the Whig militia on which he so desperately depended.) The pent-up anger of MacAlister's friends in the Light Infantry would soon find release in the upcoming battle at Briar Creek.

General Williamson effortlessly repossessed Augusta after Campbell's departure, but the American militia would be occupied for some time in operations reducing the Tory outposts that Campbell had established in the backcountry. It was these very Loyalists, however, whom Campbell faulted for the failure of the Augusta expedition. "The [Loyalist] militia of Georgia," Campbell complained, "more especially the crackers, on seeing the rebels increase on the opposite bank of the river, found many excuses for going home to their plantations. I used every argument . . . but they were deaf to reason and left me to a single man."[13]

The British failure at Augusta was early, yet compelling evidence that southern Loyalists were not as numerous, dedicated, or militarily adept as their Patriot counterparts.

Yet, no one in King George's cabinet was willing to concede this, for to do so would be to admit that the Southern Strategy was based on a flawed premise. Indeed, such an admission would have meant that the prosecution of the entire war was based on a false premise since the king's ministers had argued in Parliament that the war was worth fighting for the sake of the majority of Americans who were Loyalist.

Campbell's column marched for about four days and halted at Briar Creek, roughly halfway between Augusta and Savannah. There he was joined by about 270 Tories who had escaped slaughter at Kettle Creek.[14] They were, of course, too few and too late to prevent the British evacuation of the backcountry; nevertheless they were immediately outfitted and formed into provincial units. "The South Carolinians are put as a second battalion to Colonel Innes's," General Prevost wrote, "and the North [Carolinians] formed into a small corps by themselves agreeable to their desire."[15] The latter detachment became the North Carolina Volunteers (sometimes also known as the North Carolina Loyalists), who would play a prominent role in the upcoming campaigns. Captain John Hamilton was promoted to the provincial rank of major and assigned to command the unit. (Hamilton would later attain the provincial rank of lieutenant colonel before being captured by Lieutenant Colonel William Washington during the Charlestown campaign in 1780.)

Major General Prevost had become anxious for the safety of Campbell's expedition almost as soon as it left Savannah. American strength was increasing at Purrysburg, and it became impossible for Prevost to maintain a secure line of communication to Augusta. "Judge then," Prevost said in a letter to Campbell, "if it is not dangerous to be so far divided. I have neither carts nor harness, I cannot pretend to supply you; not now." In a second letter Prevost told the lieutenant colonel: "I always thought that our being able to keep our post at Augusta depended on the single circumstance of the back country people's joining heartily in the cause, as without that we must be certain of finding great difficulty, if not impossibility in preserving a communication to such a distance."[16]

The retreat from Augusta did not spell the end of the Southern Strategy, but it was an inauspicious beginning. The historian Kenneth Davies wrote of the campaign, "It would perhaps be too much to read into his [Campbell's] inability to hold Augusta . . . a prefiguration of Britain's future failure to overcome the southern guerillas."[17] Or maybe it is not too much, for the failure to recruit large numbers of Loyalists at Augusta had been foreshadowed by the failed Moore's Creek campaign of 1776 and would be repeated in 1781 when Cornwallis invaded North Carolina.[18]

The years Campbell spent as a prisoner in Massachusetts had left his personal affairs in shambles, and he decided that it was now time for him to return to England and put his own house in order. At the town of Ebenezer, Campbell turned over command of his troops to Lieutenant Colonel Mark Prevost (the younger brother of General Augustine Prevost). Before leaving for England, Campbell exercised the civil authority granted him by Sir Henry Clinton to appoint the younger Prevost to the post of lieutenant governor of Georgia. Then Campbell, who had done his part for the Crown, boarded ship, never to return to America. Shortly thereafter Mark Prevost would reconvene a Loyalist legislative assembly, making Georgia "officially" the only American state that was restored to the status of a royal colony with a civilian government after it declared independence.[19]

—————≫•≪—————

General John Ashe arrived at Purrysburg on 29 January 1779, after a long march from North Carolina. Ashe brought over eleven hundred troops, almost all militia. Ashe's troops were under good discipline, which was a great relief to General Lincoln's staff officers. These officers were more than a little dissatisfied with the willful South Carolina militia that had already mustered at Purrysburg; Moultrie reported that these South Carolinians were "worse than nothing, as they absolutely refuse Gen. Lincoln's orders."[20] The militia laws of South Carolina allowed for only small monetary fines for breaches of discipline. Even when South Carolina passed stricter militia regulations, they made no provision for enforcement. The result was a militia that served when, where, and how it pleased. South Carolina proved incapable of raising large numbers of professional troops and too weak-kneed to enforce greater discipline among its militia.

The arrival of Ashe's North Carolina militia tipped the scales for the Americans, who were now numerous enough—and disciplined enough—to undertake offensive operations. General Ashe had seen no military action since the Moore's Creek campaign of 1776, when he commanded a company of volunteer riflemen. Despite his inexperience, the governor of North Carolina (Richard Caswell of Moore's Creek fame) saw fit to appoint Ashe to command the important mission to reinforce General Lincoln in South Carolina in late 1778.

Ashe's troops consisted mostly of militia regiments from New Bern, Halifax, Wilmington, and Edenton, some of whom were veterans of the battle fought at Moore's Creek Bridge three years earlier. At the start of February, General Lincoln ordered the North Carolina troops to break camp and advance to join General Williamson's troops at Augusta. Ashe, weary after his journey from North Carolina, was taken aback at Lincoln's order. "It gave me much surprise," he wrote, "that troops that had marched, some of them 400 miles, harassed and without any accoutrements fit for the field, should be sent a 130 miles further in preference to the western brigade, and a number of Continental troops & South Carolina militia, who was [sic] well accoutred, and had been resting for upwards of a month at Purisburg [sic]."[21]

Despite his aggravation, Ashe followed his orders and rendezvoused with General Williamson near Augusta on 13 February. Campbell evacuated the town the following day, eventually retreating to the British base at Ebenezer. On orders from General Lincoln, Ashe followed the British as far as Briar Creek (today spelled "Bryer Creek"), which was roughly fifteen miles north of Ebenezer. Ashe made his camp near Miller Bridge, the main north-south crossing point over Briar Creek. The bridge had been burned out, but Ashe set his men about the task of repairing it.

Briar Creek juts off to the west of the Savannah River, forming an effective barrier between the Georgian low country and the piedmont. General Ashe's campsite along the road near the bridge thus blocked British access to potential backcountry Tory recruits and Indian allies. Perhaps most important, as long as Ashe remained where he was, the British could not get supplies from backcountry farmers with British sympathies (or farmers who were at least sympathetic to British hard currency). General Prevost therefore decided that Ashe would have to be dislodged from the position.

Using a plan devised by Lieutenant Colonel Campbell before he departed, Lieutenant Colonel Mark Prevost was to march most of his troops fifteen miles upstream where they would cross over Briar Creek at Paris Mill Bridge. This corps would then take a circuitous route in order to come from the north to attack the American camp in the rear. To decoy the Americans and mask the movement of the main body, a secondary force would move toward the American position from the south as if they were going to attempt to force a crossing at Miller Bridge.

The decoy force totaled about 500 men and consisted of the 1st Battalion of the 71st Regiment along with some Carolina militia. On 1 March 1779 this detachment departed Ebenezer with full pomp during broad daylight, not attempting to hide their movements. They advanced as far as Buck Creek, which was only three miles south of the American camp at Briar Creek. Meanwhile, the attack column waited until sunset and then quietly marched for the bridge at Paris Mill. This force consisted of the 2nd Battalion of the 71st Regiment, Sir James Baird's Light Infantry Corps, the Grenadier Corps of the Florida Brigade, Captain Tawse's Light Dragoons, five fieldpieces, and a detachment of about 150 "provincials, rangers, and militia."[22] The force totaled over 900 soldiers, of whom most were veteran, crack troops.

After an all-night trek, the attack column reached Paris Mill at ten o'clock the morning of 2 March; not surprisingly, they found the bridge destroyed by the rebels. A temporary bridge was constructed, but a lack of proper bridging materials resulted in a structure unable to withstand the "wide and rapid" creek.[23] A second bridge supported by pontoons proved more reliable, but it was not complete until late that evening. The delay was disturbing since the longer the column lingered at the bridge, the more likely it became that they would be discovered. Colonel Prevost ordered Baird's Light Corps (about three hundred men) and Tawse's Light Dragoons (about forty-two troopers) to ford the river that night in order to screen the main column and cut off the American path of retreat. The rest of Lieutenant Colonel Prevost's troops, including the artillery, were able to cross the pontoon bridge before sunrise the next day, 3 March 1779.

General Ashe had arrived at Briar Creek, on the west bank of the Savannah River, on 27 February. He did not have time to personally oversee the creation of the camp because he was ordered to attend a council of war with General Lincoln downriver on the eastern bank. Ashe's men lacked entrenching tools and artillery, so there was little they could do to secure the camp other than posting alert sentries. Major Ross, commanding 207 South Carolina light horse, had joined his army the preceding night. In addition, Ashe's force was reinforced by General Elbert's Georgia Continentals and some North Carolina light infantry under Lieutenant Colonel Anthony Lytle.[24] Most of Lytle's men were former Continentals or picked militiamen who had signed up for a special nine-month term as "state" troops from North Carolina. Along with Elbert's Georgians, Lytle's "nine-months men" were relatively high-quality soldiers and therefore a much needed commodity. Including the recent addition of Ross's light horse, the Americans had almost thirteen hundred troops at Briar Creek—an amount seemingly sufficient to deal with the small number of redcoats at Ebenezer.

After his meeting with General Lincoln, Ashe returned to his camp at Briar Creek on the afternoon of 2 March. Ashe was told on his arrival that enemy parties had been seen along the camp perimeter the previous night. General Bryan, commanding the North Carolina militia regiments, thought that the enemy parties were merely "horse thieves."[25] A party of forty to sixty South Carolina light horse had been sent to scout in the vicinity of Paris Mill on 1 March, but on their return on the afternoon of 2 March, General Ashe claimed not to have been informed of any unusual activity by the enemy.[26] The remainder of Major Ross's dragoons came back into camp that night around midnight after a day of foraging; however, Ashe declined to send more scouts out to Paris Mill due to the fatigue of the horsemen and because "it would be too late an hour."[27]

James Fergus was one of the troopers who had just returned from scouting near Paris Mill. In his postwar pension statement Fergus contradicted Ashe and said that his patrol informed the general that they had reliable intelligence indicating that the British had crossed Briar Creek twelve miles to the northwest near the Paris Mill Bridge. Fergus claimed to have told Ashe: "We might expect them the next day [3 March] at farthest."[28] Regardless of who is telling the truth, it is quite evident that Ashe did not believe the British to be nearby and there were no special preparations made for combat the night of 2 March.

General Lincoln described Ashe's position at Briar Creek as one of the strongest in the upcountry: Ashe's eastern flank was covered by swamps and the Savannah River, and Briar Creek protected Ashe's southern and southwestern front. "Besides," Lincoln later wrote, "[Ashe] had a party of about two hundred horse" to guard his west flank and rear.[29] However, Ashe was not using his horsemen to cover the flanks and the rear. Instead, on the morning of 3 March, Ashe sent Major Ross and 160 of his horsemen to reconnoiter over Briar Creek to the south. James Fergus and the other 40 or so troopers who had scouted Paris Mill the previous day were allowed to stay in camp and rest their horses. Fergus reported being surprised to hear that Ashe ordered Ross to patrol southward since he had told Ashe the previous day that the British were approaching from the northwest.

On the afternoon of 3 March an express rider charged into the American camp announcing that an enemy column was eight miles to the northwest and approaching fast. The British were actually much closer than that, for no more than fifteen minutes later the British columns appeared streaming toward the American camp. Accounts differ on the amount of warning time the Americans had of the British approach, but there is no disputing the fact that the Americans were forced to perform a swift and confused deployment.[30]

Ashe hurriedly ordered the drummers to beat to arms and immediately issued orders recalling Colonel Lytle's two hundred light infantry, who were stationed about a mile distant guarding Miller Bridge. General Ashe theoretically commanded almost thirteen hundred troops, but because of the detachment of Lytle's infantry and Ross's light horse, only about nine hundred men were present on the battlefield as the British approached.[31]

Despite the confusion in camp, General Ashe coolly issued orders. Some soldiers later said that they had not been informed of how to deploy in case of surprise. Ashe

disputed this claim, saying that his troops were ordered to form up as they had encamped in case of a surprise attack. In any case, the American troops scrambled to
form for battle. Colonel Perkins began moving his Edenton Regiment to its position
on the right of the battle line, but he was blocked by the deployment of the Georgia
Continentals in front of him. After the initial mix-up, within a few minutes the American troops had sorted themselves out and drew themselves up into two lines about a
quarter-mile from the camp.

The American front line consisted of the Edenton Regiment on the far right, the
Georgia Continentals in the center, and the New Bern Regiment on the left. The second line was about seventy or eighty yards behind the first and consisted of the Wilmington Regiment on the right and the Halifax Regiment on the left. The left side of
the American lines nearly touched Briar Creek, but there was a gap of about one-half
mile between the right flank of the American lines and the swamps bordering the
Savannah River. This gap would soon be exploited by the enterprising British.

Only after their hasty deployment were the American troops issued cartridges. Ashe
said that the ammunition "could not prudently have been served . . . sooner, as they
had several times received cartridges which had been destroyed and lost for the want
of cartouch boxes."[32] The militiamen were forced to carry their cartridges "under their
arms, others in the bosoms of their shirts, and some tied up in the corners of their
hunting shirts."[33] Worse yet, many of the cartridges did not match the calibers of the
soldier's guns—a fact that contributed greatly to the anxiety of the militia.

The distribution of munitions had not yet been completed when the British appeared, driving the American pickets before them. The pickets were so surprised by
the sudden appearance of the enemy that most of them never fired a shot. At about
this time the American troops realized that they were boxed in: British troops were
approaching what was now their front, while Briar Creek was at their left and rear and
the Savannah River was on their right.

The British advanced in three columns, each six abreast with the ranks drawn up
in close order. Sir James Baird's Light Infantry Corps made up the right column (facing the American left); the center column consisted of the 2nd Battalion of the 71st
Regiment; and the left column (opposite the American right) was composed of a "Carolina provincials corps," including some "rangers" (possibly some of Thomas Brown's
men, though Brown was not present). "When they came within one hundred and fifty
yards of us," Ashe reported, "they displayed their columns to the right and left to form
a line."[34] The British artillery was also deployed in the line, while Colonel Prevost kept
the Florida Grenadiers and Tawse's Light Dragoons in reserve about four hundred
yards to the rear.

James Fergus and forty of his fellow light horsemen were resting their mounts in a
nearby field when they heard the alarm in camp. "[We] had orders sent to us to get our
horses, mount them, and come into camp. This we did," Fergus wrote. "The [Ameri-
can] line was just formed as we arrived. . . . We rode close along the rear of the line
when the first general [enemy] fire was made; as we were on lower ground than the
enemy, it chiefly passed over our heads. We had got to the extremity of the right wing
where General Ashe commanded by the time the second fire was made."[35]

Fergus's deposition illustrates a common problem with British musketry of the era: overshooting. Ashe, through insight or good fortune, had positioned his troops in a "reverse-slope" deployment at the lower end of a slight grade. Troops on high ground firing at lower targets tend to fire too high. However, this serendipitous placement would not save the Americans from ultimate defeat. The Georgia Continentals and the Edenton Regiment now unleashed an ineffective volley of musketry on the redcoats. In addition, two small two-pounder swivel guns near the center of the American line added their fire, for what it was worth.

The Georgia Continentals were led by Brigadier General Samuel Elbert (recently promoted from colonel). Less than three months earlier, Elbert had led the troops from Georgia battling the British at Savannah. Elbert and Ashe were both brigadier generals. Normally the officer with the "Continental" commission would have seniority over a similarly ranked militia officer; in this case, however, the Continental contingent was so small that Elbert deferred command to Ashe, who led the much larger corps from North Carolina. General Ashe reported that the Continentals fired two or three ineffective volleys at the British before Elbert concluded that the range to the British line was too great for musketry to be effective. He therefore advanced his troops—without orders, according to Ashe—to within thirty yards of the British line. However, according to another version of the story, Ashe ordered Elbert forward, saying, "Sir, you had better advance and engage them."[36] Either way, Elbert's Georgians marched bravely forward and began a hot exchange of fire with the Highlanders to their front.

As General Elbert advanced, his troops apparently drifted or "inclined" to the left—thus unintentionally masking the fire of the New Bern Regiment, now to their left rear. At the same time, a group of British horsemen threatened the exposed American right flank. Colonel Perkins was thus obliged to shift his Edenton Regiment obliquely to the right in order to counter the possibility of being outflanked.

The leftward incline of the Continentals and the movement of the Edenton Regiment to the right created a gap in the line between the two regiments. Lieutenant Colonel Prevost took advantage of the opening in the American ranks and ordered his troops to charge. Sir James Baird's Light Infantry Corps made a swift dash forward with fixed bayonets, and the rest of the British army soon joined the headlong rush. "When the Light Infantry were running up in line to charge the rebels, one of the Highlanders called out 'Now my boys, remember poor MacAlister!': in consequence of which, this Corps spared very few that came within their reach."[37] The death of MacAlister, the safeguard murdered by Patriot militia only a few weeks earlier near Augusta, was thus avenged many times that day.

Lacking bayonets to defend themselves in close combat, the American militia immediately broke and fled at the sight of the British regulars charging with their own bayonets fixed and ready. General Ashe, who had stationed himself behind Perkins's Edenton Regiment, hastened off on horseback in a vain attempt to rally the troops: "At this instant of time the Halifax regiment, which was upon the left of the second line, broke and took flight without firing a gun. The Wilmington [regiment] (except a small part under the command of Lieut. Col. Young, who were advancing in their line to the right to prevent being flanked, and fired two or three rounds) and the New Bern [regiment] followed their example. The Edenton regiment continued for two or three discharges longer, when they gave way and took flight."[38]

Some who saw Ashe riding hard after the fleeing militia later reported that the general had fled like a coward. Other officers testified that Ashe was merely attempting to stop the flight of his fleet-footed army, and he was later cleared by a military court of the charge of personal cowardice. At this time Lieutenant Colonel Lytle, who had been guarding Miller Bridge, finally arrived on the scene accompanied by his two hundred light infantry. Lytle saw that it was too late to save the army, as the militiamen were by that time plunging headlong through the swamps and into the river.[39] The American light infantry commander therefore withdrew his regiment. While Lytle's men initially retired in good order, they were forced to swim the Savannah River in order to escape the enemy.

The only organized body of Americans left at this time on the field was General Elbert's hard-fighting Georgia Continentals. Having stood their ground while the rest of the army fled, they were now abandoned to their fate as the British enveloped their position. General Elbert later said that he did not know that "the right wing was gone till he found the enemy in his rear, killing his men."[40] After ten or fifteen minutes of valiant combat, and having himself suffered a gunshot wound during the fighting, Elbert reluctantly ordered his men to cease fire and lay down their arms. The battle of Briar Creek was over. As would be the case the following year at the battle of Camden, the bravery and discipline of the Continental troops doomed their unit after the militia fled, leaving them unsupported.

British casualties were very light: 5 killed and 11 wounded. There was never an accurate accounting of American casualties because many of the militia who escaped being killed or captured did not stop their retreat until they reached their homes in North Carolina. Colonel Prevost reported that more than 150 Americans were killed on the battlefield and an unknown number drowned attempting to swim the creek and river. The British took 227 prisoners, including nearly all of Elbert's Continentals. American casualties would have been even worse had the British soldiers not stopped their pursuit to loot the American camp. The British also took the two small two-pound swivel guns that Ashe's men had abandoned in their flight.

The Americans who escaped injury or capture had to dispose of their clothes, weapons, and other accoutrements to make the swim to safety. The right bank of the river was thus littered with hundreds of hats, canteens, and guns as the soldiers tossed their equipment aside and jumped into the river to save themselves. The loss of the military-grade muskets was particularly painful for the Americans, who were always in want of quality arms. Anthony Lytle's light corps was, for example, forced to make a decision to keep their clothes or guns as they could not swim with the weight of both: "The men who brought off their arms left great parts of their cloathing [sic] preferring to leave their hunting shirts . . . rather than their rifles."[41] For want of clothes and arms, Lytle was forced to disperse much of his corps.

Most of the defeated soldiers put the blame for the loss squarely on Brigadier General John Ashe. "The general wheeled and fled and the whole wing with him," James Fergus wrote. Allegedly, General Samuel Elbert "fully believed General Ashe betrayed us to the British, and declared that if he ever met with him, one of them should die before they parted."[42] Some American officers, including General Bryan, made accusations and inflammatory remarks against General Ashe, and a court-martial was held to determine if he was culpable of cowardice and mismanagement. Brigadier General William Moultrie presided over the court, which found Ashe innocent of cowardice but guilty of failing to secure his camp adequately.

During his court-martial, many of Ashe's officers criticized him for failing to employ his light horse as vedettes (mounted sentinels stationed in advance of the infantry pickets). A screen of vedettes would have given the Americans much greater warning than the ten or fifteen minutes they actually received. In his own defense, Ashe claimed that the quality of his troops was so poor that "had there been a day, nay, even a week's notice of the enemy's approach—the confusion would have been the same."[43] This is of course not true. If there had been a few hours' notice, Ashe would never have sent his cavalry off. With a few extra minutes Ashe could have recalled Lytle's light infantry to camp and, perhaps most importantly, the militia could have been served with the proper cartridges.

In Ashe's defense, it has to be admitted that the militia he commanded—lacking bayonets, cartridge boxes, and proper ammunition—was no match for well-equipped British regulars. Ultimately, General Lincoln must bear much responsibility for the defeat. He failed to keep his forces concentrated, thus inviting the British counterattack at Briar Creek. In addition, Ashe was entirely correct in criticizing Lincoln for sending his tired and poorly equipped militia to confront a force of seasoned regulars while the well-rested South Carolina Continentals and militia sat idle at Purrysburg.

For the British, Briar Creek appeared on the surface to be an unmitigated success. Lieutenant Colonel Mark Prevost received well-deserved praise from his older brother Augustine in dispatches to Clinton and Germain. Archibald Campbell had created the plan that Lieutenant Colonel Prevost followed, but there is no question that Lieutenant Colonel Prevost executed that plan brilliantly.

It was a satisfying triumph bought at little cost, but the British knew that Briar Creek was merely a temporary check on the momentum of the Americans, whose numbers continued to increase at Purrysburg and Augusta. It is interesting that, even in the face of catastrophic defeat at Briar Creek, the Americans still managed to find more militia recruits, whereas the Loyalist defeat at Kettle Creek seemed to squelch British recruiting prospects. Even worse, the British commissary in Savannah now reported that food stocks in the city had begun to be depleted. The victory at Briar Creek reopened British communications to the piedmont, but the supposedly "Loyalist" farmers in the backcountry failed to send any supplies.

Lieutenant Colonel Mark Prevost complained that "even after so decisive a blow" he was unable to assert any control over the backcountry. "Incursions and depredations on the plantations of such of the inhabitants who had taken protection at the time Colonel Campbell was at Augusta made the rest apprehensive of joining us heartily and led many of them to turn zealous supporters of the rebel cause."[44] Having only recruited a fraction of the expected number of Tories, the British lacked the manpower to mount a renewed campaign against Augusta. They had no choice but to fall back to

Ebenezer and abandon the backcountry to the Americans. The British victory at Briar Creek was thus quite hollow. Campbell's Augusta expedition and the battle of Briar Creek marked the beginning of a pattern of tactical victory followed by strategic withdrawal that would plague British operations throughout the war in the South.

ORDER OF BATTLE: BRIAR CREEK
Georgia, 3 March 1779

American Forces
Brig. Gen. John Ashe

	MEN	ARTILLERY
Brig. Gen. Bryan's North Carolina		
Militia Brigade[45]	800	
New Bern Regiment		
Halifax Regiment—Col. Eaton		
Wilmington Regiment		
Edenton Regiment—Col. Perkins		
Georgia Continentals—Gen. Samuel Elbert	70	
N.C. Light Infantry—Lt. Col. Anthony Lytle	200	
Light Horse (detachment from		
Major Ross's command)	40	
Cannons (4-lb.)		1
Cannons (2-lb.)		2
Total	**1,110**	**3**

British Forces
Lt. Col. Mark Prevost

	MEN	ARTILLERY
Grenadier Corps of the Florida Brigade[46]—		
Maj. Beamsly Glazier	100	
71st Regiment		
Light Infantry Corps[47]—Sir James Baird	299	
2nd Battalion	400	
Light Dragoons—Capt. Thomas Tawse	42	
Carolina "provincials, rangers, militia"[48]	150	
Cannons (6-lb.)	10	2
Howitzer (5.5")	5	1
Cannons (3-lb.)	10	2
Total	**ca. 1016**	**5**

Casualties

	AMERICAN	BRITISH
Killed	ca. 150	5
Wounded	?	11

	AMERICAN	BRITISH
Missing	n/a	–
Total Casualties	**ca. 150**	**16**
Captured	ca. 227	–
Total Losses[49]	**ca. 377**	**16**

American Detached Force
   (not engaged—south of Briar Creek)

	MEN	ARTILLERY
S.C. Light Horse—Maj. Francis Ross	167	
Total	**167**	**0**

British Decoy Force
   (not engaged—at Miller Bridge)

	MEN	ARTILLERY
1st Battalion, 71st Regiment—Maj. McPherson	356	
Carolina "volunteers and irregulars"[50]	150	
Total	**506**	**0**

EIGHT

Charlestown, 1779

"We will fight it out!"

THE CONQUEST OF CHARLESTOWN was the ultimate goal of General Prevost's British "Southern Army" (as it was now often called). Charlestown was the most populous southern city and the financial and cultural capital of the region. The South could not be conquered without its possession. Lord Germain's Southern Strategy called for large numbers of Loyalists, drawn from the backcountry of Georgia and the Carolinas, to facilitate an invasion of South Carolina. However, Lieutenant Colonel Archibald Campbell's expedition to Augusta was a failure. To make matters worse, there was a paradoxical dwindling of Tory activity in Georgia after the British victory at Briar Creek. As a result, the British did not have the strength to directly confront the American army in South Carolina. How strange, then, that in the spring of 1779 the numerically inferior British Southern Army was able to outmaneuver its larger American counterpart and nearly force the submission of South Carolina and its prestigious capital.

General Prevost made his first attempt to invade South Carolina in February 1779 when he attacked the town of Beaufort with three companies of light infantry of the Florida Brigade. Beaufort is on Port Royal Island about thirty-five miles southwest of Charlestown and thirty miles northeast of Savannah. Major William Gardner[1] led the small amphibious invasion, which was designed primarily as a diversion to draw American attention away from Lieutenant Colonel Archibald Campbell's expedition to Augusta. Major Gardner's mission was to capture the town of Beaufort, which lay at the north end of Port Royal Island. If successful, the outpost could be used to facilitate a larger invasion of South Carolina later in the year. Tory informants told General Prevost that Beaufort had a large Loyalist population that would help take and hold the island; but this intelligence proved to be only wishful thinking.

After Major Gardner landed, he was confronted on 3 February 1779 by several companies of Carolina militia led by Brigadier General William Moultrie. In a hotly contested firefight that lasted nearly three-quarters of an hour, the Americans forced the British to withdraw. Gardner's small force was badly cut up in the engagement, suffering forty killed and wounded, and twelve taken prisoner. By comparison, the Americans only suffered seven killed and eighteen wounded.[2] Gardner regained his ships with difficulty, and Prevost blamed him for the failure of the operation. "I am sorry to say," Prevost wrote, "that Major Gardner's imprudence in quitting his boats to go a place seven miles from them had nearly been the cause of the loss of the whole detachment. The retreat was cut off and but for the great bravery of the troops they must have been taken."[3]

The skirmish at Port Royal was notable as a victory of American militia over a like number of British regulars. It also failed Prevost in two other ways: First, it failed to draw General Lincoln's attention away from British operations in the Georgia piedmont; second, it showed how dangerous it was to rely on Tories to facilitate military operations —not one Tory raised a hand to help Gardner.

Despite the reverse at Briar Creek, the Americans were able to retain control of Augusta and the backcountry. "It is a matter of great importance," Lincoln wrote, "to prevent the Enemy from getting into the upper part of the Country from which we draw many of our supplies [and] in which are many unfriendly persons."[4] Without reinforcements and supplies from backcountry Loyalists and British-allied Indians, the British could not extend their operations beyond the environs of Savannah.

The losses of arms and material at Briar Creek curtailed American military operations until mid-April, when a supply of weapons and ammunition from the Dutch colony of St. Eustatia arrived at Charlestown.[5] After distributing new muskets and gunpowder to the army, Lincoln held a council of war on 19 April to decide on a strategy for retaking Georgia. The officers in the council agreed on Lincoln's plan to "take some strong ground in Georgia; prevent, if possible, the enemy from receiving supplies from the back part of the country, circumscribe their limits, prevent their junction with the unfriendly, and savages in Georgia, and in the back part of the state."[6]

To execute his strategy, Lincoln decided to march with the greater part of his army to Augusta. There, Lincoln could put an end to the minor Tory uprisings that had been troubling the backcountry since Lieutenant Colonel Archibald Campbell's expedition a few months earlier. In addition, a reconstituted Patriot legislature for Georgia was going to convene in Augusta in late April. Lincoln's movement to the city would serve to guard this important meeting and bolster the confidence of the Patriot legislators and civilians. The plan involved risk as it meant that South Carolina would be practically unguarded after the main army departed.

Notwithstanding his officers' agreement on the plan, Lincoln's strategy was both vague and unsound. Augusta had been secured by General Williamson's militia as soon as the British had evacuated the town in mid-February. The marauding handfuls of Tory partisans in the area hardly represented a threat worthy of the attention of Lincoln's entire army. In addition, the British had received almost no worthwhile reinforcements from the Georgian backcountry—only a small party of Creek warriors and a handful of Tories. Preventing supplies from being sent downriver to Savannah was certainly a worthwhile cause, but that task was already being effectively accomplished by Williamson's militia.

So what could Lincoln have been thinking? It might be argued that he was proactively moving to eliminate a latent threat before it matured into a significant one. However, it is hard to maintain that the nebulous danger posed by backcountry Tories was serious enough to warrant sending the bulk of the American southern army deep into the interior of the country. It is certainly true that the convention of the Georgia legislature deserved protection; but was it so important as to leave all of South Carolina with only minimal defenses? Lincoln failed to grasp the fact that the British could not mount a major expedition into the backcountry as long as he kept his army at Purrysburg, which threatened the line of communication between Savannah and Augusta.

Lincoln's plan to go to Augusta must have resulted from his inability to invent anything more substantial for his army to do. Savannah was the most significant target in Georgia, but the Americans lacked sufficient artillery to besiege the city. A better choice than moving his army to Augusta would have been for Lincoln to attack the British-held town of Ebenezer. This town sat at a critical Georgian crossroads that lay across the Savannah River nearly opposite the American camp at Purrysburg. The British were using Ebenezer both as a defensive bulwark and as a staging area for offensives into the backcountry. (The attack on Briar Creek, for instance, had been launched from Ebenezer.) Lincoln ignored this logical target, however, possibly out of apprehension of attacking a fortified position. One might argue that this is hindsight, but it is difficult to justify a plan that ignored the strategic target of Ebenezer, sent the American army into a remote region where the British army was not present, and left South Carolina with only scanty defenses.

General Lincoln began his march to Augusta on 20 April, leaving Brigadier General William Moultrie behind with about 1,000 militia and 220 Continentals to guard South Carolina. Lincoln knew that this force was insufficient to stop the British should they invade South Carolina, but he thought it unlikely that they would do so. After reaching Augusta on 22 April, Lincoln sent Moultrie these orders: "Keep, as long as you have it in your power, a post at Purisburgh [sic]. If the enemy should discover an inclination to attempt you in force, and to move toward Charlestown; you will please as soon as possible to possess yourself of the several passes, and delay them as much as is in your power, and give time for us to come up."[7]

The "passes" Lincoln mentioned were the fords and bridges over the various rivers and creeks that lay between Georgia and Charlestown. Lincoln saw his defensive orders to Moultrie as purely precautionary, and it probably surprised him more than anyone that these orders would actually be put to the test.

———————

Despite the advantages brought by the twin victories at Savannah and Briar Creek, the situation of the British army in Georgia during spring 1779 was anything but ideal. The American army in South Carolina was now numerically superior to the British in Georgia, and only a few hundred southern Tories had volunteered to take up arms. Worse yet, a supply convoy from England to Savannah had been intercepted by American privateers, resulting in acute shortages in the British commissary. (American privateers proved a critical scourge against British shipping throughout the war.) The lightly populated countryside near Savannah had already been stripped of its scant available forage, and the American partisans had prevented the British from foraging in the piedmont and from trading with backcountry Loyalists and Indians. General Prevost was therefore in a quandary about how to supply his army, which was now critically short of provisions.[8]

Prevost's supply situation was particularly embarrassing because one of the hoped-for benefits of invading Georgia was that it would prove a source of supply for the British forces in the Caribbean. The reality was that, far from being able to supply anyone else, the British garrison in Savannah faced the possibility of starvation. Fortunately for Prevost, word came in late April that General Lincoln was moving the greater part of his army toward Augusta. It was the break that Prevost needed. South Carolina's rich lowcountry plantations, brimming with cattle and rice, were perfect targets for a foraging expedition. Prevost decided to invade the Palmetto State. If Lincoln's army returned to South Carolina, then Prevost would simply backtrack to Georgia— his soldiers' bellies full of Carolina rice and beef. If Lincoln did not turn about quickly, then Prevost could spend even more time living off the land and denying his opponent forage; there was even the remote possibility that Charlestown might be threatened by the expedition. Either way, this would prove an excellent opportunity to test the enthusiasm of South Carolina's Tories to support restoration of Crown rule.

Prevost's plan was not without its dangers. Lincoln might attack toward Savannah while the British army was away in South Carolina, or the Americans might make a sudden move to cut Prevost off from his base in Georgia. In addition, since the rebels in Georgia had never been fully pacified, they would certainly take advantage of the British army's absence to cause all sorts of mischief. The restored royal governor of Georgia, Sir James Wright, would later write that Georgia "was being totally lost [to Patriot partisans] while the army was carrying on their operations in South Carolina."[9] The fact that Prevost was willing to accept these risks serves to illustrate not only how desperate his supply situation had become, but also how logistics impact military operations and command decisions.

On 29 April 1779 Prevost quietly ferried two thousand men across a deep swamp to the northern side of the Savannah River near Purrysburg, South Carolina. The swamp was thought by most to be impassable, but Prevost wrote that his men "with their usual spirit got over every difficulty."[10] At ten o'clock in the morning the British struck. The light infantry and the 1st Battalion of the 71st Regiment attacked Purrysburg, then guarded by only one hundred men of the 5th South Carolina Continentals. The Continentals withdrew after a brief skirmish, leaving two dead and several taken captive. Prevost had acted to take advantage of Lincoln's absence faster than the Americans had thought possible. Moultrie's little force was in no way prepared to defend against the British incursion. Only the rain-swollen Savannah River gave the Americans any respite, delaying Prevost's advance two days while the British field artillery and provisions were ferried over to the South Carolina side.[11]

Moultrie made use of Prevost's forty-eight-hour river crossing to retreat with all his force (about 950 militia and 250 Continentals) to the fords over the Coosawhatchie; at the same time he sent an urgent request to Lincoln asking him to "repair to Charlestown with your army as soon as possible."[12] Moultrie received a dispatch on 1 May from

General Stephen Bull—whose militia had recently fought at Beaufort—informing him that Bull was coming with 600 men.

General Bull's message eased Moultrie's mind, and he sent a second dispatch to Lincoln refining his request for help. Moultrie told Lincoln that one thousand men "would be sufficient to prevent their [the British] going to Charlestown."[13] Indeed, Moultrie thought that if Bull's reinforcements arrived quickly enough, he might not need Lincoln's help at all. Unfortunately, they never did arrive. As Prevost's army advanced into South Carolina, the militiamen of Bull's brigade became afraid for the safety of their families, whose farms and homes were in the path of the British advance. Some of the militiamen refused to leave their homes, while others took their families off their farms to more secure parts of the state. Either way, few reported for duty.

For his part, Lincoln did not seem concerned for the fate of Charlestown and did not wish to abandon his expedition into the backcountry: "The enemy, I think, cannot mean to attempt Charlestown with the few troops they have thrown over the Savannah."[14] Instead of detaching a force from his own army, Lincoln simply directed that the state militia, which Governor John Rutledge was then gathering at Orangeburg, should move to reinforce Moultrie after they were assembled.

Moultrie claimed that the Coosawhatchie was very low at that time, allowing for numerous fords, and was thus not a good defensive barrier.[15] Sizing up the position, Moultrie thought it better to move a few miles eastward to a bridge over the Tullifiny River; there a large hill overlooked the bridge and made for better defensive ground. On 1 May, Moultrie left a rear guard of 100 men at the main ford over the Coosawhatchie while he reorganized his army at Tullifiny. Two days later he received word that the enemy was advancing. Moultrie immediately sent Lieutenant Colonel John Laurens to the Coosawhatchie River with 150 riflemen and 100 infantry along with orders to retrieve the guard at the ford.

Lieutenant Colonel John Laurens had only joined Moultrie's command two days earlier. He was the son of Henry Laurens, one of the premier statesmen of South Carolina and former president of the Continental Congress. John Laurens was regarded as one of the most beloved and experienced officers in the Continental Army. If John Laurens had a fault, it was that he was often too reckless, earning him the reputation among some in the army as a widow maker.

John Laurens had served as Washington's aide-de-camp and was a veteran of numerous battles, including Brandywine, Germantown, and Monmouth Court House (he had been wounded in the latter two battles). Returning to South Carolina in 1779, John Laurens had only just been elected to the South Carolina assembly when he received word that Prevost's army had invaded the state. The aspiring politician immediately abandoned the statehouse for the field and offered his services to General Moultrie.

On his arrival at the Coosawhatchie ford, instead of pulling the 100-man rear guard back as he had been ordered, Laurens sent the detachment across the shallow river to confront the British advance guard.[16] Apparently wishing to make an impression on the British before retreating, Laurens also sent across the 250-man escort that Moultrie had given him (making for a total of 350 men across the river). The British troops detected Laurens's advance and occupied several houses on a hill close to the ford. From this advantageous position the British poured musketry and artillery fire down on the vulnerable Americans. "In this situation," Moultrie says, "did he [Laurens] expose his men to their fire, without the least chance of doing [the British] any injury." After losing several men to British sniping and cannonballs, Laurens took a bullet in an arm and had his horse shot from beneath him. Nursing his wound, Colonel Laurens put Captain Thomas Shubrick in command while he rode back to Moultrie's camp. Laurens told Shubrick "to stay a little longer and then to bring off the men." Quite sensibly, Shubrick did not wait but withdrew immediately, which Moultrie claims saved the detachment from being cut off.[17]

At about two o'clock in the afternoon on 3 May, Moultrie heard the sound of the action at the Coosawhatchie and assumed the rear guard to be making its way to him. Instead of the guard, however, Lieutenant Colonel Laurens arrived at Tullifiny Hill by himself.

"Well Colonel," Moultrie asked Laurens, "what do you think of it?"

"Why sir," Laurens responded, "your men won't stand."

"If that be the case," Moultrie replied, "I will retreat."[18]

After Captain Shubrick arrived with the rest of the men, Moultrie fell back over the Tullifiny River and destroyed the bridge behind him.

Moultrie was somewhat surprised that Laurens, whom he knew to be "a brave and experienced officer," would nearly have botched what should have been a routine operation. Moultrie claimed that his orders were clear: retrieve the rear guard and rejoin the main army. Moultrie blamed Colonel Laurens's unauthorized attack at the Coosawhatchie ford for spoiling the plans he had made for the defense of the Tullifiny crossing. However, Moultrie never made entirely clear why Laurens's actions prevented him from regrouping and fighting a second action at the Tullifiny—or for that matter at some other spot. In fact, the short combat at the Coosawhatchie ford proved to be the only delaying action fought by Moultrie's troops during their long withdrawal toward Charlestown.

As Moultrie's militia fell back, they destroyed the bridges and felled trees across the roads to impede the British advance. Despite these obstructions, the British moved swiftly, staying always just a few miles behind the Americans. This hot pursuit compelled Moultrie to make forced night marches to stay ahead of Prevost. As the British advanced, their scouts fanned out ahead of the main column, burning and looting homes indiscriminately. Even the Episcopal church in Prince Williams Parish was burned. Rather than galvanizing the Carolina citizenry to combat the invaders, these acts of rapine and vandalism demoralized the South Carolina militiamen, who were anxious for the safety of their families and homes. "Above all," South Carolina native David Ramsay wrote, the South Carolinians were in "dread of the royal auxiliaries, the Indian savages." A small contingent of Creek Indians—perhaps 70 to 120 warriors—accompanied Prevost's army, and their reputation for frontier savagery terrified the lowcountry citizens.[19]

Moultrie's militia now began to depart by companies and even battalions in order "to take care of their families and property." The desertion of the militia placed Charlestown in real jeopardy and prompted Moultrie to write to General Lincoln again: "I must beg you would hasten to our assistance, or I fear the town is in danger. My little army decreases, everyone running to look after his family and property. The enemy carry everything before them with fire and sword."[20]

Lincoln received Moultrie's desperate entreaties with sangfroid that bordered on disinterest. He simply refused to believe that Prevost's invasion was anything more than a feint designed to draw him back from Georgia. Lincoln sent a token force to Charlestown that consisted of 250 mounted light infantry commanded by Colonel Harris. The paltry size of the relief force demonstrated Lincoln's skepticism that South Carolina was seriously endangered. To his credit, Lincoln did make a precautionary move a few miles downriver from Augusta, where he kept a flotilla of bateaux close by on the Savannah River in case he needed to return to South Carolina.

As late as 6 May, Lincoln still appeared unconcerned about the British incursion, even though Prevost had now been in South Carolina for eight days. By this time it was irrelevant whether Charlestown was the object of the invasion or not; the fact that the British army was laying waste to the richest part of the state alone justified Lincoln's return. Even General Prevost was amazed at Lincoln's stubbornness: "It was not till some days after our progress into South Carolina that General Lincoln could be persuaded to retreat and come to the assistance of Charleston."[21]

By 8 May, Moultrie's army had so withered from desertions that he now only commanded six hundred soldiers. At that time five separate bodies of troops were winding their way toward the South Carolina capital: Moultrie's army, Governor Rutledge's militia coming from Orangeburg, Colonel Harris's detachment of Continentals, General Prevost's column, and General Lincoln's army in Georgia. In addition, civilian refugees filed away from the British in all directions, dragging children and carts full of possessions with them. "In short," Moultrie wrote, "it was nothing but general confusion and alarm. I may truly say the whole country was in motion."[22] Moultrie retreated to Dorchester, a town on the Ashley River about eighteen miles upriver from Charlestown and the place closest to the city where an army could ford the river; Bacon's Bridge was a further two miles upriver from Dorchester. Moultrie left a few hundred troops at Dorchester and Bacon's Bridge to defend the river crossings and then entered Charlestown on 9 May with the remainder of his small force.

Moultrie figured that he had about two or three days to prepare the city before the British arrived on the outskirts of Charlestown. However, on 10 May, Prevost scored a great coup: "By a rapid movement of a body of horse we made ourselves masters of the ferry at Ashley River together with all the boats there."[23] Ashley Ferry was only about seven miles from Charlestown by road and more than eleven miles downriver from Dorchester. It was an amateurish error by Moultrie not to have ordered that the boats be kept moored to the left bank of the river, where they would have been safe from British cavalry raids. Moultrie was obviously embarrassed by the incident, which he conveniently neglected to mention in his memoirs. The capture of the ferry saved General Prevost's column at least two days' march since they could now bypass Dorchester. In addition, the ferryboats gave Prevost the ability, which he otherwise would not have had, to cross and navigate the intercoastal rivers.[24]

Charlestown sits on the tip of a peninsula formed by the confluence of two large rivers, the Ashley to the south and the Cooper to the north. A series of fortifications had been erected three years earlier to protect the city against attack from the sea, but the rear or landward approaches had been neglected. As Prevost's column approached, Lieutenant Governor Thomas Bee belatedly prepared to defend the town's neglected posterior. Within a few days earthworks, artillery emplacements, and abatis stretched across the Charlestown "neck" (the narrow area behind the city that lay between the Ashley and Cooper rivers). The town's defenses were thus in tolerable shape when the British arrived to test them.

Using the boats they had captured from the Americans at Ashley Ferry, General Prevost and his men crossed the Ashley on 11 May. Prevost immediately threw over to the Charlestown neck about nine hundred men and quickly marched them to the ground before the city. Prevost left about twelve hundred men under the command of Lieutenant Colonel John Maitland five miles behind him on the right bank (southwest side) of the Ashley River. Having fewer than a thousand men before the city, no entrenching tools, and negligible artillery, Prevost had little chance of taking by force or even laying siege to Charlestown. He could only hope to bluff the Americans into submission. The game now was not chess but poker; and it had to be a quick game of bluff as Prevost assumed that General Lincoln would soon be returning from Georgia.

As the British approached within sight of the town, Captain James Moncrief, the chief engineer of the British Southern Army, went forward to reconnoiter the American defenses. He was escorted by a troop of dragoons and several hundred light infantry. Moncrief's party was immediately confronted by a force of American cavalry and infantry flying the standard of the American Legion of Brigadier General Count Casimir Pulaski. The second contest for Charlestown had begun.

<hr />

Brigadier General Count Casimir Pulaski was a flamboyant Polish officer serving in the Continental Army. He had arrived in Charlestown a few days earlier after having made the long march from the main American army in the North to reinforce the Southern Department. The count came to America in 1777 after having been recommended to Washington by Benjamin Franklin, who was then in Paris. Pulaski had been living in Europe as an exiled mercenary after having taken part in a failed revolt against the Polish Crown. After joining the American army, he commanded the American cavalry at several engagements, including Brandywine and Germantown.

Pulaski never learned to speak or understand English, so he constantly kept a translator with him. Despite this language barrier with other officers, Pulaski was generally well respected in the Continental Army. At the battle of Brandywine, Pulaski led an admirable rearguard attack, but overall his service in the army was not noteworthy. As the war progressed, Pulaski became increasingly isolated within the army and even made a few political enemies.

Pulaski asked permission of Congress in 1778 to form his own legion. The eighteenth-century "legion" was very different from its Roman namesake. Developed during the Seven Years' War in Europe, the legion was a combined arms formation consisting of several troops of cavalry and a like number of light infantry companies. This highly mobile formation was especially effective in the American theater that, unlike Europe, still had large areas of untamed wilderness. In addition, the versatility of the infantry-cavalry mix made the legion highly suited to semiautonomous operations.

Pulaski named his new unit the "American Legion"—an ironic title since a majority of the soldiers were recruited from German deserters and British prisoners of war while the officers were mostly French, German, or Polish expatriates. In any case, the unit was usually called by its unofficial name, Pulaski's Legion. General Washington disapproved of the makeup of the rank and file of Pulaski's Legion, believing that any unit consisting primarily of enemy deserters and commanded mostly by foreign officers had to have questionable loyalty. However, due to the desperate shortage of soldiers, Congress looked the other way at Pulaski's recruiting methods. Congress ordered the legion south to reinforce General Lincoln, which prompted Washington to admonish Pulaski to monitor his soldiers' discipline carefully: "Do every thing in your power to keep the men together," he wrote, "and prevent the destruction of property."[25]

Pulaski entered Charlestown on 8 May 1779 with his cavalry, and on the morning of 11 May the infantry of the legion crossed over the Cooper River from Haddrells Point. At this time Pulaski's Legion consisted of only 120 men—60 cavalry and 60 infantry. After parading down the streets of the city, the legion and a few militiamen sortied out onto the Charlestown neck to confront the British vanguard. They soon encountered Captain Moncrief and his escort of 40 British dragoons commanded by Captain Tawse. As the Americans approached, Tawse's cavalry was reinforced by several hundred infantry of the New York Volunteers and the British Light Infantry Corps. A melee immediately ensued on the grounds of the old Nightingale horse-racing track in front of the American lines. The British dragoons, supported by the light infantry, swooped down on Pulaski's outnumbered corps.

Colonel Chevalier de Rowatz,[26] a Prussian, commanded the legion's infantry contingent. According to David Ramsay, Rowatz left the protection of an advanced breastwork "from an eagerness to engage." The infantrymen were cut off and cut up by the advancing British cavalry, and Rowatz was killed. Only a handful of infantry escaped the British sabers, and the Americans then retired with difficulty behind the American fortifications. The British attempted to pursue Pulaski's cavalry as it withdrew, but they were turned back by artillery firing from the city's main gate. Although Tawse's dragoons charged the Americans three times, they only suffered two killed and four wounded in the action. Pulaski's corps had fourteen killed, forty-two taken prisoner, and some wounded, with the infantry contingent suffering the majority of the casualties and captures. The action occurred before the eyes of the townspeople. While they were disappointed by the defeat, they were impressed by Pulaski's courage. According to Ramsay, "General Pulaski had several successful personal rencounters [sic] with individuals of the British cavalry, and on all occasions discovered the greatest intrepidity."[27]

There was a great deal of confusion and disorganization in the American lines at this time. Several disparate groups of soldiers had suddenly been thrown together to defend the South Carolina capital: Governor Rutledge had come into town the previous day with the backcountry militia; Colonel Harris had just arrived with his contingent of Continental Light Infantry; and General Bull had finally arrived with the Beaufort militia. Moultrie's depleted army was of course present, as was the militia of Charles-town. No one knew his place in the lines, and many soldiers needed arms and ammu-nition. What caused the most problems, though, was the confused command structure. At one time during the afternoon of 11 May, William Moultrie was rushing through part of the American camp on horseback. He overheard one of the governor's aides telling an officer, "You are to obey the orders of the governor, of General Moultrie, and of the privy council." At this point Moultrie, without stopping his horse, turned and shouted, "No orders from the privy council are to be obeyed!" The problem of no sin-gle military commander for the garrison would soon result in tragedy.[28]

At about ten o'clock that night, movement was perceived in front of the entrench-ments. The anxious American soldiers immediately unleashed a massive fusillade into the darkness. "A few hopping shots were fired," Moultrie wrote, "and immediately after the firing [ran] almost through the lines, with cannon, field-pieces, and musketry: by which unfortunate mistake Major Benjamin Huger and 12 others were either killed or wounded."[29] It had been a terrible accident that today would be called "friendly fire." Major Benjamin Huger, the brother of Brigadier General Isaac Huger and a close friend of the Marquis de Lafayette, had been sent to close a gap in the abatis. However, no one manning the lines had been informed of the mission, and Huger's party was mis-taken for the enemy.

Moultrie was furious when he heard of the incident:

> I expressed myself with some warmth and asked, "Who gave the orders for those men to go without the lines?" Some one replied, "The Governor." He being near at hand denied his giving any such orders, upon which I said "Gentlemen (addressing myself to the governor and the council, they being all together), this will never do. We shall be ruined and undone if we have so many commanders; it is absolutely necessary to chuse [sic] one to command. If you leave the command to me, I will not interfere in any civil matters you may have to do with the enemy, such as par-lies, capitulations, etc. I will attend only to the military department."[30]

The governor and council members agreed to the terms, allowing Moultrie to as-sume sole command of the armed forces in the city. However, the agreement had a legal gray area that would soon be tested. At about three o'clock in the morning on 12 May, Governor Rutledge called on General Moultrie at his quarters. A strange conversation took place between the two senior defenders of the city. The governor, whose spirit in defense of his state had been steadfast, now suddenly seemed despondent. Rutledge wanted a parley with the enemy. He said that the American fortifications were too weak and the garrison too small to withstand the British. Rutledge was afraid that if the British stormed the lines there would be great carnage among the civilian population. Moul-trie attempted to reassure Rutledge that they possessed sufficient strength to withstand the British, but the governor was not convinced. Having relinquished to the governor the power of capitulation, Moultrie reluctantly sent an emissary to General Prevost ask-ing what terms would be granted if the town's leaders were inclined to surrender.

At 11 o'clock in the morning on the 12th, the Americans received a reply from Lieutenant Colonel Mark Prevost, the victor of Briar Creek, who now commanded the British advance guard before the city. The letter gave the Americans four hours to surrender, essentially unconditionally, or face an assault. The letter provoked a spirited debate between the city's civilian and military leadership, who had met in the governor's house. General Moultrie, Count Pulaski, and Lieutenant Colonel Laurens argued for standing firm. The military men estimated the British to be about 4,000 strong. They calculated the defenders of Charlestown to number at least 3,180—more than enough to defeat the British should they decide to attack, considering they had the advantage of the city's defensive works. Nevertheless, the governor, backed by a majority of the Privy Council, argued for capitulation. Rutledge thought that there were only 2,500 American defenders at most and believed that the British numbered between 7,000 and 8,000. Though Americans in town did not know it, there were actually fewer than 1,000 British troops before the town and only another 1,200 enemy troops at Ashley Ferry.

What followed next was one of the most controversial episodes of the Revolutionary War in the South. Five of the eight members of the Privy Council were "moderates" led by Governor Rutledge. Among these moderates, the cause of independence from England and the desire for unity with the other states were less important than the welfare of the citizens and their property in Charlestown. A group of three "radicals," led by Christopher Gadsden, made up the remainder of the council. These men were utterly committed to the cause of independence from England and to national unity with the other states. Governor Rutledge, backed by the moderates, decided that it was pointless to provoke the British to assault; he chose to send the following vaguely worded proposition to Lieutenant Colonel Prevost: "To propose a neutrality, during the war between Great-Britain and America, and the question, whether the state shall belong to Great Britain, or remain one of the United States be determined by the treaty of peace between those two powers."[31]

Moultrie opposed the proposition, and yet he admitted that South Carolina had a grievance with Congress that lent some legitimacy to the neutrality proposal. "The other states have no reason to complain," Moultrie said, "as they had not fulfilled their engagements to it [South Carolina] in giving it aid and assistance, from which promise that State came into the Union."[32] Even so, Moultrie saw no need to make such a proposal because he was completely confident that the British could not take the city. However, having yielded the power of parley, he had no choice but to send the message.

Lieutenant Colonel John Laurens was told to carry the proposal to the British, but the young firebrand refused and another courier had to be sent. The "neutrality proposal" instantly ignited a storm of controversy. John Edwards—a "radical" member of the Privy Council—was affected to weep, asking, "What? Are we to give up the town at last?"[33] Christopher Gadsden informed the supporters of independence in the South Carolina General Assembly of Governor Rutledge's proposal. Backed by a large number of assemblymen, Gadsden is said to have threatened the governor and council moderates with violence; but Rutledge refused to rescind his offer of neutrality.

Lieutenant Colonel Prevost's response to the proposal came into the city about noontime on 12 May. He refused the offer. He said that he did not come in a "legislative" capacity, that "he had nothing to do with the governor, that his business was with General

Moultrie, and as the garrison was in arms, they must surrender prisoners of war."[34] The contemporary soldier-historian Henry Lee asserted that it was a mistake for Prevost to have rejected the proposal, which would have removed South Carolina from the war and freed British troops for operations in other parts of the country. However, Prevost probably made the correct decision. It must have been tempting to accept the offer as he knew he could not take the city; however, the terms of the neutrality would have been complex and probably impossible to enforce. What of the status of Charlestown's port? If it were neutral, then the occupation of the city would have been worthless to the British. Would British and American troops have the right to travel or fight in South Carolina? What would the status of the South Carolina Continentals and militia be in such an arrangement? Did Governor Rutledge, despite his vast dictatorial powers, really have the right to negotiate South Carolina's belligerency or neutrality without the permission of the United States Congress? The Articles of Confederation —signed by representatives of all the states in 1777 but not officially in force until 1781 when Maryland finally ratified it—explicitly stated that the states had entered into a "perpetual" union, while Articles 6 and 9 reserved all power of negotiations with foreign states to Congress. Indeed, Article 6 explicitly forbade individual states from entering "into any conference, agreement, alliance or treaty" without the permission of Congress. In any case, Lieutenant Colonel Prevost certainly understood that he did not have the authority to negotiate the terms of such a far-sweeping treaty. Even if he had accepted the offer, he would have gained little immediate advantage and would have simply complicated the legality of future British military operations in the South.

In any case, General Moultrie made his decision: "Upon this [receiving the enemy's reply] the governor and council looked very grave and stedfastly [*sic*] on each other and on me, not knowing what I would say. After a little pause, I said to the governor and council, 'Gentlemen, you see how the matter stands. The point is this: I am to deliver you up prisoners of war, or not?' Some replied, 'Yes.' I then said 'I am determined not to deliver you up prisoners of war . . . WE WILL FIGHT IT OUT!' Upon my saying this, Colonel Laurens jumped up and said, 'Thank God! We are on our legs again!'"[35]

Moultrie summarily sent a message to Lieutenant Colonel Prevost rejecting his terms. Since the British commander had threatened to assault the town in his earlier communiqué, the Americans stood to their arms expecting the British to attack at any time. The prospect of the impending attack took its toll on the morale of the townspeople and the militia. At one point four men accused of deserting were taken just outside the American lines and were brought back into the town. Governor Rutledge happened by just then. When asked what should be done with the deserters, he replied: "Hang them up to the beam of the gate." This was done, "and there they hung all day."[36]

The next morning, 13 May, sunrise illuminated an empty plain before the Charlestown gate. The British had departed! Count Pulaski and his cavalry were sent out of the city. They made a quick circuit of the grounds where the British had been encamped and returned to say that there was no sign of the redcoats. Mark Prevost's bluff had been called by Moultrie. Knowing that he could not take the city by storm, there was little Prevost could now do but withdraw. In addition, the elder General Prevost had intercepted an American communiqué indicating that Lincoln and his army were approaching fast by way of forced marches. On receipt of this intelligence, General Prevost chose to evacuate his army from the Charlestown neck before it could become trapped between the city and Lincoln's army.

General Prevost could retire with honor, having accomplished more and penetrated farther into South Carolina than most—including General Lincoln—would have thought possible with such a small force. The British commander had fulfilled his primary mission to forage on enemy territory and refill his depleted commissary. Nevertheless, there was a downside to his expedition. The Creek warriors who accompanied Prevost's expedition won few friends to the royal cause. In fact, David Ramsay claimed that British support of Indians in the war turned many Tories against the Crown.[37] Prevost's troops proved particularly rapacious on campaign, and the British commander had done little to restrain his men from wanton looting that created resentment among South Carolina's citizens—Patriots and Tories. Most importantly, Prevost's quick retreat from Charlestown did not inspire confidence among the colony's Loyalists, who had fresh memories of Lieutenant Colonel Campbell's hasty abandonment of Augusta just a few months earlier.

When General Clinton's troops arrived in the vicinity of Charlestown the next year, they asked one supposed Tory why he had not supported the king more vigorously, to which the Tory replied: "Last summer the very weak army under the English General Prevost appeared, which did nothing more than plunder friend and foe. While we were scarcely overjoyed to see ourselves protected by them against the demands of Congress, General Prevost had to retreat again in greatest haste, because of the superior army of General Lincoln."[38]

While the threat to Charlestown had ended for the moment, few in the American military could take pride in their accomplishments during this episode. General Lincoln lacked a coherent strategy for confronting the British in Georgia, despite having numeric superiority. Even worse, the civilian government, led by Governor Rutledge, proved to be less than steadfast. Faced with what the politicians thought was an overwhelming military threat, they were embarrassingly eager to offer neutrality and even capitulation, fearing the loss of civilian lives and property if they persisted in resisting. Apologists for John Rutledge would have us believe that the offer of neutrality was a cleverly designed ruse that allowed the governor to draw out talks with the British long enough for General Lincoln to come to the relief of the city. However, it is painfully clear from Moultrie's and Laurens's memoirs that the offer of neutrality was authentic.[39]

The fact that Congress had as yet sent little help to South Carolina to fight the British caused feelings of despair and abandonment in the state. Rutledge knew there was little hope in resisting the British without help from the national government, yet apparently no help was forthcoming. Could Congress blame him if he sought a separate peace given their apparent disinterest in aiding his state?[40] Nevertheless, the offer of neutrality does reveal a flaw in Rutledge's character, and in that of the other moderates in South Carolina—a flaw that was not evident in the character of leaders of other cities that came to be occupied by the British during the course of the war. The events of May

1779 therefore reinforced the British belief that the South was more open to the prospect of reconciliation than was the North.

Some historians say that Rutledge "still dreamed of reconciliation with the parent country."[41] Yet, Rutledge's actions defy easy explanation. It is paradoxical that Rutledge would stand so firm against British attacks in 1776 but then nearly surrender his state when faced by a weaker threat in 1779. Were Rutledge and his supporters hypocrites? Probably not. Rather, these men were first and foremost concerned with the safety and well-being of the people of South Carolina. Governor Rutledge had repeatedly shown his dedication to the American cause, but when he erroneously came to believe that the British had arrayed overwhelming forces against Charlestown, he saw no reason to risk the lives and property of the citizens when he thought there was no hope of success.

The "siege" of May 1779 provided a prophetic preview of how the civilian leadership of South Carolina would react when Charlestown finally came under a truly serious threat in 1780. The neutrality proposal also exposed the fact that South Carolina felt a weaker attachment to the union than might have been expected, and so it foreshadowed the state's secession in 1860.

Moultrie, too, had set a precedent when he gave up to the state government the authority to parley and capitulate. This was not something that he, as a Continental officer reporting to the Continental Congress, was actually authorized to do. Perhaps Moultrie misunderstood his duty, or perhaps his friendship with Governor Rutledge prompted him to yield more authority than he should have.

Moultrie had made mistakes during this campaign, but his refusal to be intimidated saved the city. Despite the fainthearted actions of the civilian leadership, Moultrie credited the Charlestonians for steadfastness: "In justice to the citizens, they knew nothing of what was going forward in the council: they all seemed firm, calm, and determined to stand to the lines and defend their country."[42] During his later imprisonment following the fall of Charlestown in 1780, the British offered Moultrie a commission to command British troops in the West Indies, but he characteristically refused. Moultrie preferred to remain a prisoner in an American uniform than to live free in a red coat. In a time when other American generals, for instance Benedict Arnold and Charles Lee, were sacrificing their honor in hopes of winning British favor, Moultrie's loyalty to the newborn American nation was no small matter. Moultrie's successful defense of Charlestown in 1776 and 1779 would prove to be his lasting contribution to the cause of American independence.

Order of Battle: Charlestown, 1779
South Carolina, 11–12 May 1779

American Forces
Brig. Gen. William Moultrie

	MEN	ARTILLERY
Continentals		
1st S.C. Continentals— Col. Charles Pinckney	ca. 150	

Order of Battle: Charlestown, 1779 (*continued*)

	MEN	ARTILLERY
2nd S.C. Continentals—Col. Isaac Motte	ca. 150	
4th S.C. Regt. of Continental Artillery—		
Col. Barnard Beekman	60	
5th S.C. Continentals—		
Lt. Col. Alexander McIntosh	190	
Col. Harris's Light Infantry		
(detachment of Continentals)	250	
Pulaski's American Legion—		
Brig. Gen. Casimir Pulaski	120	
Militia		
Charlestown Militia—		
Col. Maurice Simons	600	
French Company—Marquis de Brétigny[43]	50	
Charlestown Militia & "Country" Militia—		
Gov. John Rutledge	780	
Grimball's Charlestown Artillery	150	
Beaufort Militia Brigade—		
Gen. Stephen Bull	400	
Col. Neal's Regiment	150	
"Raccoon" Company—		
Capt. John Allston	ca. 50	
Sailors	50	
Cannons		?
Total	**ca. 3,150**	**?**

British Forces
Maj. Gen. Augustine Prevost

	MEN	ARTILLERY
At Ashley Ferry—Lt. Col. John Maitland		
1st Battalion, 71st Regiment	356	
Regiment von Wissenbach—		
Lt. Col. Fredrick von Porbeck	448	
2nd Battalion DeLancy's (from New York)	160	
North and South Carolina provincials	200	
Total	**1,164**	**0**

At Charlestown—Lt. Col. Mark Prevost		
Grenadier Corps of the Florida Brigade—		
Maj. Beamsly Glazier	100	
Regiment von Wöllwarth (detachment)—		
Lt. Col. von Kettle	ca. 220	

	MEN	ARTILLERY
Light Dragoons—Capt. Thomas Tawse	42	
Light Infantry Corps—		
Capt. Sir James Baird	300	
New York Volunteers—		
Col. John Trumbull	234	
Creek Indians	70	
Cannons[44]		ca. 6
Total	ca. 966	ca. 6
British Grand Total	ca. 2,130	ca. 6

Casualties	AMERICAN	BRITISH
Killed	17	2
Wounded	>11	4
Missing	–	–
Total Casualties	>28	6
Captured	42	–
Total Losses[45]	>70	6

NINE

Stono Ferry

*"A pause ensued; and the order for
charge was renewed. Vain attempt!"*

MAJOR GENERAL AUGUSTINE PREVOST left the Charlestown neck on 13 May 1779, chased away by the numerically superior army of Major General Benjamin Lincoln. Prevost withdrew his forces by way of the coastal islands of South Carolina. The British could not retreat to Georgia the same way they had come because they had stripped that route of forage during their advance. Prevost had invaded South Carolina to restock his larder, and the coastal islands were well stocked with rice and cattle. In addition, the coastal islands were convenient locations for British warships and transports that could resupply or otherwise support Prevost's marauding column.

Prevost initially occupied James Island, just across the Ashley River from Charlestown. The British camped so close to the city that the Americans were able to keep watch of their movements from a church steeple in town. Fort Johnson on James Island guarded the southern approaches of Charlestown harbor, but it had been abandoned and its cannons spiked before the British could occupy that location.

In addition to ample supplies, the coastal islands afforded the British army relatively secure campgrounds since the inlets that separated the islands from the mainland prevented the Americans from easily attacking the British positions. Despite these advantages, General Prevost knew that it was dangerous to remain isolated on the South Carolina coast for an extended time. Using the boats captured at Ashley Ferry the previous month, Prevost planned to hop from island to island until he was safely back in Georgia—filling his commissariat's stores with Carolina rice and beef along the way.

Though the immediate goal of reprovisioning the British army had been fulfilled by the invasion of South Carolina, the expedition had failed to capture Charlestown or otherwise achieve a strategic advantage. The secretary of state for the American colonies, Lord George Germain, had based his entire Southern Strategy on the notion that the majority of southerners were Loyalists. It was thought that a small force of regulars would be sufficient to inspire southern Tories to rise up and break the shackles of Congress. The British army had made appearances at Savannah, Augusta, Beaufort, and now

Charlestown, and yet they had not met with the flocks of Loyalists they had been told to expect. The restored royal governor of Georgia, Sir James Wright, said that the British had enrolled only about four hundred men in the Loyalist militia from Georgia's thirty-six thousand white inhabitants. Even worse, Wright believed that only three hundred Loyalists would actually turn out under arms when called upon.

In early June 1779 General Prevost was moved to write Germain in London about his frustration with the Loyalists:

> I think it is my duty to mention that, notwithstanding the success which His Majesty's troops obtained over the rebels in the affair with General Ash [*sic;* at Briar Creek] . . . and that since obtained [by] the unmolested progress of His Majesty's troops to the gates of Charleston, that very few and those of little influence joined the King's standard. The laws framed by the rebellious provinces are so severe and awful in execution, with such spirit of faction and barbarity, that the most zealous amongst them to the King's cause are deterred from attempting to join the army. Our successes must depend on the exertions of the King's troops; their numbers are at present too small to create a necessary confidence in the inhabitants to raise at once and shake off the yoke under which they are oppressed.[1]

Prevost's disappointment was not limited to the Tories—he was equally frustrated with the southern Indians who were theoretically British allies. The British victory at Briar Creek had supposedly opened lines of communications with the Creeks and the Cherokees in the Georgian backcountry. However, few Indians had seen fit to answer the royal summons. The Crown had given large sums of money to the southern Indian nations in expectation of their support, but Prevost reported that the Crown was not receiving a satisfactory return on that investment. "I am sorry to inform your lordship," Prevost wrote, "that the assistance expected from the several Indian tribes . . . has proved so extremely trifling that not above one hundred have joined the army, that those were shortly reduced to about seventy who are really so very cautious that no real service can be had of them."[2]

General Prevost's message was clear: The Tories and the Indians could not be relied on, and additional regular soldiers were required to make progress in the South. The irony of Prevost's report was that the Southern Strategy was designed to decrease the demands on English regular forces, not increase them. Prevost's message echoed Lieutenant General Sir Henry Clinton's complaints to Lord Germain. For months Clinton had been petitioning the American secretary for more troops to confront George Washington in the northern theater. Now Major General Prevost was saying he needed more redcoats to bring the southern provinces into submission.

Lord Germain was seemingly oblivious to the bad news contained in Prevost's reports, and instead he preferred to see the glass as half full. He argued that the "feeble resistance" Prevost's troops encountered on their march into South Carolina was "indisputable proof of the indisposition of the inhabitants to support the rebel government." Germain was convinced that "the majority of the inhabitants" of South Carolina were Loyalists and that "the reduction of Charlestown" would soon prove this true. Germain believed that a second venture against Charlestown—with a larger army accompanied by naval support—would certainly meet with success. That was a fine plan for the future, but Major General Prevost was living in the present, and for now that meant he was running away.[3]

Prevost had moved a large portion of his troops to Johns Island by the last week of May 1779. This island was separated from the mainland and James Island by the Stono River.[4] The American army under General Lincoln had left Dorchester three days previous and now closely shadowed the British. On 24 May, Lincoln's advance guard fought a sharp skirmish with British pickets guarding a bridge that spanned a small rivulet called the Wappoo Cut. American riflemen were able to drive the British defenders away, and Lincoln's army crossed over to James Island on 25 May.

The British fortified their camp and made ready to defend against an American attack. Lincoln ordered his troops to form a line of battle, but he was hesitant to assault the British works. General Pulaski was preparing to storm one of the enemy redoubts when Lincoln ordered the army to break off the attack and retire. Pulaski was reportedly "exceedingly disappointed and angry" with Lincoln's decision to withdraw.[5] His disagreement with Lincoln became common knowledge in the army, which negatively affected the morale of the troops.

The South Carolina men were especially eager to engage the enemy in order to prevent further pillaging of their homeland. During General Prevost's invasion of South Carolina, more than three thousand tidewater slaves ran away to join the British army as camp followers in a futile effort to obtain their freedom. Even Governor Rutledge's plantation southwest of Charlestown had been pillaged and at least three hundred of the governor's slaves taken—though many were later recovered. "Thousands of the Negroes followed the British army . . . tho' every harsh treatment was offer'd to them," wrote Lieutenant Colonel Mark Prevost.[6] The British were unable to prevent the slaves from following their army because those slaves feared punishment from their former masters.

It was not the intention of the British at the time to abolish slavery. Their mission was to restore the authority of the Crown. To free the slaves would alienate and offend the Tory slave owners, and their support was critical to the British strategy to retake the South. Therefore, few—if any—of the runaways were granted their freedom; the British instead took them back to Georgia where most were resold to local Tories or, even worse, to British sugar plantations in the West Indies. "I have been credibly informed," wrote Lieutenant Colonel Prevost in June 1779, "that a most unlawful and iniquitous practice has of late prevailed in carrying off slaves from this province to the West Indies foreign markets and other places."[7] Despite their best efforts, British officials were unable to curb the illegal traffic of slaves "liberated" from Patriot plantations to the Caribbean.

Many runaway slaves fled to Otter Island, where, according to the historian Benson Lossing, many hundreds of them died of "camp fever."[8] A handful of blacks were armed to serve as scouts for the British. The presence of these black soldiers struck terror in the white plantation owners, who feared that the British might try to foment a slave insurrection—or at the very least provoke their slaves to mischief. In fact, some runaway slaves, in hopes of favorable treatment or in exchange for a portion of the booty, did tell plundering British soldiers where their former masters kept valuable possessions hidden.

The depredations that the British visited upon South Carolina sometimes included attacks on women. Lossing claims, "in a few cases females were violated by the brutal [British] soldiery."[9] This claim is substantiated by the firsthand account of Eliza Wilkinson, an ardent Patriot who lived near Stono Ferry during Prevost's invasion of South Carolina. In her letter journal of those days, Wilkinson detailed several occasions of plundering by British soldiers. There was a terrifying incident when several British dragoons raided her home and robbed everyone present, including her sister. "They demanded her ring from her finger," Wilkinson wrote; "she pleaded for it, told them it was her wedding ring, and begged they'd let her keep it; but they still demanded it, and presenting a pistol at her, swore if she did not deliver it immediately, they'd fire."[10]

Most British officers attempted to curb their soldiers' excesses, and the dragoons who terrorized Mrs. Wilkinson were supposedly later whipped for their offenses. Nevertheless, there was much plundering on the expedition. Prevost pushed hundreds of heads of stolen cattle in front of his column. In addition, cartloads of stolen goods left South Carolina with Prevost's men. The destruction caused by Prevost's army was said to have been worse than that committed by Clinton's forces in 1780—though the soldiers of both expeditions plundered wantonly; and even South Carolina's Tories were apparently not spared the English rapaciousness as they "plundered friend and foe."[11]

As the number of homes and plantations sacked by the British increased, public dissatisfaction with General Lincoln's handling of the war also increased. Lincoln's critics in Charlestown reported that he let the British lay waste to South Carolina while he tramped uselessly about in northern Georgia. Lincoln believed strongly in civilian control over the military, and the reproaches of South Carolina's politicians troubled him greatly. Adding to Lincoln's despondency was the fact that the terms of service of most of the troops would be expiring later that summer, at which time he would be left with a mere shell of an army. The term of the North Carolina militia would be up on 10 July 1779, while that of Colonel David Mason's Virginia militia would expire five days later on 15 July. North Carolina's nine-months regulars would be leaving Lincoln's army on 10 August. Lincoln warned Congress, "If no provisión has been made to keep up this army it will, in a short time, be reduced to a mere name." Lincoln told Washington bluntly: "I tremble for this state as there will be great danger of its being lost."[12]

Lincoln had earlier petitioned Congress for permission to return to the North for the ostensible reason that the southern climate exacerbated pain from injuries he suffered at Saratoga. When Lincoln finally received congressional approval to depart, the forlorn general told Governor Rutledge and Major General Moultrie of his intention to resign. He also mentioned that Congress had selected Moultrie to succeed him as commander of the Southern Department. In a letter to Moultrie, Lincoln explained his decision to leave: "It appears, from the unkind declarations daily thrown out in your Capital, that I have lost the confidence of the people; (whether justly or not must be determined in some future day) without which I can render little service to the public. I ought to retire; for whenever this happens to be the case, I think, a man should sacrifice his own feelings to his country's good, and resign the command into the hands of those who will render them more essential services."[13]

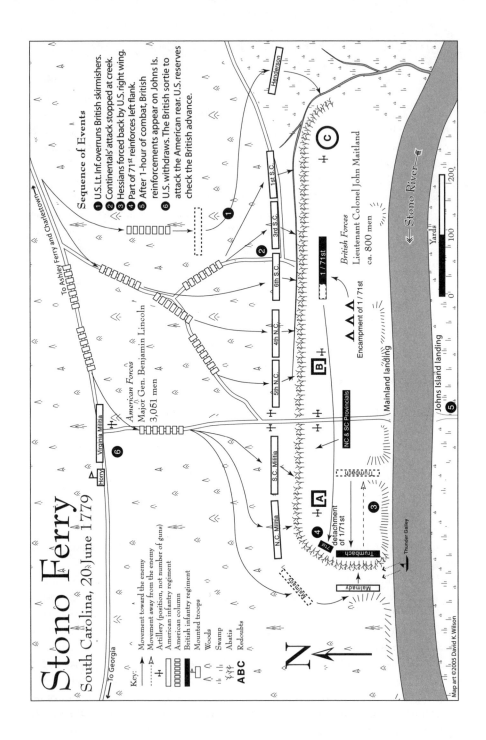

Stono Ferry
South Carolina, 20 June 1779

Map art ©2005 David K. Wilson

Sequence of Events

1. U.S. Lt. Inf. overruns British skirmishers.
2. Continentals' attack stopped at creek.
3. Hessians forced back by U.S. right wing.
4. Part of 71st reinforces left flank.
5. After 1-hour of combat, British reinforcements appear on Johns Is.
6. U.S. withdraws. The British sortie to attack the American rear. U.S. reserves check the British advance.

To Ashley Ferry and Charlestown

To Georgia

Key:
- → Movement toward the enemy
- ⇢ Movement away from the enemy
- ✝ Artillery (position, not number of guns)
- ▢ American infantry regiment
- ▢ American column
- ▬ British infantry regiment
- ▲ Mounted troops
- ⸙ Woods
- ⸯ Swamp
- ⥿ Abatis
- **ABC** Redoubts

American Forces
Major Gen. Benjamin Lincoln
3,051 men

Henderson

1st S.C.

3rd S.C.

6th S.C.

4th N.C.

5th N.C.

S.C. Militia

N.C. Militia

71st

detachment of 1/71st

Trumbach

Trumbach

Malmady

NC & SC Provincials

Encampment of 1/71st

1/71st

British Forces
Lieutenant Colonel John Maitland
ca. 800 men

Stono River

Mainland landing

Johns Island landing

Thunder Galley

Virginia Militia

Horry

N

Yards
0   100   200

Lincoln's letter is indicative of his democratic ideals. To the general's surprise, however, both Governor Rutledge and General Moultrie were unwilling to let the Saratoga veteran depart without an argument. They implored Lincoln to stay, rightly claiming that if he were suddenly to leave, it would crush the army's morale. At about the same time in early June, Lincoln received some encouraging news: The French were coming. Vice Admiral Jean-Baptist Charles Henri Hector Théodat le Comte d'Estaing (the Count of Estaing) had agreed to sail to the aid of South Carolina and Georgia with a fleet of more than twenty warships and an army of four thousand French regulars. They could be expected to arrive near the end of the summer. This news, along with the entreaties of Rutledge and Moultrie, bolstered Lincoln's spirit. He decided to stay. D'Estaing would not arrive for several months, but Lincoln needed this time to resolve the situation in South Carolina so that the French could focus on retaking Georgia.

By the end of May, Major General Prevost had moved his entire army from James Island and onto Johns Island. The primary British encampment was a fortified bridgehead on the mainland side of the Stono River at Stono Ferry, about eighteen miles from Charlestown. The position was advantageous because it allowed access to the mainland for the purposes of foraging and looting—and Prevost's army used the bridgehead for this purpose for several weeks. The disadvantage to the station was that it put a river to the backs of the troops. The British placed their fortifications on the mainland side in order to maintain easy access to the mainland and because the opposite bank was "a deep marsh" that prevented construction of any sort.[14]

The position was well manned and protected: It had three redoubts in a line parallel to the river, and the troop encampments were interspersed in between them. Several artillery pieces were distributed inside the defensive perimeter, and a line of abatis surrounded the whole works. A bridge of boats (the same boats captured at Ashley Ferry the previous month) was constructed at the ferry to allow a means of reinforcing the bridgehead in case of attack or a means of retreat across the Stono if the situation so required. On 30 May, Lincoln moved his army to within one-half mile of the bridgehead with the intention of making an assault. Pulaski conducted a reconnaissance of the position and reported to Lincoln. Believing the enemy to be too well entrenched and too numerous, Lincoln once again declined to attack, and once again the American army's morale dipped lower.

The British army in South Carolina numbered only about twenty-two hundred troops—the majority of whom (about sixteen hundred men) were encamped at the Stono Ferry bridgehead. The remainder were dispersed at various posts guarding the other river crossings to the island. By 10 June, General Augustine Prevost decided the time had come to gather his scattered army and continue his retreat toward Georgia. General Prevost went ahead to scout out the route, leaving his younger brother, Lieutenant Colonel James Mark Prevost, in command of the bridgehead at Stono.

On 16 June, General Prevost sent orders to his brother to join him with a portion of the Stono garrison. The younger Prevost complied immediately, breaking up the bridge of boats so that he could use the vessels to take half his force downriver. After Colonel Prevost's departure, command of the eight hundred men remaining at Stono Ferry fell on Lieutenant Colonel John Maitland of the 71st Regiment. Maitland was the eighth son of the Earl of Lauderdale and a former member of Parliament. Having pre-viously served in the Royal Marines, Maitland had taken command of the 1st Battal-ion of the 71st just in time to take part in Archibald Campbell's attack on Savannah in 1778.

Lieutenant Colonel Maitland was left in a precarious tactical situation by the Prevost brothers: His soldiers occupied an isolated encampment with a river at their backs and the enemy all around. The only "vessel" available to Maitland was a small, armed flat-boat capable of carrying only twenty men at a time. With the bridge of boats disman-tled, Maitland's men had no way to escape if they were pressed by a serious attack. Maitland therefore made the sensible decision to prepare to evacuate the exposed post so that when the orders to leave arrived there would be no delay in departure. He spent the next few days slowly ferrying across the river "all the sick and wounded, the negroes and Indians, with the baggage and horses belonging to the garrison."[15]

Remaining with Maitland at the bridgehead were roughly 350 men of the 1st Bat-talion of the 71st Regiment, about 200 men of the Hessian Regiment von Trümbach (formerly named von Wöllwarth),[16] and 200 to 250 Tories of the North Carolina Vol-unteers under Lieutenant Colonel John Hamilton and the 1st Battalion of the South Carolina Royalists. Both the 71st Regiment and the Hessian battalion were veterans of the 1778 attack on Savannah. The battalion of North Carolina Volunteers was formed mostly from North Carolinians who had survived the battle of Kettle Creek, but there were also present in the unit some Tories recruited from South Carolina and Georgia. In all, Maitland commanded about 800 British troops at the position.[17]

On the evening of 19 June, a spy entered the American camp from behind the enemy lines and told General Lincoln that the British were about to evacuate Stono Ferry. The spy reported that there were only six hundred men in the garrison and that the forti-fications of the post were "inconsiderable."[18] This intelligence jibed with reports from British deserters, and so Lincoln considered it accurate. Lincoln immediately held a council of war and proposed to attack the Stono bridgehead. The council agreed that an attack should be made without delay, lest Maitland complete his evacuation of the post. The fact that in less than a month all of the North Carolina and Virginia militia would be leaving probably also factored into Lincoln's decision to take action against the British at this time. Lincoln ordered Lieutenant Colonel Henderson to march his battalion of light infantry to the ferry immediately in order to secure the route to the position and screen the main army's advance. By express messenger Lincoln sent orders to General Moultrie telling him to ferry his troops over to James Island; Lincoln hoped to distract the British so that they would not reinforce the Stono bridgehead during the attack.

Lincoln's army—encamped only a few miles from Stono Ferry—eagerly prepared for the next day's action. The soldiers, especially the Continentals, felt that the army had been "mouldering [sic] away"[19] in camp too long. Desertions had become rife in many of the militia outfits. However, the prospect of action changed everything; now militia-men and regulars alike hustled to make ready for combat. Cartridges were dispensed, ammunition wagons loaded, and the artillery limbered. Lincoln issued last-minute orders to the Continentals. He told them to rely on the bayonet rather than the musket to win the day, as any hesitation in the attack would give the advantage to the entrenched defenders. Then brigades and regiments formed into columns, and all of the men fit for duty—approximately twenty-eight hundred troops out of more than three thousand present—broke camp and marched at midnight on 19 June. (Historians have universally reported in the past that Lincoln attacked with only twelve hundred men; this is incorrect, however, as the returns in Lincoln's papers indicate that his entire army was engaged. See "Author's Notes and Historiography" for more information on the size of the American army at Stono Ferry.)

⇒◆⇐

At seven o'clock in the morning on 20 June, the main body of the American army arrived near the Stono bridgehead, where they found Lieutenant Colonel Henderson's 2nd Light Infantry Battalion waiting at the designated rendezvous point. (Henderson's troops had marched ahead of the main army acting as pathfinders.) The sun had already been up about an hour when Lincoln divided his army into two wings. South Carolina native Brigadier General Isaac Huger commanded the American left, which consisted of the brigades of the North and South Carolina Continentals. General Jethro Sumner, a former North Carolina tavern keeper and a veteran of Brandywine and Germantown, commanded the Carolina militia brigades that made up the right wing of the army. Colonel David Mason's battalion of Virginia militia formed the reserve along with a small force of South Carolina light horse commanded by Lieutenant Colonel Daniel Horry. Colonel Owen Robert's 4th South Carolina Regiment of Artillery supported the whole army with eight four-pound fieldpieces.

General Huger's Continentals were certainly the most experienced American troops present, and as such they deserved the traditional "place of honor" on the American right. However, Lincoln decided to go against form on this occasion because he wanted to be sure the Continentals engaged the best British troops—the 71st Highlanders—which Lincoln correctly assumed would be positioned on the British right (the American left). Huger and many of the Continental troops under his command had been present at the American defeat at Savannah the previous December, and they were now eager to engage the British on more favorable terms.

The bridgehead at Stono Ferry sat in the middle of an empty field about half a mile wide. A few small buildings had dotted the ground near the ferry, but Maitland had destroyed these to create clear fields of fire in all directions. Two square earthwork redoubts, one about one hundred yards to the left and the other the same distance to the right of the road, straddled the road leading to the ferry. A round redoubt, flanked by a few small breastworks, anchored the right flank of the British fortifications about five hundred yards to the right of the road. Each redoubt was manned by about forty men. A line of abatis (pointed stakes and tree branches) formed a perimeter around the bridgehead in the shape of an elongated rectangle about eight hundred yards wide and one hundred yards deep. Maitland had only six light artillery pieces. Two fieldpieces were stationed to the left of the first square redoubt, while one five-and-one-half-inch howitzer and one fieldpiece were placed on the road between the two square redoubts; the other two pieces were stationed in between the second and third redoubts.

The Americans advanced in column to the designated deployment area that was located in some light woods about three-quarters of a mile from the British works.[20] Four field guns accompanied the Continental brigade, two supported Sumner's militia, and two more were kept in reserve with the Virginia militia. Two battalions of light infantry covered the army's flanks and screened the advance of the main American line. Following the model of the British army, American light battalions were elite but ad hoc formations made from detachments on temporary loan from other units. Lieutenant Colonel John Henderson's 2nd Light Infantry battalion covered the advance of the Continental brigades on the left. It consisted of light troops drawn from the South Carolina Continental and militia regiments as well as Mason's Virginia militia. The advance of the militia on the right was covered by the 1st Light Infantry battalion under Lieutenant Colonel Francis Malmady, a French national in Continental service. Malmady's battalion was composed of two light companies on loan from the North Carolina Continental regiments, the remnants of the Georgia "brigade" of Continentals (about one hundred men), and about two hundred North Carolina militia on detached duty from General John Butler's brigade.

Sumner's right wing was ordered to march to the attack first, with Malmady's troops forming the vanguard. Lincoln's plan was for the militia wing to hit the enemy's left in order to draw strength from the British right before the Continentals attacked. However, the advance of Sumner's wing was impaired by thick undergrowth in a densely wooded field. The left wing advanced more easily "as the ground over which they passed had never been cleared and was wooded only with full grown, tall, and stately pines."[21]

At about half a mile from the British works, the left wing—now well in front of the right—encountered the British pickets in the woods. A scattered firing of musketry ensued, but the pickets were quickly pushed back by Henderson's men. On hearing the gunfire, Lieutenant Colonel Maitland immediately called the British garrison to arms. Maitland was unsure what was happening in the woods, which was due in large measure to General Lincoln's decision to place his light infantry in front of his army's main body. Lincoln had been sending parties of light troops to skirmish with the garrison at Stono Ferry for the past few days. The American general now hoped that his light infantry would be considered by the British to be just another skirmishing party, and so mask the fact that he was launching a major assault.[22]

The plan worked. Maitland saw movement in the woods and ordered Captain Campbell of the 71st Regiment to take two companies of Highlanders and confront what he thought was an American probe. Had Maitland realized that Lincoln's entire army was approaching, he certainly would not have ordered anyone out of his lines. Major John Grimké, an officer in the 4th South Carolina Regiment of Artillery, was a witness to the event: "Our light troops soon drove in their picquets, who made little or no resistance; and the [light infantry] battalion commanded by Lieut. Col. Henderson on our left, in endeavoring to gain his position, fell in with two companies of the 71st regiment. . . . Lieut Col. Henderson, who was in column when he first perceived the Highlanders, formed under their fire very deliberately, and returned it. Then, ordering a charge with bayonets, drove the enemy with great precipitation into their works, leaving nearly half of their men killed or wounded on the field."[23]

Charles Stedman wrote of the skirmish: "This detachment [of Highlanders] had proceeded only a little more than a quarter of a mile when it fell in with the left wing of the provincial army already formed: An engagement immediately commenced, which was so obstinately maintained by the highlanders against so great a superiority of force, that they did not retreat until all of their officers were either killed or wounded; and of the two companies, only eleven men were able to make good their retreat."[24]

One of the wounded Highlander officers was lying with his back against a tree when a Continental soldier approached with the intention of finishing him with the bayonet. Another, more humane, American officer deflected the stroke and admonished his cruel compatriot. Lieutenant Colonel Henderson rode up at that moment and proclaimed, "That is too brave a fellow to die."[25] Henderson then ordered the very man who would have killed the Highlander to guard and keep well the prisoner on pain of his own death.

Leaving scores of dead and severely wounded Highlanders in the woods behind them,[26] the American columns now advanced to within three hundred yards of the British fortifications, where they deployed in line with their artillery. Historian Henry Lee described what happened next: "Our troops advanced with alacrity; and the enemy waited their approach until they got within sixty yards of the abatis, when a full fire from the artillery and small arms was delivered. Disobeying orders [to rely on their bayonets], our line returned the fire, which was continued on both sides for half an hour."[27]

As the Continentals approached the bridgehead, they were surprised to find that a marshy creek protected the front of the British lines on their right. This discovery stopped General Huger's troops in their tracks. The Americans were aware before the battle began that a supposedly impassable marsh protected the British far-right flank. It is likely that this creek was part of the same marsh. Huger's line companies were unwilling to advance, probably for fear of being mired in the stream while under fire. Instead, Huger's troops stood on the banks of the stream and exchanged multiple volleys with the Highlanders who were positioned in and around the small round redoubt on the right of the fortifications.

While the advance of Huger's wing stopped at the creek, the American right wing under General Sumner approached to within sixty yards of the two square redoubts. Following Lincoln's battle plan, Sumner extended his line to the right in order to envelope the left of the British bridgehead. Colonel Malmady's light infantry battalion swung around the British left until its right flank almost touched the river. Once in position, Sumner's brigade unleashed a series of furious volleys on the Carolina Loyalists who occupied the two square redoubts and the understrength Hessian Regiment von Trümbach, which guarded the extreme left of the bridgehead. It was a vicious firefight, and even the British officers admitted that the attack was "supported by the provincials with more than usual firmness."[28]

Perceiving advantage, Sumner's troops advanced to the line of the British abatis. The militiamen, despite their lack of bayonets, were not afraid to close with the Hessian grenadiers. Casualty returns of the battle show that the militia took losses equal to or exceeding those of Malmady's light infantry, who were mostly Continental troops equipped with bayonets. After braving the brutal fusillade for half an hour, the heavily outnumbered Hessians could stand no more—they broke and ran pell-mell through the camp.

The moment of decision had come: The British left flank was collapsing. Lieutenant Colonel Maitland realized that he had to rescue the situation or the Americans would roll up his entire bridgehead. Using the benefit of his interior lines, Maitland immediately shifted several companies of Highlanders from his secure right flank to reinforce his collapsing left.

This expeditious movement "stopped the progress of the Americans, and restored the fortune of the day" for the British. Then, through the "great exertions of lieutenant-colonel Maitland, and the officers in general, the Hessians were rallied and again brought into action." The combination of fire from the Highlanders, the Hessians, and the artillery (including one cannon on the flatboat in the river) drove General Sumner's troops out of the British lines. At the time of Sumner's repulse, Lincoln was with General Huger's troops on the American left and was apparently unaware that Sumner had nearly broken through the British defenses. Had he realized the advantage his right wing had gained, Lincoln might have attempted to support Sumner's attack by committing his reserves or shifting troops from his left.[29]

Meanwhile, Huger's attack had completely stalled. The British fortifications proved stronger than Lincoln had anticipated, the musketry of the Continentals was not having any effect, and the American artillery was too light to damage the British earthworks. Even before the battle had begun, Lincoln knew that victory could only come at the point of the bayonet, and he had issued orders for his troops not to fire before they had taken the enemy works. Unfortunately, the Continentals ignored their general's orders, and so Lincoln took it upon himself to remind them. Showing great courage, Lincoln rode before the line of Continentals and made a personal appeal for them to stop firing and storm the British works. It was a brave effort on the part of Lincoln, who certainly made a conspicuous target on his horse. "At length he succeeded," Henry Lee wrote, for "a pause ensued; and the order for charge was renewed. Vain attempt! the moment was passed; and instantly the firing recommenced." A few hours after the battle was over, Lincoln wrote, "I wish the troops had been so broken to service as that they could have been brought to charge the enemy with fixed bayonets."[30]

The American infantry and artillery continued a desultory fire for another half-hour, but without any appreciable impact on the Highlanders or their fortifications. During this time Huger's Continentals suffered heavy losses—ninety-eight killed and wounded —as the British sniped at them from behind their ramparts and abatis. With his infantry attack faltering, General Lincoln's only hope was to blast the British redoubts apart with his artillery to open a breach through which his Continentals could charge. However, the British artillery maintained an effective counterbattery fire against the American guns, forcing the American artillerymen to divert their attention from pounding the redoubts in order to respond to the British cannonade. The American and British cannons dueled at close range—about sixty yards—and consequently the artillery corps of both sides suffered heavily. Several times the British were driven from their guns, and all three commissioned Royal Artillery officers present were wounded, one mortally.

The American artillery corps also suffered. The commander of the 4th South Carolina Regiment of Artillery, Colonel Owen Roberts, was mortally wounded during the action. The highest-ranking American officer killed during the battle, Roberts was well known and well loved for helping inexperienced American officers learn the military arts, and his loss was mourned by all in Lincoln's small army. Dr. David Ramsay described the brave officer's last moments on the battlefield: "In the short interval between his being wounded and his dying, he was visited on the field of battle by his son Capt. Roberts, of his own regiment. The expiring father presented his sword to his son, with an exhortation to behave worthy of it, and to use it in the defence [*sic*] of liberty and country. After a short conversation he desired him to return to his proper station, adding for reason 'that there he might be useful, but to him he could be of no service.'"[31]

About fifty-six minutes into the action, a large British relief column marched into view on Johns Island. According to Lincoln's plan, the presence of General Moultrie's militia on James Island should have diverted some of the British reinforcements. However, Moultrie failed to ferry his troops to the island by the time of Lincoln's attack, and so nearly all of the British army was rushing to Maitland's aid without distraction. Moultrie has long been considered by most historians as the one responsible for losing the battle; however, the fact is that Lincoln's attack had stalled long before British reinforcements arrived. The failure of Moultrie's diversion did not therefore materially affect the outcome of the engagement.[32]

Given that the American artillery was making no impression on the British fortifications, Lincoln decided that to stay any longer was pointless. "It would have been sporting with the lives of the men to continue the attack, the enemy being under cover [of the redoubts] and our troops naked," Lincoln said.[33] "The order for retreat was not given until the causeway, which is three-fourths of a mile long, and twenty-eight feet wide . . . was completely covered . . . with British reinforcements."[34] Several American accounts of the action, including that of General Lincoln, state that the Stono Ferry garrison received a large reinforcement from Johns Island (one Patriot newspaper account reported five hundred men) during the course of the battle. However, since Lieutenant Colonel Prevost had left the post only one flatboat capable of carrying twenty men at a time, it is unlikely that the Stono Ferry garrison received a significant reinforcement during the hour-long engagement. This conclusion is confirmed by General Prevost, who stated that the Americans retreated "just as the troops were ferrying over to reinforce it [the post]."[35]

The British artillery attempted to keep up a steady fire on the retiring Americans, but they were running low on ammunition. Captain Moncrief, the chief of Prevost's engineering corps, volunteered to remedy the situation. Moncrief had been on Johns Island when the battle had started, but when he heard the sound of gunfire he rode to the ferry and crossed over to the bridgehead. As the last charges were loaded into the British cannons, Moncrief sortied from the fortifications at the head of a group of twenty soldiers. During the turmoil of the American withdrawal, Moncrief seized an American ammunition wagon and brought it back into the British lines. This action allowed the British artillery to continue their cannonade.

Captain Moncrief survived his daring escapade unscathed. This was a good thing for the British army because the talented engineer would play a critical, and successful, role in fortifying Savannah during that city's siege by the French and Americans the following October. Moncrief would then go on to supervise the successful British investment of Charlestown in 1780.

Though harassed by British cannon fire, the Americans conducted an orderly withdrawal. The dead and wounded were placed in empty wagons and removed from the field. The artillery was loaded onto limbers and brought off successfully. Lt. Colonel Maitland, however, was unwilling to allow the Americans to withdraw unmolested. With the bulk of the British army coming to his aid, the heavily outnumbered Maitland felt confident enough to mount a pursuit! Red-coated Highlanders, blue-coated Hessians, and homespun-clad Tories sallied forth from their fortifications to give chase.

Lincoln reported that his army withdrew "in an orderly and regular manner, our platoons frequently facing about and firing by word of command upon their pursuers."[36] The British became dispersed because their "zeal in pursuit had thrown them into loose order."[37] When the British troops were about four hundred yards outside their fortifications, Lincoln ordered his reserves (Colonel Mason's three hundred Virginia militia and fifty South Carolina light horse under Colonel Daniel Horry) to advance and check his pursuers. "The cavalry (Pulaski was not present) were ordered up by the American general to charge the enemy. . . . This was gallantly executed; but Maitland closed his ranks as the horse bore upon him, and giving them a full fire from his rear rank, the front, holding its ground with charged bayonets, brought this corps (brave but undisciplined) to the right about. [Colonel] Mason, with his Virginia brigade, now advanced, delivering a heavy fire. The enemy drew back; and our retreat was effected in tolerable order."[38] After having their noses bloodied by the American rear guard, the British gave up the pursuit and retired into their works. The battle had ended.

Maitland reported heavy casualties for his small command: 26 killed, 103 wounded, and 1 missing—all totaled about 16 percent of the 800-man garrison. The Americans lost 34 killed, 112 wounded, and 9 missing, or a total of about 5 percent of their nearly 3,000 men engaged. Several American officers, including General Isaac Huger, were hit by enemy fire. Also among the ranks of the wounded was a twelve-year-old Andrew Jackson, who was serving as a message rider in this, his first real stand-up battle. Jackson's older brother, Hugh, was also wounded in the battle, and he died shortly after the action. Andrew Jackson—a South Carolina native and the future seventh president of the United States—would later earn immortal fame in 1815 leading the victorious American army at the battle of New Orleans.

While Stono Ferry was a tactical success for the British, it did not change their unfavorable strategic situation. The action hastened the British departure from the area, and on 23 June 1779—three days after the battle—the post at Stono Ferry was abandoned. General Prevost continued island hopping with his army along the South Carolina coast until 12 July, when he reached the town of Beaufort on Port Royal Island. An eight-hundred-man garrison was deposited there, once again under the command of Colonel Maitland. Prevost then proceeded on to Savannah with the rest of the army.

Prevost intended to use the post at Beaufort as a foothold in South Carolina that could be used later as a launching point for a new invasion of the province.

Following the British movements, General Lincoln transferred his army to the town of Sheldon in the southwestern part of South Carolina. From there he could observe the British in Georgia, block further incursions from that state, and keep an eye on Maitland's garrison in Beaufort. When the temperature rose to oppressive levels in late July, military operations ceased and both sides took up summer quarters. Everyone was content to wait for cooler weather to renew the war.

Despite having lost the battle, General Lincoln and the other American officers took a great deal of pride in the courage of their troops. Without flinching, they had stood eye-to-eye with some of the British Empire's finest soldiers. The Americans suffered from an underdog syndrome during the whole of the Revolutionary War; as a result, any action in which their troops performed well was regarded as a victory of sorts.

Of course, the Americans had come close to actual victory when the Hessians gave way under Sumner's assault. However, Lincoln had become so caught up in the affairs of the Continental brigade on his left that he had lost touch with the progress of his army's right wing. If Lincoln had kept better track of developments on his right, he might have seen fit to commit his reserves in order to sustain Sumner's advance; had he done so, the day would almost certainly have been his. Such are the fortunes of war, though, for if Lincoln's personal intervention with the Continentals had inspired them to charge through the British defenses, his generalship would be worthy of praise instead of censure. Hence, the role of the general on a battlefield—whether to be forward inspiring the troops or back controlling the army—is one of the great dilemmas that all commanders have to face.

Major General Augustine Prevost and his brother, Lieutenant Colonel Mark Prevost, had left the Stono garrison extremely vulnerable. Before removing the bridge of boats at Stono Ferry, Mark Prevost should have evacuated the entire garrison from the mainland side of the bridgehead to Johns Island, where they would have been perfectly secure from assault. To remove the bridge, leave only one small flatboat as a ferry, and reduce the garrison by half was an open invitation for an attack that the Americans were eager to accept. Lieutenant Colonel John Maitland was the only commander on either side who could be said to have commanded skillfully. His inspiring leadership and well-timed deployments saved his command despite the numerous disadvantages heaped on him by his superiors. Maitland's performance at Stono Ferry increased his popularity not only with his own troops, but also with the army in general. Friend and foe alike admired him as a worthy and honorable soldier.

Maitland's command at Stono Ferry amounted to one-third of the British forces in the South, and they were some of the best soldiers in the British Southern Army. Had General Lincoln been able to destroy or capture the garrison at Stono, he would have crippled General Prevost's army and probably made the British position in Georgia untenable even before the French arrived in September. As it was, most of these soldiers survived to play a critical role in the upcoming siege of Savannah, and Lieutenant Colonel Maitland would soon have the opportunity to prove his courage and ingenuity again.

South Carolina, 20 June 1779

American Forces[39]

Maj. Gen. Benjamin Lincoln

	MEN	ARTILLERY
Left Wing—Brig. Gen. Isaac Huger		
2nd Batt. Light Infantry[40]—		
Lt. Col. John Henderson	ca. 115	
S.C. Continental Brigade—		
Col. Wm. Thompson		
1st S.C. Cont. Regt.—		
Col. Charles Pinckney	215	
3rd S.C. Cont. Regt.—		
Col. Wm. Thompson	402	
6th S.C. Cont. Regt.—		
Lt. Col. Wm. Henderson	164	
N.C. Continental Brigade—		
Col. James Armstrong		
4th N.C. Cont. Regt.—		
Lt. Col. James Thackston	282	
5th N.C. Cont. Regt.—		
Col. James Armstrong	315	
4th S.C. Artillery (4-lb.)—		
Col. Owen Roberts[41]	ca. 26	4
Right Wing—Gen. Jethro Sumner		
1st Batt. Light Infantry[42] Francis Malmady	358	
S.C. Militia Brigade—		
Gen. Andrew Williamson	417	
N.C. Militia Brigade—Gen. John Butler	400	
4th S.C. Artillery (detachment, 4-lb.)	ca. 12	2
Reserve		
Virginia Militia Brigade—		
Col. David Mason	283	
S.C. Light Horse—Lt. Col. Daniel Horry	ca. 50	
4th S.C. Artillery (detachment, 4-lb.)	ca. 12	2
Total	**ca. 3,051**	**8**

British Forces[43]

Lt. Col. John Maitland

	MEN	ARTILLERY
71st Regiment—Maj. Duncan McPherson	ca. 350	
1st Battalion		
2nd Battalion		

	MEN	ARTILLERY
Regiment von Trümbach		
(formerly von Wöllwarth)	ca. 200	
Provincials	ca. 200–250	
North Carolina Volunteers—		
Lt. Col. John Hamilton		
1st Batt. South Carolina Royalists		
Artillery		
Cannons (6-lb.)		2
Howitzers (5.5")		1
Cannons (3-lb.)		3
Total	**ca. 800**	6

Casualties[44]

	AMERICAN	BRITISH
Killed	34	26
Wounded	112	103
Missing	9	1
Total Casualties	**155**	**130**
Captured	–	–
Total Losses	**155**	**130**

AMERICAN CASUALTY RETURN: STONO FERRY, 20 JUNE 1779

Manuscript document in the Benjamin Lincoln Papers, Massachusetts Historical Society.

	Return of Killed							Return of Wounded							Return of Missing							
	Colonels	Lt. Colonels	Majors	Captains	Subalterns	Sgts.	Rank & File	Colonels	Lt. Colonels	Majors	Captains	Subalterns	Sgts.	Rank & File	Colonels	Lt. Colonels	Majors	Captains	Subalterns	Sgts.	Rank & File	
1st Batt. Light Infantry	=	=	=	=	=	=	5	=	=	=	=	=	=	9	=	=	=	=	=	=	=	14
2nd Batt. Light Infantry	=	=	=	=	=	=	3	=	=	=	1	2	=	8	=	=	=	=	=	=	=	14
S° Carolina Con.Brgd	=	=	=	1	=	=	5	=	=	=	1	3	1	19	=	=	=	=	=	=	7	37
N°. Carolina Con.Brgd	=	=	=	=	1	=	10	1	1	1	1	1	5	26	=	=	=	=	=	=	=	47
N°. Carolina Militia	=	=	=	=	=	=	2	=	=	=	2	1	=	17	=	=	=	=	=	=	=	22
S°. Carolina Militia	=	=	=	=	1	1	=	=	=	=	=	2	=	3	=	=	=	=	=	=	2	9
Virginia Militia	1	=	=	=	=	=	=	=	=	=	=	=	=	=	=	=	=	=	=	=	=	=
S°. Carolina Artillery	=	=	=	=	=	=	3	=	=	=	1	=	=	5	=	=	=	=	=	=	=	10
Light Horse (S°. C.)	=	=	=	=	=	=	1	=	=	=	=	1	=	=	=	=	=	=	=	=	=	2
Total	1	=	"	1	2	1	29	1	1	1	6	10	6	87	=	=	=	=	=	=	9	155

View of the bridge at Great Bridge drawn in 1848. From Benson Lossing, A Pictorial Field Book of the Revolution *(New York: Harper & Brothers, 1859).*

Major General Charles Lee. From John Grafton, The American Revolution: A Picture Sourcebook *(New York: Dover Publications, 1975).*

Colonel William Moultrie, 28 June 1776. Courtesy, National Archives and Records Administration, College Park, Md.

Sergeant William Jasper at Fort Moultrie, 28 June 1776. From author's collection. Steel engraving from G. R. Hall, Defense of Fort Moultrie *(New York: Martin, Johnson, & Co., 1858).*

Major General Sir Henry Clinton. From John Grafton, The American Revolution: A Picture Sourcebook.

Major General Benjamin Lincoln. From John Grafton, The American Revolution: A Picture Sourcebook.

Brigadier General Casimir Pulaski. From John Grafton, The American Revolution: A Picture Sourcebook.

Count Henri d'Estaing. From John Grafton, The American Revolution: A Picture Sourcebook.

Pulaski's final charge at Savannah, 1779. From John Grafton, The American Revolution: A Picture Sourcebook.

The storming of the Spring Hill redoubt, 9 October 1779. Courtesy, National Archives and Records Administration, College Park, Md.

Charlestown in 1780. From Benson Lossing, A Pictorial Field Book of the Revolution.

┿═TEN═┿

The Siege of Savannah, 1779

"Poor fellows, I envy you!"

THE SOUTHERN CAMPAIGN had become a stalemate in the late summer of 1779. General Prevost's thrusts into Georgia's backcountry and South Carolina's tidewater territories had been parried—if somewhat clumsily—by the numerically superior army of General Lincoln. Having failed to recruit more than a few hundred Tories in the backcountry, Prevost had few options for expanding his dominion outside the environs of Savannah. The small British post on Port Royal Island was isolated and posed no threat to American control of South Carolina. Likewise, General Lincoln had no effectual plan to force the British from Georgia. His numeric advantage had evaporated when the enlistment terms of many of his troops expired in July and August, and the Americans lacked sufficient artillery and naval assets to threaten the British base at Savannah effectively. To break the stalemate required outside intervention.

That intervention would come in the form of Vice Admiral Jean-Baptist Charles Henri Hector Théodat le Comte d'Estaing (henceforth d'Estaing). A well-connected member of the French aristocracy, Count d'Estaing commanded the French expeditionary forces in the American theater. Shortly after the British captured Savannah at the end of 1778, the Americans in Charlestown sent letters to d'Estaing requesting his assistance in retaking Georgia. The count's petitioners included Governor John Rutledge, General Lincoln, and Monsieur de Plombard (the French consul in Charlestown); but it is said that d'Estaing was most impressed by the entreaties of the Marquis de Brétigny, "an old musketeer of the King [Louis]" who now served as a colonel in the Continental Army. "The English had neglected to fortify Savannah," Brétigny told the count. "They were without the means of defending themselves, and had but few troops."[1]

In addition to detailing British weaknesses, Brétigny also wrote frankly of American problems in the theater: "Never has this country been in greater need of help. It is necessary to defend it against itself and against the enemy. All here is in frightful confusion; very few regular troops, no help from the north, a feeble and badly disciplined militia and the greatest friction among the leaders."[2] Even so, Brétigny told the count: "If he had no other special expedition in contemplation he could make this one *en passant,* and that it would occasion him but little delay."[3] Brétigny's description of British vulnerability convinced d'Estaing that the expedition would be worthwhile, and he accepted the assignment.

France had entered into its military alliance with the United States in spring 1778 following the American victory at Saratoga in autumn 1777. King Louis XVI saw the war as France's opportunity to pay England back for its defeat in the Seven Years' War (known as the French and Indian War in America). If Britain could be stripped of its American colonies, that would weaken France's main European rival. In addition, King Louis thought that he might be able to regain some of the colonial possessions that France had ceded to England at the end of the last war. With this in mind, Count d'Estaing had been assigned to help the Americans and at the same time watch for opportunities to seize some of England's valuable sugar islands in the Caribbean. However, this resulted in two sets of distinct objectives for d'Estaing: one to help the Americans, and the other to regain territory in the West Indies. The Americans would soon begin to wonder where the count placed them on his list of priorities.

D'Estaing's first attempt at military cooperation with the United States was at the siege of Newport, Rhode Island, in August 1778. This venture ended ignominiously for the American and French allies when d'Estaing retired from the siege prematurely, leaving the American forces isolated and without naval support. The British summarily raised the siege and chased the Americans from the island. D'Estaing insisted that he had to depart because of storm damage to his ships. The American commander at Rhode Island, Major General John Sullivan, did not regard this explanation as valid and all but accused the count of cowardice—in a *public* letter! It was the general impression among the Americans that the French had abandoned them at Newport. There were injured egos on both sides, and much damage was caused to the Franco-American alliance by this incident.

Excessive ego was perhaps the most salient aspect of d'Estaing's character. This is a trait common to generals of any era, but it still irritated the count's friends and foes alike. D'Estaing was intelligent and brave, but he was also dictatorial. He apparently made few friends in the armies and navies he commanded, and his impulsive nature annoyed many. "The ambition of Count d'Estaing is easily excited," one of his officers wrote. "Filled with the sole idea of success, he is inclined to undertake any expedition, however dangerous it may be."[4] Count d'Estaing was also known for his intelligence and wit, though the latter was not always appreciated. An artillery officer complained that his commander, "always knows how to make jokes in the least amusing circumstances."[5]

The fifty-year-old count did have the positive qualities of vigor and decision; one of his officers said that d'Estaing had the "enthusiasm and fire of a man twenty years of age." This same officer noted the count's inexhaustible energy: "The sailors believe him inhuman. Many died upbraiding him with their misery, and unwilling to pardon him; but this is a reproach incident to his austere mode of life, because he is cruel to himself. We have seen him sick and attacked with scurvy, never desiring to make use of any remedies, working day and night, sleeping only an hour after dinner, his head resting upon his hands, sometimes lying down, but without undressing. . . . There is not a man in his fleet who would believe that he has endured all the fatigue which he has undergone."[6]

The Americans in Charlestown received a letter in June 1779 from d'Estaing informing them that he would arrive at the end of the summer to help reduce Savannah. Before returning to America, d'Estaing fought several actions in the West Indies during the spring and summer of 1779, with the conquest of Grenada in July 1779 being the bright spot of his Caribbean campaign. Personally leading a charge against a heavily fortified British position, d'Estaing inspired his men shouting, *"Soldats en avant, suivez-moi! Vive le Roi!"*[7] After Grenada, d'Estaing refit his fleet and reinforced his army by embarking regiments from various French colonies in the West Indies, and then he headed for Georgia.

On 1 September 1779 the French armada of twenty-two ships of the line, nine frigates, and several dozen transports arrived off the Georgia coast. Five of the fastest frigates were immediately dispatched to Charlestown carrying d'Estaing's second in command, Major General Viscount François de Fontanges, who was to work out the operational details with the American leaders. On 4 September, Fontanges arrived in Charlestown, where he received a rapturous welcome. A council of war was called so that the French general could confer with all of the key political and military figures in the city. Native inhabitants of Georgia indicated to the viscount the best spots for disembarking the troops, and a location was agreed on for a rendezvous with the American army.

The council fixed 11 September 1779 as the date that the French and American armies would make contact before Savannah. Fontanges told the Americans that the French fleet was badly in need of food, water, and wood planking for repairs. Monsieur de Brétigny "gave his word to Count d'Estaing that the disembarked troops and the squadron should want for nothing."[8] In fulfillment of this promise, four American schooners filled with beef, rice, and lumber were sent to the French fleet. Numerous other small American galleys, both armed and unarmed, also joined the French fleet gathering at the mouth of the Savannah River.

When Fontanges returned to d'Estaing's flagship, the count was shocked to hear that Major General Lincoln only had one thousand regular troops at his immediate disposal. The Americans insisted that perhaps a few thousand militia would gather at Savannah by the appointed rendezvous date, but they would make no guarantees. In addition, Lincoln's army possessed almost no artillery—the essential article for siege warfare. The Americans were obviously in need of more than "slight assistance" in retaking Georgia.

Fully informed of the weakness of the Americans, d'Estaing contemplated abandoning the operation. Originally, d'Estaing had agreed to stay off the coast for only eight days. "That was almost like saying that I could not undertake anything there, for in a week little can be done." If it were not for the fact that many of his ships had been damaged by a severe gale on 2 September 1779, he might well have departed the American coast without firing a shot. As it was, d'Estaing now had to stay at least a month fixing his ships. "I remained at anchor for quite a long time, waiting for the delivery of wood," d'Estaing later wrote; and it seemed impossible that he could remain idle offshore, while receiving American help repairing his ships, and yet do nothing to help the Americans

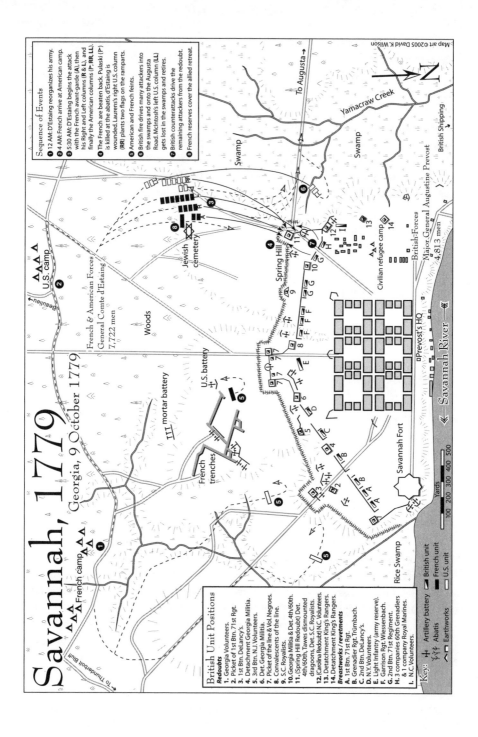

Savannah, 1779

Georgia, 9 October 1779

Map art ©2005 David K. Wilson.

Sequence of Events

1. 12 AM: D'Estaing reorganizes his army.
2. 4 AM: French arrive at American camp.
3. 5:30 AM: D'Estaing begins the attack with the French avant-garde (A), then his Right and Left columns (R & L), and finally the American columns (P, RR, LL).
4. The French are beaten back. Pulaski (P) is killed at the abatis, d'Estaing is wounded. Laurens's right U.S. column (RR) plants two flags on the ramparts. McIntosh's left U.S. column (LL) gets lost in the swamps and retires.
5. American and French feints.
6. British fire drives many attackers into the swamps and onto the Augusta Road. British counterattacks drive the remaining attackers from the redoubt.
7. French reserves cover the allied retreat.

British Unit Positions

Redoubts
1. Georgia Volunteers.
2. Picket of 1st Btn. 71st Rgt.
3. 1st Btn. DeLancy's.
4. Detachment Georgia Militia.
5. 3rd Btn. N.J. Volunteers.
6. Det. Georgia Militia.
7. Picket of the line & Vol. Negroes.
8. Convalescents of the line.
9. S.C. Royalists.
10. Georgia Militia & Det. 4th/60th.
11. (Spring Hill Redoubt) Det. 4th/60th, Tawes dismounted dragoons, Det. S.C. Royalists.
12. (Carolina Redoubt) N.C. Volunteers.
13. Detachment King's Rangers.
14. Detachment King's Rangers.

Breastworks / revetments
A. 1st Btn. 71st Rgt.
B. Grenadier Rgt. Trumbach.
C. 2nd Btn. DeLancy's.
D. N.Y. Volunteers.
E. Light Infantry (army reserve).
F. Garrison Rgt. Wiessenbach.
G. 2nd Btn. 71st Regiment.
H. 3 companies 60th Grenadiers & 1 company Royal Marines.
I. N.C. Volunteers.

Key:
- Artillery battery
- Abatis
- Earthworks
- British unit
- French unit
- U.S. unit

French camp
U.S. camp
To Thunderbolt Bluff
→Beaulieu
To Augusta →
Yamacraw Creek
Swamp
Swamp
British Shipping
French & American Forces
General Comte d'Estaing
7,722 men
Woods
Jewish cemetery
Spring Hill
III mortar battery
U.S. battery
French trenches
Rice Swamp
Savannah Fort
Civilian refugee camp
Prevost's HQ
British-Forces
Major General Augustine Prevost
4,813 men
Savannah River

Yards
100 200 300 400 500

on land. "Thus, if I had not attacked Savannah, I would have been considered a coward." Having been charged with timidity the previous year when he abandoned the siege of Newport, d'Estaing had both a personal and a political need to prove Gallic courage now: "London, America, and even Paris would have done more than dishonor me. They would have supposed that I had secret orders not to assist the Americans. It would have created an inexhaustible source of complaint, of suspicions between two nations; perhaps even a rupture of relations would have been the result. This justification was important, but the only truly decisive one was the likelihood of success."[9]

D'Estaing's expedition included the first free black regiment serving in the French Army: the Volunteers of San Domingo, who with their white officers made up one contingent of the French colonial troops from various islands in the Caribbean. D'Estaing's army also had soldiers from the "metropolitan" regiments of mainland France, such as Foix and Auxerrois, as well as hundreds of Irish expatriates serving in Count Arthur Dillon's regiment. American troops included militia and Continentals from Georgia, South Carolina, and Virginia. But there was also Pulaski's Legion, which had British and German deserters in its ranks, and officers from Poland and other Eastern European countries.

The British army was just as heterogeneous. There were troops from Scotland and England, freed blacks serving under arms for the first time in significant numbers in the Deep South, not to mention local Tory militiamen serving alongside Loyalists from North Carolina, New Jersey, and New York. As d'Estaing's ships edged closer to the Georgia coastline, the stage was now set for what was probably the most cosmopolitan military campaign ever fought in America.

⟫⟩•◆•⟨⟪

In early September 1779 the troops under Major General Augustine Prevost's command were in summer quarters, idly awaiting cooler weather to start active campaigning again. Prevost was making ready to return to England. He had some months earlier sent his resignation to his boss, Sir Henry Clinton. Prevost believed that a younger man was needed to command in the vast southern theater. Clinton approved Prevost's resignation, and he sent a replacement (Brigadier General George Garth) from New York aboard HMS *Experiment* to Savannah.

Any hope that Prevost had of quietly finishing out his term was dashed by the unexpected sighting of five French ships off Tybee Island on 4 September 1779. (These were the ones conveying Viscount de Fontanges to Charlestown.) Prevost immediately sent word to all his outposts to make ready to abandon their stations and join him in Savannah. Lieutenant Colonel John Maitland's one-thousand-man command was twenty miles away at the town of Beaufort on Port Royal Island when the French ships arrived. It was of critical importance to the safety of Savannah that Maitland's troops be recalled at once. If Maitland's troops could not be brought back, Prevost would have a hard time mounting an effective defense against a determined attack. Accordingly, General Prevost ordered Maitland to evacuate his post and repair to Savannah.

The first letter that Prevost sent to Maitland was intercepted by rebel partisans. Prevost only learned of this on 5 September, but by then a day had passed with no new sightings of French ships. Prevost now thought that the appearance of the French near his shores was perhaps, "only accidental." The frantic dispatches sent out earlier now seemed embarrassingly anxious. Prevost sent new orders to Maitland directing him to remain at Beaufort but to hold himself "in constant readiness to come away on the shortest notice." When the French fleet reappeared off Tybee Island on 6 September, Prevost's uncertainty was finally swept away. Yet another messenger dashed off to Beaufort with orders telling Maitland to repair to Savannah "without loss of time."[10]

Express riders were also sent out of the British headquarters to recall the garrison at Sunbury. Prevost tried to get word out concerning his situation by sending couriers overland to British outposts in Florida and by a sloop sent directly to Sir Henry Clinton in New York. Over the next few days d'Estaing's fleet began to gather a few miles off the coast near the lighthouse on Tybee Island. On 7 September, British observers reported seeing twenty French ships. The next day more than forty ships were visible from the lighthouse, and on 9 September, British observers counted fifty-two enemy vessels hovering menacingly off the coast.

———◈◆◈———

Major Thomas Pinckney was a member of the well-respected Pinckney family of South Carolina. He and his older brother, Colonel Charles Cotesworth Pinckney, had been educated in Europe, and both were serving with distinction in the South Carolina Continental line. Thomas learned French during his schooling in Europe, and the bright young officer had recently served as aide-de-camp to General Lincoln at Stono Ferry. Lincoln recognized Major Pinckney as the perfect man to represent his and American interests with the French. Pinckney was ordered, along with two other French-speaking American officers, to accompany the Viscount de Fontanges back to the French fleet. There he would act as translator and aide to Count d'Estaing.

Major Pinckney met d'Estaing aboard the frigate *Languedoc*. The count was eager to get operations under way. It was hurricane season, and several French ships had already been damaged by strong winds. (The hurricane season in Georgia lasts from June through November, with August, September, and October being the peak months.[11]) The waters off Georgia were known to be dangerous at that time of year. Captured British sailors warned the French captains that during hurricane season, "an English squadron had never dared to remain for eight hours even in the most beautiful weather."[12]

Major Pinckney informed d'Estaing that the best landing area was at the Beaulieu plantation in Ossabaw Sound, some twelve miles south of the Savannah River opening. D'Estaing agreed to the landing site, but he also needed to bottle up the British ships at Savannah. To this end d'Estaing decided to mount an amphibious operation to capture the fort on Tybee Island, which controlled the entrance of the river.

On the afternoon of 9 September, d'Estaing ordered the longboats brought alongside his frigate, and hundreds of troops were soon heading toward the island. D'Estaing and his staff also boarded a boat and set off toward land, accompanied by the three

American aides and a small bodyguard of twenty marines. The longboats, made heavy by the dozens of sailors aboard, moved slowly through the strong offshore currents. D'Estaing's boat, having fewer troops aboard, moved faster and subsequently landed first on Tybee. Once on land, Major Pinckney observed a strange episode that revealed the levels of disrespect and disharmony existing between d'Estaing and his senior officers: "We marched near half mile [*sic*] in the direction of the fort, when d'Estaing, looking back and seeing only his slender escort, asked the Adjutant General, where were the troops to reduce the British post? M. de Fontanges answered that he had received no directions to order any troops for the occasion. The General appeared much irritated, replying that he had informed him of the object he had in view, and that it was his duty to have brought with him the number of troops necessary for the occasion."[13]

While d'Estaing and Fontanges argued on the beach, almost seven hundred French soldiers waited impatiently in the river—no one having sent orders for them to land. The exasperated d'Estaing then found out from two black slaves passing by that the British had abandoned and burned Fort Tybee. The operation therefore turned out to be unnecessary. It was too late to turn the boats around, so the decision was made to proceed with landing the troops. By nightfall two hundred troops had come ashore on Tybee, although high winds and strong tides prevented most of the longboats from reaching the beach. The remainder of the landing force—at least five hundred men— were thus forced to spend a night trapped in the uncomfortable and crowded longboats. Rumor was rife in the ranks that d'Estaing had forgotten them, a story that reinforced the count's reputation among his men for being aloof and self-absorbed.

The next day, 10 September 1779, d'Estaing departed Tybee leaving only a small guard behind. The remainder of the troops returned to the ships. All of the transports and a few escorting frigates, carrying all the troops of the expedition, were then dispatched south to Ossabaw Sound. On 11 September a host of small craft was deployed to scout up the river. At two o'clock in the afternoon the troops were ordered into the long-boats as the army made ready to land. Many ships in the flotilla had difficulty passing the bar into the river, however, leaving about fifteen hundred men to spend another miserable night in crowded longboats offshore. It was four o'clock in the afternoon of 12 September when the landing operation finally got under way.

The original date to set to rendezvous with the Americans, 11 September 1779, had come and gone, so operations were already behind schedule. The next morning, 13 September, the French were met by a force of American cavalry led by Count Casimir Pulaski. The Polish hussar informed d'Estaing that General Lincoln's main army had been delayed crossing the Savannah River; therefore, no significant American force was ready to reinforce the French army on its beachhead.

D'Estaing has been universally criticized for not attacking Savannah as soon as he landed. Even the British later admitted that had d'Estaing marched on Savannah immediately he probably would have overrun the city without much difficulty. However, d'Estaing's situation on disembarkation was not as favorable to an attack as most seem to have believed. Bad weather hampered French landing operations considerably, leaving d'Estaing with few men ashore and no artillery. Indeed, far from being ready to march on Savannah, many French soldiers were afraid that the British might attack and drive them back into the sea. One French officer wrote: "With fifteen hundred men having only their guns, some rounds of ammunition, and three days rations, destitute of tents and baggage, exposed to a constant rain, and near enough to the enemy to apprehend an attack each instant. Fortunately the enemy was ignorant of the situation of our troops."[14]

The French continued to land troops during lulls in the bad weather on 13 and 14 September. In the meantime d'Estaing expanded the beachhead and dispatched reconnaissance forces to scout the roads to Savannah. Each soldier carried a three-day supply of water and provisions, but when those supplies ran out, the men had to look elsewhere for sustenance; thousands of hungry French soldiers were soon ravaging the countryside. Captain Jean-Rémy de Tarragon said that the better-disciplined regiments did not loot but that the reward for their restraint was that they were "left in want of everything." The less disciplined regiments, on the other hand, "pillaged indiscriminately." They slaughtered the valuable livestock of the locals while their officers, "too feeble to make any opposition," looked on with indifference. A French officer in the Agenois regiment said, "We shut our eyes to looting." While this pillaging was going on, suspected Loyalists in the area were systematically "hunted down at once and handed to the Americans."[15]

The supply situation ashore improved only briefly when the French navy fought and captured HMS *Victory* (not the same ship that would later be commanded by Nelson at Trafalgar) and HMS *Experiment*. Three transports being escorted by *Experiment* were also taken as prizes. Each ship carried substantial amounts of supplies, including much-needed foodstuffs. According to d'Estaing, capture of these ships "was manna from heaven for us"; they provided "wheat, meat was very abundant, everyone had fresh bread."[16] The capture of *Experiment* was especially fortuitous. Not only was this ship carrying Brigadier General Garth, the replacement intended for Major General Prevost, but it was also carrying thirty thousand pounds meant for paying the troops in Savannah. News of the surrender of *Experiment* was also welcome in Charlestown, as this was one of the fifty-gun frigates that blasted Fort Sullivan in June 1776.

The captured foodstuffs did not last long, however, and French supply problems were never fully remedied. Food was always in short supply and, even when available, was often spoiled. The troops ashore suffered from both hunger and dysentery, while aboard the fleet sailors complained that their meager bread rations were two years old, stale, and so worm-eaten that even cats and dogs aboard the ships refused to consume it.

Adding to the misery of the French was the steadily worsening weather. Over the next few days strong winds and rain lashed the area, and few supplies or troops could be landed during these storms. The severe weather forced the fleet to break contact with d'Estaing's ground forces and make for open seas in order to avoid being dashed against the coast by gales. The fleet suffered increasing damage to rudders and masts in the storms, and two longboats and their crews were lost. On 15 September the weather finally broke and the bulk of the army was landed. D'Estaing now ordered the army to break camp and advance on Savannah, which they reached late that afternoon.

The French vanguard advanced quite close to the town, establishing its right flank on the river at Brewton's Bluff above the old Girardeau plantation, where Lieutenant

Colonel Archibald Campbell had landed his troops in 1778. By the close of day on the 15th only two companies of grenadiers, a company of chasseurs (light infantry), and two hundred infantrymen from the Volunteers of San Domingo were in the vicinity of Savannah. The French had no artillery ashore yet, unless one counts six small swivel guns that the infantry was using for support. After sentries were posted, a new camp was established in the woods four miles southeast of the city. Most of the French soldiers had to sleep on the ground that night as few regiments had received their tents from the ships yet.

The next morning, 16 September, General Lachlan McIntosh of the Continental Army met with d'Estaing. The general from Georgia told d'Estaing that he should attack the city immediately while the British defenses were incomplete. The count rejected McIntosh's advice, arguing that General Prevost probably had twice as many troops inside the city as he presently commanded outside. In addition, the French had not yet brought their artillery ashore, nor had their frigates yet approached close enough to the city to provide fire support.

Most historians have been highly critical of d'Estaing for not attacking right away, but this is partly a result of the fact that nearly all historians have grossly underestimated the number of British soldiers at Savannah. They usually put the number at about twenty-four hundred men (including the Beaufort garrison). However, British commissary reports and General Prevost's dispatches prove conclusively that the British army in the South actually consisted of over four thousand soldiers at this time—a figure, it should be noted, that is consistent with the size of the British army in the South prior to the arrival of the French. By the end of the siege General Prevost would draft or recruit several hundred black slaves and white Tories to bring his effective total to more than forty-eight hundred men, about twenty-four hundred of whom were British and Hessian regulars. Given this revelation regarding the strength of the British garrison and the fact that a portion of the French army had not yet landed, d'Estaing's decision to forgo an immediate assault—while still debatable—is less decisively unwise than it used to seem.

While opposed to making an immediate assault, d'Estaing was not against trying to bluff the British into surrendering. To this end, the count sent the following message to Prevost: "Count d'Estaing summons his excellency, General Prevost, to surrender to the arms of his majesty the King of France. He apprises him that he will be personally responsible for all the events and misfortunes that may arise from a defense, which, by the superiority of the force which attacks him, both by sea and land, is rendered manifestly vain and of no effect."[17]

D'Estaing's letter made the usual promise of clemency if the defender capitulated immediately, and it was accompanied by the normal threat of terrible consequences if the defender forced a prolonged siege. It was nearly midday before Prevost finally responded: "I hope your Excellency will have a better opinion of me, and of British troops, than to think either will surrender on general summons, without specific terms. If you, Sir, have any [terms] to propose, that may with honour be accepted by me, you can mention them, both with regard to civil and military; and I will then give my answer."[18]

Prevost's reply was the model of eighteenth-century politeness, but it was also unconventional because it asked the French, the besiegers, to propose terms. That afternoon d'Estaing replied to Prevost, stating—quite correctly—that it was the usual custom in European warfare for the besieged to propose terms of surrender. The besieger would then either accede to or deny each term. D'Estaing also told Prevost that he was breaching protocol by continuing to improve his fortifications during their negotiations. Soon d'Estaing received a note from Prevost requesting a twenty-four-hour truce. Prevost claimed that he needed the time to confer with the civilian leaders of the city on terms for surrender. By d'Estaing's own admission, a truce would be "entirely in [Prevost's] favor," and yet he acquiesced anyway.[19]

Sometime during the late evening hours of the 16th, d'Estaing sent a letter to Prevost granting a truce that would last until seven o'clock in the evening of the next day. Unbeknownst to Count d'Estaing, four hundred men of Colonel Maitland's Beaufort garrison had rowed into Savannah at about noon that day. All of General Prevost's negotiations to that time had thus been a disingenuous effort at buying time for Colonel Maitland to reach the city—and the deception had succeeded brilliantly. The remainder of Maitland's command (another four hundred men fit for duty) would take another day to arrive—hence the reason why Prevost requested a twenty-four-hour truce. Receiving reinforcements and improving defensive works were violations of a truce, and yet Prevost did both unceasingly and unabashedly. British sentries even shot at French scouts, "not much regarding," Prevost wrote, "whether the truce was broke or not."[20]

At nine o'clock at night on 16 September, Viscount de Fontanges sent a letter to d'Estaing stating that the Americans had seen boats filled with men entering Savannah. At daybreak on the 17th Count d'Estaing and General Lincoln went to the French post on Brewton's Hill to verify the reports. From the high bluff the two allied commanders could see a string of boats filled with soldiers snaking its way upriver and into the city. "I have had the mortification," d'Estaing wrote, "of seeing the troops of the Beaufort garrison pass under my eyes."[21] The count then noted with condescension, "General Lincoln, who could and should have prevented this misfortune, saw it and fell asleep in an arm chair."[22] This was undoubtedly the most noticeable manifestation of Lincoln's sleep apnea during his career.

By the afternoon of 17 September all of Maitland's fit-for-duty men had arrived in the city. The reinforcement of Savannah was fait accompli. General Prevost sent a new message to Count d'Estaing that revealed a dramatic change in the British demeanor: "We cannot look upon our post as absolutely inexpugnable, yet that it may and ought to be defended; therefore, the evening gun to be fired this evening at an hour before sundown, shall be the signal for recommencing hostilities."[23]

Thanks to Colonel Maitland's intrepidity and General Prevost's deceitful negotiations, there would be no quick end to affairs at Savannah. D'Estaing had been thoroughly and decisively outwitted. The count later wrote that he knew that Maitland's arrival in the city had sealed the fate of the campaign and yet he chose to persist in the siege to demonstrate to the Americans his commitment to the alliance. With Maitland's crack troops now manning the lines and additional cannons being mounted hourly in the British batteries, the idea of a coup de main was dismissed. There was little for d'Estaing to do now but issue orders for the sailors to unload the artillery and for the *sapeurs* to start digging siege works.

———◆———

To crack a stronghold such as Savannah, a besieging army needed to construct a series of trenches running parallel to the enemy defensive lines (hence the term "siege parallels"). These parallels were connected by a series of saps, or small trenches, that zigzagged toward the city. The zigzags prevented the cannons of the besieged from firing directly down the trenches. By this method, perfected decades earlier by a French marshal and engineer named Sébastien de Vauban, a besieging army could construct trenches and gun batteries that would eventually extend to the very doorstep of a defender. Vauban's techniques did not guarantee victory to the besieger, but they did promise that—given sufficient time and resources—almost any line of defense could be breached.

Well-made defensive works could help to undermine or substantially delay an attacker. On 10 September, Captain James Moncrief, Prevost's chief engineer, broke ground on a series of new redoubts and gun batteries. There were only four dilapidated redoubts surrounding the city when the French first arrived off the coast. By the end of the siege Moncrief had constructed nine new reinforced redoubts and strengthened the four old ones. Between the redoubts fifteen artillery batteries were constructed; they contained seventy-six cannon-throwing balls variously weighing eighteen, nine, and six pounds. The British also possessed numerous four-pounders as well as five brass fieldpieces. Trees were felled to construct around the city a formidable abatis—a barrier of sharpened tree branches that looks like a wall of sharp stag horns—and a few feet outside the abatis Moncrief had a deep trench dug.

To help build the defenses, General Prevost pressed into service between two hundred and three hundred black slaves. Under Captain Moncrief's watchful eyes the slaves labored unceasingly for weeks until the earthworks were completed in early October. Construction never truly ceased, however, because Moncrief countered French and American movements outside the city with the construction of new redoubts and batteries. "If the Allied army would once resort to the spade," Captain Moncrief was said to have proclaimed, "he would pledge himself for the success of the defense."[24]

Prevost had recalled his outpost garrisons, and the first to arrive was Lieutenant Colonel John Cruger's Sunbury garrison (1st Battalion, DeLancy's Regiment), which came into the city on 10 September. Cruger brought in 148 of his New York Tories, but he had left behind 142 men who were too sick to make the thirty-mile march. (These invalids, under the command of Captain French, were taken prisoner a few weeks later by a handful of Americans under Colonel John White.)

Prevost learned of the French landings at Beaulieu on 11 September but declined to interfere with the debarkation: "Our numbers [are] too few and [there is] too much work to do to admit of detaching a force sufficient to obstruct them; distance thirteen miles."[25] Having too few troops to attempt to hold anything but the capital, Prevost made the defense of the town his "sole object."[26] Without the men of Colonel Maitland's command it would be a difficult task. Prevost had been without word of the Beaufort garrison for almost a week. Since it was at most a three-day journey from Savannah from Port Royal Island, Maitland was overdue. What delayed his departure is not known, but Maitland did not leave Beaufort until 13 September.

By this time the overland route off the island was blocked by American militia at Port Royal Ferry, and French warships controlled the sea lanes to Savannah. Fortunately for Maitland, he knew of a little-used third way to Georgia's capital: the intercoastal waterways. The French were blockading the mouth of the Port Royal River with two frigates, *Le Sagittaire* and *Le Fier Rodrigue,* but ships' American pilots refused to take them over the bar of the river, leaving the intercoastal route unguarded. Departing in the late afternoon of 13 September, Maitland's little fleet floated down the Beaufort River and then crossed west over the Port Royal Sound to Hilton Head Island (then sometimes called Tench's Island). A small rivulet known as Skull Creek allowed access to the Daufuskie River, which lay behind Hilton Head.

Maitland's flotilla consisted of the light frigate *Vigilant,* two row galleys, a gunboat, and three transports. The army garrison consisted mostly of the same men who had recently fought the successful rearguard action at Stono Ferry: the 1st Battalion of the 71st Regiment, a portion of the North Carolina Volunteers, and the Regiment von Trümbach (formerly named Regiment von Wöllwarth). A detachment of light infantry had also joined Maitland to bring the total number of men of his command up to about one thousand soldiers, not counting the crews of the ships. Maitland and his men were then able to navigate the Daufuskie River unhindered all the way to Tybee Island.

Not daring to alert the French fleet at the entrance of the Savannah River, Maitland stopped at Buck Island on the southwest side of Hilton Head. There *Vigilant* and the rest of the ships were parked in an out-of-the-way anchorage. All of the sick and wounded were debarked onto Buck Island, including 170 convalescents of the 71st Regiment and an unspecified number of sick Hessians. About 30 healthy Hessian artillerymen were also left at Buck Island as there was apparently not enough room for them in the boats.[27] Meanwhile, all of Maitland's able-bodied soldiers (800 men) crowded aboard a string of small rowboats and galleys and continued their odyssey. The traditional story of what happened next is as follows: "Finding the passage up the river in possession of the French, he [Maitland] was obliged to resort to some other way of getting into the town. While he was embarrassed in this difficulty, fortune threw into his hands some negro fishermen, who were well acquainted with all the creeks through the marsh, and informed him of a passage called Wall's cut, through Scull Creek, by which small boats could pass at high water."[28]

Certainly the story of Maitland's chance encounter with the black fishermen is romantic and dramatic, but the truth is that Colonel Maitland probably knew of and planned to use Wall's Cut long before he ever left Beaufort. This is substantiated by records indicating that General Prevost expected Maitland to use Wall's Cut to reach the city, and two British ships were sent to cover their approach by that route.

Maitland's men rowed their boats up Wall's Cut until the creek finally became too shallow. The men then dragged their boats overland until they reached the spot where the cut met the Savannah River. French warships were making their way up the Savannah River at this time, but they were slowed by the need to sound the river as they traveled. When Maitland's men began putting their boats in the Savannah, the French warships were still seven miles downriver.

Aided by a thick fog, Maitland's first few boats were able to enter the city of Savannah undetected just before noon on the morning of 16 September. As already noted, General Prevost had cleverly stalled Count d'Estaing while waiting for Maitland's arrival. "We have no objections to gaining a little time," Prevost wrote. "We know the troops from Beaufort are at hand and their arrival every instant looked for."[29]

Early in the afternoon of 16 September, the boats carrying the four hundred men of Maitland's first division arrived safely in the city. Maitland told Prevost on his arrival that the remainder of his command would arrive by the next day. The British general therefore sent a message to d'Estaing requesting a twenty-four-hour truce. Count D'Estaing graciously granted the request, and over the next twenty-four hours the remaining four hundred men in Maitland's convoy arrived in the city. The effect on British morale was immediate and dramatic. "The most pleasing confidence [was] expressed in every face," Prevost wrote. "The sailors [could] not be prevented from giving three cheers."[30]

Maitland's boats were immediately sent back to Daufuskie Island to transport the men left behind, but by the time the boats reached the island on 18 September, two French frigates and several American galleys had gotten above Wall's Cut, closing that route to the island. The remainder of Maitland's troops would therefore remain trapped on Daufuskie until the French retired from Georgia. Several French vessels, led by the frigate *La Truite,* had been driving upriver since 11 September, but the necessity of sounding the river to avoid becoming grounded slowed them considerably.

The French and the Americans of course blamed each other for letting Maitland through the allied noose. The Americans insisted that Viscount de Fontanges agreed at Charlestown that the French were to guard Port Royal Island; Fontanges denied this and instead claimed that the Americans had been given that responsibility. Moreover, according to d'Estaing, an American pilot assured him that once the mouth of the Savannah River was taken, there was no way the British at Port Royal could reach Savannah by water. The truth is that both sides shared accountability. Quite simply, the Americans and the French thought that there were only two routes off Port Royal Island: one by land and one by sea. That the intrepid Scottish colonel would be able to find a third way —via the little-known intercoastal passages at Skull Creek and Wall's Cut—was a circumstance his opponents did not foresee.[31]

⟫•⟪

At the same time that Maitland was entering Savannah, the main American army under General Benjamin Lincoln had also arrived before the town. To his chagrin, Lincoln discovered that d'Estaing had been negotiating with the British without first consulting him. This was a breach of protocol, considering that the Americans and the French were engaging in a joint operation on American territory. Even worse, d'Estaing had demanded that the British surrender to "the King of France," with no mention of the Continental Congress—a political faux pas indeed.

On learning of the American arrival, d'Estaing sent General Prevost the following message: "I have not been able to refuse the army of the United States uniting itself with that of the King. The junction will probably be effected this day. If I have not an answer immediately, you must confer in [the] future with General Lincoln and myself."[32] This was an odd statement: *not been able to refuse the army of the United States.* Many Americans wondered what d'Estaing could have meant by it. Why would he want to refuse the arrival of his supposed ally? The most obvious conclusion was that the count was in a rush to complete negotiations before Lincoln arrived. D'Estaing had been described as "covetous of glory,"[33] and it is likely that the egocentric French aristocrat did not wish to share the triumph of a British surrender with the Americans.

The Americans were the junior partners in this alliance, and so there was little Lincoln could do about d'Estaing's haughty manner. Lincoln's position in relation to the French was further undermined by the weakness of the ragtag army he commanded. At this time he led only a thousand regulars, a few hundred militia, and no siege train worthy of the name. American morale was—to put it mildly—not at its peak. The army of the Southern Department had suffered a string of defeats starting at Savannah in December 1778 and ending at the recent reverse at Stono Ferry in June 1779. In July the terms of service of the North Carolina Continental regiments had expired and they left for home; and by August all the out-of-state militiamen had departed as well. Lincoln was left commanding a shell of an army consisting of only the understrength South Carolina Continental regiments. The remnants of the American southern army passed the miasmic summer months encamped in the town of Sheldon opposite the British outpost at Beaufort.

During the summer the South Carolina Assembly debated legislation that was designed to enhance the numbers and effectiveness of the regulars and the militia. In an attempt to revitalize the ailing army, a proposal was submitted by John Laurens, on the advice of Congress, to raise battalions composed of slaves who would be emancipated at the end of their service. Predictably, the measure was rejected. "It was received with horror by the planters," Dr. David Ramsay wrote, "who figured to themselves terrible consequences."[34]

General Lincoln also proposed a law that would have allowed the Continentals to complete their battalions by making drafts on the militia. This measure had been adopted in other states with success, but South Carolina's legislators would have none of it. Instead, the assembly enacted a law that gave a bounty of one Negro slave and one hundred acres of land to each man who enlisted in the state's Continental regiments. Even with this inducement, South Carolina's Continental rosters were never properly filled. Dr. Ramsay bemoaned the lack of patriotic enthusiasm in his native state: "Money will not procure soldiers. The militia will not submit to a draught. . . . Most people expect the enemy here in October or November, and yet we are half asleep. . . . Our back country is much disaffected especially at the high prices of salt,[35] which is 60 dollars a bushel. . . . A spirit of money-making has eaten up our patriotism. Our morals are more depreciated than our currency."[36]

The flagging morale of the South Carolinians was revived only with news of the French expedition's arrival: "This information [of d'Estaing's arrival] put us all in high spirits. The legislature adjourned, the governor and council and military joined heartily in expediting everything that was necessary. Boats were sent to Count D'Estaing's fleet to assist in taking the cannon and stores on shore. Every one was cheerful, as if we were sure of success, and no one doubted but that we had nothing more to do than march up to Savannah and demand a surrender."[37]

General Lincoln was quick to capitalize on the newfound ardor of the Charlestonians by filling up the rosters of the Charlestown militia. "The militia were draughted," Moultrie wrote, "and a great number of volunteers joined readily to be present at the surrender and in hopes to have the pleasure of seeing the British march out and deliver up their arms."[38]

When word spread into the South Carolina piedmont of the French arrival, Brigadier General Andrew Williamson was able to gather several companies of militiamen who wanted to be in on the British surrender. Lincoln marched to Georgia with the South Carolina Continentals, arriving at Zubly's Ferry on the Savannah River on 11 September. There he discovered that the British had withdrawn, destroying all the ferryboats left behind. Lincoln had ordered that boats be sent downriver from Augusta, but they had been delayed. One small canoe was found to have escaped the British axes, and Pulaski was ordered to use it to send a troop of cavalry over the river immediately. This was accomplished by "sending one man at a time, with his accouterments, in this canoe and swimming the horse alongside."[39]

Riding through a heavy rain, this lone troop of Pulaski's Legionnaires pushed hard to reach the outskirts of Savannah the next day. Once there, they joined up with General Lachlan McIntosh, whose "brigade" of four hundred Georgia militiamen and Continentals had been operating in the vicinity for some days. On the morning of 13 September, General Pulaski and the rest of his legion arrived at McIntosh's headquarters, where he heard that the French were landing at Beaulieu. Pulaski immediately rode south to meet them. When Pulaski encountered Count d'Estaing the two generals "cordially embraced and expressed mutual happiness at the meeting."[40]

Meanwhile, Lincoln was busy getting his army across the Savannah River. Several more large canoes and boats that could carry up to thirty men each were found, and Lincoln also ordered the construction of a large flatboat. Using these vessels, Lincoln was able to transport the bulk of his fifteen-hundred-man army across by 12 September, and almost the entire army was inside Georgia by 13 September. On 14 September the army bivouacked at Ebenezer, where they were joined by Colonel Richard Parker's 1st Battalion of Virginia Continental Levies and the 1st Regiment of Virginia Light Dragoons, commanded by Major John Jameson. General George Washington had ordered these units to reinforce the southern army earlier in the year, and they had been operating in upper Georgia since mid-August.

On 15 September, Lincoln marched his troops from Zubly's Ferry to Cherokee Hill, which lay about seven miles from Savannah. By the afternoon of 16 September, Lincoln's army had marched to within three miles of the city, where they found General

McIntosh's camp at Miller's plantation. Lincoln's officers were stunned to find out that d'Estaing had unilaterally agreed to a twenty-four-hour truce with General Prevost. On hearing the news, Colonel Francis Marion is said to have shouted: "Who ever heard of anything like this before!—first allow an enemy to entrench and then fight him!"[41] Lincoln, who was disappointed after receiving a written copy of Count d'Estaing's negotiations with Prevost, wrote: "I then remonstrated to the Count against his summoning them to surrender to the arms of France only, while the Americans were acting in conjunction with him."[42] D'Estaing immediately agreed that all future negotiations would be done in both of their names. Despite his irritation, Lincoln made a point not to show any unhappiness with the French before his men. He knew that the French alliance was the key to winning independence for the United States. Good relations with France were paramount—even more important than victory in battle.

In the early morning hours of 17 September, a rumor filtered through the American camp that Colonel Maitland had eluded the French squadron guarding the river and had entered the city. Several hotheaded American officers blamed the French for the debacle, arguing that it was the clear responsibility of the French to have guarded the waterborne routes into Savannah. The French countered that the Americans neglected to inform them about the intercoastal route off Port Royal Island.

The French dismissed Lincoln's ragtag soldiers as "insurgents" who lacked energy and military disposition. While d'Estaing's officers held the Continentals in generally high regard, they were particularly scornful of the American militia, whom they derided as "badly armed, badly clothed, and I must say so badly commanded."[43] The Americans likewise regarded the French as haughty and overbearing. Thus, even before the joint venture against the British had properly begun, the two "allied" armies were clashing over politics and protocol, and trading recriminations over military failures. This was not a good way to begin a siege of a determined and united enemy.

The city of Savannah sat then, as today, on the southern bank of the Savannah River about twenty miles from the Atlantic Ocean. The city was laid out in an orderly fashion with pleasant streets and squares forming a grid pattern in a seven-hundred-yard by four-hundred-yard rectangle. The whole city rested on a sandy bluff overlooking the river at a height of about forty feet. At various times in the forty-four-year-old city's life the Americans had built fortifications around the city, but all of these works had fallen into disrepair by the time of the Revolution.

When the French ships were first sighted on the coast, Savannah's defenses were no better than when Lieutenant Colonel Archibald Campbell captured the place in December 1778. There were only four redoubts mounting a measly thirteen cannons. However, as soon as Prevost realized that Savannah was the target of the French fleet, he set Captain Moncrief about the task of fixing the shortcomings of the city's fortifications. The chief engineer immediately began improving the fortifications on the vulnerable southeastern and southwestern sides of the town. On 10 September, Moncrief broke ground on a new series of earthworks to protect the perimeter of the city; he anchored the flanks of the new defensive line against the swamps that formed natural defensive barriers on the city's western and eastern sides. Moncrief also ordered expansion and improvement of the abatis that ringed the city.

To provide the labor force that Moncrief needed, Governor Sir James Wright impressed into service hundreds of black slaves from Savannah's neighboring rice plantations. Along with rotating crews of white soldiers, these slaves worked day and night building new redoubts, gun batteries, and ramparts. Critically short of troops, General Prevost also resorted to arming several hundred black slaves, forming them into an ad hoc infantry corps. The terms that Prevost granted the slaves in exchange for their service are not known, but it is unlikely that anything short of emancipation would have induced a slave to risk his life in battle. Prevost's action could not have met with approval from the white Loyalists in Savannah. Like their Patriot counterparts, many Loyalists were slaveholders who had a vested interest in keeping the status quo with regard to the black population. In 1775 Governor Dunmore garnered almost universal contempt from the white population of Virginia—both Whigs and Tories—when he issued an emancipation proclamation and formed several hundred of Virginia's slaves into an armed battalion. That General Prevost was similarly willing to risk alienating the white population of Georgia and South Carolina shows the degree of his desperation.

Starting on 11 September, Prevost ordered the small number of armed vessels in Savannah's harbor to dismount their cannons for use in the batteries onshore. On 13 September the captains of the Royal Navy vessels agreed to make all their men and artillery available for use in defense against a landward attack. The Royal Marines in the fleet were disembarked and joined with the grenadier company of the 60th Regiment. By 16 September—when the French and American armies finally arrived before the city—Captain Moncrief had made substantial progress on his defenses. However, the British did not have sufficient numbers of troops to man the extensive defensive perimeter fully until Lieutenant Colonel Maitland and his Beaufort garrison came into town.

On 20 September several French frigates and armed American galleys took up position in the river near the city. Captain Moncrief fashioned fire rafts to discourage the approach of enemy ships. Two British vessels, *Rose* and *Savannah,* were sunk in the river's channel to block the approach of the larger enemy vessels. The French countered these moves on 21 September by preparing fire rafts of their own to send against the town. The British response was to erect a boom across the river just east of the city's harbor, which they protected with the light frigate *Germain.* These measures proved sufficient to protect the town from the threat posed by the French fire rafts, though the city was still in range of the French and American ships' guns.

After the French ships secured the river, d'Estaing was able to move his primary disembarkation point from the plantation at Beaulieu (thirteen miles from Savannah) to Thunderbolt Bluff on St. Augustine Creek, which was less than two miles from the French encampment. This move dramatically shortened the supply lines from the French beachheads and facilitated the landing of the heavy siege cannons. Though no large actions had yet been fought, there had been much skirmishing, and d'Estaing established a hospital at Thunderbolt Bluff to care for the wounded.

On 22 September the French moved their camp to within one mile of the British lines in preparation for beginning "regular approaches" or siege trenches against the city. Along their flanks the British burned buildings that the enemy might use for cover, even though many of the houses were "unfortunately [the] property of friends."[44] At nine o'clock that evening a company of picked grenadiers from the Noailles division attempted to capture a British forward outpost, but they were repulsed by a "very lively fire of artillery and musketry."[45]

At seven o'clock in the evening on 23 September, the French opened saps (trenches) about three hundred yards from the British lines. It was possible to open the siege works so close to the British lines because a thick wood and natural defilade protected the French approaches. The French trenches faced the southeastern edge of town, which was the most vulnerable part of the city because it had a large open field before it. French sappers were hampered in their efforts by a lack of proper entrenching equipment. According to Captain Tarragon, "The Americans promised tools, which they did not possess. The few they furnished, together with what we had already, could not suffice beyond the employment of 300 workmen."[46]

Despite these problems, the French made excellent progress that night extending one trench out fifty yards and another twenty-five yards. Protecting the sappers as they worked were three companies of grenadiers and chasseurs (light infantry) from the metropolitan regiments: "The grenadiers and *chasseurs* were placed in front lying down, having, further, small posts in front of them to within thirty paces of the enemy's sentinels, who happily did not patrol in the night."[47]

After the fog cleared on the morning of 24 September, General Prevost was surprised to discover that the French had opened their siege lines so close to his own. Prevost decided that a sortie was in order to reconnoiter the enemy works and possibly draw the French into the open where they would be vulnerable to the British artillery. Prevost chose Major Colin Graham of the 16th Regiment (Buckinghamshire) to lead this dangerous mission. Major Graham led a Light Infantry Corps that consisted of the light companies of the 16th, 60th, and 71st regiments. At half past eight in the morning the British batteries opened fire on the enemy trenches. The British guns ceased fire at nine o'clock. Major Graham and 97 of his troops rushed out of the British lines and attacked the nearest French trench. About 150 Highlanders of the 2nd Battalion, 71st Regiment moved up to the barracks on the southwest edge of the city in order to support Graham and cover his retreat.

The sortie came as a complete surprise to the French, who did not expect the British to react so quickly to their opening of siege works. Captain Phillipe Séguier de Terson, who commanded the grenadier company of Agenois, said that the British "ambushed us when we least expected it. They were in the rear of our trenches before we realized it, and we were caught by surprise." Monsieur Laurent François de Rouvray commanded the forward trenches, which were occupied that morning by three grenadier companies (Armagnac, Auxerrois, and Agenois) and three companies of chasseurs (Armagnac, Champagne, and Gatinois). The French troops had to leave their trenches because no firing steps had yet been made.[48]

The British infantry fired their first volley against the chasseurs, which held the French left. Confusion filled the French ranks. "M. O'Dunne, Lieut. Colonel of the entrenchment shouted 'Forward' with all his might; the other [Lieut. Colonel] had the retreat beaten." Captain Terson took his company of Agenois grenadiers and, joined by a company from the Gatinois regiment, ran to reinforce the chasseurs: "I led my company to that point immediately and counterattacked furiously, making the English fall back." The French grenadiers "fell like a foraging party" on the British, who immediately withdrew to the cover of the barracks. In their zeal the French grenadiers pursued their quarry too closely. Lieutenant Colonel Humphrey O'Dunne ran forward and told the French grenadiers to fall back. However, as soon as the British infantrymen were safe inside their fortifications, the British artillery opened fire with grapeshot, which savaged the French ranks. "M. de Rouvray . . . played into their [British] hands by ordering out the six companies; scarcely had they got up than 20 pieces of cannon loaded with cartridges beat upon them. . . . In this sortie we had 4 officers killed, 9 wounded, and 104 soldiers killed or wounded; if we had not gone out of the trenches we should not have lost a man."[49]

While some blamed Rouvray for the heavy losses, others said that Lieutenant Colonel O'Dunne was responsible: "M. O'Dunne was drunk. His natural courage and the excitement caused by the wine carried him beyond the proper limits which had been prescribed."[50]

From General Prevost's point of view, the action was a great success: "Dashing out with amazing rapidity, he [Graham] was in an instant in the enemy's nearest works which he kept possession of till two solid columns at length were very near gaining his flanks and till the whole French camp was in motion. He then ordered a retreat, which being as rapid as the advance left the heads of the enemy's columns in an instant exposed to the fire of our artillery which galled them severely and soon obliged them to retire behind their works. Our loss, one subaltern, two sergeants, and three rank and file killed, 15 r. and f. wounded."[51]

This sortie was the first substantial ground combat in America between the French and the British during the Revolutionary War. The British currently had the advantage in artillery, which took a heavy toll on the French troops who left their trenches. However, d'Estaing's soldiers were working hard to equalize this imbalance. General Lincoln described the effort to move the cannons from the new disembarkation point at Thunderbolt as "a work of difficulty";[52] this was because the guns were mounted on naval carriages whose wheels were meant for rolling on a ship's deck, not a dirt trail. Traveling carriages and trucks had to be improvised to move the artillery pieces. In order to fire through the embrasures of the batteries, the low-slung naval guns had to be raised on a barbette (platform). This made the weapons more vulnerable to British fire and also left the gunners more vulnerable because they had to stand on the platform to serve the guns, which left them exposed from the waist up. A type of firing pit was made to help protect the gunners, but the awkwardness of the arrangement slowed the rate of fire for the French artillery.[53]

Nevertheless, on the morning of 25 September the first two eighteen-pounders were placed in the battery, and at first light they began firing at the city. After a brief flurry of counterbattery fire from twenty British cannons, the two French guns were knocked from their barbette and the battery blown to pieces. During their short cannonade the French guns had little effect on the low, sandy British earthworks. The commander of the battery, Monsieur de Sané, was killed. The young officer had never been in a siege before, and he opened fire without orders. After this episode d'Estaing ordered that no guns should fire until all of their artillery was in place. To help speed the deployment of the guns, d'Estaing offered one hundred crowns to the gun crews for each eighteen-pounder they dragged up to the batteries from the supply depot at Thunderbolt. Because of this incentive, the next day six more eighteen-pounders and six twelve-pounders were deployed into the left battery—which was manned by gunners from the French navy.

The British did not allow the French to work unimpeded. On the evening of 26 September, General Prevost ordered one hundred marksmen deployed inside the abatis so that they could snipe at French workers during the night. The next day Prevost ordered Major Archibald McArthur of the 71st Highland Regiment to make another sortie. At half past midnight (the morning of 28 September) McArthur sallied forth with a detachment of Highlanders and closed to within musket range of the French lines. After "amusing" the French with several volleys of musketry, McArthur's men withdrew, taking three of their own wounded back with them. No casualties were caused by British fire; however, later that night nervous French troops mistook their own work parties for the enemy and fired into them, killing and wounding seventeen.[54]

On 28 September the French frigate La Truite (some sources call it an armed store ship) moved into the north channel close to Savannah and threw a few cannon shots into the town. Although this fire caused no real damage, the event prompted American Brigadier General Lachlan McIntosh to write to General Prevost asking that the women and children of the town be allowed to leave if they so desired. McIntosh's stake in this was his own wife and children, who were detainees in the city. Prevost declined McIntosh's entreaty in the hope that the presence of the women and children might restrain the allies from bombarding the city.

From 28 September to 1 October the two sides busied themselves with improving their siege works and building batteries and redoubts; and on this day the British finished tearing down the large barracks near the center of their lines, the rubble of which they used to build a formidable redoubt. Only occasionally did the sound of skirmishing or cannon fire disturb the labors of the work parties. On 2 October La Truite and two American galleys opened fire on the city with an even heavier bombardment; however, General Prevost said that the attack did little but furnish the British with "plenty of twelve-pound shot, of which we had none before." Consequently, the British placed two formerly useless twelve-pounders in the river battery so that they could return the allied shots—literally![55]

Prevost ordered Captain Moncrief to construct a new fifteen-gun battery to the left of the ruins of the large barracks (now a formidable redoubt) in order to counter the French batteries that were nearing completion. Moncrief finished this battery on 3 October. As the British placed each gun onto the platform, its crew began firing at the French guns opposite them. However, the British fire had little effect, and by nightfall on 3 October the French work crews completed the placement of all the guns in the siege batteries.

With his newly placed batteries, d'Estaing had arrayed an impressive amount of fire-power against Savannah. The French left battery held six eighteen-pounders and six twelve-pounders; the right battery had five eighteen-pounders and eleven twelve-pounders. The French also had a mortar battery of nine guns, each six to nine inches diameter. The Americans built a separate battery of four small four-pounders. (This little battery was actually meant to help protect the French mortar battery from attack, rather than to bombard the city.) All told, the allied batteries mounted forty-one artillery pieces of various types and caliber—far fewer than the British but of greater weight.[56] (The French and Americans had several other pieces—mostly four- and six-pound fieldpieces—but they were not mounted in a battery and are not included in the former total.) The French frigates and American galleys added another sixteen guns of twelve-pound throwing weight to bring the total number of allied guns aimed at the Georgian capital to fifty-seven. The stage was now set for a full-scale bombard-ment, the likes of which would not be seen again in Georgia until the American Civil War over eighty years later.

———◆———

At midnight on 3 October, a succession of fiery red flashes lit up the dark night out-side Savannah. A few seconds later the deep booming sound of the French mortars echoed across no-man's-land announcing to the inhabitants of Savannah that the bom-bardment had begun. Soldiers and civilians alike looked up to see the meteorlike shells arcing high overhead with cometary trails of sparks following behind them.[57] The shells hit the ground with loud thuds and then exploded a few seconds later—the French ord-nance officers had timed the bombs' fuses so that they might roll or crash through to the city's cellars before exploding, and thus cause greater casualties.

The French fired three hundred "firebombs" that night. However, not all the shells landed in the city. Many of the French rounds fell short and hit their own siege lines. General Louis Marie de Noailles, brother-in-law of Lafayette, commanded the forward trenches. For several hours the general dodged the friendly shellfire; but at two o'clock in the morning Noailles finally decided that he had had enough and ordered the mor-tar battery—manned by gun crews on loan from the fleet—to cease firing. This incident served to stir up some bad feelings between the French army and the French navy: "This bad firing was occasioned by a mistake of a ship's steward," a French army offi-cer wrote, "who had sent to the cannoneers a keg of rum instead of a keg of beer."[58] Another infantry officer—understandably annoyed at the poor performance of the mortar crews—wrote: "The artillery and part of the camp blamed Count d'Estaing for having entrusted such important batteries to the Navy."[59]

At five o'clock in the morning on 4 October, the French reopened their bombard-ment. This time they fired every gun they could bring to bear on the city, including those in their primary cannon batteries, the mortar battery, and even the little Ameri-can battery. These forty-one landward guns were then complemented by the sixteen cannons firing from naval vessels in the river. Smoke and fog hindered the allies from evaluating the results of their fusillade, but the general assumption was that the British would stand no more than a few hours of such shelling before acquiescing. "It was believed the noise would intimidate the English," Captain Tarragon wrote, "and that they were only waiting for that to surrender."[60]

The French bombardment proceeded with unremitting fury for three hours. A halt was then called in order to repair the gun platform of the left battery, which had been shaken apart by the concussion of the eighteen-pounders on its deck. Over the next four days the French fired on the city for long intervals both day and night. Mortar shells caught the city on fire nearly every day, though the fires never spread due to the efficiency of the fire brigades organized by General Prevost. "In the Americans' opinion," d'Estaing wrote, "the mortars were the alliance's ark of the covenant. They would make the walls of Jericho fall. I hoped so; but I was skeptical."[61]

The British artillery conserved its strength and returned fire only occasionally. Most of the British cannons were withdrawn from the embrasures (cannon ports) so as not to risk their crews, and there were few casualties among the soldiery. Unfortunately, the civilians suffered more. There was not sufficient cellar space to provide shelter for all the civilians. Even those in the cellars were not entirely safe as most of the spaces were not "bombproof" and were therefore still vulnerable to plunging mortar shells. Several civilians were reported killed while sheltering in their cellars. General Prevost wrote that the casualties consisted almost entirely of "helpless women and children and some few Negroes and horses."[62]

Seeking escape from the deluge of flying metal, Governor Sir James Wright joined General Prevost at his headquarters, which was safe below the bluff adjacent to the river. The French cannonade continued each day, remitting only long enough to let the gun barrels cool and allow the artillery crews some rest. Even as the shells and cannonballs continued to fly, both sides kept hard at work improving their earthworks. The French extended their trenches to their left, while the British repaired the damage done to their defenses by the French fire.

While this military activity continued, several thousand citizens of Savannah—Tories and Whigs alike—attempted to stay as safe as possible. Anthony Stokes, the royal chief justice of Georgia, was staying in a particularly dangerous part of town since his house was in a direct line of fire from the main French batteries. Stokes composed a letter to his wife that stands today as a vivid document of the siege. "The French kept up a brisk cannonade and bombardment," he wrote; "the shot frequently struck near us and the shells fell on each side of us with so much violence, that in their fall they shook the ground, and many of them burst with a great explosion." Soon enough a shell hit Stokes's quarters: "I thought I heard the cry of people in distress. We all jumped up, and before I could dress myself, my quarters were so much in flames that I could not venture further than the door. . . . As soon as the French observed the flames, they kept up a very heavy cannonade and bombardment, and pointed their fire to that object to prevent any person approaching to extinguish the flames."[63]

"The bombs set on fire two houses," Captain Tarragon wrote; "all the batteries directed [were] on this fire [and they] discharged case shot for two hours and killed in the town forty women or children of various colors, but not a soldier."[64] In the days that followed, the French mortars would occasionally throw "carcasses" (incendiary shells filled with turpentine) into the city. While only a few homes were set afire, the whole city was being ripped apart from the cannonade. "The appearance of the town afforded a melancholy prospect," Stokes wrote, "for there was hardly a house which had not been shot through, and some of them were almost destroyed."[65]

Stokes's home was destroyed by a mortar shell that also killed one of his slaves. Abandoning downtown, Stokes sought shelter in a makeshift refugee camp that had been established near Yamacraw Creek. "This place was crowded," Stokes wrote, "both inside and out with a number of whites and negroes who had fled from the town. Women and children were constantly flocking there, melting into tears and lamenting their unhappy fate." Yet these women were the lucky ones; Justice Stokes had earlier seen a woman who had been "almost shot in two by a cannon ball."[66]

Other civilians sought safety by fleeing to ships in the river and to Hutchinson's Island, which lay just north of the city in the river. "But neither the ships nor island were places of security," Chief Justice Stokes wrote, "for many shells fell into the river, and some into the shipping."[67] The Chevalier du Rumain, captain of *La Chimère* and commander of the French naval force in the Savannah River, landed with some troops on Hutchinson's Island in an attempt to compel anyone on the island to return to the city. (The French wanted the civilians to stay in the city in order to deplete British food stocks.) Rumain's men were driven off, according to Stokes, by a party of armed blacks.

General Prevost now reconsidered General McIntosh's offer of asylum for the women and children of the town. At eleven o'clock in the morning of 6 October, Prevost sent a letter to Count d'Estaing requesting permission to send the women and children out of the city on board ships, where they would remain under the protection of French warships. Prevost noted that his own "wife and children, with a few servants, shall be the first to profit by the indulgence."[68]

Despite the apparently innocent and humane nature of the application, Count d'Estaing and General Lincoln suspected duplicity. After all, in the last round of negotiations General Prevost had used the period of truce to improve his defenses and receive reinforcements. In addition, granting Prevost's request would make it easier for the British to endure a long siege, since they would no longer have to support the civilian population from their stocks of food in the city. After considering the matter for three hours, a letter was returned in the names of both Count d'Estaing and General Lincoln refusing Prevost's request. In the letter the two allied generals told Prevost that he was "personally and alone responsible for the consequences of [his] obstinacy."[69] Prevost said that he found the reply "insulting."

Some of the more daring women of Savannah were determined not to be pawns of the generals. Taking their children with them, they marched over the trenches and passed across no-man's-land to the French camp, where they demanded asylum. "It was necessary for us to take good care of them," a French officer wrote, "as they were unwilling to return."[70]

A few British deserters came into the French camp daily. They reported that the bombardment had taken a terrible toll on the civilians but that the British soldiers were relatively unscathed and in high spirits. These reports deflated the French morale: "We begin to lose confidence upon discovering that all this heavy firing will not render the assault less difficult. We should not have constructed works. In doing so we afforded the English time to strengthen theirs. We regret we did not attack on the very first day."[71]

The British earthworks—constructed of sand and with low, sloping sides—seemed impervious to French fire. "The [cannon]balls made no holes," a French officer observed, "but simply buried themselves."[72] A few months after the battle a Hessian jaeger named Captain Johann Hinrichs toured the field and made the following observations of the French artillery emplacements: "Even less can I approve of his [d'Estaing's] works. His main battery lies about four hundred paces from the enemy works. For a breach battery it is too far away, and for a demounting and ricochet battery it is too close. If he had used ricochet fire (and the ground between permits of it), he would have certainly done great damage. But at this distance a point-blank shot would go over the lines into the empty houses, or, if aimed lower, would strike into the sand and die."[73] Even d'Estaing later admitted, "The placement and construction of this [main] battery have been justifiably criticized. The primary defect of its position compromised its effectiveness."[74]

It became obvious that the bombardment was not, by itself, going to force a British capitulation within the limited period d'Estaing had envisioned. The French artillery batteries were composed of guns and crews borrowed from the warships. Two-thirds of the fleet's equipment was ashore, one French naval officer claimed; if a British fleet were suddenly to make an appearance, the French would hardly be able to fight back. The soldiers on land were suffering greatly from fatigue (but, surprisingly, not by sickness as d'Estaing noted that there were only 158 sick in the entire army). Most importantly, the sailors were suffering greatly from scurvy and a lack of fresh water and supplies. There was also the ever-present concern that to remain on the coast much longer meant risking destruction in a storm. Thus pressure to conclude operations was greater than ever.[75]

According to almost all previous histories of the siege of Savannah, at this point d'Estaing made his decision to make an assault rather than continue the siege. However, close inspection of documentary evidence shows that when d'Estaing first landed in Georgia he made a secret decision to attack on 9 October in the event that the bombardment failed to bring about British capitulation. It was now 7 October, and d'Estaing called a council of war, during which he asked his chief engineer, Antoine O'Connor, how much longer it would be before they would breach the British defenses. The engineer replied that it would take ten more days of digging to penetrate the British lines. This was too long. D'Estaing informed General Lincoln that they must either raise the siege or make an assault. "The assault was decided upon," d'Estaing wrote; "General Lincoln demanded it."[76]

Though the French continued to bombard the city and dig trenches on 7 and 8 October, this activity was merely a ruse to mask their preparations for the attack that was planned for the 9th. D'Estaing fixed the position of the assault on the large redoubt near a small rise called Spring Hill on the British right (so called because of a nearby freshwater spring). On being informed of the plans for the assault, Major Pierre Charles L'Enfant—an officer in John Laurens's elite Corps of Light Infantry who would later achieve fame as the architect of the city of Washington, D.C.—volunteered to lead a mission to clear away the abatis that formed the outer crust of the British defensive ring.

In the early morning hours of 8 October, Major L'Enfant and five American soldiers crept to the edge of the British lines armed with pitch and flaming torches. Braving a hail of British musketry, L'Enfant and his men tried to ignite the sharpened tree limbs by coating the wood with burning pitch. While they managed to kindle several parts of the abatis, the misty air and the fact that the trees were newly felled and still green conspired to put out the flames.

Later that day Count d'Estaing held a final council of war to discuss the details of the next day's assault with his officers. The meeting was contentious, which is not surprising given d'Estaing's discordant relationship with his officers. General Viscount de Noailles told d'Estaing that he and the other senior officers believed the British defenses of Spring Hill to be formidable and that he was ill-advised to assault the position. D'Estaing scoffed at Noailles's misgivings, saying, "his conclusions were those of an old man." Noailles replied: "The General would see him go under fire like a young man, but that from the observations which he had made together with officers whose experience was well known, they all regarded the [planned] attack as impracticable, and that they were astonished that the point of attack was not decided by the place where the trenches had been opened."[77]

Dismissing the objections of his officers, d'Estaing proclaimed the Spring Hill redoubt to be "the least fortified, the one where we are least perceived in advance by the enemy and the preferable one for an attack in force." Moreover, d'Estaing argued, deserters from the British camp had said that the lines on the British right were manned only by militia. Most of d'Estaing's officers argued that the attack should be made against the British left or center, where the ground was most firm and where their artillery had been softening the British defenses. D'Estaing countered that their artillery had not made much of an impression against the British fortifications and that it was therefore better to attack the enemy at a place they were least expecting it. "To take them by surprise was the main point," d'Estaing wrote. "In my eyes everything depended on that." The French commander ended the debate saying that "he owed it to his fidelity to the Americans, [and] to the honor of the King's arms . . . not to raise the siege ignominiously, without striking a vigorous blow, and that his decision was taken."[78]

The officers filed out of the council puzzled at the purpose behind it: "Being so firmly set on the attack as he himself had planned it, one fails to understand why he put the matter up for discussion. It only made particularly evident all the defects of its realization."[79]

<hr />

Captain Moncrief designed Savannah's defenses in five layers. First, the area around the city had been cleared as much as possible for several hundred yards in order to provide open fields for artillery fire in every direction. A thick ring of abatis, bordered front and back by ditches, formed the second layer of the city's defenses. About fifty yards behind the abatis was the third defensive layer, consisting of a series of redoubts flanked by artillery batteries; each redoubt had high earthwork walls surrounded by a deep ditch. A line of earthworks about fifty to one hundred yards behind the redoubts formed the fourth defensive layer, where the majority of the garrison was positioned.[80] Fifth, a tactical reserve (Major Graham's Light Infantry Corps and a handful of dragoons) was kept near the center of the defensive lines ready to reinforce a threatened sector or to help close a breach in the lines. Captain Moncrief had designed each layer of defense to slow, encumber, and/or disorganize attackers, making them vulnerable to fire or counterattack from the next layer of defense. Events would soon prove that Moncrief was, as Henry Clinton later put it, "an engineer who understood his business."[81]

General Prevost manned the redoubts mostly with militia and provincial troops, supplemented here and there by a handful of regulars. Prevost believed that the militia and provincials—less experienced soldiers than the regulars—would fight better from within the all-round fortifications. Prevost wanted the militia and provincials to take the starch out of any attacking force, making them vulnerable to counterattack by his regulars that were stationed in the earthworks behind the redoubts.

The British defenses were formidable but not impregnable. At the conclusion of the council of war held in the French camp on 8 October, d'Estaing passed out written orders of attack to his officers. The plan was supposedly developed with General Lincoln's input, though d'Estaing said that Lincoln possessed "no opinions of his own." D'Estaing did not hold his American counterpart in high esteem, but he did concede that Lincoln had courage: "General Lincoln is brave. He amused himself reconnoitering the Augusta road, to prove to me that he was not afraid of cannon fire."[82]

The plan for the attack called for the French to divide into four divisions: an avant-garde to the army, a right column, a left column, and a reserve. The avant-garde was a battalion-sized unit of elite grenadier and light infantry companies drawn from all the regiments of the army. These men were to attempt to take the redoubt by scaling the ramparts; failing that, they were to go around the redoubt's right side and attempt to enter it through the opening or gate at its rear.

The right column was commanded by Count Arthur Dillon, an Irish expatriate in the service of France's Catholic monarchy. Like the army's avant-garde, Dillon's column was composed of elite grenadier and light infantry companies drawn from the army's best regiments. This column was assigned to "support the vanguard" and attack the redoubt by moving around its left side.

Baron de Steding commanded the left column, which was made up of the line or "fusilier" companies of the army.[83] Steding's men were to march past the Augusta road and proceed more to the left of the avant-garde and Dillon's men. "As soon as this column has passed the place where we believe the abatis ends . . . it will march abruptly to the right to break through the entrenchment if there is one." Therefore, this column was not meant to attack the Spring Hill redoubt at all; instead it was to pass on the left side of the redoubt, penetrating the batteries and fortifications there. If successful, all the French attack columns were to proceed toward the barracks in the center of town, sweeping the opposition before them. The army reserve under Noailles, with a few fieldpieces, was to hold up at a Jewish cemetery near the edge of the woods outside town. This location would also serve as a rallying point for the army if they met with defeat.

General Lincoln also issued written orders to his officers. He divided his army into two columns, a right one and a left one, each with roughly half as many men as the

French columns. It is important to note that the plan of attack did *not* call for the American troops to attack the Spring Hill redoubt. Instead, Lincoln's forces were to conduct their operations to the left of the French army, who held the "position of honor" on the right. Lincoln instructed his men to "endeavor to penetrate the enemy's lines *between the battery on the left of the Spring-hill redoubt and the next [redoubt] toward the river* [emphasis added]." Lincoln admonished his men to "move to the left of the French troops, taking care not to interfere with them." To underscore this point, d'Estaing's orders of attack to the French troops said that the Americans "shall enter the town by the houses. . . . This column will take in the rear the batteries which are on its left, the nearest to the swamp or the river."

Count Pulaski's cavalry brigade (composed of his own American Legion, the South Carolina Light Dragoons, and the 1st Regiment of Virginia Light Dragoons) was to precede the American columns as a vanguard. Colonel John Laurens commanded the right or assault column, which consisted of the American light infantry and other picked units. These men were "to enter the redoubt on the left of the Spring-hill, by escalade if possible; if not by entrance to it." The American militia was placed under General Isaac Huger's command. Huger was responsible for prosecuting a feint attack on the British left, while French auxiliaries were to carry out another feint against the British center. Yet another feint was to be mounted by French marines in boats on the river.

At midnight a massive French artillery discharge marked the beginning of the operation. D'Estaing intended the noise of the batteries to mask the sound of the French and American armies assembling. The French troops formed into columns, leaving behind a camp guard and their sick troops to keep the campfires burning in order to deceive the British. The French immediately fell behind in their schedule as the officers and soldiers began to bicker over the dispositions of the troops.

The Volunteers of San Domingo, free black militia troops with white officers from what is presently Haiti, were responsible for prosecuting the feint in the center. This was the first time that free black troops were to participate in a battle with the French army. However, this militia unit had been formed only about six months earlier by d'Estaing and was therefore inexperienced. D'Estaing wanted to bolster the militia with some grenadiers from the regular metropolitan regiments in order to make the feint in the center more vigorous and disciplined, and therefore more convincing. "We saw with some concern," Captain Tarragon wrote, "militia officers of St. [*sic*] Domingo bearers of orders from Count d'Estaing to take volunteers from our companies, even from the *chasseurs*. The soldiers, prejudiced against the militia uniform, refused to go willingly."[84] It is worth noting that according to Captain Tarragon the regulars were prejudiced against the militia *uniform*, not the men themselves. In other words, Tarragon characterizes this incident as one of regulars versus militia and not white versus black. D'Estaing ended the controversy by personally intervening and ordering the metropolitan grenadiers in question to join the militia companies temporarily.

The argument between the militia officers and the regulars was only the beginning of French troubles that night. Even more disruptive was d'Estaing's order to reorganize his army only hours before the battle. Instead of having the French troops march as part of their familiar regiments, he ordered a restructuring of the entire army into a series of grenadier, light, and line battalions. This was done by stripping from each regiment its grenadier company in order to form ad hoc grenadier battalions; the same was done with the chasseur (light infantry) and the fusilier or line companies, which were respectively formed into ad hoc light or line battalions.

While it was normal for eighteenth-century armies to form light infantry and grenadier battalions in this manner, it was unusual for this to be done on such a large scale and at such a late hour before battle. Without any warning the French soldiers were placed under officers whom they did not know and grouped with men with whom they had not trained:

> In accordance with instructions given by M. D'Estaing, arrangements were made during the night by M. de Fontanges, Major General of the army and Colonel of the Volunteers of the Cape. He has generally been blamed for having, at two o'clock in the morning, and at the moment of marching, divided and subdivided the companies of Grenadiers, placing over them officers, strangers to the corps, and with whom they had no personal acquaintance. Major [Thomas] Brown of Dillon's regiment, in representing the consequences, condemned the general order of attack. His advice was not taken. The result proved that he was correct, but he himself lost his life on the occasion.[85]

D'Estaing wanted his best troops—the grenadiers and light infantry companies—grouped together so that their natural élan could be concentrated. However, the way he went about it only succeeded in scrambling and confusing the troops just hours before they were to go into combat. Indeed, d'Estaing should have ordered the formation of these elite assault battalions days or weeks earlier.

Due to the reorganization, it took the French army three hours to muster, and the men were not ready to march until three o'clock in the morning. Meanwhile, the U.S. troops were waiting impatiently for their French allies, who were supposed to rendezvous with them at the American camp no later than two hours after midnight. The American muster, in contrast to the querulous French gathering, had few problems. The army formed by platoons and was in parade formation by one o'clock in the morning. As planned, General Lincoln divided the American assault force into two columns: The right column was led by Lieutenant Colonel John Laurens and his elite Corps of Light Infantry; the left column was commanded by General Lachlan McIntosh. While Lincoln did reorganize his brigades for the attack, he mostly left the regiments—the standard unit of maneuver—intact. While the French light infantry and grenadier battalions had been formed only hours earlier, the men of Laurens's Corps of Light Infantry had been training together for weeks. Lincoln supplemented Laurens's corps with the grenadier company of the Regiment of Charlestown Militia.

Following behind these men was Colonel Francis Marion's veteran 2nd South Carolina Regiment, which had attached to it Colonel Richard Parker's battalion of Virginia Continental Levies. Forming the rear of the first column were the battalion companies of the Regiment of Charlestown Militia. The 1st, 5th, and 6th South Carolina Continental regiments comprised the left American column commanded by General McIntosh.

The French army did not arrive at the American camp until nearly four o'clock in the morning—far behind schedule and about the time the assault was supposed to have been under way. The count later tried to shift the blame for his tardiness on General Lincoln, saying that he had to send someone to find the American commander. Yet, even d'Estaing had to admit: "I should have arrived at Colonel Laurens's camp much earlier."[86]

Once both allied armies were joined—nearly five thousand men including the French reserve column—they marched at an "easy . . . and leisurely" gait toward their assembly areas.[87] The charismatic Count Pulaski led the American contingent out of camp. His cavalry brigade consisted of his own American Legion, the 1st Regiment of Virginia Light Dragoons under Major John Jameson, and Lieutenant Colonel Daniel Horry's South Carolina Light Dragoons. Flying from a lance at the head of his column was the battle flag presented to him by the Moravian Sisters of Bethlehem, Pennsylvania.[88]

American officers were assigned as guides to the French columns, but according to French accounts they were not helpful. Captain Tarragon claimed that the American officer assigned to conduct the French right column "did not know the road, and at the first musket shot he disappeared." The American assigned to guide the French left column was apparently just as useless. "This officer assured us that he had built the defenses of Savannah and was well acquainted with all its environs." However, on arriving near the British lines, the American guide told his French colleagues that "he knew nothing beyond his own command, that he was unacquainted with the surroundings of the city, that the works had been altered since the enemy had taken possession of them, and that he would act as guide no longer."[89]

Despite these difficulties, after an hour's march the allied army arrived at the assembly area near the British right flank. The troops were concealed from enemy view by the darkness and some thin woods. "The whole army then marched towards the skirt of the wood in one long column, and as they approached the open space were to break off into the different columns, as ordered, for the attack."[90]

At five o'clock General Noailles, commanding the French reserve column, took up position on a slight rise about four hundred yards beyond the British fortifications, just to the left of the Jewish cemetery that had been designated as the rallying point for the allied army in case of a severe repulse. From this position Noailles could observe the entire battlefield. The rest of the army took up position in some woods just in front of Noailles's reserves, where they began assembling into platoons for the attack. The heads of the columns then advanced close to the edge of the woods to take up position at what would today be called the start line for the attack. From the edge of the woods to the British lines was an open no-man's-land about three hundred yards wide.

According to d'Estaing's orders, the attack should "begin *at the latest* [emphasis added] at 4 o'clock in the morning."[91] Yet, an hour and one-half after that deadline only the French avant-garde battalion had taken its place in the line. Curiously, the feint attacks that were to have started at four o'clock had not yet begun either. Perhaps it was just as well because Count Dillon's column had not finished forming to the vanguard's left and Steding's column was still snaking its way through the twisting trails to its designated position. The Americans, marching behind the French, were of course even further out of place.

At this point "the stillness of the pre-dawn was broken by the eerie skirl of bagpipes." The sound had often been heard wafting from the camps of the Scottish 71st Regiment during the siege. D'Estaing described the bagpipes as "the saddest and most remarkable of instruments"; he also believed that their sound was an indication that the enemy knew they were coming. "Certainly when I heard the unexpected sound of these peripatetic bagpipes, I would have decided to call off the attack," d'Estaing claimed. However, he decided he could not, lest his indecision "furnish ample material for a joke."[92]

The plan called for the attack to begin in darkness so that the British musketry and artillery would be reduced in effectiveness; but as the light of predawn began to break on the eastern horizon, this advantage was evaporating like the morning mist. "Day begins to dawn and we grow impatient," a French officer in Steding's left column wrote.[93] Count d'Estaing shared the anxiety of his army. Not all of his troops were in position, but if he waited much longer, the daylight would reveal his position to the British.

Events then overtook d'Estaing as the American and French militiamen finally began their feint attacks: "At half past five o'clock we hear on our right and on the enemy's left a very lively fire of musketry and of cannon upon our troops from the trenches who had commenced the false attack. A few minutes afterwards we are discovered by the enemy's sentinels who fire a few shots."[94]

The French army had been discovered by the British, and d'Estaing knew it was now or never. If they waited to attack, the British could shift reinforcements to counter the assault. Placing himself at the head of the vanguard, d'Estaing turned to the troops and commanded them to "advance at the double quick, to shout 'Vive le Roi' and to beat the charge."[95] "Without waiting until the other columns had arrived at their position," wrote Major Thomas Pinckney, d'Estaing "placed himself at the head of the first column and rushed forward to the attack."[96]

Not including the French reserve, there were about four thousand men in the formations assigned to attack. The plan called for all the French and American columns to charge simultaneously. What actually happened was a confused piecemeal attack in which one relatively small battalion after another attacked individually. The French vanguard, ostensibly led by Colonel Jules Béthisy but in fact now commanded by Count d'Estaing, left the tree line by itself at half past five o'clock. The right column under General Dillon soon followed, but there was a substantial gap between it and the charging vanguard. The French left column took even longer to begin moving, while the two American columns had not even deployed when d'Estaing began his charge. Because of the piecemeal nature of the allied assault, the British could concentrate all of their fire on individual attacking formations as they emerged from the wood line.

The French avant-garde battalion consisted of three companies of grenadier volunteers picked from all the regiments of the army. These men were supported by four additional companies: two companies of grenadiers from the regiments Armagnac and Agenois, and two companies of chasseurs from Armagnac and Gatinois, for a total of 435 men. There were two British gun batteries on either side of the Spring Hill redoubt, each with five or six cannons. These batteries immediately began firing grapeshot at the onrushing French. Though the vanguard suffered galling casualties, the French soldiers did not slow down until they encountered the jagged tree limbs of the abatis. As the soldiers hacked their way through the tangled barrier with hand axes, they came under intense musket fire from the British infantry manning the Spring Hill redoubt, which was only fifty yards away.

In negotiating the abatis Count d'Estaing was slightly wounded in the arm by a musket ball (he would later receive a more serious injury to his leg). Despite the pain, d'Estaing stayed at the front urging his troops forward. The French made easy targets as they were under orders not to shoot back until they had taken the Spring Hill redoubt; the punishment for violating this order was death. Both d'Estaing and Lincoln agreed on this harsh penalty because they believed that only by the bayonet alone could they force the enemy from their fortified positions. (Lincoln had fresh memories of Stono Ferry, where his Continentals became bogged down exchanging musketry with the entrenched British instead of charging as ordered.)

The Spring Hill redoubt was garrisoned by 110 British troops. Contrary to American and French reports after the battle, the soldiers inside the redoubt were not the "elite" of the army but rather were, more or less, average soldiers. There was a contingent of 54 men of the South Carolina Royalists, 28 dismounted troopers of Captain Thomas Tawse's light dragoons (former infantrymen drafted from the 71st Regiment), and 28 "battalion men" of the 4th Battalion of the 60th Regiment.[97] "By special order" all the troops in the Spring Hill redoubt were commanded by Captain Tawse. Lieutenant Colonel Friedrich von Porbeck of the Hessian Wissenbach regiment was also present, being field officer of the day in charge of the entire British right wing.[98] It should also be noted that the fighting for the Spring Hill redoubt also included attacks on the fortified gun emplacements on each flank of the redoubt.

The ground sloped upward toward the British fortifications, forming a glacis that made the redoubts even more formidable. As the three companies of volunteer grenadiers approached, the British "fired a volley which stretched them flat on the ground." The four companies of grenadiers and chasseurs following the volunteers "found themselves exposed" as their compatriots hit the dirt. The grenadiers and chasseurs hesitated, then charged over the glacis, ran up the ramparts, and "penetrated the redoubt." The fighting now became hand-to-hand as the French, with their bayonets only, attempted to force from the position the British, who fought back with both bayonets and point-blank musketry. Colonel Jules Béthisy, who commanded the vanguard, received three gunshot wounds as he made his way into the redoubt. Unsupported, the vanguard fell back only to be "mown down by the right battery which took them in the flank." Despite appalling casualties, the grenadiers regrouped and in a few moments were again flinging themselves at the ramparts. D'Estaing was later critical of his advance troops' failure to turn to the redoubt's flank when their attempts to scale the walls proved futile.[99]

French courage was soon evidenced by the hundreds of killed and wounded on the field. At the foot of the redoubt dozens of bodies filled the ditch. When a French regular fell, ghastly red bloodstains exploded onto his clean white uniform. Amidst this gruesome scene the French right column under Count Dillon finally arrived to support d'Estaing's foundering attack. Dillon's troops had also braved murderous grapeshot as they crossed no-man's-land, and they too had sustained grievous losses as they negotiated the abatis. Many historians have incorrectly said that Dillon's column was misdirected and became bogged down in the swamps on the French left flank, contributing nothing to the battle. This is a grievous historical error as exactly the opposite really happened. According to Captain Tarragon and Major Thomas Pinckney (both of whom were participants in the battle), Dillon's column assaulted the redoubt and fought the hardest of all the French units.

Count Dillon's right column consisted of two ad hoc battalions: one of select grenadier companies, the other of grenadier and chasseur companies. A company of sixty picked volunteers served as an avant-garde to the column, led by Major Thomas Brown of Dillon's Irish Regiment. Brown and his men now penetrated the redoubt, and once again French grenadiers and chasseurs were engaged in a furious melee with the British defenders on Spring Hill. The expatriates of Dillon's Irish Regiment—wearing the bright red coats given to Irish soldiers in French service—particularly distinguished themselves at this time.[100] Major Brown was shot down on the parapet; he had the unfortunate distinction of being the highest-ranking French officer killed that day. Having earlier decried d'Estaing's battle plan, Brown nevertheless gave his life attempting to execute it.

The French left column commanded by Baron de Steding now entered the action. The left column was preceded, as was the right column, by an avant-garde of picked volunteer infantrymen. An officer in that column described its advance: "The column of M. de Steding, which moved to the left, while traversing a muddy swamp full of brambles, loses its formation and no longer preserves any order. . . . The firing is very lively; and, although this column is here most severely injured, it crosses the road to Augusta that it may advance to the enemy's right which it is ordered to attack. On this spot nearly all of the Volunteers are killed. The Baron de Steding is here wounded."[101]

Captain Tarragon, who was in the French right column, said that the left column "threw itself upon the right column and got mixed with it." However, according to a French officer in the left column, the right column had drifted left because of the British fire, thus falling into the left column. Major Thomas Pinckney of the American army said that as the French columns charged they were each "severely galled" by grapeshot and musketry. As a result, large numbers of French soldiers from both columns "got into confusion and broke away to their left toward the wood in that direction." The majority of French troops never actually made it to the redoubt; instead, they were forced by the intensity of the British fire into the wooded swamp to their left. The retrograde movement had the effect of dissolving all unit integrity. "Utter confusion" reigned, a French officer wrote; "at this moment everything is in such disorder that the formations are no longer preserved." Yet another French soldier said, "Most soldiers, not acquainted with their new chief officers, did not obey their orders. Whole companies stood still, under the briskest firing, on the spot they occupied."[102]

The road leading from Augusta into Savannah ran northwest from the Spring Hill redoubt. French soldiers began gathering in clumps on the roadway because it was elevated above the swamps and therefore consisted of solid ground. Those who stepped into the swamps were literally bogged down—a position no one wanted to be in while exposed to the British grapeshot. One French officer described the scene:

The road to Augusta is choked up [with French troops]. . . . We are crowded together and badly pressed. Two [British] eighteen pounder guns, upon field carriages, charged with canister and placed at the head of the road, cause terrible slaughter. The musketry fire from the entrenchments is concentrated upon this spot and upon the swamps. Two English galleys and one frigate [the armed brig *Germaine*] sweep this point with their broadsides, and the redoubts and batteries use only grapeshot which they shower down upon this locality.

Not withstanding all this, our officers endeavor to form into columns this mass, which does not retreat, and the soldiers themselves strive to regain their ranks. Scarcely have the commenced to do this, when the General orders the charge to be beaten. Three times do our troops advance en masse up to the entrenchments which cannot be carried. An attempt is made to penetrate through the swamp on our left to gain the enemy's right. More than half of those who enter are either killed or remain stuck fast in the mud.[103]

"The marsh attracted them," d'Estaing wrote; "they soon ended up by plunging into it. . . . The order was broken, the different corps intermingled; they were rallied rather than regrouped." The chaos on the battlefield was infectious. As each body of fresh French troops arrived on the field they were quickly thrown into confusion by the swirl of battle. D'Estaing, still nursing his wounded arm, "encouraged the soldiers to commence another attack." At the same time Major General Viscount François de Fontanges, who was second in command of the French army and also wounded, "cried out that they must retreat."[104]

At this point the Americans made their presence felt on the field. Count Casimir Pulaski's cavalry brigade rode forward attempting to pierce the British abatis. Major Rogowski, an officer in Pulaski's Legion, left what is probably a romanticized version of the cavalry action, but it serves to show what it must have been like to ride with Pulaski on his final charge:

For half an hour the guns roared and blood flowed abundantly. Seeing an opening between the enemy's works Pulaski resolved, with his Legion and a small detachment of Georgia cavalry, to charge through, enter the city, confuse the enemy, and cheer the inhabitants with good tidings. General Lincoln approved the daring plan. Imploring the help of the Almighty, Pulaski shouted to his men "Forward," and we, two hundred strong, rode at full speed after him, the earth resounding under our hoofs of our chargers.

For the first two minutes all went well. We sped like Knights into the peril. Just, however, as we passed the gap between the two batteries, a cross fire, like a pouring shower, confused our ranks. I looked around. Oh! sad moment, ever to be remembered! Pulaski lies prostrate on the ground. I leaped towards him, thinking possibly his wound was not dangerous, but a canister shot had pierced his thigh, and the blood was also flowing from his breast, probably from a second wound. Falling on my knees I tried to raise him. He said in a faint voice, "Jesus! Maria! Joseph!" Further, I knew not, for at that moment a musket ball grazing my scalp blinded me with blood, and I fell to the ground in a state of insensibility.[105]

Count Pulaski fell, according to Major Thomas Pinckney, near the abatis. Command of the cavalry then devolved to Lieutenant Colonel Daniel Horry of the South Carolina Light Dragoons. Horry rode over to the prostrate count as he was about to be removed from the field and asked for the general's orders. "Follow my Lancers," Pulaski replied, "to whom I have given my order of attack."[106] Horry attempted to comply, "But the Lancers were so severely galled by the enemy's fire, that they also inclined off to the left and were followed by all the cavalry, breaking through the American column who were attacking the Spring Hill redoubt."[107]

At about the same time that Count Pulaski was making his ill-fated charge, the first American infantry column had entered the fray led by the indomitable native South Carolinian Lieutenant Colonel John Laurens. The son of Henry Laurens, the former president of the Continental Congress, John Laurens had distinguished himself as an aide-de-camp to George Washington in the northern campaigns. He was known as a brave man of action, but he also had a reputation for impulsiveness. In 1778 Laurens wounded General Charles Lee in a duel when the latter cast aspersions on his mentor Washington. Alexander Garden, an early nineteenth-century historian of the Revolution, wrote of John Laurens: "His gallantry, in action, was highly characteristic of his love of fame. The post of danger was his favourite station. Some, indeed, may style his display of intrepidity, at every risk, the height of rashness.—Strictly speaking, it was so. But, at the commencement of the war, when the British Officers were persuaded, or affected to believe, that every American was a coward, such total disregard of personal safety, on the part of Laurens, such display of chivalric intrepidity, that equally excited their surprise and admiration, was, essentially, beneficial to our cause."[108]

Some American officers considered Laurens a widow maker and, according to Garden, refused to serve under him. William Moultrie claimed that Laurens had disobeyed his orders the previous May during General Prevost's abortive invasion of South Carolina. According to Moultrie, instead of bringing off a rearguard attack as instructed, Laurens rashly took the guard and attacked the head of Prevost's column. The small guard was needlessly cut up as a result.

Laurens's characteristic aggressiveness now came into play at Savannah. General Lincoln had ordered Laurens to assault what the British called the "Carolina redoubt," which was the redoubt to the *left* or northwest of Spring Hill, closer to the river, and not the Spring Hill redoubt. This order of attack was decided on so that the American troops would not interfere with the thousands of French troops to their right. However, when the impulsive lieutenant colonel saw that the French attacks had been repulsed, he chose to ignore his orders and lead the American right column directly against the Spring Hill redoubt. Laurens's assault column was comprised of his own Corps of Light Infantry (about 173 men) and the grenadier company of the Charlestown Militia (about 31 men); following these units was Colonel Francis Marion's 2nd South Carolina Continental Regiment (about 260 men) and the remainder of the 1st Battalion of Charlestown Militia (about 206 men). Laurens's command thus totaled 670 men who were certainly the flower of the American southern army.

The Charlestown Militia attached to Laurens's command was quite unlike most American militia units. The men were well uniformed, well equipped, and competently led. Moreover, the Charlestown Militia had drilled regularly and possessed an esprit d'corps that made it equal to many of the regular regiments in the Continental Army. Even d'Estaing was impressed by this unit: "The Charleston militiamen were all incomparably better armed and uniformed than the other troops, for almost all of them had cartridge pouches, bayonets, socks and shoes. Once they charged the trenches with a bravery and order that surprised me."[109]

As Laurens's Corps of Light Infantry charged, they were disrupted by Pulaski's cavalry as the horsemen retreated through their ranks. Nevertheless, the light infantrymen pressed their attack. Because the British artillery batteries were already engaged in close combat with the French, the Americans, as they dashed across the open fields and punched their way through the abatis, suffered far fewer casualties than the French. At the Spring Hill redoubt Laurens's troops stormed through the ditch—which was now filled with hundreds of dead and wounded French soldiers—and quickly charged up the earthwork berm of the redoubt. Yet again vicious and bloody hand-to-hand combat ensued as the American light infantry attempted to push the British from the fort with their bayonets. Lieutenant Colonel Laurens led his men from the front but was unable to force a breach. Soon, the light infantry was joined by Colonel Francis Marion's 2nd South Carolina Continental Regiment and Colonel Maurice Simons's 1st Battalion of Charlestown Militia. Colonel Richard Parker's Virginia Continental Levies and Colonel William Thompson's 3rd South Carolina Continentals also threw themselves wholeheartedly into the fray.

On 28 June 1776 the 2nd South Carolina Regiment had successfully defended Fort Sullivan in Charlestown harbor in a grueling, day-long British naval bombardment. Many veterans of that action were still with the 2nd South Carolina as it now made a ferocious assault on the parapet of Spring Hill. They suffered heavily for the effort, with ten of the regiment's officers and dozens of enlisted men killed or wounded at the redoubt. "On their attack upon the Spring-hill battery," William Moultrie wrote, "they were so crowded in the ditch, and upon the berm, that they could scarcely raise an arm; and while they were in this situation, huddled up together, did the British load and fire upon them very deliberately, without any danger to themselves."[110]

A Homeric drama unfolded on the ramparts as Lieutenants Bush and Hume, of the 2nd South Carolina Regiment's color guard, carried their regiment's two standards to the top of the redoubt. The flags, one red and one blue, had been given to the 2nd South Carolina by Mrs. Susannah Elliot in 1776 following the action at Fort Sullivan (later renamed Fort Moultrie). Soon after planting the flags on top of the berm, both color bearers were cut down dead by British musket balls. Lieutenant Gray, who had survived being wounded at Fort Sullivan in 1776, now leaped up and held the standards erect. However, a short time later Gray was also hit by a British musket ball, and he too fell mortally wounded.[111]

At this moment Sergeant William Jasper came to the rescue of the honor of the regiment. The brave sergeant had been given a sword by Governor Rutledge for his courage in saving the flag of Fort Sullivan in 1776. Grasping that sword, Jasper now retrieved the red standard from Lieutenant Gray's dying hands before he, too, was shot down with a mortal wound. Jasper, still clutching the flag, was carried back to the American camp. Among his alleged last words were, "Tell Mrs. Elliott I lost my life supporting the colors she presented to our regiment."[112]

The official British account of the destruction of the 2nd South Carolina's color guard is only slightly different from the American version:

> Lieutenant Bush being wounded handed the blue colour to Sergeant Jasper. Jasper, who had already received a bullet, was then mortally wounded, but returned the colour to Bush, who the next minute fell, yet even in the moment of death attempted to protect the flag which was afterwards found beneath him. No one could have done more, and the colour hallowed by the blood of Bush and Jasper, deserves to be deposited under a consecrated roof. . . . After the action it [the blue standard] was picked up under Bush's body by the Royal Americans [60th Regiment] and handed to their Colonel-Commandant, General Prevost, in the possession of whose grandson it remained as late as 1913.[113]

Whatever the details of the event, all agree that Sergeant Jasper and Lieutenants Bush, Hume, and Gray gave their lives bravely in defense of their unit's standards. Today a statue of William Jasper stands in Savannah's Madison Square as a monument to his courage and that of his fellow standard bearers.

The destruction of the 2nd South Carolina's color guard signaled the ebb tide of the American assault. "The parapet was too high for them to scale it under so heavy a fire," Major Pinckney reported, "and after much slaughter they were driven out of the ditch." The American troops fell back in disarray. Lieutenant Colonel Laurens lost track of parts of his command and was reduced to asking Major Pinckney if he "had seen them."[114] As Laurens finally turned and walked away from the redoubt, he is said to have looked back on his fallen comrades and, throwing his sword to the ground, exclaimed: "Poor fellows, I envy you!"[115]

While the first American column under Laurens was assaulting the Spring Hill redoubt, the second American column, consisting of the 1st, 5th, and 6th South Carolina regiments under Brigadier General Lachlan McIntosh, had yet to be committed to action. Given that nothing had gone according to plan, McIntosh sought out d'Estaing for new orders.[116] McIntosh and his aide, Major Pinckney, found the count in front of the Spring Hill redoubt: "Count d'Estaing was wounded in the arm, and endeavoring to rally his men, a few of whom with a drummer he had collected. General M'Intosh did not speak French, but desired me [Major Pinckney] to inform the Commander-in-chief that his column was fresh, and that he wished his directions, where, under present circumstances, he should make his attack. The Count ordered that we should move more to the left, and by no means to interfere with the troops he was endeavoring to rally."[117]

General McIntosh obeyed d'Estaing's orders and marched his column left of and past the mass of soldiers vying for possession of the Spring Hill redoubt. In fact, McIntosh essentially followed his original orders to make for the Carolina redoubt to the left (northwest) of Spring Hill and closer to the river. The British called this the "Carolina redoubt" because it was defended by Lieutenant Colonel John Hamilton and ninety of his North Carolina Volunteers (formed from the survivors of the Kettle Creek affair seven months earlier) along with seventy-five Tory militiamen from Georgia. However, McIntosh's troops became bogged down in the Yamacraw swamp, which protected the long flank of the British defenses in that quarter. Stuck in the swamp, McIntosh's column came under fire from the troops in the Carolina redoubt and fieldpieces in the battery between the Carolina and Spring Hill redoubts. The armed brig *Germaine* also annoyed the Americans' left flank with grapeshot from the river, though the distance was too great for this too have much effect. McIntosh's men were still slogging through the quagmire when word came that the rest of the army had retreated. General McIntosh summarily withdrew his men, having contributed little to the battle. Many historians incorrectly say that McIntosh's column attacked the redoubt and that Dillon's column got lost in the swamps. These scholars have obviously confused the two columns as it was McIntosh who got lost and Dillon who attacked.[118]

While McIntosh's men were struggling through the swamps, d'Estaing attempted to rally a group of grenadiers for another assault on Spring Hill. The French troops formed amid the firestorm, but to no avail. "With sixty men from different regiments," a French grenadier wrote, "I stayed between the abatis and the redoubt for almost fifteen minutes, taking all the enemy fire and waiting for reinforcements. Many of the soldiers were already retreating."[119]

At this point a British marksman shot and wounded d'Estaing seriously in the leg. The count's white uniform was already soaked in blood from the wound in his arm; after this second, more serious wound the general had to be carried from the field. D'Estaing's second in command, the Viscount de Fontanges, had also been wounded and removed from the field. Command of the army now devolved to the Irish general, Count Arthur Dillon. With his own column smashed and the situation obviously hopeless, Dillon wasted no time in ordering a general withdrawal: "Half of the officers were killed or wounded, the soldiers uncertain, the columns broken and intermingled without order; to retire was the general idea. . . . All that remained of the troops rushed into the swamp. The disorder was so complete that not ten soldiers out of the same company returned into the camp together."[120]

The Spring Hill redoubt lay about fifty yards in front of the main line of British earthworks. On seeing the tide of the enemy assault turned, the troops in these lines were ordered to counterattack the French and American troops. "Major Glasier of the 60th," General Prevost wrote, "with the 60th grenadiers [three companies] and the marines [one company] advancing rapidly from the lines charged (it may be said) with a degree of fury. In an instant the ditches of the redoubt and a battery to its right [and] rear were cleared, the grenadiers charging headlong into them and the enemy drove into confusion over the abatis and into the swamp."[121] Three companies of the 2nd Battalion of the 71st Regiment were soon ordered to help Major Glasier and his men, but by the time the Highlanders arrived on the field the enemy had fled.

The advance of the British grenadiers prompted Major General Viscount de Noailles to order his reserves to advance into no-man's-land to threaten another attack. Noailles's troops covered the withdrawal of the battered French army. The viscount also thought that the presence of a large body of organized French troops on the battlefield would discourage the British from mounting a pursuit of the defeated attack columns. The maneuver appeared to have the desired effect as Major Glasier did not pursue the retreating forces further than the abatis. Noailles's troops were now, however, within range of the British artillery, which immediately opened fire on the new targets. Noailles was wounded at this time, and his column suffered some casualties before retiring back into the woods.

Several French officers credited Noailles with saving the army that day. This was not d'Estaing's opinion, however; D'Estaing told Noailles he had no valid reason for advancing and therefore needlessly took casualties. It was strange criticism from a man who had just led more than eight hundred French and American soldiers to the slaughter for little reason other than personal and national pride.

<hr />

"Such a sight I never saw before," a British officer wrote. "The Ditch was filled with Dead, and in Front, for 50 Yards, the Field was covered with Slain. Many hung dead and wounded on the Abattis [sic]; and for some hundred Yards without the Lines, the Plain was strewed with mangled Bodies, killed by our Grape and Langridge [chain shot]."[122]

The battle had lasted slightly less than an hour. At ten o'clock in the morning the French and the Americans sent forth white flags requesting a truce so that they could retrieve their wounded and bury their dead. General Prevost granted the request only for those "who lay at a distance or out of sight of our lines." According to Prevost's official report to Lord Germain, the British buried 203 French and American dead on their right flank (near Spring Hill) and 28 dead on their left where General Huger had attacked. The British also captured 116 enemy injured, of whom Prevost said the "greatest part" were mortally wounded.[123]

The official French casualty return, signed by the Viscount de Fontanges, lists 11 officers killed and 35 wounded along with 140 rank and file killed and 335 wounded, for a total of 521 casualties. This number seems somewhat low, considering that the British claimed to have recovered about 347 enemy killed and mortally wounded. Captain Tarragon listed French casualties at 59 killed and 526 wounded, while another French officer put French losses as high as 377 killed and 444 wounded. General Dillon's account (related in the Pechot diary) said that 60 officers and 600 soldiers were casualties.[124]

The official American casualty return for 9 October 1779 lists 56 killed and 178 wounded, for a total of 234 casualties. This figure also appears to be somewhat low. Other sources, such as William Moultrie's memoirs, state that American casualties were as high as 457 killed and wounded. Not surprisingly, the worst casualties were suffered by the Continental units that attacked the redoubt. The cavalry suffered little, lending some doubt as to their aggressiveness and effectiveness (there was no mention of enemy cavalry in any British account of the assault). Interestingly, the Virginia Continental Levies suffered most heavily of all the American units, having sustained 60 casualties. Having started the battle with only around 150 to 200 soldiers, the levies had a casualty rate something on the order of 30 to 40 percent. We cannot know whether they suffered so because they were untrained or because they were young and felt they had something to prove and so fought like lions. Whatever the case, it is doubtful that they sustained such losses running away: these levies fought hard.[125]

The attack on the Spring Hill redoubt was quite sanguinary by any standard. The French attacked with approximately 2,585 troops in three columns. Using Captain Tarragon's casualty figure of 585 gives the French a loss rate of 22.6 percent of their troops engaged, or 12.8 percent of the French army as a whole. About 1,500 American troops attacked the British right; taking the official figure of 234 casualties yields a loss rate of 15 percent of those engaged, or 7.4 percent of the entire American army. However, using William Moultrie's higher casualty figure of 457, the loss rate may have been as high as 30 percent of those engaged, or 14.5 percent of the whole American army. Combined allied casualties were thus on the order of 20 to 30 percent of those engaged, or 10.6 to 16.3 percent of the entire allied force.

Most of the allied troops walked or limped away from the battlefield certain that they had been betrayed. Popular rumor had it at the time that a soldier of the Charlestown Militia—one Sergeant Major James Curry—had defected the night before the assault and betrayed the details of the plan of attack to the British.[126] (Tradition also holds that Curry was captured by the Americans after the battle of Hobkirk's Hill in 1781 and hung as a traitor.) However, if a defector gave the British any advance intelligence of the attack, General Prevost declined acting on it. No special precautions were taken against an attack on their right, and all parts of Savannah's perimeter were defended uniformly. Indeed, the fact that the French had opened their trenches in the British center led Prevost to believe—as d'Estaing had anticipated—that the primary thrust of any enemy attack on their lines would be against their center or left, where the ground was more open. "On our left," Prevost wrote, "the ground being firm and clear it was that on which we rather thought regular troops would choose to act and here therefore we looked for the French, and the Americans only on our right."[127]

The two feint attacks mounted against the British left and center successfully pinned British troops in position throughout the hour-long battle. According to General Prevost, when the enemy attack began, "it was still dark and rendered still more so by a very thick fog which made it impossible to determine on the sudden where the real attack was intended or how many. No movement was therefore attempted but the troops coolly at their posts waited for the enemy."[128]

General Huger led five hundred militiamen against the British left flank. A thick cloud of smoke and fog covered their approach, but the British heard the approaching column and managed to beat off Huger's attack with grapeshot and musketry from the 1st Battalion of DeLancy's New York Loyalists under Lieutenant Colonel John Cruger (while their regimental band played music, it was said![129]). The feint in the center met a similar fate: The small force of French militia (the Volunteers of San Domingo supplemented by a few metropolitan grenadiers) made little impression on the British and German defenders—although by all accounts the American feint was prosecuted with more vigor than the French feint in the center. The French feint on the river was botched so badly that it made no impression at all. The feints served their purpose, however, keeping General Prevost unsure of allied intentions. As a result, Prevost did not commit any reserves to support the Spring Hill redoubt until nearly an hour after the attack had begun, by which time the issue had already been decided.

When the allies attacked on 9 October 1779, the British defensive machinery worked exactly as it was designed to work. The French and American attackers were hit by grapeshot from the British batteries as they charged across the cleared ground, and dozens were shot down by artillery and musketry from the redoubts as they cleared a path through the abatis. Once the attack was stopped at the redoubt, the British troops in the entrenchments counterattacked and drove the enemy from the field. At this time the reserves were committed, but they were not needed.

The Franco-American plan of attack might have succeeded had it been better executed. Major Thomas Pinckney, who was a participant in the disaster, wrote a cogent postmortem of the defeat:

> Thus was this fine body of troops sacrificed by the imprudence of the French General, who, being of superior grade, commanded the whole. If the French troops had left their encampment in time for the different corps to have reached their positions, and the whole attacked together, the prospect of success would have been infinitely better, though even then it would have been very doubtful on account of the strength of the enemy's line, which was well supplied by artillery.
>
> But if Count d'Estaing had reflected a moment, he must have known, that attacking with a single column before the rest of the army could have reached their position, was exposing the army to be beaten in detail. In fact the enemy, who were to be assailed at once on a considerable part of their front, finding themselves only attacked at one point, very deliberately concentrated their whole fire on the assailing column, and that was repeated as fast as the different corps were brought up to the attack.[130]

British losses for the day, according to General Prevost's official report, were only sixteen killed and thirty-nine wounded, for a total of fifty-five casualties. Among those killed was Captain Tawse, who commanded the Spring Hill redoubt. Prevost eulogized him as "a good and gallant officer and who nobly fell with his sword in the body of the third he had killed with his own hand."[131] Tawse had previously led his dragoons in the successful action at Briar Creek. Tawse and his dragoons had also bested Count Pulaski's Legion at Charlestown the previous May.

In addition to the 110 soldiers manning the Spring Hill redoubt (which the British called the "Ebenezer Road" redoubt), 31 sailors manning the artillery batteries participated in the fight; also engaged were 74 grenadiers of the 60th Regiment and 37 Royal Marines, for a total of 252 active British combatants. One might also include the 165 defenders of what the British called the "Carolina redoubt" to the northwest of Spring Hill (90 North Carolina Volunteers and 75 Georgia Loyalists). This position was not stormed directly, but the troops manning it added their fire to the battle, although the range was too great for their muskets to have much effect. In any case, an astoundingly small number of defenders prevailed, considering that they were assailed by nearly 4,000 French and American soldiers. That the assault was made piecemeal and in daylight certainly gave the defenders great advantage. Even so, it was an astonishing action that must have been awesome to behold. Captain Tawse's defense of the Spring Hill redoubt deserves to be remembered as one of the great achievements in the history of the British army.

—⟫·◈·⟪—

The allied army wore a dreadful appearance after the battle. The French, who had suffered more than the Americans, were badly disorganized. "At midday," Captain Tarragon wrote, "little groups of men who had lost their way in the swamp were still coming back into camp."[132] The sympathetic Americans lent the French two carriages to convey their wounded to the hospital at Thunderbolt Bluff. The wounded in the French hospital were described as having been "cut to pieces by the grape shot," the British having fired from their cannons "packets of scrap-iron, the blades of knives and scissors, and even chains five and six feet long."[133]

The large numbers of wounded overwhelmed the limited resources of the French medical corps. "All the wounded were conveyed to Thunderbolt Bluff," Captain Tarragon wrote. "[The] want of linen and of surgeons prevented their wounds being dressed; those only have been saved who were slightly wounded, the rest were abandoned and are dead."[134]

Having suffered a bloody repulse, d'Estaing told General Lincoln that he was going to raise the siege and evacuate Georgia with all speed. "No argument could dissuade him," Lincoln lamented.[135] It was a popular decision with the French soldiery, but not with the Americans. "That the siege will be discontinued is inconceivable," a Charlestonian said in a letter to Lincoln. "Sorry I am to observe that the people seem in general disposed to think, if the Count abandons the siege that, since Congress has exerted itself so little to our [South Carolina's] support in men, we ought to accept the best terms that can be obtained [from the British]."[136]

Despite his disappointment, General Lincoln seemed satisfied with French efforts in Georgia and was understanding of the count's decision to leave. "Count d'Estaing has undoubtedly the interest of America much at heart," Lincoln wrote to Congress. "When the Count first arrived he informed us that he would remain on shore eight days only. He had spent four times that number; his departure, therefore, became indispensable; and to embark his ordnance and stores claimed his next attention."[137]

The American militia, disheartened after the defeat and demoralized by news that the French were going to withdraw, began to desert in droves. Most simply returned to their homes in South Carolina or upper Georgia, but a few went over to the enemy. The Chevalier du Rumain, captain of the frigate *Chimere,* made a conciliatory gesture to Prevost by sending a renewed offer of truce for the women and children of Savannah to evacuate the city. The chevalier told Prevost that his wife and children would be welcomed by him aboard his ship. It was a laughable offer now that the French were evacuating. Prevost rejected it, saying, "What had once been refused and with some degree of insult was not worth the acceptance."[138]

On 10 October the French began disassembling their artillery batteries. Once again one hundred crowns was given to each crew that could draw its gun overland to the landing at Brewton Hill overnight; and so as quickly as the batteries had been established they were dismantled. The Americans aided the French withdrawal by supplying horses to pull the guns to the landing.

The Americans proposed that the French army retreat with them to Charlestown. This plan was advantageous to both sides, it was argued, because it would discourage the British from attacking the Americans during their withdrawal and would also give the French a secure place from which they could evacuate the continent. D'Estaing rejected the plan as too time-consuming; he wanted to get the fleet away from the coast as quickly as possible. In addition, d'Estaing was afraid that Dillon's Irish troops would desert in droves on the march to Charlestown.[139]

The majority of the French army officers, however, favored the American proposal. The Army officers thought that d'Estaing was sacrificing their interests to those of the navy. In a written protest Count Arthur Dillon criticized d'Estaing's choice of Thunderbolt Bluff as the debarkation point. Dillon's letter was generally critical of his commander's judgment and argued strongly to accept the American proposal to retreat via Charlestown.

Tired of his officers' constant protestations, Count d'Estaing threatened to remove Dillon from command of his corps and replace him with Captain Louis Antoine de Bougainville—a navy officer—if he did not cease his dissension. This incident is yet another example of the lack of cooperation and respect within the expeditionary force. This disharmony existed not only between d'Estaing and his officers but also between the French army and the French navy, between the regulars and the militia (Volunteers of San Domingo), and between the French and the Americans. In light of this friction, it is not surprising that the expedition met with disaster.

In concession to the overwhelming opinion of his officers, Count d'Estaing agreed to change the point of departure from Thunderbolt Bluff to the more defensible Causton's Bluff. There was only one narrow road leading to Causton's, with impassable swamps on either side. Thus, any attempt by the British to attack the French army while it was embarking could easily be stopped on the road.

From 11 to 17 October the artillery and wounded were embarked on boats and rowed out to the fleet waiting near Tybee Island. During this time some disgruntled French soldiers deserted to the English; Count Dillon told d'Estaing "'*le moimeme*' [obedience] is no longer known by your troops."[140] Much to the astonishment of the beaten French, General Prevost allowed them to retreat unmolested.

On 18 October the rear guard of the French army (the Volunteers of San Domingo) decamped and took up position at Causton's Bluff to make ready to depart while covering the last of the evacuation. The Americans departed for South Carolina the same day and by the 19th had reached their destination. Fortunately for the French, the weather was much more cooperative during their withdrawal than it had been during their disembarkation a month earlier. They spent the whole of 19 October shuttling troops in landing craft down St. Augustine Creek, then down the Savannah River and out to the fleet at Tybee. By the evening of 20 October "not a person remained on shore."

Count D'Estaing laid the blame for the failure at Savannah entirely on Colonel Maitland's relief of the city, and he blamed that event entirely on General Lincoln and the

Americans. After the catastrophe at Savannah, d'Estaing returned to France and never again commanded an army in combat. It was an ignominious end to a miserable campaign. One of d'Estaing's soldiers summed up the count's contribution at Savannah with the pointed remark: "He conducted himself as a brave grenadier but a poor general in the affair."[141]

Despite his disappointments in America, Count d'Estaing remained a staunch supporter of the American alliance. After returning to France in 1780, he argued strongly for another expedition to be sent back to aid America. A second French mission was soon sent under the command of the more militarily competent Count de Rochambeau. D'Estaing's failure as a soldier was counterbalanced by his success in French royal politics. Unfortunately for the count, his popularity with court luminaries such as Marie Antoinette would ultimately prove to be his undoing. In 1794 the haughty and autocratic d'Estaing fell victim to the Reign of Terror, losing his head to Madame Guillotine. Ironically, the French Revolution that cost d'Estaing his life was inspired by the American Revolution for which he had fought and bled.

>—•—<

On 1 November 1779, a week after the last French topsails disappeared from Savannah's horizon, Major General Augustine Prevost sent his official report of the campaign to Lord Germain in London. Prevost wrote: "On the great scale of the war the transactions of a detached corner like this may not be of great importance, yet to us who were on the spot they were interesting." Prevost was being modest, for he well knew that the victory at Savannah was of great strategic importance. Much of the credit for the victory must be given to General Prevost and his commissary because the British were never short of provisions during the ordeal. The British stocks had been filled to the limit during the raid into South Carolina made earlier in the year. A return of provisions made after the battle showed that the garrison had sufficient flour in the city to last six thousand men at least into January and enough beef and pork to last to March 1780.[142]

Had Savannah been repossessed by the Americans, Sir Henry Clinton would have called off his planned invasion of South Carolina. While still awaiting news of the outcome of the siege, Clinton wrote the following letter to Lord George Germain: "In the case of Georgia being yet in the possession of His Majesty, the projected invasion of Carolina will be pursued with whatever attending diversions will be advisable. Should that province [Georgia] have been reduced, your lordship will be sensible of the severity of the blow and of its forcible counteraction of whatever was in agitation against Carolina. It will then behove [*sic*] us to concentrate our force and perhaps to risk in proportion to our danger."[143]

Given the consequences of failure, it is not surprising that Clinton said of Prevost's victory: "I think this is the greatest event that has happened the whole war."[144] General Prevost graciously gave credit for the victory to the soldiers, "whether British, Hessian, provincial or militia." He also made special mention of the services of Captain Moncrief, his chief engineer, who supervised the construction of Savannah's defenses. "All I can express," Prevost wrote of Moncrief, "will fall greatly short of what this gentleman deserves."

Strangely absent from the list of officers recognized by General Prevost for their endeavors during the campaign was Lieutenant Colonel Maitland's name. Maitland deserved at least as much credit as Prevost had heaped on Captain Moncrief. Yet Maitland, at the apogee of his career, would not live to reap any laurels. During one of his tedious marches in the southern swamps, Maitland took ill of malaria; he died on 25 October 1779—only a few weeks after the siege ended. Who knows what course the southern campaigns might have taken had this exceedingly capable officer lived.

Also conspicuously missing from General Prevost's report was mention of the nearly three hundred black auxiliaries who served in the lines. These soldiers did not see any significant combat during the campaign, but they did chase a group of French marines off Hutchinson's Island. Black soldiers also skirmished with American partisans in Savannah's suburbs during the allied withdrawal. However, what happened to the blacks who bore arms for King George at Savannah after the battle is a mystery. At least a few were employed as scouts and pioneers (armed workmen) during the 1780 Charlestown campaign, but there is no subsequent mention of large numbers of black soldiers serving with the British in the South. It seems logical that white Tories would have wanted the majority of the "former" slaves disarmed. Writing thirty years after the event, the historian Hugh McCall made reference to this, stating that for the British to disarm them required "shedding much of their blood"; McCall provided no details other than to say, "Policy forbids a narrative of the circumstances."[145]

Intoxicated with victory, General Prevost told Lord Germain in London that his men, after a rest, would be ready for further activity "and, we hope, offensive service." Dismissing his own recent failed invasion of South Carolina, Prevost wrote that it was his "real opinion, now more than ever" that the Patriots in the Carolinas "will not make any great resistance to any adequate force that is sent against them." In some ways this was not an inaccurate observation, but it ignored the real strategic difficulties that Prevost had failed to overcome in his recent operations in South Carolina and Georgia.[146]

The British leaders, with the possible exception of Sir Henry Clinton, were all too ready to ignore the military lessons of the southern campaign of 1779. Victory at Savannah had camouflaged all the deficiencies of the British strategic policy in Georgia. The campaigns of 1779 proved that southern Tories were too few in number and too dispirited to be relied on as the primary means of securing the southern states. The battle of Savannah had likewise shown how vulnerable the isolated British garrisons in the South were to sudden and unpredictable French naval attacks. Additional professional troops would obviously be needed to conquer the South, and the British would require a potent naval presence in southern waters if their armies were to operate securely in the theater. The British leadership failed to grasp the lesson, however, and continued to campaign in the southern states without strong naval protection. The single squadron of the Royal Navy assigned permanently to American waters operated primarily out of New York for the remainder of the war.

The military leadership of the United States and France learned more in defeat than Britain did in victory at Savannah. They knew that someday circumstances similar to those at Savannah would arise again, and they would have yet another opportunity to prove the value of their alliance. It was therefore altogether fitting that many of the soldiers who fought at Savannah—British, German, French, and American—would meet again, and that would be at Yorktown.

ORDER OF BATTLE: SAVANNAH, 1779

Georgia, 9 October 1779

American Forces[147]

Maj. Gen. Benjamin Lincoln

	MEN	ARTILLERY
Cavalry (advance guard)—		
Brig. Gen. Count Casimir Pulaski		
Pulaski's American Legion	125	
1st Regt. of Virginia Light Dragoons—		
Maj. John Jameson	166	
S.C. Light Dragoons—		
Lt. Col. Daniel Horry	ca. 50	
Right (assault) Column—		
Lt. Col. John Laurens		
Lt. Col. John Laurens's Light Corps		
Corps of Light Infantry	190	
Grenadier Company,		
Charlestown Militia	31	
2nd S.C. Continental Regt.—		
Col. Francis Marion	ca. 166	
3rd S.C. Continental Regt.—		
Col. Wm. Thompson	210	
1st Virginia Continental Levies—		
Col. Richard Parker	ca. 166	
1st Battalion, Charlestown Militia—		
Col. Maurice Simons	206	
Left Column—Brig. Gen. Lachlan McIntosh		
1st S.C. Continental Regt.—		
Col. Charles Pinckney	125	
5th S.C. Continental Regt.—		
Lt. Col. Alexander McIntosh	ca. 166	
6th S.C. Continental Regt.—		
Lt. Col. Wm. Henderson	103	
Brig. Gen. Isaac Huger's Column		
Georgia Militia		
Col. Wm. Few	64	
Col. John Dooly	135	
Col. John Twiggs	116	
Col. Robert Middleton	58	

Order of Battle: Savannah, 1779 (*continued*)

	MEN	ARTILLERY
Col. Leonard Marbury	30	
South Carolina Militia		
Col. Wm. Skirving	246	
Col. Wm. Harden	109	
Lt. Col. Benjamin Garden	129	
Brig. Gen. Andrew Williamson's Brigade		
of S.C. Militia		
"Independent Companies"	56	
Col. Hammond	42	
Col. Thomas	37	
Col. Williams	62	
Col. Reed	110	
Col. Brandon	68	
2nd Battalion, Charlestown Militia	88	
Reserve—Maj. Gen. Benjamin Lincoln		
4th S.C. Regt. of Continental Artillery—		
Col. Barnard Beekman	101	
Cannons (4-lb.)		8
Cannons (6-lb.)		2
American Total	ca. 3,155	**10**

French Forces[148]

Gen. Le Comte d'Estaing

	MEN	ARTILLERY
Avant-Garde of the Army—Col. Jules Béthisy		
Volunteer Grenadier Company—		
Capt. Aubery	60	
Volunteer Grenadier Company—		
Capt. Herneville	60	
Volunteer Grenadier Company—		
Capt. De Veone	60	
Grenadier Company of Armagnac	49	
Chasseur Company of Armagnac	53	
Grenadier Company of Agenois	73	
Chasseur Company of Gatinois	80	
Right Column—Comte Arthur Dillon		
Avant-Garde		
Volunteer Grenadier Company—		
Capt. Moëdermotte	60	
Battalion of Grenadiers		
Grenadier Company of Auxerrois	57	
Grenadier Company of Foix	83	

	MEN	ARTILLERY
Grenadier Company of Dillon	94	
Grenadier Company of Guadeloupe	50	
Chasseur Company of Guadeloupe	51	
Battalion of Grenadiers and Chasseurs		
Grenadier Company of Cambresis	88	
Grenadier Company of Haynault	85	
Chasseur Company of Champagne	67	
Chasseur Company of Le Cap	50	
Chasseur Company of Port au Prince	47	
Dragoons of Condé and of Belzunce		
(dismounted)	30	
Left Column—Baron de Steding		
Regiment of Fusiliers		
Fusilier Company of Armagnac	175	
Fusilier Company of Auxerrois	134	
Fusilier Company of Foix	203	
Fusilier Company of Dillon	256	
Fusilier Company of Walsh	26	
Regiment of Fusiliers		
Fusilier Company of Cambresis	94	
Fusilier Company of Haynault	208	
Fusilier Company of Le Cap	47	
Fusilier Company of Guadeloupe	135	
Fusilier Company of Port au Prince	87	
Dragoons of Condé and of		
Belzunce (dismounted)	23	
Reserve Column—		
Gen. Le Vicomte Louis Marie de Noailles		
Corps de reserve (drawn from first		
two columns)	400	
Artillerymen (fieldpieces, 6-lb.)	60	2
Troops Remaining Entrenched—		
Maj. Jean-Claude-Louis de Sablières		
Volunteer Chasseurs (mulattos)		
of San Domingo	540	
Volunteer Grenadiers (mulattos) of		
San Domingo—Maj. Des Français	66	
Royal Corps of Marines	337	
Chasseur Company of Martinique	52	
Fusilier Company of Martinique	36	
Dragoons of Condé and of Belzunce—		
M. Dejean	20	
Gunners and Cannoneers	163	

Order of Battle: Savannah, 1779 (*continued*)

	MEN	ARTILLERY
Troops Remaining in the Batteries		
Right Battery		
Royal Corps of Marines	108	
Cannons (18-lb.)		5
Cannons (12-lb.)		11
Left Battery		
Gunners	100	
Volunteer Chasseurs of San Domingo	40	
Cannons (18-lb.)		6
Cannons (12-lb.)		6
Mortar Battery		
Bombardiers of the Navy	30	
Volunteer Chasseurs of San Domingo	30	
Mortars (6"–9")		9
French Total	**4,567**	**39**
Allied Grand Total	**7,722**	**49**

British Forces[149]
Maj. Gen. Augustine Prevost

	MEN	ARTILLERY
71st Regiment—Lt. Col. John Maitland		
1st Battalion—Maj. Archibald McArthur	282	
2nd Battalion—Maj. McDonald	407	
Light Corps—Maj. Colin Graham		
16th Regiment	11	
Light Infantry		
(light companies of 16th, 60th, 71st)	331	
60th Regiment		
2nd Battalion	50	
3rd Battalion	65	
4th Battalion	116	
Royal Artillery	109	
Cannons (18-lb.)		ca. 2
Cannons (12-lb.)		ca. 2
Cannons (9-lb., 6-lb.)		ca. 72
Cannons (4-lb., 3-lb.)		ca. 8
Light Dragoons—Capt. Thomas Tawse		
1st Troop	25	
2nd Troop	27	
Grenadier Regiment von Trümbach		
(formerly Wöllwarth)	293	

	MEN	ARTILLERY
Garrison Regiment von Wiessenbach—		
Lt. Col. Friedrich von Porbeck	529	
Royal Marines	40	
New York Volunteers—Maj. Sheridan	220	
DeLancy's Regiment		
1st Battalion—Lt. Col. John Cruger	148	
2nd Battalion—Lt. Col. DeLancy	228	
3rd Battalion, "Skinner's" New Jersey		
Volunteers —Lt. Col. Allen	302	
British Legion	24	
King's "Florida" Rangers—		
Lt. Col. Thomas Brown	178	
South Carolina Royalists (a.k.a. Innes's		
Carolina Loyalists)—Col. Alexander Innes		
,1st Battalion	276	
2nd Battalion	109	
South Carolina Volunteers	32	
North Carolina Volunteers—		
Lt. Col. John Hamilton	126	
Georgia Loyalists and Volunteers—	111	
Maj. Wright		
Georgia Loyal Militia	175	
City of Savannah Loyal Militia	200	
Volunteer Negroes	218	
Black Pioneers	59	
Seamen	117	
Misc. troops	5	
Total	**4,813**	**ca. 84**

Casualties Occurring 9 October 1779

	U.S.	FRENCH	(ALLIED)	BRITISH
Killed	58	59	(117)	16
Wounded	181	526	(707)	39
Missing	–	–	–	–
Captured/Deserted	–	–	–	–
Total	**239**	**585**	**(824)**	**55**

Casualties Occurring 15 September–9 October 1779

	U.S.	FRENCH	(ALLIED)	BRITISH
Killed	ca. 58	63	(121)	40
Wounded	ca. 181	639	(820)	63

Order of Battle: Savannah, 1779 (*continued*)

	U.S.	FRENCH	(ALLIED)	BRITISH
Missing	–	–	–	4
Captured/Deserted	–	–	–	189
Campaign Grand Total	**ca. 239**	**702**	**(941)**	**296**

FRENCH ORDERS OF ATTACK: SAVANNAH, 9 OCTOBER 1779

Count d'Estaing's orders for the attack on Savannah, given to his officers on 8 October 1779. From Captain Jean Rémy de Tarragon's "Pechot Diary," in Facsimiles of Manuscripts in European Archives Relating to America, 1773–1783, *translated and edited by B. F. Stevens (microfilm edition, University of Texas at Arlington, item 2010).*

Orders

9 Oct. 1779

Watchword—St. Remi and Rheims.

Rally for the French and Americans—Louis.

The troops intended for the attack on Savannah will be divided into four parts.

The first, made up of volunteer grenadiers, will form the first vanguard.

The second part of the troops will form the right column; it will have a vanguard of its own.

The third, also having a vanguard, will form the left column.

The fourth part of the troops will form the reserve corps with 60 artillerymen, and some field pieces.

These four corps will be formed before leaving the camp according to the above arrangement.

They will march in knots of 12 file. They will get under arms at midnight covered by the noise of the battery. The muster-rolls called, and the formation secured, they will start by the right to march towards the left and proceed in front of the camp of the Americans.

Each division will leave the guard and the sick in its camp, and the camp guard will keep up the fires as usual.

The four divisions will rest in front of the camp of the Americans. Small posts will be sent to mark out by means of sentinels the last position which is to be taken up before the attack; it will be pointed out by officers of the staff. The march will be commenced two hours after midnight at the moment Count d'Estaing or General Lincoln shall name.

It has been agreed between the two generals that the second column, formed of the élite of the American troops, with the cavalry of General Pulasky [*sic*] at its head, will march after the left column of the French troops. The field artillery will be with the reserve corps, which will follow the right column. The noise of the feigned attacks will serve as a signal for the real one, which will begin at the latest at 4 o'clock in the morning.

The first vanguard will proceed to the capital of the Spring Hill redoubt. If it cannot escalade it, it will turn it so as to enter by the communication of the said redoubt. This communication is at the angle which commands the side of the intrenchments [*sic*].

The right column will support the vanguard by proceeding more to the left so as to pass, if possible, between the redoubt and the battery, with the redoubt on its right and the battery on its left, or so as entirely to turn the battery towards the left, which the column would then have on its right.

Deserters have intimated that there were two posts, of 20 men in all, guarding the road on the right of the redoubt and on the left of the battery.

The left column will march as if it were to proceed to a large house which is seen on the bank of the river and nearly in the same line with the redoubt. As soon as this column has passed the place where we believe the abatis ends, and when it is far enough from the right column not to be confused with it will march abruptly to the right to break through the intrenchment if there is one.

The movement of the first vanguard and the two columns must be to march to the left so as to march back to the right, and to preserve distance enough not to get mixed, and draw up in order of battle when they receive the command.

The left will take care not to get into the swamp and to pass on the inside of the spring where it begins.

It has been agreed that the American cavalry with the third column shall enter the town by the houses. When they think it is advisable to form, they will open out to 20 fathoms from the river. This column will take in the rear the batteries which are on its left, the nearest to the swamp or the river.

The redoubt having been taken and its intrenchments forced, the first vanguard, remaining in column, will march on the barracks by the inside of the enemy's intrenchments. The two columns will follow the same manoeuvre; they will deploy according to the space, the circumstances and the orders that will be given, having their right towards the inside of the enemy's intrenchments and their left towards the houses. In all cases, however, the grenadiers and chasseurs of the right column will remain in *column* [original emphasis], as well as the first vanguard, and will be ready to drive out whatever they find in the enemy's intrenchments, they will seize by way of the gorge, the batteries and redoubts which have already been turned; a position will be taken up at the barracks in communication with the trenches, and notice will be given of this by cheers for the King and by a detachment.

It is forbidden to fire, under penalty of death, before having taken the first redoubt and having formed within the intrenchments.

It is forbidden, under the same penalty, to leave the ranks in order to pillage before having received permission to do so.

The redoubt of Spring Hill and of the other intrenchments will be occupied, according to orders given, by the rear of the columns or the reserve corps.

There will be two consecutive attacks, both by the troops from the trenches, the first on the battery dismounted by our right battery, and the second on the barracks; there will also be a feigned attack by galleys and troops. A body of Americans will also make a feigned attack as near to the river as it can be made.

In case of retreat after having taken the Spring Hill redoubt, it [the rallying point] will be from behind that redoubt, which will have been closed on the enemy's side and opened on the opposite side. The second rallying-point will be at the cemetery where

French Orders of Attack: Savannah, 9 October 1779 (*continued*)

the reserve corps should be. If these two points of retreat are not available it must be by the left of the camp of the Americans and after that to the depot of the trenches, the defiles of which we should place in front of us. All the soldiers of the allied troops will wear a white cockade.

[D'Estaing's orders continued with a detailed order of battle ("order of attack" in the manuscript) for his army that is substantially the same as that given in the order of battle for the French earlier in this volume.]

AMERICAN ORDERS OF ATTACK: SAVANNAH, 9 OCTOBER 1779

General Benjamin Lincoln's orders for the attack on Savannah, given to his officers on the evening of 8 October 1779, in William Moultrie, Memoirs of the American Revolution, *2 vols. (1802; reprint, New York: New York Times and Arno Press, 1968), 2:37–40.*

Evening Orders, by Gen. Lincoln.

WATCH WORD . . . LEWIS.

The soldiers will be immediately supplied with 40 rounds of cartridges; a spare flint; and have their arms in good order.

The infantry destined for the attack of Savannah will be divided into two bodies: the first composed of the light troops, under the command of Col. Laurens; the second of the continental battalions, and the first battalion of the Charlestown militia, except the grenadiers, who are to join the light troops: the whole will parade at 1 o'clock, near the left of the line; and march by the right, by platoons.

The guards of the camp, will be formed of the invalids, and be charged to keep the fires as usual, in camp.

The cavalry, under the command of Count Pulaski, will parade at the same time with the infantry, and follow the left column of the American light troops; they will endeavor to penetrate the enemy's lines, between the battery, on the left of the Spring-hill redoubt, and the next towards the river: having effected this, they will pass to the left, towards Yamacraw; and secure such parties of the enemy, as may be lodged in that quarter.

The artillery will parade at the same time; follow the French artillery, and remain with the corps de reserve, until they receive further orders.

The whole will be ready by the time appointed, with the utmost silence and punctuality; and be ready to march, the instant Count D'Estaing and Gen. Lincoln shall order.

The light troops, who are to follow the cavalry, will attempt to enter the redoubt, on the left of the Spring-hill, by escalade, if possible, if not, by entrance to it; they are supported, if necessary, by the first South Carolina regiment: in the mean time, the column will proceed with the lines to the left of the Spring-hill battery.

The light troops, having succeeded against the redoubt, will proceed to the left, and attempt the several works between that and the river.

The column will move to the left of the French troops, taking care not to interfere with them.

The light troops, having carried the works towards the river, will form on the left of the column.

It is expressly forbidden to fire a single gun before the redoubts are carried, or for any soldier to quit his rank, to plunder, without an order for that purpose: any who shall presume to transgress, in either of these respects, shall be reputed a disobeyer of military orders, which is punishable with death.

The militia of the first and second brigades; Gen. Williamson's and the second battalion of the Charlestown militia, will parade immediately, under the command of Gen. Huger, after draughting 500 of them; the remainder of them will go into the trenches, and put themselves under the commanding officer there; with the 500, he will march to the left of the enemy's lines, and remain as near them as he possibly can, without being discovered, until 4 o'clock in the morning, at which time, the troops in the trenches, will begin an attack upon the enemy: he will then advance, and make his attack as near the river as possible; though this is only meant as a feint, yet should a favorable opportunity offer, he will improve it, and push into the town.

In case of a repulse, after having taken the Spring-hill redoubt, the troops will retreat, and rally in the rear of the redoubt; if it cannot be effected that way, it must be attempted by the same route at which they entered.

The second place of rallying (or the first, if the redoubt should not be carried) will be at the Jew's burying ground, where the reserve will be placed: if these two halts should not be effectual, they will retire towards camp.

The troops will carry on their hats, a piece of white paper, by which they will be distinguished.

British Commissary Return: Savannah, 11–20 October 1779

The return below was prepared by Peter Paumier, a member of General Prevost's staff. This manuscript document is in the Clinton Papers, Clements Library, University of Michigan, and is remarkable in that it records the numbers of women, children, and slaves who were drawing rations from the British commissary. No doubt, many of the women were camp followers—wives and girlfriends—and most of the children were members of the soldiers' families. To the modern reader, the idea of taking wives and children along on a military campaign is inconceivable, and yet this was common in the era under study. Using this document, one can determine that almost 7 percent of the total number being supplied by the British commissary at Savannah consisted of women and children associated with or attached to the army. Part of this document, but not reproduced here, is a table of the commissary stores available in the city. The table indicates that there was enough beef on hand to feed six thousand people through March 1780.

Abstract of the Number of Men, Women and Children, Negroes, and Prisoners Victualled [sic] at the Commissary General's Stores at Savannah from 11th to 20th October 1779

	MEN	WOMEN	CHILDREN	NEGROES	PRISONERS
16th Regiment	11	10	–	6	–
2nd Batt. 60th Regiment	50	7	7	–	–
3rd Batt. 60th Regiment	65	–	–	1	–
4th Batt. 60th Regiment	116	–	–	9	–

British Commissary Return: Savannah, 11–20 October 1779 (*continued*)

	MEN	WOMEN	CHILDREN	NEGROES	PRISONERS
1st Batt. 71st Regiment	274	32	20	1	–
2nd Batt. 71st Regiment	407	5	6	7	
Royal Artillery	109	8	14	27	–
Light Infantry	331	12	–	–	–
1st Troop Light Dragoons	25	3	–	5	–
2nd Troop Light Dragoons	27	3	–	5	–
New York Volunteers	220	50	35	10	–
1st Batt. General DeLancy's	148	11	5	–	–
2nd Batt. General DeLancy's	228	17	20	18	–
3rd Batt. New Jersey Volunteers	302	48	48	18	–
4th Batt. New Jersey Volunteers	1	–	–	–	–
Maryland Loyalists	1	–	–	–	–
Volunteers of Ireland	2	–	–	1	–
British Legion	24	–	–	1	–
King's Rangers	178	6	2	11	–
1st Batt. South Carolina Royalists	276	–	–	13	–
2nd Batt. South Carolina Royalists	109	–	–	12	–
South Carolina Volunteers	32	–	–	–	–
1st Batt. Royal North Carolina Volunteers	119	10	4	–	–
2nd Batt. Royal North Carolina Volunteers	7	–	–	–	–
Carolina Light Dragoons	1	–	–	–	–
Georgia Loyalists	104	10	3	10	–
Georgia Volunteers	7	–	–	2	–
Georgia Militia	375	–	–	2	–
General de Trumbach's Regiment	293	2	–	3	–
General de Wissenbach's Batt.	529	20	10	20	–

	MEN	WOMEN	CHILDREN	NEGROES	PRISONERS
Commissary					
General's Department	17	–	–	1	–
Quarter Master					
General's Department	32	–	–	–	–
Barrack Master					
General's Department	17	–	–	10	–
Inspector					
General's Department	1	–	–	1	–
Engineers General's					
Department	39	–	–	41	–
Cattle Department	5	–	–	14	–
Negroes Employed					
in Redoubts	–	–	–	54	–
Volunteer Negroes	–	–	–	218	–
Black Pioneers	–	–	–	59	–
Negroes in Service					
of Government	–	–	–	2	–
King's Boat	–	–	–	6	–
His Majesty's					
Ship *Fowey*	108	–	–	–	–
His Majesty's					
Ship *Rose*	182	–	–	15	–
His Majesty's					
Armed Brig *Keppel*	46	–	–	–	–
Seamen	77	–	–	15	–
Marines	40	–	–	–	–
Refugees	9	2	–	–	–
Town Adjutant	2	–	–	–	–
Anthony Stokes					
Esq. Chief Justice	4	–	–	–	–
Lieutenant Barclay					
on half pay list	1	–	–	–	–
Commissary					
of Prisoners	4	–	–	–	–
Rebel Officers					
on Parole	29	–	–	–	–
Provost Martial	3	–	–	–	–
Prisoners in Provost	–	–	–	–	15
Prisoners in Main Guard	–	–	–	–	17
Prisoners in					
General's Redoubt	–	–	–	–	2
General Hospital	11	–	–	–	–
Hornet Galley	18	–	–	–	–

British Commissary Return: Savannah, 11–20 October 1779 (*continued*)

	MEN	WOMEN	CHILDREN	NEGROES	PRISONERS
Seamen in Jamaica Battery	40	–	–	–	–
Brigade Major Skelly	1	–	–	2	–
Honorable Colonel Maitland	8	–	–	–	–
French Officers	8	–	–	–	–
Thunder Galley	24	–	–	–	–
Gun Boat	11	–	–	–	–
Surgeons of Navy Hospital	4	–	–	–	–
[Totals]	5,112	256	174	620	34

ERRORS EXCEPTED
SAVANNAH THE 24TH NOV. [17]79
/SIGNED/ PETER PAUMIER

AMERICAN CASUALTY RETURN: SAVANNAH, 9 OCTOBER 1779

Manuscript document in the Emmet Collection, Manuscripts & Archives Section, New York Public Library.

	Killed							Wounded								Total
	Colonels	Lt. Colonels	Majors	Captains	Subalterns	Sergeants	Rank & File	Colonels	Lt. Colonels	Majors	Captains	Subalterns	Sergeants	Drums & Fifers	Rank & File	
1st. Regt. So. Carolina	"	"	"	"	"	1	"	"	"	"	"	"	2	"	5	8
2d. ditto	"	"	1	"	3	1	11	"	"	"	1	2	2	1	19	41
3d. ditto	"	"	1	"	1	"	10	"	"	"	1	2	2	"	24	41
6th ditto	"	"	"	"	"	"	"	"	"	"	1	"	"	"	"	1
Virginia Levies	"	"	"	"	"	2	7	"	"	"	"	2	2	"	47	60
Light Infantry	"	"	"	"	"	"	7	"	"	"	3	2	2	"	15	29
Georgia Militia	"	"	"	"	"	"	1	"	"	"	"	1	1	"	8	11
So. Caro. do. of Huger's brgd	"	"	"	"	"	"	"	"	"	"	"	1	"	"	2	3
do. of Williamson's do.	"	"	"	1	"	"	5	"	"	"	1	1	1	"	8	17
do. of Colo Simons'	"	"	"	1	"	"	"	"	"	"	"	1	1	"	6	9
So. Carolina Artillery	"	"	"	"	1	"	1	"	"	"	"	"	1	"	4	7
	"	"	2	2	5	4	42	"	"	"	7	12	14	1	138	227
Of the Cavalry	"	"	"	"	"	"	1	"	"	2	"	"	"	"	4	7
[Totals with Cavalry]	"	"	[2]	[2]	[5]	[4]	[43]	"	"	[2]	[7]	[12]	[14]	[1]	[142]	[234]

s/ Edm. M. Hyrne
Ad. Genl. J.D.

American Forces

Maj. Gen. Benjamin Lincoln

	MEN	ARTILLERY
McIntosh's (a.k.a. 1st) Brigade—		
Brig. Gen. Lachlan McIntosh		
1st S.C. Continental Regt.—		
Col. Charles Pinckney	125	
3rd S.C. Continental Regt.—		
Col. Wm. Thompson	210	
6th S.C. Continental Regt.—		
Lt. Col. Wm. Henderson	103	
Georgia Militia—Col. Wm. Few	64	
Georgia Militia—Col. John Dooly	135	
Georgia Militia—Col. John Twiggs	116	
Georgia Militia—Col. Robert Middleton	58	
Georgia Militia—Col. Leonard Marbury	30	
Huger's (a.k.a. 2nd) Brigade—		
Brig. Gen. Isaac Huger		
Continentals	ca. 500	
2nd S.C. Continental Regt.—		
Col. Francis Marion		
5th S.C. Continental Regt.—		
Lt. Col. Alexander McIntosh		
1st Virginia Cont. Levies—		
Col. Richard Parker		
S.C. Militia—Col. Wm. Skirving	246	
S.C. Militia—Col. Wm. Harden	109	
S.C. Militia—Lt. Col. Benjamin Garden	129	
Williamson's Brigade—Gen. Andrew Williamson		
S.C. Militia "Independent Companies"	56	
S.C. Militia—Col. Hammond	42	
S.C. Militia—Col. Thomas	37	
S.C. Militia—Col. Williams	62	
S.C. Militia—Col. Reed	110	
S.C. Militia—Col. Brandon	68	
Corps of Light Infantry—Col. John Laurens	173	
Charlestown Militia Regiment—		
Col. Maurice Simons		
1st Battalion	237	
2nd Battalion	88	
4th S.C. Artillery Regiment—		
Col. Barnard Beekman	101	

	MEN	ARTILLERY
Cannons (4-lb.)		8
Cannons (6-lb.)		2
Cavalry & Legionary Troops—		
Brig. Gen. Count Casimir Pulaski		
Pulaski's American Legion		
Dragoons	ca. 125	
Legion Infantry	ca. 125	
1st Regt. of Virginia Light Dragoons—		
Maj. John Jameson	166	
S.C. Light Dragoons—		
Lt. Col. Daniel Horry	ca. 50	
Total	ca. 3,265	10

French Forces

Gen. Le Comte d'Estaing

	MEN	ARTILLERY
Division de Noailles—Gen. Noailles		
Regt. de Champagne	95	
Regt. d'Auxerrois	216	
Regt. de Foix	292	
Regt. de Guadeloupe	236	
Regt. de Martinique	88	
Division de Comte d'Estaing—Gen. d'Estaing		
Regt. de Cambresy	188	
Regt. de Hainault	360	
Regt. d'Agénois	97	
Regt. de Gâtinais	99	
Regt. de Le Cap	102	
Regt. de Port au Prince	156	
Artillerymen	151	
Division de Dillon—Gen. Dillon		
Dillon's (Irish) Regiment	373	
Regt. d'Armagnac	338	
Grenadier Volunteers	240	
Dragoons of Condé and of Belzunce—		
M. Dejean	73	
Volunteer Chasseurs (Mulattos)		
of San Domingo—M. De Rouvray	610	
Volunteer Grenadiers (Mulattos)		
of San Domingo—M. Des Framais	156	
Volunteers of Valbel	21	
Royal Corps of Marines	445	

American and French Camp Organization: Savannah, 1779 (*continued*)

	Men	Artillery
Bombardiers of the Navy	30	
Cannons (18-lb.)		11
Cannons (12-lb.)		17
Mortars (6"–9")		9
Fieldpieces		2
French Total	**4,366**	**39**
Allied Grand Total	**ca. 7,631**	**49**

ELEVEN

The Siege of Charlestown, 1780

"It was our last great effort, but it availed us nothing."

CHARLESTOWN was the southern colonies' greatest strength and its great-est weakness. The economic power of Charlestown made it indispensable to the southern region of the young United States; yet—as with any impor-tant asset—its very value made it a coveted target for the enemy. The defense of South Carolina therefore proved a paradox for American strategists. Like every American port city, Charlestown was easier for the British, with their powerful navy, to attack than it was for the Americans to defend. Yet, the leaders of South Carolina were men of money and property whose wealth was focused in Charlestown. They were there-fore understandably loath to give up the city without a fight. However, to defend the city the Americans would have to sacrifice the advantage of interior mobility—the one strategic advantage they had over the British.

In 1776 General George Washington attempted to defend the city of New York against an overwhelming British attack. After nearly losing his entire army in a futile defense, Washington learned that there was no one fixed point in America equal in value to his army. When faced with a similarly powerful British attack on Philadelphia in 1777, Washington attempted to defend that city in a blocking action at Brandywine Creek. After being defeated, Washington did not allow his army to be trapped. Instead, he withdrew to the interior of the country. This strategy surrendered Philadelphia to the British but prevented them from expanding their dominion into the countryside. While the Americans were deprived of a valuable economic center, they were likewise able to deny the British access to the food-producing areas of the countryside—thus keeping the British dependent on supply convoys from England that were now threat-ened by the French navy. After deciding that their resources were stretched too thin, the British chose to evacuate Philadelphia in 1778.

Having received intelligence of Clinton's preparations to attack South Carolina, Major General Benjamin Lincoln was faced with planning his own defense of the South's major urban center. Washington's Philadelphia campaign should have presented a successful strategy for Lincoln to emulate. Likewise, his commander's disastrous New York cam-paign should have deterred Lincoln from contemplating making a stand with his army inside Charlestown. Lincoln's choice of what to do should have been simple. However, military decisions are rarely made without political consideration, and southern politics would play a greater role in Lincoln's command decisions than he would have preferred.

It was indeed for political reasons that Major General Lincoln was assigned to the southern theater in the first place. The previous commander of the Southern Department, General Robert Howe, had sufficiently bad relations with the civilian government that he fought a duel with one of the region's leading politicians. Lincoln was brought in to smooth things over between the civil and military departments. On his arrival in Charlestown in December 1778 Lincoln said that he hoped he would never "be forced to the hard necessity of altercating with the civil power, than which nothing would be more disagreeable."[1]

In this mission Lincoln had proved successful and the rift between the civilian government and the Continental Army was mended. Unfortunately, Lincoln had not been nearly as successful on the battlefield. The general from New England oversaw failure after failure of American arms in 1779: the destruction of Brigadier General John Ashe's corps at Briar Creek in March, the near capitulation of Charlestown in May, the humiliating reverse at Stono Ferry in June, and the unmitigated catastrophe at Savannah in October. In short, Lincoln had lost every battle in which his armies had been engaged. Lincoln was an able administrator, and he would serve capably as secretary of war after the war ended. However, his mishandling of the Briar Creek and Charlestown campaigns in the spring of 1779 demonstrated a lack of strategic sense at the theater and operational level. Unfortunately, Lincoln's conduct of the Charlestown campaign of 1780 would only serve to cement the conclusion that he was out of his element as a theater commander.

All of the defeats suffered in 1779 created an atmosphere of despair in South Carolina and Georgia. After the departure of d'Estaing from the theater, the South Carolinians felt abandoned, and not just by the French. Many southerners thought that Congress had done almost nothing on their behalf except send them a Yankee general who had won no battles. People in Charlestown began to speak openly of abandoning the war effort. "Sorry I am to observe," one of Lincoln's friends in Charlestown wrote, "that the people seem in general disposed to think . . . since Congress has exerted itself so little to our support in men, we ought to accept the best terms that can be obtained [from the British]."[2]

Lincoln had to take such talk seriously. After all, when the British threatened Charlestown in May 1779, the civilian government of the city offered to declare the state neutral for the duration of the war if General Prevost would leave the city unmolested. If it had not been for General Moultrie's determination to "fight it out," the civilian government almost certainly would have surrendered the city. Dr. David Ramsay, a prominent physician and politician in Charlestown (and later one of America's first historians), complained of the state's low morale in a letter to William Drayton, the president of Congress: "Money will not procure soldiers. The militia will not submit to a draught. . . . The patriotism of many people is *vox et praterea nihil* [a voice and nothing more]. You know the importance of Charlestown; it is the vinculum [bond] that binds three states to the authority of Congress. If the enemy possesses themselves of this town, there will be no living for honest Whigs to the southward of [the] Santee. . . . A spirit of money-making has eaten up our patriotism. Our morals are more depreciated than our currency."[3]

The planters of South Carolina dominated the government, and they were apparently primarily interested in preserving their property and commerce. With little to no help coming from Congress, it seemed that they had to look out for themselves. To make matters worse for the beleaguered U.S. cause, the American economy had collapsed in 1779. No one had foreseen that the war would last more than three years at its outset in 1775. When the war entered its fourth year in 1779, the U.S. government ran out of money. Congress knew that to print more paper money instead of issuing specie would result in inflation, but there was little choice as they had no power to tax. Soon it took wheelbarrows of Continental script to buy a coat, and the phrase "Not worth a Continental [dollar]," became synonymous with "worthless." The Continental currency was under even more pressure in the South, where the loss at Savannah had ushered in an atmosphere of defeatism.

Measures to improve recruiting mentioned in the last chapter—such as signing bonuses of land grants—did not have the desired effect of increasing enlistments in South Carolina's Continental regiments. Lincoln wrote to George Washington in November 1779 bemoaning his situation: "With regard to this State [South Carolina], they have not, in their five regiments, seven hundred men fit for duty; and we have no reason to expect that their number will be much augmented, considering the aversion the people have for service here. . . . For, after solemn debate in the House Assembly, they resolved that the militia should not be drafted to fill up the Continental battalions, and that the militia, when in the field, should not be under the Continental articles of war; and [the Assembly] refused . . . the recommendation of Congress to raise any black corps."[4]

Lincoln was therefore left with no choice but to consolidate South Carolina's five understrength infantry regiments into three full-strength ones (or at least fuller strength units since there were still too few men for even three complete regiments). Thus, at the close of 1779 the 5th and 6th South Carolina Continental regiments of foot were dissolved and their remaining personnel merged into the 1st, 2nd, and 3rd regiments. (The 4th South Carolina Regiment was of artillery and often called the Regiment of South Carolina Continental Artillery.) This reorganization made it easier for Lincoln to make the best use of his officer corps, and it simplified equipping and supplying the army.

General Lincoln had problems other than insufficient manpower. His troops lacked ammunition, tent cloth, blankets, clothes, and other necessary military articles. Most importantly, Charlestown was "in a very defenseless situation." The city had begun fortifying itself when General Prevost approached the city in May 1779, but without an immediate threat to spur their actions, the civilian legislature procrastinated finishing the city's defenses. Lincoln lamented his predicament: "Many more [fortifications] are necessary to be constructed but from the want of negroes (the only laborers in this country), the matter is neglected. They have been sent for into the country, but from some deficiency in the law they are not brought in. Fort Moultrie . . . is supposed to be the key of the harbour, is in a very decayed state, and without a ditch, pickets, or abatis to it. The repairs of that, also, are delayed from the same cause. Two floating batteries have been recommended to cover the bar. . . . These, also, though indispensably necessary to the safety of the harbour, are unprovided."[5]

Responding to General Lincoln's entreaties, the Continental Congress set about trying to remedy South Carolina's deficient military situation. In November 1779 Congress sent a supply of war materials and artillery stores from Philadelphia to Charlestown by schooner. Among other items, the package included many articles useful for building fortifications, including one thousand fascine hatchets, five hundred felling axes, and seventy-two pickaxes, not to mention three hundred mortar shells and two "traveling forges" for making cannonballs and hot shot. To make use of these materials Lincoln had at his disposal Colonel Louis Cambray of the Continental Engineers, whom Congress had sent to Lincoln's aid the previous spring.

Congress also ordered both the Virginia and North Carolina lines (Continental brigades) to reinforce General Lincoln with all haste. Many newly raised Virginia state units (or "detachments," as they were sometimes called) were already in or were on their way to South Carolina, but General William Woodford's veteran brigade of Continentals—the "Virginia Line"—would have to make its way south from its quarters in Morristown, New Jersey. By summer of 1779 the North Carolina Line had also been ordered to depart New York for South Carolina. The progress of both brigades was slow not just because of the long distance the men had to march but also because both brigades had to reorganize and resupply themselves on the journey southward. (It took Pulaski's Legion almost three months to make the journey from New York to Charlestown in early 1779.) Even as late as December 1779 the bulk of the Virginia troops had only made it as far south as Philadelphia.[6]

Congress also sent to South Carolina a "squadron" of three Continental Navy vessels under the command of Commodore Abraham Whipple. It was generally believed that these ships, combined with the battle-tested guns of Fort Moultrie, would be sufficient to protect Charlestown harbor, given its natural defensive advantages. Morale in South Carolina began to improve with the prospect of the North Carolina and Virginia Continental lines coming, not to mention the presence of Commodore Whipple's flotilla in the harbor. It was perhaps none too soon since the Americans began to receive "frequent intelligence"[7] of a large fleet gathering off Sandy Hook in New York. No one in South Carolina doubted where that fleet was destined.

⟫◆⟪

To say that Lieutenant General Sir Henry Clinton was overjoyed when he heard the news of General Prevost's victory at Savannah is an understatement. "I think," Clinton wrote at the time, "this is the greatest event that has happened the whole war."[8] Clinton received the news on 19 November 1779 in the form of a letter from Patrick Tonyn, the royal governor of Florida. The letter came aboard the British privateer *Rosebud*, which had taken a month to arrive in New York after sailing out of St. Augustine, Florida. Even before Clinton had Tonyn's letter, word of the victory had already spread from

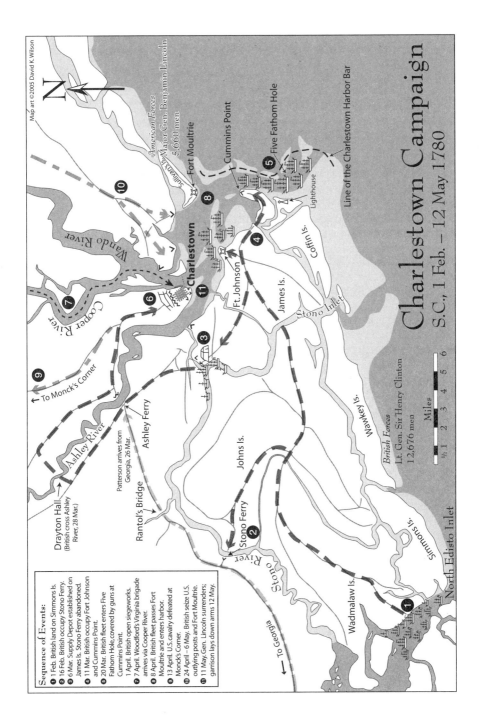

Charlestown Campaign
S.C., 1 Feb. – 12 May 1780

Map art ©2005 David K. Wilson

American Forces
Major Gen. Benjamin Lincoln
5,660 men

British Forces
Lt. Gen. Sir Henry Clinton
12,676 men

Miles
½ 1 2 3 4 5 6

Sullivan's Is.
Fort Moultrie
Cummins Point
Five Fathom Hole
Lighthouse
Line of the Charlestown Harbor Bar
Coffin Is.
Cummins Point
Charlestown
Wando River
Cooper River
To Monck's Corner
Drayton Hall
(British cross Ashley River, 28 Mar.)
Patterson arrives from Georgia, 26 Mar.
Ashley Ferry
Ashley River
Rantol's Bridge
Stono Ferry
Johns Is.
Ft. Johnson
James Is.
Stono Inlet
Wawkey Is.
Stono River
Wadmalaw Is.
Simmons Is.
North Edisto Inlet
To Georgia

Sequence of Events:

1 Feb. British land on Simmons Is.
16 Feb. British occupy Stono Ferry.
6 Mar. Supply Depot established on James Is. Stono Ferry abandoned.
11 Mar. British occupy Fort Johnson and Cummins Point.
20 Mar. British fleet enters Five Fathom Hole, covered by guns at Cummins Point.
1 April. British open siegeworks.
7 April. Woodford's Virginia brigade arrives via Cooper River.
8 April. British fleet passes Fort Moultrie and enters harbor.
13 April. U.S. cavalry defeated at Monck's Corner.
24 April – 6 May. British seize U.S. outlying posts and Fort Moultrie.
11 May. Gen. Lincoln surrenders; garrison lays down arms 12 May.

sailors on the privateer to the soldiers of the New York garrison. Many of the garrison's officers assembled their men and ordered them to discharge a *feu de joie* to commemorate the happy news, and soon the sound of celebratory musketry was echoing all over the island of Manhattan.

Clinton had been in a sort of strategic paralysis on learning of the arrival of Count d'Estaing's ships off the American coast. In August, Clinton had dispatched Lord Charles Cornwallis to Jamaica with four thousand troops to defend the island against d'Estaing and his fleet. Soon after departing New York, however, the expedition encountered a British privateer, whose crew informed them that d'Estaing's fleet was off the Bahamas headed for Georgia. Cornwallis consequently returned to New York bearing this news for Clinton.

Much to Clinton's chagrin, the British Caribbean fleet failed to follow d'Estaing into North American waters. Vice Admiral Marriot Arbuthnot's squadron in New York was no match for d'Estaing's fleet, which meant that Clinton now had to face an enemy with naval superiority. Clinton did not care for this predicament and chastised the Royal Navy severely for its inability to keep the French navy in check. For all Clinton knew, d'Estaing's fleet might strike any spot on the Atlantic seaboard from Florida to Nova Scotia. He therefore ordered the vulnerable British post at Rhode Island abandoned, and he strengthened the fortifications around New York. Clinton asked Vice Admiral Arbuthnot to send several ships to defend Halifax. It was actually something of a relief to Clinton when word came in early November that d'Estaing had laid siege to Savannah: at least French intentions were fixed to Georgia.

Clinton had been concerned for the safety of Georgia for some time. His anxiety was fueled by letters from Sir James Wright, the royal governor of Georgia, who had expressed his frustration with General Prevost's command decisions in the southern theater. Clinton became convinced that taking Charlestown was the key to creating security in the South. "If we do not conquer South Carolina," Clinton told Germain, "everything is to be apprehended for Georgia." It was therefore the *failure* of the Southern Strategy, at least as it was planned, that compelled Clinton to make ready a new expedition to South Carolina. Clinton was not altogether sanguine about the prospects of Loyalist support: "We have flattering hopes of assistance from the inhabitants . . . though I cannot say that in my opinion the conquest would have the same serious influence which would have been the case at an earlier period of the war."[9]

Clinton put his southern expedition on hold while waiting for the outcome of the crisis in Georgia. Only after receiving General Prevost's report on his victory over the French and Americans did the commander in chief resume preparations to invade South Carolina. After a few weeks of preparation, a British fleet of 88 transports, 30 men-of-war, and 8,708 soldiers sailed on 26 December 1779 for South Carolina.[10] Clinton used as a basis for his strategy a plan sketched years earlier by Lord Germain in a letter dated 8 March 1778. Instead of the frontal assault made in 1776, Germain advised Clinton to land on James Island, cross the Ashley River upstream from Charlestown, and approach the city from behind, where, Germain claimed, "the town is entirely open, if no resistance is to be expected."[11] Clinton would follow these instructions closely as the campaign progressed.

The voyage south was, according to Clinton, "most harassing and tempestuous." He wrote, "Scarcely a single day during the voyage passed without being marked by the foundering of some transport or other or the dispersion of the fleet, while we had the vexation at the same time of seeing ourselves hurried by the Gulf Stream to the eastward."[12] After four weeks of rough sailing, the battered fleet reached Georgia near the end of January 1780. Not all of the ships arrived at once, and over the next six weeks stragglers would arrive from time to time. All the surviving ships were accounted for by 20 March 1780. The *Anna*, a transport carrying two hundred Hessian soldiers, had been blown so far off course that it ended up in England instead of South Carolina![13] Other vessels, detached by the severe winter winds from the protection of the convoy, fell prey to American privateers. Of the vessels that foundered in the storms, almost all of the sailors and passengers were able to abandon their ships without injury, but their cargoes—including most of the army's horses and all the heavy artillery—were lost to the sea.

Of the fourteen hundred horses embarked in New York, only three hundred survived the journey southward. The English transports, beset by storms and kept at sea for much longer than planned, were obliged to throw the remaining eleven hundred horses overboard for lack of fodder or to save the vessels from foundering. The lack of horses would affect not only the cavalry (an arm considered invaluable in the open grasslands of the South) but also the support services that depended on horses for pulling supply carts and dragging artillery. Even more crippling was the loss of the ordnance ship *Russia Merchant*, which had aboard all of the British siege artillery. "Permit me to hope," Arbuthnot wrote to Clinton, "that stores of such consequence were not trusted, at the season we set out for this place, in a ship which the master protested was unfit for sea."[14] Fortunately for Clinton, he was able to borrow the heavy artillery he needed from Arbuthnot's fleet to make up the loss of the army's supply, though the stubborn naval commander only grudgingly parted with his big guns.

After spending a week regrouping off Tybee Island, the ships of Arbuthnot's fleet were once again ready for action. Clinton now called a council of war consisting of all his senior officers in order to decide the next step. Clinton told the council that he thought it prudent to gather every available man and make straight for Charlestown. Lord Cornwallis and the rest of the council thought it advisable to send an expedition to Augusta in hopes of drawing some of the American army away from Charlestown. Clinton yielded to Cornwallis on the matter, and most of the army's light troops were drawn off to form a "flying" column of almost 2,000 men (1,400 infantry and all of the cavalrymen whose mounts were lost at sea). General James Patterson was assigned to command the column, and he had brought along 130 "Guides and Pioneers" just for such wilderness operations. Patterson's orders were to secure Augusta as quickly as possible and then march to rejoin the main army at Charlestown.

The unusual deference that Clinton showed to Cornwallis was a consequence of Clinton's expectation that he would soon be headed home. Several months earlier Clinton had sent a letter of resignation to London. Clinton did not believe that he was being allocated sufficient numbers of men to conquer America. Despite repeated promises of reinforcement, London was never able to provide Clinton the number of soldiers he thought necessary to win the war. Clinton argued, with much justification, that the government's expectations of him were too high. General Howe had been unable to conquer America in 1776 and 1777 when the British had complete naval superiority and no threat of foreign intervention. Why did the government now believe that Clinton could win the war with fewer men, an enemy with a powerful navy, and more commitments across the continent? Assuming that the king would accept his resignation, Clinton informed Cornwallis of his intention to resign and began to defer more decisions to him. Cornwallis—an aggressive, self-confident officer by nature—of course began to act more and more as the expedition's commander and less as Clinton's subordinate—an attitude that bruised Clinton's delicate ego.

In any case, after Patterson's corps left Savannah for Augusta, planning for the invasion of South Carolina began in earnest. Captain Keith Elphinstone, a bright young naval officer who had been operating with the Royal Navy in Savannah since 1778, suggested that the fleet make for the North Edisto Inlet, twenty-five miles southwest of Charlestown. Admiral Arbuthnot disagreed with Elphinstone and argued that the troops ought to be landed closer to Charlestown on Johns Island. The admiral's plan had the advantage of placing the army only a few miles from the capital, but it would take an extra day's traveling by sea to get there.

Clinton worried that the extra time it would take to sail to Johns Island would leave the fleet vulnerable to another storm. Much to the admiral's chagrin, Clinton put his weight behind Captain Elphinstone's plan and insisted that the landings take place on the Edisto River. It was a terrible embarrassment for Arbuthnot to be overruled by an army general in favor of a junior naval officer, and the piqued admiral no doubt kept this incident in mind when Clinton later needed favors from him.

On the morning of 11 February 1780 the fleet departed Savannah, sailed past the lighthouse on Tybee Island, and headed north. By evening the fleet was approaching the entrance of the North Edisto Inlet. Late that night about two thousand grenadiers and light infantry of the British flank corps disembarked on Simmons Island (modern Seabrook Island). Despite some foul weather, the landings were uneventful and unopposed. The following day the remainder of the army debarked a short distance to the north on Wadmalaw Island. For the third time in the war Charlestown was under threat, but this time the British were serious in a way they had never been before. The sovereignty of South Carolina, Georgia, and perhaps all the southern states was now at stake.

⎯⎯⟩•⟨⎯⎯

On 12 February 1780, only hours after the British had landed, General Lincoln called a council of war at his quarters in Charlestown. After reviewing the army's returns, Lincoln put a question to his officers: "Do you think it expedient that all, or any part of our army go out and meet the enemy and attack them, as we may have opportunity on their march to town?" The notes of the meeting record, "Answered in the negative by all but Colo. Malmady." The council probably thought it unwise to send troops onto the islands when the enemy had both numeric and naval superiority, and where any U.S. forces deployed onto the islands could easily have been cut off and surrounded by the British. Lincoln instead ordered Brigadier General Moultrie to take the army's cavalry, supported by two companies of light infantry, to "harass the enemy on their march as occasion offered." Lincoln also sent orders to Colonel Richard Parker in Augusta to bring his 1st Detachment of Virginia Continentals to reinforce Charlestown.[15]

The British landing site was slightly more than twenty miles from Charlestown as the crow flew, but it was further by road. The British were at least thirty to thirty-five miles from the capital by way of Ashley Ferry and more than fifty miles away by way of Dorchester or Bacon's Bridge. Clinton now began a methodical advance over the coastal islands. Meeting little or no resistance, the British troops concentrated on securing the bridges and ferries that connected the coastal islands to each other and the mainland. As the British forces pushed further inland, the loss of the quartermaster and commissary horses began to have a great effect on operations. Other than requiring most of the officers to walk, there was no way to send supplies overland without horse-drawn carts. The British were able to overcome this problem by using row-galleys to transport supplies to the troops at the front via the numerous waterways that surrounded South Carolina's coastal islands. For a few weeks the Stono River served as the main supply line to the most advanced elements of the army. It was a workable expedient, but the advance was certainly slowed greatly.[16]

General Moultrie had positioned his force at Bacon's Bridge, which was eighteen miles above Charlestown. He sent his troops to skirmish with the forward elements of Clinton's army but told them not to risk a serious engagement. Moultrie's command amounted to 379 dragoons and 227 light infantry drawn from the various Continental regiments in the city. Colonel Francis Marion commanded the light infantry. (Colonel Laurens, who normally commanded the light infantry, was at this time in charge of the marines aboard Commodore Whipple's ships.) The Southern Department's cavalry consisted of the 1st Virginia Continental Dragoons under Colonel William Washington (cousin of George Washington) and Pulaski's Legion, now under Major Pierre François (Paul) Vernier, who had taken command of the unit after the death of Pulaski at Savannah. The remnants of Colonel Theodorick Bland's regiment of cavalry had also recently been consolidated into Washington's dragoons.

Since the British had lost most of their horses at sea, they were initially unable to counter the American advantage in cavalry. This allowed the Americans to use hit-and-run tactics with relative impunity against the slow-moving British columns. On 16 February 1780 the British crossed over the Stono River and reoccupied the old earthworks at Stono Ferry. This became a critical position because the British needed the post to protect the passage of their supply galleys up the river. Swamps flanked the river along most of its length, but the dry ground around Stono Ferry would allow anyone who controlled the post to control passage along the waterway.

General Moultrie therefore ordered his light troops to skirmish with the British in and around Stono Ferry. In one clash at Rantol's Bridge, Lieutenant Colonel William Washington's cavalry killed seven men of the North Carolina Volunteers and captured the unit's commander, Lieutenant Colonel James Hamilton, along with seven other prisoners. This insult was simply the latest blow to this particular corps of North Carolina Loyalists, which consisted of the survivors of the Kettle Creek affair.

Major Vernier, commander of Pulaski's Legion, directed many of the American actions here. Vernier was a French veteran of the Seven Years' War in Europe, and he still carried a bullet in his thigh from that conflict. Vernier called himself a chevalier (knight), though he probably had no legitimate claim to the title. Amiable and dashing, he was an excellent choice to lead the hit-and-run operations that General Lincoln was conducting against the advanced British battalions. Through his bold actions and chivalrous personality, Vernier quickly earned the goodwill of the lowcountry citizens and the respect of his British and German opponents.

For six weeks following the British landings, Vernier's troops engaged in numerous brush fights and skirmishes with British light infantry and Hessian jaeger detachments. An excellent example of this skirmish warfare occurred on 24 February 1780. That day a detachment of fifty men from the 7th and 23rd fusilier regiments marched out from their camp at Stono Ferry on a plunder raid. The company was led by a captain and two lieutenants who were, unfortunately for their men, not skilled in the ways of partisan warfare and light-infantry tactics. Captain Johann Ewald described in his diary what happened:

> The Chevalier Vernier was informed at once [of the British raid] by the country people, who were devoted to him, while they hated us from the bottom of their hearts because we carried off their Negroes and livestock. After he had observed these people for a long time, marching like a changing of the guard, Vernier followed alongside them on their return march until they were inside the narrow approaches between the ponds. Since they had not seen or heard anything of the enemy on their way out, they marched back in all tranquility and without formation. Suddenly Vernier attacked them on all sides and killed and wounded nearly half of these people, who had their impertinent and unskilled officers to thank for their misfortune.
>
> As soon as we heard the firing every jäger grabbed his rifle and hurried to their assistance with all speed. By luck we arrived just in time, when the enemy had cut off the whole detachment and was about to finish them off. The chevalier, who seemed certain of his prey, now in turn received rifle fire from all directions and withdrew. The English detachment was rescued, but they had ten killed and nine wounded. Afterward we surely killed and wounded just as many of the enemy. In addition, we captured one noncommissioned officer, four soldiers, and two lancers, and took three horses.[17]

Captain Hinrichs, another articulate Hessian jaeger, left this account of the same action:

> Vernier and his cavalry had lain in ambush at Wallace's road, at a place where two roads meet and where on both sides there are marshes and dense brushwood forming a very narrow defile, with a bridge about half way. He had ordered half of his cavalry to dismount. The English were coming down the road, as usual without rear guard and without having loaded their muskets, men and livestock in confusion. The cavalry charged and wounded three fusiliers with their lances before our men had loaded a single musket.

I happened to be strolling in front of our post. Quickly I gathered eight jägers and hurried toward this motley crowd of English, rebels, and livestock. Captain Ewald came with a platoon from another direction, and although Lieutenant Colonel Webster called us to halt, we nevertheless rushed to the bridge, for we knew the lay of the land. We arrived in the nick of time, for the dismounted cavalry coming down the road right and left had begun to fire. A few rifle shots made them halt and retire. The British had six wounded. Lieutenant Colonel Webster gave us his thanks.[18]

Hinrichs's and Ewald's casualty figures conflict, but whatever the losses were it is clear that the British were lucky to have any fusiliers walk out of the ambush alive. Just as often, however, it was the Americans falling for a baited trap. Vernier's troops were probing the perimeter of the Stono Ferry defenses on the afternoon of 4 March 1780 when Captain Ewald decided to take advantage of their curiosity:

I placed a corporal with six Scots and six jägers in two ambuscades in the outlying pine woods along the main road [to Stono Ferry]. My plan was quite correct. Toward seven o'clock in the evening a small party of about fifteen to twenty men appeared. The signal for the ambuscades was the firing of a double post [two sentries] which I had placed right in the open in front of the works. The sight of these two men was so pleasing to Vernier's gentlemen that they surrounded them in such a way that they thought they had cut them off. These well-chosen jägers allowed the enemy to play with them until it became serious. They fired the signal, the ambuscades attacked, and the enemy was nearly all shot or stabbed to death. Since night fell, some of them escaped.[19]

This type of desultory skirmishing continued at Stono Ferry until the beginning of March, when General Clinton established a large supply depot on James Island near Hudson's House at the junction of the Stono River and Wappoo Creek. This depot eliminated the need for sending supplies up the western branch of the Stono River, and Clinton on 6 March ordered the post at Stono Ferry abandoned and the defensive works there destroyed.

To many in the American army it seemed that Lincoln was not being aggressive enough in his defense, but he did not have the manpower to offer more resistance. Lincoln had to maintain a defensive line starting at Fort Moultrie on his left and ranging twenty-five miles to Bacon Bridge on his extreme right. The North Carolina line under Brigadier General James Hogun arrived in the city in the last days of February, but even with this reinforcement Lincoln could only muster thirty-five hundred men —far too few to man his extensive lines properly.

The shortage of men was in great part due to the failure of the South Carolina "country" militia to report as ordered. There had been a minor smallpox outbreak in Charlestown in November 1779 (part of an epidemic that was sweeping North America at the time). The outbreak was rapidly contained, and within a few weeks the disease had been eradicated in the state. Despite this fact, a rumor continued to circulate in the countryside that the "pox" was present in the city. This rumor was, as General Moultrie put it, "a very good pretense for the militia not coming into town." The state militia stayed away from the city in violation of orders for them to assemble and report for duty. "Not one militiaman [is] at this place on duty," Moultrie wrote at his post at Bacon's Bridge on 22 February. "They are apprehensive of the small-pox breaking out, when the weather grows warmer, and they are cooped up in town, would be worse to them than the enemy."[20]

General Lincoln was exasperated by these reports. "[I] am much surprised," he wrote, "to find the militia so unreasonable as to wish to avoid this town: are not the North Carolinians here, who have not had the small-pox? Have they views and interests to support that the inhabitants of this state have not? Surely no!" Lincoln wanted it known that the militia had "nothing to apprehend from the small-pox. There has been this day the strictest inquiry by the commissioners of the town, the surgeons of the hospitals, and the officers of the army; and they report to me that it is not in this place."[21]

Governor John Rutledge was, if anything, more miffed than Lincoln was regarding the militia's apprehension to turn out. Having been given dictatorial powers by the state assembly, the governor was also able to do something about it. At the beginning of March, Rutledge issued a proclamation that insisted the militia turn out as ordered or suffer the confiscation of their property and possible imprisonment. He also sent strongly worded letters to those militia commanders who failed to bring in their men, as this example shows: "You are to order one-half of your regiment immediately to this town, and transmit to me as soon as possible a list of those who are, or may be drafted or ordered to march, to the end that it may be known who are the defaulters. . . . People may be satisfied that the small pox is not in town, but if it was, I should not admit the circumstance as an excuse for the militia not coming down when ordered; if they will not come, they must abide the present and future consequences. I repeat in the most positive and preemptory terms that I must have one-half of your regiment here with the utmost expedition."[22]

When General Andrew Williamson's entire brigade failed to report for duty, the situation with the militia became a crisis. Williamson commanded the backcountry militia near Augusta. His men said that they were willing to serve in their own district to defend against Indian raiders and Tory bandits, but they had no inclination to go to Charlestown. For some time the Patriots in the backcountry had been feeling neglected and taken for granted. The high price and scarcity of salt (an essential food preservative in this era) was proving an enormous hardship to the citizens of the backcountry, and the government of South Carolina had done little to help ease their suffering. The collapse of the American economy only made the situation worse as the militia was not paid in a timely fashion.

Even before the British landed in February, one backcountry militia commander had written the following letter to General Williamson: "I am about to try to embody a part of the regiment to send to town; how they will turn out I can't tell, but I fear but poorly. I have made it as public in these parts, as possible, about the Governor promising to get salt for the back country; and it has given some satisfaction to the people— but at present it is bad, for many a poor man is obliged to turn out his hogs for the want of salt. To my knowledge some people must suffer greatly."[23]

All of General Williamson's five militia "regiments" (more akin in size to companies) refused to go to Charlestown, and Williamson made no effort to force them. These men could hardly be called cowards since they had faithfully served the Patriot cause since 1775 and had served dutifully at the recent siege of Savannah. However, defeat, despair, poverty, and fear of disease had drained them of the fighting spirit. The backcountry militiamen said that they would serve the American cause by "doing patrol duty in their own districts,"[24] but they refused to participate in another losing battle to save a doomed city. Call it fear of disease or mutiny, the result was the same: They stayed away.

Things got even worse for the Patriots when, on 24 March, about seven hundred North Carolina militiamen under Brigadier General Alexander Lillington (of Moore's Creek Bridge fame) left the city after their terms of service expired. However, about two hundred to three hundred North Carolina militiamen under Lieutenant Colonel Anthony Lytle (who had seen action at Briar Creek) stayed on to the very end.[25]

Eventually the threats, assurances, and entreaties of Governor Rutledge "persuaded" some of the country militiamen to report, but far fewer showed up than had reported in earlier crises. Only one thousand South Carolina country militiamen had reported for duty at Charlestown by the end of March—far fewer than had turned out to defend the city in either 1776 or 1779. Many of the militiamen who did show up were greatly dispirited, as would later become evident as the fighting intensified. The garrison's strength was now at about forty-five hundred men; but would this be enough for General Lincoln's needs?

———————————

Clinton had almost 11,000 men under his command at the beginning of March; this number included the 8,708 soldiers he had brought with him from New York and another 2,000 he had drawn from the Savannah garrison. This would seem to be plenty of soldiers to do the job, but two things led Clinton to believe that his force was insufficient. First, Clinton thought that Lincoln had far more men than was actually the case. Clinton estimated that there were 7,000 Americans guarding Charlestown. (Lincoln actually only had 4,500 at the time, though by the end of the campaign in May there would be over 5,600 Americans under arms in the city.) In late March, Clinton could only muster 5,000 fit-for-duty men in his main body; the rest were guarding scattered posts or were sick. The British commander therefore requested an additional 2,500 reinforcements from General Wilhelm Knyphausen in New York. At the same time Clinton recalled General Patterson and his 2,000-man corps from upper Georgia, even though Augusta had not yet been subdued.

Skirmishing on the right bank of the Ashley River continued as the British column advanced inland. Much courage and daring were shown on both sides during this time. In a skirmish on 25 March a sergeant in the American light infantry corps came too close to the British lines trying to gather intelligence. A German jaeger spotted him and put a rifle bullet in his belly. In his last moments the dying sergeant spoke to Captain Ewald: "He begged me to ask the surgeon whether his wound was mortal, and when he heard that it was he quietly lay down like a brave man, clasping his hands, saying: 'Well, then, I die for my country and its just cause.' Captain Hinrichs handed him a glass of wine. He drank it down with relish, and died like a man."[26]

It took General Patterson's troops about a week to work their way to Clinton's army from the Georgia backcountry. Patterson's column arrived at St. Andrew's Episcopal Church on 26 March; there it rendezvoused with the advanced elements of the main British army. Patterson's corps had to fight its way across the backcountry to join Clinton, each river crossing being disputed by American militia. According to Ewald, Patterson lost "two officers and perhaps one hundred men" during his march. Ewald also said that Patterson's column plundered its way through the backcountry taking many "Negroes, horses, and cattle" as it marched.[27] In this way, the British cavalry with Patterson's corps was able to procure mounts.

The arrival of Patterson's troops allowed Clinton sufficient manpower to cross the Ashley River. Clinton ordered the bulk of the army to assemble five miles above Ashley Ferry at the Drayton plantation. On 28 March, Clinton had seventy-five flatboats sent up the Stono River. Captain Elphinstone guided the boats into the Ashley River via the Wappoo Cut on the night of 28–29 March. The long column then made its way upriver past several American artillery batteries. The boats were able to pass the batteries undetected in the dark of night and because the sailors had muffled the oars (wrapped the oars in cloth to reduce their noise).

About an hour before daybreak the British army decamped and marched to the river landing at the plantation, near the manor house of Drayton Hall. At daybreak Captain Elphinstone directed the loading of the boats and set them rowing to the opposite bank of the river. "About eight o'clock," Captain Ewald wrote, "the light infantry and the jägers climbed up the left bank of the Ashley River at Benjamin Fuller's plantation, opposite Drayton's house."[28] A group of American cavalrymen spotted the British landings but made no effort to interfere. Lincoln apparently decided that there was no reason to risk attacking the British beachhead. It would be better, he believed, once again to yield the initiative and fight the British from behind fortifications and under protection of the numerous cannons that lined the city walls. Leaving only a small rear guard of light infantry and cavalry to hinder the British advance, Lincoln withdrew the troops guarding Ashley Ferry and Bacon's Bridge into the city.

The British beachhead expanded rapidly, and soon the army had formed in a column marching south along the road to Charlestown. Though the American light infantry and dragoons skirmished constantly with the column, they did little to slow the pace of the British advance. The British overran the abandoned earthworks at Ashley Ferry the afternoon of 29 March, and at nine o'clock that evening they camped near the Quarter House, an ancient tavern only a little more than four miles from Charlestown.

Having now taken both sides of Ashley Ferry, British flatboats were soon busily employed transporting men, materials, and artillery across the river there. Clinton reported that his forces only faced "an ineffectual scattering fire"[29] during their advance down the Charlestown neck. However, when the British column reached the Gibbes plantation on 30 March, the army's vanguard entered into a heavy skirmish with American forces. Four companies of Continental light infantry under Lieutenant Colonel John

Laurens attacked British light troops about a mile in front of the city's main defensive works. Lincoln ordered Laurens "not to engage seriously but skirmish with advanced parties, retiring slowly and orderly towards town, as there was no object in maintaining any advanced post and the advantages of a serious affair were all on the side of the enemy."[30]

The British vanguard numbered somewhere between four hundred and five hundred troops, while Laurens's corps was about three hundred to four hundred men strong.[31] Captain Ewald was among those involved in the action:

> The jägers were ordered to attack slowly, since the generals were afraid of an ambuscade in this area, which was intersected by deep ditches and short bushes. Meanwhile, the enemy was forced back from one ditch to another up to an advanced flèche which lay almost under the cannon range of the [American] fortifications, where severe firing occurred. Captain Bodungen, who led the vanguard, went around the flèche, whereupon it was abandoned by the enemy. But we hardly mastered it, and had scarcely formed a little, when we were attacked again with considerable violence and driven back, whereby three jägers were stabbed with bayonets. The light infantry came hurrying to our support, and the enemy was driven back beyond the flèche for a second time. . . .
>
> The enemy, perceiving that his maneuver was not successful, attacked the jägers and light infantry once more with a complete brigade supported by six guns. At this time the English artillery arrived [two twelve-pounders] and opened fire on the enemy, who withdrew into the city.[32]

The fight lasted two or three hours and ended only when darkness fell and both sides retired to their respective camps. The jaegers suffered nine killed, five missing, and eleven wounded. "The light infantry probably had lost just as many," Ewald wrote. This made for about twenty-five to fifty total British casualties. The five missing jaegers were eventually found, all killed by bayonets. "One of them," Ewald reported, "had his eyes cut out, which showed that the enemy was very angry and must have lost many men." Ewald claimed that he counted thirty dead Americans on the field, although the official American account listed only one killed (Captain Bowman of North Carolina) and eight wounded.[33]

The whole of the Charlestown neck now belonged to the British. During the night of 30 March 1780 the British engineers broke ground for the first siege parallel about eight hundred yards from the American fortifications. The siege had begun. However, the Americans still commanded the Cooper River and thus maintained a communication with the countryside. Clinton was depending on the Royal Navy to cut off that avenue of escape and succor, but things in that department were not progressing as he had hoped.

———✦◆✦———

Given that naval operations were so critical to both sides in the Charlestown campaign, it is surprising that both navies proved so ineffective during the siege. Neither Vice Admiral Arbuthnot nor Commodore Whipple cooperated effectively with his respective ground commander; and it often seemed that both General Lincoln and General Clinton had a better grasp of naval strategy than did their naval counterparts. Even though British naval power made the siege possible, it was truly a land-centric campaign. The Royal Navy did the minimum duty possible to conduct a successful siege; likewise, the Continental Navy proved to be of negligible value to the defense.

In this contest of lackluster admirals, Commodore Abraham Whipple turned in the most disappointing performance. At great expense the Continental Congress had sent three good ships to defend Charlestown: two thirty-two-gun frigates, *Boston* and *Providence*, as well as *Ranger*, a twenty-gun sloop once commanded by John Paul Jones. This force was supplemented by South Carolina state navy ships: *Queen of France* of twenty-eight guns and the brigs *General Lincoln* and *Notre Dame*, each of sixteen guns. Count d'Estaing had left a few French frigates at Charlestown: *La Bricole* of forty-four guns and *L'Aventure* and *Trieste*, each of twenty-six guns; these frigates were also put under Whipple's authority. The number of guns carried by the combined American fleet was impressive, though only the cannons of the *Bricole*, *Boston*, and *Providence* carried reasonably heavy metal: twenty-four-pounders. The other vessels carried primarily lightweight cannons (six- to twelve-pounders).

Some today might think that it was unreasonable to ask a small Continental squadron to compete with the large and powerful Royal Navy. However, Whipple was not being asked to go forth and engage Arbuthnot on the high seas; his mission was only to keep British ships from entering Charlestown harbor. Given this limited goal, Whipple's squadron was considered by most observers at the time to be adequate for the task. Indeed, had it not been, Congress would not have sent the backbone of the Continental Navy—a valuable and irreplaceable asset—into harm's way.

The harbor was thought defensible because of the sandbar at its entrance. The bar was low enough for most merchant vessels to pass over but was too shallow to permit passage of warships carrying full loads of cannons. Just behind the bar was a deeper area called Five Fathom Hole in which warships could anchor even fully laden with their guns. In order for the British men-of-war to enter the harbor they would have to shed many of their guns in order to raise their drafts to pass over the bar. Once lightened, they would have to wait for an easterly wind that would allow them to move into Five Fathom Hole. (The east wind also created a swell that would help bring the ships over the bar.) Nor could Admiral Arbuthnot send all of his ships through at once, but rather only a few at a time. The general expectation was that Commodore Whipple would station his ships in Five Fathom Hole and blast the British as they came over the bar without their full complement of cannons. Arbuthnot could send some of his smaller brigs and sloops fully armed into Five Fathom Hole first, but these vessels would be at a disadvantage against the American frigates. Some thought that the British would not risk the encounter.

Assuming that the British ships could force their way over the bar and into Five Fathom Hole, most expected that the American squadron would then fall back to a second line of defense in front of Fort Moultrie. With the American ships cooperating with that battle-proven fort, it was believed that the British would once again face a tough challenge getting into the harbor. In short, there were high expectations in the

American camp that the harbor could be defended. The British were deathly afraid of the challenge they faced in forcing a passage over the bar, as is indicated by this letter that Clinton sent to Germain: "Now, my Lord, the Continental frigates only, anchored within distance of defending the bar, are at least formidable, if not superior to any naval force that can be brought against them. Your Lordship is well informed that nothing larger than frigates can enter with their guns aboard, and even these must approach singly, and be successively subject, for a considerable time, to the broadsides which will rake them fore and aft, whilst the least movement [of the British ships] is sufficient to throw them on the breakers."[34]

Before Commodore Whipple's ships arrived in Charlestown, it had been Lincoln's plan to construct floating batteries that would be anchored in Five Fathom Hole. These batteries would have proved quite vulnerable to the weather and dedicated attack, but this shows that General Lincoln understood the importance of engaging the vulnerable British ships as they passed over the bar. It was presumed that if Whipple could keep control of the harbor, the city would be able to maintain communication with the north shore of the Cooper River and thus always have a means of resupply, reinforcement, and—if necessary—escape.

"It was the general if not universal opinion," Lincoln wrote, "that armed ships lying before the bar of Charlestown would effectually secure its pass." Yet, at the end of January 1780 Commodore Whipple told Lincoln that the bar could not be defended. He said that when an easterly wind blew, any American ships anchored in Five Fathom Hole would necessarily have to turn to face the wind and incoming tidewaters. At this point they would be unable to have their broadsides facing the enemy as they came over the bar. Lincoln was astounded by Whipple's statement. First, he wondered why Whipple, who had been on station at Charlestown for many weeks, had not earlier given "even one intimation that to occupy a station near the bar would be attended with hazard." Lincoln then let Whipple know what he expected of the Continental Navy: "You were sent as a protection to this part of the United States. . . . Your duty will be if possible to prevent the enemy from entering the harbor [and] if that should be impracticable you will in the next place oppose them at Fort Moultrie."[35]

The captains of the Continental vessels said that even if they were to forgo the advantage of having their broadsides to the enemy as the latter crossed the bar, the British would have the advantage of being under full sail as they crossed the bar. Since the Continental ships would either be at anchor or without sail as they waited for the enemy, the British ships could therefore speed past the Americans at full sail and get into position in front of Fort Moultrie before the American ships could catch them.

Lincoln was frustrated with the navy men. Would they not have the advantage that the British ships would not have all their guns? Surely the defense of the bar was worth some risk. The Continental Navy officers argued that even if they wanted to take up such a hazardous position, Five Fathom Hole did not always have enough water, depending on the wind and tide, for them to float their deep draft frigates, and they could not risk being grounded. "This was so new an idea," Lincoln wrote, "and if true the ships would be rendered of so much less use than was expected that I called upon the sea officers with the pilots to make the critical examination into the matter & report."[36]

Lincoln might also have told Whipple that the British did not have trouble anchoring in Five Fathom Hole in 1776 (nor would they have a problem anchoring in the hole after they took the passage again in 1780).

Whipple submitted a report to Lincoln confirming that the Continental frigates "could not lye in five fathom hole *beyond the reach of batteries from the shore*" [emphasis added]. This, then, was the critical difference between 1776 and 1780: Five Fathom Hole had sufficient depth for the frigates, but only in areas that were within reach of likely positions for British shore batteries. By this time Lincoln had lost confidence in Whipple, who seemed to be looking for any excuse possible not to engage the British at the bar. Lincoln therefore decided to sound Five Fathom Hole: "I did not content myself without spending two days in a boat on this business." After this excursion Lincoln acquiesced to Whipple's findings, "the truth of which was verified by my own observation." Whipple now proposed to defend the ship channel beneath Fort Moultrie, and Lincoln grudgingly accepted the offer.[37]

General Clinton was having just as much trouble with Vice Admiral Arbuthnot as Lincoln was having with Commodore Whipple. With all his siege artillery having been lost at sea, Clinton had to borrow from Arbuthnot's ships the ordnance necessary to reduce Charlestown's defenses. However, Arbuthnot refused to unload any guns until he found shelter for his ships, which had suffered heavily in winter storms. (The sixty-four-gun man-of-war *Defiance* had been lost in a gale off Tybee Island shortly after arriving in the theater.) The large warships finally gained respite from the wicked weather after taking up station in Beaufort harbor at the beginning of March. Arbuthnot now agreed to lend Clinton the guns and ammunition he needed; but to Clinton's great annoyance, the vice admiral did so only "with a sparing and sometimes reluctant hand." Only after weeks of repeated requests and entreaties did Clinton finally receive all the guns, shot, and powder he needed from the Royal Navy.[38]

On 11 March, Clinton occupied the remains of Fort Johnson on James Island. (The fort had been destroyed by the Americans in 1779 to prevent its use by General Prevost.) Clinton built a redoubt next to the ruins and, using the naval guns lent him by Arbuthnot, constructed a small battery overlooking Rebellion Road, the ship channel leading to the city. Under the cover of this battery, a battalion of the 71st Regiment along with two twenty-four-pounders were landed on Lighthouse Island (Morris Island today), which lay east of James Island at the entrance to the harbor. A two-gun battery was then established on Cummins Point overlooking Five Fathom Hole.

Covered by these guns, Admiral Arbuthnot was finally able to send several small boats to sound a passage over the bar. Several American galleys loosed a few shots at the boats but did not seriously interfere with the British operations. In a few days the channel was marked with buoys for the British fleet to follow. The warships *Renown* (fifty guns), *Roebuck* (forty-four guns), and *Romulus* (forty-four guns) had shed "guns, provisions, and water" in order to raise their draft sufficiently to pass over the bar.[39] These ships remained sixteen days in this vulnerable condition waiting for a favorable east wind that would facilitate their passage over the bar. The lightened, overly buoyant ships were in danger not only from surprise by a French or Spanish fleet but also from sudden storms that might capsize them.

On the morning of 20 March seven British ships crossed over the bar and into Five Fathom Hole. Most Americans still believed that Fort Moultrie, with the aid of Commodore Whipple's squadron, would stop or at least severely maul the British ships as they tried to force their way past. "We expect in a day or two," Moultrie wrote, "to see some smart firing between them and our vessels and Fort Moultrie: we have seven ships and three gallies [*sic*] to oppose them. If they will lay any time before the fort, I will engage we beat them, but it is generally thought they will pass as fast as they can, and endeavor to take their stations above the town in [the] Cooper or Ashley rivers."[40]

On 21 March, just when everyone expected to see a climactic battle between the two fleets, Whipple abandoned his position before Fort Moultrie and withdrew his ships into the Cooper River. Whipple's official explanation for this action was that the British had gotten over the bar "a force far superior to what was expected and with which our ships could by no means cope."[41] Put more bluntly, Whipple lost his nerve; he had no stomach for engaging the British men-of-war. Few Americans could understand the commodore's retreat, least of all William Moultrie: "[Whipple's] second position, when he was to lay a little above Fort Moultrie within point blank shot of the fort, with his ships across to rake the channel: in that situation it would have been impossible for them [the British] to pass without losing some of their ships. I scarcely think they would have attempted it."[42]

The American ships fell back to the Cooper River. Whipple ordered several of the South Carolina state vessels to dismount their guns for use in the siege lines. The commodore then sank several of the less seaworthy ships across the entrance of the river to serve as a cheval-de-frise (barricade) to block any British attempt to pass that way. A boom was later anchored to the masts of the sunken ships to further obstruct the entrance to the Cooper. Shore batteries mounting numerous large cannons were positioned to rake any British ship that might try to cut its way into the river. It has often been reported that the Continental vessels were sunk to form the boom chain, but this was not the case. Only some of the South Carolina state vessels were sunk; the Continental ships (*Ranger, Boston,* and *Providence*) and the best French frigate, *L'Aventure,* were kept intact and did some minor service harassing the British troops on the Charlestown neck.

The British now had a powerful fleet of warships and store ships in Five Fathom Hole. After rearming their vessels the British remained idle for three weeks until 8 April, when Arbuthnot finally decided to sortie past Fort Moultrie.[43] Eight warships came in column down the channel: First was the forty-four-gun *Roebuck* with Admiral Arbuthnot aboard; then came *Richmond* (thirty-two guns), *Romulus* (forty-four guns), *Blonde* (thirty-two guns), *Virginia* (thirty-two guns), *Raleigh* (thirty-two guns), and *Sandwich* (number of guns unknown), with the fifty-gun *Renown* bringing up the rear. Following these men-of-war were several armed transports. "It was the most majestic and beautiful spectacle that one can imagine. The fort was veiled in fire and smoke, and the roar of forty-three heavy guns resembled a terrible thunderstorm. Despite all the dangers threatening the fleet, it sailed quite slowly past the fort with colors flying proudly, one ship behind the other, without firing a shot. As soon it had passed the enemy fort, each ship made a sudden turn, fired a broadside, and sailed to its designated anchoring place [next to Fort Johnson]."[44]

No casualties were reported at Fort Moultrie, which was defended at the time by the 1st South Carolina Continentals under Colonel Charles Pinckney. The fleet suffered twenty-seven killed and wounded. Several ships sustained minor damage, and the fore-topmast of the *Richmond* was shot away. According to Arbuthnot, "the ships in general sustained damage in their masts and rigging; however not materially in their hulls."[45] The fact that most of the damage to the British ships was in their rigging indicates that the American gunners were wisely attempting to slow or stop the warships by disabling their sails. If Pinckney's men had succeeded, the British ships would have been exposed to American gunnery for a longer time, which might have proved their undoing. Though ineffective, it was a smart tactic.

Bringing up the rear of the British column was *Renown*. This vessel remained engaged with the fort somewhat longer than the other ships: "When she arrived at the fort she lay to, took in her sails, and gave such an unrelenting, murderous fire that the whole ship seemed to flare up."[46] After the column of warships passed the fort, a series of armed store ships made their way into the harbor. When the store ship *Aeolus* ran aground under the guns of the fort, it was mercilessly cannonaded by the Americans. The crew had to abandon ship, and they set fire to the vessel in an attempt to scuttle her. The fire did minimal damage, however, and the Americans were able to salvage several guns and some stores from the hulk.

According to the historian James Buchanan, "American gunnery that day made a mockery of the word."[47] This is, however, an unfair statement. The British had learned from their last encounter with Fort Sullivan in 1776, when Sir Peter Parker anchored his ships for ten hours within four hundred yards of the fort. This had allowed the Americans ample time to aim their guns at the stationary British ships and pummel them mercilessly. This time Admiral Arbuthnot made the wise decision to run his ships swiftly by the fort. The British vessels then took up position near British-occupied Fort Johnson, out of range of Fort Moultrie's guns.

Arbuthnot said that his column of eight ships took two hours to get into position off Fort Johnson; this meant that Colonel Pinckney's gunners had less than fifteen minutes to engage each vessel as it passed.[48] The Americans tried to slow the British ships by firing at their rigging but failed in the attempt. In addition, the smoke from the guns on the ships and onshore helped to obscure the ships as they passed, making it more difficult for the gunners on both sides to hit their targets. Therefore, if American gunnery was a "mockery," as Buchanan put it, the British gunnery was even worse, given that the Americans sustained no mentionable damage or casualties in the action. The event was a massive disappointment to the Americans, who had hoped for a repeat of the 28 June 1776 battle; but it was not a disgrace to the defenders of the fort. The disgrace belonged entirely to Commodore Whipple, who declined to make good on his promise to defend the ship channel beneath the fort.

The citizens of Charlestown were understandably afraid that the British warships would soon bombard the city. They could not have guessed that the British vice admiral would let his ships sit idle near Fort Johnson for the remainder of the campaign from fear of engaging the American shore batteries in Charlestown. According to Captain Hinrichs, the depression of the Americans following Arbuthnot's entry into the harbor was palpable: "Horror, astonishment, fear, despondency, and shattered hopes seemed to befog their eyes, ears, and hearts to such an extent that they did not fire a single shot at our men, who had jumped upon the parapets of the works!"[49]

Clinton wanted Admiral Arbuthnot to send his ships into the Cooper River in order to complete the encirclement of the city. While Arbuthnot initially agreed to this maneuver, he stalled and procrastinated for weeks. Clinton reported, "I therefore made use of every argument I could think of to impress the Admiral with conviction of its importance, but I could only obtain from him reiterated promises that he would very shortly comply with my desire—not withstanding which I had the mortification to be disappointed, as no attempt was *ever* [original emphasis] made by him to send ships into the Cooper to the end of the siege."[50]

Near the end of the campaign Clinton believed that he was going to have to assault the city because Lincoln was unwilling to capitulate on fair terms. Arbuthnot offered to provide fire support for this endeavor but later changed his mind. "Unless it is intended to land a body of troops under the fire of the ships' guns," he said, "I confess it would be against my better judgment to place the ships against the enemy's batteries."[51]

With Arbuthnot thus unable (or unwilling) to force an entrance into the Cooper River or engage the city with his ships, the Royal Navy served little purpose during the siege except to blockade enemy shipping from entering or leaving the harbor. Since a blockade could have been easily effected from outside the bar, Arbuthnot need not have forced his way past Fort Moultrie to enter the harbor. His sacrifice of *Aeolus* and twenty-seven sailors was thus unnecessary.

In *A Gallant Defense: The Siege of Charleston, 1780,* Carl P. Borick claims that Arbuthnot's crossing of the Charlestown bar was the critical moment of the siege. Borick argues that by entering the harbor, Arbuthnot's fleet was able to cover the rear of Clinton's army, thus allowing Clinton to free up enough manpower to encircle Charlestown. In fact, Borick claims that "had a stout defense of the bar forced Arbuthnot to withdraw, Clinton would have also had to retire" (84). However, Borick's conclusion in this case is incorrect.

Arbuthnot did assume responsibility for the British defenses on James and Morris islands shortly after the admiral entered the harbor on 8 April. Sailors and Royal Marines from the fleet took over positions then manned by the Royal Army on James and Morris islands, freeing up sufficient soldiers for Clinton to send a contingent of troops across the Cooper River. However, it was the *manpower* Arbuthnot lent to Clinton, not the presence of the ships in the harbor, that allowed Clinton his increased freedom of movement. Of course, Arbuthnot could have lent these men to Clinton without pushing his ships into the harbor. So in this respect Borick overrates the importance of the Royal Navy's crossing the bar and entering the harbor because Arbuthnot could have lent Clinton manpower from the fleet at any time.

Many of the troops assigned to the harbor defenses, such as the battalion of the 71st stationed at Cummins Point on Morris Island, were there exclusively to help facilitate the movement of the British ships into the harbor and protect them once they were there. Of course, Clinton would never had bothered to deploy his manpower in this fashion had he known that Arbuthnot would do nothing with his ships once they were in the harbor. In addition, the British were able to supply their army using the Stono

River and the depot near Hudson's House on James Island. Thus, control of Charleston harbor was not needed to supply Clinton's forces.

Clinton needed the Royal Navy inside Charlestown harbor not to cover the rear of his army, but rather to take control of the Cooper River. Had Arbuthnot managed this, the garrison would have been cut off from escape, reinforcement, and resupply. Secondarily, the Royal Navy could have provided fire support if Clinton were forced to storm the city walls, but Arbuthnot was unwilling for his ships to serve that role too.

Therefore, poor leadership on both sides rendered the opposing navies nearly useless during the campaign. Why had the Continental Navy been sent to Charlestown if not to defend the harbor? The South Carolinians could have blocked the entrance of the Cooper River without Commodore Whipple's help. And why did Vice Admiral Arbuthnot force a passage of the bar and risk his ships before Fort Moultrie if he never intended to do more than let them sit idle in the middle of the harbor? The simple explanation is that both naval commanders believed that the contest for Charlestown was going to be decided by the land campaign. With the Royal Navy in unquestioned strategic control of the seas around the city, neither Arbuthnot nor Whipple saw much reason to risk his sailors to gain what he saw as a minor tactical advantage for the benefit of the land troops. Of course, Lincoln and Clinton were exasperated with their naval counterparts, and Clinton said that he never again wanted to serve "with such an old woman" as Arbuthnot.[52]

Captain James Moncrief had overseen the hasty construction of Savannah's defenses that succeeded brilliantly in repulsing the massive French and American assault on 9 October 1779. That achievement had earned the thirty-six-year-old Scotsman a brevet promotion to major in December of that year. It had also gained him the notice of General Clinton, who now put him in charge of engineering the siege works at Charlestown. All who knew Moncrief spoke highly of his courage and character. At the battle of Stono Ferry in June 1779, he personally led a group of men on a daring charge during which they stole an American powder wagon. He now boldly reconnoitered the front lines at Charlestown to plan his engineering works, escorted only by a small bodyguard. Moncrief had certainly earned the trust of many senior officers such as Clinton, who referred to him as an engineer "who understood his business."[53] However, Captain Johann Ewald, while personally fond of Moncrief, found him wanting as an engineer: "I surely believe that for his courage and tireless zeal he would come off badly against any other army in Europe, and that he would not capture a dovecot in a European war. For the excellent men of the English army are as poor besiegers as they are brave soldiers in the field."[54]

Some British and German soldiers complained that Moncrief included too few angles and too few traverses in his trenches and siege works. These shortcomings allowed the Americans to fire their cannons directly down the length of a trench from their flank batteries. Soldiers in the lines also protested that too few saps were dug to allow troops to pass to their duty stations in the trenches without coming under fire from the American batteries.[55]

On 1 April an artillery park was established at the Gibbes plantation (about a mile from the city). This plantation was also the location of the army's supply depot on the Charlestown neck. All the items necessary to conduct the siege were ferried from Linning's Creek on the mainland across the Ashley to the landing at the Gibbes plantation. Soon this spot was a bustling center of activity as boats came and went carrying artillery pieces, entrenching tools, fascines, and other articles of war. "For lack of horses," Captain Ewald wrote, "the sailors and Negroes were used to drag these things to their places." Hundreds of mantelets had been brought from New York and were now assembled at the Gibbes plantation. The mantelets were essentially large wooden shields that would serve as backing for the earthwork redoubts to be constructed. Each mantelet stood on three legs, was six feet high and twelve to sixteen feet long, and required eighteen men to move it. Each redoubt was constructed with sixteen mantelets, each fronted by twelve feet of earth.[56]

At sunset on 1 April, Major Moncrief ordered the work parties (composed of the army soldiers, rather than Negroes) to break ground for three redoubts—one on the main road leading into town and two to the east of the road, at eight hundred yards out from the American lines. The work parties were protected by five hundred light infantrymen who occupied a ditch to their front, while another five hundred grenadiers stood by as a reserve in case the Americans attempted to interfere. Over five hundred workers labored at each redoubt through the night. On the morning of 2 April the Americans awoke to find three sturdy earthwork redoubts in front of their defensive lines on the neck. The American batteries opened fire against the British earthworks but made little impression. The work on the redoubts continued throughout the day, with troops and work parties being relieved by fresh men. However, the majority of work occurred at night when the besiegers were more or less safe from the aimed fire of the American cannons.

The society women of Charlestown still regarded the siege with novel fascination; after all, the town had not yet come under fire from the British artillery. "The women walk out from the town to the lines," General Moultrie noted at the time, "with all the composure imaginable, to see us cannonade the enemy, but I fancy when the enemy begin [to fire] they will make themselves pretty scarce." A few days later an American brigantine "whose deck was crowded with both sexes" brazenly sailed up the Cooper River to fire a few desultory shots at the British earthworks before retiring back to the city.[57]

On the night of 2 April the British constructed a trench that connected the three redoubts made the previous day, and the crews finished a new redoubt west of the road that led into the city. At noon on 3 April the Americans began firing a few artillery pieces, but again without any significant effect. During the night of 3 April the British extended their trench (or "parallel") east to the edge of the Cooper River, where they began building a battery for nine artillery pieces. At the same time they extended the parallel to the west, ending the line with a redoubt and another battery for nine guns;

the last redoubt to the west did not reach the Ashley River but instead was anchored against a swampy creek that emptied into the river.

The Americans responded to the British activity with an all-day bombardment on 4 April. Over six hundred shots were fired from the city's batteries, and the Continental Navy put in a rare appearance in support of the attack. Two American frigates, the *Boston* and the *Providence,* sailed a short way up the Cooper until they were abreast the British redoubt that was against the river. From this position they began firing into the flank and rear of the redoubt. "These vessels surely would have succeeded in destroying the work," wrote Captain Ewald, who was in the redoubt at the time. To rescue the situation, Major Moncrief had eighty sailors drag two twelve-pounders and a howitzer to a promontory that overlooked the river. A few well-placed shots from this ad hoc battery into the hull of the *Boston* convinced the Americans to withdraw, as they could not elevate their guns sufficiently to respond to the British fire. Later that night Moncrief had the redoubt on the river closed in the rear to protect against flanking fire from the river.[58]

While this sortie of the Continental Navy was ineffective, it nevertheless underscored the vulnerability of the British left flank as long as command of the Cooper River remained in American hands. Clinton wanted Arbuthnot to send ships into the Cooper in order to "cover the left of our lines, which was otherwise liable to be enfiladed by the galleys and armed vessels that might run up it [the river] from the town."[59] Arbuthnot assured Clinton that he would send ships into the Cooper, but he never made a serious effort to fulfill this promise.

On 5 April the Americans unleashed an incessant fire that lasted all day and into the night. Captain Hinrichs counted over seven hundred shots fired from American cannons into the British trenches. Though the bombardment wounded only six British soldiers, it did interfere with the crews working on the lines. At about nine o'clock that night General Clinton ordered his battery on Fenwick's Point (nine thirty-two-pounders), directly across the Ashley River from the city, to fire on Charlestown. The guns of this battery were supplemented by those of the galleys and gunboats in the Ashley. "It was a furious cannonade," Captain Hinrichs wrote, "the 32-pounders causing a fearful confusion in the city. One heard nothing but 'Oh, murder! Oh, Lord!'" Captain Ewald confirmed the apparent suffering in the city: "A terrible clamor arose among the inhabitants of the city, since the firing came entirely unexpectedly. During this time I had approached quite close to the city to discover the effect of the batteries, and in the short intervals between the shooting I could hear the loud wailing of female voices, which took all the pleasure out of my curiosity and moved me to tears." Despite the apparent ferocity of the attack, William Moultrie reported only one man killed in the city that night.[60]

As night fell on 6 April, the Americans again attempted to interfere with the British work parties by unleashing a deadly fusillade. The British responded with all their batteries, supplemented by armed galleys in the Ashley River. This compelled the Americans to slack their fire, but not before a British gun at Fenwick's Point was dismounted by an American cannonball from a distance of half a mile. Throughout the siege, both British and German soldiers were impressed at the accuracy of the American fire, which

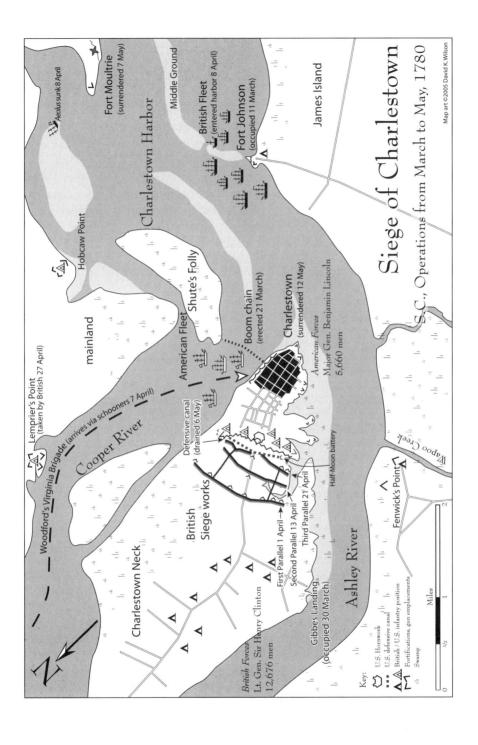

Siege of Charlestown

S.C., Operations from March to May, 1780

Map art ©2005 David K. Wilson

Key:
- U.S. Hornwork
- U.S. defensive canal
- British / U.S. infantry position
- Fortifications, gun emplacements
- Swamp

Miles

0   1/2   1   2

Fort Moultrie (surrendered 7 May)

Aeolus sunk 8 April

Middle Ground

British Fleet (entered harbor 8 April)

Charlestown Harbor

Fort Johnson (occupied 11 March)

James Island

Hobcaw Point

Shute's Folly

American Fleet

Boom chain (erected 21 March)

Charlestown (surrendered 12 May)

American Forces
Major Gen. Benjamin Lincoln
5,660 men

Half-Moon battery

Wappoo Creek

Lemprier's Point (taken by British 27 April)

mainland

Woodford's Virginia Brigade (arrives via schooners 7 April)

Cooper River

Defensive canal (drained 6 May)

Charlestown Neck

British Siege works

British Forces
Lt. Gen. Sir Henry Clinton
12,676 men

First Parallel 1 April
Second Parallel 13 April
Third Parallel 21 April

Gibbes Landing (occupied 30 March)

Ashley River

Fenwick's Point

frequently ravaged redoubts, killed and wounded men, and dismounted guns. "Their artillery was better than ours," Captain Hinrichs confessed after the battle.[61]

At two o'clock in afternoon on 7 April the British were presented with an unexpected and unwelcome sight: "Eleven American schooners and sloops loaded with troops sailed down the Cooper River to the city right before our eyes."[62] It was Brigadier General William Woodford's brigade of Virginia Continentals: close to 900 veterans of Brandywine, Germantown, and Monmouth Court House (not to mention the skirmish at Great Bridge, where Woodford had commanded his first action five years earlier).[63] In addition, 150 North Carolina militiamen under Colonel Harrington joined Woodford's column on the way, making for a total reinforcement of over 1,000 men. Lincoln thus nearly doubled the number of Continentals under his command. The addition of Woodford's and Harrington's men brought Lincoln's total strength up to his "final" figure of about 5,600 troops including the city militia.

Lincoln's greatest worry was that Clinton would cross over the Cooper River and cut his communications with the mainland. Now Lincoln could do something about the threat, as he previously had insufficient manpower to fortify his flanks. "Since the arrival of Genl. Woodford," John Laurens wrote, "Genl. Lincoln will have it in his power to execute his plan of establishing the necessary posts for this purpose on the eastern shore of the river."[64] American morale began to wax higher for the first time in many months, and many who had despaired inside the city now allowed themselves the luxury of hope.

The American celebration of Woodford's arrival was loud enough to be heard by the British in their trenches. "The enemy expressed their joy by firing all their batteries at retreat [sundown], while the garrison gave three huzzahs from their works. From eight to ten [o'clock] in the evening all the bells in the city rang out." The clamor from the American lines was so intense that many British officers thought an attack was under way: "None of us doubted but that the enemy had made a sortie," Captain Hinrichs wrote. "Hence we ran for our arms. Soon, however, came information as to the cause of the enemy's rejoicing."[65]

General Woodford was suitably proud of his men at the completion of their long trek from New Jersey. "After a forced march of 505 miles which we performed in thirty days," Woodford wrote, "I had the pleasure of throwing my troops into town in good health and spirits by the only passage now left open. We arrived the 7th at two o'clock to the great joy of the garrison. Our embarkation was made on the east side of [the] Cooper River, distant from town nine miles."[66] Woodford claimed to have marched 505 miles from Petersburg, Virginia, to Charlestown in thirty days—a prodigious average 16.83 miles a day! Indeed, Woodford claimed to march 20 miles a day when he was not "plagued with a ferry."[67]

Despite their rapid march, there were many desertions among the Virginians as they marched south. This was because many of the soldiers had the not-unfounded belief that South Carolina and Georgia were "unhealthy" and rife with malaria and yellow fever.[68] Common soldiers of that age feared disease more than enemy guns. The aversion most soldiers had to "southern" service was therefore well understood and anticipated by their officers, who sought to decrease desertions through watchful discipline.

General Clinton dismissed the importance of Woodford's arrival: "With respect to the reinforcement, I rejoice at it. They will now defend their town and when we take it, we shall take all in it."[69] Regardless of Clinton's bravado on the matter, it had never been his plan to allow the Americans to freely reinforce the city. Woodford's veterans would dramatically improve Lincoln's ability to defend the town if Clinton was forced to the extremity of an assault. It is notable that Clinton omits mention of the reinforcement in his postwar memoirs. It is also interesting to note that Admiral Arbuthnot, after sitting idle for three weeks in Five Fathom Hole, chose to push his way past Fort Moultrie on 8 April—the day after Woodford's entry into the city. It seems obvious that the arrival of Woodford's brigade (riding comfortably and safely on ships in the Cooper River) finally forced Arbuthnot to acquiesce to Clinton's demand that the fleet enter the harbor in order to help cut off Charlestown from further reinforcement.

⋖⬥⋗

The British had more or less completed the first of the customary three parallels on 9 April 1780. This fact, and the presence of Arbuthnot's squadron in the harbor, seemed reason enough for Clinton to summon General Lincoln to surrender. The correspondence was in the traditional form: an offer of clemency if the city surrendered quickly, coupled with a threat to unleash "the resentment of an exasperated soldiery" if they continued to resist. Lincoln fired back a defiant reply: "Sixty days have passed since it was known that your intentions against this town were hostile in which time has been afforded to abandon it, but duty and inclination point to the propriety of supporting it to the last extremity."[70]

After anchoring inside the harbor, the Royal Navy took over the defense of various harbor posts, such as Fort Johnson on James Island. This freed up sufficient manpower for Clinton to send Lieutenant Colonel James Webster with fourteen hundred men on a mission to cross the Cooper and complete the encirclement of the city. This force consisted of the 33rd and 64th regiments, Lieutenant Colonel Patrick Ferguson's "corps of marksmen," and Lieutenant Colonel Banastre Tarleton's British Legion. Webster was ordered to march thirty-two miles upriver to Monck's Corner and attack the American cavalry that guarded the pass there. This corps, commanded by Brigadier General Isaac Huger, was assigned to protect the American lines of communication from Charlestown to the interior of the state.

Colonel Webster's force started for Monck's Corner on 12 April. Lieutenant Colonel Tarleton commanded the cavalry that formed the vanguard of Webster's column. On the night of 13–14 April, the youthful and energetic Tarleton performed a brilliant night attack on Huger's ill-prepared troops. This action will be examined in full detail in the next chapter; however, it is sufficient to say for the moment that the Americans were easily routed. The British captured a large number of supply wagons and many badly needed cavalry horses after the action. Most importantly, the American "flying" corps was decimated and the passes over the Cooper River secured. The main body of Webster's column was now able to cross over the river into St. Thomas Parish, where they served to threaten or cut off all communications between Charlestown and the rest of the country.

While this important operation was under way, the British were also preparing for a major effort on the Charlestown peninsula. They spent 11 and 12 April building up stockpiles of ammunition and mounting cannons in their batteries, and on Thursday, 13 April, the British opened a fierce cannonade and bombardment at about nine o'clock in the morning. The British fire lasted, with only a few short interruptions, until midnight. For the first time the guns mounted in the batteries of the first parallel were unleashed in full fury, along with the large guns at Fenwick's Point. It was the first effective artillery bombardment the British had made in the siege, and it had a sobering effect on the American defenders.

"An embrazure [sic] at redan No. 7 [was] destroyed," Moultrie recorded. "A sergeant and private of the North-Carolina brigade killed; a twenty-six pounder destroyed, and one eighteen pounder dismounted. . . . Some women and children killed in town."[71] Three houses in the city were set ablaze by hot shot fired from the British lines. General Clinton was not trying to destroy the city, however, and he "let the fire of the batteries get weaker and weaker, giving the enemy time to extinguish the fires."[72] Clinton was later to write that he thought it barbaric to destroy a city that one was attempting to capture. Up to this time the American artillery had been superior to that of the British. However, the intense and accurate British cannonade unleashed on 13 April reduced the effectiveness of American counterbattery fire, and the advantage in gunnery now began to shift toward the British.

During the night of 13 April the British opened their second parallel "1,300 feet in front of their first, 500 feet from the enemy's abatis and wet ditch, and 880 feet from [the Americans'] central fortification."[73] The new trench was within rifle range of the American works, and beginning on 14 April, German jaegers and American riflemen would constantly skirmish attempting to suppress the other side's artillery, interfere with enemy construction parties, and—of course—kill each other. By 20 April the British trenches had been extended to within 250 yards of the American works. The British artillery again unleashed intense and accurate cannon and mortar fire against the city, hitting two American powder magazines, which exploded violently. On the afternoon of 21 April an American drum was heard to beat a parley. All the fighting stopped, and a rumor swept through the British army: The Americans were submitting terms for their surrender.

When the British first crossed the Ashley and took up position on the Charlestown neck, Lincoln became anxious for the safety of his lines of communication on the east side of the Cooper and Wando rivers. There was nothing to prevent the British from portaging their flatboats over the Charlestown peninsula in order to ferry troops across the Cooper and so cut the city's supply lines to the countryside. Lincoln therefore developed a plan to safeguard his communications by securing and fortifying certain key passes over the Cooper and Wando rivers, including Lampriers Point directly across from the city, Cainhoy meetinghouse on the Wando (where the Americans already had a hospital for military invalids), and Monck's Corner and Biggin's Bridge on the upper reaches of the Cooper.[74] Supply depots were established at Cainhoy and Monck's Corner to support operations in the country.

Although the plan was theoretically sound, Lincoln did not have nearly enough manpower to make it work. Before Woodford's brigade arrived, Lincoln could not even adequately man the fortifications of the city. He certainly did not have sufficient forces to defend a series of posts reaching thirty miles or more into the countryside. After Woodford entered the city on 7 April, Lincoln finally had enough troops to establish his post at Lampriers Point, but he still needed more men to guard the other passes. At that time the only American presence worth mentioning in the countryside was General Huger's "flying corps" of four hundred cavalry and a handful of militia—a force obviously inadequate to the task of guarding such a long frontier.

The only solution to the shortage was to draft more militiamen. Few of the country militiamen had reported for duty in the city (despite repeated orders to do so) because they feared smallpox in the town—or at least that was their excuse. Lincoln urgently sought a compromise. If the country militiamen would not serve in the city, would they be willing to defend the river passes outside the town? In pursuit of this goal Lincoln implored Governor Rutledge to leave the city and personally recruit and organize the state militia.

Initially Rutledge refused to depart the town, believing that "the citizens would say he left them in a time of danger."[75] Lincoln finally wrote a letter to the governor, signed by him and all the senior Continental officers, requesting him to leave immediately for the sake of the army and the city. Rutledge relented to Lincoln's entreaty, acknowledging that he was the only one with sufficient authority and moral presence to command in the countryside. On 13 April, Governor Rutledge left the city, taking the three moderate members of the privy council along to help him in his duties (and so that it would appear less as though Rutledge alone were abandoning the town). Before departing, Rutledge appointed his political rival Christopher Gadsden to the post of lieutenant governor pro tem. The four other "radical" members of the privy council remained behind with Gadsden to run the civil government in Charlestown. Gadsden and his radicals were stalwart believers in American independence. They had opposed Rutledge's offer to surrender the city the previous year and were not about to abandon the town now. The twentieth-century historians Stanly Godbold and Robert Woody wrote, "[Gadsden] had said many times that he would give his life for the cause of American liberty, and he probably believed that the city might survive the attack."[76]

Once Rutledge was safely outside Charlestown, he sent letters to the militia commanders telling them to rendezvous on the north bank of the Santee River. "Meet me there with as many volunteers as you can collect," the governor told one officer. Rutledge directed that the militiamen should turn out "cheerfully and speedily on this occasion, especially as the circumstances to which the country militia seem averse, viz. —the being confined in town, will not happen—for I don't mean to lead them thither." The Patriot militia was unimpressed by Rutledge's pleas, and over the next few weeks the tone of the governor's summonses became more threatening. "I expect to be met by the full number which I have called for," Rutledge wrote. "Every defaulter may be assured that my Proclamation of last month [to confiscate a shirker's property] shall most certainly be carried into execution against him." Yet even these threats did not bring out the state militiamen in large numbers.[77]

Only after the fall of Charlestown did the full value of Governor Rutledge's efforts became realized. "It was very fortunate for the province," Moultrie said in later years, "that the governor was not made a prisoner in town. His presence in the country kept everything alive, and gave great spirits to the people to have a man of such great abilities, firmness, and decision amongst them. He gave commissions, raised new corps, embodied the militia. . . . In short, he did everything that could be done for the good of the country."[78] It seemed that as long as Governor Rutledge was in the field, the government of the state lived on in him. It is probable that without Rutledge's efforts the famed partisan corps of Francis Marion—the "Swamp Fox"—and Thomas "Gamecock" Sumter would never have been formed. (The story of those successful campaigns is outside the scope of this narrative.) In this way Governor Rutledge redeemed himself for his less stalwart behavior when Charlestown had been threatened by General Prevost the previous year.

The same day that Rutledge left the city, Lincoln held a council of war at which he reviewed the strategic situation for his officers. The situation was bleak. The garrison was outnumbered at least two or three to one, and only half of the American force was composed of regulars. The Royal Navy was in the harbor, and its presence threatened the city's last communication with the mainland over the Cooper River. Worst of all, the Continental engineers said that the city's fortifications were "only field works . . . and could not hold out but few days more." Thus, Lincoln put the question to his officers: Should they consider "evacuating the garrison?" Brigadier General Lachlan McIntosh of Georgia was the first to respond: "I gave it as my own opinion that as we were so unfortunate as to suffer ourselves to be penned up in the town & cut off from all resources . . . we should not lose an hour longer in attempting to get the Continental troops at least out, while we still had one side open yet over the Cooper River, upon whose safety, the salvation not only of this state but some other will probably depend."[79]

The other officers present acquiesced to the brigadier's argument, but Lincoln hesitated. The deliberative general told his officers that "he only desired now that we should consider maturely of the expediency & practicability of such a measure by the time he would send for us again."[80] Lincoln would find out the next day (14 April) that General Huger's cavalry at Monck's Corner had been attacked and routed.[81] While the Americans held Lampriers Point they could still evacuate the city. However, because of the presence of British troops east of the Cooper, the garrison could no longer escape into the interior of the state without a fight. Lincoln thought that he had time to consider withdrawal, but it was probably now already too late.

For the next few days the British continued their methodical advance on the city. The Americans resisted by building rifle pits to annoy the British work parties and repositioning their cannons to counter the British approaches. Despite the Americans' best efforts, British operations were not impeded to any noticeable degree. A new two-gun battery built by the Royal Navy on James Island proved especially accurate and bothersome to the Americans. A ball from this battery hit the steeple of St. Michael's Church in the center of town, which the Americans were using as an observation post. The structure had been painted black in a futile effort to make it less visible, but the British reported that this actually made the tower "more conspicuous than ever."[82]

Despite the intensity of the British attacks, civilian casualties were relatively light. This was of little comfort to the families of those killed and wounded in the constant bombardment. Almost every day citizens and soldiers in the city were hit, with particularly poignant examples being a child and its wet nurse killed on 13 April and a man killed and a woman wounded while asleep in bed together on the 17th.[83] Nevertheless, by all accounts the civilians at Charlestown fared much better during the siege than those at Savannah had during the French and American siege and bombardment of that city in 1779. This was in large part due to the humanity of Sir Henry Clinton, who spared the city the full wrath of his artillery, although he hit the town enough to make the inhabitants' situation sufficiently uncomfortable.

On Tuesday, 18 April 1780, about forty Virginia dragoons of General Huger's command straggled into the city by way of the ferry over the Cooper River at Lampriers Point. Though he already had news of the defeat of Huger's cavalry, General Lincoln now heard from these refugees the full extent of the debacle at Monck's Corner. With a force of British infantry and cavalry now on the "Hobcaw" or "Wando" neck—only a few hundred yards from the city east of the Cooper River—Lincoln could feel the noose being tightened. He sent General Charles Scott and the Corps of Light Infantry over to Lampriers Point with "private orders" to secure an "advantageous bridge [over Hobcaw Creek] for the retreat of the army and to keep open the communication."[84]

Meeting at General Moultrie's quarters on 20 April, many officers openly lamented the fact that the garrison had not withdrawn seven days earlier when a retreat was first proposed and there were no enemy troops east of the Cooper. Any attempt to escape now would obviously be contested. Lincoln's hesitation had cost them dearly. The Americans did not have enough boats to get all their troops over the river in one movement; therefore, any evacuation would take many hours, increasing the chance of its being discovered. If the British perceived an American withdrawal, they would certainly open fire on the American boats with gunboats they had dragged into the Cooper River. Most importantly, one had to assume that General Clinton would immediately storm the city and attempt to destroy the American army while its back was against the river.

General McIntosh proposed leaving the militia to hold the fortifications until the Continental troops withdrew. It was a logical solution but not a pragmatic one. It was foolish to believe that the militiamen—the amateur soldiers—would sacrifice themselves on the battlements while the Continentals—the professionals—ran away. Even if the militia did not lay down their arms as soon as their blue-coated brethren dipped their oars, they would certainly take to their heels at the first huzzah of Clinton's grenadiers. The American officers had to face the reality that there was no hope for victory and little hope for escape. Was it now time to capitulate? Championing the case for surrender was Colonel Jean Baptiste Joseph de Laumoy of the engineers. They were surrounded, he argued, making retreat "impractical." Moreover, according to Laumoy, the city's fortifications, "if they were worthy of being called so," could not hold out for "many days longer." Surrender, Laumoy said, was the only sensible option.[85]

The conference took an unexpected turn when Lieutenant Governor Christopher Gadsden "happened to come in," as Lachlan McIntosh put it, "by accident or design." Given that the surrender of the city was being contemplated, it seemed conspicuous that no civilian leaders were invited to advise or at least observe the council proceedings. An embarrassed General Lincoln presently asked Gadsden to sit as a member of the council, though there was no legal requirement for a civilian to participate in a military council. Accepting the invitation, Gadsden said that he was "surprised and displeased" that the military officers "had entertained a thought of capitulation or evacuating the garrison."[86]

Gadsden proceeded to "use the council very rudely." He unleashed a lengthy tirade against the Continental officers and was especially disrespectful of General Lincoln. "The militia were willing to live upon rice alone rather than give up the town on any terms," Gadsden said. He then added, "Even the old women were so accustomed to the enemy's shot now that they travelled the streets without fear or dread." Meanwhile, the four remaining members of the privy council—Thomas Ferguson, Richard Hutson, Benjamin Cattell, and David Ramsay—had somehow managed to find the meeting place and now joined the debate. Councilman Ferguson said that he had seen the boats the Continentals were gathering to make good their escape. He then declared that if an evacuation were attempted, "He would be among the first who would open the gates for the enemy and assist them in attacking us before we got aboard."[87]

In a final affront to General Lincoln for the evening, Colonel Charles Cotesworth Pinckney, commander of the 1st South Carolina Continental Regiment, forgot "his usual politeness [and] addressed Genl. Lincoln in great warmth and [in] much the same strain as the lt. governor."[88] To be abused by civilian politicians is to be expected by military officers, but Lincoln was Pinckney's superior officer. Lincoln tolerated the insubordination with dignity; but one must ask at what point the admirable qualities of patience and tolerance become the undesirable qualities of indecision and weakness.

"I was myself so much hurt by the repeated insults given to the commanding officer," General McIntosh wrote, "in so public a manner—and obliquely to us all through him—that I could not help declaring [that since] it was thought impracticable to get the Continental troops out, I was for holding the garrison to the last extremity." Colonel Laumoy objected, saying, "We were already come to the last extremity, or if we were not of that opinion, desired to know what we called the last extremity." Nevertheless, McIntosh's proposal to continue the fight was approved by the council, and the daylong debate finally ended.[89]

Clearly there was a power struggle between the civilian leaders and the military authorities occurring at the council. However, the struggle was also one between a Charlestown faction and a national or Continental faction, as was indicated by the verbal attack of South Carolina native Colonel Pinckney on General Lincoln. The prime goal of the national faction was to preserve the army to fight another day, while the Charlestown faction placed the security and property of the state capital as paramount.

Gadsden and the councilmen have been characterized as hotheads who would not give up the fight. However, this is an oversimplification of their position. Gadsden made it clear that he supported continued resistance, but he also said that if the military was "determined to capitulate he had his terms in his pocket ready."[90] In other words, Gadsden was not against surrender per se—he even had terms ready if that was what Lincoln wanted—but he was adamantly against the abandonment of the city by the Continentals. In addition, it was the possibility of evacuation by the Continentals—*not surrender*—that prompted the outright seditious statements by Councilman Ferguson as well as Colonel Pinckney's insubordination. As far as Gadsden was concerned, fighting on was preferable, surrender was acceptable, but the withdrawal of the garrison was entirely out of the question.

Gadsden, Pinckney, and the other councilmen believed that letting the Continentals leave would mean disaster for the town. If the British detected the Continentals attempting to escape, Clinton would surely make an assault in an attempt to stop them. The possibility of street fighting was inconceivable to the civilian leadership. The British might even burn the city in their wrath. Even if it had been possible for the Continentals to leave undetected, the civilian leadership would not have allowed it. This was because the only way the city could get favorable terms during surrender negotiations was for the Americans to threaten to continuing fighting. Without the Continentals, the city would be open for the British to take without terms, and the lives and property of the Patriot citizens would be without protection. In other words, the Continental Army was the only bargaining chip the city fathers had, and they were not about to let it go.

General Lincoln understood Gadsden's position all too well, which is why he began preparations to withdraw in secret—an aspect of this campaign that has gone largely unreported by historians. It could never have been far from Lincoln's thoughts that Governor Rutledge had nearly surrendered the city (and the state!) less than a year earlier to General Prevost. Everyone who attended Lincoln's councils was sworn to secrecy, and the main topic at each of Lincoln's councils was the subject of evacuation. It was certainly no accident that civilian leaders were omitted from the councils.[91] During the "siege" of 1779 General Moultrie yielded the power of parley and capitulations to Governor Rutledge. General Lincoln did not make any such concessions to the civilian government now.

On 18 April fourteen additional British ships appeared just off the Charlestown bar. These ships carried twenty-five hundred reinforcements from New York that Clinton had requested two months earlier. Clinton now had enough troops to secure his lines of communications over the Cooper River and reinforce the fourteen hundred troops under Webster with enough force to prevent any American breakout. The next day, 21 April 1780, cannon fire from the British guns on the Charlestown neck managed to hit and ignite two American powder magazines. No one was hurt in the spectacular explosions that followed, but the hits demonstrated the increasing accuracy and effectiveness of the British batteries on the neck. That night British sappers began construction of the third and final parallel. "We have now approached so close," Captain Ewald wrote, "that one could easily throw a stone into the advanced ditch on the other side, which is dressed with pointed trees [abatis]."[92]

The increasing accuracy of the enemy's guns, the proximity of the British siege works, and the news of British reinforcements induced Lincoln to call another council of war. Once again purposefully leaving the civilian leadership out, Lincoln asked his officers a third time if they should evacuate or capitulate. "Colo. Lamoy still insisting upon the impossibility of holding out the garrison much longer," McIntosh reported, "and a retreat seeming to him impractical, proposed that . . . [honorable] terms of capitulation should first be offered, which possibly might be accepted by Genl. Clinton, or, if it did not succeed that we might then attempt a retreat if we thought it could be accomplished."[93]

With the sails of the British reinforcement fleet looming on the horizon, it seemed that Colonel Laumoy would have his way. The officers present voted to propose terms for surrender—they pretended that if the terms were refused they might still attempt to evacuate later. At about three o'clock in the afternoon on Friday, 21 April, Lincoln ordered a drummer up to the parapet to beat a parley. The drum's patter drifted across no-man's-land, and both sides ceased their fire. An American messenger then crossed to Clinton's camp carrying a note from Lincoln that requested a six-hour truce—which Clinton granted—so that the Americans could draft terms for their surrender.

Calling only Colonel Jean Baptiste Ternant of the engineers to his quarters to collaborate, Lincoln drew up the terms and in a few hours submitted them to Clinton and Arbuthnot. To say that Lincoln's terms expressed wishful thinking is an understatement. Lincoln proposed surrendering Charlestown to the British on the condition that the American troops be allowed to freely exit the town carrying their arms, artillery, and baggage. Clinton later wrote, "The articles proposed by the rebel General were . . . so much beyond what we thought he had a right to expect that we immediately rejected them."[94]

Receiving Clinton's refusal, Lincoln put the question to his officers once again: Should they evacuate? "It was unadvisable," they said, "because of the opposition made to it by the civil authority and the inhabitants, and because, even if they could succeed in defeating a large body of the enemy posted in their way, they had not a sufficiency of boats to cross the Santee [River] before they might be overtaken by the whole British army."[95] At about nine o'clock that evening the British batteries recommenced their fire, which was responded to in kind by the Americans. Both sides kept up the exchange all night.

The next day, Saturday, 22 April, the British continued to advance their siege works, making significant encroachments in front of the "Half-Moon" battery on the American left. On Sunday, 23 April, the British pushed their trenches to within twenty yards of the American defensive canal. The threat posed by the rapid British advances over the weekend necessitated some response by Lincoln, who determined that it was time to mount a sortie. A successful sortie would also help Lincoln in his negotiations: Showing that the Continental troops still had plenty of fight in them might help win more favorable terms from the British.

Just before dawn on 24 April 1780, a detachment of nearly three hundred picked light infantrymen from the Virginia and South Carolina regiments assembled behind the Half-Moon battery, the farthest left and most advanced redoubt of the American fortifications. A smaller group of soldiers formed behind the main gate in the Hornwork in the center of the lines.[96] Lieutenant Colonel William Henderson of the South Carolina Continentals commanded the force, having previously proved his ability to lead light troops in the Stono Ferry battle. At daybreak Henderson led his men silently out of the Half-Moon redoubt and the Hornwork. There was just enough light so that Henderson could make his way forward, but it was not yet bright enough for accurate musketry. It was the perfect time to make an attack on a fortified position. The British third parallel had trenches on both wings that did not yet meet in the middle, where a large gap of solid ground existed between the wings.[97] Part of the American force charged over this gap, while Colonel Henderson led the rest into the trench on the British right, which was guarded by a group of twenty-five British light infantrymen and thirty jaegers under Lieutenant von Winzingeroda.

The British guard had just been changed when someone yelled, "D[amn] me the rebels are there!"[98] Lieutenant Colonel Henderson's troops attacked, "bayonet in hand, without firing a shot."[99] To insure that his troops would not fire (and so hold up the advance), Henderson had them uncock their guns and remove their primings. As the Americans approached Lieutenant von Winzingeroda's position, his jaegers unleashed a scattered volley from their short German rifles. As the Americans had anticipated, it was too dark for the jaegers to aim accurately, and so not one of Henderson's men was hit; nor did the jaegers have enough time to reload their rifles before the Americans were upon them. The Continental light infantrymen leaped into the trench and bayoneted several Hessian and British soldiers. The ferocity of the American attack unnerved the British light infantrymen, who fled the trench and ran for the safety of the second parallel a hundred yards behind them. Lieutenant von Winzingeroda and his thirty jaegers were thus left "to pay for the feast," as Johann Ewald later put it.[100]

Captain Hinrichs was in command of the left wing of the British third parallel during the American sortie, and he was in an excellent position to see the action to his right. "The enemy was upon them too quickly," Hinrichs wrote. "They could not make a stand with discharged rifles against bayonets." With only their hunting swords to defend themselves, several of the Hessians were killed and several more were captured. The remaining jaegers abandoned the trench and ran back to the safety of the second parallel.[101]

Meanwhile, Captain Hinrichs ordered his troops—thirty Hessian jaegers and twelve Scottish grenadiers of the 42nd Black Watch Regiment—to fire on the flank of Americans who had overrun the right wing of the third parallel. In addition, British troops in the second parallel began firing on the Continentals. With the British now alert to the attack, Lieutenant Colonel Henderson chose to withdraw. As the Americans began falling back, the British soldiers in the second parallel rose up and charged after them. At that moment the American artillery opened fire, forcing the British back into their trenches.

The whole sortie lasted only a few minutes. Returning to their lines, Henderson's troops suffered one killed and two wounded. The single fatal casualty was Captain Thomas

Moultrie, the younger brother of General William Moultrie, who had been serving in the South Carolina light infantry. The Americans estimated that they killed about fifteen to twenty in the trenches with bayonets, while they captured twelve British and Germans, seven of whom were wounded. Ewald put British/German losses at two killed, four wounded, and ten captured. Hinrichs said that there was one killed, seven wounded, and three captured, but his figures are obviously too low. In this case the American estimates are probably correct.

Following the sortie the two sides exchanged massive amounts of small arms and cannon fire in a daylong firefight. At eight o'clock that evening Colonel Parker of the 1st Virginia Detachment and several of his men were looking over the parapet of the Half-Moon battery when a platoon of Hessian jaegers fired a well-aimed volley at them. Parker, who had led his regiment during its bloody assault on the Spring Hill redoubt at Savannah, was instantly killed. Two Virginians at his side were also shot dead, and seven others were wounded. One of Parker's officers later wrote, "He died immediately. His character is so well known, it need not be said how much he is regretted."[102]

Around midnight the British work crews and their supporting infantrymen saw, or thought they saw, about twenty or thirty Americans gathering in front of the Horn-work where Henderson's men had sortied that morning. Thinking that the Americans were preparing to attack again, the British infantry began firing while the work crews gave the alarm, which was to shout "Hurray!" three times.[103] "A fatal signal, indeed!" Captain Hinrichs wrote. "Everyone repeated the signal; the workmen ran back; the second parallel saw them coming, heard the 'Hurray!' believed they were enemies, and fired. Within a short time there was a tremendous fire of musketry, cannon, and shell on both sides. It was two o'clock in the morning before everyone realized that it was a mistake. We had an officer killed (71st) and more than fifty killed and wounded. Besides, our working parties could accomplish little or nothing during the night."[104]

Lieutenant Colonel Henderson's sortie was thus successful in causing British casualties, both directly and indirectly, through the friendly-fire incident. In addition, the anxiety and confusion in the British trenches prevented any progress on the siege lines that day. The sortie also accomplished Lincoln's goal of showing Clinton that the American troops (the Continentals, at least) still had plenty of fight left in them. Despite the success of the raid, this was the only sortie that Lincoln would order during the siege. David Ramsay argued that Lincoln could not make more sorties because he had too few men to risk, but this explanation is not satisfactory. General Prevost, for example, had made two sorties at the siege of Savannah the previous year even though he had fewer troops than Lincoln did at Charlestown. "I cannot understand why General Lincoln makes hardly any sorties," wrote Captain Ewald at the time.[105]

Strategically the most significant event of 24 April was not Henderson's sortie; rather it was the movement of Lord Cornwallis across the Cooper River with twenty-four hundred troops. This brought the number of British troops on the east side of the Cooper up to almost four thousand—more than enough to prevent any possible break-out by Lincoln's army. The next afternoon Cornwallis took control of the American post at Mount Pleasant (a.k.a. Haddrells Point) after a brief skirmish. American communication with the mainland was now under greater threat than ever.

This event prompted Lincoln to recall his Continental troops from his outlying posts, replacing them with militiamen. Lincoln left no explanation for this action, but it may be assumed that by this time he knew the end was near and did not want his best troops wasted in peripheral actions. Strangely, Lincoln only withdrew about half of the 1st South Carolina Continentals from Fort Moultrie, leaving the fort's defense to Lieutenant Colonel William Scott, who commanded about 100 Continentals and 150 South Carolina militiamen.

On 26 April, Brigadier General Louis Duportail, commandant of the Corps of Engineers for the Continental Army, managed to slip into the city after a three-week journey from Philadelphia. Duportail (formally, Louis le Begue de Presle du Portail) had been sent by Congress to aid Lincoln in his defense of the city. After giving Duportail some time to view the city's fortifications, General Lincoln called another council of war to discuss the chief engineer's observations as well as dispatches he brought from Congress.[106] The news from Philadelphia was not encouraging: No more reinforcements were coming from Washington's main army (then at Morristown, New Jersey). Congress had, Duportail said, only recently recommended to General Washington that he send the Maryland line southward, but the commander in chief had yet to act on the resolution.

As for the city's defensive works, Duportail was unimpressed. Echoing Colonel Laumoy's arguments of past councils, Duportail said that the defensive works were only "field lines" that could provide protection for only a few more days.[107] According to William Moultrie: "As soon as General Du Portail came into the garrison and looked at the enemy, and at our works, he declared they were not tenable and that the British might have taken the town ten days ago. He wished to leave the garrison immediately, but General Lincoln would not allow him because it would dispirit the troops."[108] Duportail's report (not to mention his desire to depart!) was discouraging, to say the least. The atmosphere now became even more melancholy within the American camp with the feeling that "nothing was left for us [to do] but to make the best terms we could."[109] Attempting to make himself useful, Duportail set about doing what he could to improve the American defenses. His primary contribution was ordering the Hornwork and other redoubts to be closed at the rear so that they could not be taken easily from behind. General Lincoln also set Duportail about the task of turning the Hornwork into a kind of inner keep where the entire army could retreat if they were forced from their lines. Apparently Duportail ordered the garrison to light barrels of turpentine along the front lines to prevent a surprise attack at night, which was done from this time until the end of the siege.

The next day, 27 April, Lord Cornwallis moved against an American redoubt at Lampriers Point. Colonel Francis Malmady commanded seventy-five North Carolina militiamen in the redoubt. Malmady's Revolutionary War career was generally marked by energy and spirit; in this case, however, he withdrew his men into the city without firing a shot. Fortunately, Malmady did find time to spike the four eighteen-pounders in the redoubt before evacuating. The giving up of this critical post—the city's most practical point of communication with the mainland—caused great consternation in Charlestown. The mainland side of the harbor and rivers was now entirely in the hands of the enemy, and Fort Moultrie was now the only post held by the Americans outside the narrow confines of the city.

Many American officers, including General Lincoln, were apparently none too pleased that Malmady yielded the post to Cornwallis without a fight. Lincoln demanded a written report of the incident from Colonel Malmady. The reality is, given the low state of morale in the garrison at the time, there was no way that Malmady, with only a handful of disillusioned militiamen, could have been expected to defend Lampriers Point. (A few days earlier Lincoln had withdrawn the Continental light infantrymen who had been guarding the post.) Nevertheless, the French colonel became an unpopular figure in the garrison and was encouraged by Lincoln to leave. Malmady and several other supernumerary officers who had no commands left the city but were soon captured by the British. Malmady was apparently exchanged within a few months and, according to Mark Boatner's *Encyclopedia of the American Revolution*, continued to serve in the theater leading partisan operations against the British occupation forces (670).

Matters now began to devolve quickly toward the inevitable conclusion. The British continued to work on their third parallel, which they completed on 29 April. The British sappers then pierced the dam on the right of the American defensive canal, though it took almost a week to empty the water from it. For the next few days both sides continued to improve their works. The British continued to advance and build batteries in their third parallel, while the Americans continued to improve their defenses and dig counterapproaches.

Vicious firefights involving small arms, cannons, and mortars became increasingly common as the distance between the two sides narrowed at places to only a few yards. Contemporary journals paint a vivid picture of the fighting: At one point a cannonball struck a group of seven German jaegers as they marched to their positions in the trenches. "One of them lost a leg, a second received a wound in the thigh (from the same shot), and the other five were injured by splinters of a felled tree against which the ball struck."[110] An American journal records of this time: "Severe firing of cannon, mortars, and small arms continued on both sides. Lt. Campen and Ensign Hall of No. Caro. [were] wounded badly [along with] Lt. Philips of the Virginians; privates killed and wounded not known—there are so many."[111]

The German jaegers were successful in reducing the effectiveness of the American artillery. "The jägers, to be sure, kept them sufficiently under control," Captain Hinrichs wrote, "so that they could not open their embrasures often and could fire only a furtive shot from some gun or other. . . . I had my men fill three hundred sandbags in the course of the day, and with them they made regular rifle embrasures on the parapet, opening on those of the enemy." According to William Moultrie, "When the enemy's third parallel was completed, we had sandbags placed on top of our lines for the riflemen to fire through. The sandbags were about two feet long and one foot thick. We laid down first two of them, three or four inches one from the other, and a third laid upon the top of the two, which made a small loophole for the riflemen to fire through, the British immediately followed our example: many [of the enemy] were killed and wounded through these holes."[112]

Despite the impressive resistance by the Continental riflemen on the front lines, the American situation was rapidly degenerating. The draining of the defensive canal was complete on 6 May, and the next day Fort Moultrie surrendered to a party of Royal

Marines. By this time the defenses of the fort were being maintained at a minimal level, its garrison consisting only of some three companies (118 men total) of the 1st South Carolina Continental Regiment of Foot and 100 South Carolina militiamen. The fort's commander, Lieutenant Colonel William Scott, surrendered the post without firing a shot. However, by this time the fort was serving little purpose in the defense of the city. William Moultrie said, "After the British fleet had passed Fort Moultrie, it was no longer of use to us, but rather a dead weight."[113] Nevertheless, the civilians in Charlestown looked at the fall of the fort as a bad omen: "This fort by many people was reckoned impregnable. . . . The affair damp'd the spirits of the citizens, tho not of the Army."[114]

There had been no access to live cattle on the mainland since the British had taken Lampriers Point, and by 8 May the remaining small amount of meat in the city had been depleted. The army's butcher had not properly salted the army's beef stocks, and the meat had spoiled; this man was now "very roughly handled" by some of the soldiers.[115] The garrison's rations were reduced to rice, sugar, and coffee only. It was not long before the supply of sugar and coffee ran low, and false rumors began to spread that the rice was nearly gone. There were actually ample supplies of rice in the city—802,000 pounds according to the commissary return of 5 May—but the soldiers did not consider rice to be adequate fare by itself.[116] As one soldier put it, there were "hungry guts in the garrison."[117]

The spirit of the Americans, which had held up well under the combat, began to collapse because of empty stomachs. General Clinton now sent a messenger with a rather sternly worded letter to Lincoln: "The fall of Fort Sullivan [i.e., Moultrie], the destruction on the sixth instant of what remained of your cavalry, the critical period to which our approaches against the town has [*sic*] brought us, mark this as the term of your hopes of succor, could you have framed any, and as an hour beyond which resistance is temerity. By this last summons therefore, I throw to your charge whatever vindictive severity exasperated soldiers may inflict on the unhappy people, whom you devote by persevering in a fruitless defense."[118]

General Lincoln received the letter on 8 May and, for the first time, consulted with Lieutenant Governor Christopher Gadsden on the matter of drafting terms of surrender. As was his gentlemanly manner, Clinton graciously extended the period of cessation of hostilities to the late afternoon in order to give Lincoln time to consult with the civilian leadership. At about four o'clock Lincoln sent his terms to Clinton, which were much less demanding than before. Lincoln now understood that the Continental troops, at least, would be surrendered prisoners of war and the city turned over in its entirety to the British.

However, Lincoln was still seeking unusual concessions for the militiamen and the propertied townspeople. Specifically, article 4 of the terms asked for the militia to be "permitted to return to their respective homes, and be secured in their persons and properties," rather than remain prisoners of war along with the Continental soldiers. Article 10 was the most peculiar, though, and clearly shows the influence of Christopher Gadsden and the propertied interests he represented: "Art. 10. That twelve months time be allowed all such as do not choose to continue under the British government, to dispose of their effects, real and personal, in the state without any molestation whatever;

231

or to remove such part thereof as they choose, as well as themselves and families, and that during that time, they, or any of them, may have it in their option to reside occasionally in town or country."[119]

This article would have allowed all the Patriots the right to live anywhere they wanted, move their families and property in and out of the city at will, and sell or relocate their property as they saw fit. In short, the Whigs were to be given free reign for at least a year after the occupation of the city by the British. It was a ludicrous proposal, and Clinton knew it. If this article were granted, the Americans would no doubt declare all the property in the city privately owned and not subject to confiscation. Clinton would have no more of this nonsense: The British had won the city and would have what was in it. The British commander had already established an unprecedented "Commissary of Captures" for the very purpose of "legally" and equitably disposing of captured property for the benefit of the soldiers and the army. Patriot merchant vessels at the docks were an especially lucrative asset that the British were not about to let escape under the excuse that they were private property. The next day, 9 May, Clinton sent his counterproposal to Lincoln. On article 4 Clinton made the generous offer to allow the militiamen to return home, but only as prisoners of war on parole. As for article 10, Clinton rejected it out of hand.[120]

General Lincoln held another council of war to discuss the British proposal. "Some persons were clear for opposition," a soldier wrote, "and insisted upon such terms as they were certain would not be complied with, yet ignorant of the most distant means of succor or resource. These people consisting chiefly of those who were possessed of property in the town, joined by only two Continental land and one Naval officer."[121] The council thus refused Clinton's counteroffer and proposed that a commission be appointed to discuss the matter further, but Clinton was in no mood for talk. He felt that his terms were more than fair but that the Americans were obviously "not yet sufficiently humbled to accept them."[122]

"While these flags were passing," Moultrie wrote, "the militia looked upon the business as settled, and without orders, took up their baggage and walked into town, leaving the lines quite defenseless."[123] Even when the negotiations broke off and the men were called back to their arms, many militiamen refused to serve again. The men who did report to duty were greatly disgruntled, and some among them began to grouse that General Lincoln had deceived them about the quantity of stores available to feed the garrison.

At eight o'clock in the morning on 9 May, the cease-fire ended. The Americans gave a loud cheer. "At length," Moultrie wrote, "we fired the first gun, and immediately followed a tremendous cannonade. . . . About 180 or 200 pieces of cannon fired off at the same moment." The British responded in kind. Both sides being so close now, it was the most intense artillery exchange of the siege. "The mortars of both sides threw out an immense number of shells; it was a glorious sight, to see them like meteors crossing each other and bursting in the air. The fire was incessant almost the whole night, cannonballs whizzing and shells hissing continually amongst us, ammunition chests and temporary magazines blowing up, great guns bursting, and wounded men groaning along the lines. It was a dreadful night! It was our last great effort, but it availed us nothing."[124]

The British work crews, despite the volume and intensity of the fire, managed to complete a sap to the American canal. The British had double-barreled muskets distributed along the front lines together with boxes of ammunition in order to keep a constant fire of musketry on the Americans. The pace quickened, and on the night of 10 May, British work crews advanced to the very edge of the American works. "Last night we constructed a gallery [earth bridge, or rampart] over the canal, broke through the abatis under the most terrible fire, and built a lodgment [covered earthwork] about thirty paces from the main fortifications; another one was constructed through the advanced ditch.... Cannon and musketry fire was horrible and certainly almost every minute cost the lives of several men. Without noticing it, due to the frightful musketry fire, the besieged were lucky enough to demolish all our dismantling and breach batteries."[125]

"I begin to think," Clinton wrote, "these people will be blockheads enough to wait the assault. *Je me'en lave les mains* [I wash my hands of them]."[126] Indeed, it was unlikely that Clinton could wait much longer for the Americans to be "humbled" enough to accept reasonable terms. General William Dalrymple had arrived from London on 10 May carrying a letter warning that a French fleet carrying a sizeable land force had left Brest and "might daily be expected on some part of the North American coast."[127] Clinton therefore needed to wrap up matters quickly in South Carolina before the French could intervene in the siege or attack some other British post in America. The average foot soldier also desired to make an assault so that, as Captain Ewald put, "the disagreeable task might come to an end. For the dangers and difficult work were the least of the annoyance: the intolerable heat, the lack of good water, and the billions of sandflies and mosquitoes made up the worst nuisance."[128]

At about nine o'clock on the morning of 11 May, Clinton ordered hot shot to be fired into the city. Several houses were set on fire, "the sight still more terrible and melancholy, whereupon the enemy fire weakened somewhat. The Commander in Chief, who pitied the city being reduced to ashes, issued orders about ten o'clock to stop the firing of red-hot shot, and granted the besieged time to reconsider."[129] That morning no rations were served out to the American soldiers in Charlestown; rice was still available, but military discipline had so broken down that the commissary was unable to distribute the food. There were increasing reports of looting in the city by soldiers, and the militiamen now began to desert in great numbers. A petition signed by numerous militia officers was at this time presented to General Lincoln. It implored him to surrender and said that the soldiers were satisfied with being sent home prisoners of war on parole. Seeing the hopelessness of his situation, Lincoln decided to capitulate before order broke down in the city altogether.

At noon on 11 May the Americans sent forward a white flag. However, amid the intense small-arms fire and the powder smoke on the field, the flag was not seen, and the messenger had to return to the lines. The firing continued until about two o'clock in the afternoon, at which time the Americans were compelled to raise a much larger white flag above the Hornwork. The guns suddenly became silent, and the sound of a drum was heard beating for a parley. Lincoln sent a letter to Clinton stating that, at the request of the townspeople, he was now prepared to accept the terms he previously had rejected: The Continentals were to be taken as prisoners of war, while the militia-men were to be considered prisoners of war on parole and allowed to return to their homes. Article 10 was left rejected. There would be no one-year grace period for Patri-ots to dispose of their property and settle affairs as they saw fit.

The wealth of many South Carolinians existed in the form of black slaves, who un-fortunately received indifferent treatment at the hands of Clinton's army. The histo-rian Edward Lowell wrote: "The slaves of the rebels were confiscated. On the 31st of May ten slaves were given to each regiment starting for New York. The negroes formed part of the booty of the campaign, and thousands of them were shipped to the West Indies to be sold." In addition, Johann Ewald said that General Patterson's corps brought many black slaves as plunder from his short venture into upper Georgia; and Major Moncrief was later accused of being a war profiteer for selling eight hundred slaves captured at Charlestown to Jamaica plantations and pocketing the money for himself.[130]

The morning of 12 May about sixteen hundred to eighteen hundred Continental troops marched out in front of the Hornwork, grounded their arms, and surrendered. "The British then asked," according to William Moultrie, "where our second division was? They were told that these were all the Continentals we had, except the sick and wounded [about six hundred in the hospitals]; they were astonished and said we had made a gallant defense."[131] The Continentals were denied the usual right to march to the surrender with their flags flying and playing an enemy march in defiance. Instead they marched out with their colors cased (rolled up), playing a Turkish march.[132] The Americans had to face the fact that they had reached their lowest point in the war since Washington had been chased out of New York in the winter of 1776.

Only five hundred militiamen marched out that afternoon and grounded their arms. The British rightfully suspected that there were many more militiamen in the city and threatened strict punishment if they did not turn out. "This threat," Moultrie said, "brought out the aged, the timid, the disaffected, and the infirm, many of whom had never appeared during the whole siege, which swelled the number of militia pris-oners to at least three times the number of men we ever had upon duty. . . . However, they would do to enroll on a conqueror's list."[133] Captain Hinrichs observed the sur-render ceremonies with satisfaction. "As soon as the enemy had piled arms," he wrote, "the royal colors were hoisted on the gate and a salute was fired from our encampment with twenty-two cannon. Thereupon the 7th and 63rd Regiments marched into the city with music and flying colors."[134]

Despite the length of the siege and the volume and intensity of the artillery exchanges, the official casualty toll was extremely light on both sides. Official British returns show 76 killed and 189 wounded, for 265 total casualties, or 2 percent of 12,996 in the army. The Americans reported 89 killed and 140 wounded, for 229 total casualties, or 4 per-cent of the 5,660 men engaged. Nearly all of the casualties were Continentals. The Continental officers were held prisoner at the barracks at Haddrells Point, while the Continental soldiers were mostly confined to prison ships. According to David Ramsay, only twenty civilians were killed in the siege.[135] The British took 5,611 prisoners and seized over three hundred cannons. Fewer than one hundred of these guns were pointed at the British on the Charlestown neck, the rest being in storage as spares or in batteries facing the British fleet. Large quantities of stores, gunpowder, foodstuffs, and other items were also taken. The Continental frigates *Ranger, Providence,* and *Congress* were taken, renamed, and made part of the British fleet, along with the French frigate *L'Aven-ture.*[136] The South Carolina navy vessels that escaped being made into a river barrier by the Americans were deemed to be of too poor condition to salvage and so were sunk off the coast.

Soon after all the surrenders had taken place, a careless British soldier threw a loaded musket onto a pile of arms, setting off four thousand pounds of gunpowder in an American magazine. The blast destroyed several houses and killed many Americans and British alike. The primary American magazine with ten thousand pounds of gunpowder was next to the explosion but, being in a bombproof shelter, did not ignite. As it was, about two hundred to three hundred people were killed in the blast, including Captain Collins of the Royal Artillery, who had been twice rescued from drowning on the *Russia Merchant,* "only to be burned to death" in the explosion. At least fifty to sixty British infantrymen and artillerymen guarding the magazine were killed.[137] "The entire siege did not cost us so many artillerymen," Captain Hinrichs later remarked. Civilians in town made up the remainder of the casualties. In addition to the loss of life, two thousand to three thousand muskets were destroyed "which were intended to arm the backcountry people, all of whom are loyalists, or at least pretend to be."[138] This massive blast, anticlimactic and unintentional though it was, truly signaled the end of the siege of Charlestown.

⟫⋯⟪

A month after the surrender General Lincoln, Commodore Whipple, and a small entourage of American officers were allowed to leave Charlestown on parole with the usual condition that they not take part in hostilities until exchanged. Lincoln arrived in Philadelphia on 24 June 1780. From there he wasted little time in returning to his wife and family at his ancestral home in Hingham, Massachusetts (about fifteen miles southeast of Boston). Lincoln immediately set about writing an apologia on his defense of Charlestown. In the apologia, dated 17 July 1780 and addressed to George Washington, Lincoln denied responsibility for the loss of the city. Few blamed him for it, in the sense that all knew that Charlestown would be taken when the king decided to put sufficient resources into that mission. However, Lincoln *was* blamed for the loss of the Southern Department's army. To the question of "Why the army, stores, etc. were not brought off when it appeared that the town could no longer be maintained," Lincoln responded that if he had been supplied all of the troops promised him by Congress and the state governors, he could have held the town at his leisure until he wanted to withdraw. He continued: "The expectation that our succors, when arrived, would so cover up our right [the line of the Cooper and Wando rivers] as to render an evacuation practicable when it should become expedient had been an argument in leading us to attempt a defense. That we had every reason to expect these succors is apparent from the assurances I received from [Congress, and the states of North and South Carolina]." It was not until the defeat of his cavalry at Monck's Corner, Lincoln said, that the situation proceeded beyond his control. "Previous to this unhappy event," Lincoln wrote, "and while we were expecting such ample succors, I leave your Excellency [Washington] to judge whether we could have retreated with honor—and whether the moment of doing it with a probability of success was not lost, or at least, that it could not then be attempted with propriety."[139]

Lincoln's argument is not convincing, however, because by mid-March it was painfully evident that he was not going to be reinforced by anywhere near the number of militiamen promised to him. Even if Lincoln had received the reinforcements pledged, it is foolish in the extreme to believe that groups of ill-armed and inexperienced militia could have held the series of isolated posts along the Cooper that Lincoln needed to protect his flank. Clinton's large, professional army would certainly have swept the militia aside. In short, Lincoln had no business risking his most valuable asset—the army of the Southern Department—on the basis of "hoped-for" or "promised" militia brigades to guard a line of fixed positions that, realistically, could not be held by militia.

In reality, Lincoln's army was captured because of his own indecision and because of South Carolina's turbid politics. The journals of Lachlan McIntosh and William Moultrie make it clear that political pressure from Charlestown's civilian and military leaders is what truly trapped the Continental garrison in the city. Lieutenant Governor Christopher Gadsden practically vetoed the removal of the garrison from the city, and the dissension of Colonel Pinckney and some members of the privy council bordered on mutiny. In the written statement of the war council held on 21 April 1780, the first reason given for not attempting to evacuate the garrison was that "the civil authority was utterly averse to it and intimated in council if it was attempted they would counteract the measure."[140]

Publicly, George Washington never indicted Lincoln—a man he liked and respected —for his command decisions at Charlestown. However, in a private letter to John Laurens dated 26 April 1780 (fifteen days before Lincoln's capitulation), Washington questioned Lincoln's decision to remain in the city. Washington based his criticism on his belief that, once the British fleet penetrated the bar protecting the entrance to the harbor, the city was indefensible: "The impracticability of defending the bar, I fear, amounts to the loss of the town and garrison. At this distance it is difficult to judge for you, and I have the greatest confidence in General Lincoln's prudence; but it really appears to me that the propriety of attempting to defend the town depended on the probability of defending the bar, and that when this ceased, the attempt ought to have been relinquished. In this, however, I suspend a definitive judgement and wish you to consider what I say as confidential."[141]

The above statement by Washington deserves some additional comment, due to the fact that it has often been quoted and deferred to by historians. The presence of an enemy flotilla in Charlestown harbor *should* have rendered the defense of the city impractical; however, most historians seem to forget that once Admiral Arbuthnot's ships passed the bar, they actually contributed little to the battle. Washington wrote his comments while the campaign was still under way; he could never have predicted that the British would allow their ships to perform so little service during the siege. Had they been put to better use, Washington's observation would have been quite correct. As it was, the Royal Navy did not help block American supply lines over the Cooper River, nor did the ships ever fire on the city. It is true that the British warships helped restrict American movements by their presence in the harbor, but this was a minimal contribution. William Moultrie cogently observed: "The [British] fleet was of little service to the besiegers in blocking up our port, as all the reinforcements that we got, or could expect to have, came in by land."[142]

These facts do not diminish Washington's insight, however, because the salient point of his comments is that Lincoln should have given up the defense of the city if and when it was no longer defensible. Lincoln had to have known that to remain in the city would eventually doom his garrison. Lincoln neglects to mention in his apologia that his officers recommended that they evacuate the city as early as 13 April. Had Lincoln heeded their advice immediately, he might have saved the garrison. Instead he procrastinated, and by the time Clinton made the utterly predictable move across the Cooper River to encircle the city, it was too late to escape. Surprisingly, Lincoln's reputation survived the campaign, and Congress never even held a committee of inquiry on the matter.

The British released Lincoln from his parole in October 1780 in exchange for the release of Generals William Phillips and Friedrich Riedesel, both of whom had been captured by the Americans at Saratoga in 1777 (a battle Lincoln helped to win). General Washington was happy to have Lincoln serve as his second in command at the siege of Yorktown in 1781. It was no doubt a sweet moment for Lincoln when Washington insisted that the same humiliating terms granted the Charlestown garrison regarding the honors of war be imposed on the defeated British garrison at Yorktown. The British army had to march out with their colors cased and their drums beating a British or German march. (Cornwallis chose "The World Turned Upside Down," a popular British tune at the time.)

The victory at Charlestown was Sir Henry Clinton's greatest triumph. He had overcome both enemy opposition and lack of cooperation from the Royal Navy, and he had accomplished his mission with minimal casualties. However, one must question whether Clinton's slow and deliberate approach would have worked as well against an opponent who commanded greater resources or showed more creativity in the defense. James Moncrief also earned accolades in the victory. Though some soldiers questioned his ability, results are what count in the history books. The brilliant defense of Savannah and the efficient investment and reduction of Charlestown earn Moncrief an honored place in the annals of British military engineering. Moncrief would lose his life in battle with the French while serving as chief engineer at the British siege of Dunkirk in 1793.

With the fall of Charlestown, the United States lost not only the center of commerce in the South, but also the logistic infrastructure of the Southern Department. For the first time in the war a major American army had been captured. Including William Moultrie, William Woodford, Charles Pinckney, Francis Malmady, Barnard Beekman, and William Thompson, almost all the officers and soldiers who had fought the war in the South for the last five years were now in British custody. Woodford, along with hundreds of other prisoners captured at Charlestown, would die in captivity before the war ended. The debacle at Charlestown erased the South Carolina and Georgia Continental regiments from the American order of battle, and the North Carolina and Virginia Continental lines never fully recovered from the blow.

Certainly, Charlestown was an outstanding British success, but the Southern Strategy's principal of economy of force was abandoned to make the conquest possible. Germain's original plan was for General Prevost's forces in Georgia to marshal enough Loyalist support (six thousand backcountry Tories) to take South Carolina unaided by further reinforcements. However, this plan had failed so completely that the capture of Charlestown was made possible only by Clinton's infusion of more than ten thousand additional British soldiers into the theater. Indeed, the danger that Georgia would soon be lost necessitated Clinton's invasion of South Carolina. Victory had been achieved, but the British should not have looked at it as vindication of the Southern Strategy; it remained to be seen if the British could take the fruits of victory in the southern backcountry, where it was still hoped and believed that a Loyalist majority resided.

ORDER OF BATTLE: CHARLESTOWN, 1780

South Carolina, 1 February–12 May 1780

American Forces[143] (in Charlestown at the time of its surrender)
Maj. Gen. Benjamin Lincoln

	MEN	ARTILLERY
Brig. Gen. Charles Scott's Brigade		
2nd S.C. Continental Regt.—		
Col. Francis Marion	246	
3rd S.C. Continental Regt.—		
Col. Wm. Thompson	258	
1st Virginia Continental Detach.—		
Col. Richard Parker,		
then Lt. Col. Samuel Hopkins	258	
2nd Virginia Continental Detach.—		
Col. Wm. Heth	232	
N.C. Militia—Col. Anthony Lytle	193	
Brig. Gen. James Hogun's Brigade		
1st N.C. Continental Regt.—		
Col. Thomas Clark	293	
2nd N.C. Continental Regt.—		
Col. John Patten	301	
3rd N.C. Continental Regt.—		
Lt. Col. Robert Mebane	162	
Brig. Gen. Wm. Woodford's Brigade		
1st Virginia Continental Regt.—		
Col. Wm. Russell	336	
2nd Virginia Continental Regt.—		
Col. John Neville	306	
3rd Virginia Continental Regt.—		
Col. Nath. Gist	252	

	MEN	ARTILLERY
Charlestown Brigade—Col. Maurice Simons		
Charlestown Militia		
1st Battalion—Lt. Col. Roger Smith	352	
2nd Battalion—Lt. Col. John Huger	485	
French Company—Marquis de Brétigny	92	
Brig. Gen. Lachlan McIntosh's		
Brigade of Country Militia	1,038	
Nonbrigaded Units		
1st S.C. Continental Regt.—		
Col. Charles Pinckney	231	
Light Dragoons	41	
Armed Citizens	40	
Misc. Continental Officers	52	
Brigade of Artillery—Col. Barnard Beekman		
S.C. Regt. of Continental Artillery		
(4th S.C. Continental Regt.)	93	
N.C. Regt. of Continental Artillery	64	
Charlestown Battalion of Artillery	168	
Company of Cannoneers	167	
Artillery Ordnance[144]		
Land-side batteries		79
Water-side batteries		95
Fort Moultrie		30
Mobile fieldpieces (4-lb. and 6-lb.)		17
Total	ca. 5,660	221

British Forces[145]

Lt. Gen. Sir Henry Clinton

	MEN	ARTILLERY
First Debarkation (departed New York		
23 Dec. 1779, arrived Tybee Island 1 Feb. 1780)		
British Forces		
Light Infantry Corps		
1st Battalion	622	
2nd Battalion	623	
Grenadier Corps		
1st Battalion	613	
2nd Battalion	536	
7th Regt.	411	
23rd Regt.	425	
33rd Regt.—Lt. Col. James Webster	398	
63rd Regt.	350	

Order of Battle: Charlestown, 1780 (*continued*)

	Men	Artillery
64th Regt.	360	
Royal Artillery	256	
Gen. James Patterson's		
Guides and Pioneers	104	
Provincial Forces		
British Legion[146] Col. Banastre Tarleton		
Legion Infantry—		
Maj. Charles Cochrane	ca. 201	
Legion Cavalry	ca. 200	
17th Light Dragoons	69	
Lt. Col. Patrick Ferguson's		
American Volunteers	180	
German Forces		
Jaegers—Maj. Wurmb	287	
Grenadier Regt. von Minnigerode		
(later von Schuler)	424	
Grenadier Regt. von Linsing	433	
Grenadier Regt. von Lengereke	421	
Grenadier Regt. von Graff	423	
Garrison Regt. von Huyne	574	
German Artillerists	127	
Second Debarkation[147] (departed New York		
25 Mar. 1780, arrived Stono Inlet 19 Apr. 1780)		
42nd Highland Regt.	701	
Queen's Rangers	482	
Prince of Wales's Loyal		
American Volunteers	385	
Volunteers of Ireland	565	
Hessian Regt. von Dittfurth	596	
Troops from the Savannah Garrison:		
71st Highland Regt.		
1st Battalion—		
Maj. Archibald MacArthur	487	
2nd Battalion—		
Maj. Alexander MacDonald	533	
South Carolina Royalists—		
Col. Alexander Innes	307	
North Carolina Volunteers—		
Lt. Col. John Hamilton[148]	127	
New York Volunteers—		
Col. George Turnbull	183	

	MEN	ARTILLERY
Maj. Graham's Light Infantry Corps—		
Maj. Colin Graham	273	
Artillery Ordnance		
32-lb. cannons		12
24-lb. cannons		ca. 14
12-lb. cannons		est. 24
6-lb. cannons		ca. 4
13" mortar		ca. 1
9" mortars		ca. 4
9" howitzer		ca. 1
7" howitzer		ca. 1
Total	ca. 12,676	ca. 61

Casualties

	AMERICAN	BRITISH
Killed	89	76
Wounded	140	189
Missing	n/a	n/a
Total Casualties	229	265
Captured	ca. 5,611	–
Total Losses	ca. 5,700[149]	265

⊬TWELVE⊨

Waxhaws

"I expect an answer to these propositions. . . .
If you are rash enough to reject them, the blood be upon your head."

THE LOSS OF THE CITY was not what made the American defeat at Charlestown so devastating. The Americans had suffered the capture of major cities
before. Boston, Philadelphia, Newport, New York, and Savannah had all been
taken by the British, and the last two were still occupied. Yet, because the Americans
had always managed to preserve their field army after the loss of each city, the British
were never able to extend their control much into the countryside. The capture of the
army of the Southern Department was a new development in the war that would allow
the Southern Strategy to be put fully to the test.

If the British could pacify the interior of the state, they could raise a Tory militia
and begin to draw supplies from the backcountry farms, thus reducing or eliminating
their dependence on supply convoys from England. Without this dependence, the threat
of a French fleet gaining local naval superiority would be less problematic; and the
problem posed by American privateers that frequently intercepted British supply ships
would likewise be diminished. In this respect, the pacification of the interior of South
Carolina was a high-stakes game that could affect the strategic balance in the American
theater.

To accomplish this important task, Sir Henry Clinton appointed his second in command, Lord Cornwallis, to the command of the British Southern Army. Cornwallis
had to rely heavily on his cavalry arm to accomplish his mission, which meant that he
would depend on the services of his cavalry commander, Lieutenant Colonel Banastre
Tarleton—a man "whose name would become anathema to southern patriots."[1] The
twenty-six-year-old Tarleton would soon set the precedent for the rest of the war in the
South: It would be fast-paced, hard-hitting, and—above all else—cruel. Few, if any, at
the time would have predicted that this relatively obscure lieutenant colonel would have
such an impact on the war.

Banastre Tarleton was born in 1754 to a wealthy family in Liverpool, England. His
father held a relatively high place in society and was mayor of Liverpool for a time.
After his father's death, young Tarleton inherited a large sum of money, but he quickly

squandered most of his inheritance gambling. He was studying law at Oxford when his mother purchased a cornet's commission for him in the King's Dragoon Guards. After some brief training in the cavalry, Tarleton volunteered for service in America, where he was sent in 1776 at the age of twenty-two. (He accompanied the troops of the 1776 Charlestown expedition that left from Cork, Ireland, headed to North Carolina.) Tarleton quickly gained a reputation for energy and daring after participating in a raid that captured American Major General Charles Lee at a tavern in New Jersey in December 1776 (though he did not lead the raid, as has often been reported).[2] Tarleton attemped a similar kidnapping of Henry "Light Horse Harry" Lee in 1778 but failed and was nearly shot off his horse.

In June 1778 Sir Henry Clinton authorized the formation of two new provincial units recruited from recent Irish and Scottish immigrants in New Jersey and Pennsylvania. Clinton placed the Irish nobleman Lord Francis Rawdon in command of the Volunteers of Ireland and the Scottish Lord William Cathcart in charge of the British Legion in order to influence immigrants from the two Celtic states to join their respective national regiments. The tactic was successful. "These two corps filled fast," Clinton later wrote.[3] Cathcart was a captain in the 17th Light Dragoons, but he was given the "provincial rank" of colonel to command the British Legion.[4] By the end of 1778 Cathcart's "British" Legion was well established, and twenty-four-year-old Captain Tarleton was appointed second in command of the unit and given the provincial rank of lieutenant colonel "commandant." British officers were commonly appointed to command newly raised provincial units, though their ranks in the provincial units were not considered equivalent to the same ranks in the "regular" establishment.

The ethnic makeup of the British Legion is important as other historians have used the fact that it was a "Loyalist" unit to emphasize the nature of the war in the South as a "civil war." It is technically correct to call the British Legion a Loyalist or Tory regiment. However, this is usually done in a way that misleads one to assume that the soldiers of the legion had the same ethnic makeup and were raised from the same region as the southern Patriot militiamen. Of course, while the soldiers of the legion were "Americans," they were almost all recent immigrants from Scotland who were recruited in the North.

While immigrants made up a large number of soldiers on both sides, it was well understood at the time that recent immigrants were more likely to be Loyalists and that the Patriot militia was largely made up of native-born Americans or longtime residents of America. In short, the soldiers of the British Legion, born in Scotland and recruited in the northern states, were not the "boys next door" to the typical South Carolinian. They seemed as "foreign" to the average southerner as did any other British or Hessian soldier and were distinguishable from the latter only by the green coats of their provincial uniforms.

As previously mentioned, the eighteenth-century legion was a combined arms unit, usually consisting of at least two troops of cavalry and two companies of infantry. The infantry would usually ride doubled up with the cavalry—or they would ride on their own horses acting as mounted infantry—making the whole formation highly mobile and flexible. The legion was particularly suited for independent operations in the large and sparsely populated southern theater. Unlike the northern colonies, the South had a temperate climate with moderate temperatures even in winter. Wide savannah provided satisfactory (if not ample) grazing grounds and fodder for horses. It was obviously more difficult to care for large numbers of horses in the cold, rocky, and often snow-covered regions of the North. The relatively open plains of the southern piedmont and the mobility of horses also acted as a "force multiplier" for cavalry units. A single regiment of horsemen could control an area that would take many times as much infantrymen.

Mounted troops were particularly well suited to pursuing the relatively small pockets of American regulars and militia (often no more than a few hundred men) that operated in the southern backcountry. In addition, American militiamen in the South were loath to give up their horses (despite the frequent difficulty of procuring sufficient fodder for them). Thus, southern militiamen functioned more or less as mounted infantry, and the British needed highly mobile forces of their own to counteract that mobility. In addition, cavalry was especially effective against militia because militiamen lacked good discipline and bayonets. Without bayonets, militiamen were at a distinct disadvantage against dragoons' sabers (the close-quarters weapon of the cavalry).

By the time of the 1780 invasion of South Carolina, Lord Cathcart had taken on an administrative role in the army, leaving the daily command of his legion to young Tarleton. What was still called "Cathcart's" Legion on the ship manifest did not arrive at Savannah until mid-March 1780. Once there, Tarleton found that nearly all the horses of the army, including his cavalry mounts, had been lost at sea. Having heard that there were many horses on Port Royal Island, Tarleton had his men transported there by ship; he intended to "collect at that place, from friends and enemies, by money or by force, all the horses belonging to the islands in the neighborhood."[5] Tarleton was thus able to "acquire" mounts for his legion, which included a troop of the 17th Light Dragoons that was more or less permanently attached to Tarleton's command.[6] These mounts, though inferior in quality to the trained cavalry horses lost at sea, allowed Tarleton's Legion (as it was now commonly called) to serve in proper form.

Tarleton's men screened General James Patterson's flying corps as it marched through Georgia and South Carolina. The legion fought a few desultory skirmishes with William Washington's cavalry during this time but otherwise did not see any significant action. When the siege of Charlestown began, the legion moved into reserve at the rear of the army on the Charlestown neck.

As discussed in the last chapter, Brigadier General William Woodford's Virginia Continentals entered Charlestown on 7 April 1780, bringing a desperately needed boost to the defensive manpower of the forlorn city. This event prompted Sir Henry Clinton to send troops across the river to complete the job of encircling the city. Underscoring the importance of this maneuver, Clinton had just received intelligence that a supply column "loaded with arms, ammunition, and clothing"[7] was approaching from the north. This was in fact Woodford's baggage train that had been following five or six days behind him. Clinton ordered Colonel James Webster to take a fourteen-hundred-man corps, including the British Legion, to the headwaters of the Cooper River more than thirty miles inland. There they could cross to the left bank (east side) at Biggin's Bridge. For this maneuver to work, General Isaac Huger's flying corps of cavalry, then

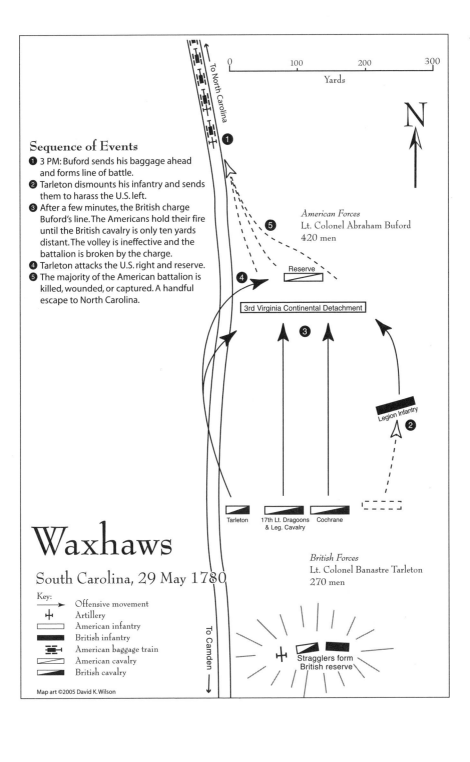

Sequence of Events

❶ 3 PM: Buford sends his baggage ahead and forms line of battle.

❷ Tarleton dismounts his infantry and sends them to harass the U.S. left.

❸ After a few minutes, the British charge Buford's line. The Americans hold their fire until the British cavalry is only ten yards distant. The volley is ineffective and the battalion is broken by the charge.

❹ Tarleton attacks the U.S. right and reserve.

❺ The majority of the American battalion is killed, wounded, or captured. A handful escape to North Carolina.

To North Carolina

0   100   200   300

Yards

N

American Forces
Lt. Colonel Abraham Buford
420 men

Reserve

3rd Virginia Continental Detachment

Legion Infantry

Tarleton   17th Lt. Dragoons   Cochrane
            & Leg. Cavalry

Waxhaws

South Carolina, 29 May 1780

British Forces
Lt. Colonel Banastre Tarleton
270 men

Key:
→ Offensive movement
✛ Artillery
▭ American infantry
▬ British infantry
⊞ American baggage train
▱ American cavalry
◣ British cavalry

To Camden

Stragglers form British reserve

Map art ©2005 David K. Wilson

stationed at Monck's Corner near Biggin's Bridge, had to be defeated or it would threaten Webster's supply lines and therefore the success of the mission.

Tarleton and his men had been resting at the Quarter House, an ancient tavern about five miles from Charlestown, when Webster arrived there on 12 April 1780. Webster temporarily attached Lieutenant Colonel Patrick Ferguson's "corps of marksmen" to the legion and then ordered Tarleton to ride ahead and screen his advance. Colonel Webster followed behind Tarleton's troops with two regular regiments, the 33rd and the 64th.

Monck's Corner, about thirty-two miles from Charlestown, was twenty-seven miles from Tarleton's position at the Quarter House. On the afternoon of 12 April, Tarleton marched five miles to Goose Creek, and Webster arrived at the same position the next morning. At Goose Creek, Tarleton's men captured a black slave who was conveying a letter from General Huger's camp to General Lincoln in Charlestown. The letter, combined with information purchased from the slave "for a few dollars," gave Tarleton complete intelligence on General Huger's dispositions at Monck's Corner. "It was evident that the American cavalry had posted themselves in front of [the] Cooper River," Tarleton wrote, "and that the militia were placed in a meeting house which commanded the bridge, and were distributed on the opposite bank." Armed with this valuable information, Tarleton continued his march in order to attack the Americans at Monck's Corner on the night of 13–14 April. "An attack in the night was judged most advisable," Tarleton wrote, "as it would render the superiority of the enemy's cavalry useless and would, perhaps, present a favourable opportunity of getting possession of Biggin bridge, on [the] Cooper river, without much loss to the assailants."[8]

"Profound silence was observed on the march," Tarleton wrote. "At three o'clock in the morning the advanced guard of dragoons and mounted infantry, supported by the remainder of the Legion and Ferguson's corps, approached the American post." Swamps lay to either side of the road leading to the American camp. Because of this fact, a single American patrol posted a few miles from the camp on the road could have easily detected Tarleton's advance; yet this measure had been neglected. Tarleton gave the order to charge: "The order was executed with the greatest promptitude and success." The Americans' "grand guard on the main road" was swiftly overrun, and a pursuit continued into Huger's camp.[9]

"The Americans were completely surprised," Tarleton wrote. "Major Vernier, of Pulaski's Legion, and some other officers and men who attempted to defend themselves were killed or wounded. General Huger, Colonels Washington and Jameson, with many officers and men, fled on foot to the swamps [that were] close to their encampment where, being concealed by the darkness, they effected their escape." Lieutenant Anthony Allaire, an officer in Ferguson's Corps of Marksmen, contradicted Tarleton and said that the Americans were not surprised: "Luckily for them, they were under marching orders, which made them more alert, when the alarm was given, than usual, which alone prevented their being all taken completely by surprise." Allaire agreed, however, that the Americans "made off with great expedition."[10]

Tarleton then ordered Major Charles Cochrane, who commanded the infantry contingent of the legion, to secure Biggin's Bridge and the meetinghouse that overlooked it. Cochrane and his men charged these positions with fixed bayonets and quickly dispersed the defending American militiamen, who were in no mood to fight. The British recovered fifteen American dead and captured sixty-three, of whom eighteen were wounded. The remainder of the American force fled precipitously. The British also captured forty-two supply wagons and a large quantity of arms, ammunition, and other baggage. Perhaps most importantly, Tarleton captured many horses that he could use for his legion. About 184 horses were captured, 82 of which were cavalry mounts. The horses were "a valuable acquisition," as Tarleton put it. The price paid for this windfall was only three men wounded and five horses killed and wounded.[11]

The defeat of Huger's cavalry was of strategic importance because it allowed Colonel Webster's forces to cross the Cooper and occupy the Hobcaw peninsula. This cut Charlestown's communications with the countryside, preventing reinforcement of the city and blocking any escape by the garrison. Clinton's plan was well conceived, and Tarleton exceeded expectations in executing it. However, the British victory can be equally credited to American incompetence. "The injudicious conduct of the American commander," Tarleton wrote, "who besides making a false disposition of his corps by placing his cavalry in front of the bridge during the night and his infantry in the rear, neglected sending patrols in front of his vedettes." Clinton later gloated in his memoirs that despite "weak, undersized, ill-appointed, and untrained horses, that active and gallant young officer [Tarleton] effectually depressed, at least for the present, this much vaunted flying corps, on which the rebels had rested all their hopes of forwarding supplies and succors to Charleston and keeping alive the spirit of rebellion in the upper country." The victory was not as complete as Tarleton claimed, however, because in just two weeks about three hundred American cavalrymen had regrouped north of the Santee River —*fully mounted*—and again threatened British forces in the area.[12]

Moultrie called the defeat at Monck's Corner "a shameful surprise."[13] It is evident that the officers of the Southern Department had learned little from the affair a year earlier at Briar Creek, where the Americans similarly failed to utilize their superior cavalry to prevent surprise. Though brave and dedicated, most American officers in the South at this time were clearly second-rate when compared with their experienced and skillful British counterparts. (This situation would change only after the arrival of Nathanael Greene and Daniel Morgan in the theater later that year.)

At Monck's Corner, Tarleton demonstrated all the energy and daring that made him an excellent leader of light cavalry. However, the aftermath of the battle demonstrated weaknesses in his command style that would make him detested among the Americans. One incident recorded by Charles Stedman and another by Anthony Allaire (both *British* officers) demonstrate that Tarleton failed to exercise proper control over his soldiers. The first of these incidents was the inhumane treatment of Major Paul Vernier during and after the battle. Vernier, the daring cavalier who had skirmished effectively with Clinton's light troops during their advance on Charlestown, had been mortally wounded during the action. According to Stedman: "Major Birnie [*sic,* Vernier] was mangled in the most shocking manner; he had several wounds, a severe one behind his ear. This unfortunate officer lived several hours, reprobating the Americans for their conduct on this occasion, and even in his last moments cursing the British for their barbarity in having refused quarter after he had surrendered. The writer of this [Stedman], who was ordered on this expedition, afforded every assistance in his power and had the major put upon a table in a public-house in the village, and a blanket thrown over him. The major, in his last moments, was frequently insulted by the privates of the legion."[14]

However, this was not the only atrocity that the soldiers of the legion perpetrated that day. Stedman continued: "Some of the dragoons of the British Legion attempted to ravish several ladies at the house of Sir John Collington, in the neighborhood of Monk's [sic, Monck's] Corner. Mrs. ——— the wife of Doctor ——— of Charlestown, was most barbarously treated; she was a most delicate and beautiful woman. Lady ——— received one or two wounds with a sword. Miss ———, sister to Major ———, was also ill treated. The ladies made their escape, and came to Monk's Corner, where, by this time, Colonel Webster had arrived and taken the command."[15]

Lieutenant Allaire confirms the violent incident: "Three ladies came to our camp in great distress: Lady Colleton, Miss Betsy Giles, and Miss Jean Russell. They had been most shockingly abused by a plundering villain. Lady Colleton badly cut in the hand by a broadsword, and bruised very much. After my friend, Dr. Johnson, dressed her hand, he, with an officer and twelve men, went to the plantation, about one mile from camp, to protect Mrs. Fayssoux, whom this infamous villain had likewise abused in the same manner."[16]

Major Patrick Ferguson—who would soon be made inspector of militia for South Carolina—was in favor of "putting the dragoons to instant death." Instead, Lieutenant Colonel Webster sent the offenders to Clinton's headquarters, where they were later "tried and whipped."[17] This incident reveals much about both British policy regarding the conduct of their soldiers and Lieutenant Colonel Tarleton's command style. First, it should be recognized that the British officers present—Stedman, Ferguson, Allaire, and Webster—disapproved of the legionnaires' dishonorable actions. The gallant Ferguson, destined to lose his life to American rifles atop King's Mountain in less than six months, was the most outraged. This means that it was not British policy to terrorize the population and that the offenders in this case were punished by their officers.

The question one must ask about these incidents is, where was Tarleton? His absence in Stedman's and Allaire's narratives is conspicuous. Where was the regiment's commander while his dragoons were hacking up Major Vernier, insulting him in his last moments, and abusing the women of the village? Giving Tarleton the benefit of the doubt (not done often nowadays), the best that can be said of him is that he did not exercise proper control of his forces during or after the action. However, it is not as if Tarleton had just taken command of these men. He had more than a year to instill a proper sense of discipline in his troops; that they acted in this manner now is indicative of Tarleton's failure to make discipline a priority in his regiment. On the other hand, Major Ferguson's troops made no transgressions; indeed, they were forced to deploy into the village to defend the civilians from Tarleton's troops.

When news of the legion's excesses at Monck's Corner reached headquarters, Lord Cornwallis was prompted to scold the young cavalry commander in a written order: "I must recommend it to you in the strongest manner to use your utmost endeavours to prevent the troops under your command from committing irregularities, and I am convinced that my recommendation will have weight, when I assure you that such conduct will be highly agreeable to the commander in chief [Clinton]."[18]

By the end of April the American cavalry began to regroup north of the Santee River under the command of Lieutenant Colonel Anthony White, who had recently arrived in South Carolina with a small contingent of Virginia cavalry. White's troopers were joined by Lieutenant Colonel Daniel Horry's South Carolina dragoons and the survivors of Monck's Corner under Lieutenant Colonel William Washington. The American cavalry then united with Colonel Abraham Buford's 3rd Virginia Detachment, which was operating in central South Carolina.

On 5 May, White's cavalry crossed the Santee River at Dupui's Ferry, where they encountered a group of 18 British "mounted light infantry" foraging under the command of Lieutenant Lovett Ash. The Americans quickly captured the enemy party, and Colonel White sent word back to Colonel Buford to collect a quantity of boats and meet him at Lenud's Ferry. While this was occurring, Lieutenant Colonel Tarleton and 150 of his dragoons were riding to Lenud's Ferry on a reconnaissance mission. On the road to the ferry Tarleton happened across a Tory, who told him about White's capture of the British soldiers. This report "stimulated Tarleton to push forward his patrole [*sic*] with the greatest expedition."[19]

When Lieutenant Colonel White arrived at Lenud's Ferry, he was disappointed to find that the boats were not "felt or seen."[20] The American commander drew up his men on the banks of the Santee, posted vedettes, and waited for Buford's men to bring the boats he needed to cross the river. By midafternoon some of Buford's regiment arrived, and a few boats were thrown over to the south bank. Lieutenant Colonel White put his eighteen prisoners along with a small guard into the boats and started them crossing the river. At the same time Tarleton and his legion arrived at the ferry. "At three o'clock in the afternoon, the advanced dragoons of the English arrived in [the] presence of [the American] videttes [*sic*]: Tarleton instantly forming his troops, ordered them to charge the enemy's grand guard, and to pursue them into the main body. The [American] corps being totally surprised, resistance and slaughter soon ceased."[21]

At Lenud's Ferry, Tarleton applied the same tactics he had previously used at Monck's Corner successfully. In particular, he charged with his entire regiment immediately on encountering the enemy vedettes. This prevented the vedettes from providing much warning of Tarleton's approach as the British cavalry arrived in the American camp just behind them. (Tarleton may have in fact followed the vedettes to the American position!) The result was another rout: "Colonels White, Washington, and Jamieson [*sic*, Major John Jameson], with some other officers and men, availed themselves of their swimming to make their escape while many who wished to follow their example perished in the river." Henry Lee put the American losses at between thirty and forty killed and wounded; British sources say that forty-one Americans were killed or wounded and that sixty-seven men were captured along with one hundred dragoon horses. The remaining two hundred American troopers fled into "Hell-hole Swamp," while some few swam the Santee to escape to the north bank of the river. Tarleton also managed to rescue the eighteen captive British light infantrymen. "Seeing the Legion descending the hill to the attack," Clinton wrote, the men of the light infantry "immediately threw the rebel guard out of the boat and, rowing back to the shore, rejoined their friends."[22]

Tarleton sustained only two dragoons and four horses killed in the action—a testament to the totality of American surprise. The secret of Tarleton's success was riding his horses hard and fast, up to and beyond the animals' endurance. Tarleton wrote, "Returning to Lord Cornwallis's camp the same evening, upwards of twenty horses expired with fatigue."[23] Cavalrymen are known for the esteem they have for their mounts. It perhaps reveals something of Tarleton's character that he did not care if he rode his horses to death. In any case, this repeat victory over the American cavalry proved that Tarleton's earlier success at Monck's Corner was not a fluke and established him, as Henry Lee put it, as "an officer rising fast in military reputation."[24]

———⊰•⊱———

Governor Rutledge had left Charlestown in mid-April in an attempt to rally the state's militia, which had been hitherto reluctant to turn out—ostensibly for fear of smallpox in the city. Rutledge and General Lincoln had devised a new plan to overcome this fear, which was to have the militia only guard the passes over the Cooper, Santee, and Wando rivers outside the city. Despite the limited nature of the service requested, Rutledge was able to rally only a few militiamen to his camp, mostly because they were convinced that the American cause in South Carolina was doomed without additional help from Congress or Washington's army.

After the defeat of the American cavalry at Monck's Corner and Lenud's Ferry, a large force of twenty-five hundred British soldiers under Cornwallis crossed the Cooper to begin securing the interior of the state. The South Carolina militia had no stomach to fight Cornwallis's professional soldiers, and most of them gave up the river passes without a fight. "Above 300 militia have deliver'd up their arms & return'd to their houses on parole," a Scottish officer wrote.[25] "They had no [notion] of running the risque [sic] of being taken in arms," an American lieutenant said. They instead preferred to return to their homes, "where they could procure protections from the commanding officer, Lt. Col. Webster." Some of the Patriot militiamen even took loyalty oaths to the Crown to save their property.[26]

The fighting around Charlestown continued until 11 May 1780, when Lincoln finally yielded at the urgings of the citizens and the militia, who no longer had the will to continue the fight. Clinton was eager to conclude the business in South Carolina so that he could return to New York. On 10 May a letter from Lord Germain arrived at Clinton's headquarters. The letter said, "A considerable French armament . . . might daily be expected on some part of the North American coast."[27] The British commander had drained the New York garrison of its manpower in order to conquer South Carolina, and the majority of the Royal Navy's American squadron was with Arbuthnot at Charlestown. This left the British commander in chief anxious for the safety of the primary British base in America: "[Since] my presence might be wanted at New York, I prepared with all diligence to finish the arrangements I had proposed for the security and good government of the province we had reclaimed, that I might be able to accompany the Admiral thither with such troops as Lord Cornwallis and I had agreed might be safely and commodiously spared from its defense in the present emergency."[28]

Clinton ordered Cornwallis to divide his command into three columns and fan out to secure the backcountry of Georgia and South Carolina. Lieutenant Colonel Thomas Brown guided one column up the Savannah River to Augusta; the second column under Lieutenant Colonel Nisbet Balfour made its way to Ninety Six; while Lord Cornwallis personally led the largest column of twenty-five hundred men along the north bank of the Santee. The earl's mission was to destroy the final remnants of the Continental Army in South Carolina then operating near Lenud's Ferry and Hell-hole Swamp.

Clinton ordered Cornwallis to engage and defeat the 3rd Virginia Continental Detachment under Lieutenant Colonel Abraham Buford. This regiment was part of the Continental brigade raised by Brigadier General Charles Scott in 1779. Most of Scott's brigade was captured at the fall of Charlestown. However, Buford's regiment suffered delays while being outfitted and was unable to march into South Carolina with the rest of Scott's brigade.

Buford's men were still at Petersburg waiting for their equipment when Brigadier General William Woodford's veteran brigade of Virginia Continentals passed through the town in early March headed south. In order to quicken his march to Charlestown, Woodford chose to leave his field artillery and most of his baggage with Buford.[29]

Lieutenant Colonel Buford left Petersburg about a week after Woodford, leaving behind a few of his companies that still had not been equipped. Buford escorted a long column of wagons that included Woodford's baggage and artillery train (two six-pounders and two small "royals"). Before entering Charlestown on 7 April, Woodford left orders for Buford to stop at Camden "till General Lincoln's pleasure is known."[30] Lincoln apparently thought it better for Buford's men to remain outside the city, and he ordered the regiment to take up position in the vicinity of Lenud's Ferry on the Santee River. At this post Buford's regiment operated in support of Brigadier General Isaac Huger's cavalry. Buford's men also acted as a bodyguard for Governor Rutledge while he attempted to raise the militia in the backcountry.

The American dragoons who escaped death or capture at Monck's Corner and Lenud's Ferry joined up with Buford north of the Santee by the end of April. After finally being uniformed and outfitted, the last few straggling companies of Buford's regiment arrived at Camden after their long march from Virginia. Thus, Buford's regiment was close to full strength by the end of the first week of May 1780. About this time Richard Caswell—hero of Moore's Creek Bridge, former governor of North Carolina, and now a brigadier general in the state militia—came down from North Carolina with 800 militiamen. Caswell's troops combined with the 450 or so men of Buford's regiment brought the American infantry outside Charlestown up to a respectable strength of over 1,250 soldiers. However, the American troops were inexperienced, ill-equipped, and still dramatically outnumbered by the troops that Cornwallis commanded in the countryside.

Clinton mentions that he had intelligence of a rebel force (Caswell's militia) headed to Georgetown in mid-May; however he seemed unaware that this corps had joined up with Buford on the Santee. On 12 May news of Lincoln's surrender reached General Huger, who had taken command of the American forces in the interior of the state. Knowing that the British would soon be moving to secure the backcountry, Huger ordered Caswell and Buford to decamp and march north to Camden, which they reached on 24 or 25 May. Caswell then marched with his militia back into North Carolina by way of the Pee Dee River. General Huger then spent two days consulting with Governor Rutledge, who was also at Camden, while Buford's Virginians guarded the town.[31]

Cornwallis reached Nelson's Ferry on 22 May 1780, following the road on which Buford had withdrawn northward ten days earlier. On 27 May, Cornwallis sent Tarleton's Legion ahead; he hoped that it could intercept Buford before he reached North Carolina. Even for the legionnaires on horseback it would be difficult to overtake the Americans, who had a substantial lead (although the lead was not as great as the British thought, given Buford's two-day stop at Camden). Tarleton's force was inferior to Buford's 3rd Virginia Detachment, which outnumbered the legion. However, if Tarleton could at least force Buford to slow his march, then perhaps Cornwallis could catch up and bring his nearly twenty-five hundred infantry into decisive action against the retreating Americans.

Tarleton rode hard on the road to Camden, which was also a primary thoroughfare to North Carolina.[32] Tarleton's relentless pace caused many of his men and horses to straggle and drop out of the march. The lifeless carcasses of horses marked the passing of Tarleton's column, a significant number having dropped dead "in consequence of the rapidity of the march, and the heat of the climate."[33] Tarleton made up his losses by "impressing" (or, as the Patriots saw it, stealing) horses along the road, which allowed him to keep up his exhausting pace and still maintain his manpower.

On hearing of Tarleton's approach, General Huger ordered Lieutenant Colonel Buford to continue his march north on the Salisbury road, while he escorted Governor Rutledge out of the state on the road to Charlotte, North Carolina. Buford sent his baggage and artillery ahead so that they would not be in the rear of his column if the British overtook him. On the morning of 28 May, Tarleton entered Camden, where he learned that Buford was rushing north to meet Continental reinforcements then in North Carolina headed south. "This information strongly manifested that no time was to be lost," Tarleton wrote, "and that a vigorous effort was the only resource to prevent the junction of the two American corps."[34]

Tarleton rested his men much of the day at Camden, which also allowed many of the stragglers to catch up. At two o'clock in the morning on the 29th, Tarleton cracked his riding crop and resumed the pursuit. He arrived at Rugeley's Mill at daybreak, covering the 13 miles between there and Camden in about five hours (moving at an impressive 2.6 miles per hour during a night march). At Rugeley's, Tarleton learned that Lieutenant Colonel Buford was 20 miles distant. Tarleton now decided to attempt "a stratagem to delay the march of the enemy: Captain David Kinlock, of the legion, was employed to carry a summons [to surrender] to the American commander, which, by magnifying the number of the British, might intimidate him to submission, or at least delay him whilst he deliberated on an answer."[35]

Unaware of the proximity of Tarleton's Legion, Buford had stopped to rest and water his horses at Waxhaw Creek, about nine miles north-northwest of present-day Lancaster, South Carolina, in an area generally known as "the Waxhaws." "The repose of the American troops had been disturbed by a young man, who, riding forward from Rugeley's Mill, warned them of the detachment which was pursuing them."[36] Heeding the young patriot's warning, Lieutenant Colonel Buford decamped posthaste and started his battalion on the road north, again sending his artillery and baggage to the head of his column. The Americans had only proceeded two miles up the road when Captain Kinlock approached. Because Kinlock refused to speak with anyone but Buford, the American commander was obliged to stop his march to open negotiations. Buford ordered his battalion to form a line of battle in a field near the road. Kinlock then presented Buford with Tarleton's summons.

Tarleton offered terms for surrender that were "nearly the same as were accepted by Charles town." The terms stated that all the militiamen were to be paroled to their homes (though there was no militia present), while all the Continental soldiers were to be made prisoners of war and taken back to Charlestown. In one respect Tarleton's terms were exceptionally generous in that they allowed all the American officers, regular or militia, to be paroled back to their homes. (At Charlestown all the officers were held as prisoners of war until exchanged.) Tarleton ended his summons with a sanguinary epigram: "I expect an answer to these propositions as soon as possible; if they are accepted, you will order every person under your command to pile his arms in one hour after you receive this flag: If you are rash enough to reject them, the blood be upon your head."[37]

The American commander gave Kinlock a laconic note to take back to Tarleton: "I reject your proposals, and shall defend myself to the last extremity." Buford's veteran officers gave their "general approval of the course he had adopted," and they now set about preparing their green recruits to receive the legion in battle.[38]

When Kinlock returned with Buford's defiant reply, Tarleton immediately prepared to attack. It is interesting to note that Tarleton did not stop his advance while his flag was being considered—a violation of the rules of war. Tarleton claims that Buford did not stop his march either while negotiating with Captain Kinlock; but this is not the case as Buford actually stopped his march on Kinlock's arrival, never to resume it.

At three o'clock in the afternoon the leading elements of Tarleton's column encountered Buford's rear guard consisting of five dragoons. Tarleton's troops quickly cut up the American pickets and took them captive. Dr. Robert Brownfield, a surgeon with Buford's regiment, vividly described the attack and its human cost:

In a short time Tarleton's bugle was heard, and a furious attack was made on the rear guard, commanded by Lieut. Pearson. Not a man escaped. Poor Pearson was inhumanely mangled on the face as he lay on his back. His nose and lip were bisected obliquely; several of his teeth were broken out in the upper jaw, and the under completely divided on each side. These wounds were inflicted after he had fallen, with several others on his head, shoulders, and arms. As a just tribute to the honour and Job-like patience of poor Pearson, it ought to be mentioned, that he lay for five weeks without uttering a single groan. His only nourishment was milk, drawn from a bottle through a quill. During that period he was totally deprived of speech, nor could he articulate distinctly after his wounds were healed.[39]

When Tarleton reached Buford's position, many of his cavalry and mounted infantry-men were "totally worn out . . . the horses of the three pounder were likewise unable to proceed." Nevertheless, Tarleton urged his men on in an effort to prevent Buford from reaching North Carolina and the reinforcements that were waiting for him there. Unable to bring his single three-pounder into range, he placed the piece on a small hill that overlooked the road, opposite the American center. Tarleton designated the hill a rallying point in case his assault was repulsed. He ordered the stragglers to form "something like a reserve" on the hill as they arrived. Meanwhile, he deployed Major Cochrane on his right flank with sixty dragoons and "nearly as many mounted infantry." At his center Tarleton placed the forty horsemen belonging to the 17th Light Dragoons along with "a part" of the legion cavalry under Captains Kinlock and Corbet. Tarleton positioned himself on his own left flank with "thirty chosen horse and some infantry." Tarleton's description of his deployment implies that a substantial portion of his force, specifically his "reserve" of stragglers, did not engage the enemy. Tarleton must have known that his troops were outnumbered, but he was confident in the ability of his men, most of whom were veterans with several years of service and all of whom had recently seen combat.[40]

Buford—having sent his artillery ahead—chose not to interfere with the British deployment, though they were only three hundred yards away. Buford now adjusted his order of battle. "He chose his post in an open wood," Tarleton observed, "to the right of the road. He formed his infantry in one line [double-ranked], with a small reserve; he placed his colours in the center; and he ordered his cannon, baggage, and [wagons] to continue their march."[41] Buford's infantry numbered about 380 raw recruits with no combat experience—most having served only a few months in the army. However, Buford did command a veteran cadre of officers cobbled together from the remnants of previously disbanded Virginia Continental regiments. The reserve was composed of a detachment of Lieutenant Colonel William Washington's Virginia dragoons—probably about 40 troopers who had escaped capture at Lenud's Ferry a few weeks earlier. (William Washington was not present.)

Tarleton began the attack by ordering Major Cochrane to dismount his infantry-men and, along with his dragoons, "gall the enemy's flank, before he moved against their front with his cavalry." Tarleton then ordered Kinlock and Corbet to charge the American center with their cavalry, "whilst Lieutenant-colonel Tarleton, with thirty chosen horse and some infantry, assaulted their right flank and reserve." The British horses would have easily traversed the three hundred yards to the American line in less than a minute. Buford ordered his troops to hold their fire until the British were in point-blank range. "On their arrival within fifty paces, the Continental infantry presented, when Tarleton was surprised to hear their officers command them to retain their fire till the British cavalry were nearer." Only when the British charge was within ten yards of the American line did Buford's officers give the order to fire. The American line lit up in one mass volley, but the fire was ineffectual. "Some officers, men, and horses, suffered by this fire; but the [American] battalion was totally broken, and slaughter was commenced before Lieutenant-colonel Tarleton could remount another horse, the one with which he led his dragoons being overturned by the volley."[42]

Buford's regimental surgeon, Dr. Robert Brownfield, said that Tarleton's initial charge was "received with firmness, and completely checked, until the cavalry were gaining the rear."[43] However, if this was the case why did the American reserve not check the British flanking movements? The fact that Buford's reserve apparently played little role in the action lends credence to Tarleton's claim that the main American line was broken on the first impact of the British charge: in that situation there would have been little the reserve could have done to rescue the situation. Tarleton's claim that the American line was broken with the initial charge is also more in line with the one-sided casualties, which will be examined in more detail below.

According to Dr. Brownfield, Buford's regiment was "well appointed and equipped."[44] It is therefore reasonable to assume that Buford's men had bayonets, which were standard issue for Continental troops at this time. Since it is difficult for men to load their weapons with the bayonets fixed, it was often the practice when receiving a cavalry charge to have the front rank kneel with fixed bayonets while the rear rank prepared to fire without bayonets being fixed. However, there is no mention of Buford adopting this expedient. It is therefore possible that Buford had his entire regiment ready to fire their weapons without fixed bayonets, but this is impossible to prove.

Assuming that Buford's men had bayonets and at least the front rank had them fixed, it is unlikely that a frontal cavalry charge could have broken the American line *provided* the Continentals held fast in their resolve. However, the historian John Keegan makes the cogent observation that a cavalry charge against infantry is more a contest of will than of steel: "A horse, in the normal course of events, will not gallop at an obstacle it cannot jump or see a way through, and it cannot jump or see a way through a solid line of men. . . . Equally, a man will not stand in the path of a running horse: he will run himself, or seek shelter, and only if exceptionally strong-nerved and knowing in its ways, stand his ground. . . . For the 'shock' which cavalry seek to inflict is really moral, not physical in character."[45]

Since Buford's rank and file consisted of raw recruits, it is likely that these young men were intimidated by the onrushing horses, their green-coated riders flailing their sabers over their heads while shouting "horrid yells of infuriated demons." This is sufficient explanation for the poor aim of the American volley, and for the infantry's breaking and running as the dragoons came down upon them as described by Tarleton.[46]

Tarleton claims that his horse was shot in the initial American volley, while Brownfield says that this event occurred during an American attempt to surrender (which Tarleton makes no mention of). The historian Henry Dawson, referencing Adjutant Henry Bowyer's account, asserts also that the Americans attempted to surrender: "Colonel Buford, perceiving that farther resistance would be useless, directed Adjutant Bowyer to advance with a flag to Lieutenant-colonel Tarleton, and to say that he [Buford] would accept the terms which had been offered in the morning. The action, not withstanding this flag, continued on both sides, and while Lieutenant-colonel Tarleton was conversing with Adjutant Bowyer, his horse was shot in the head, and fell with his rider under him. Indignant at this violation of their own flag, by the Americans, an indiscriminate slaughter was immediately commenced by the enemy."[47]

Bowyer's and Brownfield's accounts agree that Buford attempted to surrender during the engagement.[48] However, Bowyer's account says that Buford did not offer to surrender unconditionally, but rather wanted to yield under the same terms that Tarleton had offered him before the action began. If true, this was a perfectly ridiculous condition, given the circumstances. Since that battle had been joined and complete victory was within grasp, there was no reason for Tarleton to accept anything but unconditional surrender from his enemy. Buford should have understood that once the dragoons were in his midst, the time for negotiating terms had passed.

Tarleton wrote his own postmortem of the battle, which historians ever since have echoed:

> The complete success of this attack may, in great measure, be ascribed to the mistakes committed by the American commander: If he had halted the waggons [*sic*] as soon as he found the British troops pressing his rear, and formed them into a kind of redoubt, for the protection of his cannon and infantry against the assault of the cavalry, in all probability he either would not have been attacked, or by such disposition he might have foiled the attempt: The British troops, in both cases, would have been obliged to abandon the pursuit, as the country in the neighborhood could not immediately have supplied them with forage or provisions; and the continentals might have decamped in the night, to join their reinforcements. Colonel Buford, also, committed a material error, in ordering the infantry to retain their fire till the British dragoons were quite close; which when given, had little effect either upon the minds or bodies of the assailants, in comparison with the execution that might be expected from a successive fire of platoons or divisions, commenced at the distance of three or four hundred paces.[49]

Tarleton's criticisms came easy as the victor, and historians have seen little reason to contradict him. Tarleton refers to firing "by platoons or divisions," a tactic that called for every other platoon to fire in sequence while the others reloaded their weapons. Using this technique, a battalion could maintain a more or less constant stream of fire against an opponent. Tarleton's claim is that had Buford utilized this tactic, the British cavalry would have been faced with fire from the moment they began to move and the effect of sustained fire over the course of the charge would have disrupted the attacking cavalry more effectively than the massed volley that Buford actually offered.

That the American massed volley was ineffective is not in dispute; however, it was common practice then, and for decades to come, for troops with muzzle-loading firelocks to hold their fire until an attacking force was in close range and then to discharge one massive volley (perhaps holding a division in reserve). This was especially true of infantry defending against a cavalry charge, in which situation they would likely have time for only one or two shots before the enemy was upon them. For Buford's regiment to begin firing "at three or four hundred paces [yards]" would have been ill-advised since the effective range of their weapons was only eighty yards. It took less than a minute for Tarleton's men to cross the three-hundred-yard no-man's-land. Any platoons that fired their weapons would likely have had little time to reload for another volley. In addition, the smoke generated from the first volley would have served to reduce the effectiveness of later volleys fired at closer ranges; and each successive firing of a flint-lock weapon increased the chance of the piece's being fouled and misfiring, thus making the first fire from a flintlock in combat the most effective. Therefore, it must be concluded that whatever mistakes Lieutenant Colonel Buford made, having his men hold their fire for one massed volley at close range was not one of them.

Tarleton is correct, however, in saying that Buford mistimed his fire. Normal practice would have been for defending infantry to fire at attacking cavalry from a distance of thirty to fifty yards. Waiting until the British horses were only ten yards distant would have meant that many of Buford's green troops were probably already flinching at the sight of the charging steeds and their saber-wielding riders. Fear and flinching would have thrown off the infantry's aim, and this explains why the American volley was so ineffective and why it was so easy for Tarleton's cavalry to penetrate the American line.

Those familiar with the Napoleonic Wars might wonder why Buford did not form a square with his battalion. Suffice it to say that, while this tactic would prove universally popular in Europe in fifteen or so years, it simply did not exist in the British or American tactical playbooks of the Revolutionary War era.[50] Buford used the accepted method at the time, which was to post a strong reserve that could respond to flanking movements by the enemy cavalry behind his main line.

What of Tarleton's claim that Buford should have built "a kind of redoubt" using his wagons and artillery? According to Dr. Brownfield, Buford did indeed consider this option but rejected it because Buford and his officers assumed that if they stopped and improvised a fort, Tarleton would simply take up a position nearby and await reinforcements from Cornwallis (who in fact was only about two days away).

Buford's defeat was ultimately the result of the inexperience of his troops, and of his own mistake in holding his fire a few seconds too long. However, what is most controversial about the battle at Waxhaws is whether a massacre took place after the surrender and, if so, whether Tarleton ordered or condoned it. Brownfield's, Bowyer's, and Tarleton's accounts all agree that a slaughter began after Tarleton was unhorsed. Dr. Brownfield's dramatic account of the battle's aftermath is now one of the most famous and most often referenced pieces of prose regarding the Revolutionary War in the South: "The demand for quarters, seldom refused to a vanquished foe, was at once found to be in vain;—not a man was spared—and it was the concurrent testimony of all the survivors, that for fifteen minutes after every man was prostrate. They went over the ground plunging their bayonets into every one that exhibited any signs of life, and in some instances, where several had fallen one over the other, these monsters were seen to throw off on the point of the bayonet the uppermost, to come at those beneath." Equally memorable is Brownfield's description of Captain John Stokes's wounding:

> He received twenty-three wounds, and as he never for a moment lost his recollection, he often repeated to me the manner and order in which they were inflicted.

Early in the sanguinary conflict he was attacked by a dragoon, who aimed many deadly blows at his head, all of which by the dextrous [*sic*] use of the small sword he easily parried; when another on the right, by one stroke, cut off his right hand through the metacarpal bones. He was then assailed by both, and instinctively attempted to defend his head with his left arm until the forefinger was cut off, and the arm hacked in eight or ten places from the wrist to the shoulder. His head was then laid open almost the whole length of the crown to the eye brows. After he fell he received several cuts on the face and shoulders. A soldier passing on in the work of death, asked if he expected quarters? Stokes answered I have not, nor do I mean to ask quarters, finish me as soon as possible; he then transfixed him twice with his bayonet. Another asked the same question and received the same answer, and he also thrust his bayonet twice through his body. Stokes had his eye fixed on a wounded British officer, sitting at some distance, when a serjeant [*sic*] came up, who addressed him with apparent humanity, and offered him protection from further injury at the risk of his life. All I ask, said Stokes, is to be laid by that officer that I may die in his presence. While performing this generous office the humane serjeant was twice obliged to lay him down, and stand over him to defend him against the fury of his comrades. Doct. Stapleton, Tarleton's surgeon, whose name ought to be held up to eternal obloquy, was then dressing the wounds of the officer. Stokes, who lay bleeding at every pore, asked him to do something for his wounds, which he scornfully and inhumanely refused, until peremptorily ordered by the more humane officer, and even then only filled the wounds with rough tow, the particles of which could not be separated from the brain for several days.[51]

Tarleton does not deny that a slaughter occurred, but he obviously differs as to the cause. "The loss of officers and men was great on the part of the Americans," Tarleton said, "owing to the dragoons so effectually breaking the infantry, and to a report amongst the cavalry, that they had lost their commanding officer, which stimulated the soldiers to a vindictive asperity not easily restrained." Tarleton goes on to say that the wounded of each side were looked after "with all possible dispatch, and treated with equal humanity."[52] This statement of course contradicts Dr. Brownfield's account.

So what really happened? The casualty figures given by Tarleton in his official report to Cornwallis tell the real, unbiased story. Tarleton reported that the Americans suffered 113 killed "on the spot";[53] 150 wounded were "unable to travel, and left on parole";[54] and a mere 53 Americans were taken prisoner. Henry Lee says that "Lieutenant-Colonel Buford, with the horse, escaped, as did about eighty or ninety of our infantry, who fortunately being advanced, saved themselves by flight."[55] Assuming that Buford had about 40 dragoons and about 380 infantrymen, the total American force would have numbered about 420; with the killed and wounded amounting to 263, this would yield an astonishing casualty rate of over 60 percent. Even worse, if we assume (as most do) that those taken prisoner were also wounded, the total casualty figure is 316—a staggering 70 to 75 percent casualty rate. Contrast Buford's losses with those of Tarleton, who reported only 5 killed and 12 wounded—a total of 17 casualties. This amounted to a mere 6 percent of his total force of 270 men (not all of whom were engaged).

A one-sided battle with heavy casualties is not, in and of itself, proof of massacre. However, given that such casualty rates were practically unheard of in Revolutionary War battles, the casualty figures serve to reinforce the universal American claim of massacre. Moreover, Tarleton admits that his men were out of control because a false rumor that he had been killed "stimulated the soldiers to a vindictive asperity not easily restrained."[56] Tarleton also noted that the 150 American wounded were so badly hurt as to be "unable to travel." It was normal in Revolutionary War battles for some percentage of the total injured to be unable to travel, but it was again unprecedented for *all* those reported as wounded to be unable to travel.

But did Tarleton order a slaughter or refuse the Americans quarter after they attempted to surrender, as some have claimed? There is no evidence of this. Also, the American attempt to surrender—based on Adjutant Bowyer's account at least—was conditional and therefore not one that Tarleton was obligated to accept once battle had been joined. In addition, as has often been pointed out by Tarleton's defenders, the fact that 53 prisoners were taken and the 150 wounded were left alive on the field is unequivocal proof that quarter was given. This fact is sufficient to indemnify Tarleton of having issued orders to kill everyone. Nevertheless, that quarter was given to *some* should not be construed as proof that quarter was given to *all* who attempted to surrender. In addition, even if Tarleton did not order a massacre, this does not mean that the legion's soldiers did not effect a massacre on their own initiative.

Even though Tarleton may be innocent of ordering an atrocity, he is certainly guilty of failing to restrain his men once the engagement ceased to be a battle and became a simple slaughter. Charles Stedman, who was serving as chief of Cornwallis's commissary on this expedition, said of the battle: "The king's troops were entitled to great commendation for their activity and ardour on this occasion, *but the virtue of humanity was totally forgot*" [emphasis added].[57] This condemnation, coming from a British officer who served alongside Tarleton and his legion, serves as authoritative confirmation of the American accusations of brutality leveled against Tarleton and his troops after this battle.

The massacre at Waxhaws was also consistent with previous incidents of malicious and unlawful behavior committed by Tarleton's troops. Major Paul Vernier said with his dying breath that the British troops continued to molest him after he had surrendered at Monck's Corner. Acts of rapine committed after that action also indicate a lack of humanity and discipline among Tarleton's troopers. Of course, Tarleton had previously received a written reprimand from Cornwallis for failing to prevent his soldiers' transgressions at Monck's Corner.

George Washington said that the only difference between an army and a mob is discipline. Since it is the duty of the officers to create discipline, the guilt for the mass murder and mayhem that occurred at Waxhaws can only lie with Banastre Tarleton—his crime being that he never instilled a sense of professionalism and discipline in his officers and soldiers during his years as their commander. Though it was not British policy to terrorize the population, Cornwallis did not take sufficient action to restrain or punish Tarleton and his men. This makes him culpable, if not equally so, in the atrocities that Tarleton's troops committed.

The horror of the Waxhaws battle roused the ire of the American citizens and soldiers, who now thirsted for vengeance. "This tragic expedition sunk deep in the American breast," Henry Lee wrote, "and produced the unanimous decision among the [American] troops to revenge their murdered comrades whenever the blood-stained corps should give an opportunity."[58] Overnight the commander of the legion earned his sobriquet "Bloody Tarleton," and the term "Tarleton's Quarter" became a byword for murder that remained in common usage in the South for decades to come.

The battle at Waxhaws thus epitomized the British military's fixation on tactical victory and their insufficient regard for the strategic implications of their actions. In any war in which the victor hopes to reconcile with the population after subduing it, the manner in which victory is achieved is just as important as victory itself. After overwhelming success at Charlestown, the British should have concentrated on impressing the South Carolinians with their magnanimity. Instead they pursued a program of ruthlessly crushing all opposition. It was a course of action that had far-reaching consequences.

Order of Battle: Waxhaws

South Carolina, 29 May 1780

American Forces
Lt. Col. Abraham Buford

	MEN	ARTILLERY
3rd Virginia Continental Detachment—		
Lt. Col. Abraham Buford	ca. 380	
Virginia Light Dragoons	ca. 40	
Artillery		
Cannons (6-lb.)		2
Cannons ("royals")		2
Total	ca. 420	4

British Forces
Lt. Col. Banastre Tarleton

	MEN	ARTILLERY
British Legion		
Legion Infantry—Maj. Cochrane	100	
Legion Dragoons—Capt. Corbet	130	
17th Light Dragoons—Capt. Kinlock	40	
Artillery		
Cannons (3-lb.)		1
Total	270	1

Casualties

	AMERICAN	BRITISH
Killed	113	5
Wounded	150	12
Missing	n/a	–
Total Casualties	**263**	**17**
Captured[59]	53	–
Total Losses	**316**	**17**

‡⇒THIRTEEN⇒‡

The End of the Beginning

"I will never bear arms against my country . . .
I do not mean to desert the cause of America."

C ONTROL OF SOUTH CAROLINA and Georgia's backcountry could be represented by the possession of three towns: Camden, Ninety Six, and Augusta. Lieutenant Colonel Banastre Tarleton's triumph at the Waxhaws on 29 May 1780 secured Camden for the British. Soon thereafter British soldiers under Lieutenant Colonel Thomas "Burntfoot" Brown occupied Augusta without opposition. (After having been run out of the town four years earlier wearing Patriot-tailored tar and feathers, Brown no doubt relished returning to the city at the head of a British army.) Meanwhile a column of troops under Lieutenant Colonel Nisbet Balfour bloodlessly seized Ninety Six. Though Brigadier General Andrew Williamson and his brigade of backcountry Patriot militia were nearby, they stood strangely idle as Balfour's men occupied the town. Williamson then surrendered to Balfour, and soon all his troops were back in their homes as prisoners of war on parole. "His inactivity and supineness gave rise to suspicions of treason," wrote the historian William Willcox of Williamson.[1] This charge is reinforced by the fact that Williamson never brought his brigade to Charlestown during the city's long besiegement, despite having orders to do so. The backcountry brigadier summarily refused to serve again on either side for the remainder of the war. Traitor or not, "the submission of General Williamson at Ninety-Six had put an end to all resistance in every district of South Carolina."[2] The cause of American independence in the South had reached its nadir.

Until the capture of Charlestown, Sir Henry Clinton had resisted the temptation to call into service any Tory militia in the region. Even when the general felt himself short of manpower, he sent to New York for additional reinforcements of regulars rather than appeal to the local Tory population for help. Clinton wrote: "I . . . judged it to be imprudent, for many obvious reasons, to encourage the friends of [Royal] government to take any steps which might expose them to the malevolence of their enemies before I was fully certain of success, or a stroke of consequence had already taken place against the town whereby a permanent establishment might be attained to enable me to afford them proper protection."[3] In this respect, Clinton showed a far better understanding

262

of local politics than had previous British leaders in the South; the latters' efforts to raise armies of southern Loyalists had met with disaster.

Only after the occupation of Charlestown did Clinton issue a handbill calling for South Carolina's Tories to form Loyalist militias to support the Royal Army. The handbill explained how Clinton expected all able-bodied men of the province to join one of two militia forces. Men with families would serve as a home guard, assembling in their own districts "when required, under officers of their own chusing [*sic*], for the maintenance of peace and good order."[4] The young men of the province without families would form into a separate militia that would act in conjunction with the regular army in offensive operations. These men were required to serve up to six months out of the ensuing twelve months, after which they would be released.

A short time later, on 22 May 1780, Clinton issued a proclamation stating that all who continued to subvert or oppose royal government, or encourage others to do so, would "be treated with that severity so criminal and hardened an obstinacy will deserve, and his or their estates will be immediately seized, in order to be confiscated."[5] Clinton's policies were designed to reestablish Crown rule in South Carolina. All men were required to be in the Royal militia, and those who continued to oppose "legal" government were branded outlaws with no property rights.

Clinton was sensitive to the American fear of being impressed into the British regular army, and he gave written assurances to the South Carolinians that this would not be the case. In the current climate, Clinton's mandates were generally well received. "To men disposed to continue upon their farms," the historian Henry Lee wrote, "and to obey the existing powers, the proffered conditions could not be unacceptable." Some Patriots, however, could not reconcile themselves to abide by the new law, which would force them to serve in the Crown militia against the American cause. "These of course fled the state, determined never to arm against a cause which they believed to be the cause of right."[6]

Clinton appointed Major Patrick Ferguson as inspector of militia for the southern district. Ferguson's chivalric nature was well known. At the Battle of Brandywine in Pennsylvania, he lost the use of his right arm to a Patriot musket ball. Yet, in the same engagement he let pass an opportunity to take a shot at George Washington because, "it was not pleasant to fire at the back of an unoffending individual who was acquitting himself very coolly of his duty."[7]

Ferguson was charged by Clinton to both "embody and discipline" the militia. The appointment of Ferguson was an acknowledgment by Clinton that it was necessary to have someone of unimpeachable character in charge of the southern Loyalists. "You will pay particular attention," Clinton wrote on 22 May 1780 to Ferguson, "to restrain the militia from offering violence to innocent and inoffensive people, and by all means in your power protect the aged, the infirm, the women and children of every denomination from insult and outrage."[8] Clinton's orders and the appointment of Ferguson are proofs that there was no British policy to terrorize the civilian population of the South. While there is no denying that British troops committed excesses at Monck's Corner, Waxhaws, and other places, it is important to vanquish the notion that such acts were ordered or sanctioned by the British high command.

Militarily, the British were now the unquestioned masters of South Carolina and Georgia. The coastal cities of Savannah and Charlestown were now firmly in British control, as were the backcountry towns of Augusta, Ninety Six, and Camden. However, fulfillment of the Southern Strategy called for more than military victory; many citizens had to "volunteer" for service as auxiliaries to the Royal Army.

Droves of South Carolinians came into Charlestown to pledge their allegiance to the king. Over time, more than four thousand South Carolinians enlisted in the royal militia rolls, although nothing close to this number actually shouldered arms in military units. In addition, not all who pledged themselves to the Crown did so with enthusiasm. Many former Patriots joined Clinton's militia, but they did so reluctantly in order to save their property from being confiscated. "[Their] conviction that the rebels can never recover this country have induced them to surrender themselves," Clinton wrote. "They seemed at first to boggle at the idea of arming against the Congress, but with respect to the French and Spaniards they seem to say they are willing to join most heartily against them. In the northern provinces this is all I would ask; but we seem so totally masters here that I insisted on their being ready [to fight for the Crown] on the first call."[9]

That these "former" rebels agreed to bear arms for the king was no doubt a great victory for the British, and a seeming vindication of the Southern Strategy, but many such "Loyal" militia units had to have suspect allegiance. Clinton took the precaution of giving all units "loyal officers," yet one must ask how much any British officer would have trusted such men not to desert the first time a Continental regiment camped nearby. "I do not trust these people," Captain Johann Ewald said of one group of so-called Loyalists, "for what can such a handful of men undertake? I believe they are carrying out a deception to obtain arms and ammunition and to use them against us."[10]

At the time, however, the state of affairs in South Carolina appeared so favorable to the British that Clinton seemed to forget his earlier reservations regarding the power of the Loyalists in the South. In early June, just before he was to leave for New York, Clinton issued a bold edict designed to root out the most inveterate rebels and either force them to submit or make them flee the province.

> The spirit of rebellion in South Carolina being now very nearly subdued, and numbers of the inhabitants of both town and country daily offering their services and soliciting to be admitted to the conditions of British subjects, I judged it proper to release from their paroles all the persons who had surrendered or were taken prisoners before the capitulation of Charlestown (excepting such as had served in the military line or were actually in confinement at the taking of that town and Fort Moultrie) and to call on the inhabitants of the province indiscriminately to take an active part in settling and securing His Majesty's government. I therefore issued a proclamation on the 3d of June to that purpose, and threatened in it to treat as rebels and enemies to their country all those under the above description who should afterward neglect to return to their allegiance.[11]

After turning over command of the British Southern Army to Lord Charles Cornwallis, Clinton departed for New York on 6 June 1780—an event that marked the apogee of British fortunes in the South. Clinton wrote with justifiable satisfaction of the apparent completeness of his victory: "In most cases paroles were exchanged for protections, accompanied with a renewal of allegiance; and for some weeks an universal calm succeeded the agitations with which the province was lately distracted."[12]

Unfortunately for the royal cause, many southern Patriots took the British oath of allegiance only as a convenience and had no intention of serving in an armed capacity against America. The case of Isaac Hayne, a colonel in the South Carolina militia, is one of the best examples of this phenomenon. Colonel Hayne was told that if he did not take the British oath of allegiance, he would be dispossessed of his property. The Patriot officer relented and took the oath but wrote that at the time he did so only for the sake of his "wife and family." Hayne said, "I declare that it [taking the oath] is contrary to my inclination and forced upon me by hard necessity. I will never bear arms against my country . . . I do not mean to desert the cause of America."[13] When the British finally demanded in 1781 that Hayne join a British militia outfit, he fled and took up arms with the Patriots. Hayne was later captured by the British and hung for violating his oath—some calling him the Nathan Hale of the South.[14]

Clinton's revocation of the paroles was illegal by the "rules of war" since it broke the contract made when the Patriot militiamen willingly surrendered. The British officer and historian Charles Stedman observed the effects of Clinton's proclamation firsthand. He reported that many former rebels in South Carolina had hoped "to live quietly upon their estates, as prisoners upon parole, and enjoying a kind of neutrality during the remainder of the war." However, Stedman said that these "neutrals" were "very early disgusted by the proclamation of Sir Henry Clinton, which, without their consent, abrogated the paroles that had been granted, and, in one instant, converted them either into loyal subjects or rebels." Henry Lee wrote, "This arbitrary change of an understood contract affected deeply, and sorely, all to whom it applied. . . . It demonstrated unequivocally that the hoped-for state of neutrality was illusory, and that every man capable of bearing arms must use them in aid or in opposition to the country of his birth." Stedman said, "It was not long before the seeds of discontent appeared, which, when fully matured, produced a counter-revolution in the minds and inclinations of the people as complete and as universal as that which succeeded the fall of Charlestown."[15]

General Clinton's policy errors were entirely consistent with the fundamental flaws in Germain's Southern Strategy. Clinton thought that his edicts would be accepted by the populace because the British leadership took it for granted that "the majority of the inhabitants" were Loyalists—despite abundant evidence to the contrary that had accumulated by that point in the war. This basic miscalculation led Clinton, Cornwallis, and Germain to underestimate the manpower necessary to secure the southern colonies. When he left for New York, Clinton took with him almost five thousand soldiers—most of them regulars. This left Cornwallis with little more than eight thousand troops (regulars and provincials) to garrison South Carolina and Georgia, and to form a field army to continue the war into North Carolina.[16]

To be fair to Clinton, he issued his edicts under great pressure from Lord Germain to "arm and embody the loyal inhabitants of the country." Germain told Clinton: "Notwithstanding the great exertions this country has made and the prodigious force sent out for subduing the rebellion I am convinced our utmost efforts will fail . . . if we cannot find means to engage the people of America in support of a cause which is equally their own and ours, and when their enemies are driven away or subdued [we must] induce them to employ their own force to protect themselves."[17]

Over the summer and fall of 1780, groups of Tories, supported by the regulars and provincials of Cornwallis's army, battled with the remnants of American militia forces throughout South Carolina. Obscure names such as Black Mingo Creek, Blackstocks, and Hanging Rock became burned into South Carolina's historical subconscious as places of violent defiance. However, these sanguinary skirmishes produced no evidence that the Loyalists outnumbered the Patriots in the South. Instead, the continuing violence in Georgia and the Carolinas demonstrated the resilience of the Americans, who, despite the devastation of their earlier battlefield defeats, continued to raise armies and resist.

In October 1780 about one thousand South Carolina Loyalists under Major Ferguson suffered a crushing defeat at King's Mountain by a like number of Patriot militiamen. The Tory cause in the Carolinas never recovered from this demoralizing blow, and never again did southern Loyalists take up arms in such large numbers again. This contrasts sharply with the southern Patriots, who had suffered similar defeats (the capture of Savannah in 1778, Briar Creek in 1779, the siege of Savannah in 1779, Charlestown in 1780) and yet were always able, in time, to recover.

Depending on Loyalists was the core value of the Southern Strategy: a value of economy. The British leadership proved unable to disassociate their operations from this plan. To change the plan and rely on increased numbers of British regulars rather than Loyalists would increase the costs and call into question why a Southern Strategy was pursued at all. The 1779 siege of Savannah also proved that British forces in the South were vulnerable without strong naval protection. Nevertheless, when Clinton left for New York, he also took the majority of the British fleet with him, leaving Cornwallis with only minimal naval assets. Clinton and Cornwallis seemed to have made no provision or contingency plan to deal with the possibility of a sudden French attack—an omission that would have fatal consequences for the Southern Strategy at Yorktown in 1781.

When Sir Henry Clinton left South Carolina in the early summer of 1780, the war in the South was far from over; yet, the pattern for its conclusion had already been set. Despite the apparent completeness of the British victory in South Carolina and Georgia, critical flaws in strategy and policy served to undermine British success. The war would continue, being fought on southern battlefields such as Camden, King's Mountain, Cowpens, Guilford Court House, Ninety Six, and Eutaw Springs, and culminating in the final defeat of the British Southern Army at Yorktown. The Patriots may not have won every battle, but the occupation of the Carolinas was hardly as "easily maintained" as Lord Germain had predicted earlier; and while the British often achieved tactical success on the battlefield, it was the Americans who edged closer to strategic victory after nearly every engagement. Therefore, the apparent success of the Southern Strategy in the summer of 1780 did not mark the beginning of the end of the war in the South, but merely the "end of the beginning."

Author's Note and Historiography

While there have not been numerous modern studies of the southern campaigns, there have been a few excellent ones. Ira Gruber's essay "British Southern Strategy" is an outstanding overview of the fallacy of British policy in the South during the Revolution, and the inspiration for this work. Gruber makes the convincing case that Lord Germain was duped by the royal governors of Virginia and North Carolina into believing that the South was a hotbed of Loyalists. In *Loyalists and Redcoats: A Study in British Revolutionary Policy,* Paul H. Smith argues that false expectations of Loyalist support resulted in the British failure to commit enough troops to ensure the Southern Strategy's success. The key of the British failure, Smith believes, was the lack of a consistent policy toward the American Loyalists. In his essay "British Strategy for Pacifying the Southern Colonies, 1778–1781," John Shy that says Lord Germain's shifting strategic priorities, as well as his failure to check the threat posed by the French navy, helped doom the Southern Strategy.

John S. Pancake's *This Destructive War: The British Campaign in the Carolinas, 1780–1782* is probably the best military history available that also provides significant insight into how individual military engagements related to the overall British Southern Strategy. (Pancake's work concentrates on the period after the fall of Charlestown, of course.) It is also worth mentioning that while I argue with and disagree with many scholars in this book, I have the utmost respect for their work. It simply makes more sense to reconcile the differences I have with other historians than repetitiously to state my agreements —as always, we all stand on the shoulders of giants.

In the course of researching this book, I found great value in creating detailed orders of battle for each engagement. The research involved in creating the orders of battle served to reveal the truth of what happened on the battlefields better than if I had relied solely on narrative sources. In the case of three engagements studied (Moore's Creek Bridge, Stono Ferry, and the siege of Savannah) the new figures are so dramatically different from the traditionally accepted numbers that a complete reevaluation of the battles is required.

Accurate orders of battle also help to clarify the role of British Loyalists and American militiamen in the South. Many modern historians argue that the Revolutionary War in the South was primarily a partisan conflict. However, the orders of battle in this study reveal that southern Loyalists comprised a minority of the troops present in most of the battles studied in this volume. This fact works against the argument that the war in the

South was principally a partisan war, although partisan operations would take on greater importance in the phase of the war after the fall of Charlestown. The orders of battle for the period up to the fall of Charlestown reveal that even when Loyalists comprised a substantial portion of the troops present, there were often more *northern* Loyalists than their southern counterparts present, and British regulars and their professional German allies bore the brunt of the fighting.

Issues in Stono Ferry Historiography

Several aspects of the battle of Stono Ferry require critical examination with regard to the existing scholarship. The first is the reason for the Continentals' failure to charge; the second—and most controversial—is how culpable William Moultrie was in the defeat; the third is how many troops fought on the American side at Stono Ferry; and the fourth is the location of Stono Ferry.

Before the battle of Stono Ferry, Major General Benjamin Lincoln instructed Brigadier General Isaac Huger's Continental troops to forgo firing on the enemy and instead charge them with fixed bayonets. In spite of these orders, the Continentals never did make a charge and instead stood and exchanged volleys of musketry with the British. Lincoln wrote a letter to William Moultrie on the day of the battle describing the day's action. Initially, Lincoln said, "I wish the troops had been so broken to service as that they could have been made to charge the enemy with fixed bayonets." One can infer from this statement that Lincoln felt the Continentals failed to charge because of a lack of experience and professional discipline. Later in the same letter, however, Lincoln excused the Continentals, stating: "There was a creek on the right of the enemy's works, which ran in front of the redoubts . . . which was the real reason why our continental troops did not storm the works as was intended: We were wholly ignorant of there being such an obstruction in the advance of the troops, otherwise, our order of attack would have been reversed."[1]

According to Henry Lee in *The American Revolution in the South,* the Continentals were guilty of disobeying orders when they returned the British fire instead of storming their works. Lee also says that about midway through the battle Lincoln managed to stop the Continentals from firing and ordered them to charge once more, but again the troops failed to obey. If this is true, then the creek must have been surmountable, for it seems unlikely that Lincoln would have ordered a suicide attack.

Neither Henry Lee nor Charles Stedman mentioned a creek in their narratives of the battle, and a detailed map of the battle drawn by an engineer with Prevost's army shows a marsh but no creek on the right of the British fortifications. It may be concluded, therefore, that the creek was a relatively minor obstacle that was actually part of the marsh on the British right and that the Americans were already aware of this creek before the battle began. Indeed, Henry Lee reports that part of Henderson's light infantry did pass through the marsh—which supposedly was impassable—in an attempt to gain the British right flank.

It was probably out of a sensible desire for self-preservation that the Continentals failed to charge. The marsh and creek were surmountable obstacles, but troops passing through them would have been bogged down and thus made excellent targets for the muskets and cannons of the Highlanders. If the Continentals had been more disciplined, they might have charged as ordered; but one can only guess at the outcome.

⋙◈⋘

The role of Brigadier General William Moultrie in the defeat at Stono Ferry is also controversial. The contemporary historians Henry Lee and David Ramsay put either some or all of the blame for the defeat on Moultrie, and modern historians have followed their lead. However, this narrative nearly ignores Moultrie's role in the battle because I do not think that his presence on James Island would have materially affected the outcome of the engagement.

Moultrie has been blamed for failing to gather a sufficient number of boats to transport a brigade of Charlestown militia to James Island before the battle. This movement was meant to divert British attention away from Stono Ferry and so reduce or prevent the reinforcement of the Stono garrison during the battle. According to Ramsay, Moultrie's delay in getting his troops across the river was due to "mismanagement and a delay in providing boats."[2] The criticism of Moultrie has primarily stemmed from two assumptions on the part of Ramsay and Lee. The first is that it was Moultrie's responsibility to gather the necessary boats for the operation; the second is that the arrival of British reinforcements caused the American defeat. However, neither of these assumptions is correct.

In May 1779 all the American bateaux at Ashley Ferry had been captured by the British. By early June the Americans had reestablished a quantity of boats at Charlestown —though it was an amount insufficient to transport more than a few hundred men at one time. On 6 June, Lincoln sent the following order to Moultrie: "If the boats which were, a few days ago, at Ashley-Ferry, have been sent to town, I wish that you would give orders for all of them to immediately return to the Ferry."[3] The boats remained at Ashley Ferry until 19 June, when Lincoln ordered Moultrie to move his garrison of militiamen out of Charlestown and over to James Island to support Lincoln's attack at Stono Ferry. However, the boats needed for the operation were still five miles away at Ashley Ferry, as Lincoln had ordered two weeks earlier.

Moultrie lost a great deal of time sending for the boats and waiting for them to make their way to the city. In fact, Moultrie made it a point to mention in a dispatch written at eight o'clock on the night of 19 June that the boats had not yet arrived at the city docks. The early morning hours of the 20th saw the movement of troops from Charlestown to James Island incomplete and proceeding slowly. Moultrie again wrote to Lincoln stating that transport of the troops had been slowed by a "high wind." He then added pointedly, "the boats not coming from Ashley Ferry has retarded our movements very much."[4]

The hours lost waiting for the boats could have been spent ferrying Moultrie's troops to James Island. Lincoln should have anticipated the need to have the boats at Charlestown and sent appropriate orders to the ferrymen. In fact, the messenger carrying Lincoln's orders to Moultrie that evening would almost certainly have gone by way of Ashley Ferry to reach Charlestown! Lincoln could therefore have sent orders to the ferrymen

269

with the same messenger by whom he sent orders to Moultrie. If Lincoln had not ordered the boats from the city two weeks before, then Moultrie's movement may have been more readily facilitated. Ultimately, the late hour at which Lincoln made his decision to attack (the evening of the 19th) precluded a timely movement of Moultrie's militia out of Charlestown.

British records—Prevost's report of the battle to Germain—prove that only an insignificant number of reinforcements had crossed from John's Island to the bridgehead before Lincoln made his decision to retreat. However, it should be noted that Lincoln —unlike many historians—did not blame Moultrie for failing to move his troops to James Island in time to make the diversion. Lincoln seemed perfectly understanding of Moultrie's difficulties, and the commander of the Southern Department had the strength of character to avoid the temptation to make Moultrie the scapegoat for the defeat.

Perhaps the most significant new finding regarding the battle of Stono Ferry is the number of men engaged on each side. The total number of British troops is relatively easy to determine. General Augustine Prevost said in his official report to the American secretary in London that there were eight hundred troops under Lieutenant Colonel John Maitland's command at Stono Ferry on 20 June 1779. According to the contemporary British historian Charles Stedman, that garrison did "not much exceed five hundred men, really effective, and fit for duty,"[5] which implies that there were more troops present but that they were unfit due to illness or injuries. The American spy whose report instigated the American attack estimated the strength of the garrison before the battle at about six hundred men.[6] Prevost said that there were eight hundred British and Hessian troops present, and from the other sources we can conclude the fit-for-duty total to be about six hundred or seven hundred men.

The amount of American manpower at Stono Ferry is substantially more difficult to ascertain. Since Dr. David Ramsay published his *History of the American Revolution* in 1789, it has been generally accepted that Benjamin Lincoln attacked "with about 1,200 Americans on six or 700 of the British."[7] In his landmark work, *The War of the Revolution*, Christopher Ward criticized Lincoln for taking such a small force against the British bridgehead: "This affair reflected little credit upon Moultrie's [*sic,* Lincoln's] generalship. To take only 1,200 men, largely militia, against 900 British and Hessian regulars strongly entrenched, when he had five or six times that number available, was certainly poor judgment."[8]

Ward states incorrectly that at the time of the battle Lincoln had "between 6,000 and 7,000 men in Charlestown."[9] This claim is not substantiated by the facts. In a dispatch written on 4 June 1779, Lincoln cited the strength of his field army at 2,780 present and fit for duty, not including "about one hundred of the Artillery and the Light Horse, a return of the latter I have not received." In addition to his field army, Lincoln put the strength of the Charlestown garrison at "about eighteen hundred men, including the militia of that town." That brought the total strength of Lincoln's army to 4,680 troops, a figure confirmed by the manuscript returns in the collection of Benjamin Lincoln's

Papers preserved at the Massachusetts Historical Society in Boston. Lincoln's force in the field actually appears to have accrued to over 3,000 troops by the time of the battle.[10]

The order of battle that I created for Stono Ferry lists the American army's strength at Stono Ferry at 3,051 troops—or nearly all of Lincoln's field army in South Carolina. This determination is based on the fact that the primary source accounts of the battle (such as Major Grimké's narrative contained in William Moultrie's memoirs) indicate that the entire field army participated. The casualty returns for Lincoln's army made on 21 June 1779 confirm this finding: *every brigade* of Lincoln's field army was present at the engagement, *and nearly all took casualties.* (See "American Casualty Return for Stono Ferry, 20 June 1779" at the end of chapter 9.) The question thus becomes whether Lincoln left large portions of his brigades behind. This is unlikely. In order to come close to the 1,200 American troops that Ramsay says attacked at Stono Ferry, Lincoln would have to have left behind more than half of each brigade (since we know that all the brigades participated in the action). This would have been a highly irregular procedure for armies of that or any era.

Lincoln never specifically mentioned in any of his dispatches the number of troops he commanded at the engagement. I believe the reason for this is because he had mentioned the strength of his force in previous dispatches, and because Lincoln took it for granted that the recipients of his letters would correctly assume that he attacked with his entire field army. The only reference Lincoln made to the number of troops he employed at Stono is contained in a dispatch made on 21 June 1779. He wrote, "We moved yesterday morning with the principal part of our troops."[11] Since Lincoln used the phrase "principal part" we can assume that he left some of his troops behind as a camp guard —almost certainly those who were listed as "sick present" on the strength returns. Those listed on returns as "sick absent" or "sick in hospital" were obviously so ill that they had been removed from camp and thus can safely be omitted from orders of battle (those "on furlough" are similarly omitted). Lincoln probably brought only the fit-for-duty men to the battlefield, which would have been about twenty-eight hundred troops, i.e., "the principal part" of his force.

It can be noted that there were about twelve hundred Continental troops in the action, and Ramsay may have erroneously assumed that this was the total of the American forces. Moultrie reported that he had moved seven hundred troops to James Island by the afternoon of 20 June 1779. However, close inspection of the manuscript note that he sent to inform Lincoln of his position shows that the number "700" is crossed out and the figure "1400" has been substituted. This indicates that Moultrie moved nearly his entire eighteen-hundred-man garrison out of Charlestown. The "700" figure was probably the number of men who were ferried across in the first wave, and by the time the note was received most of the garrison had made it across. (Most historians say that Moultrie only moved seven hundred men, but they did not see the manuscript correction.)

—————⊱◈⊰—————

There is a minor controversy regarding the location of Stono Ferry. An overwhelming amount of evidence indicates that the ferry was located on the northwest side of Johns

Island forming a communication with the mainland. A contemporary map drawn by a British engineer accompanying Prevost's army so indicates the ferry's position.[12] Numerous firsthand accounts (including Eliza Wilkinson's diary, Benjamin Lincoln's letters, and William Moultrie's memoirs) leave no doubt that this indeed was the site of the ferry and the battle. The entry on Stono Ferry in Mark Boatner's *Encyclopedia of the American Revolution* says that Maitland's bridgehead was actually on James Island and not the mainland.[13] Boatner is mistaken, however; he probably got this erroneous position from a map drawn in 1780 and published by William Faden of James Island, which illustrated Clinton's attack on Charlestown. On this map "Stono Ferry" is a crossing between Johns Island and James Island. Clinton's map, however, is not made with reference to the action fought on 20 June 1779, but rather to the route that Clinton's army took to complete its investment of Charlestown in 1780. There were at least three ferries across the Stono River—some to James Island and some to the mainland. The location indicated on the map of the engagement included with this volume is therefore the correct position of Stono Ferry.

Issues in Savannah Historiography

There are several important controversies in the historiography of the 1779 Savannah campaign that can now be resolved. Perhaps the most salient issue is the number of troops present on all sides. Colonel Maitland's odyssey from Beaufort to Savannah is another subject that requires close examination. Some of the other matters that will be investigated include the role black soldiers played on both sides, as well as how many and whose flags were planted at the Spring Hill redoubt.

Traditional sources have underestimated the numbers of all the combatants at Savannah. More importantly, they have misstated the ratio of attacking troops to defending troops. Using Alexander Lawrence's *Storm over Savannah*—a typical traditional source—yields an allied total of 5,983 men versus 2,360 British, or a ratio of 2.53 to 1. If this ratio was accurate, it would appear that the allies had a substantial numerical advantage over the British—nearly the accepted 3 to 1 ratio that most military experts stipulate as needed for an attacking force to overcome a fortified opponent. The order of battle in this volume lists 7,722 Franco-American troops versus 4,813 British: a ratio of just 1.6 to 1—not a significant advantage. In fact, an attacker-to-defender ratio of 1.6 to 1 is so low that most modern military experts would not regard it to be sufficient to justify attacking an entrenched opponent unless the attacker had a significant qualitative edge in men or weaponry, which was not the case at Savannah.

The actual strength of the Savannah garrison (4,813) was roughly twice the number that most historians have allowed. The figure of 4,813 is derived primarily from the commissary return of 20 October 1779 present in the Henry Clinton Papers in the William Clements Library, the University of Michigan, Ann Arbor. I also referenced General Prevost's strength return of 16 October 1779 (B. F. Stevens Facsimiles, C.O.5. bundle 182, Library of Congress, Manuscripts Division). The commissary and strength returns do not differ significantly for the strengths of most units, and so the two sources serve to confirm each other. However, the commissary return is generally more satisfactory and complete, mostly because it includes the black soldiers and pioneers serving in the lines, while the strength return only lists the white troops serving in the lines: British and Hessian regulars, provincials, and militia.

Prevost's strength return lists 3,668 officers and enlisted men in regular and provincial regiments, 253 militiamen, 283 sailors serving the batteries, and 67 Royal Artillerists, for a total of 4,271. Prevost lists 1,189 as sick, for an invalid rate of about 28 percent. The commissary return includes all the troops "victualed" in the city from 11 October through 20 October 1779. A commissary return, unlike strength returns, does not differentiate between those sick and those fit for duty and includes officers; it is therefore certain that the figure of 4,813 does not represent a fit-for-duty total. Using the invalid rate of 28 percent mentioned above, it can be estimated that there were about 3,466 fit-for-duty men in the garrison.

Other historians have almost universally underestimated the size of the British garrison. The contemporary British historian Charles Stedman wrote: "The force in Savannah, under General Prevost, did not exceed two thousand five hundred of all sorts, regulars, provincial corps, seamen, militia, and volunteers." Sir James Wright, the British governor of Georgia who was in Savannah during the siege, agreed with this number. Dr. David Ramsay—an American doctor who was also present at the siege—wrote, "The force of the garrison was between 2 and 3000, of which 150 were militia." A British officer, quoted in Franklin Hough's *Siege of Savannah,* said: "Our whole force—regulars, militia, volunteers, and sailors—*on duty* did not exceed 2,350 men" [emphasis added]. A map of the battle published by William Faden states, "Total number fit for duty including soldiers, seamen, and militia: 2360."[14]

French estimates came closer to the real mark. A French officer on d'Estaing's staff made an order of battle, based on the testimony of British deserters, that put British strength at about 3,790 (not including 1,000 black laborers). Lieutenant François d'Auber de Peyrelongue, one of three French artillery officers at the siege, estimated that there were 4,500 British troops present, of which 2,500 were regulars. This was a *remarkably* accurate estimate, based on what is known today.[15]

The early-twentieth-century British historian Sir John Fortescue put the garrison's strength at 3,700 men, "of whom twenty-two hundred were fit for duty." In 1951 Alexander Lawrence wrote in *Storm over Savannah* that 2,360 men were present and fit for duty under Prevost's command, while the historian Christopher Ward said that there were 3,200 British soldiers at Savannah. Later historians have generally followed the lead of Lawrence on the matter, although he did not document his source for the total.[16]

It would have been odd for the British to have only 2,360 armed defenders in Savannah—the most often repeated figure—given that the British had invaded Georgia only nine months before with over 3,000 men under Lieutenant Colonel Campbell and they were joined by another 1,000 from Florida under General Prevost. The British certainly would have suffered some attrition from sickness and desertion. However, the British had taken few battle casualties and had actually increased their numbers by recruiting Tories and drafting blacks.

In his memoirs Sir Henry Clinton said, "[Prevost's] garrison did not consist of more than four thousand, of which not above twenty-four hundred were regimented [i.e., regular] troops."[17] Clinton's statement that 2,400 *regulars* were present is almost identical to the figure of 2,360 *total* troops present that is given most often. Therefore, it is safe to assume that at some point shortly after the battle it was revealed that the British had about 2,400 *regular* troops at Savannah; it became a common misconception that this figure included all the troops present—militia, provincials, sailors, and so forth.

Another myth that most modern historians have repeated is that the majority of the Savannah garrison was made up of Loyalists. This misinformation was probably originated by Christopher Ward in his generally excellent *War of the Revolution*. "Exclusive of Negroes," Ward wrote, "Prevost's force numbered 2,360 rank and file. It will be noticed that the great majority of the garrison was made up of American Loyalists, a fact emphasizing the character of the conflict in the South as a civil war."[18] Ward's inaccurate statement is based on his flawed figures for the strength of the garrison. Of the 4,813 armed defenders of Savannah, 2,407 were either British or Hessian regulars, or Royal Navy sailors. Of those remaining, 922 were northern Loyalists serving as professional soldiers in provincial battalions from New York and New Jersey; excluding blacks, this left only 1,207 white southern Loyalists—about one-quarter of the garrison.

Even adding the northern and southern Loyalist contingents together, this constituted only 2,129 men, or 44 percent of the garrison—as opposed to the "great majority" of the garrison that Ward claims they comprised. Without doubt, 44 percent is a substantial percentage for Loyalists participating in a major battle, but these figures do not serve to emphasize, as Ward puts it, the "character of the conflict in the South as a civil war," given that nearly half of the Loyalists present were from the North. Indeed, the order of battle for Savannah serves to prove how few Loyalists there were in the South, and how helpless they were without British and Hessian regulars to support them.

Traditional computations of the number of allied troops besieging Savannah are also imperfect, but not as dramatically as they have been for the British. A figure of about 4,384 French soldiers present can be derived by analyzing three excellent sources: the "Pechot" diary, the order of battle in Alexander Lawrence's *Storm over Savannah*, and the order of battle in Charles C. Jones's *Siege of Savannah*. Of these, the Pechot diary is by far the most detailed and the best French primary source available.

Alexander Lawrence identifies "Pechot" as the nom de plume of Captain Jean-Rémy de Tarragon. We can deduce from the text of his diary that Captain Tarragon helped lead the attack on the Spring Hill redoubt with the right French column under Count Dillon. Tarragon's order of battle is a true one in that it lists actual troop dispositions at the time of attack. This means that several of the units listed by Tarragon are the ad hoc formations created only a few hours before the attack on 9 October 1779. By cross-referencing the figures of Lawrence, Jones, and Tarragon an approximate size for each regiment can be better ascertained. "American and French Camp Organization: Savannah, 1779," included at the end of chapter 10, is an amalgamation of these sources, relying heavily on Tarragon's "Pechot" diary for the bulk of the data and arbitrarily balancing some figures that were contradicted by Lawrence in *Storm over Savannah*. The figures for the American and French camp organization differ slightly from the order of battle; this is because it was impossible to reconcile completely Tarragon's order of battle, which included ad hoc units, to the actual regiments.

The number of American troops present was more difficult to determine. Most historians put that number at about 2,000; the higher estimates allow 2,500 and the lowest give Lincoln a mere 1,350 men under his command. However, by utilizing strength returns scattered among several research libraries I was able to revise this figure upward to about 3,265—or almost 60 percent higher than most earlier estimates. The strength returns utilized were for individual regiments and brigades and were found in the manuscript archives at the William L. Clements Library in Ann Arbor, Michigan; the Thomas Addis Emmet Collection, Manuscripts and Archives Section, New York Public Library; and the Benjamin Lincoln Papers held at the Massachusetts Historical Society in Boston.

The contemporary British historian Charles Stedman came up with the grossly exaggerated figure of 10,000 total allied troops at Savannah, but his total is the upper extreme of the contemporary estimates. Other contemporary sources such as the *Paris Gazette* said that there were 3,524 French and 2,000 Americans at Savannah; while a British officer who fought at Savannah, quoted in *Rivington's Royal Gazette*, estimated the French numbers at 3,500 and the Americans at 2,500. In *Siege of Savannah,* the reputable nineteenth-century historian Charles C. Jones calculated the number of French at 4,456 (a remarkably accurate total for the time) and the Americans at 2,127. In 1952 Christopher Ward said that there were 3,500 French and only 1,350 Americans (600 Continentals and 750 militia). Alexander Lawrence extensively researched the French military archives in Paris and arrived at the number of French soldiers present as 3,883 —somewhat too low according to the detailed Pechot diary; Lawrence also wrongly concluded that there were only 2,100 Americans present during the siege.[19]

There is an oft-repeated quote from a French officer: "The American column advanced, in good order, to its point of attack. At the first discharge of a gun, two-thirds of the Virginia militia detach[ed] themselves from it."[20] But is this what really happened?

Based on the documentary sources, it is unlikely that the Virginians ran as the French officer described on the day of the assault. This is because the casualty return for 9 October 1779 showed that the regiment of "Virginia Levies" suffered nine killed and fifty-one wounded, for a total of sixty casualties—more than any other American regiment present. Only a regiment that was heavily engaged would have suffered such high casualties.

There were actually two contingents of Virginia troops in Georgia during the siege: Colonel Richard Parkers's 1st Virginia Levies and Colonel Theodorick Bland's 1st Regiment of Virginia Continental Light Dragoons. (Bland was not present, and the unit was commanded by Major John Jameson.) Both of these units consisted of regular troops, but it has been documented that they lacked proper uniforms and so could easily have been mistaken for militiamen. Parker's regiment was part of a new brigade of Virginia Continentals recently recruited by Brigadier General Charles Scott.

General Scott had been authorized to raise a brigade of three regiments of infantry in early 1779 for service in the Continental Army. Originally these troops were meant to supplement the main U.S. army under George Washington in New York; however, the desperate pleas of General Lincoln for additional manpower to reinforce the Southern Department compelled Washington and Congress to redirect these troops southward. To fill the ranks of his brigade, General Scott recruited volunteers from the twelve militia districts in Virginia; but when volunteers could not be had, Scott was authorized to draft militiamen in order to meet the quota set by the state assembly.

Even with his authorization to draft men, General Scott found it difficult to complete his brigade. According to the historian Lee A. Wallace, this was because the men feared service in South Carolina and Georgia, which were considered "sickly" regions rife with yellow fever and malaria. Scott probably never recruited more than 1,200 soldiers out of an authorized strength of 2,216; however, by mid-May he had gathered enough men to begin active operations.[21]

Before they marched south, Scott's soldiers were divided into regiments that were usually referred to as the 1st, 2nd, and 3rd Virginia regiments even though Continental formations already existed with these designations in the main army under General Washington. General Scott's units were therefore sometimes referred to as "detachments" or "levies." The historian Lee Wallace says that clothes and shoes were hard to come by for these troops, so they may have had the appearance of average militiamen even though they were regulars.

After a delay caused by British raids on Portsmouth in the spring of 1779, the first contingent of Virginia's Continental Levies started south on 27 June. This regiment of about three hundred to four hundred raw recruits was commanded by Colonel Richard Parker, who was soon followed by the 1st Regiment of Virginia Continental Light Dragoons under Major Jameson. By midsummer these troops had arrived in upper Georgia, where they took up position at Augusta on 15 August.[22]

In September 1779 the Virginians moved south to join General Lincoln's army, which was on its way to invest Savannah in cooperation with Count d'Estaing's expeditionary forces. At the town of Ebenezer, twenty-three miles north of Savannah, Colonel Parker's troops were brigaded with Brigadier General Isaac Huger's troops, including the 2nd South Carolina Continentals under Lieutenant Colonel Francis Marion. The strength returns for Huger's brigade during this period did not list individual regiments but instead lumped all of the Continentals together into one figure. This method of reporting hampers our ability today to get an accurate picture of how many and whose troops were actually present.

Let us return now to the question of what role the Virginians played in the battle on 9 October 1779. The manuscript strength return for the 1st Virginia Continental Light Dragoons dated 10 October 1779 states that there were approximately 166 Virginia cavalrymen present at the time of battle. Only a few narratives mention the Virginia cavalrymen, and those only briefly. However, we can safely assume that the Virginian dragoons were brigaded with General Pulaski's men—since we know that Pulaski commanded all of the cavalry in the American army. The 10 October strength return for the Virginia dragoons lists three wounded and one killed—presumably casualties from the previous day's combat. Nevertheless, the casualty return for the army does not mention any casualties for the dragoons—an apparent omission by Lincoln's staff.

General Huger was in command of most of the American militia, which attacked the British left flank. The Continentals and the Charlestown militia were organized into two columns under Colonel Laurens and General McIntosh to attack the British right at the Spring Hill redoubt. Placing Parker's Virginians therefore requires some deductive reasoning: Parker's men sustained the heaviest casualties of any regiment; therefore, his regiment must be placed at a point where significant action occurred. Major Thomas Pinckney's journal of the battle makes it clear that General McIntosh's column saw little combat and sustained only a handful of casualties. It can therefore be concluded that the Virginians did not march with McIntosh's column.

The Virginians were ill-clothed and inexperienced, and they therefore might have been mistaken as militia: Could they thus have been with Huger's militia attacking the British left? No, because Huger's troops only sustained about thirty casualties and Parker's regiment alone sustained sixty casualties. Having eliminated Huger's and McIntosh's columns as possibilities for the placement of Colonel Parker's regiment, we can therefore place the Virginians with the main attack column, grouped with Francis Marion's 2nd South Carolina Regiment and Colonel John Laurens's Corps of Light Infantry. This also makes sense because Lincoln had grouped all of his Continentals in the right column; even though the Virginians were just raw levies, they still qualified as Continentals. Lee Wallace reports that one of Colonel Parker's officers, Major Richard Clough Anderson, sustained a sword thrust in the shoulder, which indicates that the Virginians were in the thick of the vicious hand-to-hand melee that took place on the ramparts of the Spring Hill redoubt. The fact that Major Anderson (father of Robert Anderson, who surrendered Fort Sumter in 1861) was wounded by a sword indicates that he was personally engaged with a British officer, possibly the commander of the redoubt, Captain Thomas Tawse.

The 2nd South Carolina Regiment usually gets all the credit for the assault on Spring Hill. However, it in no way diminishes the honor of that unit to at long last acknowledge the valor of all the troops who fought atop the berm of the Spring Hill redoubt that day: Colonel Parker's Virginia Levies, Colonel William Thompson's 3rd South Carolina Regiment, the Charlestown Militia, and Lieutenant Colonel John Laurens's Corps of Light Infantry. They all fought with valor equal to that of the 2nd South Carolina, and all suffered significant casualties. It is especially important to debunk the single comment of a French officer who said that the Virginia "militia" fled. The casualty records indicate that the Continental soldiers of Virginia fought bravely atop the Spring Hill redoubt on 9 October 1779.

—⇒∘◆∘⇐—

The role that the American cavalry played at Savannah is another perplexing issue. The question boils down to this: Did the horsemen charge the British fortifications on 9 October 1779? Answering this question will at the same time solve the question of Pulaski's death: Did he die near the British batteries, as one participant account claims, or at the abatis?

The American and French orders of attack state that the cavalry was to attempt to penetrate the British lines. The light troops were to attack and force a breach that the cavalry might charge through and, as d'Estaing put it, "create fear by charging through the streets at open rein, after the way had been opened for it; it could outflank foot soldiers and cut them down from behind."[23]

Having established what the cavalrymen were *supposed* to do, what did they *in fact* do? Little went according to plan on 9 October 1779. Did Brigadier General Pulaski ignore orders, as Colonel Laurens did, and attack into the British defenses at Spring Hill? Obviously a cavalry charge against fortifications seems foolhardy, and yet several primary-source accounts—including those of Major Thomas Pinckney and Major Rogowski (of Pulaski's corps)—state that this is exactly what Pulaski attempted. In *Storm over Savannah*, Alexander Lawrence says that Captain Paul Bentalou—a soldier in Pulaski's Legion—contradicted this view and said that Pulaski kept his cavalry within the tree line. Franklin Hough supports this view in *Siege of Savannah*, saying that Pulaski left Colonel Horry in charge of the cavalry while he and Captain Bentalou rode forward by themselves (and perhaps a small party?) to see if they could help Count d'Estaing rally his troops. Bentalou's name appears on numerous strength returns for the outfit, and he is listed among the ranks of American officers wounded at Savannah. It is generally accepted that Rogowski was also present in the combat, but as there is no complete roster for the regiment, it is difficult to confirm this as fact.[24]

Major General Lincoln's casualty return for the army reported few casualties among the cavalry: only one man killed (Pulaski) and six wounded, including two officers. Including the casualties of the 1st Virginia Continental Light Dragoons brings the numbers up to only two killed and nine wounded—extremely light casualties. These figures, however, serve only to bring up more questions. If the cavalry did not leave the tree line, as Captain Bentalou claims, why did they sustain casualties at all? On the other hand, that there were so few casualties is strange, given the testimony of those who say that the charging cavalrymen were severely "galled" (in the words of Thomas Pinckney) by the enemy fire.

Shedding more light on the affair is the fact that no British account reported a cavalry attack that day (surely a memorable event, had it occurred). Colonel Daniel Horry was in command of the South Carolina Light Dragoons who, as Pinckney noted, followed the Lancers. The Virginia Dragoons are not specifically mentioned in these accounts, but it may be assumed that they were attached to Colonel Horry's command. Had the cavalry actually been "between" two British gun batteries where the fire was like "a pouring shower," as Major Rogowski claims, it is almost certain that they would have taken more casualties than the two killed and nine wounded reported later. In addition, Thomas Pinckney's account says that a severe fire caused them to incline left, meaning that the cavalry would have been receiving strong fire only from their right— i.e., they were not subjected to a cross fire. According to Alexander Lawrence, d'Estaing said that Pulaski died "by his own fault in placing himself where he should not have been at the moment." In his memoir of the siege d'Estaing said that the Polish general had "prematurely advanced in order to avail himself more promptly of the passage we were to open for him."[25]

Taking all of these accounts together, it is safe to conclude that the role of the cavalry in the battle was generally as Major Pinckney described it: The cavalry advanced only partway toward the abatis before getting turned back by artillery fire. Bentalou's and d'Estaing's testimonies indicate that Pulaski probably advanced with a small party of officers further than most of his force up to the line of the abatis, at which position most of the sources agree Pulaski was killed. (Another controversy surrounds what happened to Pulaski's body after the battle, but I choose not to become embroiled in that question.) Pinckney's version of events is the most logical scenario, given the light casualties the cavalry sustained: if they had charged between the British batteries, as Rogowski claims, where they were subjected to a cross fire, they would have had many more casualties.

The story of the color-bearers of the 2nd South Carolina at Savannah is at once one of the most romantic and most tragic of the Revolution. One physical remnant of the story still exists: the blue standard of the 2nd South Carolina Regiment captured by the British. It resides today in the Museum of the 60th Regiment, the King's Royal Rifle Corps, at Winchester, England.

From this fact we know that the 2nd South Carolina Regiment planted at least one of its two regimental standards atop Spring Hill and that it was captured by the British. But the historian Benson Lossing says that one of the two flags planted was French: "Regardless of the destructive storm, the gallant [allied] troops leaped the ditch, and planted the crescent and the lily upon the parapet." The "crescent" was the emblem on the banner of the 2nd South Carolina Regiment, while the "lily" was the fleur de lis of the royal standard of France. Lossing went on to state, "The French standard was raised by one of D'Estaing's aids [sic], who, with Hume and Bush, soon fell mortally wounded leaving their colors fluttering in the breeze." The historian Henry B. Dawson also says that the French briefly planted a flag on the Spring Hill redoubt.[26]

A British officer at the siege confirms that two flags were planted but states that they were both American: "Two Rebel Standards were once fixed upon the Redoubt on the Ebenezer Road; one of them was carried off again, and the other, which belonged to the 2nd Carolina Regiment, was taken." In his official report to London, General Prevost said, "Two stand of colours were actually planted and several assailants killed upon the parapet." However, Prevost does not mention whether they were French or American flags.[27]

Alexander Lawrence makes the erroneous claim in *Storm over Savannah* that since the British captured a flag at Spring Hill it must be a myth that Sergeant William Jasper rescued the regiment's flag. Lawrence's confusion is caused by his failure to realize that the 2nd South Carolina had two regimental flags: one red and one blue. Therefore, there were enough flags for the men of the 60th Regiment to capture one (the blue) and Jasper to have brought off a second (the red).

It was common practice at the time for regiments in European armies to have at least two battalions, and each battalion would have a flag. Nevertheless, the 2nd South Carolina Regiment, like most American regiments in the Revolution, had only one battalion. However, when Mrs. Susannah Elliot made the regiment's flags in 1776, she could not be sure that the regiment would not increase the number of battalions later in the war, so she made two just to be safe.

The heroic march of Colonel John Maitland and his Beaufort garrison to Savannah almost certainly saved the British army in Georgia; but the adventure is still surrounded by many questions. How did Maitland manage to "sneak" out of Beaufort undetected by either the Americans or the French? Did Maitland really leave Beaufort without a plan on how to get back to Savannah, trusting only to luck that he would find a way? Did a pair of black anglers tell Maitland of a "secret" route using Wall's Cut to avoid the French ships?

It turns out that some American officers had information about Maitland's departure from Beaufort only hours after the event—but they neglected to act promptly on the intelligence. Among the manuscript papers of Benjamin Lincoln is a letter from Colonel Maurice Simons of the Charlestown Militia. The letter reveals that Simons, who was in the process of marching with his men to Georgia, captured a British deserter near Port Royal Island on the evening of 13 September 1779. The deserter was a soldier in the 71st Highland Regiment, and he told Colonel Simons that Maitland had departed Beaufort earlier that day. Simons thought that the Scotsman might be a spy and dismissed the story, which he said was "not quite satisfactory."[28]

However, on 15 September an American soldier and a "sensible negro fellow" entered Simons's camp and confirmed the deserter's information: the British had evacuated the island by ship on the 13th. Colonel Simons finally conceded that there was sufficient evidence to write to General Lincoln concerning the departure of the Beaufort garrison—though it had now been two days since his first intelligence of the event. At this time Simons was still inside South Carolina camped at Great Swamp. Though he wrote to Lincoln sometime on 15 September, Simons did not send the letter until the morning of 16 September. By this time Colonel Maitland and the majority of his men were only a few hours from Savannah, which they reached at noon on the same day.

Most American officers probably did not believe that Maitland had enough boats to take a waterborne route off the island. Only two months earlier General Moultrie wrote that he was "inclined to think that they [the Beaufort garrison] mean to leave it [Port Royal Island] entirely, but are detained for want of a sufficient number of vessels."[29] Though it is perhaps too much to blame Simons for allowing Maitland to relieve Savannah, it is undeniable that had he communicated the intelligence he gained from the Scottish deserter immediately on 13 September 1779 it might have changed the course of the campaign. Given that Maitland's leaving Beaufort was hardly an unbelievable event—and was even a likely one—Simons at the very least should have taken immediate action to verify the deserter's information.

What responsibility do the French officers bear in the affair? According to the Americans, it had been agreed at Charlestown on 4 September 1779 that the Americans would guard the land route off Beaufort while the French would guard the passage by sea. Lincoln said, "The Count was to ... block up the enemy in Port Royal and Savannah, and send vessels into the southern inlets to prevent them from escaping ... to [St.] Augustine."[30] D'Estaing denied that this was the case, though, and said that no such agreement had been made: "A few days after the arrival of the Beaufort garrison he began to try to exculpate himself for this event by accusing M. de Fontanges of not telling me what had been decided at the Council held in Charleston."[31] D'Estaing said that Fontanges denied any such agreement had taken place, and d'Estaing believed him.

However, Captain Jean-Rémy de Tarragon agreed with the Americans and held d'Estaing responsible for the failure to contain Maitland: "This unfortunate junction [between Prevost and Maitland] would not have taken place if our general [d'Estaing] had marched direct to Savannah on landing or if he had sent a fifty-gun vessel into the river at Port Royal as the council of war held by the Americans at Charlestown had requested."[32]

According to Major Thomas Pinckney, he informed d'Estaing aboard the *Languedoc* on 7 September 1779 of the need to contain Maitland. "In passing before Beaufort," Pinckney wrote, "d'Estaing was apprised that Colonel Maitland, with a considerable part of the British force, was stationed at that place, and was aware of the advantages which would result from preventing his junction with the main body at Savannah." D'Estaing ordered two frigates, *Le Sagittaire* and *Le Fier Rodrigue,* to blockade Beaufort by entering Port Royal Sound. However, the frigates' pilots—supplied by the Americans at Charlestown—refused to take them over the bar of the Port Royal River. "I know," Pinckney wrote, "from the acknowledgement of the principal [American] pilot that he did refuse to carry in the vessels."[33]

Since the American pilots refused to take any ships over the bar of the river, the French could not keep close observation of Maitland's garrison at Beaufort, nor could they prevent British use of Port Royal Sound. The fact that the American pilots refused to carry the ships over the bar does not mean that the French captains could not have sounded the bar themselves—a task that should have taken only a few days at most to accomplish—and therefore does not remove French culpability in the incident. Maitland did not leave Beaufort until the morning of 13 September; the French therefore had six days to sound the bar (in small boats) and find a channel into the river. Instead, the captains of the French ships contented themselves with patrolling the ocean outside the sound. Given that both sides did not believe that there was an inland waterway to the Savannah River, the French captains and the American pilots probably thought that their post just outside the river mouth was sufficient to prevent Maitland's passage to Savannah by water. In addition, d'Estaing said that an American pilot had informed him that by taking possession of the mouth of the Savannah River the water route to Savannah from Beaufort would be blocked.

So, what really was said at the Charlestown council? It seems unlikely, if not impossible, that the Americans could have neglected to ask the French to use their navy to bottle up Maitland at Beaufort. Even if they did not, can the French, with their powerful fleet, be excused for neglecting such an obvious measure? The entire question is to a point moot, given that d'Estaing sent two ships to blockade Beaufort anyway.

It is clear that both the Americans and the French failed in several critical areas. Colonel Simons should have sent his early intelligence of Maitland's departure to General Lincoln; the American pilots should have been knowledgeable enough of the Port Royal harbor to take the French ships over its bar; and the French captains should have made a greater effort to penetrate the river after the failure of the Americans to pilot them through. However, the only important fact is that neither the French nor the Americans knew of Wall's Cut and the intercoastal route from Port Royal to Savannah. This made both the French and the Americans complacent that the measures they had taken to contain Maitland were adequate.

⊰⬦⊱

When Maitland left Beaufort, he crossed west over Port Royal Sound to Tench's Island. From there he crossed over the island into the Daufuskie River using a small rivulet called Skull Creek. Once in the Daufuskie, Maitland was able to sail behind Hilton Head Island to the mouth of the Savannah River. Popular histories of the siege tell us that Maitland, finding the mouth of the Savannah guarded by French ships, was at a loss as how to proceed; but to his good fortune he chanced upon some black fishermen who told him of a little-known passage called Wall's Cut. This passage could take him into the Savannah River upstream from the French warships and into Savannah undetected.

Hugh McCall's *History of Georgia,* published in the early 1800s, apparently contains the earliest printed version of this romantic tale: "Finding the passage up the river in possession of the French, he [Maitland] was obliged to resort to some other way of getting into the town. While he was embarrassed in this difficulty, fortune threw into his hands some negro fishermen, who were well acquainted with all the creeks through the marsh, and informed him of a passage called Wall' s cut, through Scull Creek, by which small boats could pass at high water."[34]

It is difficult to believe that Colonel Maitland arrived at the mouth of the Savannah River not knowing the river was blockaded by French ships and without a plan as how to proceed. It also seems too convenient that just when Maitland was left without a plan "fortune" threw two black fishermen his way to tell him of Wall's Cut—indeed it is doubly convenient that Maitland had led his men to exactly the spot they needed to be in order to get to Wall's Cut.

If it were not for the official report of the siege written by Captain Henry of HMS *Fowey,* the senior Royal Navy officer at Savannah, we would have little choice but to accept Hugh McCall's romantic tale at face value. Captain Henry's report—addressed to the British Admiralty—stated that on 13 September (three days before Maitland arrived at Daufuskie) the British vessels *Comet* and *Keppel* had been ordered to "place themselves below the Mud Flat, so as to cover the passage of Colonel Maitland with the King's troops from Port Royal, through Wall's Cut." Henry further stated that Maitland "had not been heard since our despatches were to him sent."[35] From these two statements we can conclude that Wall's Cut was already known to the British—hardly surprising, given the length of time the British had been navigating the river. Without having received any word from Maitland, Prevost sent naval vessels out to cover the cut since he assumed that was the route Maitland would take. Of course, if Prevost knew of the cut and expected Maitland to use it, one can presume that Maitland also knew of the cut and expected to use it even before he left Beaufort.

Captain Henry's account also makes no mention of black fishermen; instead he tells us that a Royal Navy officer led the Beaufort garrison through Wall's Cut. "The troops from Beaufort," Henry wrote, "arrived in boats from the *Vigilant* and transports, (in Callibogie Sound,) through Wall's Cut, under the direction of Lieutenant Goldensborough, of the *Vigilant*."[36] Though not romantic, it makes much more sense that Maitland knew of and planned to use Wall's Cut before he left Beaufort. This would also explain why Maitland followed the route behind Hilton Head Island in the first place: It was the only course he could have taken that would lead him to Wall's Cut.

It has been generally held that d'Estaing decided to attack the British only after the bombardment failed to force British capitulation. Most sources agree that d'Estaing called a council of war to determine the course of action after three days of bombardment: "It was the opinion of the engineers," the historian Hugh McCall wrote, "that it would require ten days more to work into the enemy's lines; upon which it was determined to try to carry them by an assault."[37] The date agreed on by the council for the attack was 9 October 1779.

However, critical examination of the documentary evidence indicates that d'Estaing set the date for the attack long before the first mortar had been fired. General George Washington wrote a letter at his headquarters in New York dated 1 October 1779 stating that an associate of his in Philadelphia "had received dispatches from the Count [d'Estaing] himself, informing him of his intention to attack the enemy on the 9th."[38]

Since d'Estaing did indeed attack on 9 October, and since Washington's letter is dated 1 October, we can conclude several things. First, Washington's information was quite good; second, since Washington was writing the letter eight days before the attack, and since it must have taken a *minimum* of two weeks for this intelligence to reach Washington in New York, d'Estaing must have set the assault date of 9 October by at least mid-September. Another point one can infer from this intelligence is that d'Estaing anticipated early on that he would have insufficient time to complete a proper siege and that an assault would ultimately be necessary.

Once again, it makes for a good story that d'Estaing impulsively decided on an assault only after his bombardment unexpectedly failed to bring about Prevost's capitulation. However, the truth makes more sense: d'Estaing knew he did not have enough time to mount a successful siege, and the date for an assault was set almost as soon as the first French boot was stuck into Georgia mud.

According to popular contemporary rumor, General Prevost made adjustments to his army's dispositions in order to better defend against the allied assault scheduled for the morning of 9 October 1779. Henry "Light Horse Harry" Lee, a Revolutionary War cavalry commander and the father of Robert E. Lee, claimed that Prevost had reinforced his right flank with picked troops. According to Lee, Prevost did this because the terrain on the British right favored an assault; however, the more popular and romantic story is that an American deserter told Prevost of the pending attack. "They knew our force was to be led to the Spring-hill battery," General Moultrie wrote, "and they prepared accordingly by filling that post with as many men as it could possibly hold; and they knew that General Huger's attack was only to be a feint, and therefore drew almost all their troops from their left to their right."[39] D'Estaing said much the same thing in his notes on the affair.

According to the nineteenth-century historian Henry B. Dawson: "The desertion, on the preceding day, of James Curry, sergeant-major of the Charleston Grenadiers, had placed the information of the intended assault in the hands of the enemy, and the flower of his [Prevost's] force, commanded by Lieutenant-colonel Maitland . . . had been placed on the right of his line to defend it."[40] After a failure in battle, it is quite common for the losing side to claim that a traitor gave away the plan. Such stories serve to remove the blame from the losing party and instead shift it to the supposed traitor, who, after the battle, is conveniently out of reach of punishment and unattainable for testimony.

The story of Sergeant Major Curry's defection as it is usually told is apocryphal. While it is possible that a grenadier of the Charlestown Militia did defect the night before the attack, there is no evidence that such a person gave away any relevant intelligence; and even if he did exist, and even if he did reveal the plan, there is no evidence that General Prevost acted on this intelligence. On the contrary, General Prevost's official report on the action specifically states that he was unsure as to where the main attack was coming on the morning of 9 October 1779, and it was not until the assault was nearly over that he dared to commit his reserves to reinforce the threatened sector of his lines.

Deserters were constantly crossing back and forth between the two enemy camps, and dozens of soldiers changed allegiance during the six-week siege. (Prevost reported forty-eight defectors just on the British side.) While defectors were a prime source of intelligence for both sides, their information could not always be believed. Low-ranking deserters often claimed to know more than they did in hopes of receiving special treatment. Both sides also had to be wary of intelligence gathered from defectors because they might in fact be spies sent to spread disinformation.

Henry Lee says that the British stationed their best troops on their right flank in anticipation of the allied assault. D'Estaing also believed this to be the case, citing the sound of bagpipes coming from the British right flank as evidence that Prevost had moved his Scottish Highlanders to cover that flank. This was not true either. Prevost had manned the "Ebenezer Road Redoubt" mostly with provincials from North Carolina and the "battalion" men of the 60th Regiment. These troops were far from elite; rather they were "average" troops. The "best" troops were the grenadiers and light infantry, who were allocated as reserves. The best battalion in Prevost's army was the 1st Battalion of the 71st Highland Regiment, and it was positioned on the left flank —far away from the Spring Hill redoubt and precisely where the British generally thought the French would attack. Part of the 2nd Battalion of the 71st was stationed near the British right flank, which explains the bagpipes that d'Estaing heard; however, that was the position these troops had already occupied, and they were not moved there as a result of any intelligence.

General Prevost stated that the ground on the British flanks favored the enemy, "notwithstanding all a good engineer could do." Prevost wrote: "On the right a swampy hollow brought him under cover to within fifty yards of our principal works, on some points still nearer. On our left, though the approach was not so well covered nor to such an extent, yet there was sufficient, and the ground being firm and clear it was that on which we rather thought regular troops would choose to act and here therefore we looked for the French, and the Americans only on our right."[41]

Pierre Ozanne's map of the battle confirms Prevost's description of the terrain on the British right. Yamacraw Creek and the swamps that surrounded it did indeed go nearly to the edge of the British fortifications. However, the creeks and swamps on the extreme British right presented more of a barrier to the allied armies than an avenue for concealed attack. Infantrymen could not advance quickly through the bogs, and so the creeks and swamps on the British right actually made for a natural defensive line. Most of the allied soldiers who entered the swamps did so by accident. General McIntosh's column accidentally became bogged down in the swamp and was unable to accomplish its mission. The armed sloop *Germain* was stationed just upriver from Savannah to cover the portion of the swamps that could not easily be seen from the British lines; from this position the *Germain* cannonaded McIntosh's column and some French troops until they were forced to withdraw.

The ground over which the main allied attack was made was south of the "Ebenezer" road, as the British called it, or the "Augusta" road, as it was called by the Americans and the French. The terrain here was clear and firm, with open fields of fire for about three hundred yards to the edge of the line of trees just south of the city. During the attack, large bodies of allied troops were forced back by the weight of the British fire. These troops ended up huddling together on the Augusta road as they were loath to enter the swamps, where they would be unable to move. British artillery took advantage of the troops' crowded position on the road and pummeled them mercilessly.

Thus, it can be observed that the terrain on the British right was in fact quite disadvantageous for attacking troops. The "swampy hollow" that General Prevost and Henry Lee claimed provided protection to attacking troops was in fact so difficult to negotiate that several French and American formations became mired in it. Troops who did enter the swamps were either cut down by British artillery or lost so much time that they failed to contribute to the battle.

<hr />

General Prevost would write in his official report that he engaged in negotiations for surrender merely "for form's sake," implying that he never intended to surrender as he knew "the unanimous opinion of the army."[42] However, numerous others state that Prevost was close to giving up before Maitland arrived. Royal Governor Sir James Wright, for example, says that he was "very happy" when, on 17 September, the decision was made in a council of war to defend the town as he had "some strong reasons to apprehend and fear the contrary."[43]

Several hearsay accounts say that it was an exhausted but defiant Lieutenant Colonel Maitland who stiffened the backbone of the defenders. According to these statements, Maitland harangued his fellow officers during a council of war held on the 17th, declaring that he "abhorred" the word "capitulation" and that he would report to the king the name of the first officer who proposed it.[44] This dramatic language may have been exaggerated by storytellers over time, but it seems likely from the evidence that Prevost was probably far less resolved to hold out to the bitter end up to the time that Maitland arrived in the city. It is quite likely, therefore, that once Maitland was there, Prevost found renewed faith and so defiantly rejected d'Estaing's summons to surrender.

Notes

Introduction

    1. William Moultrie, *Memoirs of the American Revolution,* 2 vols. (1802; reprint, New York: New York Times and Arno Press, 1968), 1:91.

Chapter 1—Making the Southern Strategy

    1. Josiah Martin to Lord Dartmouth, 30 June 1775, in K. G. Davies, ed., *Documents of the American Revolution 1770–1783,* 20 vols. (Shannon: Irish University Press, 1976), 9:213.

    2. Robert L. Scribner and Brent Tarter, eds., *Revolutionary Virginia: The Road to Independence,* 17 vols. (Charlottesville: University Press of Virginia, 1979), 5:39.

    3. Ibid., 5:42.

    4. Christopher Ward, *The War of the Revolution,* 2 vols. (New York: MacMillan Co., 1952), 2:666.

    5. Dartmouth to William Howe, 22 October 1775, in Davies, *Documents,* 11:158.

    6. Ibid., 11:159.

    7. Martin to Wm. Howe, 22 October 1775, in Davies, *Documents,* 11:160.

    8. Gregory D. Massey, *John Laurens and the American Revolution* (Columbia: University of South Carolina Press, 2000), 141.

    9. Peter Force, ed., *American Archives,* series 4, vols. 4–5 (Washington, D.C., 1853), 4:440.

    10. Sir John Fortescue, *The War of Independence: The British Army in North America, 1775–1783* (1911; reprint, London: Greenhill Books, 2001), 21.

    11. Lord George Germain to Henry Clinton, 6 December 1775, in Davies, *Documents,* 11:203.

Chapter 2—Great Bridge: The Battle for Norfolk

    1. Force, *American Archives,* 4:314.

    2. Henry Steele Commager and Richard B. Morris, eds., *The Spirit of 'Seventy-Six,* Bicentennial ed. (1958; reprint, New York: Harper & Row, 1975), 106.

    3. Benson J. Lossing, *A Pictorial Field Book of the Revolution,* 2 vols. (New York: Harper & Brothers, 1859), 2:298.

    4. This action is similar to that which occurred on Noodle Island in Boston Harbor earlier that year.

    5. Scribner and Tarter, *Revolutionary Virginia,* 5:41.

    6. The light infantry and grenadier companies were known as "flank" companies because they were usually positioned at the ends of the regiment's battle line.

    7. Lord Dunmore to Dartmouth, 18 February 1776, in Davies, *Documents,* 12:59.

8. Lossing, *Pictorial Field Book*, 2:327.

9. Scribner and Tarter, *Revolutionary Virginia*, 5:48.

10. Ibid., 5:49.

11. Captain Leslie, 1 December 1775, in Force, *American Archives*, 4:349.

12. Force, *American Archives*, 5:78.

13. Scribner and Tarter, *Revolutionary Virginia*, 5:75.

14. Davies, *Documents*, 12:60.

15. This was all of the 14th Regiment that was present in Norfolk. The other line companies were en route or were still being recruited. The figure of 163 men is the total of officers and enlisted men listed as of 1 December 1775 (Force, *American Archives*, 4:350).

16. After being taken prisoner, Lieutenant Batut told Woodford that Dunmore had said to expect only three hundred "shirtmen" (Commager and Morris, *Spirit of 'Seventy-Six*, 112). The term "shirtmen" was British slang for the Virginia Whig regulars—whose uniforms in the early period of the war consisted of hunting shirts. British soldiers in line companies were called "hatmen" after the black tricorn hats they wore (as opposed to the caps worn by the light infantry or grenadiers). Tradition has it that a slave belonging to Thomas Marshall was sent into Norfolk, where he gave Dunmore the false intelligence that there were only three hundred shirtmen present.

17. Scribner and Tarter, *Revolutionary Virginia*, 5:101.

18. Dunmore in Davies, *Documents*, 12:60.

19. Some sources spell the name "Fordice."

20. Commager and Morris, *Spirit of 'Seventy-Six*, 113.

21. Force, *American Archives*, 4:224. After Woodford was promoted to brigadier general, Alexander Spotswood became colonel of the 2nd Virginia Continentals.

22. Commager and Morris, *Spirit of 'Seventy-Six*, 113.

23. Quoted in the *Virginia Gazette* in Force, *American Archives*, 4:228–29.

24. Force, *American Archives*, 4:228–29.

25. Commager and Morris, *Spirit of 'Seventy-Six*, 112–13.

26. To spike a cannon is to render it inoperable by hammering a steel spike or nail into the touchhole.

27. Force, *American Archives*, 4:224.

28. Woodford to the President of the Convention at Williamsburg, 9 December 1775 and 11 December 1775, in Scribner and Tartar, *Revolutionary Virginia*, 5:90, 109. On the 9th Woodford reported recovering thirteen killed and eighteen wounded; in a second letter written on the 11th Woodford reported finding two additional British dead.

29. Max Calvert quoted by Woodford in Scribner and Tartar, *Revolutionary Virginia*, 5:109.

30. Dunmore to Dartmouth, 18 February 1776, in Davies, *Documents*, 12:60.

31. Frank Moore, *Diary of the Revolution*, 2 vols. (1860; reprint, New York: Arno Press, 1969), 1:181.

32. William Woodford to Patrick Henry, in Commager and Morris, *Spirit of 'Seventy-Six*, 112–13.

33. David Ramsay, *The History of the American Revolution*, ed. Lester H. Cohen, 2 vols. (1789; reprint, Indianapolis, Ind.: Liberty Fund, 1990), 1:443.

34. Benson Lossing said that this Captain Leslie was the same Captain Leslie who was killed at the battle of Princeton in 1777 (*Pictorial Field Book*, 1:328, 2:329). However, he is incorrect; Captain *William* Leslie of the 7th Regiment was killed at Princeton, and Captain *Samuel* Leslie of the 14th Regiment was in command at Great Bridge.

35. Davies, *Documents*, 12:60.

36. Dunmore's description of the engagement is in Davies, *Documents,* 12:62.

37. Commager and Morris, *Spirit of 'Seventy-Six,* 114.

38. Henry Clinton, *The American Rebellion,* ed. William B. Willcox (New Haven, Conn.: Yale University Press, 1954), 25.

39. Dunmore to Germain, 18 February 1776, in Davies, *Documents,* 12:67.

40. Ibid.

41. This order of battle is derived from Woodford's strength return of 10 December 1775 in Scribner and Tartar's *Revolutionary Virginia,* 5:101. There were fifty-one listed as sick in the 2nd Regiment and twelve sick in the Culpeper battalion.

42. The strength of the 14th Regiment is from the 1 December 1775 return in Force, *American Archives,* 4:350.

43. Colonel Woodford reported that his troops found thirteen British dead on the causeway, including Captain Fordyce, and captured eighteen British wounded, including Lieutenant John Batut, "wounded in the leg" (Woodford to the President of the Convention at Williamsburg, 9 December 1775, in Scribner and Tartar, *Revolutionary Virginia,* 5:90). Two days later Woodford wrote a letter that stated he had found two more dead grenadiers, bringing the total of British dead recovered to fifteen (Woodford to President of the Convention, 11 December 1775, in Scribner and Tartar, *Revolutionary Virginia,* 5:109). Dunmore reported seventeen killed and forty-four wounded (Dunmore to Dartmouth, 18 February 1776, in Davies, *Documents,* 12:60). I assume that Dunmore's casualty figures include the dead and wounded brought off and those left behind.

44. On his arrival Robert Howe took command due to his seniority and his commission from the Continental Congress.

Chapter 3—Moore's Creek Bridge

1. Martin to Dartmouth, 30 June 1775, in Davies, *Documents,* 9:213.

2. In French, *pied* means foot, while *mont* is mountain; thus the translation of *piedmont* is "at the foot of the mountains."

3. This is a phrase generally attributed to the twentieth-century American politician Thomas "Tip" O'Neill.

4. See Walter Edgar, *Partisans and Redcoats* (New York: HarperCollins, 2001), for more information on the South Carolina Regulator movement.

5. Modern research shows that many Regulators were also Patriots or were neutral in the Revolution. For more information, see Mark M. Boatner, *Encyclopedia of the American Revolution* (1994; reprint, Mechanicsburg, Pa.: Stackpole Books, 1996), 732–33.

6. Mary L. Medley, *History of Anson County: 1750–1976* (Wadesboro, N.C.: Anson County Historical Society, 1976), 40.

7. Thomas Brown to Patrick Tonyn, February 1776, in Davies, *Documents,* 12:69.

8. Martin to Germain, 21 March 1776, in Davies, *Documents,* 12:85.

9. Davies, *Documents,* 12:87.

10. Alex McLean in Davies, *Documents,* 12:113.

11. Hugh F. Rankin, *The Moore's Creek Bridge Campaign, 1776* (1986; reprint, Currie, N.C.: Eastern National, 1998), 14.

12. McLean in Davies, *Documents,* 12:113.

13. Ibid.

14. This is the same Dr. John Pyle who would gain his place in history as the namesake of "Pyle's Massacre," an incident in which a contingent of Tories under his command were slaughtered in action against Lee's Legion in 1781.

15. The number of Tory troops is based on Governor Martin's account of the action written to Lord Germain (Davies, *Documents*, 12:88); and Alex McLean's firsthand account of the battle of Moore's Creek (McLean in Davies, *Documents*, 12:113–14).

16. McLean in Davies, *Documents*, 12:114.

17. James Moore to Cornelius Harnett, 2 March 1776, in Force, *American Archives*, 5:62.

18. McLean in Davies, *Documents*, 12:113–14.

19. In a letter dated 24 February 1776, from a North Carolina legislator to Colonel R. Howe: "Smith . . . just now lodged seven of the leaders of the Regulators in Halifax jail. . . . He informs me that the insurrection is entirely suppressed with respect to the Regulators" (Force, *American Archives*, 4:1488).

20. Davies, *Documents*, 12:115.

21. Caswell in Force, *American Archives*, 5:62.

22. Governor Martin in Davies, *Documents*, 12:89.

23. McLean in Davies, *Documents*, 12:113–14.

24. Ibid.

25. According to Rankin, only half the planking had been removed (*Moore's Creek Bridge Campaign*).

26. George F. Scheer and Hugh F. Rankin, *Rebels and Redcoats* (Cleveland: World Publishing Co., 1957), 131–32.

27. Ibid.

28. Commager and Morris, *Spirit of 'Seventy-Six,* 115. The *Annual Register* reported that McLeod took the probably more accurate total of nine bullets and twenty-four "swan shot" (i.e., bird shot) (Scheer and Rankin, *Rebels and Redcoats,* 132).

29. Lossing, *Pictorial Field Book,* 2:382.

30. James Moore to Cornelius Harnett, 2 March 1776, in Force, *American Archives*, 5:62.

31. Caswell to the N.C. Congress, 29 February 1776, in Force, *American Archives*, 5:62.

32. Commager and Morris, *Spirit of 'Seventy-Six,* 115.

33. Rankin, *Moore's Creek Bridge Campaign*, 33; National Parks Service pamphlet, *The Battle of Moores Creek Bridge* (GPO: 1995—387-038/00227). Howard Peckham lists the total Loyalist strength at the bridge at "nearly 1,200" (Peckham, ed., *The Toll of Independence: Engagements & Battle Casualties of the American Revolution* [Chicago: University of Chicago Press, 1976], 13).

34. Force, *American Archives*, 5:62.

35. Governor Martin in Davies, *Documents*, 12:89.

36. McLean in Davies, *Documents*, 12:113–14.

37. For primary sources regarding this issue of numbers and weapons, see Davies, *Documents*, 12:85–90, 112–16; and Force, *American Archives*, 5:62–63.

38. Rankin says that the Loyalists could muster only 500 weapons on the day of the attack. This figure seems to have come from a misreading of a Patriot report stating that 150 swords and 350 firearms were captured; but this was only a partial total that did not include the 1,500 rifles mentioned earlier. See Rankin, *Moore's Creek Bridge Campaign*, 33; and Force, *American Archives*, 5:62–63.

39. Force, *American Archives*, 5:63.

40. Ibid.; Ward, *War of the Revolution*, 2:664; Henry B. Carrington, *Battles of the American Revolution* (1877; New York: Promontory Press, 1974), 174.

41. Rankin, *Moore's Creek Bridge Campaign*, 43.

42. Governor Martin to Lord Germain, 21 March 1776, in Davies, *Documents*, 12:89.

43. McLean in Davies, *Documents*, 12:113–14.

44. Clinton, *American Rebellion*, 26–27.

45. The New Bern battalion was supplemented by the militia of Craven, Johnston, Dobbs, and Wake counties. Caswell says in his official report on the engagement (Force, *American Archives,* 5:62) that Lillington's battalion was at the bridge when he arrived, but he makes no mention of Colonel Ashe's company. However, Colonel Moore says that he sent both Lillington and Ashe to the bridge: "Colonel Lillington and Colonel Ashe I ordered, by a forced march, to endeavor, if possible, to reinforce Colonel Caswell; but if that could not be effected, to take possession of Moore's Creek Bridge" (James Moore to Cornelius Harnett, 2 March 1776, in Force, *American Archives,* 5:62). In this same letter, Moore put the strength of Lillington's corps at 150 men and Ashe's company at "about one hundred." I assume that Caswell made no mention of Ashe's company because he had lumped those men together with Lillington's.

46. Governor Martin says that the force at the bridge consisted of six hundred Highlanders and one hundred Regulators (Davies, *Documents,* 12:89); whereas Alex McLean's account says that eight hundred men attacked the bridge (Davies, *Documents,* 12:116). Neither Martin nor McLean said that the number of Highlanders was ever above six hundred men.

47. British casualties are taken from the estimates of Brigadier General James Moore and Colonel Richard Caswell. According to Moore, there were "thirty killed and wounded; but as numbers of them must have fallen into the creek, besides many more that were carried off, I suppose their loss may be estimated at about fifty" (letter dated 2 March 1776, in Force, *American Archives,* 5:62). Caswell said, "The number of killed and *mortally* wounded [emphasis added], from the best accounts I was able to collect, was about thirty; most of them shot on passing the bridge. Several had fallen into the water, some of whom, I am pretty certain, had not risen yesterday evening when I left camp. Such prisoners as we have made, say there were at least fifty of their men missing" (Caswell to N.C. Congress, 29 February 1776, in Force, *American Archives,* 5:62).

The figure of 850 British troops captured is taken from a document produced by Caswell shortly after the battle (Force, *American Archives,* 5:63). This number is greater than the number of British combatants at the bridge because it is probable that many Scottish settlers who were not actually part of MacDonald's army were taken in the general sweep of the countryside by American troops.

48. British forces at campaign start figures are completely derived from Alex McLean's narrative (Davies, *Documents,* 12:114).

Chapter 4—Charlestown, 1776: The Battle of Sullivan's Island

1. Clinton, *American Rebellion,* 26.

2. Warren Ripley, *Battleground, South Carolina in the Revolution* (Charleston: The News and Courier and The Evening Post, 1983), 10–12.

3. Clinton, *American Rebellion,* 26.

4. Ibid.

5. Ibid., 28.

6. Ibid., 27.

7. Davies, *Documents,* 17:149.

8. This account of Clinton is based on the biography of the general by William B. Willcox in his introduction to Clinton's memoirs, *American Rebellion.*

9. Clinton, *American Rebellion,* 19.

10. Boatner, *Encyclopedia,* 606.

11. For more on Charles Lee, see John Alden, *Charles Lee: Traitor or Patriot* (Baton Rouge: Louisiana State University, 1951).

12. Force, *American Archives,* 5:801.

13. Ibid., 5:406.

14. Ibid., 5:404.

15. Washington to the Continental Congress, 24 September 1776, in Washington Papers, Library of Congress.

16. Force, *American Archives*, 5:721.

17. Moultrie, *Memoirs*, 1:140.

18. Force, *American Archives*, 5:720.

19. Moultrie says that Lee came into Charlestown on 8 June 1776 (*Memoirs*, 1:141); other sources say he arrived anywhere from 4 to 7 June.

20. Moultrie, *Memoirs*, 1:141.

21. Ibid.

22. Ibid.

23. Ibid. ·

24. Force, *American Archives*, 5:1186.

25. Moultrie, *Memoirs*, 1:150.

26. Force, *American Archives*, 5:1186. In 1777 Christopher Gadsden successfully built a 3,571-foot bridge to Sullivan's Island; it took months to construct and was the largest structure in America at the time (E. Stanly Godbold Jr. and Robert H. Woody, *Christopher Gadsden and the American Revolution* [Knoxville: University of Tennessee Press, 1982], 64–66).

27. Moultrie, *Memoirs*, 1:143–44.

28. Clinton to Germain, undated, in Clinton, *American Rebellion*, 372.

29. Parker to Clinton, 25 June 1776, in Clinton, *American Rebellion*, 33.

30. Commager and Morris, *Spirit of 'Seventy-Six*, 1066.

31. Force, *American Archives*, 5:1206.

32. Sources vary slightly on the number of guns aboard each British vessel. I have followed the gun ratings given by David Ramsay, *The History of the Revolution of South Carolina*, 2 vols. (Trenton: Isaac Collins, 1785), 1:144.

33. Moultrie, *Memoirs*, 1:174.

34. Ibid.

35. The estimates of the range at which the ships anchored vary among sources, with a maximum estimated range of 800 yards and a minimum of 350 yards.

36. Moultrie, *Memoirs*, 1:175.

37. Moultrie said that the fort had twenty-six guns; however, Henry Drayton gave a more detailed accounting of the fortress's weaponry, and his count is thirty-one guns. Drayton, however, accounts for many light guns that Moultrie might have ignored. British accounts of the battle insist that they plucked thirty-two-pound shot from the main mast of the *Bristol;* however, Moultrie, Ramsay, and Drayton all agree that there were no thirty-two-pound cannons at the fort.

According to Robert Gardiner, ed., *Navies and the American Revolution* (Annapolis, Md.: Naval Institute Press, 1996), 44, the British believed that the fort was armed with thirty-six-pounders from *Foudroyant,* a French warship captured in 1758 during the Seven Years' War, whose cannons were said to have been transferred to Charlestown. While it is possible that the Americans had guns from the *Foudroyant* (Moultrie did say his guns were French-made), the heaviest weapons in the fort were twenty-six-pounders.

38. Fort Sumter was named for Colonel Thomas Sumter, of the 6th South Carolina Regiment, who was then stationed at Haddrells Point. Sumter would gain his fame as the "Carolina Gamecock," a partisan leader who resisted British occupation of South Carolina in 1780 and 1781.

39. Moultrie, *Memoirs*, 1:178.

40. Ibid., 1:175.

41. Commager and Morris, *Spirit of 'Seventy-Six,* 1067.

42. Force, *American Archives,* 5:1205.

43. Davies, *Documents,* 12:170.

44. Moultrie, *Memoirs,* 1:176, 179.

45. Commager and Morris, *Spirit of 'Seventy-Six,* 1067.

46. Force, *American Archives,* 5:1191.

47. Ibid., 5:1205.

48. Moultrie, *Memoirs,* 1:179.

49. Ibid., 1:176.

50. Ibid., 1:177. Ramsay reports ten killed and twenty-two wounded (*History of the Revolution of South Carolina,* 1:147).

51. Barnard Elliot in Commager and Morris, *Spirit of 'Seventy-Six,* 1070. The name of the wounded soldier has been reported by other sources as "McDonald."

52. Force, *American Archives,* 5:1205.

53. Moultrie, *Memoirs,* 1:179.

54. Commager and Morris, *Spirit of 'Seventy-Six,* 108–9.

55. Moultrie reports that Jasper tied the flag to a sponge staff; Major Barnard Elliot said that it was a halberd; and another account says that it was a pike.

56. Moultrie, *Memoirs,* 1:179.

57. Cannonballs heated in a fire until they were red hot were called "hot shot," which was employed in naval combat and siege warfare on land to set fire to ships and buildings.

58. Force, *American Archives,* 5:1205.

59. All Royal Navy casualty figures and damage reports were taken from the letter of Sir Peter Parker to Philip Stevens, 9 July 1776, in Davies, *Documents,* 12:169–70.

60. Eric Robson says in *Letters from America* (New York: Barnes & Noble, 1950), 28n1, that Captain Scott survived his wounds but retired from service; other accounts state that Captain Scott died from his wounds.

61. Moultrie, *Memoirs,* 1:180.

62. Ibid., 1:181; Ward, *War of the Revolution,* 2:677.

63. Davies, *Documents,* 12:164. Some historians report that the British were turned back after sustaining "heavy casualties," but Clinton reports no casualties in his dispatches to London. Barnard Elliot said that the British tried to force the Breach three times R. W. Gibbes, ed., *Documentary History of the American Revolution* [Columbia, S.C.: Banner Steam-Power Press, 1853], 7).

64. Moultrie, *Memoirs,* 1:177.

65. Ramsay, *History of the Revolution of South Carolina,* 1:150.

66. Commager and Morris, *Spirit of 'Seventy-Six,* 1067.

67. Force, *American Archives,* 5:1207.

68. Moultrie, *Memoirs,* 1:144.

69. Lossing, *Pictorial Field Book,* 2:550.

70. Moultrie, *Memoirs,* 1:182.

71. Mulhenburg's regiment moved to reinforce Thompson in the afternoon of 28 June.

72. Five captured Americans aboard the British fleet "deserted" the British and escaped to Fort Johnson.

Chapter 5—Remaking the Southern Strategy

1. Germain to Clinton, 21 March 1778, in Clinton, *American Rebellion,* 87; Fortescue, *War of Independence,* 103.

2. Germain to Clinton, 21 March 1778, in Clinton, *American Rebellion,* 87.

3. Commager and Morris, *Spirit of 'Seventy Six*, 1075.

4. Davies, *Documents*, 15:61.

5. Germain to A. Campbell, 16 January 1779, in bundle 155, C.O.5, copies of Colonial Office Papers in the Library of Congress (hereafter LOC), Manuscripts Division.

6. Davies, *Documents*, 15:61.

Chapter 6—Savannah, 1778

1. Not to be confused with Colonel Robert Rogers's King's Rangers that operated out of Canada.

2. Janet Schaw in Hugh F. Rankin, *The North Carolina Continentals* (Chapel Hill: University of North Carolina Press, 1971), 18.

3. Moultrie, *Memoirs*, 1:227–28.

4. Some accounts say that the duel was fought on 13 August.

5. Godbold and Woody, *Gadsden*, 180–81.

6. Ibid., 179.

7. Regiments were the primary units of maneuver in eighteenth-century warfare. The American army was patterned after the British army. A regiment in the British army theoretically consisted of two battalions; however, in practice most British regiments in the eighteenth century had no more than one battalion. The 71st Regiment was unusual because it eventually numbered three battalions, of which the fist and second served in the South.

Simon Fraser supported the Jacobite cause in the last Scottish rebellion. He was later pardoned by the king and served in the British army during the Seven Years' War. Fraser raised the 71st Highland Regiment in 1775 but did not serve with it in America.

8. Don Troiani, Earl J. Coates, and James L. Kochan, *Soldiers in America* (New York: Stackpole Books, 1998), 43.

9. Boatner, *Encyclopedia*, 397–98. One company of the 42nd Highlanders was captured at the same time.

10. Archibald Campbell, *Journal of Lieut. Colonel Archibald Campbell*, ed. Colin Campbell (Darien, Ga.: Ashantilly Press, 1981), 29.

11. Boatner, *Encyclopedia*, 170.

12. Campbell, *Journal*, 4.

13. The Hessian regiments took their names from their unit commanders. This confusing practice makes it difficult today to trace unit lineage. Both Hessian units assigned to Campbell's army were considered "vacant" at the time, which meant that they did not have permanent commanders assigned to them. The units therefore retained the name of the last regimental commander they had, even though Messieurs von Wöllwarth and von Wissenbach were no longer commanding the regiments.

14. Oliver DeLancy was a wealthy New York Tory and head of the powerful DeLancy family of New York. DeLancy raised three battalions of troops. Two battalions served in the South, while a third stayed in New York. DeLancy's son, also named Oliver, served with distinction during the war in the regular army (Boatner, *Encyclopedia*, 326). Boatner erroneously equates DeLancy's Regiment with the New York Volunteers, another Tory regiment from New York.

15. Campbell states in a letter to Germain that he departed Sandy Hook on 27 November 1778, while in his journal he states that he departed on the 26th.

16. Mosquito-born microbial diseases such as malaria and yellow fever were attributed at the time to "miasma," or hot gases rising from the southern swamps. This resulted in the contemporary concept of "unhealthy" ground near swamps and "healthy" ground being around higher,

cooler, and drier places. The concept of healthy ground was correct, but the reason was misunderstood.

17. For a Hessian soldier's description of the tempestuous sea journey, see Ray Pettengill, trans., *Letters from America, 1776–1779* (1924; reprint, Port Washington, N.Y.: Kennikat Press, 1964), 197–204.

18. John McIntosh was the nephew of Brigadier General Lachlan McIntosh of the Georgia Continentals. John McIntosh was ostensibly colonel of the 3rd Georgia Continental Regiment; however, his regiment was terribly understrength. The Georgia Continentals were a troubled stepchild of the Continental Army. The state of Georgia being so small, it never adequately filled its quota of Continental recruits. At times the Georgia Continentals ceased to exist entirely due to enlistment expirations and desertions. See Frederick Anderson Berg, *Encyclopedia of Continental Army Units* (Harrisburg, Pa.: Stackpole Books, 1972), 45–46.

19. Commager and Morris, *Spirit of 'Seventy-Six,* 1076.

20. It is possible that Peter was purposely supplying Campbell with disinformation regarding the size of the American army in order to deceive the British.

21. Commager and Morris, *Spirit of 'Seventy-Six,* 1077.

22. Hugh McCall, *The History of Georgia* (1811; reprint, Atlanta: Cherokee Publishing Company, 1909), 377. Benson Lossing says that Elbert offered to defend the bluff with his own battalion (*Pictorial Field Book,* 2:525).

23. Campbell, *Journal,* 19–20.

24. Ibid., 11. Regular formations would consist of two or three ranks of men, each file standing shoulder to shoulder. Light formations consisted only of two ranks, with a space for one additional man left in between each file, to help them move through broken terrain more easily. In 1776 General William Howe issued orders for all British infantrymen to adopt the open formation of the light infantry. This meant that, for most of the Revolutionary War, there was little to no difference in the tactical organization of the light companies and the line companies. Like the "grenadiers," who had long abandoned the battlefield use of grenades, the "light" moniker was merely a means of designating an elite formation as the men selected for the light companies were more fleet of foot and were possessed of greater initiative.

In the British army, every regiment contained one light infantry company and one grenadier company. Together they were known as "flank" companies because, as the elite men of their regiment, they would be placed on the ends of a battle line, spots generally regarded as the most critical in the era of linear warfare. Another typical arrangement in the eighteenth century was the habit of drawing together special light infantry and grenadier corps, made from drafts of several other regiments. Although the men in these special corps still drew their pay, uniforms, and often their supplies from their "home" regiments, they would often not serve with their home regiments for lengthy periods of time while on assignment with a light infantry or grenadier corps.

25. A "forlorn hope" was a pathfinding unit. Since it was a small force, it could more easily find the best route to assault the enemy position. The remainder of the attacking force would follow the trail designated by the forlorn hope.

26. Campbell, *Journal,* 23, 24.

27. Ibid., 24.

28. Lossing, *Pictorial Field Book,* 2:525.

29. Campbell, *Journal,* 25–26.

30. Howe's order of battle (recorded in Moultrie, *Memoirs,* 1:252–53) stated that the right wing would consist of the South Carolinians formed into sixteen platoons, each with an "equal

number of files." The left wing was composed of Georgia militia formed in eight platoons each also with an "equal number of files." Howe's orders followed Steuben's drill manual to the letter, stipulating a minimum of eight platoons per battalion.

Steuben's manual also specified that companies were to form in two ranks with a minimum of ten files per platoon. Since platoons rarely reached sixteen files (the maximum specified by Bland), one can presume that a mean of thirteen files per platoon formed in two ranks created an "average" platoon of twenty-six soldiers. Since the American battle line consisted of twenty-four platoons, in theory Howe would have had 624 soldiers in line. This figure dovetails nicely with Brigadier General Isaac Huger's statement that the Americans could muster no "more than six or seven hundred men" (Moultrie, *Memoirs*, 1:252). These numbers also stand well in light of the strength return of the 3rd and 5th South Carolina regiments of 3 January 1779, which show that the S.C. regiments had fewer than 500 men. After adding the Continental artillerymen and George Walton's militia guarding the American rear, the American total comes to about 854 (see the Order of Battle).

31. McCall, *History of Georgia*, 378.

32. Campbell, *Journal*, 26.

33. Campbell in Commager and Morris, *Spirit of 'Seventy-Six*, 1078.

34. McCall, *History of Georgia*, 377.

35. Campbell, *Journal*, 27.

36. Ibid. Campbell thought that fire from his cannon caused the Americans to run away before his troops engaged the main line; in fact, Howe ordered a retreat as soon as he saw the approach of the British troops.

37. The British paroled Walton the following year, and in September 1779 he was elected the Whig governor of Georgia.

38. McCall, *History of Georgia*, 379.

39. Lossing, *Pictorial Field Book*, 2:526.

40. American strength return, 12 January 1779, Benjamin Lincoln Papers, Massachusetts Historical Society (hereafter MHS). Adding the 342 who escaped with Howe with the 94 reported killed or wounded and 453 prisoners reported by the British totals 889. This number is once again very close to the estimate of 854 troops I have made in the order of battle.

41. Lossing, *Pictorial Field Book*, 2:526n2.

42. Due to the lack of adequate medical technology and facilities, severely wounded men in the eighteenth century often died from their wounds within a few hours or days. Officers quite often reported men as wounded even though they died before the end of the battle. Therefore, for all practical purposes killed and wounded should be considered the same in evaluating the losses sustained.

43. Henry Lee, *The American Revolution in the South*, ed. Robert E. Lee (1812; reprint, New York: Arno Press, 1969), 120.

44. Campbell in Davies, *Documents*, 17:41.

45. Campbell, *Journal*, 108–9ed.n52.

46. Lee, *American Revolution in the South*, 120.

47. The figures for the South Carolina regiments are derived from the strength return of 3 January 1779 (four days after the battle); these numbers are inclusive of those listed as missing and wounded. The artillery total includes the three fieldpieces that Campbell reportedly brought off (Lossing, *Pictorial Field Book*, 2:526) and the six field guns that General Lincoln reported as being captured by the British (Lincoln to Williamson, 6 January 1779, in Benjamin Lincoln Papers, MHS). Artillery total includes only fieldpieces, and not any guns that were in battery in the city's defensive works.

48. The Light Infantry Corps included two light companies of the 71st Regiment, commanded by captains Baird and Cameron. Attached to Baird's company were 114 men of the New York Volunteers; while attached to Cameron's company were 114 men of DeLancy's 2nd Battalion and Skinner's 3rd Battalion.

49. Artillery totals for both sides include only field guns and do not count any ordnance aboard ships or "in battery" in fortifications.

50. The American casualty and captured count is derived completely from Archibald Campbell's report to Lord Germain. American returns are incomplete, but on 3 January 1779 the 3rd. S.C. listed 3 wounded and 65 missing; while the 5th S.C. listed 42 missing. On 13 January 1779, Lincoln listed 30 men present at Purrysburg as the "remnants" of Elbert's Georgia brigade—this would have made for about 170 killed, wounded, missing, or captured for that formation.

Chapter 7—Briar Creek

1. Augustine Prevost to Germain, 4 August 1779, in Davies, *Documents,* 17:176.

2. Prevost to Germain, 18 January 1779, in Davies, *Documents,* 17:43; and bundle 99, C.O.5, LOC, Manuscripts Division.

3. Campbell, *Journal,* 48.

4. Ibid., 7.

5. Samuel Elbert was the colonel in charge of the Georgia "brigade" at the first battle of Savannah in 1778. He was promoted to brigadier general in the Continental Army in 1779.

6. John C. Dann, ed., *The Revolution Remembered* (Chicago: University of Chicago Press, 1980), 178.

7. Ramsay, *History of the American Revolution,* 2:441.

8. Ninety Six received its unusual name from the fact that, at its founding, it was calculated to be ninety-six miles from an important Cherokee village.

9. Lossing, *Pictorial Field Book,* 2:506. Lossing lists only those killed and mortally wounded, and does not note the number of nonfatal casualties. Peckham's *Toll of Independence* records only seventy-five killed (57–58).

10. John Richard Alden, *The South in the Revolution, 1763–1789,* vol. 3 of *A History of the South,* ed. Wendell Holmes Stephenson and E. Merton Coulter (Baton Rouge: Louisiana State University Press, 1957), 3:235; Godbold and Woody, *Gadsden,* 171–72. Several of the newly independent American states administered what became known as "test oaths" to their citizens. Those forced to sign swore allegiance to the state, with the penalty of death or confiscation of property for those who violated the oath. South Carolina's test oath was particularly stringent and was the source of much controversy. It was never administered fully, and a public protest of it in Charlestown escalated into a low-intensity riot in June 1778.

11. Campbell, *Journal,* 63.

12. Yet another error that some historians make regarding the 1779 Georgia campaign is to assume that Georgia was completely subjugated by the British after they took Augusta. A two-week occupation hardly constitutes pacification, and Patriot militia dominated upper Georgia until mid-1780. Yet, prominent historians such as Christopher Ward, Craig Symonds, and John Keegan leave their readers with the impression that Augusta was not retaken by the Americans until 1781.

13. Campbell was joined on his march to Augusta by "irregulars from the upper country under the denomination of crackers, a race of men whose motions were too voluntary to be under restraint and whose scouting disposition in quest of pillage" (Campbell to Clinton, 4 March 1779, in Davies, *Documents,* 17:75). Thanks go to Dave Myers for helping look up the term "cracker," which apparently derives from the habit of some Georgia backcountry residents to "crack" boasts and/or to distill their own whiskey.

14. In his journal Campbell said that 270 survivors of Colonel Boyd's corps joined him (*Journal,* 66), whereas Campbell says in a letter to Germain that 300 of Boyd's corps were rescued (Davies, *Documents,* 17:75).

15. A. Prevost to Clinton, 1 March 1779, in Davies, *Documents,* 17:69.

16. A. Prevost to Campbell, 17 February 1779, in Campbell, *Journal,* 66–67.

17. Davies, *Documents,* 17:2.

18. The 1779 Augusta campaign is remarkably similar to Cornwallis's invasion of North Carolina in 1781. In both cases similarly sized British armies penetrated into the backcountry to raise the royal standard at a town that was ostensibly inside of Tory territory. In both cases the British withdrew in the face of a superior rebel army after staying less than two weeks. In both cases Tories who attempted to join the British were crushed (Kettle Creek in 1779, Pyle's Massacre in 1781). In both cases a battle was fought soon after the British withdrawal—Briar Creek in 1779 and Guilford Court House in 1781; and while both of these battles were ostensibly British victories, neither resulted in strategic advantage.

19. General Clinton hoped to reinstate civilian government in the southern colonies he liberated. This plan was a reaction to the criticisms of Loyalists such as Joseph Galloway, who had written essays criticizing the British government's failure to reestablish civilian government in reconquered provinces. See Joseph Galloway, *Fabricus* (London: G. Wilkie, 1782; Library of American Civilization microcard LAC 15696).

20. Moultrie, *Memoirs,* 1:277.

21. John Ashe to Governor Richard Caswell, 4 April 1779, in Walter Clark, ed., *The State Records of North Carolina* (Winston, N.C.: M. I. & J. C. Stewart, Printers to the State, 1896), 14:52.

22. Prevost in Davies, *Documents,* 17:78.

23. Quote from a Tory newspaper account of the action contained in Moore, *Diary of the American Revolution,* 1:139.

24. Many sources say that Lytle's first name was Archibald; however, in manuscript letters in the Benjamin Lincoln Papers, MHS, he spells his name "Anthony."

25. John Ashe in Moultrie, *Memoirs,* 1:351.

26. Fergus says there were forty horses, while Bryan and Ashe say there were sixty (Clark, *State Records of North Carolina,* 14:53).

27. Ashe to Caswell, 3 April 1779, in Clark, *State Records of North Carolina,* 14:53.

28. Dann, *Revolution Remembered,* 179.

29. Benjamin Lincoln to Governor Caswell, Purrysburg, 7 March 1779, in Clark, *State Records of North Carolina,* 14:33.

30. The messenger was from Ashe's baggage guard, stationed about eight miles upriver from the American camp at Briar Creek. When Ashe received the message, he assumed that the enemy was at least eight miles distant since that is where the baggage guard was. However, the messenger arrived only just in front of the British troops, who were just minutes behind.

31. At a council of war held on 4 March 1779 at Purrysburg, the number of troops under Ashe's command was listed as 1,260 (original manuscript document in the Benjamin Lincoln Papers, MHS).

32. John Ashe to Richard Caswell, 17 March 1779, in Clark, *State Records of North Carolina,* 14:40.

33. Clark, *State Records of North Carolina,* 14:40.

34. Ibid., 14:41.

35. Dann, *Revolution Remembered,* 179.

36. Moore, *Diary of the American Revolution,* 1:141n1.

NOTES TO PAGES 95–100

37. Campbell, *Journal,* 77.

38. John Ashe to Richard Caswell, 17 March 1779, in Clark, *State Records of North Carolina,* 14:41.

39. One American officer reported, "He heard Gen. Ashe say to some one near the brass field-piece that it was too late to rally any of the men" (Moultrie, *Memoirs,* 1:349). Since this brass field-piece was with Lytle's troops, the man Ashe was talking to was probably Lieutenant Colonel Lytle.

40. Elbert quoted by James Fergus in his pension deposition (Dann, *Revolution Remembered,* 179).

41. Lytle to Lincoln, 7 March 1779, in Benjamin Lincoln Papers, MHS.

42. Elbert quoted by James Fergus in his pension deposition (Dann, *Revolution Remembered,* 180).

43. Moultrie, *Memoirs,* 1:351.

44. M. Prevost to Germain, 14 April 1779, in Davies, *Documents,* 17:101.

45. The North Carolina Brigade consisted of the militia regiments from New Bern, Wilmington, Edenton, and Halifax. Ashe says that of the nine hundred men in General Bryan's brigade, one hundred were "waggoners [*sic*] and carters, which were always returned as soldiers"; fifty soldiers had been detached to guard the baggage; and fifty were in fatigue parties clearing a path to Matthew's Bluff. This order of battle counts the one hundred wagoners but not the men in fatigue parties or guarding the baggage.

46. The Florida Brigade consisted of the 60th and 16th regiments of foot. The Grenadier Corps consisted of the grenadier companies of both of these regiments.

47. The Light Infantry Corps consisted of the light infantry companies of the 1st and 2nd battalions of the 71st Regiment, with some light troops drafted from the New York provincial regiments (see Savannah, 1778, order of battle in chapter 6).

48. Prevost said that in addition to the regulars there were "about 150 provincials, rangers and militia, making in all 900" (Davies, *Documents,* 17:78). According to a Tory newspaper, the Loyalists consisted of "about one hundred and eighty or two hundred of the Carolina volunteers and rangers" (Moore, *Diary of the American Revolution,* 139).

49. No accurate American casualty figures exist. General Ashe claimed that no more than 150 men were unaccounted for after the battle; however this is plainly incorrect since the British captured about 227 troops. David Ramsay said that no more than 450 of the American troops present at the battle ever regrouped at Purrysburg; however, he was probably referring exclusively to the North Carolina militia and not, for example, to Lytle's light infantry or the light horsemen of Major Ross—both of whose commands survived the battle more or less intact.

The casualty figures given here are therefore those reported by General Augustine Prevost in his official report to Lord Germain, in which he reported 150 "killed on the field of battle and adjoining woods and swamps" and "near two hundred men" and 27 officers taken captive (Davies, *Documents,* 17:79). Archibald Campbell reported American losses at 100 killed and wounded, and 192 captured (Campbell, *Journal,* 77).

50. Both Prevost and Stedman refer to this group as "irregulars" and give no strength. A Tory newspaper says that this unit was composed of "about one hundred and fifty of the Carolina volunteers" (Moore, *Diary of the American Revolution,* 139).

Chapter 8—Charlestown, 1779

1. Major William Gardner of the 60th Regiment commanded the expedition. Major Valentine Gardiner of the 16th Regiment was also present but not in command. The two are often confused.

2. British casualties from Prevost in Davies, *Documents*, 17:66; U.S. casualties from Moultrie, *Memoirs*, 1:295. Peckham says that the Americans lost seven killed and twenty-five wounded (*Toll of Independence*, 57).

3. Davies, *Documents*, 17:66.

4. Lincoln to Richard Caswell, 6 February 1779, in Clark, *State Records of North Carolina*, 14:17.

5. St. Eustatia is an island in the Dutch West Indies that served as the principal source of arms and ammunition from Europe for South Carolina.

6. Minutes of the council of war held at Black Swamp, South Carolina, on 19 April 1779, in Moultrie, *Memoirs*, 1:375.

7. Lincoln to Moultrie, 22 April 1779, in Moultrie, *Memoirs*, 1:377.

8. Prevost to Clinton, 21 May 1779, in Davies, *Documents*, 17:127.

9. James Wright to George Germain, 9 August 1779, in Davies, *Documents*, 17:186.

10. A. Prevost to Clinton, 21 May 1779, in Davies, *Documents*, 17:127.

11. Prevost complained that the Savannah River was swollen with rain, which delayed his troops' crossing. On the other hand, William Moultrie said in his memoirs that it was the dry season and the rivers were low, which aided the British advance. It is impossible to reconcile the two accounts. However, Prevost's report is from a contemporary letter (Prevost to Clinton, 21 May 1779, in Davies, *Documents*, 17:127), while Moultrie's memoirs were written years after the fact. Given that May is hardly the dry season in South Carolina, I have chosen to believe Prevost's description of the weather.

12. Moultrie, *Memoirs*, 1:389.

13. Moultrie to Lincoln, 1 May 1779, in Moultrie, *Memoirs*, 1:391.

14. Lincoln to Moultrie, 2 May 1779, in Moultrie, *Memoirs*, 1:396, 397.

15. Once again, Prevost says that the rivers were swollen, while Moultrie claims they were low.

16. Henry Lee, who was not present, claims in his *Memoirs of the War in the Southern Department* that Colonel Laurens was following orders when he made a stand at the Coosawhatchie.

17. Moultrie, *Memoirs*, 1:403.

18. Ibid.

19. Ramsay, *History of the Revolution of South Carolina*, 2:22–23.

20. Moultrie, *Memoirs*, 1:404–5, 407.

21. Prevost to Germain, 10 June 1779, in Davies, *Documents*, 17:142.

22. Moultrie, *Memoirs*, 1:413.

23. Prevost to Clinton, 21 May 1779, in Davies, *Documents*, 17:127.

24. Warren Ripley asserts in *Battleground* that if it were not for the loss of Ashley Ferry, Charlestown might never have been besieged. Ripley asserts that it would have been "suicidal" for Prevost to go upriver to ford the Ashley at Dorchester. However, Prevost wrote that he expected to cross the river at Dorchester; only through his good fortune of capturing the boats at Ashley Ferry did he not pursue this course.

25. Washington to Pulaski, 8 February 1779, in John C. Fitzpatrick, ed., *The Writings of George Washington from the Original Manuscript Sources, 1745–1799*, 39 vols. (Washington, D.C.: Government Printing Office, 1931–1944; reprint, New York: Greenwood Press, 1970). Accessed online at the Library of Congress American Memory Web site: http://memory.loc.gov/ammem/gwhtml/gwhome.html.

26. Moultrie says that this soldier's name was Colonel "Kowatch" (*Memoirs*, 1:424)

27. Ramsay, *History of the Revolution of South Carolina*, 2:26.

28. Moultrie, *Memoirs*, 1:425. The privy council was a committee of eight legislators, appointed by the assembly, that served as a check on the governor's powers. Certain decisions of the governor had to be approved by the privy council, much as the U.S. Senate has to approve treaties and presidential appointments.

29. Ibid., 1:424.

30. Ibid., 1:426, 427.

31. Ibid., 1:433. The original "neutrality proposal" is lost. The version given here by Moultrie is consistent with that given by David Ramsay in *History of the Revolution of South Carolina,* 2:27, and Charles Stedman in *The History of the American War* (London, 1794), 112. However, the version recorded by John Laurens differs, stating that South Carolina would be neutral during the war but share the fate of the other states at the end of the conflict. See Massey, *John Laurens,* 137; and Edward McCrady, *History of South Carolina in the Revolution,* 2 vols. (New York: MacMillan & Co., 1902), 1:367.

32. Moultrie quoted by John Laurens in Massey, *John Laurens,* 139.

33. Moultrie, *Memoirs,* 1:432; McCrady, *History of South Carolina,* 1:373. The third "radical" councilman was Thomas Ferguson.

34. Moultrie, *Memoirs,* 1:434.

35. Ibid.

36. James Fergus in Dann, *Revolution Remembered,* 183.

37. Ramsay, *History of the Revolution of South Carolina,* 1:160.

38. Johann Ewald, *Diary of the American War,* trans. and ed. Joseph P. Tustin (New Haven, Conn.: Yale University Press, 1979), 217.

39. Richard Barry's *John Rutledge of South Carolina* (New York: J. J. Little & Ives, 1942) is a masterful piece of apologist rhetoric that all but deifies Rutledge. David Ramsay, though no political ally of Rutledge, wrote that the offer of neutrality was made "to gain time" (*History of the Revolution of South Carolina,* 2:27). Ramsay generally glossed over the neutrality proposal, probably in an attempt to save the "honor" of the state.

40. Congress had actually authorized part of the Virginia line to reinforce the Southern Department, but the time to marshal the forces was taking much longer than anticipated.

41. Godbold and Woody, *Gadsden,* 170.

42. Moultrie, *Memoirs,* 1:435.

43. It has been established that the Marquis de Brétigny commanded the French citizens in the siege of Charlestown in 1780. I have made the assumption that he commanded them at this time as well.

44. The numbers of cannons on each side were never accurately recorded. There was a substantial amount on the American side and a minimal amount on the British side—all field guns.

45. This includes only the troops killed or injured before Charlestown on 11 and 12 May 1779. The American total breaks down as follows: fourteen killed, one wounded, forty-two taken prisoner in Pulaski's skirmish; and three killed, ten wounded in the friendly-fire incident involving Huger's party. (The figures for the casualties in Huger's detachment are derived from Moultrie's statement that there were thirteen casualties and James Fergus's pension statement that there were three killed, the rest wounded.) The British casualties were sustained by Tawse's dragoons in their fight with Pulaski.

Chapter 9—Stono Ferry

1. Prevost to Germain, 10 June 1779, in Davies, *Documents,* 17:142, 143.

2. Ibid., 17:143.

3. Germain to Clinton, 27 September 1779 and 5 August 1779, in Davies, *Documents,* 17:177, 224.

4. Technically, Stono is an inlet; i.e., it is seawater and not freshwater.

5. Benjamin Lincoln to John Rutledge, 26 May 1779, Benjamin Lincoln Papers, MHS.

6. Lt. Col. James Mark Prevost to Thomas de Grey, Undersecretary of State, 27 November 1779, in bundle 182, C.O.5 copies of the British Colonial Office papers in the LOC, Manuscripts Division.

7. Lt. Colonel Mark Prevost's proclamation of 26 June 1779, in ibid.

8. Lossing, *Pictorial Field Book,* 2:555.

9. Ibid.

10. Eliza Wilkinson, *Letters of Eliza Wilkinson,* ed. Caroline Gilman (New York: Samuel Colman, 1839), 30.

11. Ewald, *Diary,* 217; Ramsay, *History of the Revolution of South Carolina,* 1:21–34; Lossing, *Pictorial Field Book,* 2:555.

12. Lincoln to John Jay, 4 June 1779; Lincoln to George Washington, 5 June 1779, in Benjamin Lincoln Papers, MHS.

13. Lincoln to Moultrie, 10 June 1779, in Benjamin Lincoln Papers, MHS.

14. Lincoln to John Rutledge, 1 June 1779, in Benjamin Lincoln Papers, MHS.

15. Stedman, *History of the American War,* 116.

16. Edward Lowell, *The Hessians* (1884; reprint, Port Washington, N.Y.: Kennikat Press, 1965), 296–97. Lowell derived this information from a manuscript journal written by a soldier in the Wissenbach regiment (241n1). The German regiments were named at this time for the officer who owned the commission for the unit. If the commission changed, so did the name of the regiment. Two regiments bore the name "Trümbach" during the war. The first held that name until 1778, when General L. von Trümbach gave up that unit's commission to General C. von Bose. General Trümbach then assumed the commission of what was the Regiment von Wöllwarth (previously Regiment von Rall) sometime in 1778. This apparently occurred after the unit had shipped out to Georgia in November 1778 as the unit retained the name Wöllwarth in the field until the summer of 1779, when it finally assumed the name Trümbach. Sometime in 1782 Trümbach became the Regiment d'Angelelli. Thus, the lineages of the two different regiments are "Trümbach-Bose" and "Rall-Wöllwarth-Trümbach-Angelelli."

Philip Katcher's *Encyclopedia of British, Provincial, and German Army Units 1775–1783* (Harrisburg, Pa.: Stackpole Books, 1973) confuses *Regiment von Trümbach-Bose* with the *Regiment von Rall-Wöllwarth-Trümbach-Angelelli.* Katcher mistakenly states that Regiment von Trümbach-Bose fought at Savannah and Stono Ferry (126), though it did not actually arrive in the southern theater until mid-1780. Katcher further confuses matters by misspelling the name Trümbach with the *ü* and *r* transposed, as Türmbach, throughout his entry for the Regiment von Trümbach-Bose.

17. Charles Stedman in *History of the American War,* 116, says that there were five hundred fit-for-duty men. A British deserter informed Lincoln that the post consisted of six hundred men. General Prevost said in a later dispatch to Germain that the post had eight hundred men (Davies, *Documents,* 18:175).

18. Benjamin Lincoln to John Rutledge, 21 June 1779, in Benjamin Lincoln Papers, MHS.

19. Major Grimké to J. Kean, 21 June 1779, in Moultrie, *Memoirs,* 1:496.

20. Major Grimké's account of the battle mentions that Henderson's light infantrymen were still in column when they first encountered the enemy in the woods in front of the fortifications. It is therefore fair to assume that the entire army was still in column at this point, waiting to display into line when the regiments were closer to the ferry (Major Grimké to J. Kean, 21 June 1779, in Moultrie, *Memoirs,* 1:498).

21. Major Grimké to J. Kean, 21 June 1779, in Moultrie, *Memoirs*, 1:498.

22. Ramsay, *History of the Revolution of South Carolina*, 2:30.

23. Major Grimké to J. Kean, 21 June 1779, in Moultrie, *Memoirs*, 1:498.

24. Stedman, *History of the American War*, 117.

25. Alexander Garden, *Anecdotes of the Revolutionary War* (Charleston, S.C., 1822), 405.

26. A full-strength company in a British regiment was about 70 men on paper, but in practice they were usually about 25 men strong. The strength of the two companies of Highlanders that advanced into the woods could have been anywhere from 50 to 150 men in strength. The consensus from both British and American sources is that most of the detachment were killed, wounded, or captured. Stedman, who gives the best British account of the affair, says that 11 men returned, but he does not say exactly how many sortied except to say two companies. According to an American newspaper, there were "twenty-seven dead, and several wounded on the ground" (*New Hampshire Gazette*, 10 August 1779, in Moore, *Diary of the American Revolution*, 1:171). Adding these numbers to Stedman's 11 who returned results in a total of at least 41 men in the two Highland companies. I would estimate that there were closer to 60, the nominal strength of two British companies.

27. Lee, *Memoirs*, 131.

28. Stedman, *History of the American War*, 117.

29. Ibid.

30. Lee, *Memoirs*, 131; Lincoln to Moultrie, 20 June 1779, in Moultrie, *Memoirs*, 1:491.

31. Ramsay, *History of the American Revolution*, 446.

32. See also "Author's Notes and Historiography."

33. Lincoln to Moultrie, 21 June 1779, in Benjamin Lincoln Papers, MHS.

34. Lincoln to Moultrie, 20 June 1779 in Moultrie, *Memoirs*, 1:493.

35. Davies, *Documents*, 17:175.

36. Lincoln to Moultrie, 20 June 1779, in Moultrie, *Memoirs*, 1:493.

37. Lee, *Memoirs*, 131.

38. Ibid.

39. The strength of the N.C. Brigade and Malmady's light infantry was derived from the 21 June 1779 strength return in the Benjamin Lincoln Papers, MHS. The strength of Williamson's militia brigade was derived from the 15 June return. The strength of Mason's Virginia militia was taken from its 8 June return. The strength of Butler's militia brigade was derived from his return of 7 June. The strength of the S.C. Brigade was derived from its 1 June return.

40. The 2nd Light Infantry battalion was made up of light troops drawn from the South Carolina Continental brigade, the South Carolina militia brigade, and the Virginia militia brigade. The numbers are derived from the "On Command" columns listed in Lincoln's 1 June 1779 strength returns: two from the 1st South Carolina, twenty-two from the 3rd South Carolina, twenty-two from the 6th South Carolina, nineteen from Williamson's South Carolina militia brigade, and an estimated fifty Virginia militiamen. These figures have been deducted from each appropriate unit in the order of battle to form the light infantry figure.

41. Major Grimké took command of the artillery regiment after Colonel Roberts was mortally wounded.

42. Malmady's 1st Light Infantry battalion drew from 77 to 120 troops (returns disagree) from the North Carolina Continentals (21 were deducted from the 4th North Carolina and 56 from the 5th North Carolina, based on the 21 June 1779 strength return of the Continental regiments), 200 troops from General Butler's North Carolina militia, and the entire 84-man "brigade" of the Georgia Continentals. The strengths of the Continental and militia units have been reduced accordingly in the order of battle.

43. According to General Prevost, the British forces consisted of "the first battalion, 71st, then much reduced, a weak battalion of Hessians, and the refugees of South and North Carolina, amounting in the whole to about eight hundred men" (Davies, *Documents*, 18:175). Stedman says that the British garrison did not much exceed "five hundred men, really effective, and fit for duty" (*History of the American War*, 116). Stedman also says that "part of the North and South Carolina regiment of provincials" was present, but he later adds that "Lieutenant-colonel Hamilton of the North Carolina regiment" particularly distinguished himself in combat (116, 118). Augustine Prevost's casualty return for the engagement lists as present at least portions of the 1st Battalion South Carolina Royalists, the North Carolina Volunteers, 1st and 2nd Battalions of the 71st Regiment, and the Trümbach Hessian regiment (Britain's Public Records Office, Colonial Office, class 5, bundle 182, copies in the LOC).

44. The U.S. casualties are from the casualty return for the engagement in the Benjamin Lincoln Papers, MHS. British casualties are from Prevost's letter on the engagement to George Germain. According to Edward Lowell (*Hessians*, 301), Trümbach's casualties were roughly nine killed and thirty-four wounded out of the total British casualties reported by Prevost.

Chapter 10—The Siege of Savannah, 1779

1. French naval officer in Charles C. Jones, ed., *Siege of Savannah* (1874; reprint, New York: New York Times and Arno Press, 1968), 58.

2. Marquis de Brétigny to Le Comte d'Estaing in Alexander Lawrence, *Storm over Savannah* (Athens: University of Georgia Press, 1951), 19.

3. French naval officer in Jones, *Siege of Savannah*, 58.

4. An unidentified French naval officer in ibid., 58, 69.

5. François d'Auber De Peyrelongue, "The American War," in *Muskets, Cannon Balls & Bombs: Nine Narratives of the Siege of Savannah in 1779*, trans. and ed. Benjamin Kennedy (Savannah, Ga.: Beehive Press, 1974), 28.

6. French naval officer in Jones, *Siege of Savannah*, 70.

7. "Soldiers in front, follow me! Long live the King!"

8. Jean-Rémy de Tarragon, "The Pechot Diary," in *Facsimiles of Manuscripts in European Archives Relating to America, 1773–1783*, ed. Benjamin Franklin Stevens, item 2010, microfilm ed. held at the University of Texas at Arlington. In *Storm over Savannah*, Alexander Lawrence identifies "Pechot" as the pen name of Captain Jean-Rémy de Tarragon.

9. Jean-Baptist Charles Henri Hector Theodat d'Estaing, "Journal of the Siege of Savannah with Some Observations by M. Le Comte d'Estaing," in *Muskets, Cannon Balls & Bombs*, ed. and trans. Kennedy, 43, 44.

10. Prevost to Germain, 1 November 1779, in Davies, *Documents*, 17:242.

11. National Oceanic & Atmospheric Administration (NOAA) Web site 1 October 2002.

12. Unnamed French naval officer in Franklin B. Hough, ed., *The Siege of Savannah* (1866; reprint, Spartanburg, SC: The Reprint Co., 1975), 64.

13. Thomas Pinckney in Hough, *Siege of Savannah*, 159–60.

14. An unnamed French army officer in Jones, *Siege of Savannah*, 67–68.

15. Tarragon, "Pechot Diary," in Stevens, *Facsimiles*; Phillipe Séguier, "Journal of Phillipe Séguier de Terson," in *Muskets, Cannon Balls & Bombs*, trans. and ed. Kennedy, 12.

16. D'Estaing, "Journal of the Siege of Savannah," 52.

17. Ronald G. Killion and Charles T. Waller, *Georgia and the Revolution* (Atlanta: Cherokee Publishing Company, 1975), 194.

18. Prevost to D'Estaing, 16 September 1779, in Killion and Waller, *Georgia and the Revolution*, 195.

19. Ibid., 196.

20. Prevost to Germain, 1 November 1779, in Davies, *Documents,* 17:243.

21. Lawrence, *Storm over Savannah,* 47.

22. D'Estaing, "Journal of the Siege of Savannah," 51.

23. Prevost to d'Estaing, 16 September 1779, in Killion and Waller, *Georgia and the Revolution,* 195.

24. McCall, *History of Georgia,* 437.

25. Prevost to Germain, 1 November 1779, in Davies, *Documents,* 17:243.

26. Ibid.

27. Prevost said that the Hessian artillerymen were left behind "by some strange neglect" on Maitland's part (Prevost to Clinton, 2 November 1779, in Clinton, *American Rebellion,* 432). However, I assume that Maitland had insufficient space in the boats for them. The boats were sent back for the Hessians, convalescents, and the crews of *Vigilant* and the other convoy ships. However, on 18 September 1779 French warships in the river managed to get above Wall's Cut and so cut off the British left at Daufuskie. These men rejoined the British army after the French fleet departed in October.

28. McCall, *History of Georgia,* 435.

29. Davies, *Documents,* 17:243.

30. Prevost to Germain, 1 November 1779, in Davies, *Documents,* 17:244.

31. D'Estaing, "Journal of the Siege of Savannah," 46, 61.

32. McCall, *History of Georgia,* 433.

33. Jones, *Siege of Savannah,* 69.

34. David Ramsay to Henry Drayton, 1 September 1779, in Gibbes, *Documentary History,* 121.

35. Salt, used as a preservative, was an indispensable food additive in the eighteenth century.

36. Ramsay to Drayton, 1 September 1779, in Gibbes, *Documentary History,* 121–22.

37. Moultrie, *Memoirs,* 2:33.

38. Ibid.

39. Jones, *Siege of Savannah,* 17; Benjamin Lincoln, "Journal of Major General Lincoln," in *Muskets, Cannon Balls & Bombs,* trans. and ed. Kennedy, 121.

40. Captain Bentalou quoted in Jones, *Siege of Savannah,* 17n1.

41. M. L. Weems, *The Life of Gen. Francis Marion* (Philadelphia: J. B. Lippincott, 1891), 60. Weems's writings are, by modern academic standards, historical fiction; yet there is much in his works that is verifiable. I include the quote here because it is part of the tradition of the battle.

42. Lincoln, "Journal of Major General Lincoln," in *Muskets, Cannon Balls & Bombs,* trans. and ed. Kennedy, 124.

43. Baron de Steding in Lawrence, *Storm over Savannah,* 66. References to French attitudes toward the Americans are from Lawrence, *Storm over Savannah,* 62–67.

44. Davies, *Documents,* 17:244.

45. French army officer in Jones, *Siege of Savannah,* 21.

46. Tarragon, "Pechot Diary," in Stevens, *Facsimiles;* Antoine François Terrence O'Connor, "Journal of the Siege of Savannah," in *Muskets, Cannon Balls & Bombs,* trans. and ed. Kennedy, 55.

47. Tarragon, "Pechot Diary," in Stevens, *Facsimiles.*

48. Séguier, "Journal," 15.

49. Ibid.; Tarragon, "Pechot Diary," in Stevens, *Facsimiles.*

50. French naval officer in Jones, *Siege of Savannah,* 63.

51. Davies, *Documents,* 17:245.

52. Lincoln to Congress, 22 October 1779, in Hough, *Siege of Savannah,* 152.

53. De Peyrelongue, "American War," in *Muskets, Cannon Balls & Bombs*, trans. and ed. Kennedy, 28.

54. British accounts state that the raid set the French and Americans firing on each other. This report has been repeated in several other contemporary and modern histories of the engagement. However, French accounts (d'Estaing, Tarragon, and Séguier) make it clear that the French were firing on themselves.

55. Prevost to Germain, 1 November 1779, in Davies, *Documents,* 17:245.

56. The number of artillery pieces given in the text is derived from Pierre Ozanne's map "Siege of Savannah" in the Ozanne Cartographic Collection, LOC. According to Ozanne, the mortars varied between six and nine inches; other sources say that the mortars were ten inches in caliber.

57. Anthony Stokes wrote that the mortar shells were less threatening than the cannonballs since one could see the mortars coming and attempt to dodge them.

58. French army officer in Jones, *Siege of Savannah,* 25.

59. Tarragon, "Pechot Diary," in Stevens, *Facsimiles.*

60. Ibid.

61. D'Estaing, "Journal of the Siege of Savannah," 59.

62. Prevost to Germain, 1 November 1779, in Davies, *Documents,* 17:246.

63. Moore, *Diary of the Revolution,* 2:226–27.

64. Tarragon, "Pechot Diary," in Stevens, *Facsimiles.*

65. Moore, *Diary of the Revolution,* 2:227.

66. Ibid., 2:225–27.

67. Ibid., 2:228.

68. Prevost to d'Estaing, 6 October 1779, in McCall, *History of Georgia,* 440. McCall also mentions that d'Estaing had refused a request by General Lachlan McIntosh on 29 September 1779 to allow his wife and children to leave the city along with other females and children who chose to depart (439).

69. D'Estaing and Lincoln to Prevost, 6 October 1779, in McCall, *History of Georgia,* 440.

70. French naval officer in Jones, *Siege of Savannah,* 64.

71. Ibid., 26.

72. Ibid., 63.

73. Johann Hinrichs in Bernhard A. Uhlendorf, trans., ed., *The Siege of Charleston* (Ann Arbor: University of Michigan Press, 1938), 169.

74. D'Estaing, "Journal of the Siege of Savannah," 56.

75. Jones, *Siege of Savannah,* 64; D'Estaing, "Journal of the Siege of Savannah," 56.

76. D'Estaing, "Journal of the Siege of Savannah," 56; McCall, *History of Georgia,* 441.

77. Tarragon, "Pechot Diary," in Stevens, *Facsimiles.*

78. Lawrence, *Storm over Savannah,* 83, 88; Tarragon, " Pechot Diary," in Stevens, *Facsimiles.*

79. Meyronnet de Saint-Marc, "Meyronnet de Saint Mark's Journal of . . . the Siege of Savannah," ed. Roberta Leighton, *New York Historical Society Quarterly* 36, no. 3 (1952): 280.

80. Most of the contemporary sources call the British works "entrenchments," but this term was often used generically for any fortification. It is more likely that the British fortifications were actually revetments, or earthworks, as contemporary maps seem to indicate. In addition, earthworks usually had trenches, or ditches, dug in front of them as additional impediment to attackers.

81. Clinton, *American Rebellion,* 150.

82. Lawrence, *Storm over Savannah,* 63; D'Estaing, "Journal of the Siege of Savannah," 52–53.

83. Most accounts, including that of d'Estaing, say that Steding commanded the left, though the order of battle in the Pechot diary says that Rouvray commanded the left (Tarragon, "Pechot Diary," in Stevens, *Facsimiles*).

84. Tarragon, "Pechot Diary," in Stevens, *Facsimiles*.

85. French navy officer in Jones, *Siege of Savannah*, 64–65.

86. D'Estaing, "Journal of the Siege of Savannah," 70.

87. French army officer in Jones, *Siege of Savannah*, 30.

88. Henry Wadsworth Longfellow wrote the poem "Hymn of the Moravian Nuns at the Consecration of Pulaski's Banner" in honor of Pulaski and the good women of Bethlehem. The original banner now resides in the Maryland Historical Society.

89. Tarragon, "Pechot Diary," in Stevens, *Facsimiles*; French army officer in Jones, *Siege of Savannah*, 29–30.

90. Thomas Pinckney in Jones, *Siege of Savannah*, 33.

91. Count d'Estaing's orders of attack in Stevens, *Facsimiles*, item 2010.

92. Lawrence, *Storm over Savannah*, 93; D'Estaing, "Journal of the Siege of Savannah," 73.

93. French army officer in Jones, *Siege of Savannah*, 30.

94. Ibid., 30–31.

95. Ibid., 31.

96. Thomas Pinckney in Jones, *Siege of Savannah*, 33n1.

97. Hough, *Siege of Savannah*, 39. "Battalion men" are troops drawn from the regular line companies, as opposed to the grenadier or light infantry companies; they are also called "hat men" for the tricorn hats they wore.

98. Many accounts say that Lieutenant Colonel Maitland was in command of the British right during the attack, but this is contradicted by General Prevost, who said that von Porbeck had command of the right that day (Davies, *Documents*, 17:247).

99. Tarragon, "Pechot Diary," in Stevens, *Facsimiles*; D'Estaing, "Journal of the Siege of Savannah," 69.

100. Dillon's Regiment was part of France's famed "Irish Brigade" formed in 1691 from the defeated remnants of James II's Irish troops (crushed by William of Orange). Originally comprised of thirteen regiments, by the 1770s the brigade had only three, of which two, Dillon's and Walsh's, saw service in America. The rank and file were both expatriates from Ireland and descendants of the original soldiers who fled Ireland ninety years earlier. See W. S. Murphy, "The Irish Brigade of France at the Siege of Savannah, 1779," *Georgia Historical Quarterly* 38, no. 4 (1954).

101. French army officer in Jones, *Siege of Savannah*, 31.

102. Tarragon, "Pechot Diary," in Stevens, *Facsimiles*; Pinckney in Hough, *Siege of Savannah*, 166; French army officer in Jones, *Siege of Savannah*, 32; Meyronnet de Saint-Marc, "Journal."

103. French army officer in Jones, *Siege of Savannah*, 32.

104. D'Estaing, "Journal of the Siege of Savannah," 69; Tarragon, "Pechot Diary," in Stevens, *Facsimiles*.

105. Rogowski in Jones, *Siege of Savannah*, 35n1.

106. Thomas Pinckney in Hough, *Siege of Savannah*, 167.

107. Thomas Pinckney in Jones, *Siege of Savannah*, 34n1.

108. Alexander Garden, *Anecdotes of the American Revolution* (Charleston, S.C., 1828), 1:73–75.

109. D'Estaing, "Journal of the Siege of Savannah," 73.

110. Moultrie, *Memoirs*, 2:40–41.

111. Lossing, *Pictorial Field Book,* 2:533.

112. Weems, *Life of Francis Marion,* 69. These are part of the statement traditionally attributed to Jasper on his death. According to Weems, Major Peter Horry encountered the wounded Jasper after his struggle atop the redoubt. However, Horry allegedly repudiated this version of events. I include the quote here because it is now part of the legend and tradition of the battle. (It is important to note that the heroism of Jasper and the color guard is not in question, only the authenticity of Jasper's final words to Horry.)

113. Edward W. Richardson, *Standards and Colors of the American Revolution* (Philadelphia: University of Pennsylvania Press and the Pennsylvania Society of Sons of the Revolution and Its Color Guard, 1982), 132.

114. Hough, *Siege of Savannah,* 166.

115. Weems, *Life of Francis Marion,* 64.

116. General Lincoln had assumed command of the reserves, leaving command of the attack to Count d'Estaing. It was therefore entirely correct for McIntosh, an officer in the Continental Army, to seek orders from d'Estaing.

117. Thomas Pinckney in Hough, *Siege of Savannah,* 168–69.

118. A few of the historians who have made this error are Henry Lumpkin, *From Savannah to Yorktown* (Columbia: University of South Carolina Press, 1981), 38; Christopher Ward, *War of the Revolution,* 2:693; and Henry Carrington, *Battles of the American Revolution,* 481. It is probable that Carrington's map of the battle, first published in 1877, popularized the mistake.

119. Séguier, "Journal," 20.

120. Tarragon, "Pechot Diary," in Stevens, *Facsimiles.*

121. Prevost to Germain, 1 November 1779, in Davies, *Documents,* 17:247.

122. T. W. Moore to his wife, 4 November 1779, in Hough, *Siege of Savannah,* 85–86.

123. Prevost to Germain, 1 November 1779, in Davies, *Documents,* 17:247.

124. Lawrence, *Storm over Savannah,* 107; Jones, *Siege of Savannah,* 46; Tarragon, "Pechot Diary," in Stevens, *Facsimiles.*

125. Moultrie, *Memoirs,* 2:41. Lincoln's casualty return of 9 October 1779 is in the Benjamin Lincoln Papers, MHS.

126. Hough, *Siege of Savannah,* 37.

127. Prevost to Germain, 1 November 1779, in Davies, *Documents,* 17:246–47.

128. Ibid., 17:246.

129. Lawrence, *Storm over Savannah,* 102.

130. Thomas Pinckney in Hough, *Siege of Savannah,* 169.

131. Prevost to Germain, 1 November 1779, in Davies, *Documents,* 17:245–46.

132. Tarragon, "Pechot Diary," in Stevens, *Facsimiles.*

133. French navy officer in Jones, *Siege of Savannah,* 65–66.

134. Tarragon, "Pechot Diary," in Stevens, *Facsimiles.*

135. Benjamin Lincoln, "Journal of Major General Lincoln," in *Muskets, Cannon Balls & Bombs,* trans. and ed. Kennedy, 127.

136. A. Timothy to Benjamin Lincoln, 13 October 1779, in Benjamin Lincoln Papers, MHS.

137. Benjamin Lincoln to Congress, 22 October 1779, in Hough, *Siege of Savannah,* 154, 155.

138. Davies, *Documents,* 17:248.

139. Tarragon, "Pechot Diary," in Stevens, *Facsimiles.*

140. Dillon to d'Estaing, in Stevens, *Facsimiles,* item 2010.

141. Séguier, "Journal," 21.

142. Peter Paumier, "Return of provisions at Savannah 24 October 1779," 24 November 1779, in Clinton Papers, Clements Library, University of Michigan, Ann Arbor.

143. Clinton to Germain, 17 November 1779, in Davies, *Documents,* 17:254–55.

144. Clinton, *American Rebellion,* 149n1.

145. McCall, *History of Georgia,* 446.

146. Davies, *Documents,* 17:249–50.

147. The American army at Savannah was reorganized on the night of 8 October 1779, just before the attack on Savannah. The brigade organization followed up to that point was set aside and regiments were reassigned to assault columns. Unit strengths for Lachlan McIntosh's brigade, the Charlestown militia, and the South Carolina artillery are based the return of 1 October in the Lincoln Papers, MHS. Isaac Huger's brigade strength is based on the return of 1 October for the militia and the return of 4 October of the Continentals. Huger returned the strength of all three of his Continental regiments (2nd S.C., 5th S.C., and Colonel Parker's 1st Virginia Levies) in one figure, making it difficult to arrive at individual unit strengths. In a completely unscientific manner, I have divided the strength of 500 Continentals that Huger listed into thirds (166 men each) to create this order of battle.

The strength of John Laurens's Corps of Light Infantry is from its return of 5 October; the Georgia Continentals were probably part of Laurens's command. The strength of the Virginia light dragoons is derived from the return of 10 October. The strength of Williamson's Brigade is taken from their return of 11 October (in the Emmet Collection, Manuscripts and Archive Section, New York Public Library).

The strength of Colonel Marbury's command was derived from Hugh McCall's *History of Georgia* (446–47). Marbury's command was never listed in any returns before the battle; however, it is listed in the casualty return of the 1st Brigade dated 10 October 1779.

The return for Pulaski's Legion dated 27 July 1779 (Benjamin Lincoln Papers, MHS) listed three troops of dragoons (156 men total, 103 fit for duty) and three companies of infantry (150 men total, 69 fit for duty). The next extant return for the legion is titled "Abstract of the Muster Rolls of General Count Pulaski's Legion in South Carolina for the Month's of August, September, October & November 1779" (Benjamin Lincoln Papers, MHS). According to this return, Pulaski's Legion detached its organic infantry contingent and converted entirely to cavalry in August 1779. The legion thereafter consisted of three troops of cavalry, each troop about 40 dragoons strong. Including officers, the legion totaled 125 men. On the last return for the unit, 61 of these 125 men were listed as "non-effective" (sick).

No mention is made in any narrative of the siege of Major John Jameson's Virginia dragoons, though the unit was present and a strength return exists for this detachment (Lincoln Papers, MHS). It is likely that Jameson's men were brigaded with the rest of Pulaski's cavalry, as one contemporary British map indicates. A return for the unit dated 10 October 1779 lists 3 wounded and 1 killed, indicating that at least a portion of Jameson's men participated in Pulaski's ill-fated charge.

The strength of Lieutenant Colonel Daniel Horry's dragoons is taken from their strength listed at Stono Ferry in June. Most accounts state that the South Carolina cavalry contingent was "small" and that together with Pulaski's cavalry totaled about 200 men. This would put Horry's strength at about 50 to 75 men.

Strength of the Charlestown Militia is from the 1 October 1779 return in Benjamin Lincoln Papers, MHS. Strength of the 1st Battalion is less the grenadier company assigned to Colonel John Laurens.

Lieutenant Colonel William Henderson's 6th South Carolina Continental Regiment is listed in the returns of the American army but is conspicuously missing from any mention in the narrative accounts of the battle and is not specifically mentioned in Lincoln's orders of attack for 9 October 1779. It is clear from the casualty returns for 9 October that the unit was not part of the assault on the Spring Hill redoubt (they suffered only 1 captain killed); it is likely that they were grouped with the column commanded by General Lachlan McIntosh.

148. The French order of battle is derived primarily from the "Pechot Diary" contained in B. F. Stevens's facsimile reproductions of documents of the American Revolution. French artillery figures are derived from Pierre Ozanne's map of the battle and the "Pechot Diary."

149. The British order of battle is derived mainly from General Prevost's commissary return for 11–20 October 1779. The commissary numbers do not make any distinction between fit-for-duty and sick. Only armed combatants are included in the order of battle above; among those not listed are engineers, commissariat workers, and black laborers (except pioneers, who might sometimes bear arms).

Miscellaneous forces include: 4th Battalion New Jersey Volunteers (1), Maryland Loyalists (1), Volunteers of Ireland (2), and Carolina Light Dragoons (1).

The British captured total includes the 74 men of the 1st Battalion of DeLancy's Regiment taken at Savages Point on 30 September 1779. Prevost's casualty return of the siege made on 18 October 1779 listed 40 killed, 63 wounded, 4 missing, and 48 deserted (original return, Clinton Papers, vol. 72, p. 24, Clements Library, University of Michigan).

British artillery figures are derived from various sources, but mostly from the map published by William Faden in 1784 "from a survey by an officer" (Don Higginbotham, *Atlas of the American Revolution*, ed. Kenneth Nebenzahl [New York: Rand McNally, 1974], 166).

Chapter 11—The Siege of Charlestown, 1780

1. Lincoln to Washington, 19 December 1778, in Jared Sparks, ed., *Correspondence of the American Revolution* (1853; reprint, Freeport, N.Y.: Books for Libraries Press, 1970), 241.

2. A. Timothy to Benjamin Lincoln, 13 October 1779, in Benjamin Lincoln Papers, MHS.

3. Ramsay to Drayton, 1 September 1779, in Gibbes, *Documentary History,* 121–22.

4. Lincoln to Washington, 7 November 1779, in Sparks, *Correspondence,* 345.

5. Ibid., 346.

6. See the letter of Richard Peters dated Philadelphia, 11 December 1779, in Benjamin Lincoln Papers, MHS.

7. Franklin B. Hough, ed., *The Siege of Charlestown* (1867; reprint, Spartanburg, S.C.: The Reprint Company, 1975), 17.

8. Clinton, *American Rebellion,* 149n1.

9. Clinton to Germain, 21 August 1779, in Davies, *Documents,* 17:189.

10. See Major Baurmeister's embarkation return in Uhlendorf, *Siege of Charleston,* plate 3.

11. Davies, *Documents,* 15:61.

12. Clinton, *American Rebellion,* 159.

13. It was said that the starving survivors on the *Anna* nearly resorted to cannibalism before they finally made landfall in England, and that the leaky ship was only just able to ground itself before nearly sinking. See Lowell, *Hessians,* for more information.

14. Clinton, *American Rebellion,* 439.

15. From Colonel Bernard Beekman's notes contained in Lachlan McIntosh's *Papers,* ed. Lilla Mills Hawes (Athens: University of Georgia Press, 1968), 112.

16. Carl P. Borick, in *A Gallant Defense: The Siege of Charleston, 1780* (Columbia: University of South Carolina Press, 2003), says that the advance of the army across the sea islands was slowed mostly by weather and from a lack of siege artillery and entrenching tools. While weather was a factor, the lack of artillery and tools did not significantly slow the British advance. By far the greatest hindrance to the British advance was their lack of horses.

17. Ewald, *Diary,* 202.

18. Captain Hinrichs in Uhlendorf, *Siege of Charleston,* 194–95.

19. Ewald, *Diary,* 204.

20. Moultrie, *Memoirs,* 2:44, 49.

21. Lincoln to Moultrie, 29 February 1780, in Moultrie, *Memoirs,* 2:55.

22. Governor Rutledge to Colonel Benjamin Garden, in Gibbes, *Documentary History,* 129. Note that Rutledge only ordered half of Garden's regiment to the city. This was normal practice in the South as at least half of the militiamen of any district had to remain near their homes to "do patrol duty, for keeping the negroes in order, and be employed in suppressing any insurrections of the disaffected [i.e., Tories]" (Gibbes, *Documentary History,* 129).

23. Colonel James Williams to General Andrew Williamson, 4 January 1780, in Gibbes, *Documentary History,* 123.

24. Moultrie, *Memoirs,* 2:49.

25. Ramsay, *History of the Revolution of South Carolina,* 2:52; McCrady, *History of South Carolina,* 1:448.

26. Ewald, *Diary,* 214.

27. Ibid.

28. Ibid., 216.

29. Clinton, *American Rebellion,* 163.

30. J. Laurens to George Washington, 9 April 1780, in George Washington Papers, Manuscript Division, LOC. Accessed on-line at the Library of Congress American Memory Web site: http://memory.loc.gov/ammem/gwhtml/gwhome.html.

31. The jaegers numbered about 274; Captain Hinrichs says that three companies of light infantry supported them in this action (Uhlendorf, *Siege of Charleston,* 237), which would have been about 180 men, for a total of 454 engaged—hence my estimate of 400 to 500 British troops engaged.

32. Ewald, *Diary,* 218–19.

33. Ibid., 220; McIntosh, *Papers,* 113; Moultrie, *Memoirs,* 2:65.

34. Clinton to Germain, 30 January 1780, in Hough, *Siege of Charleston,* 56.

35. Benjamin Lincoln et al., *Original Papers Relating to the Siege of Charleston* (Charleston, S.C.: Walter, Evan & Cogswell, 1898), 27–35.

36. Ibid., 29.

37. Ibid., 30–31.

38. Clinton, *American Rebellion,* 172, 438–40.

39. Arbuthnot to the Admiralty Office, 15 June 1780, in Banastre Tarleton, *Campaigns of 1780 and 1781 in the Southern Provinces* (1787; reprint, North Stratford, N.H.: Ayer Company Publishers, 1999), 49.

40. Moultrie, *Memoirs,* 2:59.

41. Lincoln, 17 July 1780, in Lincoln et al., *Original Papers Relating to the Siege of Charleston,* 32. Whipple said that he had only offered to act in conjunction with Fort Moultrie "when the enemies [*sic*] force off the bar did not exceed half what they now have in the harbour and when we had every assurance that a ship larger than 50 guns could not be got over the bar" (ibid., 33.) In regard to this statement, it should be observed that the British did not move any ships in the harbor larger than fifty guns.

42. Moultrie, *Memoirs,* 2:59.

43. Arbuthnot says that the British ships passed the fort on 9 April 1780, as does Captain Ewald. Clinton says it was 8 April, as does Captain Hinrichs. Moultrie and Ramsay say 7 April. There is also disagreement between contemporary sources on the weather. According to Captain Ewald, the weather was perfect: "it was the most beautiful weather in the world, with hardly any wind;

the maneuver was carried out only with the aid of the flood tide" (Ewald, *Diary*, 226). Other sources claim that there was a strong southerly (Ramsay) or southeasterly (Hinrichs) wind. Still other sources claim that there was a severe thunderstorm raging that obscured the passing of the ships for "half the time of their passing" (Henry B. Dawson, *Battles of the United States*, 2 vols. [New York: Johnson, Fry, and Company, 1858], 1:574n1). The preponderance of the evidence is that the crossing occurred on 8 April in excellent weather, with a strong south-to-southeasterly breeze.

44. Ewald, *Diary*, 226.

45. Arbuthnot to Admiralty, 15 June 1780, in Tarleton, *Campaigns*, 49.

46. Hinrichs in Uhlendorf, *Siege of Charleston*, 243.

47. John Buchanan, *The Road to Guilford Court House* (New York: John Wiley and Sons, 1997), 53.

48. Since the *Renown* took much longer to pass the fort than the other vessels did, the average time for each ship to pass was probably less than fifteen minutes except for the *Renown*. Hinrichs also claimed that most of the casualties the British took occurred on the *Renown*.

49. Hinrichs in Uhlendorf, *Siege of Charleston*, 243.

50. Clinton, *American Rebellion*, 167.

51. Arbuthnot quoted by Clinton in *American Rebellion*, 170.

52. Clinton, *American Rebellion*, 171n21.

53. Ibid., 151.

54. Ewald, *Diary*, 230.

55. Ibid., 229–36; Uhlendorf, *Siege of Charleston*, 255.

56. Captain Hinrichs says that the mantlets were constructed in New York and assembled at the Gibbes plantation (Uhlendorf, *Siege of Charleston*, 231, 233). Captain Ewald says that Moncrief tore down all the wooden buildings in the area of the Gibbes plantation to construct the mantlets (Ewald, *Diary*, 221). Hinrichs's account is more likely because it is not like the British to trust to luck that they would find the necessary wood for an article so essential for a siege.

57. Moultrie, *Memoirs*, 2:62; Ewald, *Diary*, 224.

58. Ewald, *Diary*, 224. Captain Hinrichs said that the artillery Moncrief used against the American vessel was a single brass twenty-four-pounder (Uhlendorf, *Siege of Charleston*, 237). In contrast to Ewald's account, Hinrichs claimed that the American ships "could do no damage" to the redoubt due to the extreme elevation they would need to achieve for their guns in order to hit the bluff overlooking the river.

59. Clinton, *American Rebellion*, 164.

60. Hinrichs in Uhlendorf, *Siege of Charleston*, 239; Ewald, *Diary*, 224. According to Hinrichs, just the battery on Fenwick's Point fired into the city, while Ewald reported that both the batteries at Fenwick's and Linning's Point fired. I believe that the battery on Linning's Point was probably too distant to be effective in bombarding the city and therefore choose to believe Hinrichs's account.

61. Hinrichs in Uhledorf, *Siege of Charleston*, 295.

62. Ewald, *Diary*, 226. Ewald incorrectly states that Woodford's brigade arrived on 8 April 1780 (226), while Moultrie incorrectly says that Woodford's brigade arrived on 6 April (*Memoirs*, 2:67). Barnard Beekman also said that Woodford arrived on 6 April (McIntosh, *Papers*, 114). However, it is clear from contemporary letters of General Lincoln and General Woodford that the Virginia veterans arrived on 7 April (Lincoln to Washington, 9 April 1780, and Woodford to Washington, 9 April 1780, in George Washington Papers, LOC). Captain Hinrichs's journal also says that Woodford arrived on 7 April (Uhlendorf, *Siege of Charleston*, 241).

63. Most historians say that Woodford's brigade numbered around 700 men (see, for example, Moultrie, *Memoirs,* 2:67). However, this number is only the rank and file total. Including officers and musicians, Woodford's brigade numbered 894 men according to Woodford's own strength return of 1 May 1780 (Charles H. Lesser, ed., *The Sinews of Independence* [Chicago: University of Chicago Press, 1976], 161). Woodford reorganized his ten understrength regiments into three regiments during his march south (see Woodford to Washington, 28 December 1779 and 9 April 1780, in George Washington Papers, LOC; and Lesser, *Sinews,* 163).

64. John Laurens to Washington, 9 April 1780, in George Washington Papers, LOC.

65. Hinrichs in Uhlendorf, *Siege of Charleston,* 241.

66. Woodford to Washington, 9 April 1780, in George Washington Papers, LOC.

67. Woodford to Washington, 31 March 1780, in George Washington Papers, LOC.

68. As we know today, these diseases are spread through mosquitoes that like the hot, damp conditions of the Deep South. At the time these and other diseases were attributed to "miasma" or swamp gas. This is where the contemporary concept of "healthy" and "unhealthy" ground originated. Hilly, cool areas became known as healthy ground, whereas low, hot, and wet grounds were known as unhealthy. This concept actually has some scientific basis (fewer mosquitoes in higher, cooler areas), though the mechanism was misunderstood at the time.

69. Benjamin Taliaferro, *The Orderly Book of Captain Benjamin Taliaferro,* ed. Lee A. Wallace (Richmond: Virginia State Library, 1980), 125.

70. Hough, *Siege of Charleston,* 88–89.

71. Moultrie, *Memoirs,* 2:70.

72. Hinrichs in Uhlendorf, *Siege of Charleston,* 249.

73. Ibid.

74. Lincoln to Washington, 9 April 1780, in George Washington Papers, LOC.

75. Moultrie, *Memoirs,* 2:105.

76. Godbold and Woody, *Gadsden,* 198.

77. Rutledge to Colonel Goodwyn, 24 April 1780, in Gibbes, *Documentary History,* 131–32.

78. Moultrie, *Memoirs,* 2:105–6.

79. McIntosh, *Papers,* 101.

80. Ibid.

81. Lincoln wrote that he did not hear of this rout until 16 April 1780; however, Moultrie and McIntosh say first word came on the 14th. I assume that Lincoln meant he did not have positive intelligence of the debacle until the 16th, but rumors were in the city earlier.

82. McCrady, *History of South Carolina,* 1:442.

83. Ibid.; Moultrie, *Memoirs,* 2:72.

84. McIntosh, *Papers,* 103.

85. Ibid., 104.

86. Ibid.

87. Ibid.; Godbold and Woody, *Gadsden,* 200.

88. McIntosh, *Papers,* 104.

89. Ibid., 105.

90. Ibid., 104.

91. McIntosh says that everyone who attended the councils of war were sworn to secrecy regarding both the information revealed in the council and the councils' "determinations" (*Papers,* 103).

92. Ewald, *Diary,* 232.

93. McIntosh, *Papers,* 104.

94. Clinton, *American Rebellion*, 168. Clinton's rejection included renewed offer of the terms Clinton had formerly proposed on 8 April, which Lincoln rejected.

95. Moultrie, *Memoirs*, 2:78.

96. Moultrie says there were three hundred light infantry (*Memoirs*, 2:79), as does an unidentified "orderly book" in *Documentary History of the American Revolution*, compiled by R. W. Gibbes. Lachlan McIntosh says that there were two hundred infantrymen under Henderson (McIntosh, *Papers*, 107).

The Half-Moon battery was the only American redoubt flanking the canal that formed in front of the American lines. Henderson's men could thus sortie from it without having to cross the canal. However, Captain Hinrichs says that he saw men "rushing out of the gate-work" (Uhlendorf, *Siege of Charleston*, 261), which was his term for the Hornwork, which was in the American center. Since this structure was behind the canal, we can assume that the Americans brought planks with them to use as a bridge over the canal for their sortie.

97. The description of the third parallel is from Hinrichs (Uhlendorf, *Siege of Charleston*, 262) and is confirmed by the map of the Charlestown campaign contained in Ramsay's *History of the Revolution of South Carolina*, which is by far the most detailed of the many maps available of the battle. The two wings of the trench were eventually dug up to the American canal after it had been drained, thus making the canal part of the besieger's works.

98. Uhlendorf, *Siege of Charleston*, 261.

99. Ewald, *Diary*, 233.

100. Ibid.; corroborated by Hinrichs in Uhlendorf, *Siege of Charleston*. Note that we have no account of this action from the British point of view, and that both Hinrichs and Ewald were Germans who accused the English light infantry of running away.

101. Hinrichs in Uhlendorf, *Siege of Charleston*, 265. Jaegers, who lacked bayonets and had only small hunting swords for close-in fighting, were usually paired with light infantry or grenadiers. This was so that they could retire behind the bayonet-armed troops in case an enemy charged them.

102. McIntosh, *Papers*, 118.

103. Hinrichs in Uhlendorf, *Siege of Charleston*, 265. Johann Ewald says that several French officers in the American lines shouted *"Avances, tires!"* (*Diary*, 233), which is what occasioned the alarm in the British lines—this was probably just rumor, as Lachlan McIntosh, who was in the Half-Moon redoubt that night, makes no mention of trying such a ruse.

104. Hinrichs in Uhlendorf, *Siege of Charleston*, 265.

105. Ewald, *Diary*, 233.

106. Moultrie says that the council of war called to discuss Duportail's observations was held on Wednesday, 26 April 1780 (*Memoirs*, 2:80). Lachlan McIntosh thought that this meeting occurred on Sunday, 30 April (McIntosh, *Papers*, 110). Since McIntosh expressed uncertainty regarding the date, I have gone with the date in Moultrie's account. There is actually a great deal of disagreement between McIntosh's and Moultrie's accounts as to when the civilian leaders interrupted the meetings (Moultrie says it was on 26 April, while McIntosh says it was on 19 April); however, both men are in general agreement as to what was said by the councilmen.

107. McIntosh, *Papers*, 111.

108. Moultrie, *Memoirs*, 2:80.

109. Ibid.

110. Hinrichs in Uhlendorf, *Siege of Charleston*, 279.

111. McIntosh, *Papers*, 110.

112. Hinrichs in Uhlendorf, *Siege of Charleston*, 281; Moultrie, *Memoirs*, 2:85.

113. Ibid., 2:61.

114. Unknown subaltern in McIntosh, *Papers,* 118.

115. McIntosh, *Papers,* 121.

116. Commissary return of 5 May 1780 in Benjamin Lincoln Papers, MHS.

117. Unknown subaltern in McIntosh, *Papers,* 121.

118. Clinton in Moultrie, *Memoirs,* 2:86.

119. Moultrie, *Memoirs,* 2:88, 89.

120. Clinton, *American Rebellion,* 169.

121. Unknown subaltern in McIntosh, *Papers,* 120.

122. Clinton, *American Rebellion,* 169–70.

123. Moultrie, *Memoirs,* 2:92.

124. Ibid., 2:96, 97.

125. Ewald, *Diary,* 236–37.

126. Clinton to Cornwallis, 6 May 1780, in Clinton, *American Rebellion,* 170n20.

127. Clinton, *American Rebellion,* 171 author's n22.

128. Ewald, *Diary,* 234.

129. Ibid., 237.

130. Lowell, *Hessians,* 251; Ewald, *Diary,* 214; Boatner, *Encyclopedia,* 713.

131. Moultrie, *Memoirs,* 2:108.

132. The same deprecating terms would be forced on the surrendering British at Yorktown in 1781.

133. Moultrie, *Memoirs,* 2:109.

134. Hinrichs in Uhlendorf, *Siege of Charleston,* 293.

135. Ramsay, *History of the Revolution of South Carolina,* 2:62. According to Ramsay, there were 89 killed and 138 wounded in the Continentals, 3 killed and 7 wounded among the militiamen, and 20 civilians killed.

136. John Paul Jones captained *Ranger* before he took command of *Bonhomme Richard.* Jones and patrolled the waters around England in *Ranger,* and he even launched several raids on English soil.

137. Ewald says three hundred were killed (*Diary,* 239); an unnamed subaltern says two hundred (McIntosh, *Papers,* 121). These are not recorded in the order of battle as they were not "combat" casualties.

138. Hinrichs in Uhlendorf, *Siege of Charleston,* 299.

139. Lincoln, 17 July 1780, in Lincoln et al., *Original Papers Relating to the Siege of Charleston,* 16; and Benjamin Lincoln Papers, MHS.

140. Stevens, *Facsimiles,* item 2010.

141. Washington to Laurens, 26 April 1780, in George Washington Papers, LOC.

142. Moultrie, *Memoirs,* 2:60.

143. American strength returns are primarily derived from Clinton's return of prisoners dated 12 May 1780, in bundle 99, C.O.5, copies of the British Colonial Office Papers in the LOC, Manuscripts Division; and the "Return of the Rebel Forces . . . at the surrender of Charlestown," in Moultrie, *Memoirs,* 114. Clinton's return includes invalids, musicians, and officers and contains a total of 2,643 Continental soldiers. Moultrie states on page 108 of his narrative that "we marched out between 1,500 and 1,600 continental troops, (leaving five or six hundred sick and wounded in the hospitals)," for a total of about 2,200 Continentals. A return of prisoners produced by Congress in 1780 listed 2,487 Continental prisoners.

Another accurate source for strengths of American forces in Charlestown during the siege are the captured strength returns published in Lesser, *Sinews.* While these returns are admittedly incomplete, they are the most detailed figures available. Using the methodology of counting all fit-for-duty troops along with all sick but present troops in my orders of battle, I have found that the figures given in Lesser's *Sinews* for individual regiments (especially the Continentals) and those published by the British as captured after the siege are nearly the same. Indeed some of the regimental strengths differ by only one man in the two sources. Other regiments differ by greater amounts, but most are off by only a few percent. Therefore these two sources serve to confirm each other's accuracy. (It also serves to validate the methodology of counting all fit-for-duty troops and those listed as "sick present" to figure the net strength of a unit.)

Colonel Richard Parker, who was killed on 24 April 1779, originally commanded the 1st Virginia Continental Detachment. Parker also originally commanded the brigade to which his regiment was attached before the arrival of Brigadier General Charles Scott at Charlestown.

Colonel Francis Marion commanded the 2nd South Carolina Regiment until he was evacuated from the city in late April because of an injured ankle.

The forty-one "light dragoons" listed are probably survivors of the action at Monck's Corner. Moultrie says that "40 Virginians" entered the city on 18 April 1780 (*Memoirs*, 2:72).

In the return of prisoners listed in Moultrie's memoirs, the French company is listed at 43. In the captured returns published in Lesser, *Sinews*, the same company is listed at 92 men. Johann Ewald remarked in his journal of the siege that there were at least 200 French soldiers of d'Estaing's army still in Charlestown at the surrender and that he made the acquaintance of one of d'Estaing's grenadiers there. I have therefore used the higher number listed in Lesser's *Sinews* in this order of battle.

McIntosh's militia brigade is listed as containing 1,231 men in the return of prisoners made by the British after the capture of Charlestown, but no figures for individual militia companies are contained in the British return. In the captured returns published in Lesser's *Sinews*, individual militia units are listed but are not complete. The militia regiment of Anthony Lytle is listed at 193 men in Lesser, *Sinews;* I have therefore subtracted this number from the figure of 1,231 militia given in the British return of prisoners in order to be able to show Lytle's men separately in the order of battle.

Other militia companies listed in Lesser's *Sinews* are as follows (figures include fit-for-duty and sick present):

S.C. Militia—Col. Joseph Maybank	22
S.C. Militia—Col. Benjamin Garden	97
S.C. Militia—Col. Wm. Skirving	33
Militia—Col. McDonald	98
S.C. Militia—Col. Hugh Giles	77
S.C. Militia—Col. George Hicks	20
S.C. Militia—Col. Richard Richardson	68
S.C. Militia—Col. Joe. Kershaw	38
S.C. Militia—Col. Robert Goodwin	39
N.C. Militia—Col. Henry Harrington	150
N.C. Militia—Col. Hugh Tinning	94

Totals include those sick but present. The fit-for-duty totals would be as much as 25 percent lower. The "Total Losses" figure of 5,700 for the Americans is derived by adding the captured total of 5,611 (which includes the sick and wounded) to the killed total of 89.

144. Artillery figures were derived primarily from Moultrie, *Memoirs*, 2:106–7. These figures represent artillery actually mounted in battery, and not all the ordnance possessed by the Americans in reserve and in their artillery parks. Moultrie reported the following as the weight and number of the artillery: 24-lb. guns: 15; 18-lb. guns: 31; 12-lb. guns: 43; 9-lb. guns: 68; total: 157.

The British reported the following as U.S. ordnance captured (this list probably includes pieces that were never mounted in battery): 10" mortar: 1; 9¾" mortar: 1; 7¼" mortar: 1; 5½" mortar: 3; 4½" mortar: 3; 8" howitzer: 1; 26-lb. cannons: 12; 24-lb. cannons: 12; 18-lb. cannons: 29; 12-lb. cannons: 79; 9-lb. cannons: 70; 6-lb. cannons: 28; 4-lb. cannons: 57; 3-lb. cannons: 6; ½-lb. swivels: 3; 4-lb. carronades: 2; total: 308 (Hough, *Siege of Charlestown*, 116).

145. Primary sources for the British order of battle are Clinton's strength return dated 1 May 1780 in bundle 99, C.O.5, copies of British Colonial Office Papers in the LOC, Manuscripts Division; the embarkation list sent from Major Carl Baurmeister to Baron von Jungkenn, 26 March 1780, facsimile copy in Uhlendorf, *Siege of Charleston,* plate 3; and the embarkation lists of 23 December 1779 and 25 March 1780, bundle 99, C.O.5, LOC, Manuscripts Division. These lists do not entirely agree, and each is incomplete in certain respects. To create the order of battle listed here I have had to resolve the differences between the lists and make certain assumptions about units that might be named differently in different lists. I have generally used the numbers from the 1 May 1780 strength return mostly because the return was done more closely in time to the end of the siege, and therefore should be more accurate to the date for which I am making the order of battle. I included all officers and soldiers listed as effectives, regardless of their status as sick or wounded, but I did not include those soldiers listed as "Prisoners of the Rebels" or those that were designated as "On Command or Recruiting." Troops that were "On Command" had usually been assigned to ad hoc formations such the light infantry or grenadier companies and were thus not present in their "home" regiments. Likewise, troops recruiting would likely have been in Britain or elsewhere not with the army.

The 1 May 1780 strength return lists a "detachment" of light infantry but does not mention Major Graham's Light Infantry corps, which is recorded in a strength return dated 15 May 1780 in the Clinton Papers, William L. Clements Library, University of Michigan, Ann Arbor. I assume that the "detachment" mentioned in the strength return is actually Major Graham's light corps and have listed it as such in the order of battle.

The following troops were in the first embarkation from New York but did not participate in the siege. The Hessian recruits were replacements for the two German regiments garrisoning Savannah, while the chasseurs and riflemen aboard the *Anna* were blown by a storm to England.

Recruits for Regiment von Wissenbach	50
Recruits for Regiment von Trümbach	93
Chasseurs (Hesse Cassel, Anspach)—	
Capt. Hanger	ca. 165
Althausen's Riflemen	35

The figures for the number of cannons in the British army at this time were derived mainly from the correspondence between Clinton and Arbuthnot in Clinton, *American Rebellion*, 438–40.

146. Tarleton's Legion is listed as having 470 soldiers on 1 May 1780, the embarkation list in Uhledorf, *Siege of Charleston*, plate 3.

147. This figure comes from Clinton, *American Rebellion*, 167n14. Clinton says that the reinforcement from New York numbered 2,566 effectives and 1,863 fit for duty. The strength of the 42nd Regiment was listed in Captain Hinrichs's journal as 750 (Uhlendorf, *Siege of Charleston,* 105), while a return for the Prince of Wales Loyal Americans dated 15 May 1780 listed 319 effectives and 250 fit for duty (in the Clements Library, University of Michigan, Ann Arbor).

148. Lieutenant Colonel John Hamilton was taken prisoner by Lieutenant Colonel William Washington.

149. See this chapter's note 143 for an explanation of American total losses.

Chapter 12—Waxhaws

1. Boatner, *Encyclopedia,* 1087.

2. The raid was carried out by twenty-five troopers of the 16th Dragoons and was commanded by Lieutenant Colonel William Harcourt.

3. Clinton, *American Rebellion,* 111.

4. Lord Cathcart may have used as the foundation for his legion a unit of Loyalist provincials known as the Caledonian Volunteers, who were raised and commanded by one Captain William Sutherland.

5. Tarleton, *Campaigns,* 7.

6. Lord Cathcart, who helped found the British Legion, was formerly a captain in the 17th Light Dragoons, and it is likely that this troop was previously commanded by Cathcart.

7. Tarleton, *Campaigns,* 15.

8. Ibid., 15–16.

9. Ibid.

10. Ibid., 16; Anthony Allaire, *Diary of Lieut. Anthony Allaire* (1881; reprint, New York: New York Times Press, 1968), 11.

11. Tarleton says that 400 cavalry mounts were captured; Stedman says 182, with 82 being cavalry mounts. Lachlan McIntosh says 150 horses were captured by the British.

12. Tarleton, *Campaigns,* 17; Clinton, *American Rebellion,* 166.

13. Moultrie, *Memoirs,* 2:72.

14. Stedman, *History of the American War,* 183.

15. Ibid.

16. Allaire, *Diary,* 12.

17. Stedman, *History of the American War,* 183.

18. Cornwallis to Tarleton, 25 April 1780, in Tarleton, *Campaigns,* 38.

19. Tarleton, *Campaigns,* 19.

20. Lee, *Memoirs,* 156.

21. Tarleton, *Campaigns,* 20.

22. Ibid.; Clinton, *American Rebellion,* 169; Lee, *Memoirs,* 156.

23. Tarleton, *Campaigns,* 20.

24. Lee, *Memoirs,* 164.

25. John Peebles, *John Peebles' American War,* ed. Ira D. Gruber (Mechanicsburg, Pa.: Stackpole Books, 1998), 582.

26. Unknown subaltern in McIntosh, *Papers,* 116–17.

27. Clinton, *American Rebellion,* 171n22.

28. Ibid., 177.

29. Woodford ordered his artillery and baggage to follow as soon as possible, escorted "by 140 men of Colo. Buford's regiment, which is all of that corps who can be marched at present, about 300 will be left and I see no probability for them being equipped for a march in any short time" (Woodford to Washington, 8 March 1780, in George Washington Papers, LOC).

30. Woodford to Washington, 31 March 1780 in George Washington Papers, LOC.

31. Governor Rutledge to Governor Nash, 24 May 1780, in Commager and Morris, *Spirit of 'Seventy Six,* 1117; William Dobein James, *The Life of Brigadier General Francis Marion,* ed. Alan R. Light (Charleston, S.C.: Gould and Riley, 1821; e-text version, 1997), chap. 2.

32. Over the next year several actions would be fought in close proximity to this road in northern South Carolina: Waxhaws, Rugeley's Mill, Hanging Rock, Camden, and Hobkirk's Hill.

33. Tarleton, *Campaigns,* 27.

NOTES TO PAGES 252–263

34. Ibid., 28.

35. Ibid.

36. Dawson, *Battles,* 1:583. Bowyer in Garden, *Anecdotes of the American Revolution,* 3:126–28.

37. Tarleton, *Campaigns,* 78.

38. Ibid., 79; Dawson, *Battles,* 1:584. Dr. Robert Brownfield says that Buford held a council of war with his officers before responding to Tarleton's summons (James, *Life of Francis Marion,* appendix.).

39. James, *Life of Francis Marion,* appendix.

40. Tarleton, *Campaigns,* 79. Dr. Brownfield says that Tarleton had placed his cavalry on the wings and his infantry in the center (James, *Life of Francis Marion,* appendix).

41. Tarleton, *Campaigns,* 29.

42. Ibid., 30.

43. James, *Life of Francis Marion,* appendix.

44. Brownfield in ibid.

45. John Keegan, *The Face of Battle* (1976; reprint, New York: Penguin Books, 1984), 95–96.

46. Brownfield in James, *Life of Francis Marion,* appendix.

47. Dawson, *Battles,* 1:584; referencing Adjutant Bowyer's account.

48. Brownfield, in James, *Life of Francis Marion,* says that Ensign Cruit, rather than Adjutant Bowyer, carried the white flag to Tarleton (appendix).

49. Tarleton, *Campaigns,* 31.

50. Fredrick William Baron von Steuben, *Revolutionary War Drill Manual* (1794; reprint, New York: Dover, 1985), 51–55.

51. Brownfield in James, *Life of Francis Marion,* appendix.

52. Tarleton, *Campaigns,* 30–31.

53. Ibid., 31.

54. Tarleton to Cornwallis, 29 May 1780, in ibid., 84.

55. Lee, *Memoirs,* 167.

56. Tarleton to Cornwallis, 29 May 1780, in Tarleton, *Campaigns,* 84.

57. Stedman, *History of the American War,* 193.

58. Lee, *Memoirs,* 165.

59. The British initially took 203 prisoners but paroled 150 of them because they were too severely wounded to be moved.

Chapter 13—The End of the Beginning

1. Clinton, *American Rebellion,* 174n1.

2. Cornwallis to Clinton, in Clinton, *American Rebellion,* 176. General Williamson accepted a British parole—actions that caused some Patriots to suspect that Williamson had cut some treasonous deal with the British. Williamson was later said to have passed intelligence of British operations to Colonel John Laurens while he resided in British-occupied Charlestown. This undercover work won him clemency in South Carolina after the war. See Boatner, *Encyclopedia,* 1210.

3. Clinton, *American Rebellion,* 174.

4. Ibid., 70.

5. Ibid., 72.

6. Lee, *Memoirs,* 163.

7. Boatner, *Encyclopedia,* 364.

8. Clinton, *American Rebellion,* 441.

9. Ibid., 175n3.

10. Ewald, *Diary,* 242.

11. Clinton, *American Rebellion,* 181.

12. Stedman, *History of the American War,* 197–98.

13. Elmer D. Johnson and Kathleen Lewis Sloan, eds., *South Carolina: A Documentary Profile of the Palmetto State* (Columbia: University of South Carolina Press, 1971), 205.

14. Hayne was captured during a raid to "rescue" Brigadier General Andrew Williamson from British custody. The Americans succeeded in freeing Williamson, only to lose Hayne as a captive. Ironically, Williamson returned himself over to British custody, saying that he would be violating his loyalty oath if he fought again on the American side—the same oath that Hayne was later executed for violating.

15. Stedman, *History of the American War,* 198; Lee, *Memoirs,* 168.

16. Clinton, *American Rebellion,* 177n10. The troops that returned to New York were the British grenadier and light infantry corps, 42nd Regiment, the Hessian grenadier regiments (Minnigerode, Linsing, Lengereke, Graff), the Field-Jaeger corps, and the Queen's Rangers.

17. Germain to Clinton, 5 August 1779, in Davies, *Documents,* 17:177.

Author's Note and Historiography

1. Lincoln to Moultrie, 20 June 1779, in Moultrie, *Memoirs,* 1:491.

2. Ramsay, *History of the Revolution of South Carolina,* 2:29.

3. Lincoln to Moultrie, 6 June 1779, in Benjamin Lincoln Papers, MHS.

4. Moultrie to Lincoln, 19 June 1779; Moultrie to Lincoln, 20 June 1779, in Benjamin Lincoln Papers, MHS.

5. Stedman, *History of the American War,* 176.

6. See the deposition of the American spy in the Benjamin Lincoln Papers, MHS.

7. Ramsay, *History of the American Revolution,* 2:446.

8. Ward, *War of the Revolution,* 2:686. In his account of the action at Stono, Ward mistakenly states that General Moultrie led the attack, when in fact it was General Lincoln who commanded at the ferry.

9. Ward, *War of the Revolution,* 2:686.

10. Lincoln to John Jay, 4 June 1779, in Benjamin Lincoln Papers, MHS.

11. Lincoln to Rutledge, 21 June 1779, in Benjamin Lincoln Papers, MHS.

12. This map is reproduced in Douglas W. Marshall and Howard H. Peckham's *Campaigns of the American Revolution: An Atlas of Manuscript Maps* (Ann Arbor: University of Michigan Press, 1976), 83–85.

13. Boatner, *Encyclopedia,* 1062.

14. Stedman, *History of the American War,* 127; Ramsay, *History of the American Revolution,* 2:449; Hough, *Siege of Savannah,* 43; William Faden, "Plan of the Siege of Savannah," in *Atlas of the American Revolution,* ed. Kenneth Nebenzahl (New York: Rand McNally, 1974), 167.

15. P. Gauthier, "List of English regular troops . . . ," 12 November 1779, in Stevens, *Facsimiles,* item 2010; François d'Auber De Peyrelongue, "The American War," in *Muskets, Cannon Balls & Bombs: Nine Narratives of the Siege of Savannah in 1779,* trans. and ed. Benjamin Kennedy (Savannah, Ga.: Beehive Press, 1974), 28.

16. Fortescue, *War of Independence,* 135; Lawrence, *Storm over Savannah,* 48; Ward, *War of the Revolution,* 2:690.

17. Clinton, *American Rebellion,* 150.

18. Ward, *War of the Revolution,* 2:690.

19. Jones, *Siege of Savannah,* 40; Hough, *Siege of Savannah,* 38.

20. Jones, *Siege of Savannah*, 32.

21. Taliaferro, *Orderly Book*.

22. Ibid., 10; Prevost in Davies, *Documents*, 17:241.

23. D'Estaing, "Journal of the Siege of Savannah," 66.

24. Lawrence, *Storm over Savannah*, 100; D'Estaing, "Journal of the Siege of Savannah," 72.

25. Lossing, *Pictorial Field Book*, 2:532; Lawrence, *Storm over Savannah*, 100.

26. Lossing, *Pictorial Field Book*, 2:532; Dawson, *Battles*, 1:567.

27. Hough, *Siege of Savannah*, 40; Prevost to Germain, 1 November 1779, in Davies, *Documents*, 17:247.

28. Maurice Simons to Benjamin Lincoln, 16 September 1779, in Benjamin Lincoln Papers, MHS.

29. Moultrie to Lincoln, 17 July 1779, in Benjamin Lincoln Papers, MHS.

30. Benjamin Lincoln, "Journal of Major General Lincoln," in *Muskets, Cannon Balls & Bombs: Nine Narratives of the Siege of Savannah in 1779*, trans. and ed. Benjamin Kennedy (Savannah, Ga.: Beehive Press, 1974), 121.

31. D'Estaing, "Journal of the Siege of Savannah," 61.

32. Jean-Rémy de Tarragon, "The Pechot Diary," in Stevens, *Facsimiles*, item 2010.

33. Pinckney in Hough, *Siege of Savannah*, 158–59. The two ship names mentioned as blockading Port Royal were given by a French naval officer in Jones, *Siege of Savannah*, 59; this account thus serves to confirm Pinckney's account.

34. McCall, *History of Georgia*, 435.

35. Killion and Waller, *Georgia and the Revolution*, 210.

36. Ibid.

37. McCall, *History of Georgia*, 441.

38. George Washington, 1 October 1779, in Fitzpatrick, ed., *The Writings of George Washington*. Accessed on-line at the Library of Congress American Memory Web site (http://memory.loc.gov/ammem/gwhtml/gwhome.html).

39. Moultrie, *Memoirs*, 2:42.

40. Dawson, *Battles*, 567.

41. Davies, *Documents*, 17:246–47.

42. Prevost to Germain, 1 November 1779, in Davies, *Documents*, 17:243.

43. James Wright to Germain, 5 November 1779, in Davies, *Documents*, 17:252.

44. Lawrence, *Storm over Savannah*, 50.

Selected Bibliography

Manuscript and Facsimile Manuscript Sources

Select documents, identified in the footnotes, were utilized from the following collections:

British Colonial Office Papers (Copies). Manuscripts Division, Library of Congress. Class 5 bundles 99, 155, 182. Compiled by Benjamin Franklin Stevens.

Clinton Papers. Clements Library, University of Michigan, Ann Arbor.

Hargrett Rare Book & Manuscript Library, University of Georgia.

Lincoln, Benjamin. Papers. Massachusetts Historical Society, Boston. Microfilm edition held at the University of Texas at Arlington.

Lincoln, Benjamin. Papers. Thomas Addit Emmet Collection. Manuscripts and Archives Division, New York Public Library.

Ozanne, Pierre. Map: "Siege of Savannah." Dated 1779 in the Ozanne Cartographic Collection, Library of Congress. Call number G3924.S333 1779.09 OZ22.

Stevens, Benjamin Franklin, ed. *Facsimiles of Manuscripts in European Archives Relating to America, 1773–1783.* Microfilm edition held at the University of Texas at Arlington.

Washington, George. Papers. Manuscript Division, Library of Congress. Series 3 Letter books, Varick Transcripts: Continental Army Papers 1775–83; Series 4 General Correspondence 1697–1799; and Series 6 Military Papers 1755–98. Accessed on-line at the Library of Congress American Memory Web site (http://memory.loc.gov/ammem/gwhtml/gwhome.html).

Published Primary Sources

Allaire, Anthony. *Diary of Lieut. Anthony Allaire.* 1881. Reprint, New York: New York Times Press, 1968.

Campbell, Archibald. *Journal of Lieut. Colonel Archibald Campbell.* Edited by Colin Campbell. Darien, Ga.: Ashantilly Press, 1981.

Clark, Walter, ed. *The State Records of North Carolina.* 30 vols. Winston, N.C.: M. I. & J. C. Stewart, Printers to the State, 1896.

Clinton, Henry. *The American Rebellion.* Edited by William B. Willcox. New Haven, Conn.: Yale University Press, 1954.

Commager, Henry Steele, and Richard B. Morris, eds. *The Spirit of 'Seventy-Six.* 1958. Reprint, Bicentennial edition, New York: Harper & Row, 1975.

Dann, John C., ed. *The Revolution Remembered.* Chicago: University of Chicago Press, 1980.

Davies, K. G., ed. *Documents of the American Revolution 1770–1783.* 20 vols. Shannon: Irish University Press, 1976.

D'Estaing, Jean-Baptist Charles Henri Hector Théodat. "Journal of the Siege of Savannah with Some Observations by M. Le Comte d'Estaing." In *Muskets, Cannon Balls & Bombs: Nine Narratives of the Siege of Savannah in 1779,* edited and translated by Benjamin Kennedy, 42–75. Savannah, Ga.: Beehive Press, 1974.

Ewald, Johann. *Diary of the American War.* Translated and edited by Joseph P. Tustin. New Haven, Conn.: Yale University Press, 1979.

Fitzpatrick, John C., ed. *The Writings of George Washington from the Original Manuscript Sources, 1745–1799.* 39 vols. Washington, D.C.: Government Printing Office, 1931–1944. Reprint, New York: Greenwood Press, 1970. Accessed on-line at the Library of Congress American Memory Web site (http://memory.loc.gov/ammem/gwhtml/gwhome.html).

Force, Peter, ed. *American Archives.* Series 4, vols. 4–5. Washington, D.C., 1853.

Galloway, Joseph. *Fabricus.* London: G. Wilkie, 1782; Library of American Civilization microcard LAC 15696.

Gibbes, R. W., ed. *Documentary History of the American Revolution.* Columbia, S.C.: Banner Steam-Power Press, 1853.

Hough, Franklin B., ed. *The Siege of Charlestown.* 1867. Reprint, Spartanburg, S.C.: The Reprint Company, 1975.

———. *The Siege of Savannah.* 1866. Reprint, Spartanburg, S.C.: The Reprint Company, 1975.

Johnson, Elmer D., and Kathleen Lewis Sloan, eds. *South Carolina: A Documentary Profile of the Palmetto State.* Columbia: University of South Carolina Press, 1971.

Jones, Charles C., ed. *Siege of Savannah.* 1874. Reprint, New York: New York Times and Arno Press, 1968.

Killion, Ronald G., and Charles T. Waller. *Georgia and the Revolution.* Atlanta: Cherokee Publishing Company, 1975.

Lincoln, Benjamin, et al. *Original Papers Relating to the Siege of Charleston.* Charleston, S.C.: Walter, Evan & Cogswell, 1898. (Accessed courtesy the rare book archive at the Center for American History, University of Texas at Austin.)

McIntosh, Lachlan. *Lachlan McIntosh Papers.* Edited by Lilla Mills Hawes. Athens: University of Georgia Press, 1968.

Moore, Frank. *Diary of the Revolution.* 2 vols. 1860. Reprint, New York: Arno Press, 1969.

Moultrie, William. *Memoirs of the American Revolution.* 2 vols. 1802. Reprint, New York: New York Times and Arno Press, 1968.

Peebles, John. *John Peebles' American War.* Edited by Ira Gruber. Mechanicsburg, Pa.: Stackpole Books, 1998.

Pettengill, Ray, trans. *Letters from America, 1776–1779.* 1924. Reprint, Port Washington, N.Y.: Kennikat Press, 1964.

Prevost, Augustine. "Journal of the Siege of Savannah in 1779." Translated by Charles Edgeworth Jones. In *Publications of the Southern History Association, vol. 1.* Washington, D.C.: Southern History Association, 1897.

Ramsay, David. *The History of the American Revolution.* 2 vols. Edited by Lester H. Cohen. 1789. Reprint, Indianapolis, Ind.: Liberty Fund, 1990.

———. *The History of the Revolution of South Carolina.* 2 vols. Trenton: Isaac Collins, 1785.

Robson, Eric, ed. *Letters from America.* New York: Barnes & Noble, 1950.

Saint-Marc, Meyronnet de. "Meyronnet de Saint Mark's Journal of . . . the Siege of Savannah." Edited by Roberta Leighton. *New York Historical Society Quarterly* 36, no. 3 (1952).

Scribner, Robert L., and Brent Tarter, eds. *Revolutionary Virginia: The Road to Independence.* 17 vols. Charlottesville: University Press of Virginia, 1979.

Séguier, Phillipe. "Journal of Phillipe Séguier de Terson." In *Muskets, Cannon Balls & Bombs: Nine Narratives of the Siege of Savannah in 1779,* edited and translated by Benjamin Kennedy, 3–26. Savannah, Ga.: Beehive Press, 1974.

Stedman, Charles. *The History of the American War.* London, 1794.

Steuben, Fredrick William, Baron von. *Revolutionary War Drill Manual.* 1794. Reprint, New York: Dover, 1985.

Taliaferro, Benjamin. *The Orderly Book of Captain Benjamin Taliaferro.* Edited by Lee A. Wallace. Richmond: Virginia State Library, 1980.

Tarleton, Banastre. *Campaigns of 1780 and 1781 in the Southern Provinces.* 1787. Reprint, North Stratford, N.H.: Ayer Company Publishers, 1999.

Uhlendorf, Bernhard A., trans. and ed. *The Siege of Charleston.* Ann Arbor: University of Michigan Press, 1938.

Wilkinson, Eliza. *Letters of Eliza Wilkinson.* Edited by Caroline Gilman. New York: Samuel Colman, 1839.

Secondary Sources

Alden, John Richard. *The South in the Revolution, 1763–1789.* Vol. 3 of *A History of the South.* Edited by Wendell Holmes Stephenson and E. Merton Coulter. Baton Rouge: Louisiana State University Press, 1957.

Barry, Richard. *John Rutledge of South Carolina.* New York: J. J. Little & Ives, 1942.

Berg, Frederick Anderson. *Encyclopedia of Continental Army Units.* Harrisburg, Pa.: Stackpole Books, 1972.

Boatner, Mark M. *Encyclopedia of the American Revolution.* 3rd ed. Mechanicsburg, Pa.: Stackpole Books, 1996.

Borick, Carl P. *A Gallant Defense: The Siege of Charleston, 1780.* Columbia: University of South Carolina Press, 2003.

Buchanan, John. *The Road to Guilford Court House.* New York: John Wiley and Sons, 1997.

Carrington, Henry B. *Battles of the American Revolution.* 1877. Reprint, New York: Promontory Press, 1974.

Dawson, Henry B. *Battles of the United States.* 2 vols. New York: Johnson, Fry, and Company, 1858.

Edgar, Walter. *Partisans and Redcoats.* New York: HarperCollins, 2001.

Fortescue, Sir John. *The War of Independence: The British Army in North America, 1775–1783.* 1911. Reprint, London: Greenhill Books, 2001.

Garden, Alexander. *Anecdotes of the American Revolution.* 3 vols. Charleston, S.C., 1828.

———. *Anecdotes of the Revolutionary War in America.* Charleston, S.C., 1822.

Gardiner, Robert, ed. *Navies and the American Revolution.* Annapolis, Md.: Naval Institute Press, 1996.

Godbold, E. Stanly, Jr., and Robert H. Woody. *Christopher Gadsden and the American Revolution.* Knoxville: University of Tennessee Press, 1982.

Grafton, John. *The American Revolution: A Picture Sourcebook.* New York: Dover Publications, 1975.

Gruber, Ira. "Britain's Southern Strategy." In *The Revolutionary War in the South: Power, Conflict, and Leadership,* edited by W. Robert Higgins, 205–38. Durham, N.C.: Duke University Press, 1979.

Higginbotham, Don. *Atlas of the American Revolution.* Edited by Kenneth Nebenzahl. New York: Rand McNally, 1974.

Higgins, Robert W., ed. *The Revolutionary War in the South: Power, Conflict, and Leadership.* Durham, N.C.: Duke University Press, 1979.

James, William Dobein. *The Life of Brigadier General Francis Marion.* Charleston, S.C.: Gould and Riley, 1821. E-text version, edited by Alan R. Light, 1997.

Katcher, Philip. *Encyclopedia of British, Provincial, and German Army Units 1775–1783.* Harrisburg, Pa.: Stackpole Books, 1973.

Keegan, John. *The Face of Battle.* 1976. Reprint, New York: Penguin Books, 1984.

Lambert, Robert Stansbury. *South Carolina Loyalists in the American Revolution.* Columbia: University of South Carolina Press, 1987.

Lawrence, Alexander. *Storm over Savannah.* Athens: University of Georgia Press, 1951.

Lee, Henry. *The American Revolution in the South.* Edited by Robert E. Lee. 1812. Reprint, New York: Arno Press, 1969.

Lesser, Charles H., ed. *The Sinews of Independence.* Chicago: University of Chicago Press, 1976.

Lipscomb, Terry W. *The Carolina Lowcountry April 1775–June 1776 and the Battle of Fort Moultrie.* Columbia: South Carolina Department of Archives and History, 1994.

Lossing, Benson J. *A Pictorial Field Book of the Revolution.* 2 vols. New York: Harper & Brothers, 1859.

Lowell, Edward. *The Hessians.* 1884. Reprint, Port Washington, N.Y.: Kennikat Press, 1965.

Lumpkin, Henry. *From Savannah to Yorktown.* Columbia: University of South Carolina Press, 1981.

Marshall, Douglas W., and Howard H. Peckham, eds. *Campaigns of the American Revolution: An Atlas of Manuscript Maps.* Ann Arbor: University of Michigan Press, 1976.

Massey, Gregory D. *John Laurens and the American Revolution.* Columbia: University of South Carolina Press, 2000.

McCall, Hugh. *The History of Georgia.* 1811. Reprint, Atlanta: Cherokee Publishing Company, 1909.

McCrady, Edward. *History of South Carolina in the Revolution.* 2 vols. New York: MacMillan & Co., 1902.

Medley, Mary L. *History of Anson County: 1750–1976.* Wadesboro, N.C.: Anson County Historical Society, 1976.

Morrill, Dan. *Southern Campaigns of the American Revolution.* Baltimore: The Nautical & Aviation Publishing Company of America, 1993.

Murphy, W. S. "The Irish Brigade of France at the Siege of Savannah, 1779." *The Georgia Historical Quarterly* 38, no. 4 (1954): 304–21.

Nadelhaft, Jerome. *The Disorders of War: The Revolution in South Carolina.* Orono: University of Maine at Orono Press, 1981.

Pancake, John S. *This Destructive War: The British Campaign in the Carolinas, 1780–1782.* Tuscaloosa: University of Alabama Press, 1985.

Peckham, Howard H., ed. *The Toll of Independence: Engagements & Battle Casualties of the American Revolution.* Chicago: University of Chicago Press, 1976.

Rankin, Hugh F. *The Moore's Creek Bridge Campaign, 1776.* 1986. Reprint, Currie, N.C.: Eastern National, 1998.

———. *The North Carolina Continentals.* Chapel Hill: University of North Carolina Press, 1971.

Richardson, Edward W. *Standards and Colors of the American Revolution.* Philadelphia: University of Pennsylvania Press and the Pennsylvania Society of Sons of the Revolution and Its Color Guard, 1982.

Ripley, Warren. *Battleground, South Carolina in the Revolution.* Charleston, S.C.: The News and Courier and The Evening Post, 1983.

Scheer, George F., and Hugh F. Rankin. *Rebels and Redcoats.* Cleveland: World Publishing Co., 1957.

Shy, John. "British Strategy for Pacifying the Southern Colonies, 1778–1781." In *The Southern Experience in the American Revolution,* edited by Jeffery J. Crow and Larry E. Tise, 157–73. Chapel Hill: University of North Carolina Press, 1978.

Smith, Paul H. *Loyalists and Redcoats: A Study in British Revolutionary Policy.* Chapel Hill: University of North Carolina Press, 1964.

South, Stanley. *Palmetto Parapets: Exploratory Archeology at Fort Moultrie, South Carolina.* Columbia: National Parks Service and the Institute of Archeology and Anthropology, University of South Carolina, 1974.

Sparks, Jared, ed. *Correspondence of the American Revolution.* 1853. Reprint, Freeport, N.Y.: Books for Libraries Press, 1970.

Symonds, Craig L., and William J. Clipson (cartographer). *A Battlefield Atlas of the American Revolution.* Baltimore: Nautical & Aviation Publishing Co. of America, 1986.

Troiani, Don, Earl J. Coates, and James L. Kochan. *Soldiers in America.* New York: Stackpole Books, 1998.

Ward, Christopher. *The War of the Revolution.* 2 vols. New York: MacMillan Co., 1952.

Weems, M. L. *The Life of Gen. Francis Marion.* Philadelphia: J. B. Lippincott, 1891.

Index

African Americans. *See* black and slave participation

American Civil War, 14, 153, 277

American Indians, 3, 21, 44, 47, 62; and American military, 3, 21, 47, 204; and Charlestown (1779), 101, 105, 112, 115; Cherokee War of 1776, 62, 87; Cherokees, 62, 77, 87, 117, 147, 197n8; Creeks, 62, 101, 105, 112, 115, 117; and William Moultrie, 44; Prevost disappointment in, 117; and Proclamation of 1763, 21; and Southern Strategy, 62, 91, 101, 103, 112, 117; and Stono Ferry, 122

American Legion. *See* Pulaski's Legion

American militia, 1, 7–8, 21, 24, 42, 62, 63, 243, 297n12; and Augusta–Briar Creek, 83–89, 91–98; and cavalry, 244; and Charlestown (1776), 43–44, 56–57; and Charlestown (1779), 102–6, 108–9, 111, 114; and Charlestown (1780), 203–6, 218, 221–24, 229–34, 236, 238–39, 250, 315n135, 316n143; and Clinton's occupation policies, 265–66; cooperation with Continental Army, 66–67; and depredations, 89; and drafting into regulars, 146, 194–95, 276; and Florida invasions, 66–69; and Indians, 62; and Benjamin Lincoln, 81–82; as Minutemen, 5, 7–9, 13, 17–18, 26, 30, 33–34; and Monck's Corner, 246–47; and Moore's Creek Bridge, 25–27, 29–30, 33–34; and Norfolk, 17; and Port Royal, 100–101; and Savannah (1778), 74–79; and Savannah (1779), 133, 135, 137, 144, 146–48, 159–60, 162, 166–67, 171, 177–78,

184–85, 190, 275–77, 280, 284; and Stono Ferry, 119, 122–28, 130, 132, 269–70; and threat of slave insurrection, 3, 311n22; and George Washington, 43; and Waxhaws, 251–53; and Williamson's surrender, 262

American riflemen: and Augusta–Briar Creek, 96; and Charlestown (1776), 53, 56; and Charlestown (1779), 104; and Charlestown (1780), 220, 222, 230; and Patrick Ferguson, 248; at Great Bridge, 13; at Hampton, 7–8; and Moore's Creek Bridge, 25, 27, 91; at Norfolk, 15; and Savannah (1778), 71, 75; and Stono Ferry, 118

Arbuthnot, Marriot, 226, 250, 317n145; conflict with Henry Clinton, 199–200, 210, 213–14; crossing Charlestown bar, 210; failure to enter Cooper River, 213, 216; ineffectiveness at Charlestown, 207–8, 210–14, 236; passing Fort Moultrie, 211–12, 219, 311n43; and *Russia Merchant*, 199; and Savannah (1779), 198

Armstrong, James, 56, 130

Articles of Confederation, 111

Ashe, John: and Augusta–Briar Creek, 88, 91–98, 194, 298n26, 298n30, 229n39, 229n45; and Moore's Creek Bridge, 26, 30, 34, 291n45

Ashley Ferry: and Charlestown (1779), 106–7, 110, 114, 300n24; and Charlestown (1780), 201, 206; and Stono Ferry, 116, 121, 269

Augusta, 116; and Augusta–Briar Creek, 84, 85–91, 95, 97–98, 297n12, 297n13,

Augusta (*continued*)
298n18; and Thomas Brown, 65, 251, 262; and Charlestown (1779), 100–103, 106, 112; and Charlestown (1780), 199–201, 204–5; and Kettle Creek, 86–87; and Savannah (1779), 147; and Waxhaws, 264, 276

Baird, James: and Augusta–Briar Creek, 84, 92, 94–95, 98; and Charlestown (1779), 115; and Savannah (1778), 73, 75–76, 79, 297n48
Beaufort: and Charlestown (1780), 210; and Patriot militia, 108, 114; and Savannah (1779), 137–38, 141–42, 144–46, 149, 272, 280–83; and skirmish at Port Royal, 100, 104, 116; and Stono Ferry, 128–29
Beaulieu Plantation, 138, 143, 147, 149
Beekman, Barnard: and Charlestown (1779), 114; and Charlestown (1780), 237, 239, 312n62; and Savannah (1779), 178, 190
Bellew, Henry, 15–16
black and slave participation, 43, 86, 155, 234; aiding Americans, 288; and British army, 118, 185–86; as British infantry at Savannah, 141, 149, 155, 176, 181, 187, 272–74, 310n149; building fortifications, 54, 143, 149, 273; Congress proposes slave battalions, 146, 195; and Dunmore's emancipation proclamation, 7–8; informants/scouts for British, 26, 72, 75, 118, 144, 246, 280, 282; informants/scouts for French, 139; and Royal Ethiopian Regiment, 9–11, 16; as ship pilots, 53, 144, 281; and threat of slave insurrection, 3, 118; and Volunteers of San Domingo, 137, 159; and West Indies slave trade, 118
Boyd, "Colonel" (Loyalist leader), 86–88, 298n14
Brétigny, Marquis de, 114, 133–35, 239, 301n43
Briar Creek, 172, 194, 205, 247, 266; battle of, 89–99, 298n18, 298n30; and Charlestown (1779), 101–2, 109; failure to inspire Loyalists, 97–98, 100, 117; and Thomas Tawse, 172
British 7th Regiment, 202, 234, 239, 288n34

British 14th Regiment, 2, 9–11, 13–14, 17, 288n15, 288n34
British 15th Regiment, 58
British 16th Regiment, 150, 180, 185, 299n46, 299n1
British 17th Light Dragoons, 240, 243–44, 254, 260, 318n6
British 23rd Regiment, 202, 239
British 33rd Regiment, 58, 219, 239, 246
British 37th Regiment, 58
British 42nd Regiment, 58, 227, 240, 295n9, 320n16
British 54th Regiment, 58
British 57th Regiment, 58
British 60th Regiment, 299n46, 299n1; and Augustine Prevost, 83; and regimental flag of 2nd S.C., 279; and Savannah (1779), 149–50, 163, 168–69, 172, 180, 284; at Sunbury, 71, 83
British 63rd Regiment, 234, 239
British 64th Regiment, 219, 240, 246
British 71st Regiment, 70, 294n7; and Augusta–Briar Creek, 84, 89, 92, 94, 98–99, 299n47; and Charlestown (1779), 103, 114; and Charlestown (1780), 210, 213, 228, 240; and Savannah (1778), 71–73, 75–76, 79, 297n48; and Savannah (1779), 144, 150, 152, 162–63, 169, 180, 186, 280, 284; and Stono Ferry, 121–24, 130, 304n43
British Florida Brigade, 92, 98, 100, 114, 299n46. *See also* British 16th Regiment; British 60th Regiment
British militia, 242; and Augusta–Briar Creek, 83–84, 89, 92, 98; and Thomas Brown, 65–66, 84; and Clinton's occupation policies, 262–65; and Patrick Ferguson, 248, 263; and Norfolk, 11; role in partisan war, 267; and Savannah (1779), 137, 157–58, 169, 172, 175, 181, 186, 273–74; and Stono Ferry, 117
British Parliament, 1, 5, 40, 60, 90, 122
British provincials, 2, 98, 114; Delancy's New York Regiment, 71, 79, 114, 143, 171, 181, 186, 294n14, 297n48, 310n149; "Ferguson's" American Volunteers, 219, 240, 246; King's "Florida" Rangers, 65, 66, 84, 94,

181, 186, 294n1; New York Volunteers, 71, 75, 79, 84, 108, 115, 181, 186, 240, 294n14, 297n48; North Carolina Volunteers, 90, 122, 131, 144, 168, 172, 181, 186, 201, 240, 304n43; Royal Highland Emigrants, 23–31; Skinner's New Jersey Regiment, 71, 79, 181, 297n48; South Carolina Royalists, 122, 131, 163, 181, 186, 240, 304n43; South Carolina Volunteers, 181, 186; "Tarleton's" British Legion, 181, 186, 219, 240, 243–50, 252–60; Volunteers of Ireland, 243

British Royal Marines, 2, 7; and Charlestown (1776), 47, 51, 58; and Charlestown (1780), 213, 230–31; and John Maitland, 122; and Savannah (1779), 149, 169, 172, 181, 187

Brown, Thomas (French-Irish officer), 160, 164

Brown, Thomas (Georgia Loyalist), 65–66; and Augusta (1780), 251, 262; and Augusta–Briar Creek, 84, 94; and Savannah (1779), 181

Brownfield, Robert, 253, 255–58, 319n38, 319n40, 319n48

Buford, Abraham: and Lenud's Ferry, 249; and Waxhaws, 251–58, 260, 319n38; and William Woodford, 251, 318n29

Bull, Stephen, 104, 108, 114

Burgoyne, John, 59, 82

Burke, Thomas, 42

Cameron, Charles, 73–74, 79, 297n48

Campbell, Archibald: and Augusta–Briar Creek, 81, 83–84, 86–92, 97–98, 100–101, 112, 297n13, 298n14; and John Maitland, 122; and Savannah (1778), 69–79, 141, 148, 273, 295n20, 296n36

Campbell, John, 24, 28–29, 34–35

Campbell, William, 2, 36, 50, 61

Carlisle Commission, 60–61

Caswell, Richard, 56, 91; and Briar Creek, 91; and Moore's Creek Bridge, 25–31, 33–34; and Waxhaws, 251–52, 291n45

Cathcart, William, 243–44, 318n4, 318n6

Charleston, S.C. See Charlestown, S.C.

Charlestown, S.C., 5, 14, 60, 62, 69, 82, 90, 128, 267–68, 319n2; and Augusta–Briar Creek, 84, 89; and Charlestown (1776), 36–39, 41, 43, 45–47, 50, 52, 54–57, 63, 292n37; and Charlestown (1779), 100–114, 300n24; and Charlestown (1780), 176, 193–201, 203–26, 228–29, 231, 233–40, 314n97; and Clinton's policies, 262–66; and Savannah (1778), 71–72; and Savannah (1779), 133, 135, 137, 140, 145, 147, 172, 174, 280–81; and Stono Ferry, 116–19, 121, 269–72; and test oath riots, 297n10; and Waxhaws, 242–44, 246–48, 250–51, 253, 260

Charlestown Militia: and Charlestown (1779), 114; and Charlestown (1780), 239; and Savannah (1779), 160, 166–67, 177–78, 190, 277, 280, 284

chasseurs, French, 141, 150–51, 158–59, 160, 162–64, 178–80, 183, 191

chasseurs, German, 317n145

Clinton, Henry: and 1776 southern expedition, 4, 36–37, 62; and 1778 Georgia expedition, 69–71; and 1778 Southern Strategy, 63–64; and Arbuthnot, 200, 210, 213; attempt to resign, 64, 199–200; and Briar Creek, 97; and Charlestown (1779), 117; and Charlestown (1780), 112, 119, 193, 198–201, 203, 205–10, 213–14, 216, 218–20, 223, 225–26, 228, 231–34, 236–39, 244, 250, 272; and civil authority in Georgia, 90; and civil government, 298; and Cornwallis, 200, 242; and Fort Sullivan, 36–43, 45–48, 50–51, 53–55, 58; and Lenund's Ferry, 250; and Monck's Corner, 244, 247–49; and James Moncrief, 158; and Norfolk, 16–17; in North Carolina, 32–33; and northerns, 60–61; policies for Loyalists and rebels, 262–66; raising provincial corps, 243; and Savannah (1779), 137–38, 158, 175–76, 196, 273; and Waxhaws, 251

Coercive Acts. See Intolerable Acts

Colomb, Pierre, 78

Colonial militia. See American militia

Continental marines, 201

Continental Navy, 196, 201, 208–14, 216

Coosawhatchie ford, 103–5, 300n16

Cornwallis, Charles: and Caribbean expedition, 198; and Charlestown (1776),
45–47, 54; and Charlestown (1780),
198–99, 228–30; and Henry Clinton,
199–200, 242, 251, 264; and failure of
Southern Strategy, 265–66; letter censur-
ing Tarleton, 248; and North Carolina
1781, 90, 298n18; reliance on Tarleton,
242; and Waxhaws, 250–52, 257–59; and
Yorktown, 237
Cruger, John, 143, 171, 181
Culpeper Minutemen, 7–9, 13, 17–18,
289n41
Curry, James, 171, 284

Dartmouth, Lord, 1–4, 22, 37, 39
D'Estaing, Henri: assault on Savannah,
158–65, 167–72, 178, 182, 184, 191, 279,
284; and Beaufort garrison, 145, 280–81;
and Caribbeans, 135; death in French
Revolution, 175; debate on assault location, 157; decision to assault, 156, 283;
invasion of Georgia, 121, 133–41, 147–49,
151–57, 198, 273, 276; and Benjamin Lincoln, 145–46, 148, 155, 157–58; negotiations with Prevost, 141–43, 145–46, 148,
155, 286; and Newport, 134; and Casimir
Pulaski, 147, 278–79; and Tybee Island,
138–39; withdrawal from Georgia,
173–75, 194, 208
Dillon, Arthur, 137; criticism of d'Estaing,
174; storming of Savannah, 158, 162–64,
169–70, 178, 191, 274
Dillon's Irish Regiment, 307n100; storming
of Savannah, 160–64, 169, 179, 191
disease, 67, 71, 122, 143–44, 270; and
Charlestown (1780), 205, 234,
315–316n143, 317n145; and Count d'Estaing, 134; and Donald MacDonald, 28;
and John Maitland, 176; malaria and yellow fever, 176, 218, 276, 294n16, 313n68;
and James Moore, 31; and Norfolk,
289n41; and Savannah (1779), 156, 159,
182, 273, 309n147, 310n149; smallpox,
203, 205; and Stono Ferry, 271
dueling, 67, 69, 82, 166, 194
Dunmore, Earl of: and 1776 southern expedition, 2, 4, 16–17, 36–37; emancipation

proclamation, 8, 149; and Great Bridge,
9–11, 13–14, 288n16, 289n43; and Hampton raid, 7–8; influence on Southern
Strategy, 2, 61, 63; and Norfolk destruction, 15–16, 67; Williamsburg powder
raid, 6–7
Duportail, Louis, 229, 314n106

Ebenezer, 90–92, 98, 102, 147, 276
Edwards, John, 110
Elbert, Samuel: and Augusta–Briar Creek,
84, 92, 95–96, 98, 295n22, 297n50, 297n5;
and Savannah (1778), 73–74, 77, 79,
295n22
Elliot, Barnard, 55, 69, 293n55, 293n63
Elliot, Susannah, 55, 167–68, 279
Elphinstone, Keith, 200, 206
Ewald, Johann, v; battle with John Laurens,
207; crossing Ashley River, 206; and Loyalists, 264; and James Moncrief, 214–16;
and siege of Charlestown, 216, 226–28,
233–34, 311n43, 312n56, 312n60, 312n62,
314n100, 314n103, 315n137, 316n143;
and skirmishing, 202–3, 205

Fergus, James, 87, 93–96, 301n45
Ferguson, Patrick, 219; appointed inspector
of militia, 263; and Charlestown (1780),
240; and King's Mountain, 266; and
Monck's Corner, 246, 248; and George
Washington, 263
Ferguson, Thomas, 224–25, 301n33
Five Fathom Hole: and Charlestown (1776),
45, 52; and Charlestown (1780), 208–11,
219
Fontanges, François de, 142; and attack at
Spring Hill, 165, 169–70; and
Charlestown council of war, 135, 137–38,
145, 281; friction with d'Estaing, 139; and
reorganization of French army, 160
Fordyce, Charles, 11–12, 17, 289n43
Fort Johnson: and Charlestown (1780), 43,
57, 293, 210–12, 219; and Stono Ferry,
116
Fort Morris, 71–72
Fort Moultrie: and Charlestown (1776), 43,
45–48, 50, 54, 56, 140, 167, 212, 231; and
Charlestown (1780), 195, 196, 203,

208–14, 219, 229–31, 239, 264, 311; renamed Moultrie, 55

Fort Sullivan. *See* Fort Moultrie

France: entry into war, 60–61, 63; French Revolution, 175; French ships and Charlestown, 208; war objectives, 134

French Army: Dragoons of Condé and of Belzunce, 179, 191; Regt. d'Agénois, 178, 191; Regt. d'Armagnac, 150, 162, 178–79, 191; Regt. d'Auxerrois, 137, 150, 178–79, 191; Regt. de Cambresy, 179, 191; Regt. de Champagne, 150, 179, 191; Regt. de Foix, 137, 178–79, 191; Regt. de Gâtinais, 178, 191; Regt. de Guadeloupe, 179, 191; Regt. de Hainault, 179, 191; Regt. de Le Cap, 179, 191; Regt. de Martinique, 179, 191; Regt. de Port au Prince, 179, 191; Volunteers of San Domingo, 137, 141, 159, 171, 174, 179–80, 191; Volunteers of Valbel, 191

French militia. *See* French Army, Volunteers of San Domingo

French Navy, 121, 198–99; as artillerists, 153, 156; attack on Hutchinson's Island, 155; and blockade of Port Royal, 144–45, 148, 281–82, 321n33; capture of Experiment, 140; capture of Tybee Island, 138–39; and d'Estaing's Caribbeans, 135; hurricane threat, 138; landing at Beaulieu, 139–40; need for American help, 135, 137; and Newport, 134; poor provisions, 140; and Savannah (1779), 134–35, 137–41, 144–45, 148–49, 151–52, 155, 173

French Royal Marines, 139, 159, 176, 179–80, 191

Gadsden, Christopher: bridge to Sullivan's Island, 292n26; and Charlestown (1776), 57; and Charlestown (1779), 110; and Charlestown (1780), 221, 224–25, 231, 236; duel with Robert Howe, 69

Galloway, Joseph, 298n19

Garth, George, 137, 140

Gates, Horatio, 42, 59

Georgia Continentals: 3rd Regiment, 295n18; and Augusta–Briar Creek, 84, 92, 94–96, 98; and Charlestown (1780), 237; and Savannah (1778), 72, 74–75, 77, 79; and

Savannah (1779), 147, 309n147; scarceness, 295n18; and Stono Ferry, 124

Germain, George, 78, 83, 97, 170, 175–76, 198, 209, 266, 270; and Charlestown (1776), 39–40, 42, 53; and Charlestown (1779), 116–77; and Charlestown (1780), 250; and Clinton's policies, 265–66; conflict with Henry Clinton, 40, 63; and Moore's Creek Bridge, 32–33; and southern Loyalists, 86, 100, 116–17, 238, 265, 267; and Southern Strategy of 1775, 3–4, 19, 22, 37, 39, 267; and Southern Strategy of 1778, 60–64, 238, 265, 267

German regiments: Regt. von Graff, 240, 320n16; Regt. von Huyne, 240; Regt. von Lengereke, 240, 320n16; Regt. von Linsing, 240, 320n16; Regt. von Minnigerode, 240, 320n16; Regt. von Trümbach, 122, 125, 131, 144, 180, 302n16, 304n43, 304n44, 317n145; Regt. von Wissenbach, 71, 79, 114, 163, 181, 186, 294n13, 302n16, 317n45; Regt. von Wöllwarth, 71, 75–76, 79, 114, 122, 131, 144, 180, 294n13, 302n16

Girardeau Plantation, 72–73, 77–78, 140

Glazier, Beamsly, 98, 114

Graham, Colin, 150–51, 158, 180, 241, 317n145

Great Bridge, 36, 218, 288n34; battle of, 9–18; and Moore's Creek Bridge, 24

grenadiers, American, 166, 177, 184, 284. *See also* Charlestown Militia

grenadiers, British, 287n6, 288n16, 295n24, 299n46; and Augusta–Briar Creek, 92, 94, 98; and Charlestown (1779), 114; and Charlestown (1780), 200, 215, 223, 227, 239, 314n101, 316n143, 317n145, 320n16; and Great Bridge, 9–13, 17; and Savannah (1779), 149, 169, 172, 284

grenadiers, French, 141, 150–51, 158–60, 162–64, 169, 171, 175, 178–79, 182–83, 191

grenadiers, German, 125, 180, 240, 320n16

Grimké, John, 124, 271

Gwinnett, Button, 66–67, 69

Half-Moon battery, 226–28, 314n96, 314n103

Hamilton, John: and Augusta–Briar Creek, 87, 90; and Charlestown (1780), 201, 240,

Hamilton, John (*continued*)
  317n148; and Savannah (1779), 168, 181;
  and Stono Ferry, 122, 131, 304n43
Hayne, Isaac, 265, 320n14
Henderson, John, 122–25, 130, 268, 302n20
Henderson, William: and Charlestown
  (1780), 227–28, 314n96; and Savannah
  (1779), 177, 190, 309n147; and Stono
  Ferry, 130
Henry, Patrick, 5, 7, 9, 13
Hessians. *See* German regiments
Hinrichs, Johann: and American sortie,
  227–28, 314n96, 314n97; observations
  on d'Estaing's works, 156; and siege of
  Charlestown (1780), 213, 216, 218, 230,
  234–35, 311n31, 311n43, 312n48, 312n56,
  312n58, 312n60, 317n147; and skirmish-
  ing at Charlestown (1780), 202–3, 206;
  on superiority of American artillery, 218
Hornwork, 227–29, 233–34, 314n96
Horry, Daniel: and Charlestown (1780), 56;
  and Lenud's Ferry, 249; and Savannah
  (1779), 161, 166, 177, 191, 309n147; and
  Stono Ferry, 123, 128, 130
Horry, Peter, 308n112
Houstoun, John, 67, 69, 76
Howe, Richard, 54
Howe, Robert: command of Southern
  Department, 67–69, 81–82, 84, 194; duel
  with Gadsden, 69; and Norfolk, 15, 18,
  33, 67; and Savannah (1778), 71–78; as
  womanizer, 67, 69
Howe, William, 64, 200; and Charlestown
  (1776), 37, 39; and Lord Dartmouth, 2–3;
  and Lord Dunmore, 17; and light
  infantry doctrine, 295n24; and Josiah
  Martin, 19; and northerns, 59; succeeded
  by Clinton, 60
Huger, Benjamin, 109, 301n45
Huger, Isaac: and Charlestown (1776), 56;
  and Charlestown (1779), 109; and
  Charlestown (1780), 219, 221–23; and
  Monck's Corner, 219, 222–23, 244, 246–
  47; and Savannah (1778), 71, 74, 77–78,
  296n30; and Savannah (1779), 159,
  170–71, 177, 185, 189–90, 276–77, 284,
  309n147; and Stono Ferry, 123, 125–26,
  128, 130, 268; and Waxhaws, 251–52

illness. *See* disease
indigo, 43, 56, 63
Innes, Alexander, 84, 90, 181, 240
Intolerable Acts, 1, 60
Irish Brigade. *See* Dillon's Irish Regiment
Irish Parliament, 37

jaegers: activities during Charlestown 1780
  siege, 220, 227–28, 230, 240, 311n31,
  314n101, 320n16; and Savannah (1779),
  156; skirmishing outside Charlestown,
  202, 205, 207
Jameson, John: and Lenud's Ferry, 249; and
  Monck's Corner, 246; and Savannah
  (1779), 147, 161, 177, 191, 275–76,
  309n147
Jasper, William: and Charlestown (1776), 52,
  55, 293n55; and Savannah (1779),
  167–68, 279, 308n112
Jones, John Paul, 208, 315n136

Kettle Creek, 90, 298n18; battle of, 87–88;
  and North Carolina Volunteers, 97, 122,
  201; survivors form units, 90
Kinlock, David, 252–54, 260
Knyphausen, Wilhelm, 205

Lafayette, 109, 153
Laurens, John: and Charlestown (1779),
  110–12, 301; and Charlestown (1780),
  201, 207, 218, 236; and Coosawhatchie,
  104–5, 166; and Charles L'Enfant, 156;
  and Savannah (1779), 159–61, 166–68,
  177, 184, 190, 277, 278; and slave battalions, 146; and Andrew Williamson, 319
Lee, Charles: biography and treason, 41;
  capture by British, 243; and Charlestown,
  44–48, 51, 53, 55–57; duel with John
  Laurens, 166; and Florida invasion, 66;
  and Robert Howe, 67; in New York, 40;
  in North Carolina, 42–43; in Virginia, 42
Lee, Henry: on Charlestown (1779), 111; on
  Henry Clinton's policies, 263, 265; and
  John Laurens, 300; on Lenud's Ferry, 249–
  50; and Pyle's Massacre, 289; on Savannah
  (1778), 77, 78; on Savannah (1779), 283–
  85; on Stono Ferry, 125, 126, 268, 269;
  and Tarleton, 243; on Waxhaws, 258, 260

Lee, Robert E., 283
Legge, William. *See* Dartmouth, Lord
Lemprière, Clement, 45
L'Enfant, Pierre Charles, 156–57
Lenud's Ferry, 249–51, 254
Leslie, Samuel, 10–11, 12–15, 17, 288n34
light infantry, American: and Augusta–Briar
    Creek, 93, 96–98, 299n49; and
    Charlestown (1779), 106–8, 114; and
    Charlestown (1780), 201, 205–7, 223,
    227–28, 230, 314n96; and Savannah
    (1779), 156, 159–60, 166–67, 177, 189–90,
    277, 309n47; and Stono Ferry, 122–26,
    130, 132, 268, 302n20, 303n39, 303n40,
    303n42
light infantry, British, 287n6, 288n16,
    295n24, 320n16; and Augusta–Briar
    Creek, 84, 89, 92, 94–95, 98, 299n47;
    and Charlestown (1776), 32, 36; and
    Charlestown (1779), 103, 107–8, 115; and
    Charlestown (1780), 200, 202, 206–7, 215,
    227, 239, 241, 311n41, 314n100, 317n145;
    and Lenud's Ferry, 249–50; and Norfolk,
    9–11, 17; and Port Royal skirmish, 100;
    and Savannah (1778), 72–73, 75–76, 79,
    297n48; and Savannah (1779), 144, 150,
    158, 180, 186, 284
light infantry, French. *See* chasseurs, French
light infantry, German. *See* chasseurs, Ger-
    man
Lillington, Alexander: and Charlestown
    (1780), 205; controversy with Caswell,
    33, 291n45; and Moore's Creek Bridge,
    26–27, 30–31, 33–34
Lincoln, Benjamin: assigned Southern
    Department, 69, 71, 81; attempt to resign,
    119, 121; and Briar Creek, 82, 83, 89,
    91–93, 97, 297; and Charlestown (1779),
    101–8, 112; and Charlestown (1780),
    193–96, 200–210, 213–14, 218–26,
    228–33, 235–37, 238; and Kettle Creek,
    88; and Monck's Corner, 246, 313; and
    northerns, 81–82; and Savannah (1778),
    72, 78, 296; and Savannah (1779), 133,
    135, 138, 139, 142, 145–48, 151, 155,
    156, 158–60, 163, 165, 166, 173, 174,
    177, 178, 182, 184, 190, 275–78, 280,
    281; sleep apnea, 81; and Stono Ferry,

116, 118, 121–30, 268–72; and Waxhaws,
    250–52
logistics and supply: and Augusta–Briar
    Creek, 87–91, 97; and Charlestown
    (1776), 50–51, 53; and Charlestown
    (1779), 101–3; and Charlestown (1780),
    195–96, 199, 201, 203, 209, 213–15,
    219–21, 231, 236, 247, 256; and Moore's
    Creek Bridge, 29; and Norfolk, 10; and
    northerns, 82, 193; and Savannah (1778),
    73, 78; and Savannah (1779), 140, 149,
    152, 156, 185–86; and Southern Depart-
    ment, 82, 237; and Stono Ferry, 116;
    strategic effects, 61, 63, 103, 242; and
    Waxhaws, 244, 246–47
Loyalists, 267–68; and Augusta–Briar
    Creek, 83–91, 97, 100, 299n48; British
    expectations after Moore's Creek Bridge,
    32–33, 36, 63; and British Legion, 243,
    318n4; and Charlestown (1776), 36–37,
    39; and Charlestown (1779), 100–103,
    112; and Charlestown (1780), 198, 201,
    204, 235, 238; and civilian government,
    298n19; and Henry Clinton, 16, 32, 37,
    39, 63–64, 198, 262–66; and conception
    of Southern Strategy, 2–4; and Patrick
    Ferguson, 263; and Florida, 65–66; and
    Robert Howe, 67; importance to war
    effort, 242; and Kettle Creek, 87–89, 97;
    and Lenud's Ferry, 249; and Moore's
    Creek Bridge, 19, 21–35, 290n38; and
    Norfolk, 5, 9–11, 13–17; and Augustine
    Prevost, 90, 116–17; and Pyle's Massacre,
    289n14; and Savannah (1778), 71, 73,
    78, 294n14; and Savannah (1779), 133,
    137, 140–41, 143, 149, 154, 169, 171–72,
    176, 181, 186, 273–74; and skirmish at
    Port Royal, 100–101; and slave emanci-
    pation, 8, 118, 149, 176; and Southern
    Strategy of 1778, 61–64; and Stono
    Ferry, 116–17, 119, 122, 125, 128;
    thought a majority, 1–3, 19–20, 22, 33,
    117, 235, 238, 265–67; and Tory political
    faction, 5
Lytle, Anthony: and Briar Creek, 92–93,
    96–98, 299n39, 299n49, 316n145; and
    Charlestown (1780), 205, 238; misidenti-
    fied as "Archibald," 298n24

MacDonald, Donald: assignment to N.C., 22; at Cross Creek, 23–24; march to Wilmington, 25–26; and Moore's Creek Bridge, 27–28, 30–33, 35

Maitland, John: and Charlestown (1779), 107, 114; death from malaria, 176; and Savannah (1778), 79; and Savannah (1779), 145, 148–49, 174, 176, 180, 188, 284–86, 307; and Stono Ferry, 121–30, 270, 272; trek from Beaufort, 137–38, 142–45, 272, 280–83, 305

Malmady, Francois: and Charlestown (1780), 200, 229–30, 237; and Stono Ferry, 124–26, 130

Marion, Francis, 222; and Charlestown (1776), 51, 55; and Charlestown (1780), 201, 238; evacuation from Charlestown, 316n143; and Savannah (1779), 148, 160, 166–67, 177, 190, 276–77

Martin, Josiah: and Henry Clinton, 36; and Moore's Creek Bridge (MCB), 19–24, 26, 30; origination of Southern Strategy, 1–4; responsibility for MCB defeat, 31–33; and Southern Strategy of 1778, 61, 64

McIntosh, John, 72, 295n18

McIntosh, Lachlan, 295n18, 318n11; and Charlestown (1780), 222–24, 226, 236, 239, 313n81, 313n91, 314n96, 314n103, 314n106; duel with Gwinnett, 67, 69; and Florida invasion, 66; and Savannah (1779), 141, 147–48, 152, 155, 160, 168–69, 177, 190, 277, 285, 306n68, 308n116, 310n147

McLean, Alex: agent provocateur, 22–23; and Corbett's Ferry, 26; and Cross Creek, 24, 30, 31; and Loyalist desertions, 25; and Moore's Creek Bridge, 28, 30; optimism for futures, 32

McLeod, Donald, 26, 28–29, 34–35, 290n28

Monck's Corner: atrocities at, 247–48, 259, 263; battle at, 219, 221–22, 246–47; effect on siege of Charlestown, 235; survivors of, 223, 249, 251, 316n143; and Tarleton's tactics, 249–50

Moncrief, James: and Charlestown (1779), 107–8; and Charlestown (1780), 214–16, 234, 237, 312n56, 312n58; and Savannah

(1779), 143, 148–49, 152, 157–58, 175–76; and Stono Ferry, 127–28

Monmouth Court House: and John Laurens, 104; and Charles Lee, 55; and Southern Strategy, 60–61; and Woodford's brigade, 218

Moore, James, 24–31, 34, 291n45, 47

Moore's Creek Bridge, 36, 205, 251, 267; and Augusta–Briar Creek, 86, 90–91; battle of, 26–34, 291n45; influence on Germain, 33, 63

Morris, John, 50, 52, 57

Morris, Robert, 42

Motte, Isaac, 114

Moultrie, William: and John Ashe, 97; and Beaufort, 100; and Charlestown (1776), 43–56; and Charlestown (1779), 102–6, 109–13, 194, 225; and Charlestown (1780), 201, 203, 211, 215, 216, 220–23, 228–32, 234, 236, 237; and Fort Johnson, xiii, 43; and Robert Howe, 77; and Monck's Corner, 247; and Savannah (1779), 147, 167, 170, 171, 184, 280, 284; and S.C. militia, 91; and Southern Department, 119, 121; and Stono Ferry, 122, 127, 268–72

Mulhenburg, Peter, 56, 293n71

Murray, John. See Dunmore, Earl of

Nash, Francis, 48, 56

Native Americans. See American Indians

Neutrality Proposal, 110–13, 301n31, 301n39

New York: and Augusta–Briar Creek, 86; British primary base, 59–61, 64; and Charlestown (1776), 36–37, 40–41, 54–55; and Charlestown (1780), 196, 198–99, 205, 215, 225, 234, 239–40, 312n56, 317n145, 317n147; and Clinton's S.C. policies, 262, 264–66; and DeLancy family, 294n14; and Lord Dunmore, 17; and Benjamin Lincoln, 81–82; and Savannah (1778), 70–73; and Savannah (1779), 137–38, 143, 171, 176, 181, 186, 274, 276, 283; Washington's 1776, 193, 234, 242; and Waxhaws, 250

Noailles, Louis Marie de, 150; and assault on Savannah, 158, 161, 169–70, 179,

191; dodging shellfire, 153; friction with d'Estaing, 157, 170

North Carolina, 1st Continental Regiment, 24, 34, 48, 56, 238

North Carolina, 2nd Continental Regiment, 15, 18, 24, 56

North Carolina, 3rd Continental Regiment, 57, 238

North Carolina, 4th Continental Regiment, 26, 282, 303n42

North Carolina, 5th Continental Regiment, 130, 303n42

O'Dunne, Humphrey, 151

Parker, Hyde, 77

Parker, Peter: and Charlestown (1776), 43, 45–54, 57, 63, 212; and decision to attack Fort Sullivan, 39–40; and Irish fleet of 1776, 36–37, 42

Parker, Richard: and Charlestown (1780), 201, 228, 238, 316n143; and Savannah (1779), 147, 160, 167, 177, 190, 275–77, 316n143

Patterson, James, 199–200, 205–6, 234, 240, 244

Pechot. See Tarragon, Jean-Rémy de,

Philadelphia: and Charlestown (1780), 193, 196, 229, 235; comparison to Charlestown, 242; and Moore's Creek Bridge, 30; and Savannah (1779), 283; and Southern Strategy of 1778, 59–61, 63

Pinckney, Charles, 138; and Charlestown (1779), 113; and Charlestown (1780), 212, 224, 225, 236, 237, 239; and Savannah (1779), 177, 190; and Stono Ferry, 130

Pinckney, Thomas: and Charlestown (1776), 57; and Savannah (1779), 138, 139, 162, 164, 166, 168, 172, 277, 278, 279, 281

Porbeck, Friedrich von, 79, 114, 163, 181, 307n98

Port Royal. See Beaufort

Prevost, Augustine, 83; and Augusta–Briar Creek, 84, 90, 92; and Thomas Brown, 65–66, 84; and Charlestown (1779), 100, 103–7, 109, 111–12, 114, 222, 225, 228,

300; and Charlestown (1780), 194–95, 198, 210, 238; and East Florida, 67, 71; and Kettle Creek, 90; and Loyalists and Indians, 117; and plundering, 119; and Port Royal skirmish, 100–101; and Savannah (1778), 70, 72; and Savannah (1779), 133, 137–38, 140–46, 148–52, 154–55, 158, 166, 168–76, 180, 185, 196, 273–74, 279, 281–86, 305; and Stono Ferry, 116, 118, 119, 121, 122, 127–29, 268, 270, 272; and supply shortage, 103; takes command in Georgia, 81, 83

Prevost, Mark: and Briar Creek, 92, 94–98; and Charlestown (1779), 109–11, 114; and Augustine Prevost, 90; and slaves, 118; and Stono Ferry, 121, 127, 129

privateers, 102, 199, 242

Privy Council, 109–10, 221, 224, 236, 301n28

Proclamation of 1763, 21

Pulaski, Casimir, 107; and Charlestown (1779), 107–8, 110–11, 114, 172, 196; controversy about death, 277–79; and Moravian Nuns, 307n88; and Savannah (1779), 137, 139, 147, 159, 161, 165–67, 177, 184, 191, 276, 309n47; and Stono Ferry, 118, 121, 128

Pulaski's Legion, 196, 307n88; and Charlestown (1779), 107–8, 114, 301n45; and Charlestown (1780), 201–2; makeup of, 108; and Monck's Corner, 246; and Savannah (1779), 137, 147, 159, 161, 165, 172, 177, 191, 276–79, 309n147; without Pulaski, 201, 202, 246

Purrysburg: and Augusta–Briar Creek, 77–78, 82–84, 88–91, 97, 297n50, 298n31, 299n49; and Charlestown (1779), 102–3

Pyle, John: and Moore's Creek Bridge, 24, 35; and "Pyle's Massacre," 289n14, 298n18

Ramsay, David: and Augusta–Briar Creek, 299n49; and Charlestown (1776), 292n37, 293n50; and Charlestown (1780), 224, 228, 234, 311n43, 314n97, 315n135; on Indians, 105, 112; on Casimir Pulaski, 108; and Savannah (1779), 273; and S.C. neutrality proposal, 301n31, 301n39; and S.C. patriotism, 146, 194; on size of

Ramsay, David (*continued*)
American battles, 14; and slave battalions, 146; and Stono Ferry, 127, 269–71
Regulators: and Alamance Court House, 21; and Moore's Creek, 23, 26–32, 34–35, 42; in North Carolina, 19; numbers at Moore's Creek, 291n46; Patriot suppression of, 290n19; as Patriots, 289n5; reasons for disaffection, 22; in South Carolina, 22
rice, 43, 63, 73–74, 103, 116, 135, 149, 224, 231, 233
Roberts, Owen: and Charlestown (1776), 57; and Savannah (1778), 77, 79; and Stono Ferry, 127, 130, 303n41
Rouvray, Laurent François de, 150–51, 191, 307n83
Royal Artillery, British: and Augusta–Briar Creek, 84, 92, 94, 98; and Charlestown (1780), 199, 207, 210, 215, 220, 223, 232, 235, 240; and Savannah (1778), 75–76, 79; and Savannah (1779), 103, 105, 143, 150–52, 154, 167, 170, 172, 180, 186, 285; and Stono Ferry, 123, 126–27
Royal Navy, British, 2–3, 37, 40–41, 198, 250; as artillerists, 11–13, 223, 274; and Charlestown (1776), 39–40, 45–55, 57, 63; and Charlestown (1778), 71; and Charlestown (1780), 198–200, 207–14, 216, 219, 222–23, 225, 236–37, 311n41, 311n43, 312n48; at Hampton, 7–8; "Irish" fleet of 1776, 32, 36–39; and Norfolk, 14–17; and Port Royal skirmish, 101; and Savannah (1779), 138, 140, 144, 149, 155, 176, 187, 280, 282; and Stono Ferry, 116
Rutledge, John, 118; and Charlestown (1776), 44, 51, 55; and Charlestown (1779), 104, 106, 108–14; and Charlestown (1780), 204–5, 221–22, 225, 311n22; and Continental authority, 44; and Benjamin Lincoln, 119, 121; and neutrality proposal, 110–13, 301n39; and Savannah (1779), 133, 167; and Waxhaws, 250–52

safeguards, 89, 95
salt, 146, 204, 231, 305n35

Saratoga, 59–61; and Carlisle Commission, 61; and French alliance, 59–60, 134; and Benjamin Lincoln, 69, 82, 119, 121, 237
Savannah, 14, 55, 67, 116, 128, 194, 242, 266–67, 302n16, 317n145; and Augusta–Briar Creek, 81–84, 88, 90, 95, 97; cavalry in siege, 277–79; and Charlestown (1779), 100–103; and Charlestown (1780), 196, 198, 200–201, 205, 214, 223, 228, 237, 240; color bearers in siege, 279; date of assault determined, 283; founding, 72; Maitland's relief of city, 280–82; Prevost adjusting lines before attack, 283–85; Prevost negotiations with d'Estaing, 285–86; and Savannah (1778), 70–80; and Savannah (1779), 133, 135, 137–92; and Stono Ferry, 122–23, 128–29; troop numbers in siege, 272–75; Virginia infantry in siege, 275–77; and Waxhaws, 244, 264
Scott, Alexander, 52, 57, 293n60
Scott, Charles, 223, 238, 251, 275–76, 316n43
Scott, William, 229
ships, American: *Boston*, 208, 211, 216; *General Lincoln*, 208; *Notre Dame*, 208; *Providence*, 208, 211, 216, 235; *Queen of France*, 208; *Ranger*, 208, 211, 235, 315n136
ships, British: *Acteon*, 47, 49, 52, 57; *Active*, 47–48, 57; *Anna*, 199, 310n13, 317n145; *Blonde*, 211; *Bristol*, 45, 47–48, 50, 52, 54, 57, 292n37; *Comet*, 282; *Defiance*, 210; *Experiment*, 47–48, 52, 57, 137, 140; *Fowey*, 7, 187, 282; *Friendship*, 47, 57; *Germain*, 149, 285; *Keppel*, 187, 282; *Raleigh*, 211; *Ranger*, 57; *Renown*, 210–12, 312n48; *Richmond*, 211–12; *Roebuck*, 210–11; *Romulus*, 210–11; *Rose*, 149, 187; *Rosebud*, 196; *Russia Merchant*, 199, 235; *Sandwich*, 211; *Savannah*, 149; *Solebay*, 47–48, 57; *Sphynx*, 47, 49, 57; *St. Lawrence*, 57; *Syren*, 47, 49, 57; *Thunder*, 47–49, 57; *Victory*, 140; *Vigilant*, 144, 283, 305n27; *Virginia*, 211
ships, French: *Foudroyant*, 292n37; *La Bricole*, 208; *La Chimère*, 155, 173; *La Truite*, 145, 152; *L'Aventure*, 208, 211, 235;

Le Fier Rodrigue, 144, 281; *Le Sagittaire,* 144, 281; *Trieste,* 208
sickness. *See* disease
Simons, Maurice: and Charlestown (1779), 114; and Charlestown (1780), 239; and Maitland's departure from Beaufort, 280–81; and Savannah (1779), 167, 177, 189–90, 280–81
Skull Creek, 144–45, 282
slaves. *See* black and slave participation
Smith, John Carraway, 73–74
South Carolina, 1st Continental Regiment: and Charlestown (1776), 57; and Charlestown (1779), 113; and Charlestown (1780), 212, 224, 229, 231, 239; consolidation, 195; and Savannah (1779), 160, 168, 177, 189–90; and Stono Ferry, 130, 303n40
South Carolina, 2nd Continental Regiment: and Charlestown (1776), 43, 48, 49–50, 55–56; and Charlestown (1779), 114; and Charlestown (1780), 238, 316n143; consolidation, 195; and Savannah (1779), 160, 166–69, 177, 190, 276–77, 279, 309n147
South Carolina, 3rd Continental Regiment: and Charlestown (1776), 56; consolidation, 195, 238; and Savannah (1778), 71, 74, 79, 296n30, 297n50; and Savannah (1779), 167, 177, 190, 277; and Stono Ferry, 130, 303n40
South Carolina, 3rd Rifle or Rangers. *See* South Carolina, 3rd Continental Regiment
South Carolina, 4th Continental Regiment of Artillery, 195; and Charlestown (1776), 48–49, 56–57; and Charlestown (1780), 239; and Savannah (1778), 74, 77, 79, 296n30; and Savannah (1779), 153, 178, 189–90; and Stono Ferry, 123, 124, 126–27, 130, 132
South Carolina, 5th Continental Regiment: and Charlestown (1776), 56; and Charlestown (1779), 103, 114; consolidation, 195; and Savannah (1778), 71, 74, 78, 296n30, 297n50; and Savannah (1779), 160, 168, 177, 190, 309n147
South Carolina, 6th Continental Regiment: and Charlestown (1776), 56; consolidation,

195; and Savannah (1779), 160, 168, 177, 189, 190, 309n147; and Stono Ferry, 130, 303n40; and Thomas Sumter, 292n38
southern geopolitics, 21–22
Southern Strategy, the, xi–xvi, 56, 78, 90, 100, 116, 242, 264; and Henry Clinton, 37–40, 60–64, 198, 238, 265, 266; historiography, 267–68; and William Howe, 37; making of in 1775, 1–4; and Augustine Prevost, 117–18; remaking of in 1778, 59–64
Spotswood, Alexander, 11, 13, 288n21
Squire, Matthew, 2, 8, 11
St. Augustine, Florida, 65, 67, 71–72, 81
St. Michael's Church, 223
Steding, Baron de, 158, 161–62, 164, 179, 307n83
Stedman, Charles: and Briar Creek, 299n50; and Clinton's policies, 265; and Monck's Corner, 247–48, 318n11; and Savannah (1779), 273, 275; and S.C. neutrality proposal, 301n31; and Stono Ferry, 125, 268, 270, 303n26, 304n43; and Waxhaws, 259
Steuben, Wilhelm, 296n30
Stevens, Edward, 13, 17–18
Stokes, Anthony, 154–55, 187, 306n57
Stokes, John, 257–58
Stono Ferry, 138, 194, 199, 267, 320n8; battle of, 121–31; casualties, 132; and Charlestown (1780), 201–3, 214, 227; failure of Continentals to charge, 268; Hessians at, 302n16; location of, 271–72; numbers engaged, 270–71; role of Moultrie in defeat, 269–70; and Savannah (1779), 144, 146, 163
Stuart, John, 62
Sullivan, John, 134
Sumner, Jethro: and Charlestown (1776), 57; and Stono Ferry, 123–26, 129–30
Sumter, Thomas, 56, 222, 292n38
Sunbury, 66, 71–72, 138, 143

Tarleton, Banastre, 242, 262; and Charlestown (1780), 219, 240, 243–44; and formation of British Legion, 243; and Lenud's Ferry, 249–50; letter of reprimand, 248–49; and Monck's Corner, 246–48, 318n11, 319n40, 319n48; and

Tarleton, Banastre (*continued*)
Tarleton's Quarter, 260; and Waxhaws, 252–60
Tarragon, Jean-Rémy de: a.k.a Pechot, 274; and army size, 274–75; and assault on Spring Hill, 164, 170–71, 173, 182; on French artillery, 154; on French looting, 140; on French siegeworks, 150; and Volunteers of San Domingo, 159
Tawse, Thomas: and Briar Creek, 92, 94, 98; and Charlestown (1779), 108, 115, 301n45; and Savannah (1779), 163, 172–73, 180, 277
Tawse's Light Dragoons: and Briar Creek, 92, 94, 98; and Charlestown (1779), 108, 115, 301n45; and Savannah (1779), 163, 172, 180
Tea Act, 60
test oaths, 88, 297n10
Thompson, William: and Charlestown (1776), 46–48, 50, 53, 56, 293n71; and Charlestown (1780), 237–38; and Savannah (1778), 71, 74, 77, 79; and Savannah (1779), 167, 177, 190, 277; and Stono Ferry, 130
Thunderbolt Bluff, 149, 151–52, 173–74
tobacco, 43, 56, 63
Tonyn, Patrick: and Thomas Brown, 65–66; and Charlestown (1776), 39; and Charlestown (1780), 196
Tories. *See* Loyalists
Tybee Island: and Charlestown (1780), 199–200, 210, 239; and Savannah (1778), 71–72; and Savannah (1779), 137–39, 144, 174, 278

Vernier, Paul, 201–2, 203, 246–48, 259
Virginia, 1st Continental Detachment: and Charlestown (1780), 201, 228, 238, 316n143; and Savannah (1779), 147, 177, 190, 275–76, 309n147
Virginia, 1st Continental Levies. *See* Virginia, 1st Continental Detachment
Virginia, 1st Continental Light Dragoons, 147, 159, 161, 177, 191, 201, 278
Virginia, 1st Continental Regiment, 18, 238

Virginia, 2nd Continental Detachment, 238, 276
Virginia, 2nd Continental Regiment, 7, 17–18, 238, 288n21
Virginia, 2nd State Regiment. *See* Virginia, 2nd Continental Regiment
Virginia, 3rd Continental Detachment, 249: 251–52, 260, 276
Virginia, 3rd Continental Regiment, 238

Wall's Cut, 144–45, 280, 282–83, 305n27
Walton, George, 75–76, 79, 296n30, 296n37
Wappoo Cut, 118, 203, 206
Washington, George: and Charlestown (1780), 236, 237; on discipline, 259; and John Laurens, 104, 166; and Charles Lee, 40–43, 55; and Benjamin Lincoln, 81, 82, 119, 195, 235–37; on militia, 43; on Norfolk, 5, 16; and northerns 59–61, 63, 71, 117, 193, 234; and Casimir Pulaski, 107, 108; and Savannah (1779), 283; sending reinforcements south, 147, 229, 250, 276; target of Patrick Ferguson, 263; and William Washington, 201
Washington, William: and Charlestown (1780), 201; contingent and Waxhaws, 254; and John Hamilton, 90, 201; and Lenud's Ferry, 249; and Monck's Corner, 246; and Banastre Tarleton, 244, 246
Waxhaws: and American sentiments, 260; battle of, 253–57; effects on British policy, 262–63; and Andrew Pickens, 87; proximity to other battles, 318n32; question of massacre, 257–59
weather: and Charlestown (1776), 37, 47, 53; and Charlestown (1779), 300; and Charlestown (1780), 199–200, 204, 208–10, 310n16, 311–312n43, 317n145; and Moore's Creek Bridge, 37; and Norfolk, 7; and Savannah (1778), 71; and Savannah (1779), 134, 137–40, 156, 174; and Stono Ferry, 129, 269
Webster, James: and atrocities at Monck's Corner, 248; and Charlestown (1780), 203, 219–20, 225, 239; and Monck's Corner, 219–20, 244, 246–48, 250

Whipple, Abraham: assignment to
Charlestown, 196; ineffectiveness at
Charlestown, 207–12, 214, 311n41;
and John Laurens, 201; parole of, 235
White, Anthony, 249
White, John, 143
Wilkinson, Eliza, 119, 272
Williamson, Andrew: accusations of treason,
319n2; and Augusta–Briar Creek, 84, 86,
89, 91, 101; and Charlestown (1780),
204–5; and Florida invasion, 67; and
Savannah (1779), 147, 178, 185, 189–90;
and Stono Ferry, 130; surrender to
British, 262
Wilmington, 22–23, 27, 32, 91, 299n45
women and children: and British policy,
263; and Charlestown (1780), 215, 220,
223–24; and Monck's Corner, 248;

Moravian Nuns of Pennsylvania, 307; and
Norfolk, 10, 15; and Prevost's invasion of
S.C., 119; and Savannah (1779), 152,
154–55, 173, 185
Woodford, William, 56; and Charlestown
(1780), 196, 218–19, 221, 237–38,
312n62, 313n63; and Great Bridge,
9–13, 17, 288n16, 288n21, 289n41,
289n43; and Hampton, 7–8; and Norfolk
destruction, 15, 18; and Waxhaws, 244,
251, 318n29
Wright, James: and Charlestown (1779), 103;
and Charlestown (1779), 198; and Georgia Loyalists, 117; and Savannah (1778),
74–75; and Savannah (1779), 149, 154,
273, 285

Zubly's Ferry, 77, 147